Policy Implications
of
Greenhouse Warming

Mitigation, Adaptation, and the Science Base

Panel on Policy Implications of Greenhouse Warming

Committee on Science, Engineering, and Public Policy

National Academy of Sciences
National Academy of Engineering
Institute of Medicine

NATIONAL ACADEMY PRESS
Washington, D.C. 1992

National Academy Press • 2101 Constitution Ave., N.W. • Washington, D.C. 20418

Library of Congress Cataloging-in-Publication Data

Committee on Science, Engineering, and Public Policy (U.S.). Panel on
    Policy Implications of Greenhouse Warming.
        Policy implications of greenhouse warming : mitigation,
    adaptation, and the science base / Panel on Policy Implications of
    Greenhouse Warming, Committee on Science, Engineering, and Public
    Policy, National Academy of Sciences, National Academy of
    Engineering, Institute of Medicine.
            p.   cm.
        Contains the report of the Policy Implications of Greenhouse
    Warming—Synthesis Panel published separately in 1991 under the same
    title.
        Includes bibliographical references and indexes.
        ISBN 0-309-04386-7
        1. Global warming—Government policy—United States.
        2. Greenhouse effect, Atmospheric—Government policy—
    United States
        3. Environmental policy—United States. I. Title.
        QC981.8.G56C64   1992
        363.73'87—dc20   92-11583
                                                                   CIP

POLICY IMPLICATIONS OF GREENHOUSE WARMING
SYNTHESIS PANEL

DANIEL J. EVANS (Chairman), Chairman, Daniel J. Evans & Associates, Seattle, Washington

ROBERT McCORMICK ADAMS, Secretary, Smithsonian Institution, Washington, D.C.

GEORGE F. CARRIER, T. Jefferson Coolidge Professor of Applied Mathematics, Emeritus, Harvard University, Cambridge, Massachusetts

RICHARD N. COOPER, Professor of Economics, Harvard University, Cambridge, Massachusetts

ROBERT A. FROSCH, Vice President, General Motors Research Laboratories, Warren, Michigan

THOMAS H. LEE, Professor Emeritus, Department of Electrical Engineering and Computer Science, Massachusetts Institute of Technology, Cambridge, Massachusetts

JESSICA TUCHMAN MATHEWS, Vice President, World Resources Institute, Washington, D.C.

WILLIAM D. NORDHAUS, Professor of Economics, Yale University, New Haven, Connecticut

GORDON H. ORIANS, Professor of Zoology and Director of the Institute for Environmental Studies, University of Washington, Seattle

STEPHEN H. SCHNEIDER, Head, Interdisciplinary Climate Systems, National Center for Atmospheric Research, Boulder, Colorado

MAURICE STRONG, Secretary General, United Nations Conference on Environment and Development, New York (resigned from panel February 1990)

SIR CRISPIN TICKELL, Warden, Green College, Oxford, England

VICTORIA J. TSCHINKEL, Senior Consultant, Landers, Parsons and Uhlfelder, Tallahassee, Florida

PAUL E. WAGGONER, Distinguished Scientist, The Connecticut Agricultural Experiment Station, New Haven

Staff

ROB COPPOCK, Staff Director
DEBORAH D. STINE, Staff Officer
NANCY A. CROWELL, Administrative Specialist
MARION R. ROBERTS, Administrative Secretary

POLICY IMPLICATIONS OF GREENHOUSE WARMING
MITIGATION PANEL

POLICY IMPLICATIONS OF GREENHOUSE WARMING
ADAPTATION PANEL

COMMITTEE ON SCIENCE, ENGINEERING, AND PUBLIC POLICY

---

*Term expired 6/30/90.
†Term expired 6/30/91.

The National Academy of Sciences is a private, nonprofit, self-perpetuating society of distinguished scholars engaged in scientific and engineering research, dedicated to the furtherance of science and technology and to their use for the general welfare. Upon the authority of the charter granted to it by the Congress in 1863, the Academy has a mandate that requires it to advise the federal government on scientific and technical matters. Dr. Frank Press is president of the National Academy of Sciences.

The National Academy of Engineering was established in 1964, under the charter of the National Academy of Sciences, as a parallel organization of outstanding engineers. It is autonomous in its administration and in the selection of its members, sharing with the National Academy of Sciences the responsibility for advising the federal government. The National Academy of Engineering also sponsors engineering programs aimed at meeting national needs, encourages education and research, and recognizes the superior achievements of engineers. Dr. Robert M. White is president of the National Academy of Engineering.

The Institute of Medicine was established in 1970 by the National Academy of Sciences to secure the services of eminent members of appropriate professions in the examination of policy matters pertaining to the health of the public. The Institute acts under the responsibility given to the National Academy of Sciences by its congressional charter to be an adviser to the federal government and, upon its own initiative, to identify issues of medical care, research, and education. Dr. Kenneth I. Shine is president of the Institute of Medicine.

The Committee on Science, Engineering, and Public Policy (COSEPUP) is a joint committee of the National Academy of Sciences, the National Academy of Engineering, and the Institute of Medicine. It includes members of the councils of all three bodies.

The study reported here was supported by the U.S. Environmental Protection Agency. It also received support from the National Research Council Fund, a pool of private, discretionary, nonfederal funds that is used to support a program of Academy studies of national issues in which science and technology figure significantly. The NRC Fund consists of contributions from a consortium of private foundations, including the Carnegie Corporation of New York, the Charles E. Culpeper Foundation, the William and Flora Hewlett Foundation, the John D. and Catherine T. MacArthur Foundation, the Andrew W. Mellon Foundation, the Rockefeller Foundation, and the Alfred P. Sloan Foundation and the Academy Industry Program, which seeks annual contributions from companies that are concerned with the health of U.S. science and technology and with public policy issues with technological content.

Preface

Greenhouse gases and global warming have received increasing attention in recent years. The identification of the antarctic ozone hole in 1985 combined with the hot, dry summer of 1988 in North America to provide the drama that seems to be required for capturing national media coverage. Emerging scientific results, including findings about greenhouse gases other than carbon dioxide, added to the interest.

One consequence was congressional action. The HUD-Independent Agencies Appropriations Act of 1988 (House Report 100-701:26) called for

> [an] NAS study on global climate change. This study should establish the scientific consensus on the rate and magnitude of climate change, estimate the projected impacts, and evaluate policy options for mitigating and responding to such changes. The need for and utility of improved temperature monitoring capabilities should also be examined, as resources permit.

According to subsequent advice received from members of Congress, the study was to focus on radiatively active trace gases from human sources, or "greenhouse warming." This report combines in a single volume the products of that study.

The study was conducted under the auspices of the Committee on Science, Engineering, and Public Policy, a unit of the councils of the National Academy of Sciences, the National Academy of Engineering, and the Institute of Medicine. The study involved nearly 50 experts, including scientists as well as individuals with experience in government, private industry, and public interest organizations.

The work of the study was conducted by four panels. The Synthesis Panel (whose membership is listed on page iii) was charged with developing overall findings and recommendations. The Effects Panel (whose membership is listed on page iv) examined what is known about changing climatic conditions and related effects. The Mitigation Panel (whose membership is listed on page v) looked at options for reducing or reversing the onset of potential global warming. The Adaptation Panel (whose membership is listed on page vi) assessed the impacts of possible climate change on human and ecologic systems and the policies that could help people and natural systems adapt to those changes.

The panels conducted their analyses simultaneously between September 1989 and January 1991. The chairmen of the Effects, Mitigation, and Adaptation panels were members of the Synthesis Panel. Several members of the Synthesis Panel also were members of other panels. In its deliberations, however, the Synthesis Panel considered more than just the reports of the other panels. It also heard from experts with a range of views on the policy relevance of computer simulation models, widely held to be the best available tools for projecting climate change, and of economic models used to assess consequences of policies to reduce greenhouse gas emissions. The study also drew upon the report of the Intergovernmental Panel on Climate Change, an international effort released during the course of the study. Several members of the various study panels also contributed to that effort. Finally, the study drew upon other Academy studies. For example, in its examination of sea level, the panel used analyses from the following reports: *Glaciers, Ice Sheets, and Sea Level: Effects of a CO_2-Induced Climatic Change* (National Academy Press, 1985); *Responding to Changes in Sea Level: Engineering Implications* (National Academy Press, 1987); and *Sea-Level Change* (National Academy Press, 1990). The findings and recommendations of the Synthesis Panel are thus much more than a summary of the assessments performed by the other three panels. They contain analysis that goes beyond the topics covered by the other panels.

About eight months elapsed between the initial release of the report of the Synthesis Panel and the time at which this document went to press. The response to that report and to the prepublication documents prepared by the other panels has been gratifying. Our findings and recommendations and the analyses upon which they are based have been presented to members of Congress and officials in the federal administration. They have been distributed to officials and interested individuals in other countries. Many news stories have referred to our work. We believe the study has already helped guide the national debate and demonstrated a rational approach to evaluating possible responses. We hope this document will continue to do so.

The report identifies what should be done now to counter potential greenhouse warming or deal with its likely consequences. The recommendations, if followed, should provide the United States, and the rest of the world, with a rational basis for responding to this important concern.

The Honorable Daniel J. Evans, Chairman
Policy Implications of Greenhouse Warming

Contents

Policy Implications
of
Greenhouse Warming

Part One

SYNTHESIS

1

Introduction

Greenhouse gases in the atmosphere have an important influence on the climate of our planet. Simply stated, greenhouse gases impede the outward flow of infrared radiation more effectively than they impede incoming solar radiation. Because of this asymmetry, the earth, its atmosphere, and its oceans are warmer than they would be in the absence of such gases.

The major greenhouse gases are water vapor, carbon dioxide (CO_2), methane (CH_4), chlorofluorocarbons (CFCs) and hydrogenated chlorofluorocarbons (HCFCs), ozone (O_3), and nitrous oxide (N_2O). Without the naturally occurring greenhouse gases (principally water vapor and CO_2), the earth's average temperature would be about 33°C (59°F) colder than it is, and the planet would be much less suitable for human habitation.

Human activity has contributed to increased atmospheric concentrations of CO_2, CH_4, and CFCs. The increased atmospheric concentrations of greenhouse gases may increase average global temperatures. The possible warming due to increased concentrations of these gases is called "greenhouse warming." The atmospheric concentration of CO_2 in 1990 was 353 parts per million by volume (ppmv), about 25 percent greater than it was before the Industrial Revolution (about 280 ± 10 ppmv prior to 1750). Atmospheric CO_2 is increasing at about 0.5 percent per year. The concentration of CH_4 was 1.72 ppmv in 1990, or slightly more than twice that before 1750. It is rising at a rate of 0.9 percent per year. CFCs do not occur naturally and were not found in the atmosphere until production began a few decades ago. Continued increases in atmospheric concentrations of greenhouse gases would affect the earth's radiative balance and might cause a significant amount of additional greenhouse warming.

General circulation models (GCMs) are the principal tools used to project climatic changes. At their present level of development, GCMs project that an increase in greenhouse gas concentrations equivalent to a doubling of the preindustrial level of atmospheric CO_2 would produce global average temperature increases between 1.9° and 5.2°C (3.4° and 9.4°F). The larger of these temperature increases would mean a climate warmer than any in human history. The consequences of this amount of warming are unknown and could include extremely unpleasant surprises.

During the last 100 years the average global temperature has increased between 0.3° and 0.6°C (0.5° and 1.1°F). This temperature rise could be attributable to greenhouse warming or to natural climate variability; with today's limited understanding of the underlying phenomena, neither can be ruled out.

Increases in atmospheric greenhouse gas concentrations probably will be followed by increases in average atmospheric temperature. We cannot predict how rapidly these changes will occur, how intense they will be for any given atmospheric concentration, or, in particular, what regional changes in temperature, precipitation, wind speed, and frost occurrence can be expected. So far, no large or rapid increases in the global average temperature have occurred, and there is no evidence yet of imminent rapid change. But if the higher GCM projections prove to be accurate, substantial responses would be needed, and the stresses on this planet and its inhabitants would be serious.

It is against this backdrop that prudent, necessarily international, plans should be made and actions undertaken. These plans and actions should start with responses justified by the current credibility of the threat. They also should include preparatory measures that can set the stage for more far-reaching responses if the evidence of need becomes persuasive. It is in this setting that the Synthesis Panel performed its analyses and developed recommendations for action by the United States.

The principal findings and conclusions of the panel are summarized in Chapter 8, and its recommendations are in Chapter 9. Appendix A, "Questions and Answers About Greenhouse Warming," discusses relevant issues in a format the panel believes may be especially useful to the reader.

2

Background

THE GLOBAL NATURE OF GREENHOUSE WARMING

Greenhouse warming is global in at least two respects. First, greenhouse gases released anywhere in the world disperse rapidly in the global atmosphere. Neither the location of release nor the activity resulting in a release makes much difference. A molecule of CO_2 from a cooking fire in Yellowstone or India is subject to the same laws of chemistry and physics in the atmosphere as a molecule from the exhaust pipe of a high-performance auto in Indiana or Europe. Second, the anticipated climatic effects include changes in the global circulation of air and water. Global average temperature is often used as an indicator of the various climatic effects. Climate change, however, has many facets: seasonal cycles and annual fluctuations of temperature and precipitation, wind speed and direction, and strength and direction of ocean currents. Although the results of climate change will differ from place to place, they derive from global processes.

GREENHOUSE GAS EMISSIONS FROM
HUMAN ACTIVITIES

Greenhouse warming is complicated in another, more fundamental way. The amounts released vary, of course, but virtually every form of human activity contributes some amount of greenhouse gas to the atmosphere or removes some from the atmosphere. Subsistence agriculture contributes its bit, as does modern industry and the consumption and use of modern goods and services. Growing trees remove CO_2 from the atmosphere, but burning wood for heating and cooking releases CO_2 into the atmosphere. Rice paddies and cattle contribute CH_4. Industrial activities include releases of all the greenhouse gases to varying extents. In most societies the burning of fossil fuels for electricity and transportation is a major contributor.

Since releases of greenhouse gases are connected to most economic activity, significant reductions in their emission may affect the economic competitiveness of individuals, firms, and nations. Avoiding additional greenhouse warming may be costly, it may create economic winners and losers, and it may alter trade balances.

THE EFFECTS OF WORLD POPULATION AND ECONOMIC GROWTH

The world's population today is 5.3 billion, and it is expected to continue to grow at about 1.7 percent per year at current rates of fertility. Figure 2.1 shows historical population growth and an estimate for 2000. This increasing population is one of the major factors affecting trends in greenhouse gas emissions. More people create greater demand for food, energy, clothing, and shelter. Producing such products emits greenhouse gases.

Economic growth also produces more greenhouse gas emissions. If population grows with constant per capita income, more resources are used for food, clothing, and shelter. If per capita income grows in a constant population, the demand for goods also grows, particularly for health and education services, transportation, and housing. Most nations in the world have policies to reduce population growth rates, but all nations seek to achieve rapid growth in per capita income. The reduction of greenhouse gas emissions is well served by the first objective (reducing population growth) but, depending on the means used, can be in conflict with the second (growth in per capita income).

The detailed links between population growth and greenhouse gas emissions are complex and not well understood. The developing countries that have reduced their population growth rates within the last 30 years did so only after rapidly increasing their standards of living. This often was accompanied by environmental degradation. Perhaps it will be possible to rapidly raise living standards without resulting in traditional patterns of pollution. Unfortunately, there are few examples to guide us. What is needed is a breakthrough in strategies for development, especially with respect to energy supply and demand. Developing countries experiencing rapid economic growth will need effective mitigation programs if they are to avoid substantial increases in their greenhouse gas emissions. Implementing new strategies will require funds that will probably be scarce if populations grow rapidly. Nevertheless, at any given per capita rate of greenhouse gas emissions, a smaller population means fewer emissions, as well as less stress on the environment in general.

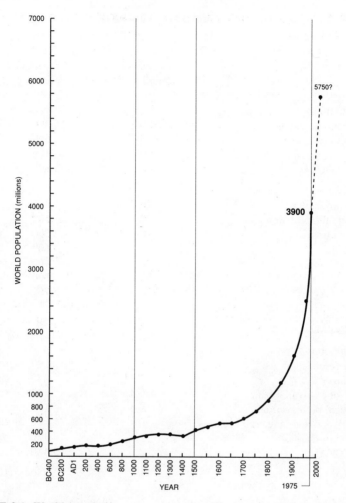

FIGURE 2.1 World population.

SOURCE: C. McEvedy and R. Jones. 1978. *Atlas of World Population History.* Middlesex, United Kingdom: Penguin. Figure 6.2.

TRENDS IN HUMAN ACTIVITIES AFFECTING GREENHOUSE GAS CONCENTRATIONS

Table 2.1 presents emission estimates for five greenhouse gases (CO_2, CH_4, CFC-11, CFC-12, and N_2O) that accounted for about 87 percent of the increase in the heat-trapping capacity of the atmosphere in the 1980s and about 92 percent of the increase over the previous 100 years. The table presents estimated 1985 emissions (in million tons per year) and converts non-CO_2

TABLE 2.1 Estimated 1985 Global Greenhouse Gas Emissions from Human Activities

	Greenhouse Gas Emissions (Mt/yr)	CO_2-equivalent Emissions[a] (Mt/yr)	
CO_2 Emissions			
Commercial energy	18,800	18,800	(57)
Tropical deforestation	2,600	2,600	(8)
Other	400	400	(1)
TOTAL	21,800	21,800	(66)
CH_4 Emissions			
Fuel production	60	1,300	(4)
Enteric fermentation	70	1,500	(5)
Rice cultivation	110	2,300	(7)
Landfills	30	600	(2)
Tropical deforestation	20	400	(1)
Other	30	600	(2)
TOTAL	320	6,700	(20)[b]
CFC-11 and CFC-12 Emissions			
TOTAL	0.6	3,200	(10)
N_2O Emissions			
Coal combustion	1	290	(>1)
Fertilizer use	1.5	440	(1)
Gain of cultivated land	0.4	120	(>1)
Tropical deforestation	0.5	150	(>1)
Fuel wood and industrial biomass	0.2	60	(>1)
Agricultural wastes	0.4	120	(>1)
TOTAL	4	1,180	(4)
TOTAL		32,880	(100)

NOTE: Mt/yr = million (10^6) metric tons (t) per year. All entries are rounded because the exact values are controversial.

[a]CO_2-equivalent emissions are calculated from the Greenhouse Gas Emissions column by using the following multipliers:

CO_2	1
CH_4	21
CFC-11 and -12	5,400
N_2O	290

Numbers in parentheses are percentages of total.
[b]Total does not sum due to rounding errors.

SOURCE: Adapted from U.S. Department of Energy. 1990. *The Economics of Long-Term Global Climate Change: A Preliminary Assessment—Report of an Interagency Task Force.* Springfield, Va.: National Technical Information Service.

TABLE 2.2 Carbon Dioxide Emission Estimates

	1960		1970		1980		1988	
	Total	Per Capita	Total	Per Capita	Total	Per Capita	Total	Per Capita
East Germany	263.6	15.4	160.6	15.8	306.9	18.3	327.4	19.8
United States	2858.2	16.1	4273.5	20.9	4617.4	20.2	'804.1	19.4
Canada	193.2	10.6	333.3	15.4	424.6	17.6	437.8	16.9
Czechoslovakia	129.8	9.5	199.1	13.9	242.4	15.8	'33.6	15.0
Australia	88.4	8.4	142.6	11.4	202.8	13.9	41.3	14.7
USSR	1452.4	6.6	2303.4	9.5	3283.5	12.5	39 32.0	13.9
Poland	201.7	7.0	303.6	9.2	459.8	12.8	4.9.4	12.1
West Germany	544.9	9.9	736.6	12.1	762.7	12.5	66).9	11.0
United Kingdom	589.6	11.4	643.1	11.4	588.9	10.3	55 .2	9.9
Romania	53.5	2.9	119.5	5.9	199.8	9.2	22(7	9.5
South Africa	98.6	5.5	149.6	6.6	213.4	7.7	284 ?	8.4
Japan	234.3	2.6	742.1	7.3	934.6	8.1	989.	8.1
Italy	110.4	2.2	286.0	5.5	372.5	6.6	359.'	6.2
France	274.3	5.9	426.1	8.4	484.4	9.2	320.1	5.9
Korea	49.1	0.4	52.1	1.5	125.8	3.3	204.6	4.8
Spain	12.8	1.5	110.7	3.3	198.7	5.5	187.7	4.8
Mexico	63.1	1.8	106.0	1.8	260.3	3.7	306.9	3.7
People's Republic of China	789.4	1.2	775.9	1.0	1490.1	1.5	2236.3	2.1
Brazil	46.9	0.7	86.5	0.7	176.7	1.5	202.4	5
India	121.7	0.4	195.4	0.4	350.2	0.4	600.6	0 7

NOTE: Emission estimates are rounded and expressed in million tons of CO_2; per capita estimates are rounded and expressed in tons of CO_2. All tons are metric.

SOURCE: Adapted from Thomas A. Boden, Paul Kanciruk, and Michael P. Farrell. 1990. *Trends '90: A Compendium of Data on Global Change.* Oak Ridge, Tenn.: Oak Ridge National Laboratory.

gases into CO_2-equivalent emissions so that their respective contributions can be compared. These projections necessarily involve uncertainties. (Note that throughout this report tons (t) are metric; 1 Mt equals 1 million metric tons.)

The United States is the world's largest contributor of greenhouse gas emissions. Table 2.2 shows total and per capita CO_2 emissions (the dominant greenhouse gas emitted by human activity) for the United States and several other countries from 1960 to 1988, in order of their most recent per capita emissions. Two of the six countries with the largest total emissions are developing countries (People's Republic of China and India). Per capita

TABLE 2.3 Carbon Dioxide Emissions per Unit of Economic Activity (1988 to 1989)

	Emissions (Mt CO_2/yr)	GNP (billions of \$/yr)	Emissions/GNP Ratio (Mt CO_2/\$1000 GNP)
China	2236.3	372.3[a]	6.01[b]
South Africa	284.2	79.0	3.60
Romania	220.7	79.8[a]	2.77[b]
Poland	459.4	172.4[a]	2.66[b]
India	600.6	237.9	2.52
East Germany	327.4	159.5[a]	2.05[b]
Czechoslovakia	233.6	123.2[a]	1.90[b]
Mexico	306.9	176.7	1.74
USSR	3982.0	2659.5[a]	1.50[b]
South Korea	204.6	171.3	1.19
Canada	437.8	435.9	1.00
United States	4804.1	4880.1	0.98
Australia	241.3	246.0	0.98
United Kingdom	559.2	702.4	0.80
Brazil	202.4	323.6	0.63
West Germany	669.9	1201.8	0.56
Spain	187.7	340.3	0.55
Italy	359.7	828.9	0.43
Japan	989.3	2843.7	0.35
France	320.1	949.4	0.34

[a]Estimates of GNP for centrally planned economies are subject to large margins of error. These estimates are as much as 100 times larger than those from other sources that correct for availability of goods or use free-market exchange rates.
[b]The emissions/GNP is also likely to be underestimated for centrally planned economies.

SOURCE: Table 2.2 above for CO_2 emissions. For GNP, entries are from World Bank, 1990, *World Development Report, 1990,* World Bank, Washington, D.C., Table 3. For centrally planned economies other than China, estimates are from U.S. Central Intelligence Agency, *World Factbook 1990.*

emissions in 1988 are lower than those in 1980 in several countries, including the United States, suggesting that some actions to reduce greenhouse warming are already being taken.

It is also informative to compare emissions to economic activity. Table 2.3 shows CO_2 emissions per unit of economic activity for recent emissions data. The table illustrates that some developing countries and centrally planned economies are large emitters of greenhouse gases per unit of

TABLE 2.4 Estimated Deforestation in the Tropics (thousand hectares)

	Number of Countries Studied	Total Land Area	Forest Area 1980	Forest Area 1990	Annual Deforestation 1980-1990
Africa	15	609,500	289,700	241,500	4,800
Latin America	32	1,263,500	825,900	753,000	7,300
Asia	15	891,100	334,500	287,500	4,700
TOTAL	62	2,754,500	1,450,100	1,282,300	15,800

NOTE: Entries cover closed tropical forests. Closed forests have trees covering a high proportion of the ground and grass does not form a continuous layer on the forest floor. The numbers are indicative and should not be taken as regional averages.

SOURCE: Committee on Forestry. 1990. *Interim Report on Forest Resources Assessment 1990 Project,* Tenth Session. Geneva, Switzerland: Food and Agriculture Organization of the United Nations.

economic activity and that the United States is in the middle of the field. It also shows France with low emissions per unit of economic activity, probably because of its extensive reliance on nuclear power as a source of electricity.

Table 2.4 shows recent estimates of deforestation in tropical forests for selected countries. About 80 percent of this wood is destroyed or used as fuel wood, and the remaining 20 percent is harvested for industrial or trade purposes. If the trees are burned, the CO_2 they have stored is added to the air, and if they are replaced with plants that grow more slowly, less CO_2 will be removed from the atmosphere.

3

The Greenhouse Gases and
Their Effects

Atmospheric concentrations of greenhouse gases are increasingly well known. Current concentrations, emission accumulation rates, and atmospheric lifetimes of key gases are summarized in Table 3.1. Past releases of these gases are less well documented. As shown in Figure 3.1, atmospheric CO_2 began increasing in the eighteenth century. Regular monitoring, begun in 1958, shows an accelerated increase in atmospheric CO_2. About a decade of data also documents rapidly increasing atmospheric concentrations of CH_4. Indirect evidence from tree rings, air bubbles trapped in glacial ice as it formed, and other sources has been used to reconstruct past concentrations of these gases.

The dispersion and transformation of greenhouse gases in the atmosphere are also fairly well understood. There is, however, one important exception: CO_2. Recent measurements indicate that about 40 percent of the CO_2 released into the atmosphere stays there for decades at least, and about 15 percent seems to be incorporated into the upper layers of the oceans. The location of the remaining 45 percent of the CO_2 from human activity is not known. Until the redistribution of newly emitted CO_2 is more thoroughly understood, reliable projections of the rate of increase of atmospheric CO_2 will lack credibility even for precisely estimated emission rates. Even so, it is probably sensible during the next decade or two to use 40 percent of CO_2 emissions as an estimate of the atmospheric accumulation rate. On a longer time scale, there is, as of now, no estimation procedure that merits confidence.

Each greenhouse gas is subject to different chemical reactions in the atmosphere and to different mechanisms of alteration or removal. Thus projections of future concentrations must account not only for emissions but also for transformations in the atmosphere. In addition, the various greenhouse gases have different energy-absorbing properties. For example, each molecule

TABLE 3.1 Key Greenhouse Gases Influenced by Human Activity

	CO_2	CH_4	CFC-11	CFC-12	N_2O
Preindustrial atmospheric concentration	280 ppmv	0.8 ppmv	0	0	288 ppbv
Current atmospheric concentration (1990)[a]	353 ppmv	1.72 ppmv	280 pptv	484 pptv	310 ppbv
Current rate of annual atmospheric accumulation[b]	1.8 ppmv (0.5%)	0.015 ppmv (0.9%)	9.5 pptv (4%)	17 pptv (4%)	0.8 ppbv (0.25%)
Atmospheric lifetime (years)[c]	(50-200)	10	65	130	150

NOTE: Ozone has not been included in the table because of lack of precise data. Here ppmv = parts per million by volume, ppbv = parts per billion by volume, and pptv = parts per trillion by volume.

[a]The 1990 concentrations have been estimated on the basis of an extrapolation of measurements reported for earlier years, assuming that the recent trends remained approximately constant.

[b]Net annual emissions of CO_2 from the biosphere not affected by human activity, such as volcanic emissions, are assumed to be small. Estimates of human-induced emissions from the biosphere are controversial.

[c]For each gas in the table, except CO_2, the "lifetime" is defined as the ratio of the atmospheric concentration to the total rate of removal. This time scale also characterizes the rate of adjustment of the atmospheric concentrations if the emission rates are changed abruptly. CO_2 is a special case because it is merely circulated among various reservoirs (atmosphere, ocean, biota). The "lifetime" of CO_2 given in the table is a rough indication of the time it would take for the CO_2 concentration to adjust to changes in the emissions.

SOURCE: Intergovernmental Panel on Climate Change. 1990. *Climate Change: The IPCC Scientific Assessment*, J. T. Houghton, G. J. Jenkins, and J. J. Ephraums, eds. New York: Cambridge University Press. Reprinted by permission of Cambridge University Press.

of CH_4 absorbs radiative energy 25 times more effectively than each molecule of CO_2, and CFC-12 is 15,800 times more effective than CO_2 on a per molecule basis and, since molecules of the two gases have different mass, 5,750 times more effective on a per mass basis. Figure 3.2 incorporates a simple extrapolation of current atmospheric transformation rates. It displays the incremental energy absorption rates that would accompany various emission scenarios. The energy absorption is given in watts per square meter (W/m^2) and, in accord with the vocabulary of this subject, changes in the absorption

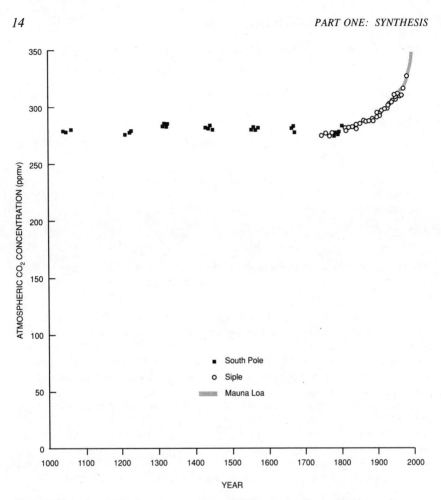

FIGURE 3.1 Atmospheric concentrations of CO_2. Atmospheric CO_2 began increasing in the eighteenth century. Direct measurements made at the Mauna Loa Observatory in Hawaii since 1958 indicate that the increase has accelerated.

SOURCE: Adapted from W. M. Post, T.-H. Peng, W. R. Emanuel, A. W. King, V. H. Dale, and D. DeAngelis. 1990. The global carbon cycle. *American Scientist* 78(4):310-326, Figure 3b.

are called "radiative forcing." The curves show the aggregate contribution of each gas for the period from 1990 to 2030.

EARTH'S RADIATION BALANCE

The climatic system of the earth is driven by radiant energy from the sun. Incoming solar radiation at the top of the earth's atmosphere has an average intensity, over the year and over the globe, of 340 W/m^2. Over the long time

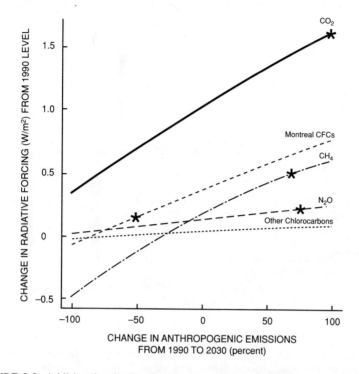

FIGURE 3.2 Additional radiative forcing of principal greenhouse gases from 1990 to 2030 for different emission rates. The horizontal axis shows changes in greenhouse gas emissions ranging from completely eliminating emissions (−100 percent) to doubling current emissions (+100 percent). Emission changes are assumed to be linear from 1990 levels to the 2030 level selected. The vertical axis shows the change in radiative forcing in watts per square meter at the earth's surface in 2030. Each asterisk indicates the projected emissions of that gas assuming no additional regulatory policies, based on the Intergovernmental Panel on Climate Change estimates and the original restrictions agreed to under the Montreal Protocol, which limits emissions of CFCs. Chemical interactions among greenhouse gas species are not included.

For CO_2 emissions remaining at 1990 levels through 2030, the resulting change in radiative forcing can be determined in two steps: (1) Find the point on the curve labeled "CO_2" that is vertically above 0 percent change on the bottom scale. (2) The radiative forcing on the surface-troposphere system can be read in watts per square meter by moving horizontally to the left-hand scale, or about 1 W/m^2. These steps must be repeated for each gas. For example, the radiative forcing for continued 1990-level emissions of CH_4 through 2030 would be about 0.2 W/m^2.

SOURCE: Courtesy of Michael C. MacCracken.

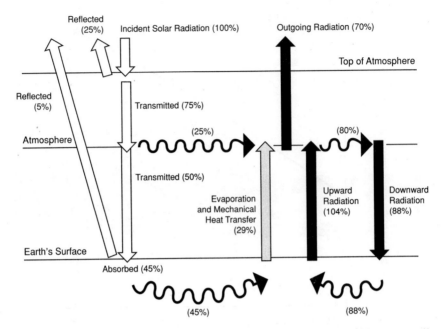

FIGURE 3.3 Earth's radiation balance. The solar radiation is set at 100 percent; all other values are in relation to it. About 25 percent of incident solar radiation is reflected back into space by the atmosphere, about 25 percent is absorbed by gases in the atmosphere, and about 5 percent is reflected into space from the earth's surface, leaving 45 percent to be absorbed by the oceans, land, and biotic material (white arrows).

Evaporation and mechanical heat transfer inject energy into the atmosphere equal to about 29 percent of incident radiation (grey arrow). Radiative energy emissions from the earth's surface and from the atmosphere (straight black arrows) are determined by the temperatures of the earth's surface and the atmosphere, respectively. Upward energy radiation from the earth's surface is about 104 percent of incident solar radiation. Atmospheric gases absorb part (25 percent) of the solar radiation penetrating the top of the atmosphere and all of the mechanical heat transferred from the earth's surface and the outbound radiation from the earth's surface. The downward radiation from the atmosphere is about 88 percent and outgoing radiation about 70 percent of incident solar radiation.

Note that the amounts of outgoing and incoming radiation balance at the top of the atmosphere, at 100 percent of incoming solar radiation (which is balanced by 5 percent reflected from the surface, 25 percent reflected from the top of the atmosphere, and 70 percent outgoing radiation), and at the earth's surface, at 133 percent (45 percent absorbed solar radiation plus 88 percent downward radiation from the atmosphere balanced by 29 percent evaporation and mechanical heat transfer and 104 percent upward radiation). Energy transfers into and away from the atmosphere also balance, at the atmosphere line, at 208 percent of incident solar radiation (75 percent transmitted solar radiation plus 29 percent mechanical transfer from the periods during which the climate is steady, the radiation from the top of the atmosphere to space has, again on average, the same intensity. As can be seen in Figure 3.3, the incoming arrows, representing the incoming intensity or energy flux, balance the outgoing arrows at the top of the atmosphere. The figure shows a similar balance at the earth's surface. The downward flow of energy at the earth's surface is 133 percent of the incident solar radiation (the 45 percent of the incident solar radiation absorbed from the incoming energy flow plus the 88 percent downward infrared radiation). The combined downward transfer of energy at the earth's surface is greater than that arriving at the top of the atmosphere because the atmosphere, since it has a temperature greater than absolute zero, also emits energy. The energy emitted by the atmosphere adds to that arriving at the surface. The energy arriving at the earth's surface is balanced by that leaving the surface (the 29 percent evaporation and mechanical heat transfer and the 104 percent upward infrared radiation). Similarly, the flow of energy into the atmosphere (incoming solar radiation not reflected from the top of the atmosphere, outbound evaporation and mechanical heat transfer, and upward infrared radiation from the earth's surface) balances the flow of energy away from the atmosphere (incoming solar radiation transmitted to the earth's surface, outgoing infrared radiation, and downward infrared radiation).

Some of the numbers shown in Figure 3.3 depend on the state of the atmosphere, for example, its temperature, greenhouse gas content, cloud distribution, and wind distribution. Others depend on the temperature of the land and ocean surfaces and/or on the ice cover. Changes in any and all of these characterizing features can produce changes in the individual heat fluxes and, in particular, changes in atmospheric and/or oceanic temperature. These can lead to changes in cloud cover and humidity that, in turn, induce further changes in the state of the atmosphere. In addition, both the interdependencies of the individual heat transfer contributions illustrated in Figure 3.2 and the (partial) list of possible changes in characterizing features just mentioned imply that increases in greenhouse gas concentrations will lead to modifications of the climate.

---

surface plus 104 percent upward radiation balanced by 50 percent of incoming solar continuing to the earth's surface, 70 percent outgoing radiation, and 88 percent downward radiation). These different energy transfers are due to the heat-trapping effects of the greenhouse gases in the atmosphere, the reemission of energy absorbed by these gases, and the cycling of energy through the various components in the diagram. The accuracy of the numbers in the diagram is typically ±5.

This diagram pertains to a period during which the climate is steady (or unchanging); that is, there is no net change in heat transfers into earth's surface, no net change in heat transfers into the atmosphere, and no net radiation change into the atmosphere-earth system from beyond the atmosphere.

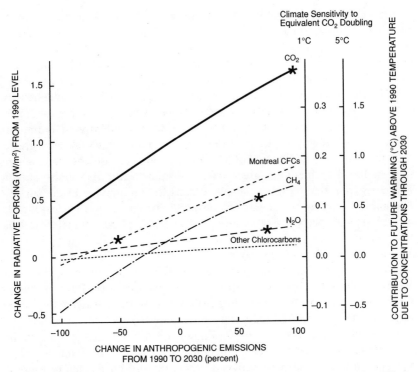

FIGURE 3.4 Commitment to future warming. An incremental change in radiative forcing between 1990 and 2030 due to emissions of greenhouse gases implies a change in global average equilibrium temperature (see text). The scales on the right-hand side show two ranges of global average temperature responses. The first corresponds to a climate whose temperature response to an equivalent of doubling of the preindustrial level of CO_2 is 1°C; the second corresponds to a rise of 5°C for an equivalent doubling of CO_2. These scales indicate the equilibrium commitment to future warming caused by emissions from 1990 through 2030. Assumptions are as in Figure 3.2.

To determine equilibrium warming in 2030 due to continued emissions of CO_2 at the 1990 level, find the point on the curve labeled "CO_2" that is vertically above 0 percent change on the bottom scale. The equilibrium warming on the right-hand scales is about 0.23°C (0.4°F) for a climate system with 1° sensitivity and about 1.2°C (2.2°F) for a system with 5° sensitivity. For CH_4 emissions continuing at 1990 levels through 2030, the equilibrium warming would be about 0.04°C (0.07°F) at 1° sensitivity and about 0.25°C (0.5°F) at 5° sensitivity. These steps must be repeated for each gas. Total warming associated with 1990-level emissions of the gases shown until 2030 would be about 0.41°C (0.7°F) at 1° sensitivity and about 2.2°C (4°F) at 5° sensitivity.

Scenarios of changes in committed future warming accompanying different greenhouse gas emission rates can be constructed by repeating this process for given emission rates and adding up the results.

SOURCE: Courtesy of Michael C. MacCracken.

It is important to recognize that these climate modifications are not in-stantaneous responses to the gas concentration changes that produce them. There is always a transient period, or "lag," before the equilibrium tempera-ture is reached. In an equilibrium condition, all of the incoming energy is radiated back to space. During the transient period, however, some of that incoming heat is still being used to heat up the deep oceans, which warm more slowly than the atmosphere. So the surface temperature of the planet is not yet at the temperature required to balance all of the incoming energy. Accordingly, the full commitment to temperature rise corresponding to the greenhouse gas accumulations at a given time may not become fully apparent for several decades (or more). The ultimate increase in global average temperature corresponding to a given increase in greenhouse gas concentra-tion is called the equilibrium global average temperature.

Figure 3.4 shows possible impacts on the global equilibrium temperature of changes in atmospheric concentrations of greenhouse gases. Two scales have been added to the right-hand side of the figure describing the radiative forcing properties of greenhouse gases (Figure 3.2). The scale labeled 5°C is associated with the hypothesis that the equivalent of doubling CO_2 would produce a 5° increase in the equilibrium global average temperature, and the 1°C scale accompanies the hypothesis that such a doubling would imply a 1° increase.

Figure 3.4 can be used to construct scenarios of changes in committed future warming resulting from policies that lead to different greenhouse gas emission rates. In particular, it can be used to produce a first approximation of the implications for greenhouse warming of policies resulting in speci-fied emission rates. This could be very helpful in establishing priorities for action. For example, the effect of reducing N_2O emissions by 10 percent is much smaller than that of reducing CH_4 by 10 percent.

Because it is so difficult to determine the extent of global warming from temperature measurements alone, it would be very helpful to monitor the radiation balance of the earth. There are currently, however, no functioning satellites capable of directly measuring outbound infrared radiation.

WHAT WE CAN LEARN FROM CLIMATE MODELS

The climate is extremely variable. Temperature, humidity, precipitation, and wind vary markedly from week to week and season to season. These natural variations are commonly much larger than the changes associated with greenhouse warming. There are also patterns to these natural variations, and it is these patterns that we think of as "climate."

The importance of greenhouse warming will be determined by the mag-nitude and abruptness of the associated climatic changes. Useful prediction requires credible quantitative estimates of those changes. Numerical computer simulations using general circulation models (GCMs) are generally considered the best available tools for anticipating climatic changes. Data from previous interglacial periods can be compared to results from computer models. Past conditions, however, are inexact metaphors for current increases in atmospheric concentrations of trace gases.

In order to simulate the intricate climatic system, GCMs themselves are complicated. They are complex computational schemes incorporating well-established scientific laws, empirical knowledge, and implicit representations. Mechanisms occurring on scales smaller than the smallest elements of the atmosphere, land, or oceans resolved in the GCM (i.e., "subgrid" scales) are represented by mathematical characterizations called "parameterizations." A typical GCM involves hundreds of thousands of equations and dozens of variables. About half a dozen different model types exist, and others are being developed.

One major drawback common to all current GCMs is that they lack adequately validated representations of important factors like cloud cover feedback, ocean circulation, and hydrologic interactions. Therefore it is unreasonable to expect the models to provide precise predictions, decades into the future, of global average temperature. This is especially so given that the expected global temperature rise is smaller than current naturally occurring regional temperature fluctuations on all time scales, daily, seasonal, and decadal.

General circulation models most commonly simulate the equilibrium climatic conditions associated with doubling atmospheric concentrations of CO_2 compared to preindustrial levels. Current GCM simulations based on these assumptions show a range of global average equilibrium temperature increases of 1.9° to 5.2°C (3.4° to 9.4°F). Many other calculations and simulations have been conducted; some with no cloud interactions, some with only a simple heat sink in place of oceans, some with no distinction between day and night. For the most part, these calculations also provide predictions within or close to this range.

The GCM results have been interpreted in slightly different ways by groups with differing perspectives. The Intergovernmental Panel on Climate Change (IPCC) used a range of 2° to 4°C (3.6° to 7.2°F) accompanying an equivalent doubling of preindustrial CO_2. The National Research Council's Board on Atmospheric Sciences and Climate used a range of 1.5° to 4.5°C (2.7° to 8.1°F), numbers receiving slightly greater usage among atmospheric scientists.

For the purposes of informed policy choice, it is crucial to acknowledge the limited capability of the GCMs. This is especially true because there is no clear connection between temperature records of the last century and the atmospheric accumulation of greenhouse gases. The temperature record for the northern hemisphere, for example, shows some rise until about 1940, a slight decrease from 1940 until the mid-1970s, followed by another rise.

There currently is no persuasive evidence that these variations were driven by growing atmospheric concentrations of greenhouse gases. The 100-year temperature record is not inconsistent with the range of climate sensitivity predicted by the GCMs, but neither is it inconsistent with the natural variability of the earth's climate.

There is another key limitation on the knowledge acquired from GCMs. In essence there are fewer than two dozen GCM simulation runs with five independent models on which to base conclusions. Every one incorporates untested and unvalidated hypotheses. They may be sensitive to changes in ways that current calculations have not yet revealed. For example, a recent examination of available computer runs shows considerable difference in the treatment of clouds. Although all runs yield similar results for a "clear sky" without clouds, their results vary substantially when clouds are included. The limited number of GCM simulations has two important consequences. First, there are too few runs to scientifically determine "most likely" values within the range. Second, it is not strictly possible to eliminate temperature changes of less than 1°C (1.8°F) or greater than 5°C (9°F).

Although GCMs cannot produce scientific "proof" in their predictions, they do map seasonal cycles of surface temperature quite well. GCMs also reasonably simulate daily and annual variability in air pressure patterns over large areas. In addition, most models represent the broad features of wind patterns, and the most recent models provide realistic simulations of winter and summer jet streams in the lower stratosphere. GCM simulations of other climate variables, such as precipitation, soil moisture, and north-south energy transport, are much less satisfactory. They do not provide credible quantitative estimates of the longer-term changes in global climate that might be driven by greenhouse gas accumulations.

The panel believes that prudent policy choices should be based on conservative assumptions in the face of large uncertainty. The panel uses a range of 1° to 5°C (1.8° to 9°F) and notes that it is broader than ranges adopted by other groups. In the panel's view, this range expresses much less unwarranted faith in the numbers produced by GCMs than does a narrower range.

Simply looking at the global average temperature associated with an equivalent doubling of preindustrial levels of CO_2 does not convey some important aspects of climate change. For example, there is no particular significance to exactly that level of greenhouse gas concentrations. In fact, unless serious efforts to limit releases of greenhouse gases are undertaken, atmospheric concentrations will exceed this level during the next century. In addition, GCMs may not produce reliable information about regional or local aspects of climate change that are of greatest interest to decision makers. These include amounts and timing of precipitation, frequency and timing of floods and temperature extremes, and wind extremes. Soil moisture content, dates of first and last frost, and timing of exceptionally hot days are all more important for plant life than is average temperature.

WHAT WE CAN LEARN FROM THE
TEMPERATURE RECORD

Global temperature data are available for the period 1890 to 1990, but those from the earlier half of the century are difficult to interpret with confidence. The most comprehensive assessment of the record of surface temperature, depicted in Figure 3.5, reveals a warming since the late nineteenth century of between 0.3° and 0.6°C (0.5° and 1.1°F). This warming is supported by several different kinds of information. Adjustments have been attempted to negate known complicating factors such as the biases introduced by the location of long-term measurement stations near urban areas with their attendant local warming.

To some extent the natural temperature variation in the climatic system makes it difficult to interpret the observational record. In particular, it is not possible to determine how much, if any, of the average global temperature rise over the last century might be attributed to greenhouse warming.

Increasing atmospheric concentrations of greenhouse gases may produce changes in both the magnitude and the rate of change of global average temperature that have few or no precedents in the earth's recent history. Figure 3.6 depicts estimates of the ranges of temperature in various periods of the past. A range of less than 1°C (1.8°F) was experienced in the last century, less than 2°C (3.6°F) in the last 10,000 years, and perhaps 7°C (13°F) in the last million years. Figure 3.6 shows these temperatures compared to a line representing an average global temperature of about 15°C (59°F), which is the global average temperature for the period 1951 to 1980. During this period the largest number of temperature recording stations were operating, and the averages for this period are commonly used as a base against which to assess global temperatures. Despite the modest decline in the average temperature in the northern hemisphere between about 1940 and 1975, we are still in an unusually warm period of earth's history. Thus the temperature increases of a few degrees projected for the next century are not only large in recent historical terms, but could also carry the planet into largely unknown territory.

Recent analyses, however, raise the possibility that some greenhouse warming could be offset by the cooling effect of sulfate aerosol emissions. Such emissions may have contributed to regional temperature variations and to differences in the temperature records of the northern and southern hemispheres.

On the geologic time scale, many things affect climate in addition to trace gases in the atmosphere: changes in solar output, changes in the

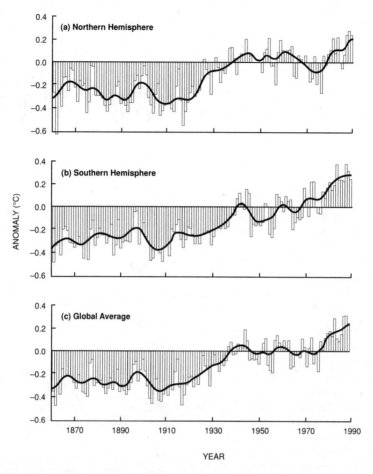

FIGURE 3.5 Combined land air and sea surface temperature relative to 1951-1980 average temperatures. Land air temperatures are typically measured 1 to 2 m above ground level. Sea surface temperatures are typically measured in the layer from the ocean's surface to several meters below.

SOURCES: Land air temperatures are updated from P. D. Jones, S. C. B. Raper, R. S. Bradley, H. F. Diaz, P. M. Kelly, and T. M. L. Wigley. 1986. Southern hemisphere surface air temperature variations, 1851-1984. *Journal of Climate and Applied Meteorology* 25:1213-1230. P. D. Jones, S. C. B. Raper, R. S. Bradley, H. F. Diaz, P. M. Kelly, and T. M. L. Wigley. 1986. Northern hemisphere surface air temperature variations, 1851-1984. *Journal of Climate and Applied Meteorology* 25:161-179. Sea surface temperatures are from the U.K. Meteorological Office and the COADS as adjusted by G. Farmer, T. M. L. Wigley, P. D. Jones, and M. Salmon. 1989. Documenting and explaining recent global-mean temperature changes. *Final Report to NERC*, Contract GR/3/6565. Norwich, United Kingdom: Climate Research Unit.

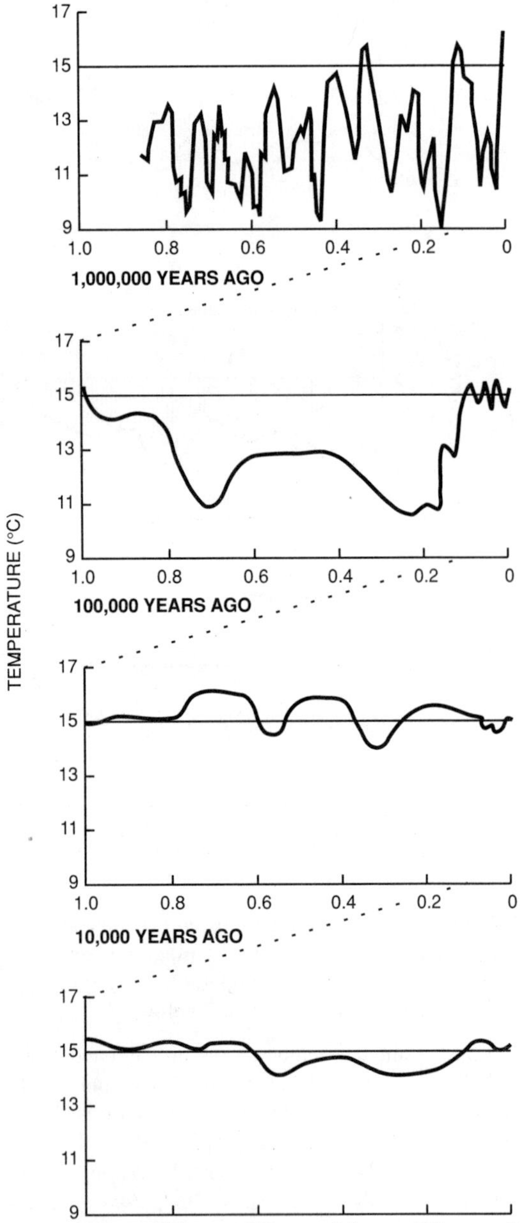

FIGURE 3.6 An approximate temperature history of the northern hemisphere for the last 850,000 years. The panels are at the same vertical scale. The top panel shows the last million years, the second panel amplifies the last 100,000 years, the third panel the last 10,000 years, and the bottom panel the last 1,000 years. The horizontal line at 15°C is included for reference and is the approximate average global temperature for the period 1951 to 1980. Considerable uncertainty attaches to the record in each panel, and the temperature records are derived from a variety of sources, for example, ice volume, as well as more direct data. Spatial and temporal (e.g., seasonal) variation of data sources is also considerable.

SOURCE: National Research Council. 1983. *Changing Climate: Report of the Carbon Dioxide Assessment Committee.* Washington, D.C.: National Academy Press. Figure 1.14.

earth's orbital path, changes in land and ocean distribution, changes in the reflectivity of the earth, and cataclysmic events like meteor impacts or extended volcanic eruptions.

These and other contributors to the earth's climate make it difficult to interpret the temperature history. Just as it is impossible to rule out natural variability, it is also impossible to rule out an underlying trend, so that the observed rise of 0.3° to 0.6°C (0.5° to 1.1°F) may be superimposed on a long-term (but nonuniform) rise or fall in global temperature.

SEA LEVEL

Average sea level of the oceans has varied throughout earth's history, and it is changing slightly today. Global sea level was about 100 m (328 feet) lower than current levels at the coldest point of the last ice age about 18,000 years ago. During the geologic past, there have been repeated variations from present sea level of more than this amount, both during times of intense glaciation and during periods in which the earth was free of ice. All of human civilization, however, has lived in a period when the average sea level was roughly as it is today.

Tide gauges measure sea level variations in relation to a fixed point on land and thus record "relative sea level" (RSL). RSL at any particular place varies over time and space. The direct causes of these variations include vertical motions of land to which the tide gauge or other measuring device is attached and changes in the volume of sea water in which the gauge is immersed. Differences in atmospheric pressure, water runoff from land, winds, ocean currents, and the density of sea water all cause variations in sea level in comparison to the global average sea surface.

Climate-related contributions to sea level change are of two kinds: variations in the actual amount or mass of water in the ocean basins (due mostly to changes in precipitation and runoff) and thermal expansion or contraction (changes in the density of water, due to variations of temperature and salinity).

The melting of the northern continental ice sheets between 15,000 and 7,000 years before the present probably accounts for most of the rise of the sea to present levels. Some have suggested that global warming due to increased atmospheric concentrations of greenhouse gases could lead to disintegration of the West Antarctic Ice Sheet, most of which is grounded below sea level. If climate warms and warmer ocean water intrudes under the ice sheet, the release of ice from the sheet would accelerate. The melting of the West Antarctic Ice Sheet is quite unlikely, however, and virtually impossible by the end of the next century. Estimates based on a combined oceanic and atmospheric GCM suggest that several hundred years would be required to achieve this amount of warming. The principal effects on sea level of greenhouse warming over the time period examined in this study will thus be due to thermal expansion.

Thermal expansion (and contraction) of the oceans, caused by a combination of increasing (decreasing) temperature and salinity, accounts for seasonal and interannual variations in sea level. These changes are not large enough, however, to account for the differences over tens of thousands of years. Warming the entire ocean from 0°C (32°F) to the current global average ocean temperature would result in a thermal expansion of about 10 m (33 feet).

In order to estimate oceanic thermal expansion from greenhouse warming, changes in the temperature, salinity, and density of the oceans have to be considered. Two types of models yield somewhat different results, depending on the assumptions made concerning transfer of heat into the deep ocean waters. The results are 20 to 110 cm (8 to 43 inches) when heat is carried downward by eddy diffusion and 10 to 50 cm (4 to 20 inches) when some downward diffusion is balanced by upwelling from the deep oceans. Both estimates are for the year 2100 and an equivalent of doubling the preindustrial atmospheric concentration of CO_2. The panel used a range of sea level rise from 0 to 60 cm (24 inches) for a doubling of CO_2.

POSSIBLE DRAMATIC CHANGES

The behavior of complex and poorly understood systems can easily surprise even the most careful observer. There are many aspects of the climate system that we do not understand well and which could provide such surprises. In particular, some radical changes that could result from increases in global temperatures must be considered plausible even though our understanding of them is not sufficient to analyze their magnitudes or likelihoods:

1. CH_4 could be released as high-latitude tundra melts, providing a sudden increase of CH_4, which would add to greenhouse warming.

2. The combination of increased runoff of fresh water in high latitudes and a reduced temperature differential from equator to pole could result in radically changed major ocean currents leading to altered weather patterns.

3. There could be a significant melting of the West Antarctic Ice Sheet, resulting in a sea level several meters higher than it is today.

Such major (and perhaps rapid) changes could be accompanied by more dramatic warming of the atmospheric and oceanic systems than is now apparent. No credible claim can be made that any of these events is imminent: nonetheless, with continuing greenhouse gas accumulations, none of them are precluded.

CONCLUSIONS

Neither the available climate record nor the limited capabilities of the climate models permit a reliable forecast of the implications of continued accumulations of greenhouse gases in the atmosphere. Neither do they permit an assessment as to whether the increase from 1890 to 1990 in global average temperature can be attributed to greenhouse gases. However, it is probable that some positive rate of warming will accompany continued accumulation of greenhouse gases in the atmosphere. An important question is: When will we have a more definite fix on the rate at which warming will occur?

It is unlikely that our understanding of such basic phenomena as the role of clouds and ocean dynamics will improve greatly over the next few years. It is also unlikely that a useful level of improvement in regional predictive capability will emerge in that time. A few decades may be required before atmospheric scientists produce the answers we seek. Some current limitations on our knowledge could be reduced by better characterization of such "subgrid" processes as precipitation and mechanical heat transfer, better coupling of atmospheric, land surface, and oceanic models, and better models of the role of ecosystems. Access to computers with greater capacity and speed would accelerate these improvements. All of these depend in large measure on progress in the scientific understanding on which the models are based.

The overall magnitude of greenhouse warming and its rate of emergence can only be inferred from several different kinds of information. The pieces of the puzzle are currently understood with varying degrees of uncertainty. Nevertheless, there is clear evidence and wide agreement among atmospheric scientists about several basic facts:

1. The atmospheric concentration of CO_2 has increased 25 percent during the last century and is currently increasing at about 0.5 percent per year.

2. The atmospheric concentration of CH_4 has doubled during that period and is increasing at about 0.9 percent per year.

3. CFCs, which are man-made and have been released into the atmosphere in quantity only since World War II, are currently increasing at about 4 percent per year.

4. Items 1, 2, and 3 are primarily direct consequences of human activities.

5. Current interpretations of temperature records reveal that the global average temperature has increased between 0.3° and 0.6°C (0.5° and 1.1°F) during the last century.

As a result, the panel concludes that there is a reasonable chance of the following:

1. In the absence of greater human effort to the contrary, greenhouse gas concentrations equivalent to a doubling of the preindustrial level of CO_2 will occur by the middle of the next century.

2. The sensitivity of the climatic system to greenhouse gases is such that the equivalent of doubling CO_2 could ultimately increase the average global temperature by somewhere between 1° and 5°C (1.8° and 9°F).

3. The transfer of heat to the deep oceans occurs more slowly than within the atmosphere or the upper layers of the ocean. The resulting transient period, or "lag," means that the global average surface temperature at any time is lower than the temperature that would prevail after all the redistribution had been completed. At the time of equivalent CO_2 doubling, for example, the global average surface temperature may be as little as one-half the ultimate equilibrium temperature associated with those concentrations.

4. A rise of sea level may accompany global warming, possibly in the range of 0 to 60 cm (0 to 24 inches) for the temperature range listed above.

5. Several troublesome, possibly dramatic, repercussions of continued increases in global temperature have been suggested. No credible claim can be made that any of these events is imminent, but none of them are precluded.

4

Policy Framework

The previous chapter clearly points out gaps in our knowledge and understanding of key physical phenomena in greenhouse warming. Nevertheless, current scientific knowledge seems to indicate that unconstrained releases of greenhouse gases from fossil fuel combustion and other sources would ultimately cause climate change. There are no specific conclusions, however, about the regional and local effects associated with increased atmospheric concentrations of greenhouse gases. Nor is there much indication about how rapidly the effects might emerge.

Our knowledge about other topics central to the analysis of the greenhouse warming problem is at least as insecure. The number of analyses of the overall impact on the economy of this country of greenhouse warming is even smaller than the number of GCM runs simulating an equivalent doubling of CO_2. Economic experts differ in their assumptions about future population and economic growth, technological change, and a host of other factors. Because the economic models must project trends far into the future, their results are likely to remain controversial.

How then, in the midst of this uncertainty, can we begin to evaluate policy options? Several concepts that can help us in that task are presented in the next two sections.

COMPARING MITIGATION AND ADAPTATION

Many different policies could be adopted in response to the prospect of greenhouse warming. In order to evaluate these policy options, it is useful to categorize them into three types:

1. Options that eliminate or reduce greenhouse gas emissions.

2. Options that "offset" emissions by removing greenhouse gases from the atmosphere, by blocking incident solar radiation, or by altering the reflection or absorption properties of the earth's surface.

3. Options that help human and ecologic systems adjust or adapt to new climatic conditions and events.

In this report the first and second types of interventions are referred to as "mitigation" since they can take effect prior to the onset of climate change and slow its pace. Mitigation options are discussed in more detail in Chapter 6 and Part Three. The third type of intervention is referred to as "adaptation" since its effects come into play primarily after climate has changed. A fuller discussion of adaptation appears in Chapter 5 and Part Four.

In comparing mitigation and adaptation, one consideration is whether a given action will, in addition to providing adaptation or mitigation benefits, also improve economic efficiency. Even progressive societies find much of their economic activity falling short of demonstrated "best practice." New, more efficient practices are being developed continually, but it takes time for them to diffuse throughout the economy. There are many obstacles to more rapid diffusion of better practice, including lack of information, insufficient supply of components or products, political interests, inappropriate incentives, and simple human inertia. In general, however, every society has many opportunities to improve its overall situation by reducing the gap between current practice and best practice. Many of the actions taken to deal with potential greenhouse warming could also improve economic well-being because they are more efficient than prevailing practice. These options should be distinguished from another class of actions: so-called "free-standing" actions, which satisfy other social or environmental objectives (and may or may not contribute to economic efficiency as such).

Figure 4.1 compares hypothetical mitigation and adaptation actions in response to potential greenhouse warming. If climate change occurs, and no mitigation or adaptation actions are undertaken, a substantial reduction in real income is likely over time. Initially, mitigation is likely to reduce real income more than either doing nothing or taking adaptation measures as climatic changes emerge. Ultimately, however, mitigation actions could result in higher real income than waiting and taking adaptation measures. In this scenario, investing in mitigation reduces consumption now, but produces advantages in the future. Expenditures on mitigation options should thus be seen as investments in the future.

Many combinations of mitigation and adaptation actions are possible. Choosing the best mix of mitigation and adaptation strategies depends in part on the discount rate applied to the investment. The higher the discount rate, the greater the case for postponement of costly actions. Use of discount rates is one way of assigning values to future outcomes.

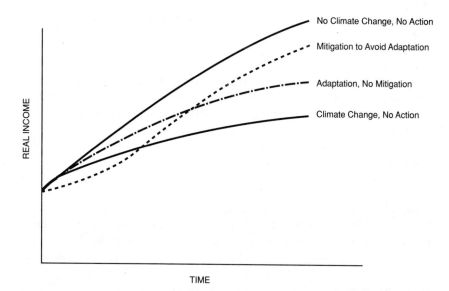

FIGURE 4.1 Schematic comparison of mitigation and adaptation. The uppermost curve plots world economic well-being, essentially the amount of real income available for consumption, assuming that there is no climate change. The lowest curve plots world economic well-being assuming that there is climate change and no actions are taken either to prevent or to cope with those changes. Notice that the axes are not defined quantitatively. Thus the curves are only relative, and this figure cannot be used to estimate the amount of economic welfare lost by expenditures on mitigation. Similarly, it cannot be used to estimate the time at which the return from expenditures on mitigation would exceed the return from expenditures on adaptation.

ASSIGNING VALUES TO FUTURE OUTCOMES

Most people have a time preference for money. They would rather have, for example, $100 to use today than $105 a year from now. Future costs and benefits are usually transformed into their "present value" by using a discount rate, which is similar to the interest on savings. Discount rates enable current and future returns to be compared.

A central, and controversial, issue is which discount rate to use in weighing the relative advantages of present and future impacts and costs. There are essentially three courses of action with regard to responding to potential greenhouse warming: (1) we can invest resources now to slow greenhouse gas emissions; (2) we can invest in other projects that might yield a higher return; and (3) we can defer any kind of investment in the future in favor of current consumption. Applying a discount rate near the yield on other investments—at least 10 percent per year in most countries, in real terms—

in evaluating responses to greenhouse warming would lead to the conclusion that our investment dollars could be most efficiently used in capital projects, education, or other sectors. It suggests that we should not take costly, low-payoff actions to reduce greenhouse gas emissions. High discount rates place a low value on future outcomes. Applying a low discount rate to greenhouse investment choices—say, 3 percent per year—would make investing now to avoid greenhouse warming more attractive. But such a low discount rate means that other investment opportunities have been exhausted or are being ignored. It is likely that there will be more investment opportunities with returns of greater than 3 percent than there are available funds. A low discount rate on resources invested in response to potential climate change is inconsistent with a high return on capital investment.

The panel makes no attempt to resolve this issue. This study uses rates of 3, 6, and 10 percent in calculations to ensure that unique circumstances that would alter assessment of the outcome are not overlooked. Because consumers sometimes act in ways that indicate an even higher discount rate in their purchases, a rate of 30 percent is also used in considering some mitigation options. For the purposes of comparing options and arriving at recommendations for action, the panel used a single real discount rate of 6 percent per year. Use of a 10 percent discount rate would decrease the present value of the low-cost options but would not change their rankings.

A METHOD FOR COMPARING OPTIONS

Using the concepts described above, we can compare options by carefully enumerating the impacts of action and inaction and then trying to find a course that minimizes the net costs of the impacts of mitigation and adaptation.

More specifically, the anticipated consequences of greenhouse warming (both adverse and beneficial) can be arrayed to produce a "damage function" showing the anticipated costs and benefits associated with projected climatic changes. The mitigation and adaptation options can be similarly arrayed according to what they would cost and how effective they would be. A well-designed response will involve balancing incremental impacts and costs. A sensible policy requires that the level of action chosen be "cost-effective," which means that the total cost of attaining a level of reduction of climate change should be minimized.

Ideally, the evaluation would consider the full costs associated with each mitigation alternative. Called "full social cost pricing," such an analysis would allocate to each option not only the costs of its development, construction, operation, and decommissioning or disposal, but also those of environmental or health problems resulting from its use. Burning coal, for example, not only emits greenhouse gases, but also contributes to a variety of health problems (for nearby residents as well as coal miners) and to environmental problems such as acid rain. All these would be included in full social cost pricing. A different example involves increasing automobile fuel efficiency by reducing the size and weight of vehicles. Reducing vehicle size results both in reduced emissions of greenhouse gases, a benefit, and in increased likelihood of injury from collisions with larger vehicles, a cost. Ideally, all costs and benefits would be considered.

In practice, such a framework can be used only in an approximate manner. It is impossible to determine all of the costs of all options today, much less of climatic changes that will not occur for 50 to 100 years. Many of the important concerns are difficult to measure and are not fully captured in prices or other market indicators. Nevertheless, the panel finds this conceptual framework to be a constructive way to organize the evaluation of policy options.

Assessing Mitigation Options

Most mitigation options considered here use currently available techniques and equipment that could be installed within 10 years. Actions that reduce or offset emissions of greenhouse gases or otherwise deal with greenhouse warming are evaluated in terms of annualized costs and annualized reduction of CO_2 emissions. Options addressing greenhouse gases other than CO_2 are translated into the equivalent CO_2 emissions. Annualized costs (or emissions) are determined by estimating the total costs in constant dollars (or emissions in CO_2 equivalent) of that option over its lifetime. This includes the so-called "engineering" costs of construction, installation, operation, maintenance, and decommissioning or disposal. The total discounted cost is divided by the number of years the option is expected to last, resulting in the annualized cost of that option. Annualized emission reductions are calculated in a similar fashion.

The mitigation options in this menu are then ranked according to their cost-effectiveness. Those achieving the reduction of CO_2 or CO_2-equivalent emissions most cheaply are ranked highest. Finally, the overall potential of each option is estimated because there are limits on how much can be achieved with each option. For example, avoiding emissions by using hydroelectric power generation might be comparatively cheap, but there are few remaining locations in the United States where dams could be built. Its overall potential is therefore relatively small.

This method has distinct advantages and disadvantages. One advantage is that it enables options with different lifetimes to be compared. The costs (and benefits) of a natural gas-fired electricity plant may accrue over 25 to 30 years, a much longer period than the periods associated with vehicle efficiency improvements, since the typical life of a car is probably not more than 10 years. A disadvantage is that because implementation of the high-priority options would change the pattern of emissions over time, the cost-effectiveness of various options during the later portion of their operating life might be different. For example, programs to use electricity more efficiently appear quite cost-effective in the panel's current analysis. If such programs were aggressively implemented, the need for new electricity generating capacity over the next few decades would be reduced. Thus the cost-effectiveness of investments in power generation in, say, 2010 could be altered by electricity conservation programs today. This study makes no attempt to account for such possibilities, but they could be examined in future studies.

Each time a new analysis is performed, a new series of "least cost" options will emerge. This circumstance allows policymakers to regularly adjust actions to ensure the most efficient use of resources.

Assessing Adaptation Options

Options intended to help people and unmanaged systems of plants and animals adapt to future climate change are more difficult to assess than mitigation programs. First, we must speculate about future climatic conditions. GCMs are currently unable to accurately predict local and regional events and conditions of greatest interest to policymakers.

Second, we must predict how the affected systems are likely to react to the changing conditions. Sensitivity to climate change depends on many things, including physiological response to temperature or moisture stress and dependency on other components of the system. A crucial concept in the assessment is the speed at which the system adjusts. If adjustments are made more rapidly than climatic conditions change, the system should be able to adapt without government assistance, although not without cost.

In the panel's analysis of adaptation options, "benchmark" costs were developed on the basis of the costs of contemporary extreme weather events or conservation and restoration programs. These estimates were used to develop a measure of the magnitude of the costs that might be associated with climate change.

But the panel recognizes that many issues cannot be quantified. This is especially true for impacts, and the impacts of concern are of three fundamentally different kinds.

First are the consequences, either beneficial or harmful, for things that are exchanged in markets. Agriculture, for example, will be affected by changes in precipitation patterns and dates of frost in ways that will be captured in prices and other market indicators. These are reasonably easy to quantify, and adding up the market effects gives a clear picture of the impacts.

Second are things whose values are not well captured in markets. Genetic resources are generally undervalued because there are few property rights in genetic resources and people therefore cannot capture the benefits of the investments they might make in preserving biodiversity. Many species are unlikely ever to have marketable attributes, and it is virtually impossible to predict which ones may ultimately have economic value. These consequences are not well identified in current accounting systems.

Third are items that some people value for reasons that have little to do with their "usefulness" or economic worth. This "ecocentric" valuation assigns intrinsic value to the living world. Species loss, in this view, is undesirable regardless of any economic value that may derive from those species. Humanity, it is held, should not do things that alter the course of natural evolution.

The panel recognizes the difficulty of measuring these noneconomic criteria in the quantitative method described above. Since such values are codified, to some extent, in laws (e.g., those to protect biodiversity), potential greenhouse warming responses must be consistent with protection of the noneconomic values. These may be among the most difficult values to accommodate if climates change substantially. In spite of the difficulties outlined above, the panel believes this cost-effectiveness approach is the most useful method for evaluating policies involving response to greenhouse warming.

OTHER FACTORS AFFECTING POLICY CHOICES ABOUT GREENHOUSE WARMING

Once policy options have been ranked, certain factors not directly related to greenhouse warming come into play in the decision-making process.

One such factor concerns risk perception. People differ in their willingness to take risks. We can expect people to differ in their reaction to the potential and uncertain threat of greenhouse warming as well. Some people may be distressed by the possibility that cherished parts of their cultural heritage or natural landscapes might be lost. Others might be unwilling to accept some aspects of proposed adjustments—perhaps abandoning their traditional homeland and moving elsewhere. In any case, people and organizations will differ in their judgments about how much society should pay to reduce the chance of uncertain climate change.

Another factor is the constraint of limited resources. The United States is a large, wealthy country. Many other nations are severely constrained in their ability to act because of limited financial and human resources.

5

Adaptation

The amount of money, labor, and equipment we are willing to expend to avoid greenhouse warming depends in part on how we view the results of climate change and how much we are willing to risk possible negative consequences. Estimating all these outcomes is difficult, however, because we cannot predict with certainty what changes will occur globally and we cannot predict at all the effects in a given region. Regardless of what the changes will be, a necessary first step in determining the proper allocation of resources is to examine the ability of natural systems and humans to adapt.

METHODS OF ADAPTATION

Humans, animals, and plants are able to adapt to different climates. Animals and plants live in the Himalayas and in Death Valley, although not all species thrive in both. Human adaptability is shown by our living and working in both Riyadh and Barrow.

Human societies can and do thrive in many different climates, but it is the rate of climate change as much as its magnitude that could pose a threat. Disasters caused by severe weather and degradation of the environment illustrate the kinds of disruptions that could accompany rapid climate change. There are five alternative human responses: (1) modify the hazard, as by channeling rivers that are prone to flooding; (2) prevent or limit impacts, as by building dikes; (3) move or avoid the loss, as by implementing flood plain zoning; (4) share the loss, as by providing insurance; and (5) bear the loss, as by losing all or part of a crop. Thus we have a large menu of potential adaptation options, some of which are best made before an event and some after.

Plants and animals will always be found regardless of climatic changes in the ranges discussed here. The threat to the natural communities of plants and animals, called ecosystems, from greenhouse warming also comes from its projected rate of change as much as its magnitude. If the climate changes as rapidly as some computer models project, the present natural ecosystems may become fragmented and break up. New communities may replace them with different mixes of species. Long-lived plants like trees, for example, might persist. If ill adapted to the new conditions, however, they would fail to compete and reproduce. Species better fitted to the new climate would immigrate, sometimes hastened by disturbances of various kinds. Species well suited to the changing conditions may become more dominant, or pioneer species that could fill a particular niche may thrive in the new conditions. Certain ecosystems might vanish if the climate that currently sustains them disappears or changes its location faster than the key species are able to migrate.

THE ROLE OF INNOVATION

Much human adaptation involves the invention and diffusion of technological "hardware" or "software." Examples of technological hardware include air conditioners that make hot days comfortable and tractors that cultivate large tracts of land in a few days if spring is late. Software includes information, rules, and procedures like weather forecasts or insurance restrictions. Knowledge and new procedures are generally indispensable for adopting new hardware. Major breakthroughs like irrigation usually consist of innovations in social organization and financing as well as new machinery.

Many past innovations in hardware and software have helped people adapt themselves and their activities to climate and variable weather. Food preservation in warm weather, refrigeration and air conditioning, antifreeze for all-weather automobile travel, and weather satellites to aid prediction all help. Such innovations can occur rapidly in comparison to the 40 to 50 years envisioned for the equivalent doubling of atmospheric CO_2. For example, in 1900 California had little crop production; in 1985 it produced twice as many dollars of crops as second-place Iowa. Penicillin was discovered in 1928; by 1945 it was saving thousands of lives.

The question frequently asked is how rapidly inventions can replace existing equipment and how fast other technology can be supplanted. About two-thirds of capital stock in most industrialized countries is in machinery, and one-third is in buildings and other structures. This capital stock turns over more rapidly than might be expected. Most current office space, for example, is in buildings built in the last 20 years. In Japan, the average period for virtually complete replacement of machinery and equipment ranges from about 22 years in textiles to about 10 years in industries like telecommunications or electrical machinery. Replacement can be fast in agriculture, too. The estimated lifetime of particular strains for five major crops in the United States is less than 10 years and is expected to be even shorter in the future.

As societies have become more affluent, they have reduced their sensitivity to natural phenomena in many ways. Overall, the trend is toward systems of transportation, communication, and energy production and use that are less sensitive to climate. Improved technology and social organization also seem to have lessened the impacts of climate fluctuations on food supply over the last 100 years. In the time frame over which the effects of greenhouse warming are felt, more societies may become more robust with respect to climate change.

ASSESSING IMPACTS AND ADAPTIVE CAPACITY

The data and analyses used in this study to assess impacts and adaptive capacity are drawn mostly, but not exclusively, from the United States. Few other countries share the United States' combination of wealth, low population density, and range of climates. Moreover, the panel recognizes that our domestic well-being is intimately tied to what happens in other countries. Major international shifts in trade flows, agricultural production, energy demand patterns, and more could profoundly affect this country. But a full analysis of such global interactions remains for future studies.

The assessment of impacts in this study examines separately the sensitivity of various human and ecologic systems to climate change. Not all interactions could be assessed, even though the panel recognizes that such interactions may be relevant. For example, unmanaged natural systems have important interactions with forestry. Although the assessment of forestry considers shifts in ranges of pests and other key species, major alterations in unmanaged natural systems may contain unforeseen problems for forestry. The assessment here is an initial appraisal of impacts and adaptive capabilities of affected human and natural systems in the United States; additional effort is necessary for a more complete understanding of these issues.

CO_2 Fertilization of Green Plants

An increasing atmospheric concentration of CO_2 would increase agricultural production by enhancing the use of sunlight and slowing transpiration in some plants. The overall production of organic material also depends on other factors such as temperature, moisture, and nutrients. It is difficult to anticipate the amount of increased organic production accompanying greenhouse warming because extrapolation from small-scale laboratory experiments to whole fields of crops or to complete systems of unmanaged plants and animals is uncertain. The increases in photosynthesis and slowing of transpiration, however, would probably be somewhat less than observed in laboratory experiments. These effects would apply to plants in agriculture, managed forests, and unmanaged ecosystems.

Agriculture

Changes in average temperature are probably less important for agricultural productivity than changes in precipitation and evaporation. Whether the projected changes are calculated as precipitation and evaporation or the resulting changes in crop yields, the different climate scenarios produced by different general circulation models (GCMs) yield large variations for agriculture. But farming has always been sensitive to the weather, and experience suggests that farmers adapt quickly, especially in comparison to the rate at which greenhouse warming would occur. Countries like the United States, which encompass many climate zones and have active and aggressive agricultural research and development, would probably be able to adapt their farming to climatic changes deriving from greenhouse warming. Poorer countries with less wealth or fewer climate zones may have more difficulty avoiding problems or taking advantage of better conditions.

Managed Forests and Grasslands

Forests and grasslands each cover more than a quarter of the United States. Trees have long lifetimes, and are unlikely to adjust rapidly enough by themselves to accommodate rapid warming. Forests, however, can be managed to preserve ample forest products. Middle-aged forests are at most risk if climate changes, since young forests can be replaced cheaply and older ones are valuable to sustain. The adaptation of valuable forests by management is possible using methods that are flexible and work in many climates.

Natural Landscape

The natural landscape consists of unmanaged ecosystems that include many species of animals, plants, and microorganisms harvested as game, fruit, or drugs. Ecosystems absorb CO_2, emit O_2, and cleanse air and water. Ecosystems also emit CO_2, CH_4, and other hydrocarbons. For a variety of reasons, the adaptation of natural ecosystems to climate change is more problematic than that of managed systems like farms or plantation forests. The principal impacts of climate change are expected to be on plants. Impacts on animals would mostly be indirect, through changes in plant functioning and vegetation dynamics, but significant direct effects of climate change are possible. Some species of birds appear especially responsive to temperature and may shift their ranges relatively rapidly. Climate change may make some species extinct, but the diversity of ecosystems would probably protect those functions that are carried out by many species. For example, diseases removed first the chestnut and then the elm from eastern forests, but the loss of their capacity to absorb CO_2 was quickly made up by other species. Some ecological processes, however, are carried out by only a few species. Only a few species enhance soil productivity by fixing nitrogen, and the grazing of a single large species may alter a landscape. If climate change removed one of these species or encouraged another, even a diverse ecosystem could be affected. Even small climatic changes resulting from greenhouse warming would be likely to alter unmanaged ecosystems. The adaptation of the natural landscape can be helped by moving species when they are in trouble, providing corridors along which those that can may move, and intervening to maintain diversity of species in key ecosystems.

Marine and Coastal Environments

Concern about coastal swamps and marshlands comes from their special ecological value and the fact that they are already under stress from human development and pollution. Wetlands have persisted in the past despite slowly changing sea levels. Greenhouse warming could induce sea level rise, however, faster than new wetlands could form. In addition, human activity could constrain such movement if wetlands are bounded by dikes, bulkheads, or other structures. Climate change also could alter upwelling of deep ocean waters or paths of major currents and thus wind and precipitation patterns. Areas of upwelling are among the biologically most productive ocean habitats, and such changes could affect fisheries substantially. We do not understand these phenomena well enough, however, to predict the ecological consequences of coastal or ocean changes with confidence. At present, the potential for human intervention to ease adaptation in marine ecosystems seems limited.

Water Resources

Climate change affects natural seasonal and yearly variations in water resources by changing precipitation, evaporation, and runoff. The first indications that the demand for water is exceeding the supply usually come during drought. Changes in water supply due to greenhouse warming could be moderated, for example, by storage (in natural aquifers or constructed reservoirs) or joint operation of water systems. Demand for water can be reduced through a variety of management techniques, including conservation and price incentives. Constructing dams, canals, and other facilities takes time, and so such adaptation actions need to be taken well in advance. Actions to deal with current variability of water supply should help prepare for the possible consequences of greenhouse warming.

Industry and Energy

Most industrial sectors, including electric power generation, are only moderately sensitive to climate change. Access to regular water supplies is the largest single problem. In most sectors, the planning horizon and lifetime of investments is shorter than the rates of change we could expect from greenhouse warming. In general, industry in the United States will likely adapt to greenhouse warming without much difficulty.

Tourism and Recreation

Tourism and recreation are more sensitive to climate change than some other sectors because part of the industry is closely associated with nature. This part of tourism and recreation will necessarily migrate as the attractive conditions and areas move. Although specific regions will be adversely or favorably affected, for a country as large as the United States, the overall effect will probably be negligible.

Settlements and Coastal Structures

Direct climatic changes of greatest importance to human settlements are changes in the extremes and seasonal averages of temperature, and in the geographic and seasonal distributions of rainfall. Although these direct climatic changes may be important, the secondary effects of greenhouse warming on the levels of water bodies are much more important. Urban areas will probably choose to protect existing sites rather than move. Adaptations can be encouraged by changing building codes and land use planning. Allowances should be made for climate change when long-lived structures or facilities are constructed or renovated.

Human Health

Humans have successfully adjusted to diverse climates. Human health could be affected by greenhouse warming because people are sensitive to climate directly as well as being susceptible to diseases whose carriers, or "vectors," are sensitive to climate. In the United States, however, the rate of improvements in health due to better technology and its application should greatly exceed the threat to health due to climate change. These improvements would not, of course, result from choices about costs and benefits of responding to greenhouse warming as such. The health consequences may be worse in countries with fewer resources.

Migration

Historical evidence suggests that migration over long distances, such as occurred in the United States during the Dust Bowl period, is not an automatic response to climate change. Migrations typically follow established routes and cover relatively short distances. While economic and other stresses will continue to provide incentives for migrants to move to the United States or other industrialized countries, there is unlikely to be climate-driven migration on a scale that could not be managed, at least in the next two decades. What happens over the course of a decade or two, however, can set the stage for developments over the longer term. Nevertheless, taking steps now to prevent future migration would not be justified given human adaptability to change and uncertainties about which areas would be affected.

Political Tranquility

Concern about political tranquility stems from fear that the occasional disaster of today might become persistent tomorrow and that accumulation of problems may become overwhelming. Countries outside the industrial world may lack the institutions or resources to manage additional environmental crises. Difficulties of organizing coordinated, multilateral responses to problems such as hunger are already evident. Greenhouse warming could aggravate present economic, political, and social problems, swamping national governments and international assistance activities and programs.

SOME IMPORTANT INDICES

The same diversity that illustrates how humanity and nature adjust to environmental conditions shows that global averages are inappropriate as foundations for thinking about impact or adaptation. Because most adaptations are local, their cost cannot be calculated until such factors as future water supply can be predicted in specific regions. Strategic indices of greenhouse warming for agencies to monitor and scientists to predict include the following:

1. Seasonal and yearly variation in regional supplies of water to streams and soils.

2. Variability of ocean currents, particularly those affecting regional habitability and coastal life.

3. Variation in regional sea level and inshore height of waves.

4. Variability of the timing of such biological events as blooms and migrations.

Since even future global averages are uncertain, we will not soon know what these four regional indices will indicate and therefore will not be able to predict local impacts and to design specific adaptations. Nonetheless, monitoring the local climate, including the water in streams and seasonal events, is crucial over time and will eventually lay the foundation for designing and selecting these specific adaptations.

EVALUATING ADAPTATION OPTIONS

It is difficult to evaluate adaptation options in the face of uncertainties. Consider a hypothetical bridge over an estuary as an example. An added meter of height above sea level might add $100,000 to current construction costs. If that additional clearance were not included at the time of construction, and the sea level rose enough to require it after 50 years, the retrofit raising of the bridge might cost $5 million. Discounted at 6 percent per year, the present value of that $5 million is $271,000. If we were certain the sea would rise, we could realize a benefit of $171,000 in this example by adding the meter of clearance today rather than waiting.

This kind of comparison of current and future investment should be performed when each adaptation option is considered. There are three key elements in this approach: the probability that the outcome will require adaptive action, the discount rate, and the time at which future spending would have to take place. Obviously, reducing our uncertainty about future climate would justify larger investments in adaptations.

Economical adaptation that lessens sensitivity to climate is desirable. Developing drought-resistant crops or using water more efficiently should enable us to deal with weather variability today and position us to cope with future climate change. Poorer countries may have greater difficulties. They typically lack money, information, and expertise. Often they are sorely stressed by current weather extremes, and additional strains accompanying climate change may make their lot worse. If greenhouse warming improves their situation, they may have difficulty taking advantage of their good fortune because of the limits on their capacity to respond.

In general, there are four limits on human responses to greenhouse warming. One is time. Time is needed for people to adapt in a location to a new climate, to design and build new infrastructures, or to adapt by moving to a region where the climate is preferred. Although time is needed to adapt managed things like farming, the historical evidence suggests that farmers can respond, especially in developed countries. The second limit is water. Some uses, like irrigation or cooling, use water in large quantities. Transporting large quantities of water over great distances is possible but expensive. The third limit, and a common one, is money. Adaptations like furnaces and air conditioners, sea walls and canals take money. The fourth limit is techniques and information that are used to make decisions and set priorities.

The recommendations in this report address these areas. It is important that we incorporate these limitations into our thinking when we imagine the effects of the climate of 2030 imposed on the people and landscape of that time.

ADAPTING TO CLIMATE CHANGE

Just as strategic planning requires ranking greenhouse warming with all the other changes ahead, it also demands sorting human activities and nature into classes of sensitivity and adaptability to greenhouse warming alone. Then the more sensitive and serious consequences of greenhouse warming can be ranked within the whole spectrum of changes, and adaptational responses can be decided accordingly. The Adaptation Panel (see Part Four) developed the classifications presented in Table 5.1, which are used here to categorize adaptation options with respect to the United States.

Activities with Low Sensitivity

Fortunately, several human activities have low sensitivity, allowing us to concentrate on others. Machinery and buildings are renewed faster than the projected pace of greenhouse warming, and so industry should have little trouble adapting. In general, the decision-making horizons in industry are shorter than the time at which most climatic impacts would emerge. Most industries in countries like the United States can thus be expected to adapt as the climate changes.

The expected climatic changes are within the range people now experience where they live and to which those who move usually learn to adapt. In industrial countries, public health should be less at risk than it is elsewhere. The pace of improvements in health from better technology and public measures can and likely will exceed any deterioration from greenhouse warming. Epidemics from causes already known, failure to control population, and chemical pollution are more serious threats to health than greenhouse warming.

Activities That Are Sensitive But Can Be Adapted at a Cost

As the most valuable outdoor human activity, farming would have the greatest impact on national income due to greenhouse warming. Average warming would not greatly affect yields, but seasonal variations in precipi-

TABLE 5.1 The Sensitivity and Adaptability of Human Activities and Nature

	Low Sensitivity	Sensitive, but Adaptation at Some Cost	Sensitive, Adaptation Problematic
Industry and energy	X		
Health	X		
Farming		X	
Managed forests and grasslands		X	
Water resources		X	
Tourism and recreation		X	
Settlements and coastal structures		X	
Human migration		X	
Political tranquility		X	
Natural landscapes			X
Marine ecosystems			X

NOTE: Sensitivity can be defined as the degree of change in the subject for each "unit" of change in climate. The impact (sensitivity times climate change) will thus be positive or negative depending on the direction of climate change. Many things can change sensitivity, including intentional adaptations and natural and social surprises, and so classifications might shift over time. For the gradual changes assumed in this study, the Adaptation Panel believes these classifications are justified for the United States and similar nations.

tation and evaporation would. Experience shows, however, that farming must continually adapt to cope with, and even exploit, the stresses and fickle nature of climate. Adaptations to climate change would be required in both rich and poor countries to protect crops, substitute new ones, and protect their foundations of soil and water.

Although less thoroughly managed than farming and growing a crop with a long life, regeneration and management techniques are available that should enable needed forest products to be sustained.

Should climate warm, most cities would try to adapt rather than abandon their sites. Although the adaptation might be costly, the costs would in most cases be lower than the cost of moving the city. By far the highest costs would be in coastal cities, where added protection would be needed in response to storms if the sea rises. Where the coast is thinly settled, protective zoning or even retreat may be sensible.

For the nation as a whole, tourism and recreation seem adaptable to greenhouse warming at little net cost. Adaptation within a country or a region, however, may entail switching a function or activity from one geographical area to another. Some regions may win a new activity, while the same activity becomes untenable and is lost in another. The gradual changes foreseen in this study will combine these pluses and minuses, with a likely small net change for a nation of our size and diversity.

Activities That Are Sensitive with Questionable Adjustment or Adaptation

In the unmanaged systems of plants and animals that occupy much of our landscape and oceans, however, the rate of change of some key processes may be slower than the pace of greenhouse warming, making their future questionable. Unmanaged ecosystems respond relatively slowly, and hence their adaptability to greenhouse warming is more questionable than that of the managed systems of crops on a farm or timber in a plantation.

This slow response comes from the long lives of some of their components, like trees that last longer than the ones planted for timber. It comes from the slow and chancy arrival of seed and birds traveling on the wind, in currents, or along corridors rather than being intentionally transported and planted by farmers. Response is slow because the replacement of plants and animals on an acre of wild land or in an estuary can take decades or centuries and because evolution takes centuries or millennia.

Greenhouse warming would not likely make land barren except at the arid extremes of existing climates if climate became drier. What *is* likely are changes in the composition of ecological communities in favor of those species that are able to move rapidly and far and the disappearance of some species that move slowly. Marine plants and animals inhabiting intertidal regions of rocky shores undoubtedly would be affected by rising sea level. Coral reefs, which are breeding and feeding areas for many of the world's tropical fisheries, could suffer because they appear to be particularly sensitive to water temperature changes.

Although the impacts of the whole range of climatic changes on the functioning of ecosystems cannot be predicted with confidence, the risk of their happening justifies some of the adaptation strategies recommended in Chapter 9 and adds to the justification for some of the mitigation strategies.

Cataclysmic Climatic Changes

Large changes in climate have happened in the past. Desperate masses of people have fled drought or flood in places with marginal farming and growing population. These disasters occurred before greenhouse gases began increasing, and they could occur again. The panel knows of no convincing attempt, however, to compute the probability of cataclysmic changes such as the stopping of the current that warms Europe. Because the probability and nature of such unexpected changes are unknown, the panel cannot project their impacts or devise adaptations to them.

CONCLUSIONS

As discussed in Chapter 3, a rise in global average temperatures in the next century above those of any period in the last 200,000 years cannot be excluded. Unfortunately, there currently is no way to reliably determine the effects of such global changes for particular regions. These changes will probably be gradual. People in the United States likely will have no more difficulty adapting to such future changes than to the most severe conditions in the past, such as the Dust Bowl.* Other countries may have more difficulty, especially poor countries or those with fewer climate zones. Some natural systems of plants and animals would be stressed beyond sustainability in their current form, a prospect some people may find unacceptable. The stronger the concern about these various changes, the greater the motivation to slow greenhouse warming.

In addition, the panel has not found it possible to rule out or rule in such major disturbances as sudden and major changes in regional climates, ocean currents, atmospheric circulations, or other natural or social phenomena. At present, it is not possible to analyze their likelihood or consequences.

Human societies and natural systems of plants and animals change over time and react to changing climate just as they react to other forces. It would be fruitless to try to maintain all human and natural communities in their current forms. There are actions that can be undertaken now, however, to help people and natural systems adjust to some of the anticipated impacts of greenhouse warming. The panel recommends action now (see Chapter 9) based on gradual climate change. Such action would be more important if climate change proved to be sudden and unanticipated rather than smooth and predictable.

---

*See dissenting statement by panel member Jessica Mathews at the end of Part One.

6

Mitigation

Greenhouse warming is a global phenomenon, an important fact with regard to mitigation because releases of greenhouse gases have the same potential effect on global climate regardless of their country of origin. An efficient mitigation strategy for the United States would allow the United States to take cooperative action in other countries; some of the most attractive low-cost mitigation options may be in the poorest developing countries.

This analysis of mitigation costs and the potential for reducing potential greenhouse warming was developed by the Mitigation Panel (see Part Three) and is derived almost entirely from experience and data in the United States. The analytical framework is general, however, and could be applied in other countries.

The application of this framework to a diverse array of mitigation options is a pioneering effort. These "first-order" analyses are meant only to be initial estimates of the cost-effectiveness of these options. They demonstrate a method that can be used in determining appropriate mitigation options. The intent is to illustrate the manner in which options should be evaluated with the best estimates available.

This analysis is a cross-sectional, as opposed to a longitudinal, analysis of options over time. It does not attempt, for example, to project future levels of economic activity and their implications for greenhouse gas emissions. The analysis does account, however, for future consequences of current actions. The direct effect of each option on greenhouse gas emissions is assessed. The panel does not examine those options under the different overall emission rates that might occur at future times. This analysis must therefore be seen as an initial assessment of mitigation options in terms of their return on investment under current conditions. A subsequent analysis should consider appropriate strategies under conditions existing at the time.

THE ROLE OF COST-EFFECTIVENESS

A mitigation strategy should use options that minimize effects on domestic or world economies. Strategies therefore should be evaluated on the basis of cost-effectiveness as well as other considerations. Care must be taken to ensure that estimates of both costs and effects are comparable. Cost calculations, for example, need to use consistent assumptions about energy prices, inflation, or discount rates. Benefits must be evaluated in standard terms, such as the equivalent amount of CO_2 emission reductions.

The cost of mitigation may include a number of components, some of which are difficult to measure. Three different kinds of costs need to be distinguished. First are direct expenditures to reduce emissions or otherwise reduce potential greenhouse warming. These include, for example, the purchasing of energy-efficient air conditioners or insulation. Second are long-term investments that increase the overall efficiency of large-scale systems. Examples include investment in more efficient electricity generation and industrial facilities. Third are possible substitutions among final goods and services that require different amounts of energy. An example is the substitution of public transit for private automobiles.

Current expenditures to reduce greenhouse warming are in principle the easiest to measure because there generally are current market transactions from which to obtain data. For longer-term capital expenditures, a discount rate must be used to calculate the present value of costs so they can be compared with costs of other options. Where major substitutions of final goods or services are required, the full costs are difficult to determine. The potential loss in value to consumers of the changes in consumption patterns must be estimated.

TECHNOLOGICAL COSTING VERSUS ENERGY MODELING

There are two choices for estimating the costs of various mitigation options: "technological costing" and "energy modeling." Technological costing develops estimates on the basis of a variety of assumptions about the technical aspects, together with estimates—often no more than guesses—of the costs of implementing the required technology. This approach can be useful for evaluating emerging technologies when it is hard to apply statistical methods to estimate costs from market data. Technological costing relies implicitly on economic assumptions, and like energy modeling assumes that direct costs are a good measure of total cost.

Energy modeling uses a variety of techniques to project energy uses and supplies by region over time. Often, energy modeling uses data on prices and quantities consumed to construct statistical behavioral relationships. Unlike technological costing, energy models strive to ensure that the projections are internally consistent by keeping track of the overall relationship between energy supplies and demands.

Neither approach is perfect. Technological costing studies are often criticized as providing overly optimistic estimates. Their main weaknesses are that they are not always consistent with observed market behavior and that they sometimes fail to allow for impacts on quantities and prices in other markets and therefore neglect "general equilibrium" effects of major actions undertaken. Energy modeling analyses are challenged because of weaknesses in model specification, measurement error, and questionable relevance of historical data and behavior for future untested policy actions.

In this study, the cost-effectiveness indicators for mitigation actions are derived mostly from technological costing rather than energy modeling analyses. In some instances, these analyses show mitigation actions yielding a net savings, implying that investment in these actions would yield a positive economic return. Realizing such net savings, however, would require a set of conditions not now in existence. In other words, achieving such savings would require overcoming private or public barriers of various kinds. If these impediments can be overcome at relatively low cost, society could achieve substantial benefits from these actions, often even if greenhouse warming were not a problem.

Technological costing and energy modeling are in rough agreement, given the large uncertainties in the best available knowledge. This enhances the credibility of the results.

PLANNING A COST-EFFECTIVE POLICY

Investment involves choosing among alternative uses of resources. Finding the least-cost mix of responses to greenhouse warming entails comparing all the different possible responses. Figure 6.1 illustrates that the least-cost plan will probably involve a mix of responses. For simplicity, only two hypothetical options are plotted. They are shown as curves giving the cost for achieving various reductions in greenhouse gas emissions (or the equivalent: removal of greenhouse gases from the atmosphere, blocking of incident radiation, or changing the earth's reflectivity). For comparability, all responses are translated into CO_2-equivalent emissions.

Both options exhibit increasing cost for increasing reductions in emission (the curves gradually bend upward). If the only alternative were to achieve the desired level of reduction by choosing one option, the clear preference would be option B. Option B produces each level of reduction at lower cost (c'') than option A (c').

If, however, it were possible to select some of option A and some of option B, the greatest payoff would come from a mixture of the two. Option B should be selected up to the point at which the cost of additional reductions with option B exceeds the cost of the first reductions with option A (shown by the dashed line). Thereafter, the most cost-effective strategy would be to select some of A and some of B until the desired level of reduction is achieved.

Figure 6.2 extends the comparison to additional options with different characteristics. Option C shows "negative cost," or net positive benefits, associated with achieving the initial reductions in CO_2 emissions. An example is energy conservation, such as better insulating of hot water heaters to reduce heat loss. The cost of insulating would be less than the cost of adding electricity generating capacity if the conservation measures were not implemented.

Option D illustrates a "backstop technology." A backstop technology provides an unlimited amount of reduction at a fixed cost. An example would be an abundant energy source that provides electricity with no CO_2 emissions at all. Where a backstop technology exists, its cost sets a ceiling on the investment in reducing emissions. Only options costing less than D should be considered, no matter how much emission reduction is desired.

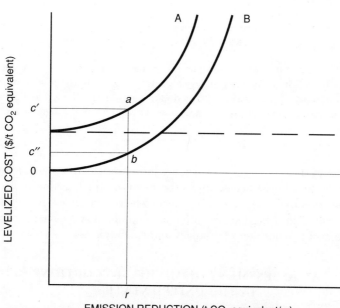

FIGURE 6.1 A comparison of hypothetical mitigation options. Curves show the costs of various levels of reduction in CO_2-equivalent emissions. Total costs for the period of the analysis are divided by the number of years, and all comparisons over time are assumed to be on the same basis.

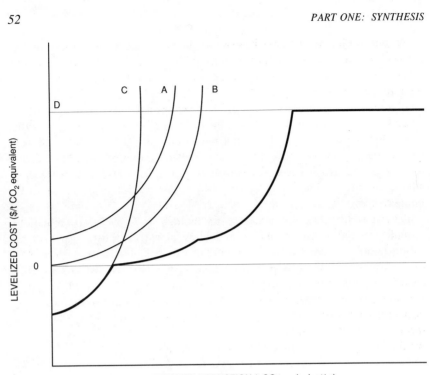

FIGURE 6.2 A comparison of multiple mitigation options. Curves show the costs of various levels of reduction in CO_2-equivalent emissions for four hypothetical mitigation options. Total costs for the period of analysis are divided by the number of years, and all comparisons over time are assumed to be on the same basis.

The heavy line in Figure 6.2 shows the cost-effective combination of options. Option C is selected up to the point at which option B becomes more cost-effective. Option A is added when it becomes cost-effective. The heavy line showing the cost-effective combination becomes horizontal when the cost reaches that of the backstop technology.

AN ASSESSMENT OF MITIGATION OPTIONS
IN THE UNITED STATES

Several premises are central to the design of a well-conceived mitigation policy. First, responses to greenhouse warming should be regarded as investments in the future of the nation and the planet. The actions required will have to be implemented over a long period of time. They must, however, be compared to other claims on the nation's resources.

Second, cost-effectiveness is an essential guideline. The changes in energy, industrial practices, land use, agriculture, and forestry that are likely to be needed to limit emissions of greenhouse gases require investments over time. These are likely to be large enough to affect the economy in various ways. The sensible guideline is cost-effectiveness: obtaining the largest reduction in greenhouse gas emissions at the lowest cost.

A true cost-effectiveness analysis of reducing greenhouse gas emissions would measure only the costs of interventions taken solely because of greenhouse warming. This is difficult in practice because many of these actions contribute to several social goals, making it hard to distinguish the costs and benefits attributable to greenhouse warming alone. There are two ways such complications might be handled: by adding benefits to reflect contributions to multiple goals or by reducing costs to reflect their allocation among different goals. For example, eliminating CFC emissions would slow both the depletion of the ozone layer and the onset of greenhouse warming. A proper accounting of reducing CFC emissions would either assign additional benefits to reflect those gained in the area of ozone depletion or reduce the cost allocated to greenhouse warming proportionate to the contribution of those actions to other goals. In either case, the cost-effectiveness ratio would be improved if multiple social goals were considered. Similarly, several actions that would reduce greenhouse gas emissions are mandated by the Clean Air Act. A full cost-effectiveness analysis would account for the fact that society has already decided to bear these costs, so that only additional costs and benefits would be included in the analysis of greenhouse warming. Limits on time and resources precluded complete analysis of these complications in this study, and the results presented here should be considered a first cut that points the way for further analyses.

Third, a mixed strategy is essential. A least-cost approach produces a variety of options. A mixed strategy, however, requires comparison of options in different sectors of the economy.

In comparing various mitigation options, this panel emphasizes three factors. The first factor is the cost-effectiveness of the option. In calculating cost-effectiveness, the panel converted reductions of all greenhouse gases into CO_2-equivalent emission reduction in order to be able to compare all options on the same basis.

The second factor is the ease or difficulty of implementation of the option. Although a particular option may be technically possible for relatively wealthy countries, it may be precluded for social, economic, or political reasons. These implementation obstacles are different for each option considered. The panel estimates emission reductions that could be achieved if explicitly defined feasible opportunities were executed. For example, one option calls for reducing energy use in residential lighting by 50 percent through replacement of incandescent lighting (2.5 interior light bulbs and 1 exterior light bulb per residence) with compact fluorescent lights. Another option calls for improving on-road fuel economy to 25 miles per gallon (32.5 mpg in Corporate Average Fuel Economy (CAFE) terms) in light vehicles by implementing existing technologies that would not require changes in size or attributes of vehicles. Each option is also evaluated in terms of an optimistic "upper-bound" (100 percent achievement) or a pessimistic "lower-bound" (25 percent) level of implementation. A brief description of the mitigation options considered in this study is found in Table 6.1.

The third factor is the interconnectedness of the option to other issues in addition to greenhouse warming, for example, destruction of the ozone layer or biological extinction. These additional factors, however, were considered only in a qualitative manner and are part of the reason that recommendations are not based solely on the cost-effectiveness calculations developed in this study.

Table 6.2 shows selected mitigation options in order of cost-effectiveness. Some options, primarily in energy efficiency and conservation, have substantial potential to mitigate greenhouse warming with net savings or very low net cost. However, they have not been fully adopted because of various implementation obstacles.

Net savings does not mean that no expenditure is required to implement these options. Rather, it indicates that the total discounted cost of the option over the period of analysis is less than its discounted direct benefit, usually reduction in energy consumption, where the discount rate is 6 percent. At higher discount rates the relative cost would rise. These are options that ought to be, and probably will be, implemented, since they are in the interests of those who implement them. The decisions to start, however, can be hastened through better information and incentives.

Table 6.2 also includes some options that are more costly, face substantial obstacles to their implementation, or have other costs or benefits that are difficult to characterize. For example, reduction of CFC consumption is also beneficial in reducing stratospheric ozone depletion, and the combined benefit derived for greenhouse warming and ozone depletion would raise CFC control options in the ranking of preferred actions. Questions about the appropriateness of current technologies and public opposition to nuclear power, however, currently make this option difficult to implement. To the extent that concern about greenhouse warming replaces concern about nuclear energy and "inherently safe" nuclear plants are developed, this option increases its priority ranking.

Table 6.3 presents what the panel calls geoengineering options. The geoengineering options in this preliminary analysis include several ways of reducing temperature increases by screening sunlight (e.g., space mirrors, stratospheric dust, multiple balloons, stratospheric soot, and stimulating cloud condensation nuclei) as well as stimulation of ocean uptake of CO_2. Several

TABLE 6.1 Brief Descriptions of Mitigation Options Considered in This Study for the United States

RESIDENTIAL AND COMMERCIAL ENERGY MANAGEMENT

Electricity Efficiency Measures

White Surfaces/Vegetation	Reduce air conditioning use and the urban heat island effect by 25% through planting vegetation and painting roofs white at 50% of U.S. residences.
Residential Lighting	Reduce lighting energy consumption by 50% in all U.S. residences through replacement of incandescent lighting (2.5 inside and 1 outside light bulb per residence) with compact fluorescents.
Residential Water Heating	Improve efficiency by 40 to 70% through efficient tanks, increased insulation, low-flow devices, and alternative water heating systems.
Commercial Water Heating	Improve efficiency by 40 to 60% through residential measures mentioned above, heat pumps, and heat recovery systems.
Commercial Lighting	Reduce lighting energy consumption by 30 to 60% by replacing 100% of commercial light fixtures with compact fluorescent lighting, reflectors, occupancy sensors, and daylighting.
Commercial Cooking	Use additional insulation, seals, improved heating elements, reflective pans, and other measures to increase efficiency 20 to 30%.
Commercial Cooling	Use improved heat pumps, chillers, window treatments, and other measures to reduce commercial cooling energy use by 30 to 70%.
Commercial Refrigeration	Improve efficiency 20 to 40% through improved compressors, air barriers and food case enclosures, and other measures.
Residential Appliances	Improve efficiency of refrigeration and dishwashers by 10 to 30% through implementation of new appliance standards for refrigeration, and use of no-heat drying cycles in dishwashers.
Residential Space Heating	Reduce energy consumption by 40 to 60% through improved and increased insulation, window glazing, and weather stripping along with increased use of heat pumps and solar heating.
Commercial and Industrial Space Heating	Reduce energy consumption by 20 to 30% using measures similar to that for the residential sector.
Commercial Ventilation	Improve efficiency 30 to 50% through improved distribution systems, energy-efficient motors, and various other measures.

(Table 6.1 continues)

TABLE 6.1 *(continued)*

Oil and Gas Efficiency	Reduce residential and commercial building fossil fuel energy use by 50% through improved efficiency measures similar to the ones listed under electricity efficiency.
Fuel Switching	Improve overall efficiency by 60 to 70% through switching 10% of building electricity use from electric resistance heat to natural gas heating.

INDUSTRIAL ENERGY MANAGEMENT

Co-generation	Replace existing industrial energy systems with an additional 25,000 MW of co-generation plants to produce heat and power simultaneously.
Electricity Efficiency	Improve electricity efficiency up to 30% through use of more efficient motors, electrical drive systems, lighting, and industrial process modifications.
Fuel Efficiency	Reduce fuel consumption up to 30% by improving energy management, waste heat recovery, boiler modifications, and other industrial process enhancements.
Fuel Switching	Switch 0.6 quads[a] of current coal consumption in industrial plants to natural gas or oil.
New Process Technology	Increase recycling and reduce energy consumption primarily in the primary metals, pulp and paper, chemicals, and petroleum refining industries through new, less energy intensive process innovations.

TRANSPORTATION ENERGY MANAGEMENT

Vehicle Efficiency	
Light Vehicles	Use technology to improve on-road fuel economy to 25 mpg (32.5 mpg in CAFE[b] terms) with no changes in the existing fleet.
	Improve on-road fuel economy to 36 mpg (46.8 mpg CAFE) with measures that require changes in the existing fleet such as downsizing.
Heavy Trucks	Use measures similar to that for light vehicles to improve heavy truck efficiency up to 14 mpg (18.2 mpg CAFE).
Aircraft	Implement improved fanjet and other technologies to improve fuel efficiency by 20% to 130 to 140 seat-miles per gallon.

TABLE 6.1 *(continued)*

Alternative Fuels

Methanol from Biomass	Replace all existing gasoline vehicles with those that use methanol produced from biomass.
Hydrogen from Nonfossil Fuels	Replace gasoline with hydrogen created from electricity generated from nonfossil fuel sources.
Electricity from Nonfossil Fuels	Use electricity from nonfossil fuel sources such as nuclear and solar energy directly in transportation vehicles.
Transportation Demand Management	Reduce solo commuting by eliminating 25 per cent of the employer-provided parking spaces and placing a tax on the remaining spaces to reduce solo commuting by an additional 15 percent.

ELECTRICITY AND FUEL SUPPLY

Heat Rate Improvements	Improve heat rates (efficiency) of existing plants by up to 4% through improved plant operation and maintenance.
Advanced Coal	Improve overall thermal efficiency of coal plants by 10% through use of integrated gasification combined cycle, pressurized fluidized-bed, and advanced pulverized coal combustion systems.
Natural Gas	Replace all existing fossil-fuel-fired plants with gas turbine combined cycle systems to both improve thermal efficiency of current natural gas combustion systems and replace fossil fuels such as coal and oil that generate more CO_2 than natural gas.
Nuclear	Replace all existing fossil-fuel-fired plants with nuclear power plants such as advanced light-water reactors.
Hydroelectric	Replace fossil-fuel-fired plants with remaining hydroelectric generation capability of 2 quads.
Geothermal	Replace fossil-fuel-fired plants with remaining geothermal generation potential of 3.5 quads.
Biomass	Replace fossil-fuel-fired plants with biomass generation potential of 2.4 quads.
Solar Photovoltaics	Replace fossil-fuel-fired plants with solar photovoltaics generation potential of 2.5 quads.
Solar Thermal	Replace fossil-fuel-fired plants with solar thermal generation potential of 2.6 quads.

(Table 6.1 continues)

TABLE 6.1 *(continued)*

Wind	Replace fossil-fuel-fired plants with wind generation potential of 5.3 quads.
CO_2 Disposal	Collect and dispose of all CO_2 generated by fossil-fuel-fired plants into the deep ocean or depleted gas and oil fields.

NONENERGY EMISSION REDUCTION

Halocarbons

Not-in-kind	Modify or replace existing equipment to use non-CFC materials as cleaning and blowing agents, aerosols, and refrigerants.
Conservation	Upgrade equipment and retrain personnel to improve conservation and recycling of CFC materials.
HCFC/HFC-Aerosols, etc.	Substitute cleaning and blowing agents and aerosols with fluorocarbon substitutes.
HFC-Chillers	Retrofit or replace existing chillers to use fluorocarbon substitutes.
HFC-Auto Air Conditioning	Replace existing automobile air conditioners with equipment that utilizes fluorocarbon substitutes.
HFC-Appliance	Replace all domestic refrigerators with those using fluorocarbon substitutes.
HCFC-Other Refrigeration	Replace commercial refrigeration equipment such as that used in supermarkets and transportation with that using fluorocarbon substitutes.
HCFC/HFC-Appliance Insulation	Replace domestic refrigerator insulation with fluorocarbon substitutes.

Agriculture (domestic)

Paddy Rice	Eliminate all paddy rice production.
Ruminant Animals	Reduce ruminant animal production by 25%.
Nitrogenous Fertilizers	Reduce nitrogenous fertilizer use by 5%.
Landfill Gas Collection	Reduce landfill gas generation by 60 to 65% by collecting and burning in a flare or energy recovery system.

GEOENGINEERING

Reforestation	Reforest 28.7 Mha of economically or environmentally marginal crop and pasture lands and nonfederal forest lands to sequester 10% of U.S. CO_2 emissions.

TABLE 6.1 *(continued)*

Sunlight Screening

Space Mirrors	Place 50,000 100-km^2 mirrors in the earth's orbit to reflect incoming sunlight.
Stratospheric Dust[c]	Use guns or balloons to maintain a dust cloud in the stratosphere to increase the sunlight reflection.
Stratospheric Bubbles	Place billions of aluminized, hydrogen-filled balloons in the stratosphere to provide a reflective screen.
Low Stratospheric Dust[c]	Use aircraft to maintain a cloud of dust in the low stratosphere to reflect sunlight.
Low Stratospheric Soot[c]	Decrease efficiency of burning in engines of aircraft flying in the low stratosphere to maintain a thin cloud of soot to intercept sunlight.
Cloud Stimulation[c]	Burn sulfur in ships or power plants to form sulfate aerosol in order to stimulate additional low marine clouds to reflect sunlight.
Ocean Biomass Stimulation	Place iron in the oceans to stimulate generation of CO_2-absorbing phytoplankton.
Atmospheric CFC Removal	Use lasers to break up CFCs in the atmosphere.

[a]1 quad = 1 quadrillion Btu = 10^{15} Btu.
[b]Corporate average fuel economy.
[c]These options cause or alter chemical reactions in the atmosphere and should not be implemented without careful assessment of their direct and indirect consequences.

options, including space mirrors and removal of CFCs from the atmosphere, are not included among those recommended for further investigation in Chapter 9.

Geoengineering options appear technically feasible in terms of cooling effects and costs on the basis of currently available preliminary information. But considerably more study and research will be necessary to evaluate their potential side effects, including the chemical reactions that particles introduced into the atmosphere might cause or alter. The data presented in Table 6.3 were developed during the course of the study and represent initial estimates. These or other options may, with additional investigation, research, and development, provide the ability to change atmospheric concentrations of greenhouse gases or the radiative forcing of the planet.

Geoengineering options have the potential to affect greenhouse warming on a substantial scale. However, precisely because they might do so, and because the climate system and its chemistry are poorly understood, these options must be considered extremely carefully. We need to know more about them because measures of this kind may be crucial if greenhouse warming occurs, especially if climate sensitivity turns out to be at the high end of the range considered in this study. Efforts by societies to restrain their greenhouse gas emissions might be politically infeasible on a global scale, or might fail. In this eventuality, other options may be incapable of countering the effects, and geoengineering strategies might be needed. Some of these options are relatively inexpensive to implement, but all have large unknowns concerning possible environmental side-effects. They should not be implemented without careful assessment of their direct and indirect consequences.

TABLE 6.2 Comparison of Selected Mitigation Options in the United States

Mitigation Option	Net Implementation Cost[a]	Potential Emission[b] Reduction (t CO_2 equivalent per year)
Building energy efficiency	Net benefit	900 million[c]
Vehicle efficiency (no fleet change)	Net benefit	300 million
Industrial energy management	Net benefit to low cost	500 million
Transportation system management	Net benefit to low cost	50 million
Power plant heat rate improvements	Net benefit to low cost	50 million
Landfill gas collection	Low cost	200 million
Halocarbon-CFC usage reduction	Low cost	1400 million
Agriculture	Low cost	200 million
Reforestation	Low to moderate cost[d]	200 million
Electricity supply	Low to moderate cost[d]	1000 million[e]

NOTE: Here and throughout this report, tons are metric.

[a]Net benefit = cost less than or equal to zero
  Low cost = cost between $1 and $9 per ton of CO_2 equivalent
  Moderate cost = cost between $10 and $99 per ton of CO_2 equivalent
  High cost = cost of $100 or more per ton of CO_2 equivalent
[b]This "maximum feasible" potential emission reduction assumes 100 percent implementation of each option in reasonable applications and is an optimistic "upper bound" on emission reductions.
[c]This depends on the actual implementation level and is controversial. This represents a middle value of possible rates.
[d]Some portions do fall in low cost, but it is not possible to determine the amount of reductions obtainable at that cost.
[e]The potential emission reduction for electricity supply options is actually 1700 Mt CO_2 equivalent per year, but 1000 Mt is shown here to remove the double-counting effect (see p. 62 for an explanation of double-counting).

TABLE 6.3 Cost-Effectiveness Ordering of Geoengineering Mitigation Options

Mitigation Option	Net Implementation Cost	Potential Emission Mitigation (t CO_2 equivalent per year)
Low stratospheric soot	Low	8 billion to 25 billion
Low stratospheric dust, aircraft delivery	Low	8 billion to 80 billion
Stratospheric dust (guns or balloon lift)	Low	4 trillion or amount desired
Cloud stimulated by provision of cloud condensation nuclei	Low	4 trillion or amount desired
Stimulation of ocean biomass with iron	Low to moderate	7 billion or amount desired
Stratospheric bubbles (multiple balloons)	Low to moderate	4 trillion or amount desired
Space mirrors	Low to moderate	4 trillion or amount desired
Atmospheric CFC removal	Unknown	Unknown

NOTE: The feasibility and possible side-effects of these geoengineering options are poorly understood. Their possible effects on the climate system and its chemistry need considerably more study and research. They should not be implemented without careful assessment of their direct and indirect consequences.

Cost-effectiveness estimates are categorized as either savings (for less than 0), low (0 to $9/t CO_2 equivalent), moderate ($10 to $99/t CO_2 equivalent), or high (>$100/t CO_2 equivalent). Potential emission savings (which in some cases include not only the annual emissions, but also changes in atmospheric concentrations already in the atmosphere—stock) for the geoengineering options are also shown. These options do not reduce the flow of emissions into the atmosphere but rather alter the amount of warming resulting from those emissions. Mitigation options are placed in order of cost-effectiveness.

The CO_2-equivalent reductions are determined by calculating the equivalent reduction in radiative forcing.

Here and throughout this report, tons are metric.

COMPARING OPTIONS

Table 6.2 shows estimates of net cost and emission reductions for several options. It must be emphasized that the table presents the Mitigation Panel's estimates of the technical potential for each option. For example, the calculation of cost-effectiveness of high-efficiency light bulbs (one of the building efficiency options) does not consider whether the supply of light bulbs could meet the demand with current production capacities. It does not consider the trade-off between expenditures on light bulbs and on health

care, education, or basic shelter for low-income families. Nor does it consider aesthetic issues about different sources of illumination.

Care must be taken in developing such a table because there is some
"double-counting" among potential mitigation options. For example,
implementation of both the nuclear and the natural gas energy options assumes
replacement of the same coal-fired power plants. Thus, simply summing up
the emission reductions of all options to give total reduction in emissions
would overstate the actual potential. The options presented in Table 6.2
have been selected to eliminate double-counting.

Finally, although there is evidence that efficiency programs can pay,
there is no field evidence showing success with programs on the massive
scale suggested here. There may be very good reasons why options exhibiting net benefit on the table are not fully implemented today.

Figure 6.3 illustrates the results of different rates of implementation of
those options. The many uncertainties in the calculations of both costs and
emission reductions have been collapsed into two lines. The line labeled
"25% Implementation/High Cost" assumes incomplete implementation of
each option (25 percent implementation of feasible opportunities) and the
high end of the range of cost estimates for that option (high cost). This line
shows a lower bound of what is reasonable to achieve. The line labeled

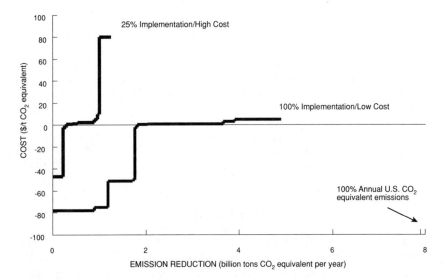

FIGURE 6.3 Comparison of mitigation options. Total potential reduction of CO_2-
equivalent emissions is compared to the cost in dollars per ton of CO_2 reduction. Options
are ranked from left to right in CO_2 emissions according to cost. Some options show
the possibility of reductions of CO_2 emissions at a net savings. See text for explanation.

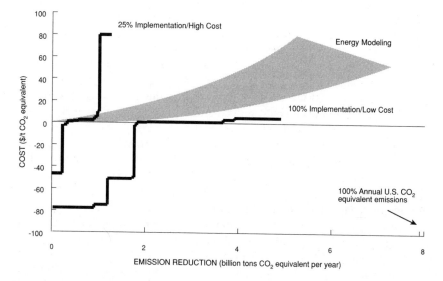

FIGURE 6.4 Comparison of mitigation options using technological costing and energy modeling calculations.

"100% Implementation/Low Cost" assumes complete implementation of each option (100 percent implementation) combined with the low range of cost estimates for that option (low cost). This line indicates the upper bound that could be achieved with all options shown. A complete analysis would calculate appropriate implementation rates for each option. That is beyond the scope of this study. It should be realistic to achieve emission reduction and cost results somewhere between the two lines in Figure 6.3.

As pointed out earlier in this chapter, technological costing and energy modeling sometimes yield different results. For this reason, both are presented in Figure 6.4. The "100% Implementation/Low Cost" and "25% Implementation/ High Cost" curves are repeated from Figure 6.3, and the range typical of energy modeling is shown. As can be seen from Figure 6.4, the United States should be able to achieve substantial reduction in greenhouse gas emissions at low cost, or perhaps even a small net savings.

IMPLEMENTING MITIGATION OPTIONS

An array of policy instruments of two different types are available: regulation and incentives. Regulatory instruments mandate action and include controls on consumption (bans, quotas, required product attributes), production (quotas on products or substances), and factors in design or production (efficiency, durability, processes). Incentive instruments are designed to influence decisions by individuals and organizations and include taxes and subsidies on production factors (carbon tax, fuel tax) and on products and other outputs (emission taxes, product taxes), financial inducements (tax credits, subsidies), and transferable emission rights (tradable emission reductions, tradable credits).

Interventions at all levels could effectively reduce greenhouse warming. For example, individuals could reduce energy consumption, recycle goods, and reduce consumption of deleterious materials. Local governments could control emissions from buildings, transport fleets, waste processing plants, and landfill dumps. State governments could restructure electric utility pricing structures and stimulate a variety of efficiency incentives. National governments could pursue action in most of the policy areas of relevance. International organizations could coordinate programs in various parts of the world, manage transfers of resources and technologies, and facilitate exchange of monitoring and other relevant data.

The choice of policy instrument depends on the objective to be served. Although this analysis of mitigation options does not include all possibilities, the panel is hopeful that it does identify the most promising options. This analysis provides the beginnings of a structure and a process for identifying those strategies that could appropriately mitigate the prospect of greenhouse warming.

CONCLUSIONS

There is a potential to inexpensively reduce or offset greenhouse gas emissions in the United States. In particular, the maximum feasible potential reduction for the options labeled "net benefit" and "low cost" in Table 6.2 totals about 3.6 billion tons (3.6 Gt) of CO_2-equivalent emissions per year. (Here, as elsewhere in the report, tons are metric.) This is a little more than one-third of the total 1990 greenhouse gas emissions in the United States and represents an optimistic upper bound on what could be achieved using these options.

A lower bound can be estimated from Figure 6.4. Arbitrarily using a cutoff of between \$10 and \$20 per ton of CO_2-equivalent emission reduction would produce a level of about 1 Gt of CO_2-equivalent emissions per year, or a little more than 10 percent of current greenhouse gas emissions in the United States.

This analysis suggests that the United States could reduce its greenhouse gas emissions by between 10 and 40 percent of the 1990 level at very low cost. Some reductions may even be at a net savings if the proper policies are implemented.

7

International Considerations

Effective action to slow greenhouse warming will require international effort regardless of policies in the United States. Many of the cost-effective options appropriate for the United States are also applicable in other countries, including developing nations. The coal resources in China and the former USSR alone ensure that without their cooperation, policies aimed at stabilizing greenhouse emissions elsewhere would probably be doomed to failure. Yet the position of the United States as the current largest emitter of greenhouse gases means that action in the rest of the world will be effective only if the United States does its share.

Developing countries may participate in the reduction of greenhouse gas emissions if the first steps are taken by the industrialized countries and if some sort of international agreement is made providing them with additional financial and technical resources to make the necessary changes.

Global population growth, which will largely take place in developing countries, is a fundamental contributor to increasing emissions of greenhouse gases. Developing countries accounted for about 17 percent of world commercial energy consumption 20 years ago, and about 23 percent today. They are expected to account for about 40 percent by 2030. Although it is the industrialized world that contributes most of the current greenhouse gas emissions, this will likely change in the future. Emissions from developing countries will become even more important as they improve their economies and consume more fossil fuels. Either increasing population or growing economic activity can increase emissions of greenhouse gases. Even with rapid technological progress, slowing global population growth is a necessary component for the long-term control of greenhouse gas emissions. Although it may not be financially costly, it is beset with other political, social, and ideological obstacles.

The long-term control of greenhouse gas emissions will require the diffusion and implementation of technology in developing countries. A real challenge will be to ensure that technologies reach those who need them, overcoming such obstacles as lack of information or inability to pay for them. The technological capabilities of developing countries need to be improved. The creation and enhancement of the infrastructure for research and absorption of technology form a precondition for this improvement. Programs in agriculture, forestry, pollution control, and housing might be used both as vehicles for the transfer of relevant technologies and for the enhancement of the research and technology infrastructure.

Similarly, reversing deforestation, to lower atmospheric concentrations of greenhouse gases in the short term, raises a host of issues other than costs. It will be important for international programs to use a broad perspective.

INTERNATIONAL ACTIVITIES

Much work has already been accomplished on the international level, and more is currently under way. Internationally, research on a variety of global change issues (including greenhouse warming) is being undertaken principally under the auspices of two complementary scientific programs: the World Climate Research Program (WCRP) and the International Geosphere-Biosphere Program (IGBP). The WCRP was established by the World Meteorological Organization in 1979 under its overall program, the World Climate Program (WCP). Its major objectives are to determine the extent to which climate can be predicted and the extent of human influence on climate. The IGBP was adopted by the International Council of Scientific Unions (ICSU) in 1986. The objective of the program is to describe the interactive physical, chemical, and biological processes that regulate the total earth system.

In 1988 the World Meteorological Organization and the United Nations Environment Programme sponsored the Intergovernmental Panel on Climate Change (IPCC). At the first IPCC meeting, in November 1988, three working groups were set up: Working Group I, to provide a scientific assessment of climate change; Working Group II, to provide an assessment of the potential impacts of climate change; and Working Group III, to consider response strategies. Hundreds of scientists from different countries contributed to the IPCC report produced in 1990.

The Second World Climate Conference was convened in late 1990 under the sponsorship of several U.N. organizations. The conference was separated into a scientific and technical session and a ministerial session. The conference discussed the results of the first decade of work under the WCP, the First Assessment Report of the IPCC, and the development of the IGBP. The scientific and technical session produced conclusions and recommendations in three areas: (1) greenhouse gases and climate change; (2) use of climate information in assisting sustainable social and economic development; and (3) priorities for enhanced research and observational systems. The ministerial declaration essentially recognized greenhouse warming to be an international problem and urged further elaboration and assessment of response strategies.

A large number of deliberations are under way concerning international negotiations on greenhouse issues. Recent experiences with the Montreal Protocol on Substances That Deplete the Ozone Layer and its subsequent elaboration in the London Protocol and with the earlier Law of the Sea provide guidance about what approaches are useful and what to avoid. It is expected, however, that negotiations about limiting greenhouse warming will be more difficult than their predecessors in the environmental area.

FUTURE INTERNATIONAL AGREEMENTS

There is a growing momentum in the international community for completion of an international agreement on climate change in time for signing at the 1992 U.N. World Conference on Environment and Development. The first meeting of the Ad Hoc Working Group of Government Representatives to Prepare for Negotiations on a Framework Convention on Climate Change was held in February 1991. The panel believes that the United States should fully participate in this process.

Identification of priority actions should take full account of their potential to reduce or offset greenhouse gas emissions and their costs of implementation. Further, the panel believes that international arrangements should allow nations to receive credit for actions taken to reduce or offset emissions in other countries. In other words, under such an arrangement countries like the United States could negotiate interventions in other countries if these proved more cost-effective than domestic actions.

OTHER ACTIONS

The importance of multilateral international agreements should not obscure the value of unilateral or bilateral action. The United States should not only adjust its own policies, but also pursue bilateral agreements and technical assistance programs that promote reforestation, protection of biodiversity, and greater energy efficiency.

In framing actions to respond to greenhouse warming, the United States should consider cooperative programs in other countries that might be more cost-effective than domestic options.

8

Findings and Conclusions

This study reviews current knowledge about greenhouse warming and examines a wide variety of potential responses. The panel finds that, even given the considerable uncertainties in our knowledge of the relevant phenomena, greenhouse warming poses a potential threat sufficient to merit prompt responses. People in this country could probably adapt to the likely changes associated with greenhouse warming. The costs, however, could be substantial. Investment in mitigation measures acts as insurance protection against the great uncertainties and the possibility of dramatic surprises. In addition, the panel believes that substantial mitigation can be accomplished at modest cost. In other words, insurance is cheap.

These responses, however, must be based on consideration of the uncertainties, costs of actions and inaction, and other factors. The panel believes they should be based on the approach outlined in Chapter 4. Actions that would help people and natural systems adapt to climate change are described in Chapter 5. Actions to mitigate greenhouse warming are described in Chapter 6.

The findings and conclusions presented here draw on the detailed assessments performed by the other three panels contributing to this study: the Effects Panel (Part Two), the Mitigation Panel (Part Three), and the Adaptation Panel (Part Four). The Synthesis Panel, however, considered additional materials in its deliberations and in the preparation of this report. These include, for example, the reports of the three IPCC working groups, the conference statement from the Second World Climate Conference, statements from other international meetings, publications of the national laboratories and other research organizations in the United States, and documents prepared in other countries. The findings and conclusions of this panel reflect additional analysis, deliberation, and judgment beyond those of the other panels contributing to this study.

POLICY CONSIDERATIONS

The phenomenon of greenhouse warming is complex, and so are the possible responses to it. First, the extent, timing, and variation of future warming and its likely impacts need to be assessed. Second, both the cost and the effectiveness of options to slow greenhouse warming must be estimated and compared to the costs of postponing action. Third, the possible advantages and disadvantages of these actions need to be evaluated in light of the extent to which people, plants, and animals are likely to adjust by themselves or with assistance to changes in the climate. Fourth, the policymaker needs to evaluate these actions in comparison to other ways resources might be used. Before acting, we need to be confident that expenditures to slow climate change make sense. Fifth, decision makers will judge all these factors in a broader context. Responses to greenhouse warming will be determined by people worried about economic growth, food supply, energy availability, national security, and a host of other problems. Many responses appear to produce sizable benefits with regard to other goals, such as reducing air pollution. This study makes no attempt to assess these additional dividends. Instead, it focuses on response to greenhouse warming as such.

Capacities of Industrialized and Developing Countries

Different countries have quite different capacities to respond to change. Poverty, in particular, makes people vulnerable to change and substantially reduces their flexibility in responding to change. Countries with low per-capita income face difficult trade-offs between stimulating economic development and alleviating environmental problems. These countries, which already have difficulty coping with environmental stresses today, will be even more sorely pressed when confronted by climate change.

This report examines response to greenhouse warming in the United States, a country richly endowed with natural and human resources, and one benefiting from a geography that encompasses many climate zones. Compared to many other countries, the United States is well situated to respond to greenhouse warming.

This panel does not attempt to view greenhouse warming from the perspective of a country less well endowed. Of course, greenhouse warming is a global phenomenon, and many global aspects must be included in any analysis. Nevertheless, most of the data utilized in this study to evaluate mitigation and adaptation options relate to the United States. A more comprehensive examination must wait for future studies.

Taxes and Incentives

Decisions about energy use and other activities that emit greenhouse gases are made daily, even hourly, by 250 million people in the United States in many different areas from transportation to hair drying. Experience here and abroad has shown the inducements of prices and taxes to be a sure way to transmit government policies to decentralized decision makers. Achieving significant reductions in greenhouse gas emissions, however, could involve considerable sacrifice and economic disruption.

There are advantages of market-incentive approaches, but they are not universal. For particular technologies, like the chlorofluorocarbons (CFCs), it may be quicker to use direct regulatory interventions such as emissions limits or caps, although buttressing these with taxes can ensure that the regulations are enforced. An alternative to taxes that has been suggested, and endorsed by several foreign governments and the United States in the Clean Air Act, is establishing emission limits. While this approach seems reasonable on the surface, it has significant shortcomings in implementation.

The major defect with regulatory actions such as emission limits is that there is no easy way that the government can directly control emissions from so many different and separate sources. However, regulation as a technology-forcing mechanism has contributed to reducing emissions of key air pollutants in the United States. It other areas it has been less successful.

Taxes and regulations can discourage or prevent people from taking actions that would increase greenhouse gas emissions; incentives of various kinds can encourage them to act in ways that reduce emissions. If interventions are needed, this panel believes that, in general, incentive-type measures are preferable.

Fundamental and Applied Research

Research is inexpensive in comparison with many other policy options that could make a difference in greenhouse warming. The federal research budget on topics related to global climate change is a little more than $1 billion for fiscal year 1991, which is small in comparison to the expected impact or costs of climate change. Although these funds have been identified as applying to greenhouse warming research, some of them contribute to other objectives as well. Policy should be designed and executed in ways that increase our understanding of the way human activity affects greenhouse warming.

Research on the actual impacts of climate change may identify vulnerabilities and highlight areas for policy action. Every year there are droughts, heat waves, severe storms, and other such phenomena. Understanding how economies and communities of plants and animals are affected by extreme climate events, and whether those responses are changing over time, could provide important guidance for policy choices.

Better understanding of how biological communities function as both sources and sinks of greenhouse gases, especially CO_2, might also help anticipate the consequences of greenhouse warming. More detailed knowledge about phenomena affecting radiative forcing, such as cloud physics and chemistry, or of key mechanisms in the global climate system, such as ocean currents and heat transfers, could help identify where actions might have greatest leverage. Research satellites capable of measuring the energy balance of the earth are necessary, as is maintaining thermometer measurement networks.

Most research up to now has emphasized climatological issues. The global climate change budget in the United States is about 95 percent on the physical phenomena of atmosphere, oceans, and so on and 5 percent on mitigation, adaptation, and impacts. We need to know more about the social and economic processes generating greenhouse gas emissions and about the costs of mitigating these emissions, especially in the energy sector. We need reviews and assessments of policy options to slow climate change, and improvements in the data base for understanding economic and environmental trends relating to global change. Because greenhouse warming is a global problem encompassing a wide range of areas, it will be important to establish programs that are interdisciplinary and examine developing countries as well as high-income countries like the United States.

A PROPOSED FRAMEWORK FOR RESPONDING TO THE THREAT OF GREENHOUSE WARMING

The analyses performed for this study show that the United States should be able to adapt to the changes in climate expected to accompany greenhouse warming. They have also identified a number of options that could slow or offset the buildup of greenhouse gases. Other options could help position us to ease future adaptations to the consequences of greenhouse warming. The fact that people can adapt, or even that they are likely to do so, does not mean that the best policy is to wait for greenhouse warming to occur and let them adapt. Waiting and adapting may sacrifice overall economic improvement in the long run.

The panel has sorted response policies into five categories: (1) reducing or offsetting greenhouse gas emissions, (2) enhancing adaptation to greenhouse warming, (3) improving knowledge for future decisions, (4) evaluating geoengineering options, and (5) exercising international leadership. The recommended options in each category are described in Chapter 9.

GENERAL CONCLUSIONS

In conducting this study, the panel first established the approach and framework described in Chapter 4. The information and data summarized in Chapters 5 and 6 were then gathered and analyzed. On this basis, the Synthesis Panel reached the collective judgment that the United States should undertake not only several actions that satisfy multiple goals but also several whose costs are justified mainly by countering or adapting to greenhouse warming. The panel believes that a systematic implementation of the complete set of low-cost options described in Chapter 9 is appropriate. The panel concludes that options requiring great expenses are not justified at this time.

9

Recommendations

Despite the great uncertainties, greenhouse warming is a potential threat sufficient to justify action now. Some current actions could reduce the speed and magnitude of greenhouse warming; others could prepare people and natural systems of plants and animals for future adjustments to the conditions likely to accompany greenhouse warming.

There are a number of mitigation and adaptation options available to the United States. This panel recommends implementation of the options presented below through a concerted program to start mitigating further buildup of greenhouse gases and to initiate adaptation measures that are judicious and practical. It also recommends a strong scientific program to continue to reduce the many uncertainties. International cooperation is essential in all areas.

The recommendations are generally based on low-cost, currently available technologies. Topics for which new information or techniques must be developed are clearly identified. In many instances, more detailed treatments can be found in Part Two, "The Science Base"; Part Three, "Mitigation"; and Part Four, "Adaptation." The numbers in parentheses refer to pages in this part where these topics are discussed.

REDUCING OR OFFSETTING EMISSIONS OF
GREENHOUSE GASES

Three areas dominate the analysis of reducing or offsetting current emissions: (1) eliminating halocarbon emissions, (2) changing energy policy, and (3) utilizing forest offsets. Eliminating CFC emissions is the biggest single contribution in the short run. Energy policy recommendations include reducing emissions related to both consumption and production. Recommendations on both global and domestic programs are included under forest offsets. The United States could reduce or offset its greenhouse gas emissions by between 10 and 40 percent of 1990 levels at low cost, or at some net savings, if proper policies are implemented.

Halocarbon Emissions

Continue the aggressive phaseout of CFC and other halocarbon emissions and the development of substitutes that minimize or eliminate green-house gas emissions. (pp. 53, 55-59)

Chlorofluorocarbons not only have a role in the depletion of stratospheric ozone, they also contribute a significant portion of the radiative forcing (i.e., the ability to "trap" heat in the atmosphere) attributable to human activities. The 1987 Montreal Protocol to the Vienna Convention set goals regarding international phaseout of CFC manufacture and emissions. The United States is a party to that agreement as well as to the London Protocol, which requires total phaseout of CFCs, halons, and carbon tetrachloride by 2000 in industrialized countries and by 2010 in developing countries. Un-less this agreement is forcefully implemented, the use of CFCs may con-tinue to intensify greenhouse warming. Every effort should be made to develop economical substitutes that do not contribute to greenhouse warm-ing.

Energy Policy

Study in detail the "full social cost pricing" of energy, with a goal of gradually introducing such a system. (pp. 32-33, 68, 69)

On the basis of the principle that the polluter should pay, pricing of energy production and use should reflect the full costs of the associated environmental problems. The concept of full social cost pricing is a goal toward which to strive. Including all social, environmental, and other costs in energy prices would provide consumers and producers with the appropriate information to decide about fuel mix, new investments, and research and development. Such a policy would not be easy to design or implement. Unanticipated winners and losers could emerge, either through improper accounting of externalities, lack of knowledge, or lack of incorporation of other concerns (such as energy security) or through cleverness and innova-tion. Phasing such a policy in over time is essential to avoid shocks caused by rapid price changes. It would best be coordinated internationally.

Reduce the emission of greenhouse gases during energy use and con-sumption by enhancing conservation and efficiency (pp. 55-59, 60), including action to:

- Adopt nationwide energy-efficient building codes
- Improve the efficiency of the U.S. automotive fleet through the use of an appropriate combination of regulation and tax incentives
- Strengthen federal and state support of mass transit
- Improve appliance efficiency standards
- Encourage public education and information programs for conservation and recycling
- Reform state public utility regulation to encourage electrical utilities to promote efficiency and conservation
- Sharply increase the emphasis on efficiency and conservation in the federal energy research and development budget
- Utilize federal and state purchases of goods and services to demonstrate best-practice technologies and energy conservation programs

The efficiency of practically every end use of energy can be improved relatively inexpensively. Major reductions could be achieved in energy use in existing buildings through improvements in lighting, water heating, refrigeration, space heating and cooling, and cooking. Gains could be achieved in transportation by improving vehicle efficiency without downsizing or altering convenience. Significant gains could also be achieved in industrial electricity use through fuel switching and improvements in process technologies. Initial calculations show that some options could be implemented at a net savings. There are informational barriers to overcome, however. For example, homeowners may not be aware of the gains to be realized from high-efficiency furnaces. There are also institutional barriers. For example, most public utility commissions disallow a rate of return to power companies on efficiency and conservation options. The panel concludes that energy efficiency and conservation is a rich field for reducing greenhouse gas emissions.

Make greenhouse warming a key factor in planning for our future energy supply mix. The United States should adopt a systems approach that considers the interactions among supply, conversion, end use, and external effects in improving the economics and performance of the overall energy system. (pp. 55-59, 60) Action items include efforts to:

- Develop combined cycle systems that have efficiencies approaching 60 percent for both coal- and natural-gas-fired plants
- Encourage broader use of natural gas by identifying and removing obstacles in the distribution system
- Develop and test operationally a new generation of nuclear reactor technology that is designed to deal with safety, waste management, and public acceptability
- Increase research and development on alternative energy supply technologies (e.g., solar), and design energy systems utilizing them in conjunction with other energy supply technologies to optimize economy and performance

• Accelerate efforts to assess the economic and technical feasibility of CO_2 sequestration from fossil-fuel-based generating plants

The future energy supply mix will change as new energy technologies and greenhouse warming take on increased importance. A "systems approach" should be used to optimize the economics and performance of future energy systems. Interactions among supply options, conversion systems, end use, and external effects should receive much more attention than they have in the past. Actions for improving energy supply systems must cover all important elements in the mix. Also, it is important to prepare for the possibility that greenhouse warming may become far more serious in the future.

Alternative energy technologies are unable currently or in the near future to replace fossil fuels as the major electricity source for this country. If fossil fuels had to be replaced now as the primary source of electricity, nuclear power appears to be the most technically feasible alternative. But nuclear reactor designs capable of meeting fail-safe criteria and satisfying public concerns have not been demonstrated. A new generation of reactor design is needed that adequately addresses the full range of safety, waste management, economic, and other issues confronting nuclear power. Focused research and development work on a variety of alternative energy supply sources could change the priorities for energy supply within the 50-year time span addressed in this study.

Forest Offsets

Reduce global deforestation (pp. 65-66), including action to:

• Participate in international programs to assess the extent of deforestation, especially in tropical regions, and to develop effective action plans to slow or halt deforestation
• Undertake country-by-country programs of technical assistance or other incentives
• Review U.S. policies to remove subsidies and other incentives contributing to deforestation in the United States

In addition to reducing the uptake of CO_2 in plants and soils and being a source of atmospheric CO_2, deforestation contributes to other important problems: loss of species and reduction in the diversity of biologic systems, soil erosion, decreased capacity to retain water in soil and altered runoff of rainfall, and alteration of local weather patterns. The United States now has increasing forest cover, but tropical forests worldwide are being lost at a rapid rate. Nearly every aspect of tropical deforestation, however, is difficult to measure. Even the amount of land deforested each year is subject to disagreement. Nevertheless, action should be initiated now to slow and eventually halt tropical deforestation. Such programs need to be developed by those countries where the affected forests are located in cooperation with other countries and international organizations. Developing countries with extensive tropical forests will require substantial technological and developmental aid if this goal is to be reached.

Explore a moderate domestic reforestation program and support international reforestation efforts. (pp. 55-59, 66-67)

Reforestation offers the potential of offsetting a large amount of CO_2 emissions, but at a cost that increases sharply as the amount of offset increases. These costs include not only those of implementation, but also the loss of other productive uses of the land planted to forests, such as land for food production. Reforesting can, at best, only remove CO_2 from the atmosphere and store it during the lifetime of the trees. When a forest matures, the net uptake of CO_2 stops. If the reforested areas are then harvested, the only true offset of CO_2 buildup is the amount of carbon stored as lumber or other long-lived products. However, the wood might be used as a sustained-yield energy crop to replace fossil fuel use. The acreage available within the United States for reforestation, and the amount of CO_2 that could be captured on these lands with appropriate kinds of trees, are controversial and may be limited. Many details remain to be resolved.

ENHANCING ADAPTATION TO GREENHOUSE WARMING

The nature and magnitude of the weather conditions and events that might accompany greenhouse warming at any particular location in the future are extremely uncertain. This panel examined the sensitivity of the affected human and natural systems to the events and conditions likely to accompany greenhouse warming. The panel's adaptation recommendations are intended to help make the affected systems less vulnerable to future climate change. Most of the recommendations, by making the systems more robust, also help them deal with current climate variability. Some, such as purchasing land or easements for specific habitats or corridors for migration, would not be needed if greenhouse warming does not occur.

Specific adaptation recommendations address agriculture, water systems, long-lived structures, and preservation of biodiversity.

Maintain basic, applied, and experimental agricultural research to help farmers and commerce adapt to climate change and thus ensure ample food. (pp. 38-39)

Farming is the preeminent activity essential to humanity that is exposed to climate. During recent decades, its successful adaptation to diverse climates and changing demand rested on vigorous research and application by both government and business. As climate changes, adapted varieties, species, and husbandry must be more promptly sought and then proven in the reality of fields and commerce. Special challenges are (1) while adapting, to sustain the natural resources of land, water, and genetic diversity that underlie farming; (2) to be productive during extreme weather conditions; (3) to manage irrigation to produce more food with less water; and (4) to exploit the opportunity of increased fertilization provided by more CO_2 in the air.

Make water supply more robust by coping with present variability by increasing efficiency of use through water markets and by better management of present systems of supply. (pp. 40-41)

Currently, weather and precipitation cause natural variability in the water supply, in soil, and in streams, and changes in climate could be expected to produce even greater variability. Fortunately, coping with the present variability makes supply more reliable or robust for future climate change when needed. In many places, supply and demand can be better matched by raising the efficiency of use through changes in rights, markets, and prices, by clever management and engineering of irrigation, and by changes in urban styles of living (e.g., water-efficient landscaping and reduced lawn maintenance). Because the joint management of supplies under the jurisdiction of several agencies can increase water yields substantially, the protracted negotiations for such cooperation should begin now.

Plan margins of safety for long-lived structures to take into consideration possible climate change. (pp. 43-44)

Margins of safety adequate for past climate may be insufficient for a changed climate. Most investments like bridges, levees, or dams have lives as long as the time expected for climate to change. The margins used in constructing such structures are generally computed from the historical frequency of extremes like storms or droughts. The possibility of greenhouse warming must now be considered in computing these margins of safety. A logical procedure for justifying investment in a wider margin of safety now involves two considerations: its cost in terms of its expected present value compared to that of retrofitting the structure when needed, and the probability that the alteration will in fact be needed.

Move to slow present losses in biodiversity (pp. 39-40, 46), including taking action to:

- Establish and manage areas encompassing full ranges of habitats
- Inventory little-known organisms and sites
- Collect key organisms in repositories such as seed banks
- Search for new active compounds in wild plants and animals

- Control and manage wild species to avoid over-exploitation
- Pursue captive breeding and propagation of valuable species that have had their habitats usurped or populations drastically reduced
- Review policies, laws, and administrative procedures that have the effect of promoting species destruction
- Consider purchasing land or easements suitable for helping vulnerable species to migrate to new habitats

Even without greenhouse warming, a series of steps to slow present losses in biodiversity are warranted. Any future climate change is likely to increase the rate of loss of biodiversity while it increases the value of genetic resources. Greenhouse warming therefore adds urgency to programs to preserve our biological heritage. Much remains to be done to ensure that key habitats are protected, that major crop cultivars are collected, and that extensive options are retained for future use. Serious initiatives have only recently been started. In most countries, the driving forces behind the degradation of biodiversity relate to the development context within which people farm; harvest forest products; utilize fresh water, wildlife, and fish; and otherwise invest in land or water. Moreover, there are policies that actually promote destruction by fostering open tillage crops, short-term timber-harvesting concessions, excessive use of water, and inappropriate fishing technology. If climate changes, existing reserves and parks may become unsuitable for species currently living there, and landscape fragmentation may make migration more difficult. Conservation efforts should give more attention to corridors for movement, to assisting species to surmount barriers, and to maintaining species when their natural habitats are threatened.

IMPROVING KNOWLEDGE FOR FUTURE DECISIONS

Data collection and applied research can make exceptional contributions in reducing uncertainties of greenhouse warming. The return on investment in research is likely to be great. The panel identifies the following areas for emphasis: collection and interpretation of data on climate change, improvement in weather forecasting, key physical mechanisms in climate change, and research on the interactions between the biosphere, human activities, and the climate system.

Continue and expand the collection and dissemination of data that provide an uninterrupted record of the evolving climate and of data that are (or will become) needed for the improvement and testing of climate models. (pp. 19-22, 22-25, 26-27)

Current data collection programs should be maintained and should be continued after the new (and different) collection systems (e.g., EOS, the Earth Observing System) have become operational. Earlier modes of collection should be phased out only when the interpretation of new and old data streams has proceeded for an appropriate time. Uncertainties in the climate record and its interpretation should not be exacerbated by change in instrumentation.

Continuous monitoring of key indices that can reveal climate change is needed for identifying adaptations that will be needed in the future. These include the supply of water in the streams and soil of a region, sea level, ocean currents, and dates of seasonal events like blooms and migrations.

Improve weather forecasts, especially of extremes, for weeks and seasons to ease adaptation to climate change. (p. 36)

If storms could be accurately forecast several days in advance, people could prepare for or escape them and hence could live in climates with greater variation and extremes. If extremely cold or dry seasons could be foreseen confidently, appropriate crops could be planted and harvested, and floods and droughts managed more effectively. Continued improvement of several-day forecasts, provision and dissemination of forecasts for additional parts of the world, and increasing knowledge of atmosphere-ocean interactions may help enhance adaptation to greenhouse warming.

Continue to identify those mechanisms that play a significant role in the climatic response to changing concentrations of greenhouse gases. Develop and/or improve quantification of all such mechanisms at a scale appropriate for climate models. (pp. 19-21, 27-28)

Some of the mechanisms already known to need such attention include those involving the role of clouds, the role of the oceans in heat transfer, the possible release of CO_2 in the oceans (i.e., into the atmosphere) with change in ocean temperature, the role of the biosphere in the storage and release of CO_2 and CH_4, and the effect of particle concentrations on cloud cover and radiative balance.

It is also necessary to improve the quantification (at a scale suitable for climate models) of processes such as precipitation, soil moisture, and run-off. Some current mathematical characterizations are unable to provide credible regional projections of these factors even when used for scenarios in which the greenhouse gas concentrations are not changing.

Conduct field research on entire systems of species over many years to learn how CO_2 enrichment alters the mix of species and changes the total production or quality of biomass. Research should be accelerated to determine how greenhouse warming might affect biodiversity. (pp. 39-40, 71)

Communities of plants and animals are complex and intricate. Simplified and controlled experiments in laboratories can help understand them better. Greenhouse warming is likely to increase the rate of loss of biodiversity, and so it adds urgency to experimental programs to preserve our biological heritage. But scientists also must learn how disparate, entire systems of species live and react to changes in their habitats and especially to changes in the concentration of CO_2. The effect of combined CO_2 enrichment and greenhouse warming on the mix of species and other attributes of natural communities cannot be determined without field research conducted over many years.

Strengthen research on social and economic aspects of global change and greenhouse warming. (pp. 70-71)

The U.S. research program has emphasized issues of atmospheric chemistry, climate modeling, and monitoring, while relatively little attention has been given to issues of impacts, mitigation, and adaptation. Major priorities should be (1) improved understanding of the costs for mitigating greenhouse gas emissions, particularly in the energy sector, (2) more detailed studies of the impacts of and adaptations to climate change, (3) a better understanding of the social and economic processes generating greenhouse gas emissions, (4) policy analysis of options and strategies relating to climate change, and (5) improvements in the data base for understanding economic and environmental trends relating to global change.

Greenhouse warming is a global problem; therefore it will be important to encourage interdisciplinary and international programs. Thorough analytical studies of the impacts of greenhouse warming currently are limited to a few relatively high income countries. Yet it is the poor countries, with a large fraction of their population and output in the farm sector, who are the most vulnerable to climate change. In the research areas listed above, it will be important to examine behavior in developing countries as well as in high-income countries like the United States.

EVALUATING GEOENGINEERING OPTIONS

Undertake research and development projects to improve our understanding of both the potential of geoengineering options to offset global warming and their possible side effects. This is not a recommendation that geoengineering options be undertaken at this time, but rather that we learn more about their likely advantages and disadvantages. (pp. 54-61)

Several geoengineering options appear to have considerable potential for offsetting global warming and are much less expensive than other options being considered. Because these options have the potential to affect the radiative forcing of the planet, because some of them cause or alter a variety of chemical reactions in the atmosphere, and because the climate system is poorly understood, such options must be considered extremely carefully. These options might be needed if greenhouse warming occurs, climate sensitivity is at the high end of the range considered in this report, and other efforts to restrain greenhouse gas emissions fail.

The first set of geoengineering options screens incoming solar radiation with dust or soot in orbit about the earth or in the atmosphere. The second set changes cloud abundance by increasing cloud condensation nuclei through carefully controlled emissions of particulate matter. Despite their theoretical potential, there is convincing evidence that the stratospheric particle options contribute to depletion of the ozone layer. The stratospheric particle options should be pursued only under extreme conditions or if additional research and development removes the concern about these problems. The cloud stimulation option should be examined further and could be pursued if concerns about acid rain could be managed through the choice of materials for cloud condensation nuclei or by careful management of the system. The third class increases ocean absorption of CO_2 through stimulating growth of biological organisms. The panel recommends that research projects be undertaken to improve understanding of both the potential of these options to offset global warming and their possible side effects. Such assessments should involve international cooperation. This is not a recommendation for implementing these options at this time.

EXERCISING INTERNATIONAL LEADERSHIP

As the largest source of current greenhouse gas emissions, the United States should exercise leadership in addressing responses to greenhouse warming.

Control of population growth has the potential to make a major contribution to raising living standards and to easing environmental problems like greenhouse warming. The United States should resume full participation in international programs to slow population growth and should contribute its share to their financial and other support. (p. 65)

Population size and economic activity both affect greenhouse gas emissions. Even with rapid technological advances, slowing global population growth is a necessary component of a long-term effort to control worldwide emissions of greenhouse gases. Reducing population growth alone, however, may not reduce emissions of greenhouse gases because it may also stimulate growth in per capita income. If the nature of economic activity (especially energy use) changes, some growth will be possible with far less greenhouse gas emissions.

Encouraging voluntary population control programs is of considerable benefit for slowing future emissions of greenhouse gases. In addition, countries vulnerable to the possible impacts of climate change would be better able to adapt to those changes if their populations were smaller and they had higher per capita income.

The United States should participate fully with officials at an appropriate level in international agreements and in programs to address greenhouse warming, including diplomatic conventions and research and development efforts. (p. 67)

There is a growing momentum in the international community for completion of an international agreement on climate change in time for signing at the 1992 United Nations World Conference on Environment and Development. The United States should participate fully in this activity and continue its active scientific role in related topics. The global character of greenhouse warming provides a special opportunity in the area of research and development. International cooperation in research and development should be encouraged through governmental and private sector agreements. International organizations providing funds for development should be encouraged to evaluate projects meeting demand for energy growth by conservation methods on an equal footing with projects entailing construction of new production capacity.

Individual Statement by a Member of the Synthesis Panel

JESSICA MATHEWS

Jessica Mathews, a member of the Synthesis Panel, disagrees with the conclusions in Chapter 5 with the following statement. "The analysis does not support the conclusion that greenhouse warming will be no more demanding than past climatic changes. If the change is unprecedented in the experience of the human species, how can it be claimed that people will have no more difficulty adapting to future changes than to those of the past?

"The reasoning used here is that human economic activities are largely divorced from nature and that modern technology effectively buffers us from climate. Combined with assumptions of gradual change, no surprises, and an olympian perspective on national costs, the result is an unduly sanguine outlook. Even as a portrayal of a best case scenario (rather than a most likely one), this is a flawed analysis.

"First, it underestimates the extent to which human societies, even affluent ones, depend on the underpinning of natural systems. While recognizing that the pace of greenhouse warming will most likely exceed the rate at which species and ecosystems can adapt, the study does not go on to examine the resulting impacts of severe ecosystem disruption on human societies.

"Also, the impacts of climate change on economic activities are considered separately, sector by sector (farming, industry, transportation, etc.). This is understandable given the difficulty of analyzing the interactions, but here the compartmentalization of impacts in both the natural and economic spheres seems to lead to the distorted view that people, economic activity, infrastructure, and natural context can be disassociated. The finding that 'expected climatic changes are within the range people now experience . . . and to which those who move usually learn to adapt,' means nothing about adaptation to greenhouse-induced change. The fact that one can move with

84

ease from Vermont to Miami has nothing to say about the consequences of Vermont acquiring Miami's climate.

"Reasoning from the experience of past adaptations is risky given that in the past societies could usually expect that climate fifty years hence would be reasonably like that of the present. This will probably not be the case during a greenhouse warming, because of the difficulties of forecasting regional impacts, the rate of expected change, and because we may be operating under conditions with which mankind has no past experience.

"Finally, it may be strictly accurate that 'pluses and minuses' will combine to produce 'small net change for a nation of our size.' But the distribution of impacts in time and space matters more than this treatment suggests. Costs that are indisputably enormous (including human suffering) begin to appear deceptively manageable when viewed solely from the perspective of their impacts on a multitrillion dollar economy. For example, in the case of cities, the study finds that while 'adaptation might be costly, the costs would in most cases be lower than the cost of moving the city.'"

Part Two

THE SCIENCE BASE

10

Introduction

During the past century, human activities have caused increases in the atmospheric concentrations of both naturally occurring and artificially introduced "greenhouse" gases. The carbon dioxide (CO_2) concentration, for example, has increased about 25 percent. Currently, these long-lived gases, some of which are more effective than others at trapping heat, combine to provide an increase in greenhouse warming over the past 100 years equivalent to that which would have been provided by a 40 percent increase in CO_2 alone.

The highly publicized concern that these greenhouse gas accumulations might lead to a significant modification of the earth's climate underlies an expanding body of literature. Much of this work deals with quantitative discussions of the greenhouse gas accumulation itself, quantitative analyses of the heat balance of the planet, and inferences from these analyses for climate change. Part Two of this report has been written by the Effects Panel with a full awareness of the deliberations that have led to much of the greenhouse warming literature, and its assessments rest on the same foundations as do several other assessments of the same questions.[1] It was not the panel's purpose to retrace these steps, but rather to assess this body of knowledge in terms of policy needs.

The panel first examined the climate record and the difficulties associated with its interpretation, as well as the available analytical tools and their limitations. It then developed a concise, objective account of the current knowledge, understanding, and predictive capability that attend the greenhouse warming question. The panel made no attempt to perform a comprehensive critical assessment from the perspective of the various relevant scientific disciplines. The report of the Intergovernmental Panel on Climate Change (1990) is comprehensive and covers in greater detail the topics that are addressed in the report of the Effects Panel. The Effects Panel's report is more constrained in scope and presents a succinct representation of data and knowledge to serve as a backdrop for current policy decisions. In doing so, it examines in depth only a few topics that illustrate the extent to which the current science base is sufficient to inform policy decisions. The panel believes the principal difference between its analysis and that of the IPCC is that in the Effects Panel's analysis a greater credence is accorded to the uncertainties in the current scientific knowledge and tools.

The task assigned to the Effects Panel did not require it to assess policy issues as such. Nevertheless, its members record here their support of the conclusions, including the need for prudent response, that are expressed in the report of the Synthesis Panel (Part One).

NOTE

1. See, for example, Intergovernmental Panel on Climate Change, 1990; U.S. Congress, Office of Technology Assessment, 1991; and National Research Council, 1983.

REFERENCES

Intergovernmental Panel on Climate Change. 1990. Climate Change: The IPCC Scientific Assessment, J. T. Houghton, G. J. Jenkins, and J. J. Ephraums, eds. New York: Cambridge University Press.

National Research Council. 1983. Changing Climate: Report of the Carbon Dioxide Assessment Committee. Washington, D.C.: National Academy Press.

U.S. Congress, Office of Technology Assessment. 1991. Changing by Degrees: Steps to Reduce Greenhouse Gases. OTA-O-482. Washington, D.C.: U.S. Government Printing Office.

11

Emission Rates and Concentrations
of Greenhouse Gases

Several atmospheric trace gases are relatively transparent to incoming solar radiation but absorb, or trap, outbound infrared radiation emitted from the earth's surface. Water vapor, one of several naturally occurring greenhouse gases (including CO_2, methane (CH_4), and nitrous oxide (N_2O)), also traps heat by mechanisms associated with mechanical transfer and convection. The trapping of heat by these gases is called the "greenhouse effect." This label emphasizes the similarity of the phenomenon to the warming that occurs in a greenhouse, although that warming is mostly associated with blocking convective heat transfer. Without the naturally occurring greenhouse effect, the earth's average temperature would be about 33°C (59°F) colder than it is now, and the planet would be much less suitable for human life. This report is not concerned with the natural greenhouse effect, but rather with additional global warming due to human-induced increases in the atmospheric concentration of greenhouse gases. This enhancement of the greenhouse effect is called "greenhouse warming." Table 11.1 presents key attributes of the principal greenhouse gases deriving, in part or entirely, from human activities.

CARBON DIOXIDE

The increase from 280 ppmv (parts per million by volume) to 354 ppmv in the atmospheric concentration of CO_2 since 1800 is well established from ice core studies (Neftel et al., 1985; Friedli et al., 1986) and direct atmospheric measurements (Keeling et al., 1989a). The error in the ice core record is probably not more (and perhaps less) than ±10 ppmv,[1] and the atmospheric record since 1957 is known to within ±1 ppmv. The emission of CO_2 into the atmosphere via the burning of fossil fuels is also well

TABLE 11.1 Key Greenhouse Gases Influenced by Human Activity

	CO_2	CH_4	CFC-11	CFC-12	N_2O
Preindustrial atmospheric concentration	280 ppmv	0.8 ppmv	0	0	288 ppbv
Current atmospheric concentration (1990)[a]	354 ppmv	1.71 ppmv	280 pptv	484 pptv	310 ppbv
Current rate of annual atmospheric accumulation[b]	1.8 ppmv (0.5%)	0.015 ppmv (0.9%)	9.5 pptv (4%)	17 pptv (4%)	0.8 ppbv (0.25%)
Atmospheric lifetime (years)[c]	(50-200)	10	65	130	150

NOTE: Ozone has not been included in the table because of lack of precise data. Here ppmv = parts per million by volume; ppbv = parts per billion by volume; and pptv = parts per trillion by volume.

[a]The 1990 concentrations have been estimated on the basis of an extrapolation of measurements reported for earlier years, assuming that the recent trends remained approximately constant.

[b]Net annual emissions of CO_2 from the biosphere not affected by human activity, such as volcanic emissions, are assumed to be small. Estimates of human-induced emissions from the biosphere are controversial.

[c]For each gas in the table, except CO_2, the "lifetime" is defined as the ratio of the atmospheric concentration to the total rate of removal. This time scale also characterizes the rate of adjustment of the atmospheric concentrations if the emissions rates are changed abruptly. CO_2 is a special case because it is merely circulated among various reservoirs (atmospheric, ocean, biota). The "lifetime" of CO_2 given in the table is a rough indication of the time it would take for the CO_2 concentration to adjust to changes in the emissions.

SOURCE: Adapted from Intergovernmental Panel on Climate Change (1990). Reprinted by permission of Cambridge University Press.

quantified over much of the last century (Marland, 1990). Other anthropogenic input rates of CO_2 are not as well known, but it is unlikely that the total of such input since 1700 has exceeded one-half of the fossil fuel inputs. The 1990 total of emissions resulting from other human activities, even with the present rate of tropical deforestation, is about one-quarter the rate from burning fossil fuels alone.

Calculating the effective atmospheric lifetime of the actual emissions is complex because CO_2 molecules are constantly exchanged between the atmosphere, the oceans, and the biosphere. Although a typical molecule stays in the atmosphere about 4 years, atmospheric CO_2 concentrations vary seasonally and between the northern and southern hemispheres. However, because of the exchange with other "sinks," the "lifetime" associated with an individual CO_2 anomaly, or surge in atmospheric concentration, is 50 to 200 years. In addition, the total natural flow of CO_2 into and out of the atmosphere is about 30 times greater than that caused by human activities. This natural carbon cycle, however, was approximately constant over the 10,000 years prior to the Industrial Revolution, even though there were changes in the biosphere—deserts emerged and forests migrated, for example. What matters for greenhouse warming is the increased concentration of CO_2 (and other greenhouse gases) in the atmosphere rather than the total annual flow into and out of the atmosphere.

The increase in atmospheric CO_2 concentration since 1860, which is approximately the beginning of the fossil fuel era, has been slightly more than 60 percent of the concentration that would be in the atmosphere if all the fossil fuel emissions had remained in the atmosphere. The results of most models of the ocean-atmosphere carbon system are consistent with this approximate 60-40 split of the total fossil fuel emissions. However, the ocean-atmosphere models cannot reproduce the observed (from direct atmospheric measurements and the derived concentrations from ice cores) CO_2 increase in this century if one adds to the fossil fuel CO_2 emissions the estimated net flux of CO_2 that results from land cover change. On the other hand, to match the ice core CO_2 record for the period 1700 to 1900, it is necessary to invoke a terrestrial source of CO_2 in addition to the fossil fuel emissions. Improved understanding of various aspects of relevant phenomena is reported from time to time (e.g., Keeling et al., 1989a,b; Kirchman et al., 1991). At present, however, there are no data indicating that much of the missing carbon is in the deep ocean (to which the transfer of CO_2 would be expected to be very slow), nor are there as yet any observations to suggest that it might have become incorporated into the soil and/or biomass of the continents.

Although there are substantial uncertainties in our understanding of the components of the carbon cycle, the atmospheric concentration of CO_2 has been steadily increasing because of human activities[2] in a manner that can be described by using a simple empirical relationship; e.g.,

increment in atmospheric CO_2 at time t =
60% of accumulated fossil fuel emissions.

However, there is no real assurance that the nature of the unknown sink is consistent with such an extrapolation, which essentially assumes the terrestrial flux from land cover change. This uncertainty is especially trouble-some in discussions of the atmospheric condition at times when CO_2 (or the equivalent in other greenhouse gases) may have become twice or more the present value.

In short, there is a clear record of recent increases in atmospheric CO_2, a reasonably good estimate of the anthropogenic emissions, and a range of CO_2 uptake by the oceans with which the scientific community seems com-fortable. However, the panel concludes that there are no data or compelling hypotheses that identify sinks and transfer mechanisms that could redress the observed very large imbalance in this century between the emissions and the known sinks.

METHANE

The atmospheric concentration of CH_4 in 1990, about 1.71 ppmv, is more than double the preindustrial value of about 0.8 ppmv (Craig and Chou, 1982; Blake and Rowland, 1988). Concentrations currently are increasing at about 0.9 percent per year (Blake and Rowland, 1988). Two main path-ways for CH_4 generation have been identified: (1) reduction of CO_2 with hydrogen, fatty acids, or alcohols as hydrogen donors and (2) transmethylation of acetic acid or methyl alcohol by CH_4-producing bacteria. The principal phenomena involved include biological processes in natural wetlands and rice paddies, burning of plant material in tropical and subtropical regions, consumption of biomass by termites, anaerobic decay of organic waste in landfills, and ventilation of coal mines. Additional sources include enteric fermentation by ruminant animals, leakage from natural gas pipelines, and venting from oil and gas wells. The amount of CH_4 currently released from these various sources, however, is not known with precision. The Intergovernmental Panel on Climate Change (IPCC) estimated 1990 total CH_4 releases to be between 400 and 600 teragrams (Tg) per year (Inter-governmental Panel on Climate Change, 1990).

Global measurements suggest that CH_4 concentrations are greatest at latitudes poleward of 30°N. The approximately 0.14 ppmv greater concen-tration of CH_4 in the northern hemisphere over the southern hemisphere is not surprising given that most CH_4 is produced over land (Wuebbles and Edmonds, 1991).

The major sink for CH_4 is reaction with the hydroxyl radical (OH) in the atmosphere. In addition, soils may be a sink for CH_4, but this has not yet been determined quantitatively. CH_4 has a relatively short lifetime in the atmosphere of 10 ± 2 years (Prinn et al., 1987). Recent work on the reac-tion of OH with CH_4 (Vaghjiani and Ravishankara, 1991) indicates a longer CH_4 lifetime (by about 25 percent) and a smaller inferred flux (about 100 Tg CH_4 per year) than was previously estimated. Reduction in the amount of global atmospheric OH may provide an explanation for 20 to 50 percent of the increase in atmospheric CH_4 concentration, but this is highly uncertain given the unavailability of reliable direct measurements of tropospheric OH concentrations (Wuebbles and Edmonds, 1991).

Methane emissions from wetlands are sensitive to temperature and soil moisture (Crutzen, 1989). Future climatic changes could thus significantly affect the fluxes of CH_4 from both natural wetlands and rice paddies. A highly uncertain but potentially large source of CH_4 is the methane hydrates stored in permafrost sediments, CH_4 trapped in permafrost, and decomposable organic matter frozen in the permafrost (Cicerone and Oremland, 1988). Future climate warming could release these sources of CH_4, thereby further adding to the warming. However, the lowering of the water table in tundra as a result of a warmer, drier climate could decrease CH_4 fluxes into the atmosphere owing to increased microbial oxidation. This might provide a negative feedback for atmospheric CH_4 (Whalen and Reeburgh, 1990). The net effect of climatic changes on atmospheric concentrations of CH_4 is highly uncertain.

In short, the atmospheric concentration of CH_4 has more than doubled over preindustrial levels. In addition to many natural sources, there are a number of anthropogenic sources of atmospheric CH_4. The extent of relevant human activities has increased over the last 100 years, and an inferred decrease in atmospheric OH during this period also could contribute to the CH_4 increase. However, the quantitative importance of each of the factors contributing to the observed increase in CH_4 is not known at present.

HALOCARBONS

With the exception of methyl chloride, most halocarbons come entirely from human activities. Atmospheric concentrations of the major anthropogenic halocarbons in 1990 are 280 parts per trillion by volume (pptv) for CFC-11; 484 pptv for CFC-12; 60 pptv for CFC-113; and 146 pptv for carbon tetrachloride (CCl_4). Their annual rates of increase over the past few years are 4 percent for CFC-11; 4 percent for CFC-12; 10 percent for CFC-113; and 1.5 percent for CCl_4 (Fraser and Derek, 1989; Intergovernmental Panel on Climate Change, 1990; Wuebbles and Edmonds, 1991). Concentrations of the fully halogenated chlorofluorocarbons (CFCs) are slightly greater in the northern hemisphere than in the southern hemisphere. This fact is consistent with the geographic distribution of releases (>90 percent from industrialized nations), a 45°N to 45°S mixing time of about 1 year, and the very long atmospheric lifetimes of these CFCs.

Halocarbons are used as aerosol propellants (CFCs 11, 12, and 114), foam blowing agents (CFCs 11 and 12), solvents (CFC 113, methyl chloroform (CH_3CCl_3), and CCl_4), and fire retardants (halons 1211 and 1301).

Methyl chloride is primarily released from the oceans and during biomass burning.

There is no significant tropospheric removal mechanism for the fully halogenated halocarbons such as CFCs 11, 12, 113, 114, and 115 or for halon-1301. They are primarily removed by photodissociation in the middle to upper stratosphere. The fully halogenated halocarbons therefore have long atmospheric lifetimes, ranging from about 60 years (CFC-11) to about 400 years (CFC-115).

Emissions of many halocarbons are governed by the Montreal Protocol on Substances That Deplete the Ozone Layer. The Protocol specifies that the production and consumption of CFCs 11, 12, 113, 114, and 115 be limited to 50 percent of their 1986 levels by 1998 and of halons to their 1986 levels after 1994. The London Protocol, adopted in June 1990, requires a total phaseout of CFCs, halons, and CCl_4 by 2000 in industrialized countries and by 2010 in developing countries. Emissions of these gases will continue after their production has ceased, however, because of their presence in refrigerants, foams, fire retardants, and so on.

NITROUS OXIDE

The 1990 average atmospheric concentration of nitrous oxide (N_2O) is about 310 ppbv and is increasing at a rate of about 0.2 to 0.3 percent per year (Khalil and Rasmussen, 1988). Ice core data suggest that preindustrial atmospheric concentrations of N_2O were about 288 ppbv (Khalil and Rasmussen, 1988). The atmospheric concentration of N_2O is about 1 ppbv higher in the northern hemisphere than in the southern hemisphere (Rasmussen and Khalil, 1986).

Denitrification in aerobic soils is thought to be a dominant source of atmospheric N_2O (Keller et al., 1986). There is, however, considerable uncertainty in the source budget for N_2O and in the causes for its increasing concentration in the atmosphere. The two possible sources that most likely account for the observed increase are (1) nitrification and denitrification of nitrogen from industrially produced fertilizers and (2) high-temperature combustion, such as from coal-burning power plants (Wuebbles and Edmonds, 1991). Some results are contradictory, however, as to whether combustion is the major source or totally unimportant (Hao et al., 1987; Muzio and Kramlich, 1988). The oceans also are a significant, although probably not dominant, source of N_2O (McElroy and Wofsy, 1986). An accurate determination of the global annual ocean flux is difficult because of uncertainties associated with quantifying the gas exchange coefficient and because the partial pressure of N_2O in the surface waters varies considerably, ranging from being supersaturated by up to 40 percent in upwelling regions to being undersaturated by a few percent in areas around Antarctica and in upwelling currents (Cline et al., 1987). It is still unclear whether N_2O is primarily produced from nitrification in near-surface waters or denitrification in oxygen-deficient deep waters. Quantification of global N_2O emissions from soils is difficult because of the heterogeneity of terrestrial ecosystems and the variability in environmental conditions. N_2O emissions from the use of nitrate and ammonium fertilizers are difficult to quantify because the N_2O fluxes depend on numerous factors, including type of fertilizer, soil type, soil temperature, weather, and farming practices. Conversion of nitrogen to N_2O ranges from 0.01 to 2 percent (Conrad et al., 1983). Leaching of nitrogen fertilizers into groundwater may result in additional fluxes of N_2O into the atmosphere.

The major atmospheric process removing N_2O is photochemical decomposition in the stratosphere. N_2O is not chemically active in the troposphere. N_2O has a lifetime in the atmosphere of about 150 years.

In short, we know that the atmospheric concentration of N_2O is now about 8 percent higher than in the preindustrial period. N_2O has a relatively long atmospheric lifetime. It is difficult to account for the source of the observed increase in atmospheric N_2O, but it is thought to be anthropogenic. The observed rate of growth indicates a 30 percent imbalance between sources and sinks (Hao et al., 1987).

NOTES

1. Some believe the error for concentrations derived from ice core data may be as large as ±20 ppmv.

2. That human activities are causing the increasing atmospheric concentration of CO_2 is known from carbon isotope studies.

REFERENCES

Blake, D. R., and F. S. Rowland. 1988. Continuing worldwide increase in tropospheric methane, 1978 to 1987. Science 239:1129-1131.

Cicerone, R., and R. Oremland. 1988. Biogeochemical aspects of atmospheric methane. Global Biogeochemical Cycles 2:299-327.

Cline, J. D., D. P. Wisegarver, and K. Kelly-Hansen. 1987. Nitrous oxide and vertical mixing in the equatorial Pacific during the 1982-1983 El Niño. Deep Sea Research 34:857-873.

Conrad, R., W. Seiler, and G. Bunse. 1983. Factors influencing the loss of fertilizer nitrogen into the atmosphere as N_2O. Journal of Geophysical Research 88:6709-6718.

Craig, H., and C. C. Chou. 1982. Methane: The record in polar ice cores. Geophysical Research Letters 9:1221-1224.

Crutzen, P. J. 1989. Emissions of CO_2 and other trace gases to the atmosphere from fires in the tropics. 28th Liège International Astrophysical Colloquium, University de Liège, Belgium, June 26-30.

Fraser, P. J., and N. Derek. 1989. Atmospheric halocarbons, nitrous oxide, and methane—The GAGE program. Baseline 87:34-38.

Friedli, H., H. Loetscher, H. Oeschger, U. Siegenthaler, and B. Stauffer. 1986. Ice core record of the $^{13}C/^{12}C$ record of atmospheric CO_2 in the past two centuries. Nature 324:237-238.

Hao, W. M., S. C. Wofsy, M. B. McElroy, J. M. Beer, and M. A. Togan. 1987. Sources of atmospheric nitrous oxide from combustion. Journal of Geophysical Research 92:3098-3104.

Intergovernmental Panel on Climate Change. 1990. Climate Change: The IPCC Scientific Assessment, J. T. Houghton, G. J. Jenkins, and J. J. Ephraums, eds. New York: Cambridge University Press.

Keeling, C. D., R. B. Bacastow, A. F. Carter, S. C. Piper, T. P. Whorf, M. Heimann, W. G. Mook, and H. Roeloffzen. 1989a. A three dimensional model of atmospheric CO_2 transport based on observed winds: 1. Analysis of observational data. In Aspects of Climate Variability in the Pacific and the Western Americas, D. H. Peterson, ed. Geophysical Monograph 55. Washington, D.C.: American Geophysical Union.

Keeling, C. D., S. C. Piper, and M. Heimann. 1989b. A three dimensional model of atmospheric transport based on observed winds: 4. Mean annual gradients and interannual variations. In Aspects of Climate Variability in the Pacific and the Western Americas, D. H. Peterson, ed. Geophysical Monograph 55. Washington, D.C.: American Geophysical Union.

Keller, M., W. A. Kaplan, and S. C. Wofsy. 1986. Emissions of N_2O, CH_4, and CO_2 from tropical soils. Journal of Geophysical Research 91:11,791-11,802.

Khalil, M. A. K., and R. A. Rasmussen. 1988. Nitrous oxide: Trends and global mass balance over the last 3000 years. Annals of Glaciology 10:73-79.

Kirchman, D. L., Y. Suzuki, C. Garside, and H. W. Ducklow. 1991. High turnover rates of organic carbon during a spring phytoplankton bloom. Nature 352:612-614.

Marland, G. 1990. Carbon dioxide emission estimates: United States. In TRENDS '90: A Compendium of Data on Global Change, T. A. Borden, P. Kanciruk, and M. P. Farrell, eds. Report ORNL/CDIAC-36. Oak Ridge, Tenn.: Carbon Dioxide Information Analysis Center, Oak Ridge National Laboratory.

McElroy, M. B., and S. C. Wofsy. 1986. Tropical forests: Interactions with the atmosphere. In Tropical Rain Forests and the World Atmosphere, G. T. Prance, ed. AAAS Selected Symposium 101. Boulder, Colo.: Westview Press.

Muzio, L. J., and J. C. Kramlich. 1988. An artifact in the measurement of N_2O from combustion sources. Geophysical Research Letters 15(12):1369-1372.

Neftel, A., E. Moor, H. Oeschger, and R. C. Finkel. 1985. Evidence from polar ice cores for the increase in atmospheric CO_2 in the past two centuries. Nature 315:45-47.

Prinn, R., D. Cunnold, R. Rasmussen, P. Simmons, F. Alyea, A. Crawford, P. Fraser, and R. Rosen. 1987. Atmospheric trends in methylchloroform and the global average for the hydroxyl radical. Science 238:945-950.

Rasmussen, R. A., and M. A. K. Khalil. 1986. Atmospheric trace gases: Trends and distributions over the last decade. Science 232:1623-1624.

Vaghjiani, G. L., and A. R. Ravishankara. 1991. New measurement of the rate coefficient for the reaction of hydroxyl with methane. Nature 350:406-409.

Whalen, S. C., and W. S. Reeburgh. 1990. Consumption of atmospheric methane by tundra soils. Nature 346:160-162.

Wuebbles, D. J., and J. Edmonds. 1991. Primer on Greenhouse Gases. Chelsea, Mich.: Lewis Publishers.

12

Radiative Forcing and Feedback

Many facets of the earth's climatic system are poorly understood. A significant uncertainty associated with the modeling of future climatic changes is due to deficiencies in the understanding of, and in the incorporation into the climate models of, several interactive climate feedback mechanisms. In this discussion of radiative forcing, the planet's heat balance, and these feedbacks and their consequences, emphasis is given to global mean quantities, since, conventionally, the concept of radiative feedback mechanisms is applied to global mean quantities associated with changes from one equilibrium climate to another. Many aspects of these feedback mechanisms are controversial. The conventional wisdom has been challenged on several points (see, for example, The George C. Marshall Institute, 1989; Lindzen, 1990), and new analyses of key issues are reported regularly (see, for example, Jenkinson et al., 1991; Kirchman et al., 1991; Ramanathan and Collins, 1991).

THE HEAT BALANCE

When the planet's climate is not undergoing change, the energy flux to the earth from the sun is in balance with the sum of the reflected portion of that solar flux and the outward infrared radiation that emerges from the top of the atmosphere. Figure 12.1 gives a schematic view of these fluxes and also depicts several of the components of the energy flow that occurs within the climatic system.

In particular, Figure 12.1 indicates that, of the 340 watts per square meter (W/m^2) that are incident on the atmospheric envelope from the sun, about 100 W/m^2 are reflected (from clouds, glaciated areas, and so on); 80 W/m^2 are absorbed within the atmosphere, and 160 W/m^2 are absorbed into the oceans and the continental land masses. Heat is returned from the oceans and the land by infrared radiation from the surface (390 W/m^2). Ninety W/m^2 are returned by nonradiative processes that lead to the upward transport of water vapor (with its latent heat) and of sensible heat. All of the 90 W/m^2 flux and a substantial part (call it B) of the 390 W/m^2 radiative flux are deposited in the atmosphere. The total energy flux to the atmosphere ($80 + 90 + B$) is necessarily in balance with the infrared emission from the atmosphere, 320 W/m^2 of which is directed downward into the ocean-land mass interface and the rest of which emerges from the top of the atmosphere (along with that fraction of the interface radiation ($390 - B$) that is not absorbed in the atmosphere). One can see that these numbers are mutually consistent by noting that the total nonreflected solar input is equal to the total (infrared) output of the system, that the total energy flux downward through the interface balances the upward flux from that interface, and that the energy received by the atmosphere ($80 + 90 + B$) plus the nonabsorbed upward flux from the interface ($390 - B$) is in balance with the radiation from the atmosphere that supplies the output of the system (at the top) and the radiative flux downward into the interface.

The interplay among the transmission of infrared radiation through the atmosphere, the absorption of infrared in the atmosphere, and the emission of infrared from the atmosphere is distributed throughout the height of the gaseous envelope. The foregoing, highly oversimplified splitting of these aspects of the infrared interchange into individual macroscopic items is needed only for the schematic presentation within this chapter. One need not choose a particular, necessarily artificial, value for B, because here a chosen value for B would not affect the conclusion drawn.

Note that, since each flux shown in Figure 12.1 is a globally averaged quantity, there is no depiction of the horizontal heat fluxes within the atmosphere and ocean that redistribute heat from one part of the planet to another. Nevertheless, such internal transfers play vital roles in the physical processes that determine the climatic state.

There are two important points to note from Figure 12.1. The first is that the 240 W/m^2 emission at the top of the atmosphere (TOA) is 150 W/m^2 less than the 390 W/m^2 emission from the surface. This radiative flux difference is the greenhouse effect of the earth's present atmosphere, and it is caused by the absorption of infrared radiation by greenhouse gases and clouds. The second important point of Figure 12.1 is that the atmospheric greenhouse gases and the clouds emit infrared radiation downward to the surface, and this direct radiative heating of the surface by the atmosphere (320 W/m^2) is twice the direct solar heating (160 W/m^2). By itself, the additional 320 W/m^2 provided by infrared surface heating produces substantial warming of the surface above the temperature that would otherwise prevail; thus it is the greenhouse effect that makes our planet habitable.

RADIATIVE FORCING

Suppose that, at time t, the state of the climatic system is that characterized by Figure 12.1. Suppose, too, that the greenhouse gas content of the atmosphere at that time is equivalent to a CO_2 content of 300 ppmv. Suppose (once more) that, just after time t, the greenhouse gas levels are changed and the subsequent concentrations are equivalent to a CO_2 concentration of 600 ppmv. This scenario is adopted here, not because CO_2 doubling has some special significance but because it is an atmospheric modification that may occur within the next century and particularly because the CO_2 doubling scenario has become the baseline case most commonly used by atmospheric scientists to compare the performance of one model with that of another. Immediately after this augmentation of greenhouse gas content, no changes in interface temperature, atmospheric temperature distribution, atmospheric moisture content, or any other component can yet have occurred. Accordingly, the only heat flux changes at that time would be those implied by an increased fractional absorption of the 390 W/m^2 of infrared radiation up from the interface. That implication (for the CO_2 doubling scenario) is a reduction of approximately 4.4 W/m^2 in the upward infrared flux through the tropopause (not shown in Figure 12.1), which, after a radiatively controlled adjustment of the state of the stratosphere that evolves on a time scale of about one month, leads to a deficit, also of 4.4 W/m^2, in the 240 W/m^2 radiation out of the top of the atmosphere. This 4.4 W/m^2 imbalance in

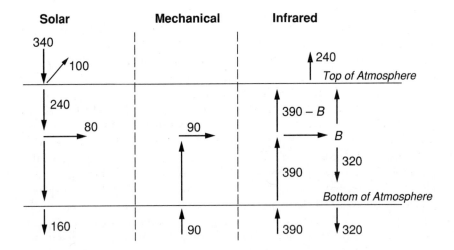

FIGURE 12.1 Schematic illustration of the radiative energy budget of the surface-atmosphere system. Horizontal arrows denote heat fluxes taken up by the atmosphere. Numbers are in watts per square meter.

the overall heat budget of the planet is the "radiative forcing" that accompanies the CO_2 doubling scenario.

Comparisons of the radiative forcing associated with various greenhouse gas emission scenarios provide quantified characterizations of the effectiveness of such scenarios, and Chapter 17 includes a more general quantitative relationship between greenhouse gas emission scenarios and the radiative forcing levels to which they lead.

RADIATIVE FEEDBACK MECHANISMS

In order to demonstrate radiative feedback mechanisms, it is convenient to assume initially that climate change is manifested solely by temperature changes within the climatic system and that all other climate parameters remain fixed at their unperturbed values. In this framework, there is no change in the climatic system's 240 W/m^2 solar absorption. Moreover, let G denote the 4.4 W/m^2 radiative forcing, and let ΔF be the change in the TOA infrared flux following the imposition of the forcing. Thus,

$$G = \Delta F = \delta F \,/\, \delta T \cdot \Delta T_s \,,$$

where $\delta F/\delta T$ is the black body rate of change of the surface radiative flux per unit change of surface temperature, ΔT_s. For the surface temperature of this calculation (288 K), $\delta F/\delta T$ is 3.3 W/m^2/°C, and therefore

$$\Delta T_s = \frac{4.4}{3.3} \cong 1.3°\mathrm{C}.$$

If it were not for the fact that this warming introduces numerous interactive feedback mechanisms, then ΔT_s = 1.3°C (2.3°F) would be a robust estimate of that global mean quantity. Unfortunately, such feedbacks introduce considerable uncertainty in ΔT_s estimates. Three of the more commonly discussed radiative feedbacks are described in the following sections. Although these phenomena are interrelated in the actual climatic system, they are discussed separately here to clearly identify their respective consequences. Additional feedback mechanisms involving land-surface hydrology are described in Chapter 15. The qualitative tools used to analyze energy transfers in the climatic system are less well developed in these latter mechanisms.

Water Vapor Feedback

The best understood, although still controversial, feedback mechanism is water vapor feedback. This phenomenon is intuitively easy to comprehend:

a warmer atmosphere can contain more water vapor, which itself is a greenhouse gas. Thus an increase in one greenhouse gas (CO_2) induces an increase in yet another greenhouse gas (water vapor), resulting in a positive (amplifying) feedback mechanism. Although it has been suggested that the water vapor feedback might be negative (Lindzen, 1990), recent combined observational and model results strongly support the conventional interpretation that water vapor provides positive feedback (Raval and Ramanathan, 1989; Rind et al., 1991). Notwithstanding the connection between water vapor and clouds in the climatic system, they are treated separately for analytic purposes (see also the "Cloud Feedback" section, below).

To be specific on this point, Raval and Ramanathan (1989) have employed satellite data to quantify the temperature dependence of the water vapor greenhouse effect. From their results, it readily follows (Cess, 1989) that water vapor feedback reduces $\delta F/\delta T$ from the prior value of 3.3 W/m^2/°C to 2.3 W/m^2/°C. This in turn increases the global warming, for a CO_2 doubling, from 1.3° to 1.9°C (2.3° to 3.4°F).

There is yet a further amplification. Because water vapor also absorbs solar radiation, water vapor feedback leads to an additional heating of the climatic system through enhanced absorption of solar radiation. With Q denoting solar absorption by the climatic system (240 W/m^2 for the present climate), this effect produces $\Delta Q/\Delta T_s = 0.2$ W/m^2/°C (Cess et al., 1990). To incorporate this into a ΔT_s estimate, extension of the previous analysis to include solar absorption yields $\Delta T_s = \lambda G$, where λ is the climate sensitivity parameter defined by

$$\lambda = \frac{1}{\Delta F / \Delta T_s - \Delta Q / \Delta T_s} .$$

It then follows that the inclusion of the solar component of water vapor feedback results in $\Delta T_s = 2.1$°C (3.8°F), so that the net effect of water vapor feedback is to amplify the initial $\Delta T_s = 1.3$°C (2.3°F) warming by the factor of 1.6.

The progressive forcing and feedback amplifications are summarized in Table 12.1. Here H denotes the greenhouse effect (150 W/m^2 for the present climate). The radiative forcing (process 1) simultaneously increases H and reduces F, so that the planet emits 4.4 W/m^2 less energy than it absorbs from the sun. It is this imbalance that causes greenhouse warming and results in $\Delta T_s = 1.3$°C (2.3°F) (process 2). Although the climatic system returns to its original radiation balance, with 240 W/m^2 both absorbed and emitted, process 2 increases further the greenhouse effect by 2.7 W/m^2 (154.4 to 157.1 W/m^2) because of enhanced surface emission resulting from surface warming.

TABLE 12.1 Forcing and Response of the Climatic System Caused by a Doubling of Atmospheric CO_2

	ΔT_s (°C)	H (W/m²)	F (W/m²)	Q (W/m²)
Present climate	0	150.0	240.0	240.0
Process				
1. Radiative forcing	0	154.4	235.6	240.0
2. Temperature response without water vapor feedback	1.3	157.1	240.0	240.0
3. Including infrared water vapor feedback	1.9	160.4	240.0	240.0
4. Including solar water vapor feedback	2.1	161.1	240.4	240.4

NOTE: See text for definition of symbols.

Process 3 incorporates the infrared consequences of water vapor feedback, with a 3.3 W/m² increase in H (157.1 to 160.4 W/m²) being simultaneously due to the increase in atmospheric water vapor and to enhanced surface emission. The TOA radiation budget is only slightly modified by process 4. An important point is that the combined effects of water vapor feedback and surface warming have amplified the 4.4 W/m² greenhouse forcing to 11.1 W/m². As Raval and Ramanathan (1989) have emphasized, this suggests that direct monitoring, from satellites, could help identify future changes in the greenhouse effect.

The most detailed climate models for the purpose of projecting climate change are three-dimensional atmospheric general circulation models (GCMs), and these models seem to depict properly the infrared component of water vapor feedback. In a recent intercomparison of atmospheric GCMs (Cess et al., 1990), it was found that 19 GCMs collectively produced

$$\Delta F / \Delta T_s = 2.3 \pm 0.2 \text{ W} / \text{m}^2.$$

Thus the models used by many investigators are mutually consistent and in agreement with the observational result of Raval and Ramanathan (1989). It must be noted, however, that a variety of phenomena, such as the role of clouds, make such interpretation difficult.

The above calculations are not dynamic and thus do not completely characterize all relevant phenomena. A recent analysis is more inclusive (Rind et al., 1991). First, a GCM predicts increased water vapor in the middle and upper troposphere. This prediction is compared to observed satellite-generated data on seasonal water vapor content in the convective western Pacific and the largely nonconvective eastern Pacific. These results suggest that water vapor feedback is not overestimated in models and should amplify the climatic response to increased concentrations of greenhouse gases.

Snow-Ice Feedback

An additional feedback mechanism is snow-ice feedback, by which a warmer earth has less snow and ice cover, resulting in a darker planet that in turn absorbs more solar radiation. While this conventional albedo feedback description is quite obvious, and by itself constitutes a positive feedback, it now appears that the retreat of snow and ice cover might activate other interactive processes.

The same set of GCMs as used by Cess et al. (1990) to investigate cloud feedback (see next section) has recently been used to interpret and intercompare feedbacks associated solely with a change in snow cover. What that study shows is that clouds can significantly influence the snow-induced change in albedo and that this effect is more subtle than a mere masking of the change in surface albedo by the clouds. For example, in some models the snow-induced planetary albedo change is *greater* when clouds are present than when they are not. The reason for this is that the cloudiness change induced by the snow retreat causes a shift in clear-sky regions from snow-covered land to snow-free land, and this by itself is a positive feedback. The snow retreat can also induce an infrared feedback, which in some models is positive and in others negative. Thus it is clear that snow-ice feedback is far more complex than the conventional interpretation that it is a direct albedo feedback.

Cloud Feedback

Feedback mechanisms related to clouds are extremely complex. To demonstrate this, it is useful to first consider the impact of clouds on the present climate. Summarized in Table 12.2 are the radiative impacts of clouds on the global climatic system for annual-mean conditions. These radiative impacts refer to the effect of clouds relative to a "clear-sky" earth. The

TABLE 12.2   Infrared, Solar, and Net Cloud Radiative
Forcing (CRF)

Component	CRF (W/m^2)
Infrared	31
Solar	−44
Net	−13

NOTE: These are annual-mean values estimated from data for
January, April, July, and October (Ramanathan et al., 1989).

presence of clouds heats the climatic system by 31 W/m^2 through increasing
the greenhouse effect. Because of the similarity of this process to trace gas
radiative forcing, this impact is referred to as cloud radiative forcing. Through
reflection of solar radiation, clouds also result in cooling of the system. As
demonstrated in Table 12.2, the latter effect dominates the former, and the
net effect of clouds on the annual climatic system is a 13 W/m^2 radiative
cooling.

Although clouds produce net cooling of the climatic system, this does
not mean that clouds will necessarily offset additional global warming due
to increasing greenhouse gases. As discussed in detail by Cess et al. (1989,
1990), cloud feedback constitutes the *change* in net cloud radiative forcing
associated with a particular change in climate. To emphasize the complexity of this feedback mechanism, three contributory processes are summarized:

• *Cloud amount:* If cloud amount decreases because of global warming,
as occurs in typical GCM simulations (e.g., Cess et al., 1989), then this
decrease reduces the greenhouse effect attributed to clouds and so acts as a
negative feedback mechanism. But there is a related positive feedback; the
solar radiation absorbed by the climatic system increases because the diminished cloud cover causes a reduction of reflected solar radiation by
clouds. There is no simple way of appraising the net sign of this feedback
component.

• *Cloud altitude:* A vertical redistribution of clouds will also induce
feedbacks. For example, if global warming displaces a given cloud layer to
a higher and colder region of the atmosphere, this will produce a positive
feedback because the colder cloud will emit less radiation and will thus
enhance the greenhouse effect.

• *Cloud water content:* There has been considerable recent speculation
that global warming could increase cloud water content, thereby resulting in
brighter clouds and hence a negative component of cloud feedback. This

may oversimplify the situation. Increases in cloud albedo can induce compensating positive infrared feedback (Cess et al., 1990), and in some models the net effect may be positive (Schlesinger, 1988; Cess et al., 1990; Rind et al., 1991). Recent analysis using both satellite and model results showed that highly reflective cirrus clouds are produced in tropical regions when sea surface temperature increases sufficiently (Ramanathan and Collins, 1991). The increased albedo may be sufficient to counter further warming due to infrared feedback.

The above discussion illustrates some of the complexities associated with cloud feedback; indeed, differences in models' depictions of this feedback largely account for the significant differences in climate sensitivity among the 19 GCMs (Cess et al., 1990). This intercomparison employed a perpetual July simulation in which the climate was changed by imposing a 4°C (7.2°F) perturbation on the global sea surface temperature while holding sea ice fixed. Since a perpetual July simulation with a GCM produces little snow cover over land, this effectively eliminates snow feedback. The details of this simulation are given elsewhere (Cess et al., 1989, 1990). The approach was chosen to minimize computer time and thus allow a large number of modeling groups to participate.

Cess et al. (1990) have summarized climate sensitivity parameters (λ as defined in the "Water Vapor Feedback" section above) for the 19 GCMs, and these results are reproduced in Figure 12.2. The important point is that

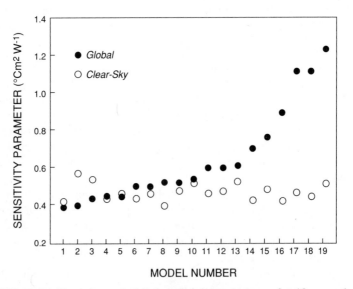

FIGURE 12.2   Clear-sky and global sensitivity parameters for 19 general circulation models.

Source: Reprinted courtesy of Robert D. Cess.

cloud effects were isolated by separately averaging the models' clear-sky TOA fluxes, so that in addition to evaluating the climate sensitivity parameter for the globe as a whole (solid circles), it was also possible to evaluate it for an equivalent "clear-sky" earth (open circles). Note the remarkable agreement of the clear-sky sensitivity parameters; this is due to the agreement of water vapor feedback components, as discussed above. There is, however, a nearly threefold variation of the global (clear plus overcast) sensitivity parameter; clearly, given the clear-sky agreement, most of the variation in the global sensitivity parameters of current models can be attributed to cloud feedback. Certainly, improvements in the treatment of cloud feedback are needed if GCMs are ultimately to be used as reliable climate predictors.

REFERENCES

Cess, R. D. 1989. Greenhouse effect: Gauging water-vapour feedback. Nature 342:736-737.

Cess, R. D., G. L. Potter, J. P. Blanchet, G. J. Boer, S. J. Ghan, J. T. Kiehl, H. Le Treut, Z.-X. Li, X.-Z. Liang, J. F. B. Mitchell, J.-J. Morcrette, D. A. Randall, M. R. Riches, E. Roeckner, U. Schlese, A. Slingo, K. E. Taylor, W. M. Washington, R. T. Wetherald, and I. Yagai. 1989. Interpretation of cloud-climate feedback as produced by 14 atmospheric general circulation models. Science 245:513-516.

Cess, R. D., G. L. Potter, J. P. Blanchet, G. J. Boer, A. D. Delgenio, M. Deque, V. Dymnikov, V. Galin, W. L. Gates, S. J. Ghan, J. T. Kiehl, A. A. Lacis, H. Le Treut, Z.-X. Li, X.-Z. Liang, B. J. McAvaney, V. P. Meleshko, J. F. B. Mitchell, J.-J. Morcrette, D. A. Randall, L. Rikus, E. Roeckner, J. F. Royer, U. Schlese, D. A. Sheinin, A. Slingo, A. P. Sokolov, K. E. Taylor, W. M. Washington, R. T. Wetherald, I. Yagai, and M. H. Zhang. 1990. Intercomparison and interpretation of climate feedback processes in 19 atmospheric general circulation models. Journal of Geophysical Research—Atmospheres 95(10):16,601-16,615.

Jenkinson, D. S., D. E. Adams, and A. Wild. 1991. Model estimates of CO_2 emissions from soil in response to global warming. Nature 351:304-306.

Kirchman, D. L., Y. Suzuki, C. Garside, and H. W. Ducklow. 1991. High turnover rates of dissolved organic carbon during a spring phytoplankton bloom. Nature 352:612-614.

Lindzen, R. S. 1990. Some remarks on global warming. Environmental Science and Technology 24(4):424-426.

Ramanathan, V., and W. Collins. 1991. Thermodynamic regulation of ocean warming by cirrus clouds deduced from observations of the 1987 El Niño. Nature 351:27-32.

Ramanathan, V., R. D. Cess, E. F. Harrison, P. Minnis, B. R. Barkstrom, E. Ahmad, and D. Hartmann. 1989. Cloud-radiative forcing and climate: Results from the Earth Radiation Budget Experiment. Science 243:57-63.

Raval, A., and V. Ramanathan. 1989. Observational determination of the greenhouse effect. Nature 342:758-761.

Rind, D., E.-W. Chiou, W. Chu, J. Larsen, S. Oltmans, J. Lerner, M. P. McCormick, and L. McMaster. 1991. Positive water vapor feedback in climate models confirmed by satellite data. Nature 349:500-503.

Schlesinger, M. E. 1988. Ocean drilling program: Early glaciation of Antarctica. Nature 333:303.

The George C. Marshall Institute. 1989. Scientific Perspectives on the Greenhouse Problem. Washington, D.C.: The George C. Marshall Institute.

13

Model Performance

Adequate prediction of global surface warming caused by increasing greenhouse gases will require coupled models of the atmosphere, oceans, ice sheets and snow fields, and biosphere. These coupled models will have to provide time-dependent simulations that adopt, as input conditions, scenarios for future emissions of greenhouse gases. And, like the proverbial chain, the validity of these coupled models is governed by the weakest of the component models. The IPCC scientific assessment (Intergovernmental Panel on Climate Change, 1990) reviewed current results in these and related topics. To date, most emphasis has been placed on the development and testing of atmospheric models. Even though policymakers would like them, current capabilities do not allow credible projections of regional effects. The panel finds that these and other aspects of climate models have even greater uncertainty than those associated with global mean temperature projections. However, for purposes of assessing their limits for policy decisions, the primary focus of the examination here is on global mean temperature.

Considerable effort has been focused on atmospheric GCM experiments in which the CO_2 concentration of the atmosphere is instantaneously doubled and the models are then allowed to achieve a new equilibrium climate. Although these simulations do not provide information on time-dependent (or "transient") climatic changes that would accompany more realistic greenhouse gas accumulation scenarios, they do allow a means of testing, understanding, and comparing atmospheric GCMs. The IPCC scientific assessment (Intergovernmental Panel on Climate Change, 1990) provided a convenient summary of these simulations. For present purposes the only simulations considered are those that utilize computed clouds; i.e., that incorporate cloud feedback.

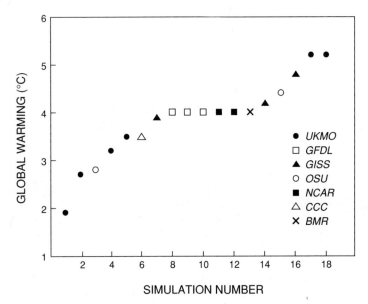

FIGURE 13.1 Global warming from 18 GCM simulations for a doubling of atmospheric CO_2. The institutional designations are United Kingdom Meteorological Office (UKMO), NOAA Geophysical Fluid Dynamics Laboratory (GFDL), NASA Goddard Institute for Space Studies (GISS), Oregon State University (OSU), National Center for Atmospheric Research (NCAR), Canadian Climate Centre (CCC), and Australian Bureau of Meteorology Research Centre (BMR).

The equilibrium global warming (i.e., ΔT_s) produced by 18 different CO_2 doubling simulations[1] is summarized in Figure 13.1. The simulation numbers are in order of increasing projection of global warming. Multiple simulations have been performed by five of the seven involved GCMs; these serve as sensitivity studies for a specific model. As an example, simulation numbers 4 and 5 (UKMO), and 8 through 10 (GFDL), respectively, proceed to a finer horizontal resolution. Note that neither model indicates a significant influence of horizontal resolution on the model-predicted global warming. The UKMO GCM produced both the greatest (5.2°C (9.4°F)) and the smallest (1.9°C (3.4°F)) global warming, and this notable variation is the consequence of differences in assumptions about cloud parameters (Mitchell et al., 1989).

The horizontal solution technique used in the seven GCMs is either finite difference (UKMO, GISS, OSU) or spectral (GFDL, NCAR, CCC, BMR). The spectral models are in much better agreement (ΔT_s = 3.5° to 4.0°C (6.3° to 7.2°F)) than the finite difference models (ΔT_s = 1.9° to 5.2°C (3.4° to 9.4°F)). This is probably coincidental. Of the 19 models in Figure 12.2, eight are finite difference and eleven are spectral, and here neither group is found to exhibit better agreement than the other. It should be noted that no persuasive comparison of model results with global warming observations has yet been constructed.

It is important to realize that the global warming results in Figure 13.1 include snow-ice feedback, whereas the sensitivity parameters in Figure 12.2 do not, and this partially explains differences between Figures 12.2 and 13.1. For example, simulation numbers 10 (GFDL) and 14 (GISS) in Figure 13.1 produce quite comparable global warming (4.0° and 4.2°C (7.2° and 7.6°F), respectively). The same GFDL and GISS models are, however, models number 12 and 19 in Figure 12.2. Relative to clear skies, Figure 12.2 shows rather modest positive cloud feedback in the GFDL model, whereas there is a very strong positive feedback in the GISS model.

That these two models agree well in Figure 13.1 is at least partially due to compensatory differences in snow-ice albedo feedback. Both modeling groups have provided feedback diagnostics so that individual feedbacks may be progressively incorporated, and this is demonstrated in Table 13.1. The two GCMs produce similar warming in the absence of both cloud feedback and snow-ice albedo feedback. The incorporation of cloud feedback, however, shows that this is a stronger feedback in the GISS model, as is consistent with Figure 12.2. But the additional incorporation of snow-ice albedo feedback largely compensates for their differences in cloud feedback. Thus, while the two models produce comparable global warming, they do so for quite different reasons.

It is emphasized that Table 13.1 should not be used to estimate the amplification factor due to cloud feedback, because feedback mechanisms are interactive. From Table 13.1 the cloud feedback amplifications for the GFDL and GISS models might be inferred to be 1.2 and 1.6, respectively, but only in the absence of snow-ice albedo feedback. If snow-ice albedo feedback is incorporated before cloud feedback, then the respective amplification factors are 1.3 and 1.8. These larger values are due to an amplification of cloud feedback by snow-ice albedo feedback.

The change in precipitation that would be concurrent with global warming is of considerable importance. Global mean precipitation change, for

TABLE 13.1 Comparison of Global Warming (°C) for the GFDL and GISS GCMs with the Progressive Additions of Cloud Feedback and Snow-Ice Albedo Feedback

Feedbacks	GFDL	GISS
No cloud or snow-ice	1.7	2.0
Plus cloud	2.0	3.2
Plus snow-ice	4.0	4.2

the same models as in Figure 13.1, is summarized in Figure 13.2 (Inter-governmental Panel on Climate Change, 1990; no value is reported for simulation number 7). Although there is considerable variability among the simulations, with reference to Figure 13.1 there is an obvious correlation between precipitation change and global warming. This is to be expected, since global warming enhances surface evaporation and hence precipitation.

To be more specific on this point, Figure 13.3 provides a scatter plot of precipitation change versus global warming. Although 17 simulations are represented here, there are four coincident points (one finite difference and three spectral). Clearly, differences among global warming simulation models are the cause of much of the variance in the predictions of global precipitation change. Note that the finite difference models exhibit a considerably stronger correlation, and there is no obvious explanation for this. The primary point of Figure 13.3 is that global precipitation change and global warming are, as would be expected, strongly coupled.

Of far more practical importance than the global averages are the regional patterns of changes in both precipitation and soil moisture. While global precipitation, for reasons discussed above, will increase with global warming, one would anticipate that there would be geographical regions where just the opposite occurs. Frequently, arid subtropics are a consequence of the descending branch of the tropical Hadley cell, and a shift in

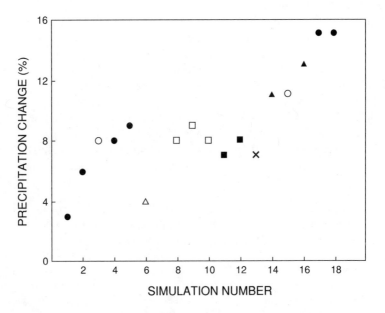

FIGURE 13.2 Global precipitation change for 17 of the global warming simulations of Figure 13.1.

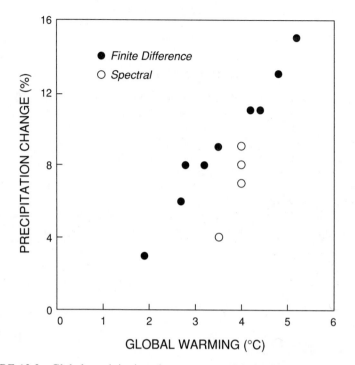

FIGURE 13.3   Global precipitation change versus global warming for the 17 simulations.   There are four coincident points.

its location should bring with it a reduction of precipitation. Regional changes in soil moisture are even more difficult to predict, because soil moisture is the difference between precipitation and evaporation plus runoff, and errors in the change of any of these quantities will produce magnified errors in the fractional change of soil moisture.

As noted at the beginning of this chapter, persuasive projections of future climatic changes will require the availability of reliable coupled atmosphere, ocean, cryosphere, and biosphere models. As of now, in most models, the role assigned to the oceans does not include any horizontal transport. In many studies, in fact, the ocean temperature has been postulated as a boundary condition, often to provide a surrogate parameter from which potentially useful insights can be drawn. Recently, more elaborate models of the ocean have been coupled to GCMs in climate change simulations (Stouffer et al., 1989; Manabe et al., 1990), but efforts at this level are in their infancy. Clearly, there is a need here for model improvements, particularly with respect to cloud-climate interactions. And, of course, the other component models, as they evolve, will have to undergo similar scrutiny.

NOTE

1. Not the same set as cited in Figure 12.2.

REFERENCES

Intergovernmental Panel on Climate Change. 1990. Climate Change: The IPCC Scientific Assessment, J. T. Houghton, G. J. Jenkins, and J. J. Ephraums, eds. New York: Cambridge University Press.

Manabe, S., K. Bryan, and M. J. Spelman. 1990. Transient response of a global ocean-atmosphere model to a doubling of atmospheric carbon dioxide. Journal of Physical Oceanography 20:722-749.

Mitchell, J. F. B., C. A. Senior, and W. J. Ingram. 1989. CO_2 and climate: A missing feedback? Nature 341:132-134.

Stouffer, R. J., S. Manabe, and K. Bryan. 1989. Interhemispheric asymmetry in climate responses to a gradual increase of atmospheric CO_2. Nature 342:660-662.

14

The Climate Record

TEMPERATURE

The clearest signal of an enhanced greenhouse effect, or greenhouse warming, that is projected by climate models is a widespread and substantial increase of surface temperature, especially over continental areas. For this reason, special attention has been given to the observed temporal and spatial variations of land surface temperatures (typically measured 1 to 2 m (3.3 to 6.6 feet) above ground level) and sea surface temperatures (typically measured in the layer from the surface to several meters below the ocean's surface). Estimates of global temperature change are credible only for measurements that have been taken since the late nineteenth century. Earlier temperature data are available, but their spatial distribution and their sparseness seriously compromise the attempts to infer global averages. Additional difficulties arise because measurements were not taken with an eye to the small and gradual global average changes that are characteristic of climate change. This problem is exacerbated when regional changes are at issue simply because the statistical amelioration of offsetting bias is not very helpful when the data are sparse.

The most comprehensive assessment of the instrumental record of surface temperature has recently been completed by the Intergovernmental Panel on Climate Change (1990). A significant warming has been observed since the late nineteenth century. Uncertainties underlie the interpretation of the data, but there is consensus that the actual rise probably lies within the range of 0.3° to 0.6°C (0.5° to 1.1°F) (see Figure 14.1). Qualitatively, an inference of global warming is supported by several independent sources of information: (1) land and sea surface temperatures are independently measured, and both depict significant warming (Figure 14.2), (2) the collective

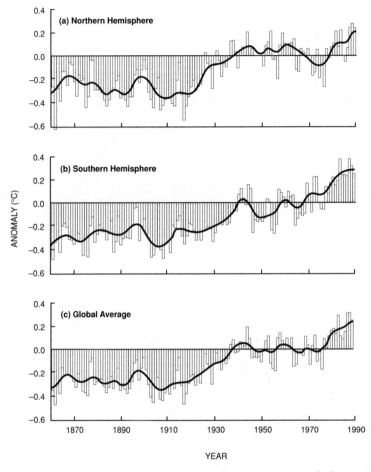

FIGURE 14.1 Combined land air and sea surface temperature relative to 1951 to 1980 average temperatures. Land air temperatures are typically measured 1 to 2 m above ground level. Sea surface temperatures are typically measured in the layer from the ocean's surface to several meters below. Smoothed curves are 11-year bimodal filters with the first and last 5 years drawn by projecting the endpoints of the series.

SOURCES: Land air temperatures are updated from Jones et al. (1986a,b), and sea surface temperatures are from Farmer et al. (1989).

behavior of many glaciers is likely to be sensitive to large-scale temperature variations, and many mountain glaciers have retreated since the end of the nineteenth century, some of them markedly, and (3) estimates of sea level variations over the past century indicate a general rise in sea level that is qualitatively consistent with the global increase of surface temperature.

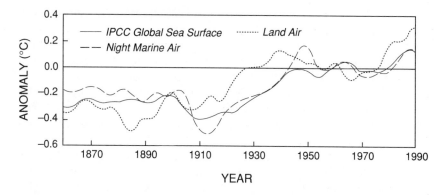

FIGURE 14.2   IPCC global sea surface (solid), night marine air (dashed), and land air (line-dots) temperature anomalies, relative to 1951 to 1980. Smoothed curves are 11-year bimodal filters with the first and last 5 years drawn by projecting the endpoints of the series.

SOURCES: Sea surface temperatures are averages from Farmer et al. (1989) and the U.K. Meteorological Office. Night marine air temperatures are from the U.K. Meteorological Office. Land temperatures are equally weighted averages of data from Jones et al. (1986a,b), Hansen and Lebedeff (1988), and Vinnikov et al. (1990).

Uncertainties in the Record

Despite the fact that there is virtually unanimous agreement that global temperatures have increased since the nineteenth century, the exact magnitude is still somewhat uncertain for a variety of reasons. For land-based surface temperatures, these uncertainties arise for the following reasons:

• Station locations have changed and thereby have introduced uncertainties into the interpretation of the temporal record.

• Many stations are located in and around cities that have increased in size and population density, thereby introducing a systematic increase in the local temperature record that is unrelated to global climate change.

Additional uncertainties for *both* land and sea surface temperatures include the following:

• The spatial coverage of the data is neither globally comprehensive nor optimally sited, and the degree of coverage changes over time.

• Changes have occurred in instruments, exposures of thermometers, observing schedules, observing practices, and other factors including land use, thus introducing artificial changes in the temperature record, sometimes of a systematic nature.

Most of these uncertainties have been assessed in various studies, as reviewed by Karl et al. (1989). Arguably the most serious of these uncertainties are the changes in observation practices related to sea surface temperature measurements. Changes in these practices have resulted in systematic biases as large as the observed warming depicted in Figure 14.1. The sea surface temperature has been measured by the use of various types of buckets lowered from the ship's deck, and more recently by the water flowing to the ship's engine intake. Various researchers have addressed this problem (Farmer et al., 1989; Bottomley et al., 1990; Folland and Parker, 1990). Differences in the assumptions, in approaches used to correct for these systematic biases, and in the input data lead to an uncertainty associated with the warming since the nineteenth century of about ±0.1°C (±0.18°F).

Urbanization effects in the thermometric record have now been assessed by various researchers for many, but by no means all, regions of the globe. Studies by Hansen and Lebedeff (1987, 1988), Balling and Idso (1989), Karl et al. (1988), Karl and Jones (1989, 1990), and Jones et al. (1989, 1990) suggest that the bias introduced into the observed warming of the land surface varies from a high of 0.1° to 0.2°C (0.18° to 0.36°F) over the United States down to negligible amounts over western areas of the former USSR and eastern China. Jones et al. (1990) estimated that the apparent global warming of the land surface record attributable to urbanization is no more than about 0.05°C (0.09°F). When one considers that the land covers about three-tenths of the global surface area, the bias due to urbanization in the global temperature record is most likely to be at least an order of magnitude smaller than observed warming. A more definitive statement awaits more comprehensive studies.

Another important consideration in the compilation of hemispheric and global temperatures is the spatial coverage of observations over both land and sea. The spatial coverage of the observations since the nineteenth century has not been uniform in time or space. For example, ships of opportunity, which provide the greatest portion of the sea surface measurements, have followed preferred navigational routes and consequently leave vast portions of the ocean inadequately sampled. The effect of spatial sampling inadequacies has been addressed for the land areas by Jones et al. (1986a,b) and for the ocean areas by Bottomley et al. (1990) and Folland and Colman (1988). These analyses suggest that changes in spatial coverage have not had a serious impact on our ability to discern changes in the global thermometric record. Because of the large-scale coherence of multidecadal climate variations, especially over the oceans, the sampling problem probably adds less than 0.1°C (0.18°F) uncertainty to the observed warming, as depicted in Figure 14.1.

Other biases and inhomogeneities in the temperature record have been directly assessed only on a regional basis, but indirectly assessed on a global basis. These include changes in observing schedules, types of instrument shelters used, and station relocations in the land-based record. Studies by Jones et al. (1986a), Karl and Jones (1990), and Parker (1990) indicate that, although these types of biases may be quite significant on a regional scale, for hemispheric and global averages many of the biases and inhomogeneities tend to cancel.

Considering all the uncertainties in the thermometric climate record, it would be most appropriate to provide a range of most likely rates of warming from the latter half of the nineteenth century to the present. This range, as given by the IPCC (Intergovernmental Panel on Climate Change, 1990), is of the order 0.3° to 0.6°C (0.5° to 1.1°F). That is, the warming rate, calculated either as a trend from the 1860 to 1890 era to the present, or as the difference in temperature for the 1980s minus the value for the period from the 1860s to the 1890s, is between 0.3° and 0.6°C (0.5° and 1.1°F). At this time, there are no compelling reasons to dispute the range given. Whether this warming is related to the greenhouse effect is discussed in the next section.

Spatial and Temporal Characteristics

The increase in temperature has occurred somewhat differently in the northern hemisphere than in the southern hemisphere (Figure 14.1). A rapid increase in temperature occurred in the northern hemisphere during the 1920s into the 1930s, whereas the increase in the southern hemisphere during this time was much more gradual. A substantial portion of the global warming observed since the latter half of the nineteenth century occurred prior to World War II. The past half-century is characterized by relatively constant global mean temperatures except for the 0.1° to 0.2°C (0.18° to 0.36°F) steplike temperature increase that occurred around 1980. This relatively constant global mean temperature is characteristic of both hemispheres, but with some evidence of cooling in the northern hemisphere during the 1960s and 1970s. Some analyses suggest that the northern hemisphere cooling may be related to sulfate aerosol emissions (e.g., Wigley, 1991). The warmth of the 1980s has continued into the 1990s.

The global mean ocean temperature and the surface air temperature of the southern hemisphere (which is predominantly water) have risen at a rate comparable to that over land (Figure 14.3a). This is not altogether consistent with time-dependent GCM simulations with enhanced greenhouse gases. These simulations generally have a slower rate of temperature increase in the southern hemisphere and over the oceans, especially the circumpolar oceans, than in the northern hemisphere (Stouffer et al., 1989; Washington and Meehl, 1989; Manabe et al., 1990). At this time, however, the large variability in transient climate simulations and the difficulty in linking these simulations to the appropriate part of the climate record prevent unequivocal statements about the consistency or lack thereof between simulations and the climate record.

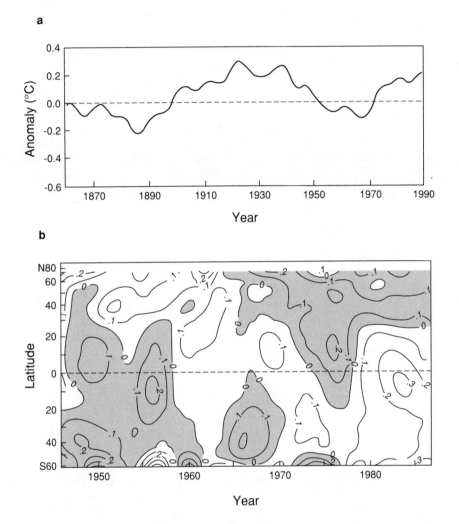

FIGURE 14.3   (a) IPCC differences between land and sea surface temperature anomalies (relative to 1951 to 1980) for the northern hemisphere, 1861 to 1989. (b) Annual anomalies of zonal average temperature over the ocean.   Shaded areas represent conditions cooler than the 1945 to 1986 zonal average. (c) Same as (b) except for land only. (d) Same as (b) except for land and ocean combined.

SOURCES: Land air temperatures are updated from Jones (1988). Sea surface temperatures are averages of the U.K. Meteorological Office and Farmer et al. (1989).

c

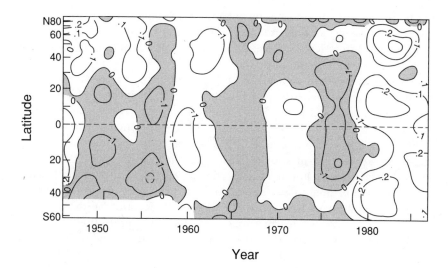

Year

d

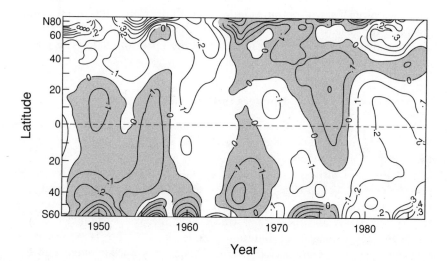

Year

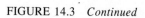

FIGURE 14.3   *Continued*

Climate models that have been allowed to reach equilibrium with 2 (sometimes 4) times preindustrial concentrations of CO_2 project temperature increases in polar and high latitudes that would be larger than those at low latitudes. These are related to the extent of land and sea ice and other factors. Currently, the largest variations in temperature are found at high latitudes (Figure 14.3). Changes of temperature as depicted in Figure 14.3d are over too short a period to reflect systematic changes in the warmth of the equatorial region relative to polar regions.

Because of the high natural variability of climate, it is pertinent to ask when we might expect to unequivocally link the greenhouse effect to the observed climate variations. Two recent studies address this question on a regional basis assuming validity of the IPCC projections. Briffa et al. (1990) used the variability in a 1400-year reconstructed tree-ring density record to address this question for Fennoscandia. Briffa et al. (1990) indicated that because of low-frequency climate variability, it will be decades before we will be able to confirm or contradict the IPCC projections in the Fennoscandia region. Karl et al. (1990) used the central North American observed climate record to determine when the IPCC projections could either be confirmed or contradicted for that region. Karl et al. (1990) indicated that if the models with a 4°C (7.2°F) (i.e., high) climate sensitivity to enhanced greenhouse gases are used, we probably should have already detected significant warming in this region, but for the low-sensitivity model (2°C (3.6°F) warming in central North America from preindustrial times to 2030) we probably will not be able to detect statistically significant warming rates for at least another two decades. Thus, at this time, no credible assertion that the recent temperature rise is the result of changes in greenhouse gas forcing is justified.

Changes in Extremes

Long-term changes and variations of extreme maximum and minimum temperatures have recently been assessed over three large land areas. These include the United States, the former USSR, and the People's Republic of China (PRC). Until now, the dearth of analyses about extremes has been due to the difficulty in transferring these observations to computer-compatible media. Recent work by Karl et al. (1991) indicates that the warming in the United States and the former USSR over the past several decades is solely due to an increase of nighttime temperatures (Figure 14.4). Furthermore, the range of extreme temperatures, especially during summer in the United States and the former USSR, has also decreased (Karl et al., 1991). Climate models with enhanced greenhouse gases cannot yet reliably predict the expected change in extremes. It has been demonstrated that in the

United States the rise in the minimum temperature is at least partially related to increases in cloud cover (Plantico et al., 1990).

The differential change of the maximum and minimum temperatures points out the limited amount of information that can be derived from changes in the mean and how cloud changes may already be influencing the observed climate record. Thus long-term consistent ancillary climatic data (such as vertical and horizontal cloud distribution) are needed in addition to basic temperature data.

Temperatures Aloft

Temperatures aloft have been measured by instruments carried by balloons and, most recently, by satellite instruments. Global records have been constructed for various atmospheric layers by Angell (1988) back to 1957 using balloon or radiosonde information. Spencer and Christy (1990) have used the space-based Microwave Sounding Unit (MSU) data to reconstruct global temperature variations back to 1979 for tropospheric layer temperatures. The global mean annual temperatures of MSU data are in excellent agreement ($r^2 = 0.95$) with the mid-tropospheric temperatures as calculated by Angell (1988). This comparison is consistent with the less complete spatial coverage of the data used by Angell (1988), at least for the past decade.

Climate models with enhanced greenhouse gases project not only increased temperatures in the troposphere but also decreased temperatures in the stratosphere (in addition to the decrease accompanying depletion of stratospheric ozone). Mid-tropospheric temperatures since 1957 have shown an increase, and stratospheric temperatures a decrease. In addition, however, temperatures in the higher troposphere have also decreased, a circumstance that is not projected by climate models that include CO_2 changes only. Furthermore, the decrease in stratospheric temperatures is primarily found in the southern hemisphere in and around Antarctica, probably related to the decrease in stratospheric ozone (Trenberth and Olson, 1989). Finally, a recent study has pointed out the danger of overinterpreting mid-tropospheric temperature trends based on short time series. Whereas previous studies showed current temperature increases compared to 1957, Elms et al. (1990) extended their examination back to 1950 and found little or no temperature change from that date.

PRECIPITATION

Unlike model projections of changes in temperature with an enhanced greenhouse effect, or greenhouse warming, regional and geographic pat-

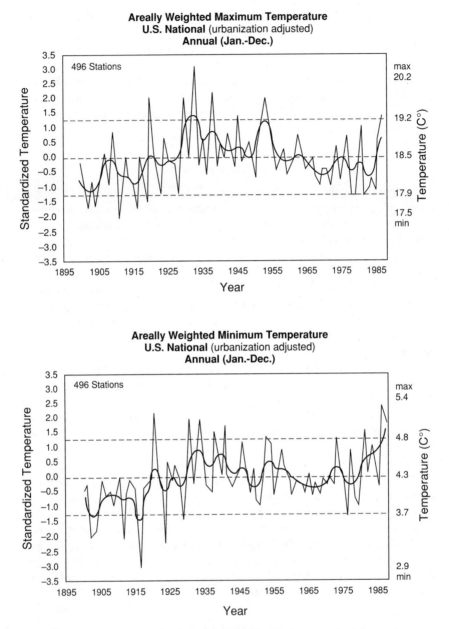

FIGURE 14.4 Changes in the annual mean daily maximum and minimum temperature in the United States (left panels) and the former USSR (right panels). A nine-
point bimodal filter was used to smooth the data.

Source: Reprinted courtesy of T. R. Karl.

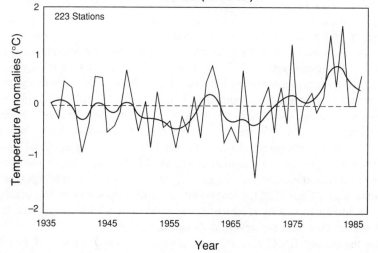

FIGURE 14.4 *Continued*

terns of precipitation change are not nearly as consistent from one model to the next. Nonetheless, some general characteristics are evident, such as (1) a global increase in precipitation; (2) significantly more precipitation at high latitudes and in the tropics throughout the year and during winter at mid-latitudes, but little change over the subtropics; and, of particular interest for the United States, (3) a suggestion in several but not all of the models of reduced summer and enhanced winter precipitation in the interior of North America.

The instrumental record related to global changes of precipitation is much more difficult to assess than the thermometric record. Nonetheless, there have been several large-scale analyses of precipitation variations over the northern and southern hemisphere *land* masses (Bradley et al., 1987; Diaz et al., 1989; Vinnikov et al., 1990), which have demonstrated that during the past several decades precipitation has tended to increase in northern hemisphere mid-latitudes and in the southern hemisphere. The increase in the northern hemisphere is predominantly due to an increase over the former USSR, and to a smaller degree over the United States (Figure 14.5). A decrease in precipitation over the past few decades has been noted over the subtropics of the northern hemisphere. This is primarily due to the decrease observed over the Sahel, and partially due to lower monsoonal rainfall over India. Changes of precipitation over oceanic regions are largely unknown.

Overall, the land data do suggest a general increase in land-based precipitation over the past few decades. This may be consistent with model projections, but quantitative inferences are difficult to defend. Precipitation varies in space and time much more than does temperature. A much higher density of stations is needed to calculate precipitation variations than is required for temperature. Such high-density data do exist, but they are not exchanged on an international basis. Furthermore, the efficiency of the collection of precipitation (both frozen and liquid) by different rain gauges varies with wind speed and raindrop size. In many countries, collection efficiency has tended to increase as operational practices have improved, often in poorly documented ways, possibly leading to an artificial upward trend in some regions (Groisman et al., 1991). Sevruk (1982) and Folland (1988) discuss the causes of the collection error. Despite these potentially serious biases, many of the important variations apparent in the precipitation records are evident in hydrological data, such as changes in lake levels and stream flow and the severe desiccation of the Sahel.

In the recent IPCC scientific assessment (Intergovernmental Panel on Climate Change, 1990) and summary report (Jäger and Ferguson, 1991), several scenarios of changes in North American precipitation were given based on various models (a decrease in summer precipitation up to 10 percent and an increase in winter precipitation up to 15 percent). Karl et al. (1990) show that even if these projections were correct, it would take decades before we could detect such changes. On the other hand, at the present time there is neither any evidence for increased aridity in the United States nor any systematic increase in winter to summer precipitation ratios (Karl et al., 1990). Furthermore, if the rate of change for the increase of winter to summer precipitation ratios suggested by the modeling reported by the IPCC were correct, we probably should have already detected such changes. All in all, the record cannot support persuasively a quantitative relationship between the greenhouse gas accumulation and the precipitation variations of the last century.

IMPROVING OUR CLIMATE OBSERVATIONS

At the present time the only reliable methods of measuring daily temperature and precipitation at the surface are the in situ measurements made at the thousands of weather stations around the world. Unfortunately, few (if any) of the stations make measurements for the purposes of detecting and monitoring climate change. The primary functions are to serve the needs of weather prediction and the weather assessment community. Such activities are quite distinct from monitoring climate change. The World Meteorological Organization is beginning to take some steps to rectify this situation (e.g., the Global Climate Baseline Data Base and the Climate Change Detection Project), but without strong support from national weather services, which currently do not operate their stations for the purpose of monitoring climate change, these programs will not succeed. That support will become important as new observing techniques and programs are brought on-line.

In the United States the National Oceanic and Atmospheric Administration (NOAA) is responsible for observing the nation's daily weather. NOAA operated 8,640 stations that monitored daily precipitation in 1967, but by 1988 the total had dropped to about 7,000. The totals for temperature monitoring dropped from 5,920 stations in 1967 to about 5,200 in 1988. The importance of these temperature and precipitation observation stations is critical, because many of them are located in rural environments, free from the urban heat island effect. This decrease in number has occurred during times of increased interest in global climate change. A dense network of stations is required to monitor the regional details of climate change, especially for precipitation, and to implement corrections for biases in the climate record. Other U.S. agencies also monitor the daily weather for a variety of purposes. At present, there is no central collection agency that can make available the full suite of weather observations made by the various U.S. agencies. This unfortunate situation should be rectified.

Furthermore, potentially new sources of bias have been and continue to be introduced into the NOAA network without an adequate means of assess-

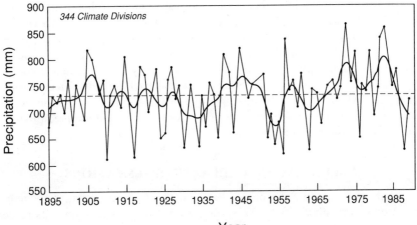

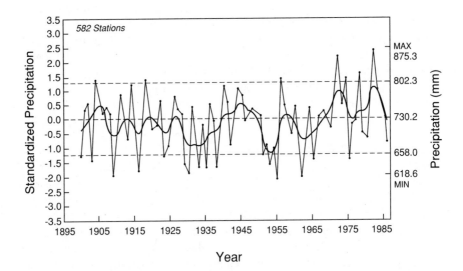

FIGURE 14.5   Changes in the annual total precipitation averaged over the contiguous United States from (a) Climate Division data, which make use of all stations with temperature *and* precipitation measurements (about 6,000 in recent decades), (b) the U.S. Historical Climate Network, which has a fixed set of higher-quality stations throughout the twentieth century, and (c) adjusted precipitation measurements over the former USSR based on optimal averaging methods (Groisman et al., 1991).

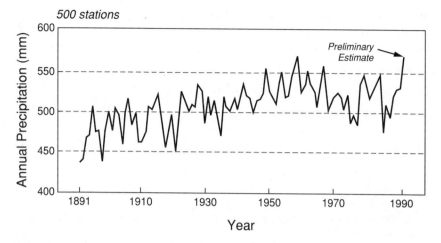

FIGURE 14.5 *Continued*

ing these biases. For example, a new thermometric instrument was installed at about half of the stations in the U.S. cooperative network between 1984 and 1988. At the present time, the bias introduced by this new instrument is significant with respect to interpreting U.S. climate change (Quayle et al., 1991). Side-by-side measurements of new and old measurement systems were not required. Such tests for a period of at least one year (the annual cycle) should be considered essential for climate monitoring. In addition, this instrument did not have the ability to retain maximum and minimum temperatures on a midnight-to-midnight basis. As a result, the opportunity was lost to eliminate many of the thermometric biases that had existed in the network because observers were understandably unwilling to remain with a fixed observation schedule over the decades.

The United States operates one of the most comprehensive networks in the world, but it needs to be improved in several ways:

1. Steps should be taken to ensure the continued operation of long-term stations in rural areas.

2. The surface observations of climate-related elements by various departments (e.g., Commerce, Interior, Agriculture, and Defense) should be integrated and made available for more comprehensive analyses.

3. Data should be assessed for biases as well as random errors on a routine basis, and corrections should accompany the disseminated data.

4. Electronic transfer of weather station observations should become routine operating procedure.

5. NOAA will soon be implementing an Automated Surface Observing System (ASOS). The methods of making observations and the locations of

many observing stations are scheduled to undergo significant change. NOAA should provide for side-by-side operation of the new and old instruments long enough to ensure that interpretation uncertainty is not introduced.

REFERENCES

Angell, J. K. 1988. Variations and trends in tropospheric and stratospheric global temperatures, 1958-87. Journal of Climate 1:1296-1313.

Balling, R. C., Jr., and S. B. Idso. 1989. Historical temperature trends in the United States and the effect of urban population growth. Journal of Geophysical Research 94:3359-3363.

Bottomley, M., C. K. Folland, J. Hsiung, R. E. Newell, and D. E. Parker. 1990. Global Ocean Surface Temperature Atlas (GOSTA). Joint Meteorological Office/Massachusetts Institute of Technology Project. London: U.K. Department of Energy and Environment.

Bradley, R. S., H. F. Diaz, J. K. Eischeid, P. D. Jones, P. M. Kelly, and C. M. Goodess. 1987. Precipitation fluctuations over northern hemisphere land areas since the mid-19th century. Science 237:171-175.

Briffa, K. R., T. S. Bartholin, D. Eckstein, P. D. Jones, W. Karlen, F. H. Schweingruber, and P. Zetterberg. 1990. A 1400-year tree-ring record of summer temperatures in Fennoscandia. Nature 346:434-439.

Diaz, H. F., R. S. Bradley, and J. K. Eischeid. 1989. Precipitation fluctuations over global land areas since the late 1800s. Journal of Geophysical Research 94:1195-1210.

Elms, J. D., T. R. Karl, A. McNab, and J. Christy. 1990. A preliminary analysis of the covariation of surface and midtropospheric temperatures. Proposed for the 41st International Astronautical Congress, Dresden, Germany. American Institute of Aeronautics and Astronautics, Washington, D.C.

Farmer, G., T. M. L. Wigley, P. D. Jones, and M. Salmon. 1989. Documenting and explaining recent global-mean temperature changes. Norwich, U.K.: Climatic Research Unit.

Folland, C. K. 1988. Numerical models of the raingauge exposure problem, field experiments and an improved collector design. Quarterly Journal of the Royal Meteorological Society 114:1485-1516.

Folland, C. K., and A. W. Colman. 1988. An interim analysis of the leading covariance eigenvectors of worldwide sea surface temperature anomalies for 1951-80. LRFC 20. U.K.: U.K. Meteorological Office.

Folland, C. K., and D. E. Parker. 1990. Observed variations of sea surface temperature. In Proceedings of the NATO Advanced Research Workshop on Climate-Ocean Interaction. Norwell, Mass.: Kluwer Academic Press.

Groisman, P. Ya., V. V. Koknaeva, T. A. Belokrylova, and T. R. Karl. 1991. Overcoming biases of precipitation measurement: A history of the USSR experience. Bulletin of the American Meteorological Society 72(11):1725-1733.

Hansen, J., and S. Lebedeff. 1987. Global trends of measured surface air temperature. Journal of Geophysical Research 92:13345-13372.

Hansen, J., and S. Lebedeff. 1988. Global surface temperatures: Update through 1987. Geophysical Research Letters 15:323-326.

Intergovernmental Panel on Climate Change. 1990. Climate Change: The IPCC Scientific Assessment, J. T. Houghton, G. J. Jenkins, and J. J. Ephraums, eds. New York: Cambridge University Press.

Jäger, J., and H. L. Ferguson, eds. 1991. Climate Change: Science, Impacts and Policy: Proceedings of the Second World Climate Conference. New York: Cambridge University Press.

Jones, P. D. 1988. Hemispheric surface air temperature variations: Recent trends and an update to 1987. Journal of Climate 1:654-660.

Jones, P. D., S. C. B. Raper, R. S. Bradley, H. F. Diaz, P. M. Kelly, and T. M. L. Wigley. 1986a. Northern hemisphere surface air temperature variations, 1851-1984. Journal of Climate and Applied Meteorology 25:161-179.

Jones, P. D., S. C. B. Raper, R. S. Bradley, H. F. Diaz, P. M. Kelly, and T. M. L. Wigley. 1986b. Southern hemisphere surface air temperature variations, 1851-1984. Journal of Climate and Applied Meteorology 25:1213-1230.

Jones, P. D., P. M. Kelly, G. B. Goodess, and T. R. Karl. 1989. The effect of urban warming on the northern hemisphere temperature average. Journal of Climate 2:285-290.

Jones, P. D., P. Ya. Groisman, M. Coughlan, N. Plummer, W-C. Wang, and T. R. Karl. 1990. Assessment of urbanization effects in time-series of surface air-temperature over land. Nature 347:169-172.

Karl, T. R., and P. D. Jones. 1989. Urban bias in area-averaged surface temperature trends. Bulletin of the American Meteorological Society 70:265-270.

Karl, T. R., and P. D. Jones. 1990. Reply to comments on "Urban bias in area-averaged surface temperature trends." Bulletin of the American Meteorological Society 71:572-574.

Karl, T. R., H. F. Diaz, and G. Kukla. 1988. Urbanization: Its detection in the United States' climate record. Journal of Climate 1:1099-1123.

Karl, T. R., D. Tarpley, R. G. Quayle, H. F. Diaz, D. A. Robinson, and R. S. Bradley. 1989. The recent climate record: What it can and cannot tell us. Reviews of Geophysics 27:405-430.

Karl, T. R., R. R. Heim, Jr., and R. G. Quayle. 1990. The greenhouse effect in central North America: If not now, when? Science 251:1058-1061.

Karl, T. R., G. Kukla, V. N. Raguvayev, M. Changeny, R. G. Quayle, R. R. Heim, Jr., and D. Fasterling. 1991. Global warming: Evidence for asymmetric diurnal trends. Geophysical Research Letters 18(12):2253-2256.

Manabe, S., K. Bryan, and M. J. Spelman. 1990. Transient response of a global ocean-atmosphere model to a doubling of atmospheric carbon dioxide. Journal of Physical Oceanography 20:722-749.

Parker, D. E. 1990. Effects of changing exposure of thermometers at land stations. In Climate Change: The IPCC Scientific Assessment, J. T. Houghton, G. J. Jenkins, and J. J. Ephraums, eds. New York: Cambridge University Press.

Plantico, M., T. R. Karl, G. Kukla, and J. Gavin. 1990. Are recent changes of temperature, cloudiness, sunshine, and precipitation across the United States related to rising levels of anthropogenic greenhouse gases? Journal of Geophysical Research 95:16617-16637.

Quayle, R. G., D. R. Easterly, T. R. Karl, and P. J. Young. 1991. Effects of recent thermometer changes in the cooperative station network. Bulletin of the American Meteorological Society 72(11):1718-1723.

Sevruk, B. 1982. Methods of Correcting for Systematic Error in Point Precipitation Measurement for Operation Use. Operational Hydrology Report No. 21. Geneva: World Meteorological Organization.

Spencer, R. W., and J. R. Christy. 1990. Precise monitoring of global temperature trends from satellites. Science 247:1558-1562.

Stouffer, R. J., S. Manabe, and K. Bryan. 1989. Interhemispheric asymmetry in climate responses to a gradual increase of atmospheric CO_2. Nature 342:660-662.

Trenberth, K. E., and J. G. Olson. 1989. Temperature trends at the South Pole and McMurdo Sound. Journal of Climate 2:1196-1206.

Vinnikov, K. Va., P. Ya. Groisman, and K. M. Lugina. 1990. The empirical data on modern global climate changes (temperature and precipitation). Journal of Climate 3:662-677.

Washington, W. M., and G. A. Meehl. 1989. Climate sensitivity due to increased CO_2: Experiments with a coupled atmosphere and ocean general circulation model. Climate Dynamics 4:1-38.

Wigley, T. M. L. 1991. Could reducing fossil-fuel emissions cause global warming? Nature 349:503-506.

15

Hydrology

Water is the most important single determinant of the earth's climate.
Water covers 70 percent of the earth's surface. The oceans store heat, and
they absorb CO_2 and other atmospheric chemicals. Snow fields, glaciers, ice
sheets, and sea ice are collectively the greatest mass of fresh water on earth.
They exercise a major influence on the planet's overall albedo (surface reflectivity). Finally, water vapor is the predominant greenhouse gas. Water vapor,
water droplets, and ice crystals are crucial elements in the climatic system.

Several aspects of the hydrologic cycle are important with respect to
climate change. As components of the climatic system begin to warm,
other factors come into play that amplify or reduce the initial warming.
Some of these are atmospheric phenomena or processes directly affecting
the earth's radiative balance (e.g., water vapor feedbacks and cloud feedbacks). Some are land-based phenomena or processes with impacts on
radiative balance (e.g., snow and ice feedbacks and feedbacks involving
surface albedo and temperature, or snow cover and soil moisture). Least
well-understood are phenomena or processes that involve the biosphere (e.g.,
evaporation and transpiration). This chapter describes mechanisms involving the movement of water through the hydrologic cycle. Related mechanisms whose functions rely more directly on exchange of energy with the
atmosphere are described in Chapter 12.

MECHANISMS INVOLVING LAND SURFACE HYDROLOGY

Precipitation

Precipitation and soil moisture content, and the resulting runoff, are important components in the climatic system. One computer simulation, which
examined a shift in ground cover in the Amazon basin from forest and

savannah to pasture, showed regional climate change with a weakened hydrologic cycle exhibiting reductions in both precipitation and evaporation (Lean and Warrilow, 1989). A realistic simulation of precipitation is an important characteristic for studies of climate change. All general circulation models (GCMs) simulate broad features of the observed precipitation pattern, but they also contain significant errors. These include inadequate characterization of the Southeast Asian summer monsoon rainfall and the summer rains in the southern Zaire basin. Recent models also show large differences in estimates of the intensity of tropical ocean rainbelts (Intergovernmental Panel on Climate Change, 1990).

Soil Moisture

Soil moisture is the "control valve" of the land surface hydrology. Soil moisture is the source of water for evaporation and thus controls heat transfer from the land surface. It also is the principal absorber of heat in the surface. Precipitation and soil moisture, and the associated runoff, are directly interconnected. Soil moisture is an important factor for vegetation, including agricultural crops, and through them affects evapotranspiration, surface reflectivity, and other aspects of the climatic system.

General circulation models appear to be quite sensitive to the proper formulation of the hydrologic budgets of the land surfaces of the earth. For example, numerical experiments reviewed by Mintz (1982) have shown that large-scale changes of land surface evaporation in GCMs produce significant changes in the predicted circulation and precipitation. Smaller and more realistic soil moisture anomalies may not produce such drastic changes, but it appears (e.g., Rowntree and Bolton, 1983) that they can have considerable impact on the climate of the region surrounding the anomaly. This and other evidence (e.g., Rind, 1982; Shukla and Mintz, 1982; Sud and Fennessy, 1984; Yeh et al., 1984) indicate that there is a critical need for sound parametric expressions for evaporation and related land surface processes over areas with typical length scales of hundreds of kilometers. While the details of most processes at local scales are well known and understood, as of now there is no agreement on how these hydrologic processes should best be parameterized at the scales appropriate for GCMs. General circulation models are complex in structure, and they involve intense and sophisticated computational schemes. Yet, in most instances their representation of the hydrology of the earth's land surfaces is crude and not well tested.

The Biosphere

Climate affects ecosystems in a variety of ways. It is an important influence on processes that determine the carbon and nutrient cycles of ecosystems. It also affects the community structure of ecosystems. Predicting how ecosystems will respond to climate change is difficult for at least three reasons. First, ecosystems contain a complex web of interactions among biological processes. Direct effects on one process may indirectly influence other processes in ways we do not yet understand. Second, the response of ecosystems to specific climatic changes depends in part on what other environmental factors are changing. A clear example is the interaction between changes in precipitation and CO_2, which functions as a growth stimulant to green plants. Third, current climate change predictions are not sufficiently detailed to permit conclusions about the consequences for the biosphere for either natural ecosystems or land management practices. For many biological processes, changes in temperature extremes and the subannual patterns of temperature and moisture are more important than changes in annual mean values. Thus it is difficult to assess the interactions between the biosphere and the climatic system.

Nevertheless, there are some clear interactions. The most important short-time-scale role of the land biosphere in the climatic system is its control of evapotranspiration. Any attempt to develop a realistic land surface parameterization must separate the functioning of vegetation from that of the soil in the hydrologic cycle. Vegetation intercepts water (when precipitation evaporates from leaves before it reaches the soil), extracts water from the soil through roots, slows the transfer of water from soil into the atmosphere, alters wind patterns in ways that affect soil temperature and rates of evaporation or evapotranspiration, and causes differences in surface reflectivity (albedo).

These and other aspects of vegetation and its effects need to be characterized in sufficiently simple terms to be incorporated in GCMs. Adequate data on vegetation cover and soils would also be required.

IMPACT OF GREENHOUSE WARMING ON THE HYDROLOGIC CYCLE

The implications of greenhouse warming for changes in the hydrologic cycle and concomitant water resources were studied by the Panel on Water and Climate of the National Research Council (1977). Much of the more recent research in the 1980s has been reviewed by Gleick (1989). Two major approaches can be distinguished to analyze the problem, namely, the direct and the indirect approach.

In the direct approach, hydrologic variables such as runoff and soil moisture are part of the primary output of a climate forecasting method. Such climate forecasting can be based on paleoclimatic records, more recent (historical) records, and GCM computations. Unfortunately, however, it appears that among all forecasting variables the specifically hydrologic variables are the ones that involve the largest degree of uncertainty. For example, even when different GCM outputs are in general agreement on changes in precipitation and temperature, they show much larger discrepancies in soil moisture and runoff. Moreover, the spatial scales of the output of the direct forecasting methods are usually one or more orders of magnitude larger than those of watersheds and catchments, which are common in hydrology.

Mainly for this reason, most hydrologists concerned with the likelihood of climate change have made use of indirect approaches. In this second class of approaches the specifically climatic outputs of climate forecasting methods are used as inputs for more detailed hydrologic models, which operate at smaller scales more appropriate for river basins and hydrologic catchments. Unfortunately, the state of the art in hydrologic modeling is probably less advanced than that of the current GCM technology. Most hydrologic simulation models, relating precipitation, runoff, and the moisture state of the catchment, are heavily parameterized and thus require an extensive data record for calibration and validation. Thus the panel concludes they cannot be trusted when they are applied to changing conditions outside their range of calibration. Furthermore, because the outputs from climate forecasting methods are generally acknowledged to be unreliable, in many instances these hydrologic models have been run with hypothetical climate scenarios as input. Usually, there is no way of knowing how internally consistent or otherwise realistic they are.

In spite of these uncertainties a few plausible results emerge from all the research so far. One is that with greenhouse warming, there is a distinct possibility over the mid-latitudes of a relative decrease in winter precipitation in the form of snow. This may in turn result in decreased water storage in the form of winter snowpack. Earlier melting of this snowpack and increased evaporation during the summer may then lead to increased aridity in many areas of the world.

In view of the potentially disastrous consequences of such scenarios, and because of the need to reduce the extreme uncertainty surrounding all this work, it is clear that a vigorous research program is urgently called for. A major effort should be directed toward a better understanding of the main hydrologic transport phenomena at scales relevant for process modeling in climate dynamics and for more regional catchment modeling in hydrology. An important component of this will be the design and execution of experiments on these scales.

REFERENCES

Gleick, P. H. 1989. Climate change, hydrology and water resources. Reviews of Geophysics 27:329-344.
Intergovernmental Panel on Climate Change. 1990. Climate Change: The IPCC

Scientific Assessment, J. T. Houghton, G. J. Jenkins, and J. J. Ephraums, eds. New York: Cambridge University Press.

Lean, J., and D. A. Warrilow. 1989. Simulation of the regional climatic impact of Amazon deforestation. Nature 342:411-413.

Mintz, U. 1982. The sensitivity of numerically simulated climates to land surface conditions. In Land Surface Processes in Atmospheric General Circulation Models, P. S. Eagleson, ed. New York: Cambridge University Press.

National Research Council. 1977. Climate, Climatic Change, and Water Supply. Panel on Water and Climate. Washington, D.C.: National Academy Press.

Rind, D. 1982. The influence of ground moisture conditions in North America on summer climate as modeled in the GISS-GCM. Monthly Weather Review 110:1487-1494.

Rowntree, P. E., and J. A. Bolton. 1983. Simulation of the atmospheric response to soil moisture anomalies over Europe. Quarterly Journal of the Royal Meteorological Society 109:501-526.

Shukla, J., and Y. Mintz. 1982. The influence of land surface evapotranspiration on earth climate. Science 215:1498-1501.

Sud, Y. C., and M. J. Fennessy. 1984. Influence of evaporation in semi-arid regions on the July circulation: A numerical study. Journal of Climatology 4:383-398.

Yeh, T. C., R. T. Wetherald, and S. Manabe. 1984. The effects of soil moisture on the short-term climate and hydrology change: A numerical experiment. Monthly Weather Review 112:475-490.

16

Sea Level

Average sea level over the oceans has not been constant throughout earth's history, and it is changing slightly today. Global sea level was about 100 m (a little more than 300 feet) lower at the peak of the last ice age, about 18,000 years ago. During the geologic past, there have been repeated variations from present sea level of more than this amount during times of intense glaciation and during periods in which the earth was free of ice. During the whole period of human civilization, however, the average sea level has been roughly as it is today. Current understanding of sea level change—especially the processes by which it occurs, the rates, and the record of past change—is described in detail in *Sea-Level Change* (National Research Council, 1990).

Tide gauges measure sea level variations in relation to a fixed point on land and thus record "relative sea level" (RSL). RSL at any particular place varies over time and space. The direct causes of these variations include vertical motions of the land to which the tide gauge or other measuring device is attached, and changes in the volume of sea water in which the gauge is immersed. Differences in atmospheric pressure, water runoff from land, winds, ocean currents, and the density of sea water all cause spatial and temporal variations in sea level in comparison to the "geoid" (the surface of constant gravitational potential corresponding, on average, to the global mean sea surface). An atmospheric pressure differential of 1 millibar is equivalent to a sea level difference of 1 cm (0.4 inch). Variation in the runoff of large rivers can result in local sea level changes of as much as 1 m (about 3 feet). In exceptional circumstances, in the North Sea, along the Chinese coast, and in the Bay of Bengal, sea level may rise by 5 m (about 15 feet) or more in a "storm surge." These changes are generally no more than a few days in duration. Both irregular and seasonal changes in temperature or salinity of the upper ocean layers cause expansion or contraction of the water volume. These relatively short-term changes in sea level may persist for a few days, several months, or even several years, and their magnitude may be as much as 5 to 15 cm (2 to 6 inches).

CLIMATE-RELATED SEA LEVEL CHANGE

Climate-related contributions to sea level change can be associated either with variations in the actual mass of water in the ocean basins or with thermal expansion (due to changing density and thus variations of temperature and salinity).

The mass of water at or near the earth's surface is practically constant for periods of 10,000 years or less. What matters for sea level is the partitioning of this mass of water among the major hydrologic reservoirs. The four major reservoirs are the oceans (1,370 million km^3), ice (30 million km^3), surface waters (8 to 19 million km^3), and atmospheric moisture (0.01 million km^3) (National Research Council, 1990). The melting of the northern continental ice sheets between 15,000 and 7,000 years before the present probably accounted for most of the rise of the sea to current levels.

Some have suggested that greenhouse warming could lead to disintegration of the West Antarctic Ice Sheet, most of which is grounded below sea level. If climate becomes warmer, and warmer ocean water intrudes under the ice sheet, the release of ice from the sheet would accelerate. Estimates suggest that several hundred years would be required to achieve this amount of warming (Bryan et al., 1988; Meier, 1990). The current estimated effect on sea level of the West Antarctic Ice Sheet is –0.6 ± 0.6 mm (–0.02 ± 0.02 inches) per year, or a net decrease. Glaciers other than the West Antarctic and Greenland ice sheets have been estimated to have contributed about 0.46 ± 0.26 mm (0.017 ± 0.01 inches) per year to sea level rise since 1900 (Meier, 1990).

Differences in water temperature, or in a combination of temperature and salinity, account very well for seasonal and interannual variations in sea level (National Research Council, 1990). This thermal expansion is not large enough, however, to account for the changes over tens of thousands of years. Warming the entire ocean from 0°C (32°F) to the current global average temperature of about 15°C (59°F) would involve thermal expansion of only about 10 m (about 30 feet).

EVIDENCE OF SEA LEVEL RISE OVER THE LAST 100 YEARS

Several studies of various periods during the last 100 years are in general agreement that mean sea level is rising (see the following reviews: Aubrey, 1985; Barnett, 1985; Robin, 1986). Estimates range from about 0.5 to 3.0

mm (0.019 to 0.1 inches) per year, with most lying in the range of 1.0 to 1.5 mm (0.039 to 0.058 inches) per year. More recent studies show similar or slightly higher estimates, ranging from 1.15 (Barnett, 1988) to 2.4 ± 0.9 mm (0.045 to 0.095 ± 0.036 inches) (Peltier and Tushingham, 1989).

There are several possible sources of error common to all these studies. First, they all use the same global mean sea level data set. Although this is based on about 1,300 stations worldwide, only about 420 have a time series of greater than 20 years. In practice, the variability is such that 15 to 20 years of data are needed to compute accurate trends, which significantly reduces the size of the data set. Second, there is a historical bias in the data set in favor of northern Europe, North America, and Japan. This geographical bias can be reduced, but not eliminated, by treating regional subsets of the data set as independent information. Finally, the most important source of error results from the difficulties in removing vertical land movements from the data set. Although efforts have been made to address each of these sources of potential bias, it cannot be said unequivocally that these factors have not systematically biased all the studies in the same direction.

PROJECTING FUTURE SEA LEVEL RISE

Various estimates of future sea level rise have been made (Intergovernmental Panel on Climate Change, 1990). In general, most of these studies foresee a sea level rise of between 10 and 30 cm (4 and 12 inches) over the next four decades. This is significantly faster than the estimated rise over the last 100 years. The IPCC (Intergovernmental Panel on Climate Change, 1990) estimates a sea level rise of between 8 and 29 cm (3 and 12 inches) by 2030, with a "best estimate" of 18 cm (7 inches) for its "business-as-usual" scenario (no reduction in emissions of greenhouse gases). By the year 2070, IPCC projects a rise of between 21 and 71 cm (8 and 28 inches), with a best estimate of 44 cm (17.6 inches).

These estimates, however, are subject to considerable uncertainty. In order to estimate oceanic thermal expansion, changes in the interior temperature, salinity, and density of the oceans have to be considered. Observational data are scant. Alternatively, estimates can be based on numerical models of ocean circulation. Ideally, detailed three-dimensional models would describe the various oceanic mixing processes and simulate transfer and expansion effects throughout the oceans. However, such models are in the early stages of development, and applications are few in number. Instead, simple box upwelling-diffusion models are used. This type of model typically represents land and oceans by a few "boxes." The complicated processes of oceanic mixing are simplified in one or more parameters. Inclusion of expansion coefficients in the model (varying with depth and possibly with latitude) allows sea level changes to be estimated as well.

Two types of box upwelling-diffusion models yield somewhat different results (National Research Council, 1990). In a "pure diffusion" (PD) model, heat is carried downward by eddy diffusion. In an "upwelling diffusion" (UD) model an upwelling rate balances some of the transfer into the deep oceans. The PD model transports heat relatively rapidly into the oceans, which slows the atmospheric temperature rise but increases the rate of sea level rise. The UD model reduces heat penetration into the ocean, allowing the climate to warm more rapidly but reducing the sea level response. Different choices of parameters in these models probably are more important than the differences in the models themselves. PD and UD models have been run assuming that the deep water of the world ocean remains relatively unchanged (ocean circulation is "surprise free") except that the deep water becomes somewhat warmer because of vertical and lateral mixing. The projected rise in sea level from thermal expansion estimated by the PD model ranges from 20 to 110 cm (8 to 44 inches) and by the UD model from 10 to 50 cm (4 to 20 inches). Both estimates are for the year 2100 and a radiative equivalent of doubling the preindustrial atmospheric concentration of CO_2.

Because of the uncertainties about key phenomena described in this chapter, this panel uses a range of sea level rise from 0 to 60 cm (about 24 inches) associated with an equivalent doubling of preindustrial levels of CO_2. There would be a lag of from a few years to several decades before the level would be reached, with a greater delay the higher the rise. This expected sea level rise is based on a combination of factors, including the possibility that the net change associated with ice at the high latitudes may be a lowering of sea level combined with the thermal expansion of the oceans. This range is slightly lower than those found elsewhere. For example, the IPCC (Intergovernmental Panel on Climate Change, 1990) anticipates a doubling of preindustrial levels of CO_2 by about 2030, and estimates a sea level rise of between 8 and 29 cm (3 and 12 inches) by 2030 and of between 21 and 71 cm (8 and 8 inches) by 2070.

REFERENCES

Aubrey, D. G. 1985. Recent sea levels from tide gauges: Problems and prognosis. In Glaciers, Ice Sheets and Sea Level: Effect of a CO_2-induced climatic change. DOE/ER/60235-1. Washington, D.C.: U.S. Department of Energy, Carbon Dioxide Research Division.

Barnett, T. P. 1985. Long-term climatic change in observed physical properties of the oceans. Pp. 91-107 in Detecting the Climatic Effects of Increasing Carbon Dioxide, M. C. MacCracken and F. M. Luther, eds. DOE/ER-0235. Washington, D.C.: U.S. Department of Energy.

Barnett, T. P. 1988. Global sea level change. In Climate Variations over the Past Century and the Greenhouse Effect. A report based on the First Climate Trends

Workshop, September 7-9, 1988. Rockville, Md.: National Oceanic and Atmospheric Administration.

Bryan, K. S., S. Manabe, and M. J. Spelman. 1988. Interhemispheric asymmetry in the transient response of a coupled ocean-atmosphere model to a CO_2 forcing. Journal of Physical Oceanography 18(6):851-867.

Intergovernmental Panel on Climate Change. 1990. Climate Change: The IPCC Scientific Assessment, J. T. Houghton, G. J. Jenkins, and J. J. Ephraums, eds. New York: Cambridge University Press.

Meier, M. F. 1990. Role of land ice in present and future sea level change. In Sea-Level Change. Washington, D.C.: National Academy Press.

National Research Council. 1990. Sea-Level Change. Washington, D.C.: National Academy Press.

Peltier, W. R., and A. M. Tushingham. 1989. Global sea level rise and the greenhouse effect: Might they be connected? Science 244:806-810.

Robin, G. de Q. 1986. Changing the sea level. In The Greenhouse Effect, Climate Change and Ecosystems, B. Bolin, B. Döös, J. Jäger, and R. A. Warrick, eds. Chichester, United Kingdom: John Wiley and Sons.

17

A Greenhouse Forcing and Temperature Rise Estimation Procedure

This chapter provides a compact estimation procedure for projecting greenhouse warming. It can be applied to a broad but simple family of emission scenarios and to either of two *postulated* climate sensitivities. Using this procedure, one can determine (1) the increment in the radiative forcing from 1990 to 2030 that would accompany the scenario under examination and (2) the equilibrium global mean temperature increase that would be consistent with that increment and the chosen forcing. Because of limitations in our understanding of the oceans, it is not possible to incorporate a simple estimation procedure for time-dependent (transient) climatic changes. But since the focus here is on the long-term implications of human actions, transient effects are less important than equilibrium effects.

Although emissions will undoubtedly continue after the year 2030 and would contribute to further climate change, the procedure presented in this chapter is limited to the next few decades. It is limited in this way both because of the difficulty of producing credible projections beyond that period and because of the panel's emphasis on practical actions that can be undertaken now. Certainly, actions or inaction during this period will have important longer-term implications that deserve attention in broader considerations of a sustainable environment. In addition, this interval was selected because 2030 is roughly the time at which the IPCC's high scenario (sometimes referred to as "business-as-usual") suggests that an equivalent doubling of the preindustrial CO_2 concentration may occur if minimal (or no) actions are taken to limit the recent, precontrol rates of increase of greenhouse gas emissions (Intergovernmental Panel on Climate Change, 1990). Beyond 2030, various approximations that are made may also become less valid.

The procedure takes into account the rate at which, following its emission into the atmosphere, each greenhouse gas is removed from the atmosphere (e.g., by transport to the oceans or by chemical reaction), but no account is taken of the extent to which one greenhouse gas (including ozone and water vapor in the stratosphere) may be affected by or introduced as a by-product of a chemical reaction that depletes another. In particular, in accord with the uncertainties attending the fate of CO_2 emissions (Emanuel et al., 1989), the procedure is approximately consistent with the observations of the past century; i.e., approximately 60 percent of the CO_2 emissions introduced into the atmosphere are removed promptly, and the remaining 40 percent contribute to long-term (i.e., several century) enhancement of the CO_2 concentration. The current concentrations, current emission rates, and lifetimes of the most important of the greenhouse gases that were considered are given in Table 17.1, and projected concentrations are shown in Figure 17.1. The radiative forcing associated with each of these gases is depicted as a function of its concentration level in Figure 17.2.

As indicated in Chapter 18, the Effects Panel agrees that it is plausible to expect that the increase in the equilibrium global mean temperature of our climatic system that might be implied by an equivalent CO_2 doubling would

TABLE 17.1 1990 Atmospheric Concentrations, Emissions, and Lifetimes of Key Greenhouse Gases

Species	1990 Atmospheric Concentration	1990 Emissions		Assumed Lifetime (years)
		Natural	Anthropogenic[a]	
CO_2	354 ppmv	—	6 Pg C/yr	—[b]
CH_4	1.72 ppmv	200 Tg/yr	340 Tg/yr	10
N_2O	310 ppbv	9.3 Tg N/yr	4 Tg N/yr	150
CCl_4	146 pptv	—	119 Gg/yr	50
CH_3CCl_3	158 pptv	—	738 Gg/yr	7
CFC-11	280 pptv	—	361 Gg/yr	60
CFC-12	484 pptv	—	428 Gg/yr	130
CFC-113	60 pptv	—	202 Gg/yr	90
CFC-114	15 pptv	—	15.7 Gg/yr	200
CFC-115	5 pptv	—	6.9 Gg/yr	400
HCFC-22	122 pptv	—	179 Gg/yr	15
Halon-1301	2 pptv	—	7 Gg/yr	110

[a]Only anthropogenic emissions are assumed to increase or decrease because of future policy and technological developments.
[b]There is no simple method for calculating CO_2 lifetime.

SOURCE: Courtesy of Michael C. MacCracken.

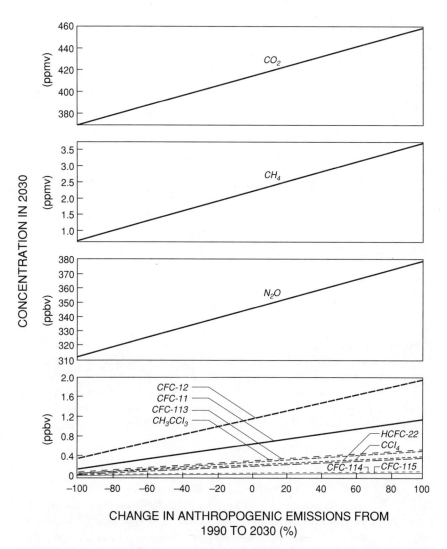

FIGURE 17.1 Projected concentrations of various greenhouse gases in the year 2030 as a function of change in anthropogenic emissions of those gases over the period 1990 to 2030.

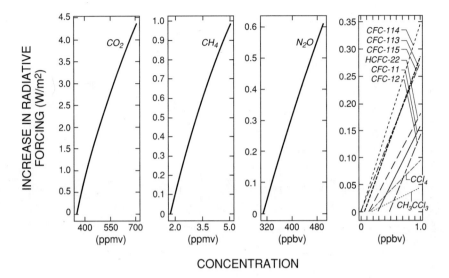

CONCENTRATION

FIGURE 17.2 Increment in radiative forcing of the surface-troposphere system over the period 1990 to 2030 for concentrations of various greenhouse gases that may occur over that period.

lie between 1° and 5°C (1.8° to 9°F). Accordingly, the change from its 1990 value of the equilibrium global mean temperature associated with the 2030 concentration of each of the greenhouse gases is calculated for the 1° sensitivity and for the 5° sensitivity.

The values of the forcing and of the change in equilibrium global average temperature that have been compiled in accord with the foregoing description can be extracted for any chosen scenario from Figure 17.3.

RESULTS

Future changes in concentration are based on changes in emissions from their 1990 baseline values. Table 17.1 lists the 1990 baseline atmospheric concentrations and estimated emissions, subdivided into natural and anthropogenic sources. These estimates are quite close to the IPCC estimates, differing slightly because of updated estimates of lifetimes and because of calibration of the model used in representing the carbon budget.

Figure 17.1 shows the atmospheric concentrations in the year 2030 resulting from linear changes in 1990 emissions over the period from 1990 to 2030. Generally, percentage changes from +100 percent to −100 percent encompass the plausible scenarios. However, CO_2 emissions could, under some scenarios, more than double over the next 40 years (e.g., see Trabalka,

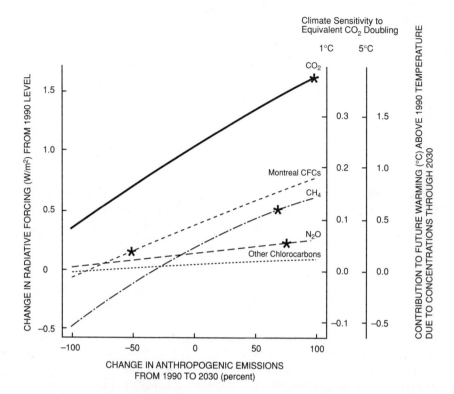

FIGURE 17.3 The incremental change to the radiative forcing of the surface-troposphere system (in watts per square meter) as a function of the percentage change in anthropogenic emissions of various species from 1990 to 2030. The asterisks indicate the projected emissions of the various species, assuming no additional regulatory policies, based on IPCC estimates and the original restrictions agreed to under the Montreal Protocol. Interactions among different species and the indirect chemical effects induced by these species (e.g., on stratospheric ozone) are not included. The right-hand vertical scales show two ranges of global average temperature responses. The first corresponds to a climate whose temperature response to an equivalent of doubling of the CO_2 concentration is 1°C (1.8°F); the second corresponds to a rise of 5°C (9°F) for an equivalent doubling of CO_2. These scales give the incremental change in temperature that is projected from the 1990 to 2030 emissions once climatic equilibrium is reestablished. To obtain the projected equilibrium change in temperature from preindustrial times through 2030, add to the value from the right-hand scale an amount equal to 55 percent of the climate sensitivity to a doubling of the CO_2 concentration. Of this total amount, a warming of 0.3° to 0.6°C (0.5° to 1.1°F) is estimated to have already occurred from the mid-nineteenth century to 1990. Assumptions are as in Figure 17.2.

1985), and emissions of hydrochlorofluorocarbons (HCFCs) and hydro-fluorocarbons (HFCs) that are being introduced as replacement compounds for those CFCs being controlled under the Montreal Protocol could increase by 1,000 percent or more from present emission levels.

The effects of the changes in emissions can then be converted into changes in the radiative forcing as a function of concentration. Figure 17.2 shows the relationships based on the formulae for estimating changes in radiative forcing as selected by IPCC, which are generally in reasonable agreement with the other results (Intergovernmental Panel on Climate Change, 1990). Note that, among the simplifications, no account is taken here of the radiative effects of the CO_2 and stratospheric H_2O that would result from chemical destruction of CH_4 and no allowance is made for changes in stratospheric or tropospheric ozone. In addition, the radiative forcings caused by the different species are not completely equivalent (Wang et al., 1991), but the approximations here are adequate for this comparative analysis.

Based on these relations, Figure 17.3 relates changes in radiative forcing to possible changes in emissions over the period 1990 to 2030 for CO_2, CH_4, N_2O, CFCs controlled by the Montreal Protocol (CFCs 11, 12, 113, 114, and 115), and halocarbons not controlled by the Montreal Protocol (including HCFC-22, CH_3CCl_3, and CCl_4). As indicated above, these estimates do not account for the climate-chemistry couplings involving species that are not directly emitted (e.g., ozone changes, stratospheric water vapor, and CH_4 conversion to CO_2), which will likely cause noticeable changes, but not so large as to change the general character of the curves.

Figure 17.3 also shows (with asterisks) the expected changes in emissions for CO_2, CH_4, and N_2O assuming a scenario similar to the IPCC high scenario. The asterisk on the CFC curve, for example, indicates a 50 percent reduction, even though stricter controls have recently been agreed upon under the Montreal and London Protocols.

To provide an indication of the potential climatic importance of the change in radiative flux, temperature change multipliers have been used to produce the vertical coordinates on the right-hand side of the figure. The commitment to future warming (i.e., the expected equilibrium temperature increase) that would occur as a consequence of emissions from 1990 to 2030 can be derived by taking the product of the multiplier and the climate sensitivity to a CO_2 doubling. This product, for two different climate sensitivities, is displayed on the vertical coordinate on the right-hand side of Figure 17.3. Thus, if the sensitivity is 1°C (1.8°F), the CO_2 contribution to future warming assuming constant emissions (0 percent change) is about 0.24°C (0.43°F). The estimates for climate sensitivity span a rather wide range, indicated in the figure by including coefficients for climate sensitivities of 1° and 5°C (1.8° to 9°F). This wide range of climate sensitivity estimates creates a large range in possible temperature changes from 1990 to 2030, demonstrating the importance of uncertainties created by our limited understanding of oceanic behavior and other phenomena.

Although the full warming due to emissions from 1990 to 2030 will not occur until a few decades thereafter, there will also be warming during the period from emissions prior to 1990. In addition, the continuing emissions beyond 2030 will lead to further warming over the longer term.

IMPLICATIONS

The results of this analysis offer several points for consideration in attempting to optimize a greenhouse gas limitation policy.

1. The slope of the N_2O curve in Figure 17.3 is so flat that even large changes in emissions would have a relatively minor effect over this period. This assumes, however, that the ozone interactions with N_2O are small. In any case, continued emissions of N_2O, over the long term, will not lead to a significant increase in warming despite its long lifetime.

2. Once CFC emissions are reduced by 50 percent, little more is gained (with respect to their greenhouse warming effect) by further reduction in the period to 2030, although a CFC buildup would continue to occur at this level of emissions. (In addition, the effects of CFCs on ozone need to be considered.) Clearly, however, a failure to implement the Montreal Protocol would have a substantial warming effect (as pointed out by Hansen et al., 1989). Unless emissions of the uncontrolled CFCs increase substantially (and they might), their greenhouse warming effect will be relatively modest over this period, although continued emissions would allow an additional concentration buildup and the associated forcing. The uncontrolled CFCs do not generally have long lifetimes.

3. Strong controls on CH_4 emissions, though perhaps difficult to implement, would produce a large effect. (Note that the potential for additional CH_4 emissions from CH_4 hydrates now tied up in permafrost has not been included.)

4. Carbon dioxide is clearly the major factor and has the steepest slope and the potential to lead to the largest temperature changes. Note, however, that 25 to 50 percent reductions in CO_2 emissions over the period 1990 to 2030 will still lead to rather substantial increases in the radiative flux (and ultimately in temperature change).

Summing the radiative flux changes assuming no change in emissions (already a rather stringent measure) produces a flux increase of about 1.6 W/m^2. This, when added to the 2.45 W/m^2 already experienced since 1765 (or the 1.95 W/m^2 since about 1900), indicates that the climate will have been committed to the radiative equivalent of a CO_2 doubling (4.4 W/m^2) by about 2030 or a little later. Any increases in emission rates will only make the changes greater. In addition, although beyond the time horizon of this report, continued emissions beyond 2030 will further increase the projected temperature change.

The extent to which changes in radiative forcing will be significant to society depends on the climate sensitivity and the consequent climatic impacts on human activities and natural systems. Given that past climates have varied substantially as a result of comparable forcings and that ecosystems under such conditions were quite different than at present, however, this schematic analysis suggests that significant climate change will be very difficult to avoid, although its rate of onset may be slowed.

REFERENCES

Emanuel, W. R., G. G. Killough, W. M. Post, H. H. Shugart, and M. P. Stevenson. 1989. Computer Implementation of a Globally Averaged Model of the World Carbon Cycle. TR010. Washington, D.C.: Carbon Dioxide Research Division, U.S. Department of Energy.

Hansen, J., A. Lacis, and M. Prather. 1989. Greenhouse effect of chlorofluorocarbons and other trace gases. Journal of Geophysical Research 94:16417-16421.

Intergovernmental Panel on Climate Change. 1990. Climate Change: The IPCC Scientific Assessment, J. T. Houghton, G. J. Jenkins, and J. J. Ephraums, eds. New York: Cambridge University Press.

Trabalka, J. R., ed. 1985. Atmospheric Carbon Dioxide and the Global Carbon Cycle. DOE/ER-0239. Washington, D.C.: U.S. Department of Energy.

Wang, W.-C., M. P. Dudek, X.-Z. Liang, and J. T. Kiehl. 1991. Inadequacy of effective CO_2 as a proxy in simulating the greenhouse effect of other radiatively active gases. Nature 350:573-577.

18

Conclusions

Despite (1) uncertainties in the interpretation of the climate record, (2) severe limitations on the predictive capabilities of the models, (3) masking effects of the natural variability of the models, and (4) masking effects of the natural variability of the climatic system, there is clear evidence and wide agreement among members of the atmospheric sciences community and the members of this panel about several basic facts:

1. The atmospheric concentration of CO_2 has increased by at least 25 percent since preindustrial times and is currently increasing at about 0.5 percent per year.

2. The atmospheric concentration of CH_4 has doubled during that period and is increasing at about 0.9 percent per year.

3. Atmospheric concentrations of CFCs, which are a result of industrial activities and have been released into the atmosphere in quantity only since World War II, are currently increasing at about 4 percent per year.

4. Items 1, 2, and 3 are primarily direct consequences of human activities.

5. Current interpretations of temperature records reveal that the global average temperature has increased between 0.3° and 0.6°C (0.5° and 1.1°F) during the last century.

As a result, the panel concludes that there is a reasonable chance of the following:

1. In the absence of greater human effort to the contrary, greenhouse gas concentrations equivalent to a doubling of the preindustrial level of CO_2 will occur by the middle of the next century.

2. The sensitivity of the climatic system to greenhouse gases is such that the equivalent of doubling CO_2 could ultimately increase the average global

temperature by somewhere between 1° and 5°C (1.8° and 9°F). This range is slightly broader than those used by other groups. Prudence dictates that the uncertainties in the science base call for wider rather than narrower ranges of projected temperatures for use in policy choices. In the panel's view, this range expresses much less unwarranted faith in the numbers produced by GCMs than does a narrow range.

3. The transfer of heat to the deep ocean occurs more slowly than the transfer of heat within the atmosphere or within the upper layers of the ocean. The resulting transient period, or "lag," means that the global average surface temperature at any time is lower than the temperature that would prevail after all the redistribution had been completed. The greater the response, the faster the warming; however, the increase in the warming rate is less than proportional to the climate sensitivity, so it will take longer for the full warming to appear. At the time of equivalent CO_2 doubling, for example, the global average surface temperature may be as little as one-half the ultimate equilibrium temperature associated with those concentrations.

4. A rise in sea level may accompany global warming, possibly in the range of 0 to 60 cm (0 to 24 inches) for the temperature range listed above. This range allows for uncertainties in estimates of current sea level change. Zero is included in the range not only because of the uncertainties but also because precipitation in the Antarctic functions to partially offset thermal expansion.

5. A wide range of potentially amplifying or moderating feedbacks have been suggested that involve atmospheric composition and climatic changes. Examples include increased CH_4 emissions as the permafrost melts, increased carbon uptake by plants at higher CO_2 concentrations, increased summer drying of continental interiors, increased continental precipitation in winter, increased hurricane frequency and/or intensity, and many more potential changes and surprises. Convincing quantitative demonstrations and confirmations of these and other potential changes are lacking, and there is no evidence that any of the changes are imminent, but none of them are precluded.

Part Three

MITIGATION

19

Introduction

Various technologies and policy options have the potential to mitigate greenhouse warming. The Mitigation Panel was given the task of evaluating the effectiveness of these interventions, with the following specific charge:

- The panel should examine the range of policy interventions that might be employed to mitigate changes in the earth's radiation balance, assessing these options in terms of their expected impact, costs, and at least in qualitative terms, their relative cost-effectiveness.
- Preliminary evaluation will help identify policy interventions for closer examination. These might include reducing emissions in primary energy production or industrial processes, transportation vehicles and systems, or agricultural processes. They might include policies aimed at reducing energy consumption or changing practices in agriculture, silviculture, or general land use. Novel global system interventions, such as removal of greenhouse gases from the atmosphere, blocking of incident radiation, or altering of the earth's albedo, should not be excluded.
- Attention should be given to factors affecting the design and implementation of potential programs at the international and regional levels, including, as explicitly as feasible, organizations that should be involved and practical impediments. In performing this task, the panel should take into account any major relationship between the particular intervention and ecological or other problems apart from global climate change.

The panel defines "mitigation policy" as including programs and specific interventions that might reduce either the rate at which the radiative balance is changing or the ultimate level at equilibrium, assuming one is reached. Mitigation policies include not only interventions designed to reduce the emission of greenhouse gases but also actions such as reforestation (or reducing deforestation), removal of radiatively active gases from the atmosphere, and altering the earth's albedo in ways that affect the earth's radiative balance.

SOURCES OF GREENHOUSE GAS EMISSIONS

This section provides a very brief summary of the magnitudes and sources of greenhouse gas emissions in order to suggest targets for mitigation strategies and some indication of the magnitude of the effort required. It is not intended to be a critical review, but relies on the recent summary compiled by the Intergovernmental Panel on Climate Change (1990, 1991). More information is available in the report of the Effects Panel (Part Two).

The greenhouse gases include carbon dioxide (CO_2), chlorofluorocarbons (CFCs), methane (CH_4), nitrous oxide (N_2O), ozone (O_3), and water vapor. Although water vapor continually cycles through the atmosphere, if there is a change in atmospheric temperature, the mean water vapor concentration could change and provide an important positive feedback (i.e., magnify the temperature change). Other gases such as carbon monoxide (CO) and nitrogen oxides (NO_x) are involved in chemical reactions in the atmosphere and affect the concentrations of greenhouse gases (in this case, O_3). Greenhouse gas emissions come from both anthropogenic (man-made) and natural sources (such as CH_4 from wetlands). Table 19.1 lists the primary greenhouse gases, the anthropogenic sources, and the relative contribution of each gas toward greenhouse warming. As shown in this table, CO_2 is the single most important greenhouse gas worldwide, but others also make a significant contribution.

Table 19.2 shows the current rates at which greenhouse gases are increasing worldwide. Figure 19.1 breaks down the current worldwide contributions to radiative forcing by source sector for emissions during the 1980s. As shown here, energy use that generates emissions of CO_2 and other greenhouse gases is the major greenhouse emission source. Table 19.3 shows a recent projection of global emissions from different sources for the years 2000, 2015, and 2050. As CFCs are phased out (presumably), under present international agreements, emissions from energy use are likely to dominate the anthropogenic influence on greenhouse warming.

Even though CO_2 contributes about half of the radiative forcing from increased atmospheric concentrations of greenhouse gases, Table 19.4 shows that once in the atmosphere, each molecule of the other greenhouse gases contributes more to global warming than does each molecule of CO_2. For example, CFC-11 has, per molecule, 12,400 times the capacity of CO_2 to trap heat.

Worldwide, the United States is at present the largest emitter of greenhouse gases (World Resources Institute, 1990). As shown in Figure 19.2, the use of energy in the form of coal, oil, and natural gas is the largest

TABLE 19.1 Global Greenhouse Gases with Their Anthropogenic
Emission Sources

Greenhouse Gas	Greenhouse Gas Contribution During the 1980s[a] (%)	Anthropogenic Emission Sources
Carbon dioxide	56	Combustion of coal, oil, natural gas, and wood for use in electric utilities and for industrial, residential, and commercial use
		Combustion of gasoline, diesel fuel, and other hydrocarbon fuels for automobiles, trucks, trains, aircraft, and ships; calcining of limestone during cement manufacture
		Deforestation, which leads to a net decrease in the mass of terrestrial organic matter
Methane	15	Decomposition of waste in landfills
		Fossil fuel use, which results in emissions during coal mining, during exploration, production, and transportation of oil and natural gas, and via incomplete combustion of natural gas
		Agricultural sources, including biomass burning, animal husbandry (cattle), and rice cultivation
Chlorofluoro-carbons	24	CFCs, which are used to make rigid and flexible foam, and as aerosol propellants, refrigerants, and industrial degreasers
		Halons, which are used in fire extinguishers and as sterilants for some medical applications
Nitrous oxide	5	Agricultural biomass burning, including use of wood as a fuel and forest clearing
		Use of nitrogenous fertilizers and probably inadvertent fertilization through atmospheric nitrate deposition
Tropospheric ozone	—	Generated from nitrogen oxides and carbon monoxide emitted

[a]The greenhouse contribution shown is the fractional contribution to the greenhouse gas alteration of the earth's radiation balance due to atmospheric concentration during the 1980s. The percent contribution is based on data from the IPCC Working Group I report (Intergovernmental Panel on Climate Change, 1990). Greenhouse gas emissions come from both anthropogenic (man-made) and natural sources (such as methane from wetlands). The contribution of tropospheric ozone to greenhouse warming is unknown at this time, according to the IPCC.

TABLE 19.2 Key Greenhouse Gases Influenced by Human Activity

	CO_2	CH_4	CFC-11	CFC-12	N_2O
Preindustrial atmospheric concentration	280 ppmv	0.8 ppmv	0	0	288 ppbv
Current atmospheric concentration (1990)[a]	353 ppmv	1.72 ppmv	280 pptv	484 pptv	310 ppbv
Current rate of annual atmospheric accumulation	1.8 ppmv (0.5%)	0.015 ppmv (0.9%)	9.5 pptv (4%)	17 pptv (4%)	0.8 ppbv (0.25%)
Atmospheric lifetime (years)[b]	(50-200)	10	65	130	150

NOTES: Atmospheric lifetimes are computed as the ratio of the atmospheric burden to net annual removal, which is estimated as emissions less atmospheric accumulation. Net annual emissions of CO_2 from the biosphere not affected by human activity are assumed to be small, as are volcanic emissions. Release and uptake from the biosphere not affected by human activity are included under emissions deriving from human activity. Emission estimates of human-induced emissions from the biosphere are controversial.

Ozone has not been included in the table because of lack of precise data. Here, ppmv = parts per million by volume; ppbv = parts per billion by volume; and pptv = parts per trillion by volume.

[a]The 1990 concentrations have been estimated on the basis of an extrapolation of measurements that go through 1988 or 1989, assuming that the recent trends remained approximately constant.

[b]For each gas in the table, except CO_2, the "lifetime" is defined as the ratio of the atmospheric content to the total rate of removal. This time scale also characterizes the rate of adjustment of the atmospheric concentrations if the emission rates are changed abruptly. CO_2 is a special case because it is a thermodynamically stable gas that equilibrates with oceanic and biospheric processes. The lifetime shown does not indicate the lifetime of the gas molecules, but rather of the perturbation of atmospheric concentrations.

SOURCE: Intergovernmental Panel on Climate Change (1990). Reprinted by permission of Cambridge University Press.

anthropogenic source of CO_2 emissions in the United States. Cement production, gas flaring, and land use change are relatively minor sources. Table 19.5 shows the history of U.S. emissions of CO_2 since 1950, indicating the U.S. percentage has been cut in half over the last 30 years, although the total has almost doubled. The major sources of CH_4 emissions (Figure 19.3) are solid waste (gas emissions from landfills), natural gas pipeline

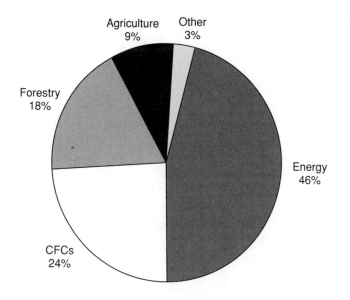

FIGURE 19.1   Estimated global contribution to radiative forcing by sector, 1980 to 1990.

SOURCE: Intergovernmental Panel on Climate Change (1991).

leakage, and livestock. The emissions of N_2O are much more difficult to estimate, and the principal cause of its increasing atmospheric concentration is unknown, but a rough approximation puts these emissions at approximately 1.4 Mt/yr.[1] This is determined by taking worldwide N_2O emissions and scaling those emissions by the land area of the United States.

With a variety of greenhouse gases being emitted to the atmosphere, it would be useful to have a single index of the relative greenhouse impact of the various gases. This would allow comparison of the relative climatic benefits of mitigation measures that address the emissions of different gases or measures that reduce emissions of one gas at the expense of increasing emissions of another (e.g., if changing the working fluid in a refrigeration system results in a less energy-efficient refrigerator). Ultimately, such an index might also let us understand the relative importance of the emissions of gases that are not themselves greenhouse gases but that because of their involvement in chemical interactions in the atmosphere influence the abundance of greenhouse gases. Because such an index would have to involve not only the infrared absorptive capacities, concentrations, and concentration changes of individual gases, but also their spectral overlaps and atmospheric residence times, exact values will be scenario dependent. A single index that meets all of our needs may not even exist. It is clear that the

TABLE 19.3   Global Greenhouse Gas Emissions from Human Activities

	1985 Emissions (Mt/yr)	Projections (Mt/yr)[a]		
		2000 Emissions	2015 Emissions	2050 Emissions
CO_2 emissions[b]				
Commercial energy	18,854 (86)	25,633 (87)	33,508 (89)	57,168 (92)
Tropical deforestation	2,628 (12)	3,241 (11)	3,388 (9)	3,728 (6)
Other	438 (2)	589 (2)	753 (2)	1,243 (2)
TOTAL	21,900	29,463	37,650	62,139
CH_4 emissions[c]				
Fuel production	58 (18)	88 (22)	124 (26)	228 (32)
Enteric fermentation	74 (23)	96 (24)	110 (23)	156 (22)
Rice cultivation	109 (34)	124 (31)	138 (29)	171 (24)
Landfills	29 (9)	40 (10)	48 (10)	100 (14)
Tropical deforestation	19 (6)	24 (6)	24 (5)	28 (4)
Other	29 (9)	28 (7)	33 (7)	36 (5)
TOTAL	320	400	477	711
CFC-11 and CFC-12 emissions[d]				
TOTAL	0.64	0.84	0.76	0.83
N_2O emissions[e]				
Coal combustion	1.0 (25)	·1.5 (26)	2.0 (29)	3.2 (36)
Fertilizer use	1.5 (38)	2.6 (43)	3.1 (44)	3.7 (41)
Gain of cultivated land	0.4 (10)	0.3 (8)	0.6 (8)	0.5 (6)
Tropical deforestation	0.5 (13)	0.4 (11)	0.7 (10)	0.8 (9)
Fuel wood and industrial biomass	0.2 (5)	0.2 (4)	0.2 (3)	0.2 (2)
Agricultural wastes	0.4 (10)	0.5 (8)	0.5 (7)	0.5 (6)
TOTAL	4	6	7	9

NOTE: Numbers in parentheses are percentages of total.

[a]Mt = megatons = million metric tons.

[b]Projection based on U.S. EPA (1989) Rapidly Changing World Scenario; assumed average annual growth rate = 1.6 percent.

[c]Projection based on U.S. EPA (1989) Rapidly Changing World Scenario; assumed average annual growth rate = 1.2 percent.

[d]CFC emission projection (from EPA) assumes no further controls beyond original Montreal Protocol; assumed average annual growth rate = 0.4 percent.

[e]Nitrous oxide projections (from EPA) assume an average annual growth rate of 1.2 percent.

SOURCE: Data are from U.S. Department of Energy (1990).

TABLE 19.4 Radiative Forcing Relative to CO_2 per Molecule Change and per Unit Mass Change in the Atmosphere for Present-Day Concentrations

Gas[a]	Change in Radiative Forcing (ΔF) Relative to Change in Temperature (ΔC)	
	per Molecule Relative to CO_2	per Unit Mass Relative to CO_2
CO_2	1	1
CH_4	21	58
N_2O	206	206
CFC-11	12,400	3,970
CFC-12	15,800	5,750
CFC-113	15,800	3,710
CFC-114	18,300	4,710
CFC-115	14,500	4,130
HCFC-22	10,700	5,440
CCl_4	5,720	1,640
CH_3CCl_3	2,730	900
CF_3Br	16,000	4,730
Possible CFC substitutes		
HCFC-123	9,940	2,860
HCFC-124	10,800	3,480
HFC-125	13,400	4,920
HFC-134a	9,570	4,130
HCFC-141b	7,710	2,900
HCFC-142b	10,200	4,470
HFC-143a	7,830	4,100
HFC-152a	6,590	4,390

[a]CO_2, CH_4, and N_2O forcings are from 1990 concentrations.

SOURCE: Intergovernmental Panel on Climate Change (1990).

relative importance of different gases will be a function of the time interval over which one chooses to integrate, with the short-lived gases appearing more important over short integration times. Evolution of such an index has occurred rapidly over the past several years, and a useful index of global warming potential (GWP) has recently been described in the IPCC Working Group I document (Intergovernmental Panel on Climate Change, 1990).

The GWP is not yet a mature concept, but it provides a preliminary basis for a simple comparison of the emissions of various greenhouse gases and has been adapted for use here. It is, by definition, "the time integrated

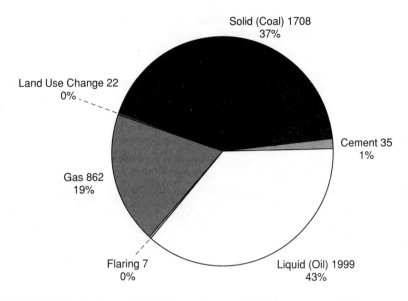

FIGURE 19.2   Sources of U.S. CO_2 emissions (1987) in megatons CO_2.
Source: Adapted from Marland (1990).

commitment to climate forcing from the instantaneous release of 1 kilogram of a trace gas expressed relative to that from 1 kg of carbon dioxide." The GWP has, in essence, units of degree years over degree years and varies considerably with the time interval of integration because of the different mean lifetimes of the gases. The indices of global warming potential for the most important gases are given in Table 19.6. The CO_2-equivalent impact of different greenhouse gases on greenhouse warming is computed by taking the emission of each greenhouse gas and simply multiplying that emission by its GWP. As shown here, CO_2 is the least effective greenhouse gas per kilogram emitted, but its contribution to global warming is the largest. CH_4 has an "indirect effect" because its ultimate decomposition products are CO_2 and H_2O. The Mitigation Panel has used the same method to determine the "CO_2-equivalent" reduction of different greenhouse gas mitigation strategies. In addition, as discussed in Part Two, the Effects Panel has developed a method of comparing the relative impact on radiative forcing and temperature rise due to greenhouse warming from reducing the emissions of different greenhouse gases on a worldwide basis.

By using the U.S. greenhouse gas emission estimates provided earlier and multiplying these emissions by the GWP of each gas, a rough estimate of U.S. emissions in CO_2-equivalent emissions is shown in Table 19.7. This provides a baseline for mitigation of U.S. greenhouse gas emissions.

TABLE 19.5 Carbon Dioxide Emissions from Fossil Fuel Burning and Cement Manufacture in the United States (Mt C/yr)

Year	Total	Solid	Liquid	Gas	Cement	Gas Flaring	Per Capita	Percentage of Global Total
1950	696.1	347.1	244.8	87.1	5.3	11.8	4.6	42.5
1951	716.8	334.5	262.2	102.7	5.7	11.7	4.6	40.4
1952	698.0	296.6	273.2	109.9	5.8	12.5	4.4	38.7
1953	714.5	294.3	286.6	115.5	6.1	11.9	4.5	38.7
1954	680.5	252.2	290.2	121.2	6.3	10.6	4.2	36.4
1955	746.0	283.3	313.3	130.8	7.2	11.4	4.5	36.4
1956	781.9	295.0	328.5	138.1	7.6	12.7	4.6	35.8
1957	775.1	282.7	325.8	147.6	7.1	11.9	4.5	34.0
1958	750.8	245.3	333.0	155.8	7.5	9.3	4.3	32.1
1959	781.4	251.5	343.5	169.9	8.1	8.4	4.4	31.6
1960	799.5	253.4	349.8	180.4	7.6	8.3	4.4	30.9
1961	801.9	245.0	354.1	187.4	7.7	7.7	4.4	30.8
1962	831.5	254.2	364.3	198.7	8.0	6.3	4.5	30.7
1963	875.6	272.5	378.8	210.3	8.4	5.6	4.6	30.7
1964	912.9	289.7	389.7	219.8	8.8	5.0	4.8	30.3
1965	948.3	301.1	405.6	228.0	8.9	4.7	4.9	30.1
1966	999.7	312.7	425.9	246.4	9.1	5.5	5.1	30.2
1967	1039.2	321.1	443.6	258.5	8.8	7.2	5.2	30.4
1968	1081.0	314.8	471.9	277.4	9.4	7.6	5.4	30.1
1969	1132.0	319.7	497.4	297.8	9.5	7.7	5.6	29.7
1970	1165.5	322.4	514.8	312.1	9.0	7.2	5.7	28.5
1971	1173.2	305.7	530.5	323.3	9.7	4.2	5.7	27.7
1972	1227.3	310.4	575.5	327.6	10.2	3.6	5.9	27.8
1973	1275.4	334.0	605.4	321.7	10.6	3.6	6.0	27.4
1974	1231.1	330.1	580.7	307.9	10.0	2.4	5.8	26.4
1975	1179.0	317.6	565.1	286.0	8.4	1.9	5.5	25.5
1976	1262.0	351.6	608.1	291.3	9.0	2.0	5.8	25.8
1977	1269.7	355.6	641.9	260.5	9.7	2.0	5.8	25.2
1978	1293.4	361.2	655.0	264.7	10.4	2.2	5.8	25.5
1979	1300.9	378.7	634.6	274.8	10.4	2.4	5.8	24.4
1980	1259.3	394.6	581.0	272.5	9.3	1.8	5.5	23.9
1981	1210.6	403.0	533.1	264.2	8.8	1.4	5.3	23.6
1982	1116.9	390.1	502.2	245.4	7.8	1.4	4.9	22.5
1983	1149.4	405.5	500.1	233.8	8.7	1.4	4.9	22.6
1984	1187.5	427.8	507.1	241.5	9.6	1.6	5.0	22.6
1985	1201.3	448.0	505.6	236.7	9.6	1.4	5.0	22.3
1986	1204.5	439.7	531.1	222.6	9.7	1.4	5.0	21.7
1987	1257.5	465.8	545.3	235.0	9.6	1.8	5.2	22.1
1988	1310.2	493.6	566.4	238.6	9.5	2.1	5.3	22.2

NOTE: Emission estimates are rounded and expressed in megatons of carbon; per capita estimates are rounded and expressed in tons of carbon.

SOURCE: Marland (1990).

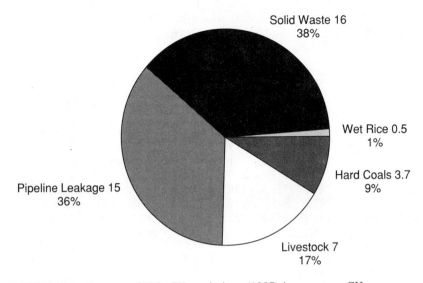

FIGURE 19.3   Sources of U.S. CH_4 emissions (1987) in megatons CH_4.

Source: Adapted from Table 24.1 in World Resources Institute (1990).

STRUCTURE OF PART THREE

The following key questions are addressed by the Mitigation Panel in this part of the report:

• Concerning the comparison of mitigation options: What technical and policy options are available to mitigate emissions and greenhouse warming? What are the costs, benefits, and distributional effects of the various policies?

• Concerning the implementation of mitigation options: What are the disadvantages and advantages of different policies and the methods of implementing those policies? How should different policy methods be implemented?

In answering these questions, the panel was charged not with deciding whether emissions should be reduced, but rather with evaluating which options have the greatest potential to mitigate greenhouse warming if the decision is made to do so. Chapter 20 discusses the panel's approach to evaluating options and the general advantages and disadvantages of different methods of implementing policies.

In Chapters 21 through 28, the technical costs and potentials of some of the mitigation options deemed to be most suitable for reducing greenhouse gas emissions are estimated by source sector:

• Residential and commercial energy management (Chapter 21)
• Industrial energy management (Chapter 22)

TABLE 19.6 Global Warming Potentials of Several Greenhouse Gases

	Time Horizon		
	20 Years	100 Years	500 Years
CO_2	1	1	1
CH_4 (including indirect)	63	21	9
N_2O	270	290	190
CFC-11	4500	3500	1500
CFC-12	7100	7300	4500
HCFC-22	4100	1500	510

NOTE: The global warming potentials (GWPs) show the relative contributions to radiative forcing (with respect to CO_2) for instantaneous injection to the atmosphere of 1 kg of gas. Because the gases have different atmospheric lifetimes, their relative importance changes with the time interval over which the radiative impact is integrated. CH_4 is thus seen to have a large impact over short times, but it is less important over longer times because of its short lifetime. The CH_4 calculation recognizes that when CH_4 is fully oxidized, CO_2 is one of its products.

SOURCE: Intergovernmental Panel on Climate Change (1990).

- Transportation energy management (Chapter 23)
- Energy supply systems (Chapter 24)
- Nonenergy emission reduction (halocarbons, agriculture, landfill gas) (Chapter 25)
- Population (Chapter 26)
- Deforestation (Chapter 27)
- Geoengineering (reforestation, sunlight screening, ocean fertilization, halocarbon destruction) (Chapter 28)

It is important to note that the panel did not formulate or analyze specific scenarios projecting emission rates into the future. The panel felt that the accuracy of such projections so far in the future was questionable (as illustrated by the accuracy of projections made in the past). Rather, it assumed that the world of the future would be roughly like the world of today and focused on potential methods for reducing emissions as if they were being applied to current (1989) emission sources. It should also be noted that the panel looked at emission reductions and other measures from a U.S. perspective—methods by which U.S. emissions could be reduced and areas in which the United States could transfer technology, support research and development, or otherwise assist other countries in reducing their emissions.

TABLE 19.7   Estimate of Current U.S. CO_2-Equivalent Emissions

Pollutant	Approximate U.S. Greenhouse Emissions (Mt/yr)[a]	GWP (100 yr)[b]	Approximate U.S. CO_2-Equivalent Emissions (Mt CO_2 equivalent/yr)[a,c]
CO_2	4800	1	4800 ± 10%
CH_4	50	21	1050 ± 20%
CFC-11	0.08	3500	280 ± 30%
CFC-12	0.14	7300	1020 ± 30%
CFC-113	0.08	4200	340 ± 30%
N_2O	1.4	290	410 ± 60%
Approximate total U.S. anthropogenic CO_2-equivalent emissions			7900 ± 20%

[a]Mt = megatons = 1 million metric tons.
[b]GWP = global warming potential. This is multiplied by the emission estimate to determine the CO_2-equivalent emissions. The 100-year lifetime integration is used in these calculations.
[c]Qualitative indications are given for the relative reliability of the emissions numbers.

SOURCE: Marland (1990) (CO_2); World Resources Institute (1990) (CH_4); personal communication from F. H. Vogelsberg, Du Pont, to Deborah Stine, Committee on Science, Engineering and Public Policy, 1990 (CFCs); U.S. Department of Energy (1990) (all gases).

The discussion in each of Chapters 21 through 27 is divided into the following sections:

• *Recent Trends.* Recent trends in emissions from the sector are described. For example, in the industrial sector, the level of energy intensity has decreased in recent years. The effectiveness of efforts to reduce emissions or improve efficiency in the sector is also discussed.

• *Emission Control Methods.* Methods that can be used to reduce emissions from the sector are discussed. These can include technical actions both on the demand side (e.g., improving end-use energy efficiency) and on the supply side (e.g., reducing emissions from power plants).

In addition, the potential emission reductions and the costs of implementing such methods are quantified. As discussed in Chapter 20, a "supply curve" of the implementation cost (dollars per ton CO_2 equivalent) and emission reduction (megatons of CO_2 per year) is developed for each option if possible. These are "first-order" analyses, meant only to be a beginning point for determining the cost-effectiveness of various mitigation options and for demonstrating a method that could be used to evaluate options.

Specifically, second-order effects, including system adjustments that change costs of greenhouse warming emissions in other sectors, in other regions of the world, or at later points in time, are not included. In other words, the analysis presented here should not be viewed as the definitive assessment of each option. Rather, the intent is to describe a manner in which options could be evaluated and to illustrate the approach with the best estimates available.

• *Barriers to Implementation.* The technical and policy barriers to achieving the potential emission reductions described in the previous section are discussed. For example, in many cases we can improve the energy efficiency with relatively short economic payback periods, and yet these energy measures have still not been fully implemented. What prevents us from achieving the energy reductions that are possible?

• *Policy Options.* A number of policy options with differing levels of effectiveness can be used to encourage the reduction of greenhouse gas emissions in a particular sector. Each policy and the positive and negative aspects of implementing it are discussed. The policies described here are not all-encompassing but are some that the panel believes are most worthwhile to consider. A key resource used in this section is the Department of Energy's (DOE) report entitled *A Compendium of Options for Government Policy to Encourage Private Sector Responses to Potential Climate Change* (U.S. Department of Energy, 1989). The DOE report includes a more comprehensive look at the range of possible mitigation policies.

Unfortunately, for many of the options, few data are available to evaluate the expected effectiveness. Evaluations of the effectiveness of comparable policies implemented in the past are sorely needed. In the absence of such studies it is difficult to determine how much of the potential reductions can actually be achieved.

• *Other Benefits and Costs.* Uncounted in the implementation cost are nongreenhouse-related benefits and costs that might derive from a particular policy. For example, on the benefit side, when energy consumption is reduced, the emissions that cause urban air pollution are also reduced. On the other hand, reductions in coal consumption could have severe economic consequences for coal-mining communities.

• *Research and Development Needs.* Research and development that is needed to remove or decrease technical and other barriers to reducing greenhouse gas emissions is described. For example, hydrogen would be an ideal transportation fuel on some counts, but technical barriers in terms of storage and infrastructure limit its application. In some cases, the barrier is cost. For example, photovoltaics could generate at least a portion of the energy supply, but high cost currently limits broad usage. In this case, continued research could improve the technology so that cost can be reduced. A key reference on research and development in the energy sector is a recent report by the Energy Engineering Board of the National Research Council entitled *Confronting Climate Change: Strategies for Energy Research and Development* (National Research Council, 1990).

Because the discussion in these chapters is at times highly technical, a glossary (Appendix S) has been provided for the reader's convenience. In addition, conversion tables (Appendix T) are provided for those who may be unfamiliar with the units of measurement used throughout this report.

The final chapter of this part, Chapter 29, summarizes the results of individual analyses and draws some general conclusions regarding the relative merits of potential interventions. This analysis should not be interpreted as all-inclusive, but it does provide semiquantitative consideration of a wide sampling of potential approaches to mitigation. The principal findings and recommendations concerning the policy choices facing the country are found in the report of the Synthesis Panel (Part One).

NOTE

1. Throughout this report, tons (t) are metric; 1 Mt = 1 megaton = 1 million tons; and 1 Gt = 1 gigaton = 1 billion tons.

REFERENCES

Intergovernmental Panel on Climate Change. 1990. Climate Change: The IPCC Scientific Assessment, J. T. Houghton, G. J. Jenkins, and J. J. Ephraums, eds. New York: Cambridge University Press.

Intergovernmental Panel on Climate Change. 1991. Climate Change: The IPCC Response Strategies. Covelo, Calif.: Island Press.

Marland, G. 1990. Carbon dioxide emission estimates: United States. In TRENDS '90: A Compendium of Data on Global Change, T. A. Borden, P. Kanciruk, and M. P. Farrell, eds. Report ORNL/CDIAC-36. Oak Ridge, Tenn.: Carbon Dioxide Information Analysis Center, Oak Ridge National Laboratory.

National Research Council. 1990. Confronting Climate Change: Strategies for Energy Research and Development. Washington, D.C.: National Academy Press.

U.S. Department of Energy (DOE). 1989. A Compendium of Options for Government Policy to Encourage Private Sector Responses to Potential Climate Change. Report DOE/EH-0103. Washington, D.C.: U.S. Department of Energy.

U.S. Department of Energy (DOE). 1990. The Economics of Long-Term Global Climate Change: A Preliminary Assessment. Report of an Interagency Task Force. Report DOE/PE-0096P. Washington, D.C.: U.S. Department of Energy.

World Resources Institute (WRI). 1990. World Resources 1990-91. New York: Oxford University Press.

20

A Framework for Evaluating
Mitigation Options

To devise a coherent strategy for mitigation of greenhouse warming, it is necessary to have an analytical framework that compares the alternatives available. This chapter develops such a framework and discusses a number of issues that arise in the development of a plan to respond to the potential effects of greenhouse warming.

Economics and engineering are central to the comparison of alternatives. The connections between human activities and their environmental consequences are technological in character; engineering is consequently required to imagine, design, and implement alternatives. Economic concepts are central to choosing among the technically feasible alternatives. A variety of social and cultural factors are also important in the interactions of humans with their physical environment, but these are not the primary focus of this inquiry.

The chain of causation from human activities, to the release of greenhouse gases, to changes in the composition of the atmosphere, and to climate change is long, often indirect, and complex. For this reason, estimating the relationship between human activities affected by policies or shifts in markets and far-removed changes in climate is a difficult technical task. Indeed, the very human difficulty of perceiving this indirect and long-term relationship is an important component of the problem of greenhouse warming.

It is easier to see the direct costs of decreasing CO_2 emissions than to estimate the benefits of doing so. There is, accordingly, an emphasis in this report on the direct costs of change rather than on the potential benefits and secondary costs of changing. Readers should bear in mind that the picture presented by the panel is skewed in this respect.

Even if the relation between human activity and climate change were readily quantifiable, there would still be the matter of selecting the most effective, least costly response strategies. Here economic concepts are central. Proposed responses to greenhouse warming include ideas that would affect national economies, international trade, and the life-styles of people in both developing and industrialized societies. Moreover, selecting some of these alternatives would mean that other highly valued objectives—such as improving economic status or national security—would have to be altered. Making choices in the face of scarcity—the problem at the heart of economic science—is inescapable.

Much of this chapter is devoted to explaining the difficulties of carrying out a conceptually straightforward approach. There are three critical problems: (1) markets are imperfect—that is, neither the prices observed nor the responses of markets are the simple result of demand and supply operating unimpeded; (2) uncertainties abound in the technical realm, in social responses to policy instruments, in environmental changes due to changing climate, and in markets; and (3) consideration of most alternatives requires comparing costs and benefits at different times, paid for or enjoyed by different people.

Although it has been possible to assemble an overview of the options for mitigating greenhouse warming, the panel urges readers to bear in mind the formidable problems of theory and practice limiting the precision of the estimates that can be provided at this time and even the qualitative accuracy of the picture that can be presented.

BACKGROUND

Greenhouse warming is a phenomenon of the atmosphere, taking place in a global "commons." Similar emissions of greenhouse gases have similar potential to affect global climate, regardless of their country of origin. Thus mitigation strategies must be global in scope, at least implicitly involving both developed and developing countries. Indeed, many of the lowest-cost mitigation options may be found at first in some of the poorest developing countries. For example, the efficiency of wood-burning cookstoves can potentially be raised at very low cost (Reid, 1989). Because these countries may be unwilling or unable to afford such policies, the developed countries may choose to underwrite such efforts. This targeted redistribution of economic resources could be efficient and less costly to the developed countries than mitigation strategies directed solely toward their domestic economies.

Because of the limited availability of information on a global basis, however, and the scope of the panel's responsibilities, the analysis of mitigation options in the chapters that follow is devoted largely to the United States. With a few exceptions, information on mitigation costs and estimates of mitigation potential are derived entirely from U.S. experience and data. Similar analyses should be effected for other countries. Indeed, the analytical framework used in this report is generally applicable to the analysis of mitigation options in a global context.

THE ROLE OF COST-EFFECTIVENESS

Principal among the objectives of policymakers in designing a mitigation strategy should be to minimize the adverse effects of mitigation on the domestic or world economy. This requires designing a strategy that is "cost-effective"—one in which the incremental costs of reducing radiative forcing are minimized. Because the cost per unit of mitigation for most options is not likely to be constant over the entire range of measures, estimates of incremental cost per unit of mitigation will depend on the degree of mitigation obtained, and may rise rapidly as measures are used more intensively. In this report, all cost estimates are based on changes from current levels of emissions, although in many cases these cost estimates are for substantial increments of potential mitigation.

The cost of mitigation may include a number of components, some of which are difficult to measure. First, there are direct expenditures, such as the increased cost of chemical substitutes for CFCs; these costs reduce CFC concentrations below what they would otherwise be and do so promptly. Direct expenditures can be measured readily when market transactions are available to provide data on the prices consumers pay for the benefits of these expenditures. Second, there are investments whose benefits are delayed. For example, higher energy efficiency in an industrial facility will return benefits in the form of reduced emissions of greenhouse gases and energy costs as the facility reduces its energy consumption over the life of the plant. In estimating the value of a stream of benefits and costs over time, a discount rate (interest rate) is used to compute the present value equivalent in order to compare alternative investments. Third, there are implicit costs and benefits in substitutions among final goods or services that imply different levels of greenhouse gas emission. For example, inducing urban commuters to switch from automobiles to mass transit would reduce an important source of greenhouse gas emissions. Yet experience in the United States suggests that such a switch would not occur at the energy prices observed in recent times. If changes in government policy are necessary to change behavior, however, the social cost would include the net loss in value to consumers of changes in their behavior that would not have occurred without changes in policy. That cost is difficult to measure because there is no market transaction that directly reflects such changes in value to customers.

Because most of the mitigation options discussed in this report involve a reduction in energy consumption, there may also be reductions in other undesirable externalities of energy production. The social and economic costs of these reductions in energy consumption may even be outweighed by their benefits. For example, the decision to limit highway speed to 55 miles per hour (mph) in the 1970s and 1980s reduced traffic fatalities considerably. In principle, these reductions in externalities should be deducted from the direct and indirect costs of mitigation. Where possible, these favorable offsetting effects are identified in the chapters that follow; however, they are not generally quantified and applied as offsets to the estimates of cost per unit of mitigation. Of course, many of the issues bear on societal and individual preferences having components that extend beyond quantifiable costs.

ENERGY MODELING

The scope of the task of cost-effective choice can be seen through a review of the work done to date by economists who have estimated the costs and, less often, the benefits of mitigating greenhouse warming. There have been relatively few attempts to estimate these costs by energy modeling. In energy modeling the energy sector of the economy is represented in terms of technological activities such as space heating or transportation services. By using a mathematical programming or other algorithm, the models then solve for the "optimal" trajectory of prices, output, fuel mix, and technologies. It can be shown that, under certain conditions, the optimal trajectory would correspond to the outcome of perfectly competitive markets. (See Appendix R for more details.) Recently, a few economists have begun to work on estimating the costs and benefits of various CO_2 reduction scenarios in this way. Most of these modeling exercises are still in rather preliminary form.

A major problem in measuring the costs of reducing emissions of greenhouse gases lies in establishing the baseline from which these reductions are to be measured. If the object is to measure the costs of restricting CO_2 emissions by some year, such as 2030, to some percentage of current emissions, it is necessary to begin by predicting unconstrained emissions for 2030. The costs of limiting CO_2 will then be dependent on the assumptions made about economic and population growth until that date; the prices of oil, natural gas, and coal; technological changes in energy-using industries; and numerous other parameters that drive emissions in the unconstrained baseline scenario.

A simpler approach is to estimate the cost of reducing CO_2 from current emission levels. This procedure eliminates the necessity for predicting unconstrained CO_2 emissions in some future year, but it does not provide estimates of the cost of restricting future emissions to some fixed level.

In either case, it is necessary for energy modelers to make assumptions about the costs of certain activities at scales outside recent experience or to predict technical change over some horizon. The estimated costs of reforestation or ocean-modification options are highly speculative. So are the estimates of additional costs of technologies to replace current fossil-fuel-based electric power generation. As a result, costs are usually estimated for various scenarios of technical change. These scenarios include a range of estimates of fuel prices, growth in gross national product (GNP), and other parameters.

There are four relatively recent attempts to model the prospective costs of CO_2 reductions: Nordhaus (1989), Manne and Richels (1990), Jorgenson and Wilcoxen (1989), and Edmonds and Reilly (1983). These provide a perspective on the current state of the art in modeling the cost of CO_2 abatement. (Another review that reaches similar conclusions is Darmstadter (1991).)

The Nordhaus Study

Nordhaus's work on global warming began in 1977. In recent papers, he has presented the beginnings of a major modeling effort designed to estimate the cost of controlling CO_2 and other greenhouse gases, assuming efficient markets and taking into account the costs and benefits of various rates of abatement. As part of this exercise, he has attempted to synthesize the results from eight studies of CO_2 abatement, which draw upon data on current practice and extrapolations into the future. A log-linear ordinary least-squares regression is fitted to these estimates and shown as a relation between CO_2 reductions and a "tax rate" per ton of carbon at 1989 prices. This tax rate purports to measure the minimum cost of reduction—an estimate of the marginal cost for the whole economy of the most efficient approach to CO_2 reduction. His results are shown in Figure 20.1.

Nordhaus also estimates the marginal costs of achieving efficient reductions in greenhouse warming through reductions in CFCs and through reforestation. He then combines the three cost curves for CFCs, reforestation, and CO_2 abatement into a single efficient marginal cost curve for greenhouse gas reductions. These results are shown in Figure 20.2. (The chart estimates, for example, that a 30 percent reduction of greenhouse gases would not be equivalent of $150/t CO_2 equivalent.)

Nordhaus's results on the costs of mitigation should be thought of as his estimate of "the best we can do" to reduce carbon usage at minimum cost, by using currently known technology or expert estimates of the technology that can reasonably be expected to be available. Because his model assumes the consumption of resources at current levels and constant exponential growth of the economy with this resource constraint, the resulting esti-

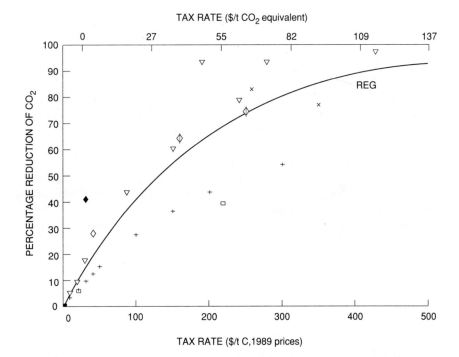

FIGURE 20.1   The Nordhaus study of the marginal cost of CO_2 reduction.   The symbols refer to estimates from different models.

SOURCE: Nordhaus (1990).

mates of mitigation costs must be viewed as tentative. Nordhaus stresses that the actual costs of regulatory approaches are likely to be higher, because government-mandated reductions in emissions are likely to be less efficient than a carbon tax.

Analyses like Nordhaus's, however, implicitly ignore institutional barriers that impede efficient economic adjustments to change. Such barriers exist because information is imperfectly distributed, there are regulatory restrictions on transactions, and buyers or sellers can possess monopolistic control over markets. For example, the adoption of such energy efficiency measures as the installation of better-insulated windows suffers from several impediments: homeowners are generally uninformed about many possible efficiency measures, and building codes may not permit the installation of windows that would be suitable. If existing barriers to adaptation can be lowered, both buyers and sellers can gain from the resulting transactions, which leads to estimates of negative costs for some mitigation steps. That does not mean that mitigation requires no monetary outlay: it is still

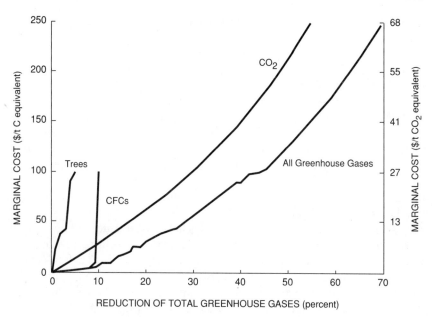

FIGURE 20.2   The Nordhaus study of marginal cost of greenhouse gas reduction.
SOURCE: Nordhaus (1990).

generally an investment, requiring the commitment of capital. It does mean that, relative to the present situation, everyone can gain from lower barriers to adaptation. There is a strong case, prima facie, for adopting such policies, although experience over the past decade suggests that resistance to doing so often exists.

The Manne and Richels Study

Manne and Richels have built simulation models of CO_2 reductions for the United States and for the entire world. These models estimate the cost of various CO_2 abatement scenarios from the present through the twenty-first century and thus include forecasts of economic growth, fuel prices, and new technology.

Manne and Richels examine the economic cost of holding carbon emissions constant from 1990 to 2000 and then gradually reducing these emissions to 80 percent of 1990 levels by 2020. Using a discount rate of 5 percent, they estimate the present value of aggregate loss to U.S. economic consumption due to this constraint under a variety of scenarios concerning U.S. energy technology and policy. The most restrictive and pessimistic scenario—one that assumes no autonomous improvements in energy efficiency, no development of low-cost nuclear power, and no cost-effective means of removing CO_2 from utility waste gases—predicts very small reductions in U.S. consumption until 2010, but sharply rising losses thereafter. The discounted present value of U.S. consumption losses through 2100 is $3.6 trillion under this scenario, or about 1 year's current consumption (i.e., less than 1 percent of total consumption during the century). Using the most optimistic combination of assumptions, Manne and Richels estimate that the present value of the cost of the carbon emission reduction through 2100 would fall to $0.8 trillion. In that case, technical progress in and wider use of nuclear power, improved CO_2 removal technology, and overall energy efficiency in the economy could reduce the cost of mitigation by 78 percent in their model.

It should be stressed that Manne and Richels's results depend heavily on their assumptions concerning U.S. economic growth, world fuel prices, and the prospects for technical progress in the energy sector. They assume a substantial slowing of U.S. economic growth from 3 percent annually in the period from 1990 to 2000 to only 1 percent annually in the last half of the twenty-first century, in the absence of a carbon constraint. A higher rate of economic growth would increase the estimated costs of a carbon constraint substantially, but probably not proportionately with future GNP.

Manne and Richels's estimate of the carbon tax required to produce a 20 percent reduction in carbon (C) emissions, compared to 1990 rates, is shown in Figure 20.3. It shows the carbon tax rising from nearly zero in 2000 to nearly $400/t C in 2010 and peaking at about $600/t C in 2020.[1] The tax falls thereafter, presumably due to a slowing of economic growth and the expansion of more efficient (lower emissions) energy supply technology.

The Jorgenson and Wilcoxen Study

Jorgenson and Wilcoxen have built a long-term simulation model of the U.S. economy to measure the effects of energy and environmental policies on U.S. economic growth. Although this model was not constructed with the goal of estimating the effects of CO_2 reductions, it can be used for this purpose. Jorgenson and Wilcoxen's model is by far the most disaggregated and complete model discussed here. It also has the most sophisticated treatment of capital formation, an important determinant of long-term economic growth.

Carbon dioxide emissions from fossil fuel consumption plus cement manufacture were virtually the same in 1972 and 1987, according to Jorgenson and Wilcoxen, in large part because of a doubling of the relative price of oil between these two years. This observation can be used to simulate the cost of a freeze on CO_2 emissions, given the central role of energy prices in the

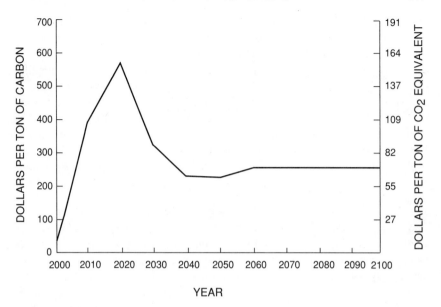

FIGURE 20.3   Manne and Richels's analysis of a carbon tax.

SOURCE: Manne and Richels (1990).

Jorgenson-Wilcoxen growth model.   An analysis prepared by the authors concludes that long-term growth of the gross domestic product in the United States was reduced by about 1.3 percent per year by the 1972-1987 doubling of oil prices (Jorgenson and Wilcoxen, 1989).

None of the three energy models described above is likely to provide precise estimates of the effects of a reduction in CO_2 emissions in the next 30 years or beyond.   Nevertheless, they are quite helpful in judging the first approximations of those effects.   Of the models described, Nordhaus's is the best for projecting the immediate costs of reducing CO_2 emission from any given current level.   Manne-Richels and Jorgenson-Wilcoxen provide longer-term simulation models of the effect of energy-environment policies, including the limitation of CO_2 emissions.

The Edmonds and Reilly Study

The Edmonds and Reilly (1983) model analyzes long-term, global emissions of CO_2 by adopting a simplified picture of an economy that generates CO_2 from fossil fuel burning.   Because it was developed early in the current cycle of attention to greenhouse warming, the model has been widely used (e.g., Lashof and Tirpak, 1991).

The model divides the global economy into nine regions, each of which is assumed to be a single market for energy. Six primary energy categories, three of which emit CO_2 in varying amounts per unit of energy consumed, are analyzed. Demand for energy is driven by a simple model of population, regional economic activity (GNPs), energy productivity (a measure of the pace of technological change), and taxes. Supply of energy is governed by regional resource availability and economic descriptions of "backstop" technologies available within each region. (A backstop technology provides the price at which unlimited quantities of energy are assumed to be available from an inexhaustible resource; in general, the backstop technology is more expensive than other resources currently available from domestic production or international trade.)

Edmonds et al. (1986) discuss the behavior of this model when a significant subset of those assumptions is systematically varied. Projected CO_2 emissions range from 5 to 20 Gt C/yr in the 400 scenarios examined. (These values cover the span between the twenty-fifth and seventy-fifth percentiles of the 400 scenarios.) Thus, by employing assumptions that are not inconsistent with current estimates, this widely used model projects a sizable uncertainty in CO_2 emissions 60 years in the future, ranging from values close to those emitted today to values 4 or more times larger.

PROBLEMS IN COMPARING OPTIONS

The energy models described above yield results that appear to be strikingly different from those presented in subsequent chapters. For example, Figure 20.4 shows a curve for energy efficiency (discussed in Chapter 21) that indicates that significant amounts of carbon mitigation are available at *negative* net costs ("net savings") to society. (Net costs in Figure 20.4 are described in two ways: dollars per ton of CO_2 saved; and costs per kilowatt-hour of electricity needed to achieve those savings.) As shown on the right-hand vertical scale, energy efficiency in the buildings sector saves money because, although energy-efficient appliances cost more than those currently in use, the additional cost (at a 6 percent real rate of interest) is less than the cost of the energy saved. Compare Figure 20.2, which estimates the carbon tax required to induce carbon emission reductions; that such a tax must be imposed to reduce emissions of greenhouse gases means that there is a *positive* net cost to society. Which perspective, if either, is correct?

The answer lies in understanding the inherent limitations of each approach with respect to the task of evaluating specific mitigation options. Energy modeling, in its current state of development, is limited in its ability to evaluate the direct reduction or offset of greenhouse gas emissions achievable by different options. The approach used in this study, which the panel

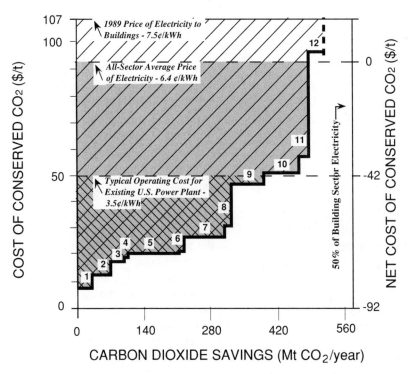

Potential Net Savings:

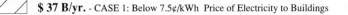

$ 37 B/yr. - CASE 1: Below 7.5¢/kWh Price of Electricity to Buildings

$ 29 B/yr. - CASE 2: Below 6.4¢/kWh All-Sector Average Price of Electricity

$ 10 B/yr. - CASE 3: Below 3.5¢/kWh Typical Operating Cost for Existing U.S. Power Plant

FIGURE 20.4 Technological costing analysis of energy efficiency in the buildings sector.

calls "technological costing," is better suited to this task but limited in its ability to assess overall consequences for the economy. Several related problems are discussed below: (1) deviations of real markets from the idealized bargaining assumed in economic theory, (2) uncertainty, and (3) comparisons of current costs with future benefits. These problems lead to the conclusion that there is no single formula or method for choosing the best alternatives, although comparisons among alternatives are necessary to make informed and prudent decisions.

Structural Assumptions

A common limitation on evaluations of mitigation options is the assumption of unconstrained markets, in which buyers and sellers can arrive at
mutually agreeable prices for the exchange of goods without external influence. Roughly half the world's energy is not sold through unconstrained
markets, however—a reflection of the widespread perception that energy is
too important to be left outside the sphere of government control. Evaluations that do not allow for such factors can produce misleading results.

Market Imperfections and Regulatory Distortions

Markets can be constrained directly by price setting, as in the policies of
the Organization of Petroleum Exporting Countries (OPEC) cartel, or indirectly, as in the regulations that limit the production of CFCs in the United
States. These are imperfect markets—one caused by monopolistic practices, the other a result of an international agreement to protect the stratospheric ozone layer. Interventions in an unconstrained market may or may
not be justified as a matter of social policy, but all such interventions move
prices away from the levels that would prevail otherwise. This creates
important complications in estimating the costs of abating greenhouse gases.

Energy prices are not what they would be without regulation—and, consequently, their levels after mitigation steps are taken become more difficult
to estimate. Other imperfections—in capital markets, building codes, subsidies, and taxes—all bend the behavior of producers and consumers away
from the equilibrium that would obtain in their absence. Moreover, consumer and commercial discount rates are generally higher than the discount
rates typically used in the societal cost-benefit analyses discussed below in
the section on rates of return (Meier and Whittier, 1982; Train, 1985; Ruderman
et al., 1987; Electric Power Research Institute, 1988; Peters, 1988; Ross,
1989; Gladwell, 1990; Koomey, 1990). Indeed, the market imperfections
already in place provide significant room for mitigation.

The analyses of potential mitigation options contained in the chapters
that follow are often addressed to such market failures. Some utilities and
governments have accumulated significant experience with such policies in
the past 15 years (Vine, 1985; Hirst et al., 1986; Vine and Harris, 1988;
Koomey and Levine, 1989; Krause et al., 1989; Rosenfeld et al., 1989;
Wilson et al., 1989; American Council for an Energy-Efficient Economy,
1990; Nadel, 1990). Experience shows that these policies can offer high
returns in the short run—greater than the cost of capital in many cases
(Geller et al., 1987; Train and Ignelzi, 1987; Geller and Miller, 1988; U.S.
Department of Energy, 1988; Krause et al., 1989; Nadel, 1990). This is the
origin of the net negative cost estimates in Figure 20.4. Note, however, that

evaluations of energy efficiency programs are usually made in terms of public utility outlays, rather than total social costs. The latter is the appropriate standard of measure of energy efficiency programs because both the benefits and the costs of energy efficiency are widely distributed, affecting firms and households that are neither shareholders in utilities nor purchasers of their energy services.

Technological Costing Versus Energy Modeling

The limitations of energy modeling indicate the need for an additional method to supplement the information provided by the energy modeling method in the effort to estimate the costs of mitigation. This approach, "technological costing," bases its estimates on a variety of assumptions about the technical aspects of the mitigation option, together with estimates—often no more than guesses—of the costs of implementing the required technology. This approach can be useful whenever there are insufficient data on the actual costs realized in markets or when it is difficult to use statistical methods to estimate the costs of future policies from the historical behavior of markets. Technological costing does not escape the limitations of economics, however, because this approach also relies implicitly on economic assumptions. The most important of these is the assumption that direct costs are a good measure of total cost.

The technological costing approach should be seen as complementary to the modeling described above, which uses simulation techniques to make inferences from economic data and assumptions about economic structure. Energy modeling studies are likely to be useful whenever observations of market behavior are available. As shown in Chapter 29, the two approaches are in rough agreement, given the large uncertainties in the best available knowledge. This lends some comfort with respect to the general validity of the results, although the degree of uncertainty limits the utility of these estimates for the purposes of making specific policy recommendations.

Neither the energy modeling nor the technological costing approach is perfect. Technological cost studies can often be criticized for scanting informational, adjustment, or managerial costs. Their main weakness is that they fail to allow for impacts on quantities and prices in other markets and therefore neglect "general equilibrium" effects of any major actions undertaken—something that the full-scale economic models allow for. Energy modeling analyses are subject to criticisms concerning model specification, measurement errors, and the relevance of historical data and behavior for future untested policy actions. In the chapters that follow, most of the cost-effectiveness measures derive from technological costing rather than energy modeling. The estimates of cost-effectiveness and emission reduction potential from the analyses in this report are combined in Chapter 29, which traces out a "supply curve" of mitigation possibilities. In some instances, these analyses find a negative cost of mitigation, implying that mitigation actions sometimes yield a positive economic return. Negative mitigation costs assumes certain current public or private market imperfections will be overcome. If such imperfections could be corrected at low enough cost, society could achieve substantial benefits from these mitigation measures even if greenhouse warming were not a problem.

The energy models set a baseline for more detailed analyses—a baseline, discussed below, that is still fuzzy. Yet energy models do attempt to capture responses to changes in technology and policy from markets reaching throughout society. Analyses that use prices only as static indicators of current value can miss dynamic adjustments of great significance on time scales of decades.

Uncertainties in Energy Modeling

Although the timing of greenhouse warming is not known with precision, it is highly likely that any effects will unfold over times much longer than the normal horizons of economic forecasting. Accordingly, mitigation efforts may have to be spread out over decades as well. Analyzing such possibilities requires extrapolation of economic conditions well into the coming century, an enterprise of doubtful accuracy given our current understanding of economic dynamics. The existence of so many uncertainties constitutes the second major problem in policy design.

There are no facts about the future. Estimates of important parameters, such as the level of carbon tax needed to induce large-scale (20 to 50 percent) reductions in CO_2 emissions, vary by large amounts. Nordhaus (1990) estimates \$40/t C (\$11/t CO_2 equivalent) of coal equivalent; Manne and Richels (1990), \$250/t C (\$68/t CO_2 equivalent). These variations illustrate the current state of the art. Not only do all models indicate large quantitative uncertainty, the narrow base of validation raises questions about the qualitative uncertainties and systematic errors that may be embodied in the models. For instance, several models incorporate a rate at which energy efficiency improvements enter the economy—an ad hoc but influential assumption. Edmonds et al. (1986) find that the exogenous energy efficiency improvement rate explains much of the variation in the behavior of the widely used Edmonds-Reilly forecasting model. Yet there is no theoretical reason to think that energy efficiency improvements should grow exponentially or that the rate of improvement is independent of government policy. The assumption appears to be made simply for convenience in modeling.

Thus, for the purpose of policy design in the near future, energy models are essential to framing a conceptually sound approach, but neither individually nor collectively do they provide comprehensive guidance on the choices to be made.

Uncertainties in Technological Costing

Although the panel believes that the technological costing approach provides the most information for evaluating the mitigation potential of current options, this approach does have certain limitations or uncertainties. Perhaps most important, such option-driven assessments do not do a good job of incorporating social responses. For example, despite the proven benefits of a variety of energy efficiency measures, consumers have been slow to adopt them. Lack of information, financial constraints on households, and a variety of other barriers impede their use. Such factors are difficult to incorporate in the technological costing approach, which leads some to criticize this approach as having too often led to optimistic estimates of options.*

A second uncertainty in the technological costing approach involves interactions among different options. Implementing energy efficiency options, for example, would likely reduce demand for energy. This, in turn, could alter the price of energy, which would affect the panel's calculations of cost-effectiveness for energy options, which assume a constant price for the cost of electricity, natural gas, gasoline, and so on.

This constant cost assumption is an additional uncertainty that affects not only the interaction among the prices of different options, but also the cost of each individual option. The technological costing approach assumes that the implementation of a particular option does not affect the cost of that option. For example, a substantial increase in the number of natural gas-fired electricity generating plants could increase demand for natural gas, and therefore the price of natural gas would likely rise. Such price increases could affect the cost-effectiveness calculation for natural gas, perhaps enough to alter its ranking.

The energy modeling approach takes such issues of demand, supply, and consumer behavior into account, whereas the technology costing approach does not. Although the panel recognizes the possibility of such interactions, it believes the technological costing approach is better suited to responding to the panel's charge of evaluating the comparative advantages and disadvantages of specific mitigation options so that it can identify and rank the available mitigation strategies. Since the panel realized that such interactions are likely, however, it developed reasonable targets (e.g., re-

---

*Panel members Douglas Foy and Robert Crandall have further views on the use of technological costing: Foy wishes to emphasize that the approach can overestimate the net social cost (i.e., social costs less the social benefits) of mitigation, because it fails to include many possible quantifiable and unquantifiable *social benefits*—such as reduced air pollution and enhanced energy security. In contrast, Crandall believes that the approach is likely to provide estimates of the *social cost* of mitigation that are overly optimistic. He believes that such excessive optimism is particularly noticeable in, but not necessarily limited to, the transportation sector, given the economic studies that reach very different conclusions from those advanced in this report.

placement of 3.5 incandescent light bulbs per household with compact fluorescent lighting) and cost assumptions in its calculations, leaving a full assessment of such interactions to future studies. In addition, the panel presents the implications of less than full implementation of those reasonable estimates.

Comparisons over Time

One important conceptual contribution of economic theory addresses the third problem in policy design: the matter of comparing benefits and costs occurring at different times. Because the time scales of greenhouse warming are long in comparison with most of the rhythms of human events, it is particularly critical to think through clearly the question of intertemporal comparisons of value.

Steps to mitigate future changes in climate are investments: we incur the costs now, and we and future generations enjoy the benefits. If our principal concern is the effects of our current actions on our grandchildren and great-grandchildren, we should compare greenhouse mitigation actions with alternative legacies that can be left to future generations. The conventional approach to making this comparison is to apply a discount rate, comparing the value of investments against the value of an equivalent sum put into an interest-bearing instrument. The discounting procedure reduces the value of future benefits, because the alternative—earning interest—steadily raises the level that must be achieved to be competitive.

Some argue that discounting may not be appropriate. For example, if taking option A today results in destruction of a particular ecosystem in 2020, whereas taking option B results in destruction of the same ecosystem in 2030, should a lesser cost be assigned to option B? The discounting procedure does so. If options A and B differ in no other respect, it would be a mistake to apply the discounting approach blindly. But as discussed below, it remains sensible in practice to require returns on investment of at least 10 percent per year, except under special circumstances. That is, mitigation actions should be compared with other investments we can make now. The availability of alternative investments establishes a minimum rate of return, which mitigation actions should yield if they are to compete favorably with these alternative choices to improve life in the future.

Rates of Return

What are the rates of return on alternative investments? Macroeconomic calculations for the United States suggest a return on capital investments of about 12 percent. The U.S. government operates under a guideline, both for government investments and for regulatory requirements on the private sector, suggesting that a project or a regulation with a prospective rate of return below 10 percent in real terms (i.e., corrected for inflation) should be rejected (Office of Management and Budget, 1974; Reischauer, 1990). The World Bank lends extensively to developing countries around the world, mainly but not exclusively for large-infrastructure projects. The informal guideline in project evaluation is that the estimated rate of return must exceed 10 percent in real terms, although in some circumstances, where nonquantifiable benefits are expected to be important, lower estimated rates of return are accepted. A survey of over 1000 projects undertaken during the 1970s and 1980s yielded an average expected return on completion of 16 percent (Pohl and Mihaljek, 1989).

Other rates of interest have been suggested for evaluating public investments. An extensive and complex literature exists that attempts to sort out which of several possible discount rates should be used in the United States, depending on whether the investment in question is deemed to displace private investment, personal consumption (where consumers are borrowing at rates higher than 10 percent to consume now), or government investment (e.g., see Hausman, 1979; Lind, 1982). Recently, the Congressional Budget Office has suggested that the appropriate rate of return for evaluating U.S. government projects is about 3 or 4 percent in real terms, the rate at which the United States is able to borrow from the rest of the world, and hence the real cost to Americans (Reischauer, 1990); however, this standard may be irrelevant to a global issue such as greenhouse warming (see the discussion of discount rates in Chapter 4, Part One).

The appropriate criterion in establishing a discount rate should be the ability to provide for future generations. Determining that rate requires deciding the scale of investment and, at any given scale, comparing each proposed investment in the future with alternative investments. What is relevant, again, is the return on feasible investments that the mitigating policies displace anywhere in the world. The World Bank experience and current criteria suggest that any proposed mitigation investment should be expected to yield at least 10 percent per year, except under special circumstances.

The time frame for global climate change, at 50 to 100 years or more, is a long one by the standards of most investments and most public policy. At a discount rate of 10 percent, the present value of a dollar 50 years from now is less than a cent, and that of a dollar 100 years from now is less than one-hundredth of a cent. In other words, far distant payoffs from current investments are worth practically nothing today.

Suppose, however, that the cost of greenhouse mitigation rises sharply from current levels as greenhouse gas concentrations increase. Does that not warrant doing something now? The answer is negative, as long as alternative investments continue to have a higher yield. Indeed, that criterion will be easier to meet if, as postulated, the cost of mitigation increases in the future and the yield from mitigation declines.

This conclusion would fail to hold only if the yield on alternative investments in the future could be expected to fall, and to fall by so much that over the total 50- to 100-year period the yield on alternative investments would be lower than the yield on mitigation actions taken in the near future. The "at least 10 percent" criterion is applicable to the late twentieth century; it might not be applicable to the mid-twenty-first century if there were a decline in the yield on alternative investments. Although this is a theoretical possibility, there is little historical evidence to support it. The world's capital stock has been growing relative to its labor force for two centuries, and although the return to capital has fallen over one or two decades in countries of exceptionally high investment such as Japan and Korea, it has not fallen significantly over the longer period of world industrialization.

Growth and Uncertainty

Two qualifications may, however, have to be introduced to the "at least 10 percent" criterion. The first derives from the fact that gross world product can be expected to grow over the next century. Because the driving forces of climate change appear to be related to economic activity in general, many components of the cost of global climate change may also be proportional to gross world product. To the extent that is true, the cost of climate change will increase with economic output. Although discounting reduces the present value of more distant costs, the possibility that they may grow over time cuts in the other direction.

It is ordinarily assumed in economic analyses that gross world product per capita will grow at a rate between 1 and 3 percent per year over the next 50 years, a magnitude that depends partly on advancing technology and partly on the rate at which existing technology is absorbed by economies that are not operating at the frontier of existing technology. If the costs of climate change are proportional to per capita gross world product, and if that quantity grows, for example, at 3 percent per year, then the yield criterion for mitigation actions drops to "at least 7 percent."

It should be noted that the costs of global climate change may not be proportional to gross world product. As change begins to be evident, societies will take adaptive action, and it is the cost of future adaptive action that is in part avoided by mitigation action now. However, the costs of some adaptive actions will not be proportional to gross world product. For example, the costs of building sea walls to protect against rising sea levels, if that should occur, may not increase with gross world product, even though flood damage in the absence of sea walls might increase with gross world product.

The second qualification concerns the uncertainty that attends predictions about future climate change and its associated costs. Uncertainty is an important topic, one that is conceptually different from comparing present costs with known future benefits. However, one aspect of uncertainty deserves mention because it could influence the choice of a discount rate, especially when the uncertainty cannot be entered directly into the cost-benefit calculation, as it should be.

The uncertainties associated with mitigating global climate change and its attendant costs are, in the current state of knowledge, at least as great as—and probably greater than—the uncertainties associated with other forms of investment that could be undertaken today. Accordingly, the investor averse to risk might conclude that costly mitigation actions should not be undertaken. However, the payoff from mitigation actions now will be greatest if the magnitude of global climate change and the associated costs turn out to be high, even if that is judged to be a contingency of low probability. Of course, if the costs associated with global climate change are low, any investment in mitigation actions will have a low return. Yet such investment may still be worthwhile as insurance against an uncertain but possibly costly contingency.

How do these considerations influence the discount rate? The precise answer is not at all straightforward, unless the uncertainty itself is related in a particular way to the passage of time. Roughly speaking, however, one can say that where an uncertain outcome (the future payoff from mitigation actions) is negatively correlated with overall economic prospects (as measured by future gross world product per capita), and where the uncertainty grows exponentially with time, some deduction from the discount rate used to evaluate mitigation actions is warranted. How much? That depends in detail on the nature of the uncertainty, an issue that remains to be clarified, and on the degree of our aversion to risk. Presumably, it was this sort of consideration that led U.S. policymakers in 1980 to stipulate a discount rate of only 7 percent for energy-related projects, 3 percent lower than the general standard for government investments.

In this report, most mitigation policies are analyzed at three different discount rates—3, 6, and 10 percent—so that decision makers may choose as they wish. In addition, the efficiency options are also analyzed at 30 percent—to represent the rate of return that studies show consumers currently need before they will invest in energy efficiency.

Generic Alternatives in a Least-Cost Strategy

Investment involves choosing among alternative uses of resources. As discussed in the preceding section, these choices are significantly influenced by policy choices, including the discount rate. With policy guidance on this and other key assumptions, it is possible to develop a cost-effective portfolio of investments in mitigation (for a similar application, see Northwest Power Planning Council, 1986).

Finding the least-cost mix of responses to greenhouse warming entails comparing all the different mitigation responses. Figure 20.5 illustrates that the least-cost plan will probably involve a mix of responses. For simplicity, only two hypothetical options are plotted. They are shown as curves giving the cost for achieving various reductions in greenhouse gas emissions (or the equivalent: removal of greenhouse gases from the atmosphere, blocking of incident radiation, or changing of the earth's reflectivity). For comparability, all responses are translated into CO_2-equivalent emissions.

Both options exhibit increasing cost for increasing reductions in emission (the curves gradually bend upward). If the only alternative were to achieve the desired level of reduction by choosing one option, the clear preference would be the hypothetical option B. Option B produces each level of reduction at lower cost than option A.

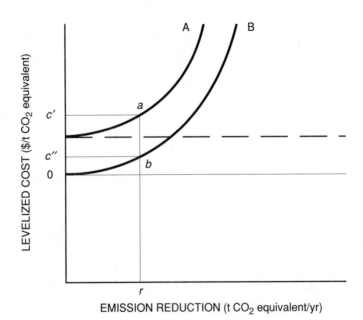

FIGURE 20.5   A comparison of hypothetical mitigation options. Curves show the costs of various levels of reduction in CO_2-equivalent emissions. Total costs for the period of analysis are divided by the number of years, and all comparisons over time are assumed to be on the same basis. Both the cost and potential emission reduction are converted to CO_2 equivalents to allow comparison across different mitigation options.

Several analysts (Edmonds and Reilly, 1986; Nordhaus, 1990) have pointed out the technical complications of making sensible comparisons among different greenhouse gases. The cost of reductions has been plotted along the vertical axis in terms of a "levelized" cost (i.e., total cost over the period of analysis, divided by the number of years). Responses to greenhouse warming should be evaluated as investments, because the benefit that is sought will generally take a long time to appear. Consequently, it is important to compare costs over time, rather than simply in the particular years in which expenditures are made. Discounting the costs and benefits allows such a comparison. As discussed above, the choice of discount rate influences the comparisons made.

Figure 20.6 extends the comparison to additional options with different characteristics. Option C shows the "negative cost," or net positive benefits, associated with achieving the initial reductions in CO_2 emissions. An example is energy efficiency, such as variable speed motors or compact fluorescent lighting. The cost of these measures would be less than the cost

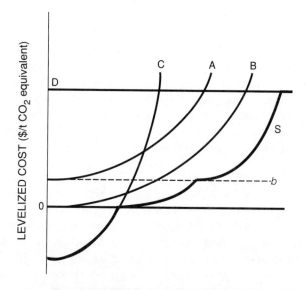

EMISSION REDUCTION (t CO_2 equivalent/yr)

FIGURE 20.6 A comparison of multiple mitigation options. Curves show the costs of various levels of reduction in CO_2-equivalent emissions for four hypothetical mitigation options. Total costs for the period of analysis are divided by the number of years, and all comparisons over time are assumed to be on the same basis. Both the cost and the potential emission reduction are converted to CO_2 equivalents to allow comparison across different mitigation options.

of adding electricity generating capacity if the conservation measures were not implemented.

Option D illustrates a "backstop technology." A backstop technology provides an unlimited amount of reduction at a fixed cost. An example would be an abundant energy source that provides electricity with no CO_2 emissions at all. Where a backstop technology exists, its cost sets a ceiling on the investment in reducing emissions. Only options costing less than D should be considered, no matter how much emission reduction is desired.

The heavy line labeled S in Figure 20.6 shows the cost-effective combination of options. Option C is selected up to the point at which option B becomes more cost-effective. Option A is added when it becomes cost-effective. S becomes horizontal when the cost reaches that of the backstop technology.

As comparison of curves A and B indicates, the cost-effective portfolio contains a mix of alternatives. The level of expenditure is established by governments, who are guided by estimates of the benefits to be derived from mitigation, as well as budgetary considerations, international commitments, and other factors. The level of expenditure translates into a number of tons of greenhouse gas reductions; the objective is to get the largest reduction for that expenditure. This is shown by curve S in Figure 20.6, which outlines the mix of investments that produces any specified reduction at the least cost. At the point labeled b, for instance, all of the pairings from options B and C below the dashed line have been obtained, and acquisition of the alternatives at the bottom of curve A is beginning to be added. Additional savings from options B and C would also be pursued as the level of spending moves upward. (This discussion assumes that curves A through D describe independent activities, so as to avoid double-counting of savings. See Chapter 29 for an additional discussion of the problems involved in double-counting.)

Curves A through C all reflect a conventional assumption: that the cost of obtaining reductions in greenhouse gas generally increases as the size of the reduction is increased. Note, however, that curve C begins below zero. As discussed in Chapters 21, 22, and 23, there may be options available that are of net benefit to society even without accounting for the benefits of reduced greenhouse warming. These include some energy efficiency measures, such as variable speed motors or compact fluorescent lighting. As mentioned above, these actions may be worth more to electric utilities than the costs of producing and installing them because the improved efficiency allows the electric utility to defer expensive additions to generating capacity. In principle, they can therefore be provided at no cost to the homeowner because they reduce the total cost of serving that customer, provided the utility can reap a reward on its investment in energy efficiency. A substantial portion of the energy savings would reduce emissions of CO_2 while simultaneously producing economic benefits. There may be other options available whose costs are lower than the cost of the energy saved, even without placing a value on the reductions in greenhouse gas emissions.

What prevents these measures from being taken now are lack of information, inadequate economic incentives for utilities, high discount rates for personal consumption, and resistance to changing established methods. However, even technically feasible measures that benefit the national economy as a whole may not benefit every individual.

Research and development should both lower and flatten the supply curves in Figure 20.6, reducing the cost of alternatives and raising the scale at which they can be economically introduced. Research and development here includes social experimentation in areas such as mass transit, marketing of energy efficiency, and planting of trees on residential property, where consumer behavior has a substantial effect on the reductions achieved. More generally, research affects uncertainty. Although the supply curves in Figure 20.6 are drawn as lines, there is actually considerable uncertainty about how much reduction is available and at what price. The lines should be bands. The distinction between two technologies may not be as clear in practice as shown for curves A and B in Figure 20.6.

Timing of Mitigation Policy and Transient Effects

As further described in Appendix B, another important consideration in designing a mitigation policy is the timing and targeting of mitigation activities so that they have the desired impact on greenhouse warming. Therefore an important distinction to make is that human activities affect both the stocks and the flows of greenhouse gas emissions.

Greenhouse gas emissions occur in one time period, with some portion of the emissions sequestered immediately by the natural system (e.g., oceans) but with the remainder augmenting the much larger stock in the atmosphere that has developed over geological time due to the natural occurrence and long lifetime of many of these gases.

The response of climate may depend in complicated ways on both stock (atmospheric concentrations) and flow (emissions and absorptions into oceans, plants, and other reservoirs). Changing both—as is done in most mitigation approaches—may therefore produce nonlinear effects. Lowering emissions by 10 Mt/yr for 10 years may not have the same effect on greenhouse warming as lowering the stock of greenhouse gases by 100 Mt in a single year. This implies that different CO_2 reduction patterns will have different effects on greenhouse warming with time and thus different benefits.

Therefore, in evaluating a prospective mitigation measure, one must examine the relationship between both the timing and duration of its reduction in greenhouse gases and the policy outcome desired.

Not only are there nonlinear effects due to the response of the natural environment, there also are important nonlinearities in social dynamics. An important body of knowledge has been accumulated on the reaction of various national economies to the energy price shocks of the 1970s. This analysis suggests that gradual change is likely to be significantly less costly than sudden imposition of a carbon tax or any other policy instrument designed to bring about a rapid change in CO_2 emissions (Jorgenson and Wilcoxen, 1991). More generally, the *transient* effects of policy can be a large fraction of the total impact of attempts to mitigate greenhouse warming, particularly if the economic changes occur on a time scale of a year or shorter.

Thus timing is an important policy consideration. Climate change is a slow process in comparison with the rates of price fluctuations or changes in the business cycle. To the extent that institutions permit slow phasing in of policies such as carbon taxes, gradual changes are likely to be less disruptive economically.

Uncertainty and Choice of Parameters

Uncertainty cannot be ignored in responding to greenhouse warming. Errors of doing too much can be as consequential as errors of doing too little; the error of trying to solve the wrong problem is as likely as the error of failing to act. Above all, errors are inevitable, whether one acts or not, but inevitable errors are also occasions to learn. Therefore policy design that incorporates these lessons of the past helps to increase the resilience of the decision-making system and to foster future learning (Holling, 1978).

An initial step is to choose the range of parameters to be used in the analysis. The case of discount rates has been discussed here at some length, illustrating the social judgments at stake in making these quantitative assumptions. Note that what is needed is a range, rather than a single "best" value. If uncertainty cannot be avoided, one needs to know what would happen under different circumstances, so that serious errors can be forestalled and affordable ones identified.

Therefore, as illustrated in Chapter 29, after using the best information that the Mitigation Panel had available to evaluate the cost-effectiveness and emission potential of the various mitigation options at discount rates ranging from 3 to 30 percent, the panel used its judgment as shown in Figures 29.1 to 29.3 to provide a range of values for the cost and potential of mitigation. This process culminates in Figure 29.5, which shows two curves: one with the highest cost and lowest emission reduction, the other with the lowest cost and highest emission reduction. This technological costing curve range is compared with the range developed using energy modeling as an accuracy check.

It is important to note that the mitigation options evaluated are merely technical choices. It is the policy judgments that are of instrumental importance, first, because a judgment of what to study shapes the kinds of conclusions that can be reached (Selznick, 1947; Kingdon, 1984) and, second, because governments are likely to be held accountable for their actions, including actions taken in analyzing large-scale changes. Both require policy-level involvement, as well as competent technical execution.

Because of this, the Mitigation Panel believes it is important to also evaluate various policy instruments that can be used in implementing the mitigation options. A list of some of the alternatives that have been proposed appears in Table 20.1. The list includes command-control instruments, economic incentives, revenue-neutral incentives, information programs, and redefinition of the mission and profits of utilities. The potential of these policy options for reducing the barriers to implementing the mitigation option is discussed in the evaluation of each option.

CONCLUSIONS

The charge to the Mitigation Panel was to "examine the range of policy interventions that might be employed to mitigate changes in the earth's radiation balance, assessing these options in terms of their expected impacts, costs, and, at least in qualitative terms, their relative cost-effectiveness." In this chapter, the panel has examined the two primary methods that can be used to evaluate greenhouse gas mitigation options: technological costing and energy modeling. While the energy modeling approach uses models that predict society's responses based on *past* societal behavior, technological costing attempts to determine the cost-effectiveness and emission reduction potential of *future* behavior and assumes that current public or private market imperfections can be overcome. The panel believes that the technological costing approach is better suited to evaluating the comparative advantages and disadvantages of specific mitigation options because current energy models do not have the specificity needed for such an analysis. For example, they look at the impact of a given carbon tax across the economy, but not the cost of specific methods for responding to that tax. However, there are reasons to be skeptical of the degree to which option-driven assessments can incorporate social responses (including market responses) to alternative courses of action. For example, although it is technically feasible at some cost to replace all coal-fired plants with nuclear power plants, social opposition to the installation of nuclear plants could prevent the option from being implemented. Yet, because energy modeling draws inferences from past behavior, the total cost of a shift to nuclear power may be overestimated, if there were to be widespread public reevaluation of the relative risks of climate change and energy technology, and if

TABLE 20.1 Potential Greenhouse Gas Mitigation Instruments

I. *Command-Control Instruments*
   A. Consumption
      1. Bans on certain products (aerosol hairsprays)
      2. Quantitative limitations on certain products
         (rationing during wartime)
      3. Mandated consumption of certain products or services
         (unleaded gasoline)
   B. Production
      1. Quotas on offending products (CFCs)
      2. Quotas on products using offending substances
         (asbestos-product phaseouts)
   C. Input choices in production
      1. Mandated fuel efficiency (Corporate Average Fuel Economy
         standards)
      2. Durability standards (automobile bumper standards)
      3. Fuel mixture standards (gasohol?)
      4. Land reforestation requirements (strip-mining regulations)
   D. Provision of public services
      1. Mass transit options
      2. Acquisition of public lands
   E. Standards for energy-efficient buildings

II. *Economic Incentives*
   A. Taxes on inputs
      1. Carbon tax levied on fuels
      2. Specific fuel taxes (gasoline, jet fuel, etc.)
   B. Taxes on outputs
      1. Emission tax
      2. Sales tax on products (gas-guzzler tax)
   C. Financial incentives
      1. Research and development tax credit
      2. Tax credits (or deductions) for improved technologies
   D. Transferable property rights
      1. Tradeable emission reductions (offset, SO_2 abatement
         credits, CFC permits)
      2. Reforestation credits (proposed less-developed country debt
         relief)

III. *Revenue-Neutral Incentives*
   A. Gas-guzzler fee combined with gas-sipper rebate for new cars
   B. Fee rebates to create a market for low emissions of NO_x, hydrocarbons,
      CO, and particulates for new cars
   C. Variable hookup fees for new buildings

TABLE 20.1 *(continued)*

IV. *Information Programs*
    A. Provision of basic data
    B. Provision of technological data
    C. Transmission of economic signals
    D. Technical assistance

V. *Redefining the Mission and Profits of Utilities*
    A. Incentives for utilities to invest in conservation and share in the
       avoided cost

VI. *Direct Actions*
    A. Direct government action (such as carrying out geoengineering
       options)

---

investments in nuclear engineering were to produce technical alternatives that were widely regarded as acceptable.

In conducting the analyses in subsequent chapters, the panel used the best and most reliable information available. But because more and better information is needed to determine the full social costs of mitigating greenhouse warming, the analysis presented in this report should be seen as a starting point on which future assessments can build. Despite the uncertainties described in this chapter, the components of a reasonable policy approach can be inferred from the discussion above:

• Although U.S. national policy is important, it is not by itself the determining factor in global greenhouse gas emissions.

• There are likely to be substantial economic impacts from controlling greenhouse gas emissions. Transient effects and transaction costs are important and potentially large, but they are highly uncertain, and methods for making usable predictions of these dynamic effects do not exist.

• Mixed strategies, aimed at cost-effective reductions of greenhouse gas emissions, are likely to be the best approach to mitigation. The timing and precise design of such a mix of policies are both significant and uncertain at present. It makes sense, accordingly, to emphasize that set of policies that is cost-effective.

• The ranking of options in terms of cost-effectiveness is strongly dependent on the choice of discount rate and a variety of uncertainties concerning technology, energy prices, and economic growth.

• The substantial uncertainties in both science and social science make errors inevitable. It is important, accordingly, to shape policies that can be resilient and that foster learning.

NOTE

1. Throughout this report, tons (t) are metric; 1 Mt = 1 megaton = 1 million tons; and 1 Gt = 1 gigaton = 1 billion tons.

REFERENCES

American Council for an Energy-Efficient Economy (ACEEE). 1990. Proceedings of the 1990 ACEEE Summer Study on Energy Efficiency in Buildings. Washington, D.C.: American Council for an Energy-Efficient Economy.

Atkinson, S. E., and R. Halvorsen. 1984. A new hedonic technique for estimating attribute demand: An application to the demand for automobile fuel efficiency. Review of Economics and Statistics 66(3):416-426.

Barker, B. S., S. H. Galginaitis, E. Rosenthal, and Gikas International, Inc. 1986. Summary Report Commercial Energy Management and Decision-making on the District of Columbia. Washington, D.C.: Potomac Electric Power Company.

Darmstadter, J. 1991. The economic cost of CO_2 mitigation: A review of estimates for selected world regions. Discussion paper ENR91-06. Washington, D.C.: Resources for the Future, Inc.

Edmonds, J. A., and J. M. Reilly. 1983. A long-term global energy-economic model of carbon dioxide release from fossil fuel use. Energy Economics 5:74-88.

Edmonds, J. A., and J. M. Reilly. 1986. The IEA/ORAU Long-Term Global Energy CO_2 Model: Personal Computer Version A84PC. Report ORNL/CDIC-16 CMP-002/PC. Institute for Energy Analysis, Oak Ridge Associated Universities. (Available from National Technical Information Service, Springfield, Va.)

Edmonds, J. A., J. M. Reilly, R. H. Gardner, and A. Brenkert. 1986. Uncertainty in Future Global Energy Use and Fossil Fuel CO_2 Emissions for 1975 to 2075. Report DOE/NBB-0081. Carbon Dioxide Research Division, Office of Basic Energy Sciences, Office of Energy Research, U.S. Department of Energy. (Available from National Technical Information Service, Springfield, Va.)

Electric Power Research Institute (EPRI). 1988. DSM Commercial Customer Acceptance, Volume 1, Program Planning Insights. Report EM-5633, Project 2548-1. Palo Alto, Calif.: Electric Power Research Institute.

Geller, H. S., and P. M. Miller. 1988. 1988 Lighting Ballast Efficiency Standards: Analysis of Electricity and Economic Savings. Washington, D.C.: American Council for an Energy-Efficient Economy.

Geller, H. S., J. P. Harris, M. D. Levine, and A. H. Rosenfeld. 1987. The role of federal research and development in advancing energy efficiency: A $50 billion contribution to the U.S. economy. In Annual Review of Energy 1987, J. M. Hollander, ed. Palo Alto, Calif.: Annual Reviews, Inc.

Gladwell, M. 1990. Consumer's choices about money consistently defy common sense. Washington Post. February 12, 1990. A3.

Hausman, J. A. 1979. Individual discount rates and the purchase and utilization of energy-using durables. Bell Journal of Economics 10(1):33-54.

Hirst, E., J. Clinton, H. Geller, and W. Kroner. 1986. Energy Efficiency in Buildings: Progress and Promise. Washington, D.C.: American Council for an Energy-Efficient Economy.

Holling, C. S., ed. 1978. Adaptive Environmental Assessment and Management. New York: John Wiley & Sons.

Jorgenson, D. W., and P. J. Wilcoxen. 1989. Environmental Regulation and U.S. Economic Growth. Cambridge, Mass.: Harvard Institute of Economic Research.

Jorgenson, D. W., and P. J. Wilcoxen. 1991. U.S. Environment Policy and Economic Growth: How Do We Fare? Paper presented to the American Council for Capital Formation Center for Policy Research, September 12, 1991.

Kingdon, J. W. 1984. Agendas, Alternatives, and Public Policies. Boston: Little, Brown.

Koomey, J. 1990. Energy Efficiency Choices in New Office Buildings: An Investigation of Market Failures and Corrective Policies. Ph.D. dissertation. University of California, Berkeley.

Koomey, J., and M. D. Levine. 1989. Policies to Increase Energy Efficiency in Buildings and Appliances. Report LBL-27270. Berkeley, Calif.: Lawrence Berkeley Laboratory.

Krause, F., E. Vine, and S. Gandhi. 1989. Program Experience and Its Regulatory Implications: A Case Study of Utility Lighting Efficiency Programs. Report LBL-28268. Berkeley, Calif.: Lawrence Berkeley Laboratory.

Lashof, D. A., and D. A. Tirpak, eds. 1991. Policy Options for Stabilizing Global Climate. Washington, D.C.: U.S. Environmental Protection Agency.

Lind, R. C., ed. 1982. Discounting for Time and Risk in Energy Policy. Washington, D.C.: Resources for the Future and Johns Hopkins University Press.

Manne, A. S., and R. G. Richels. 1990. Global CO_2 emission reductions—The impacts of rising energy costs. Preliminary draft. February 1990.

Manne, A. S., R. G. Richels, and W. W. Hogan. 1990. CO_2 emission limits: An economic cost analysis for the USA. Energy Journal 11(2):51-85.

Meier, A., and J. Whittier. 1982. Purchasing patterns of energy efficient refrigerators and implied consumer discount rates. In Proceedings of the 1982 ACEEE Conference. Washington, D.C.: American Council for an Energy-Efficient Economy.

Nadel, S. 1990. Lessons Learned: A Review of Utility Experience with Conservation and Load Management Programs for Commercial and Industrial Customers. Albany: New York State Energy Research and Development Authority.

Nordhaus, W. D. 1989. The economics of the greenhouse effect. Preliminary draft, June 4, 1989. Available from W. D. Nordhaus, Department of Economics, Yale University, New Haven, Conn.

Nordhaus, W. D. 1990. To slow or not to slow: The economics of the greenhouse effect. Paper presented at the 1990 Annual Meeting of the American Association for the Advancement of Science, New Orleans, La., February 15-20, 1990.

Northwest Power Planning Council. 1986. Northwest Conservation and Electric Power Plan. Portland, Oreg.: Northwest Power Planning Council.

Office of Management and Budget (OMB). 1974. Discount Rates to Be Used in Evaluating Time-Discounted Costs and Benefits. OMB Circular A-94. Washington, D.C.: Office of Management and Budget.

Peters, J. S. 1988. Lessons in Industrial Conservation Program Design. In Proceedings of the 1988 ACEEE Summer Study on Energy Efficiency in Buildings. Washington, D.C.: American Council for an Energy-Efficient Economy.

Pohl, G., and D. Mihaljek. 1989. Project Evaluation in Practice. Washington, D.C.: World Bank. December.

Reid, W. V. C. 1989. Sustainable development: Lessons from success. Environment 31(4):29-35.

Reischauer, R. D. 1990. Statement of the Director, Congressional Budget Office, before the Committee on Energy and Natural Resources, U.S. Senate. March 1990.

Rosenfeld, A. H., R. J. Mowris, and J. G. Koomey. 1989. Policies to improve energy efficiency and reduce global warming. Strategic Planning and Energy Management 9(2):7.

Ross, M. 1989. Improving the efficiency of electricity use in manufacturing. Science 244:311-317.

Ruderman, H., M. D. Levine, and J. E. McMahon. 1987. The behavior of the market for energy efficiency in residential appliances including heating and cooling equipment. Energy Journal 8:101-124.

Selznick, P. 1947. TVA and the Grass Roots. Berkeley: University of California Press.

Stone, D. A. 1988. Policy Paradox and Political Reason. Glenview, Ill.: Scott, Foresman.

Train, K. 1985. Discount rates in consumers' energy-related decisions: A review of the literature. Energy 10(12):1243-1253.

Train, K., and P. C. Ignelzi. 1987. The economic value of energy-saving investments by commercial and industrial firms. Energy 12(7):543-553.

U.S. Department of Energy (DOE). 1988. Technical Support Document: Energy Conservation Standards for Consumer Products: Refrigerators, Furnaces, and Television Sets. Report DOE/CE-0239. Washington, D.C.: Building Equipment Division, Conservation and Renewable Energy, U.S. Department of Energy.

Vine, E. 1985. State Survey of Innovative Energy Programs and Projects. Report LBL-19126. Berkeley, Calif.: Lawrence Berkeley Laboratory.

Vine, E., and J. Harris. 1988. Planning for an Energy-Efficient Future: The Experience with Implementing Energy Conservation Programs for New Residential and Commercial Buildings, Volumes 1 and 2. Report LBL-25525. Berkeley, Calif.: Lawrence Berkeley Laboratory.

Wilson, D., L. Schipper, S. Tyler, and S. Bartlett. 1989. Policies and Programs for Promoting Energy Conservation in the Residential Sector: Lessons from the Five OECD Countries. Report LBL-27289. Berkeley, Calif.: Lawrence Berkeley Laboratory.

21

Residential and Commercial Energy Management

The buildings sector—both residential and commercial—is the largest end-user of electricity in the United States, using more electricity than either the industrial or the transportation sectors. The buildings sector consumed a full 62 percent of the 2634 billion kilowatt hours (BkWh) generated by U.S. electric utilities in 1989 (Rosenfeld et al., 1991). The buildings sector also uses coal, oil, and natural gas for heating and appliances. In 1989 the buildings sector accounted for 36 percent of total U.S. primary energy consumption (U.S. Department of Energy, 1989b; Rosenfeld et al., 1991; see Figure 21.1).

RECENT TRENDS

Energy use in the United States has not increased in a linear fashion. The 1973 OPEC oil embargo created a powerful incentive to conserve energy. Figure 21.2 compares primary energy use in all sectors to gross national product (GNP), noting that, in the 1960 to 1973 period, energy use and economic production were increasing at nearly the same rate. However, from 1973 to 1986, while GNP grew by 35 percent, total energy use remained nearly constant, and oil and gas use decreased 1.2 percent annually (Rosenfeld et al., forthcoming). As a result, 25 exajoules[1] (EJ) of anticipated energy usage worth $165 billion was avoided annually. In 1989, GNP projected primary energy use was 118 EJ, but only 86 EJ was actually consumed, representing a savings of 33 EJ, or 38 percent of the actual amount consumed. The average *net* annual savings (cost of efficiency measures less energy cost saved) during this period (1973 to 1986) from efficiency amounted to $100 billion.

Even greater savings were realized for electricity. Figure 21.3 compares

201

electricity use to GNP and shows that, like primary energy, electricity and economic production grew at the same rate during the 1960 to 1973 period. However, from 1973 to 1989 the growth in electricity did not keep pace with GNP. In 1989, GNP projected electricity use was 4300 BkWh, but only 2634 BkWh was actually consumed, representing a savings of 1666 BkWh, or 63 percent of the actual amount consumed. U.S. electricity revenues on sales of this 2634 BkWh were $175 billion in 1989, representing annual gross savings (i.e., avoided cost) of $100 billion and an electrical savings equivalent to the annual output of 320 base load power plants (Rosenfeld et al., 1991).

Because electricity has consistently accounted for two-thirds of all primary energy consumed in buildings and three-quarters of building energy

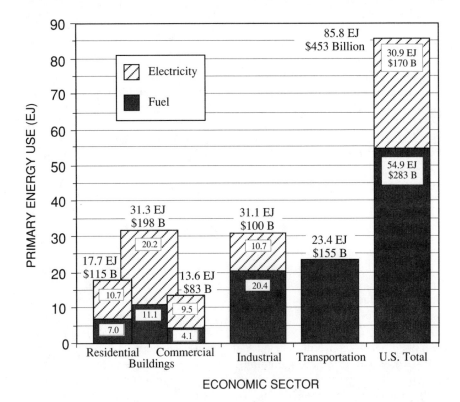

FIGURE 21.1   U.S. primary electricity and fuel use by economic sectors (1989).

SOURCES: Energy data—U.S. Department of Energy (1989c). Residential and commercial buildings data, estimated based on shares of 1987 end use—U.S. Department of Energy (1989a). Price data—extrapolated from U.S. Department of Energy (1989d).

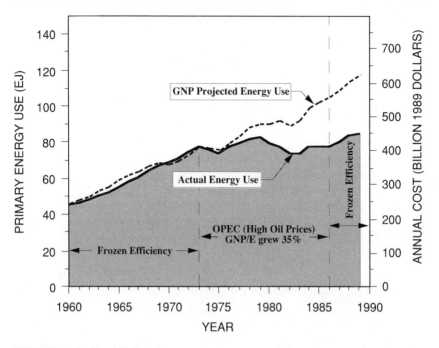

FIGURE 21.2   Total U.S. primary energy use: actual versus gross national product projection (1960 to 1989).

SOURCES: Rosenfeld et al. (1991) and Energy Information Administration (U.S. Department of Energy, 1989c).

bills, reductions in this sector's electric demand have made an important contribution to total U.S. electricity savings. Figure 21.4 shows pre-1973 annual growth rates of 4.5 percent and 5.4 percent for residential and commercial use, respectively; during the 1973-1986 period, residential energy use remained level, whereas commercial use increased at only 1.6 percent per year. Space heating intensity in new commercial buildings also declined significantly after 1973, as illustrated by Figure 21.5 (Rosenfeld et al., 1991). In addition, efficiency measures during this period avoided an increase of approximately 50 percent in emissions of CO_2, SO_2, and NO_2. Without these measures, coal use would have doubled (Rosenfeld et al., 1991).

Nevertheless, the buildings sector's need for energy—particularly electricity—is expanding. The DOE base-case forecast projects that U.S. electricity demand for all sectors will grow by nearly 33 percent before the end of the century, an average annual increase of 2.3 percent (Edmonds et al., 1989).

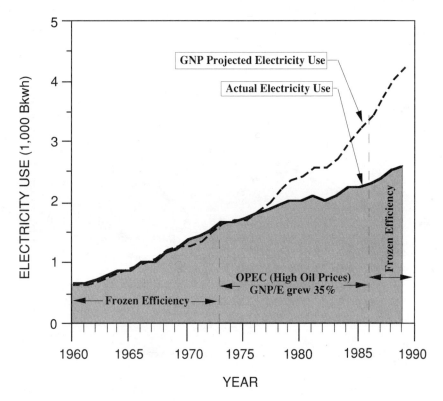

FIGURE 21.3 Total U.S. electricity use: actual versus gross national product projection (1960 to 1989). The GNP-electricity curve has been adjusted by 3 percent per year to account for increasing electrification.

SOURCES: Rosenfeld et al. (1991) and Energy Information Administration (U.S. Department of Energy, 1989c).

EFFICIENCY POTENTIAL

Recent Studies

A consensus is emerging in the engineering, utility, and regulatory communities that, even when past efficiency gains and projected population and economic expansion are considered, an additional, significant reduction can be made in U.S. residential and commercial electricity consumption. This reduction is not expected to sacrifice comfort levels and will cost less—in many cases, substantially less—than the purchase of new sources of power or of power at marginal production costs.

Potential efficiency measures are varied; taken singly, each may realize only a relatively small gain. Nonetheless, their aggregate effect can be

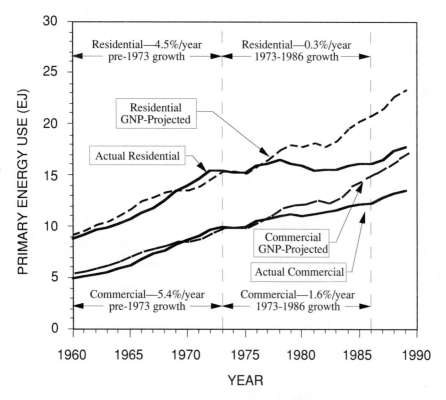

FIGURE 21.4   Primary energy use in U.S. buildings (1960 to 1989).

SOURCES: Data are from Energy Information Administration (U.S. Department of Energy, 1989c,f).

substantial. Recently, various studies have estimated the aggregate impact of applying these technologies to both new and existing uses in the residential, commercial, and industrial sectors:

• The Electric Power Research Institute (EPRI)—which is supported by the nation's electric industry—recently concluded that, by implementing existing efficiency technologies, total projected electricity use in the U.S. residential sector for the year 2000 could be reduced by 27.1 percent to 45.5 percent, with a similar reduction of 22.5 percent to 48.6 percent in the commercial sector (Electric Power Research Institute, 1990).

• Lovins (1986) found cost-effective annual electric demand savings of 73 percent in the Austin, Texas, municipal utility service territory, at an average cost of 0.87 cent per kilowatt-hour (kWh) (against a conservatively derived 2.7 cents/kWh avoided cost of operating existing plants).[2]

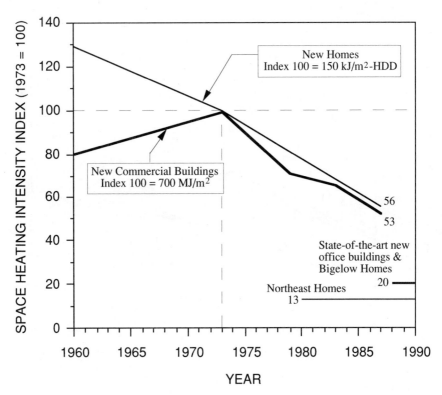

FIGURE 21.5   Space heating intensity for new U.S. buildings.

SOURCES: For new homes and new commercial buildings, U.S. Department of Energy (1989g); for new office buildings, Pacific Northwest Laboratory (1983).

• Usibelli et al. (1983) and Miller et al. (1989), in studies commissioned by DOE and the New York State Energy Research and Development Authority, estimated potential electrical savings from efficiency at 37 percent for the Pacific Northwest and 34 percent for New York.

• An American Council for an Energy-Efficient Economy (ACEEE) study in New York State found that more than one-third (34.3 percent) of projected residential sector growth in demand for electricity use, and nearly half (47.1 percent) of projected commercial sector growth in demand for electricity, could be eliminated (American Council for an Energy-Efficient Economy, 1989). The ACEEE study relied on several restrictive assumptions, taking into account only near-term technologies and basing its estimates only on existing buildings (generally, savings are greater when efficiency measures are implemented during the construction process).

Calculating Efficiency Potential on Supply Curves

Figure 21.6 is a compilation of nine conservation supply curves that depict the technical potential for electricity savings in U.S. buildings by the year 2000. Supply curves describe, in a more rigorous manner, the way in which large-scale efficiency gains and consequent dollar and carbon emission savings are aggregated from individual energy efficiency measures. The curves relate energy savings achieved by implementing a given efficiency measure to that measure's "cost of conserved energy" or CCE (Meier et al., 1983). Conservation supply curves are discussed in greater detail in Appendix C.

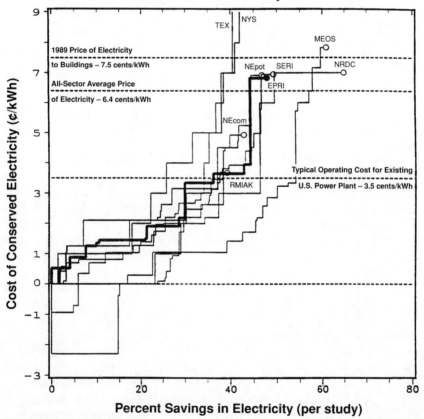

Residential and Commercial Electricity

FIGURE 21.6   Potential conservation supply curves for residential and commercial electricity.

SOURCE: Rosenfeld et al. (1991).

TABLE 21.1   "Prices" of Electricity at the Meter

	Price (cents/kWh)
1. Residential price (seen by consumer)	7.5
2. Industrial price	4.7
3. All-sector average price	6.4
4. Marginal cost of operating a coal plant and delivering 1 kWh to the meter	3.5
5. Line 3 plus externality cost: 1 to 3 cents/kWh (New York has chosen 1.4 cents/kWh for the worst coal plant)	7.4–9.4

Conserved energy may be considered a resource and plotted on a supply curve because it is liberated to be "supply" for other energy demands. Each of the energy prices described in Table 21.1 can be drawn as a horizontal line across a supply curve. All steps located below a selected price line are cost-effective, and the rational investor should take each of these steps (which are additive in effect), stopping where the staircase crosses the line. Of course, different price assumptions drastically alter estimates of dollar savings.

It should be noted that estimated savings (plotted on the *x*-axis) also present uncertainties. They are illustrated in Table 21.2, which compares the unit energy consumption of an average new 1990 refrigerator (1000 kWh/yr) on line 1 with the consumption of an optimal refrigerator (200 kWh/yr) on line 4. Although an engineer might assume potential savings to be 800 kWh/yr, to a utility forecaster or program manager, line 3 is more realistic and reflects a sales-weighted average of refrigerator efficiency that is below the optimum.

The studies on which the supply curves are based were undertaken by diverse groups and compiled at Lawrence Berkeley Laboratory (Rosenfeld et al., 1991). Electricity savings for the nine conservation supply curves in Figure 21.6 are calculated based on "frozen efficiency" (Table 21.2). The individual studies assumed real discount rates of 3 to 5 percent to calculate the cost of conserved electricity, but all nine have been corrected to 6 percent. Because the EPRI curve represents the approximate midrange of these curves, it has been highlighted in Figure 21.6 and will be the focus of the discussion below. It is replotted in Figure 21.7 for four different discount rates. The EPRI curve is also consistent with a new National Research Council study (National Research Council, 1990); however, the analysis presented there is too coarse to compile as a supply curve. That study estimates a near-term retrofit potential savings of 30 percent and a long-term retrofit potential of 50 percent (National Research Council, 1990, Table 4.12). These potential savings nicely bracket the EPRI potential savings of 45 percent.

Figure 21.7 is a sensitivity analysis showing that investing up to 7.5 cents/kWh—the average U.S. price of electricity in the residential and commercial sectors—will produce aggregate electricity savings of 45 percent for all "social" discount rates: 3, 6, and 10 percent. Potential savings are insensitive to the differences among 3 percent, 6 percent, and 10 percent, but at a 30 percent discount rate, savings drop from 45 to 30 percent. At the short-term marginal cost of providing electricity from an existing base

TABLE 21.2 Unit Energy Consumption for a New Refrigerator

	Base (kWh/yr)	Target (kWh/yr)
1. Average new 1990 refrigerator consumption "frozen" until year 2000[a]	1000	—
2. Anticipated efficiency resulting from the 1993 National Appliance Standards for refrigerators[b]	700	—
3. Better efficiency in year 2000 achieved by 1980s-type utility efficiency programs	—	600
4. Most efficient refrigerator in year 2000, including all technical improvements with cost of conserved energy (CCE) less than 6 cents/kWh[c]	—	200

[a]The average refrigerator sold in 1990 must meet the National Appliance Standards of about 1000 kWh/yr as mandated by the National Appliance Energy Conservation Act of 1987 (P.L. 100-12).

[b]The 1993 appliance standards will require that the average refrigerator use no more than about 700 kWh/yr (refer to 10 CFR Part 430, Vol. 54, No. 221, 11/17/89, p. 47918).

[c]Technical potential of about 200 kWh/yr for an 18-ft^3 (21-ft^3 adjusted volume) top-mounted, auto-defrost refrigerator-freezer, at an average CCE of less than 6 cents/kWh (based on estimated incremental cost of $720 (1990 dollars), compared to the 1990 standard of about 1000 kWh/yr, using a real discount rate of 3 percent and 20-year life). Earlier analysis by DOE gave a technical potential of only 490 kWh/yr for the same size and type refrigerator-freezer, and an average CCE of less than 5 cents/kWh (based on an estimated incremental cost of $400 (1990 dollars) and the same assumptions as above). (See U.S. Department of Energy, 1989e, p. 3-37, Table 3.17.) For discussion of why 200 kWh/yr is selected for the technical potential, as opposed to the proposed standard of 700 kWh/yr, see discussion of household appliances in this chapter, American Council for an Energy-Efficient Economy (1986, p. 3-8, Table 1), and Rosenfeld et al. (1991).

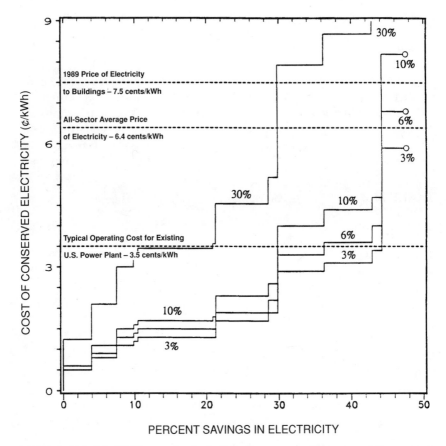

FIGURE 21.7 The EPRI curve for the buildings sector, sensitivity to real discount rate. SOURCE: Rosenfeld et al. (1991).

load power plant (3.5 cents/kWh), the 10 percent discount rate reduces energy savings to 30 percent, and at the 30 percent rate savings drop to 20 percent. However, for any price equal to or higher than the all-sector (residential, commercial, and industrial) average avoided cost of 6.4 cents/ kWh (see Table 21.1), variations in discount rates below 10 percent have little effect.

Aggregate Annual Savings: $10 Billion to $37 Billion

Figure 21.8 displays the costs and technical potential of the 11-step EPRI conservation supply curve (which includes technologies that are commer-

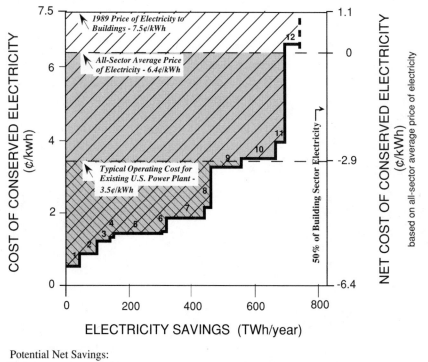

FIGURE 21.8   Cost of conserved electricity for buildings.

cially available or that have been developed and tested), with an additional first step for white surfaces/vegetation to save air conditioning. The 12 steps, identified in Table 21.3, encompass a cumulative savings of 734 BkWh (at 7.5 cents/kWh avoided cost), which is 45 percent of 1989 residential and commercial buildings sector use of 1627 BkWh. At 3.5 cents/kWh avoided cost, savings decline to 667 BkWh, which is 41 percent of buildings sector use. Table 21.3 lists the cost per kilowatt hour of each of the EPRI measures (plus white surfaces/vegetation) and notes that each of these measures would save energy and atmospheric carbon at a net negative cost—that is, while saving money as well.

Three cases representing different annual net savings in billions of dollars are shown in Figure 21.8.

TABLE 21.3 Cost of Saving Electricity and CO_2 Through Conservation in Buildings

	A CCE $d = 0.06$ (cents/kWh)	B Net CCE $(A - 6.4)$[a] (cents/kWh)	C Net CC CO_2 $(10 \times B/0.7)$[b] ($/t)	D Potential U.S. Electricity Savings, Cumulative (BkWh/yr)	E Potential U.S. CO_2 Savings, Cumulative (Mt CO_2/yr)
1. White surfaces/vegetation[c]	0.5	-5.9	-84	45	32
2. Residential lighting[d]	0.9	-5.5	-79	101	71
3. Residential water heating	1.3	-5.1	-74	139	97
4. Commercial water heating	1.4	-5.0	-72	149	104
5. Commercial lighting	1.5	-5.0	-71	315	221
6. Commercial cooking	1.5	-4.9	-70	322	225
7. Commercial cooling	1.9	-4.5	-64	437	306
8. Commercial refrigeration	2.2	-4.2	-60	459	321
9. Residential appliances	3.3	-3.1	-44	562	393
10. Residential space heating	3.7	-2.8	-39	667	467
11. Commercial and industrial space heating	4.0	-2.4	-35	689	482
12. Commercial ventilation	6.8	1.4	6	734	514
TOTAL U.S. buildings sector 1989 use				1627	1140

NOTE: d = discount rate; Mt = megatons.

[a] All-sector average price of electricity = 6.4 cents/kWh.

[b] Carbon emissions from Edmonds et al. (1989) using 1990 fuel inputs to electricity, 1 kWhe = 0.7 kg CO_2.

[c] From Akbari et al. (1988, 1989).

[d] EPRI measures 2 through 12 have been converted from 5 percent discount rate to 6 percent discount rate by multiplying EPRI/CCE values by 1.05. EPRI values for "Potential U.S. Electricity Savings, Cumulative" have been expanded by a factor of 1.4 to account for EPRI's failure to include improvements for which they had no cost data (residential appliances and commercial miscellaneous equipment) and to adjust the EPRI savings, which were compared to utility projections that included 9 percent naturally occurring efficiency improvements, to frozen efficiency. (See also Rosenfeld et al., 1991.)

• Case 1: Price of electricity equal to or below 7.5 cents/kWh (price of electricity to buildings). This case illustrates the highest annual net savings. Here all 12 steps are cost-effective, so all 734 BkWh is saved. The gross savings in electric bills is then $55 billion (734 BkWh × 7.5 cents/kWh). The white area underneath the curve ($18 billion) is the annualized cost of investments for the 12 steps. The light hatched area is the difference between the gross bill savings and the annualized cost of the measures. This amounts to $37 billion per year.

Case 1 applies to those regions of the United States in which the power glut is ending and utilities are contemplating building or buying new, relatively expensive capacity that will raise the price of electricity. In this case, society profits from all investments in which the cost of conserved energy is less than 7.5 cents/kWh. From the viewpoint of policy, such investments should be encouraged. This can be accomplished by making them more profitable to the utility than purchasing power or building power plants. An option discussed and recommended below is to restructure the profit rules for utilities; such measures have already been taken in New England, New York, Wisconsin, and California.

• Case 2: Price of electricity equal to or below all-sector average of 6.4 cents/kWh. This case represents annual net savings between the two extremes of cases 1 and 3. Here the first 11 steps are cost-effective, and the potential net savings (shaded hatched area) become $29 billion. The case 2 price is used for savings tabulated in the overall energy efficiency supply curve.

• Case 3: Price of electricity equal to operating cost of existing U.S. power plant equal to or below 3.5 cents/kWh. In this case, the last three steps are not cost-effective, and savings drop to 562 BkWh. At this extremely low electricity price,[3] net savings from each step drop sharply, adding up to a potential net savings (cross-hatched area) of only $10 billion per year.

Nonetheless, it must be emphasized that, when any potential assumption about electricity pricing is used, these nine steps with CCE lower than 3.5 cents/kWh are always profitable to society and, if the relevant jurisdiction has updated its profit regulations, to electric utilities as well.

Transforming Electricity to Carbon

At this point, electricity savings can be transformed into units of avoided CO_2, to derive Figure 21.9 from Table 21.3. Figure 21.9 is the same as Figure 21.8, with the x-axis converted to CO_2 savings (1 BkWh = 0.7 Mt CO_2) and the y-axis converted to cost of conserved CO_2 (1 cent/kWh = $14.3/t). Figure 21.9 reveals a potential cost-effective savings of 514 Mt CO_2/yr.[4] This is approximately 10 percent of the total U.S. 1989 emissions

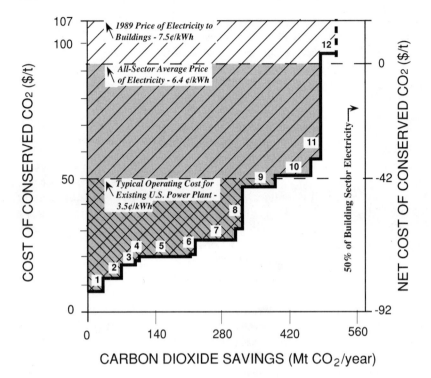

Potential Net Savings:

$ 37 B/yr. - CASE 1: Below 7.5¢/kWh Price of Electricity to Buildings

$ 29 B/yr. - CASE 2: Below 6.4¢/kWh All-Sector Average Price of Electricity

$ 10 B/yr. - CASE 3: Below 3.5¢/kWh Typical Operating Cost for Existing U.S. Power Plant

FIGURE 21.9   Net cost of conserved carbon dioxide (CC CO_2) for electric efficiency in the buildings sector.

of 5 Gt CO_2 and 45 percent of the total 1139 Mt CO_2/yr generated as a by-product of the electricity used in 1989 in the U.S. buildings sector. At a 6.4-cent/kWh price of avoided electricity, the 1989 savings are $29 billion, corresponding to a (negative) average cost of conserved CO_2 of –$57/t CO_2.

ENERGY EFFICIENCY MEASURES

Each energy efficiency measure expected to contribute substantially to the savings estimated above is described in more detail in this section.

These descriptions are followed by brief discussions of the additional savings that can be obtained from fossil fuel efficiency measures and by switching certain end uses from electricity to other energy sources. Discussion of major electricity efficiency measures will attempt to follow the order of their cost of conserved energy, from lowest to highest, as set forth in Table 21.3; Table 21.4 lists primary energy consumption by fuel type for both

TABLE 21.4 Primary Energy Consumption for Commercial and Residential Buildings by Fuel Type, 1986 (in quadrillion (10^{15}) Btu)

	Electricity[a]	Gas	Oil	Other[b]	Total	Percent
Residential Sector						
Space heating	1.81	2.87	1.00	0.39	6.07	39.8
Water heating	1.61	0.82	0.10	0.06	2.58	16.9
Refrigerators	1.44				1.44	9.4
Lighting	1.04				1.04	6.8
Air conditioners	1.08				1.08	7.1
Ranges/ovens	0.64	0.21	0.00	0.03	0.88	5.8
Freezers	0.45				0.45	2.9
Other	1.19	0.54			1.72	11.3
TOTAL	9.27	4.43	1.10	0.48	15.28	100.0
Commercial Sector						
Space heating	1.00	1.83	0.79	0.18	3.80	32.4
Lighting	2.96				2.96	25.2
Air conditioning	0.98	0.12			1.11	9.4
Ventilation	1.49				1.49	12.7
Water heaters	0.37	0.19	0.08		0.64	5.5
Other	1.37	0.24	0.01	0.11	1.73	14.7
TOTAL	8.17	2.38	0.89	0.29	11.73	100.0
TOTAL residential[c] and commercial consumption 1986	17.44	6.81	1.98	0.77	27.01	100.0

[a]Represents value of primary energy inputs in production of electricity (11,500 Btu/kWh).

[b]For residential: coal and liquefied petroleum gas. For commercial: coal, liquefied petroleum gas, and motor gasoline (off-road use). Excludes estimated 0.8 quad of energy from wood fuel in residential sector.

[c]Totals for residential and commercial consumption from Energy Information Agency (U.S. Department of Energy, 1989f). Distribution between end uses based on Lawrence Berkeley Laboratories residential end-use model and Oak Ridge National Laboratory/Pacific Northwest Laboratories Commercial End-Use Model. Latest period for which data are available is 1986.

SOURCE: U.S. Department of Energy (1989a).

major appliances and other uses in the residential and commercial segments of the buildings sector.

In the residential and commercial building sectors, electricity efficiency technologies include such measures as

• more efficient fluorescent lamps, high-frequency ballasts, reflectors, and occupancy and daylight sensors that, together, can save up to 84 percent of lighting energy in commercial buildings while maintaining the same level of useful light (Lovins, 1986);

• superefficient appliances that, through a variety of complementary technologies, achieve the same level of performance while consuming far less energy; and

• building shell measures such as insulation, trees that shade windows, white roof and pavement surfaces that reflect sunlight, and heat-reflective windows that retain heat in winter and deflect it in summer.

White Surfaces and Vegetation

Planting vegetation and painting roof and road surfaces white can save approximately 50 BkWh/yr of the total U.S. air conditioning use of 200 BkWh/yr. Of the 50 BkWh/yr, about 25 BkWh/yr are direct savings from decreased air conditioning needs in buildings that have light-colored roofs and are shaded by properly placed deciduous trees. Indirect savings of another 25 BkWh/yr are realized once vegetation, light-colored roofs, and light-colored roadways are in place, cooling "urban heat islands" in the summer. "Urban heat islands" is the term used by meteorologists to describe the fact that in summer most cities are 2° to 5°C hotter than their surroundings. The cause is solar heat absorbed by dark surfaces, and the removal of trees that would have cooled the air by evapotranspiration. The total savings including indirect savings from the cooler cities could equal 50 BkWh/yr (Akbari et al., 1990).[5]

Electrical Appliances

Residential and Commercial Lighting

Lighting is the largest end use in the commercial sector (257.4 BkWh/yr in 1986) (U.S. Department of Energy, 1989a) and about 11 percent of all residential electricity (90.4 BkWh/yr in 1986) (U.S. Department of Energy, 1989a). The efficiency of existing lighting can be improved through the use of compact fluorescent lamps (CFLs). Today's efficient CFLs have long life, good color, and reduced maintenance cost. Two types of CFLs are available: one with separate ballast and the other with "integrated" built-in ballast. Each can fit into a standard light socket (Lawrence Berkeley Laboratory, 1990).

Because CFLs are 4 times as efficient as incandescent bulbs and last a minimum of 10,000 hours, one 16-W CFL replaces a series of thirteen 60-W incandescents over its lifetime. It is expected that CFLs will penetrate first the commercial and then the residential markets, thus saving 50 percent of the 200 BkWh currently used annually by incandescents. By late 1990, about 50 million CFLs had been sold in the United States. These are installed mainly in some of the 300 million recessed fixtures in commercial buildings, where there appears to be no major barrier to their complete market saturation. Incandescents in these 300 million fixtures now typically use a total of 60 BkWh/yr; at least 50 BkWh/yr will be saved by the CFLs. Residential applications, which are expected to increase following market saturation in the commercial sector, will save half of the current residential lighting use, or 50 BkWh/yr. This 100-BkWh/yr savings is equivalent to 3.8 percent of the total 1989 U.S. electricity demand of 2630 BkWh. Table 21.5 compares the cost of compact fluorescents to incandescent bulbs currently in use and shows that one of the former can, by replacing 13 comparable incandescents over its lifetime of 40 months, save $28 and pay for itself on average in 7 to 21 months (Lawrence Berkeley Laboratory, 1990).

Residential and Commercial Water Heating

Some 20 to 30 percent efficiency savings can be achieved over 1987 residential practice by increasing insulation and using low-flow devices and thermal traps. Alternative water heating systems, using heat pumps or solar energy, can increase savings to 70 percent. Commercial savings, using residential measures as well as heat pumps and heat recovery systems, are estimated at 40 to 60 percent (Electric Power Research Institute, 1990).

Cooking

Electric range efficiency measures include additional insulation, seals, improved heating elements, reflective pans, reduced thermal mass, and reduced contact resistance. They are expected to increase efficiency from 1987 residential levels by 10 to 20 percent and from 1987 commercial levels by 20 to 30 percent (Electric Power Research Institute, 1990).

Commercial Cooling

The electricity required by commercial cooling—the second highest category of use in this sector—can be reduced by 30 to 70 percent from 1987 levels by a combination of efficiency measures, including heat pump technologies, high-efficiency chillers, chiller capacity modulation and downsizing, window treatments, and radiant barriers. Lighting efficiency can increase estimated high-end savings by another 10 percent (Electric Power Research Institute, 1990).

TABLE 21.5 Simple Payback Calculations for a 16-W Compact
Fluorescent Lamp (CFL)

	Prices ($)			
	Wholesale[a]		Retail	
	Low	High	Low	High
1 CFL	7.00	10.00	9.00	20.00[b]
Price of initial incandescent	0.75	0.75	0.75	0.75
Net first cost of CFL	6.25	9.25	8.25	19.25
Monthly savings using CFL (electricity savings plus avoided incandescent cost)	0.93	0.93	0.93	0.93
Simple payback time (months)	6.7	10.0	8.9	20.7
Lamp life (months)	40.0	40.0	40.0	40.0

NOTE: The following assumptions are made:

• CFL/incandescent ratio: One 16-W CFL replaces thirteen 60-W incandescents. One CFL lasts approximately 10,000 hours; thirteen incandescents, at 750 hours each, last 9750 hours.

• Lifetimes: It is estimated that the lifetime of approximately 10,000 hours is spread over 40 months at 250 hours per month (58 hours/week) for typical usage in a commercial or office space.

• Monthly electricity savings: Replacing a 60-W incandescent with a 16-W CFL saves 44 W at the meter. Over its lifetime of 10,000 hours, the CFL saves 440 kWh. With the all-sector average price of electricity of 6.4 cents/kWh, the CFL saves 440 × 6.4 cents/kWh = $28.00. This results in monthly savings of $0.70.

• Monthly avoided incandescent cost: The initial incandescent costs $0.75, and the remaining 12 incandescents are calculated to cost $0.23 per month (12 × $0.75 = $9.00 divided by 40 months).

[a]Wholesale prices have been included because innovative methods are being used by some utilities to make CFLs available to customers at wholesale prices, allowing the customers to realize the largest savings on efficiency.
[b]For less-developed countries such as India, high import fees raise this cost to $35.00.

Household Appliances

Refrigerators use more electricity than any other residential appliance, and refrigeration is the second largest use of residential electricity (146.6 BkWh/yr, with an additional 59.8 BkWh/yr for freezers (1987) (Electric Power Research Institute, 1990)). The ACEEE reports that refrigerators sold in 1986 consumed an average of 1074 kWh/yr, that the best available mass-produced units in 1988 used 810 kWh (meeting the new U.S. appliance efficiency standards of about 1000 kWh/yr), and that advanced units in the near-term would use 699 kWh (American Council for an Energy-Efficient Economy, 1989).[6] Therefore an efficient refrigerator that meets upcoming U.S. appliance efficiency standards is projected to save approximately 264 kWh/yr and sell at a premium of about $66 (note that this does not include the cost of CFC phaseout discussed in Chapter 25). The cost of energy saved is 2.5 cents/kWh, compared to an average residential electricity cost of 7.5 cents/kWh (Rosenfeld et al., 1991).

Further improvement, by using such existing technologies as double gaskets, more efficient compressors and fans, and additional insulation, could reduce usage to 463 kWh/yr at a cost of 1.43 cents/kWh (Krause et al., 1988). Higher-efficiency components, including dual evaporators and evacuated-panel or low-emissivity insulation, or aerogels, could permit refrigerators to use as little as 180 kWh/yr (Table 21.2, and American Council for an Energy-Efficient Economy, 1986). In short, improved technology could increase the efficiency of new refrigerators by 4.5 times over 1990 levels, and nearly 4 times over the ACEEE advanced level. It is estimated that their retail cost would be in the range of 3.5 to 5 cents/kWh saved, well below the current U.S. average for new supply, 7.5 cents/kWh.

In addition, dishwasher efficiency improvements of 10 to 30 percent relative to 1987 residential stock are expected from models with no-heat drying cycles and from reductions in hot water usage (Electric Power Research Institute, 1990).

Office Equipment

Office equipment—computers, printers, copiers, and telephones, for example—probably use half of the more than 1.37 quads of electricity consumed annually by the commercial sector's "other" category (see Table 21.4 for 1986 data). Currently, all office equipment of this type, including that used in homes (which is reflected in residential sector use) is estimated to consume more than 60 BkWh/yr; demand is growing rapidly and more research is required to establish its current level (Lovins and Heede, 1990). It is estimated that existing technology and advanced management techniques could reduce total electric input for office equipment by 60 to 70 percent in the short term, and by up to 90 percent in the longer term (Lovins and Heede, 1990).

Building Shell Efficiency

Space heating, at 157.4 BkWh/yr (1986) (U.S. Department of Energy, 1989a), represents the largest use of electricity in the residential subsector. There, energy efficiency requires measures for specific regions of the country, based on their climate and building practices (National Association of Home Builders Research Foundation, Inc., 1985; Energy Information Administration, 1988). Building shell efficiency can be improved through thicker or more efficient wall, ceiling, floor, and pipe insulation; "low-E" (high reflectivity to heat) glazing or superwindows; and caulking and weatherstripping. Indeed, 36.6 percent of all single-family households in the United States lack insulation in their roofs or ceilings (Energy Information Administration, 1987).

Passive solar techniques can also be used in existing and new buildings. These measures include concentration of window area toward the south to maximize collection of solar heat during cold months and construction of overhangs to provide shade during the summer (U.S. Department of Energy, 1989b).

Potential Fossil Fuel Savings in Buildings: $20 Billion per Year

As shown in Figure 21.1, the buildings sector consumes primary energy that has not been converted into electricity—mainly oil and natural gas. This also represents a source of savings from energy efficiency measures.

In 1989, residential and commercial buildings used about 12.6 quads (10^{15} Btu; see note 1) of fuel—7.7 quads of natural gas, 2.7 quads of oil, 0.2 quads of coal, and about 2 quads of wood (wood is not discussed here because it produces no net CO_2). Natural gas and oil are interchangeable in commercial furnaces and water heaters, so they are grouped together to estimate potential fuel savings. This fixes the base case ("frozen efficiency") for fuel use at 10.4 quads/yr.

There have been only two thorough efficiency studies of fuel use in buildings, a study of the U.S. residential sector by the Solar Energy Research Institute (SERI, 1981) and a study of the California residential sector by Meier et al. (1983). Both were conducted in the residential sector, involved natural gas, and used a discount rate of 6 percent. However, oil and gas are interchangeable in commercial applications, and the technologies that use oil or gas in residential applications are very similar in design. Figure 21.10 shows that about 50 percent of all residential natural gas use can be saved at a cost of less than the current average natural gas price of $5.63/MBtu. Extrapolating this estimate to cover all gas and oil use in buildings yields savings of about 5.2 quads; after subtracting the $10 billion annualized cost of the efficiency investment, net savings are nearly $20 billion per year.

To transform fuel savings to CO_2 savings, it is necessary to convert the *x*-axis in Figure 21.10 to avoided CO_2. This is done by adding the CO_2 that oil and natural gas contribute to base-case fuel use in buildings.[7] Weighting these fuels by their respective carbon contents (based on their relative use) yields an estimate that 1 MBtu "fuel" is equivalent to 16 kg carbon and 59 kg CO_2, and, further, that 1 quad "fuel" is roughly 59 Mt CO_2. The *y*-axis

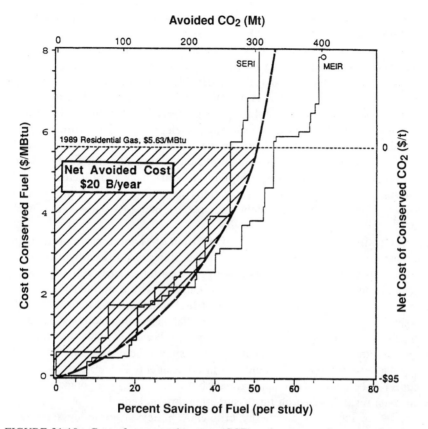

FIGURE 21.10 Cost of conserved energy (CCE) and net cost of conserved carbon dioxide (CC CO_2) for the residential sector.

is converted by dividing by 6, so $1/MBtu = $17/t CO_2. The net CC CO_2 is shown in the right-hand scale of Figure 21.10, running down from 0 to -$95/t CO_2. The average CC CO_2 is about -$70/t CO_2. The potential carbon savings are about 300 Mt of avoided CO_2. This is about 6 percent of the total U.S. 1989 emissions of 5 Gt CO_2.

Fuel Switching

In industry an observed tendency exists to substitute fuel for electricity, but in buildings, fuel switching primarily involves replacing electric resistance heat with on-site combustion of natural gas. This can reduce operating expense and CO_2 emissions by about one-third for the U.S. mix of fuel used for electricity generation.

Fuel switching is the least well-studied conservation option in the U.S. buildings sector. This is so because, first, under the existing regulatory regime governing utilities—at least until recently in some jurisdictions—electricity sales lost through fuel switching invariably reduced the utility's revenue and profits. Second, the geographic distribution of fuel switching potential is uneven and thus is not tabulated in DOE's Residential Conservation Survey (Rosenfeld et al., 1991). Geographic distribution depends on recent competitive marketing programs by electric and gas utilities. Thus, in California, most homes have gas heat and gas on the premises, but in northern California, only 22 percent of homes have gas clothes dryers versus 60 percent in southern California. If Pacific Gas and Electric (PG&E) had the same gas appliance saturations as Southern California Edison, PG&E's peak demand could be reduced by 360 MW (Rosenfeld et al., 1991).

Switching hot water heaters from electricity to natural gas represents the largest potential of this type in the United States. A 1988 Michigan study demonstrated that 400,000 homes with gas heat but electric resistance water heaters could be switched to gas hot water heat, with a simple payback time of 2 years (Krause et al., 1988) and that fuel switching in Michigan had the potential to save about 20 percent of residential electricity. However, Michigan appears to have a higher fraction of homes with gas available than does the rest of the United States, so the results shown here may not be widely applicable. A 10 percent reduction in all residential electricity use would appear to be a reasonable approximation for fuel switching potential nationally; the results, based on this assumption, are presented in Table 21.6.

Fuel switching as an energy efficiency policy is attracting interest in several locations. In Vancouver, Canada, BC Hydro gave subsidies to consumers to replace electric water heaters with gas units. Several utilities in Vermont are developing or considering the development of fuel switching programs aimed at space and water heating to reduce peak winter demand.[8] Massachusetts utility regulators recently ordered utilities in that state to consider this option.[9] In Wisconsin, the Public Service Commission has directed utilities to encourage fuel switching where cost-effective.

New Buildings

Discussion so far has focused on retrofitting existing buildings, developing more efficient appliances, and installing more efficient equipment in both existing and new buildings. However, efficiency gains can also be realized during the construction process. New buildings can be designed and constructed to conserve both electricity and fuel, primarily as they are used for space heating. Nonetheless, both potentials are surprisingly small (Rosenfeld et al., 1991).

Currently, fuel use in buildings amounts to about 10 quads/yr, with a

TABLE 21.6 Fuel Switching Example of Saving 10 Percent of a Building's Electricity by Switching Water Heaters from Electric Resistance to Gas Heat (discount rate = 6 percent)

	1989 Use	1989 Potential Savings
Electricity		
BkWh (10 percent of building's BkWh)	1,627	163
Mt CO_2 (1 kWhe = 0.7 kg CO_2)	1,139	114
Net dollars (6 cents/kWh x 163 BkWh)	—	9.8 billion
Gas		
Quads (1 kWhe = 0.0043 MBtu)	10.4	−0.7
Mt CO_2 (1 quad = 57 Mt)	600	−40
Dollars (at average $4.20/MBtu)	—	−3.0 billion
Net		
Mt CO_2	1,739	74
Dollars	170 billion	6.8 billion
Net CC CO_2 ($/t)	—	−92

retrofit potential of about 5 quads. Making new buildings more fossil fuel efficient than current practice is expected to save only about 0.5 quad/yr after a decade of construction, or 2 quads/yr after 40 years, the longest time horizon used in a recent study (Rosenfeld et al., 1991). The potential savings in electric space heating per decade of construction are slightly smaller than for fuel, because little electricity is used for space heating.

The reason for this surprising result is that new buildings—with better insulation, better windows, and fewer drafts—now use very little space heat. It is interesting that new homes are being added to U.S. stock at about 2.2 percent per year, and old homes are being retired at about 0.7 percent per year (i.e., about 3 times more slowly). Yet each of the old homes consumes about 3 times as much gas for space heat as each of the new ones, so there is little net increase; a similar finding applies to commercial buildings. Optimal new homes need only one-quarter as much space heat as the average home built in 1989, and optimal office buildings use almost no space heat at all, so there is not much heat left to save. Efficiency gains in new buildings are discussed further in Rosenfeld et al. (1991) and Bevington and Rosenfeld (1990).

Summary of Potential Savings in the Buildings Sector

Combined savings in the buildings sector are 850 Mt of CO_2 (513 Mt CO_2 for electricity, 300 Mt for fuel, and 74 Mt for fuel switching). This is equivalent to about 50 percent of the total CO_2 emitted into the earth's atmosphere as a result of energy use in the nation's buildings sector, and 17.1 percent of U.S. annual emissions of 5000 Mt CO_2. Annual net dollar savings are $29 billion for electricity, $20 billion for fuel, and $4.3 billion for fuel switching—a total of $53 billion. This is equivalent to 12 percent of the total 1989 U.S. energy bill of $450 billion. These results are summarized in Table 21.7.

Nonetheless, it is unlikely that this potential will be fully achieved in the absence of effective policy tools and particular incentives (discussed below) to make energy efficiency more profitable to utilities than burning increasing quantities of fossil fuel, especially coal.

TABLE 21.7 Summary of the Potential Savings of Electricity, Fuel (Gas and Oil), and CO_2 for Existing Buildings (discount rate = 6 percent)

	1989 Use	1989 Potential Savings
Electricity		
BkWh	1,627	734
Mt CO_2 (1 kWhe = 0.7 kg CO_2)	1,139	513
Dollars (at 7.5 cents/kWh)	112 billion	—
Net dollars (at 6.4 cents/kWh)	—	29 billion
CC CO_2 ($/t)	—	−57
Fuel (gas and oil)		
Quads	10.4	5.2
Mt CO_2 (1 MBtu = 57 kg CO_2)	600	300
Dollars (at $5.63/MBtu)	58 billion	—
Net dollars (at $5.63/MBtu)	—	20 billion
CC CO_2 ($/t)	—	−70
Fuel switching—Net savings from switching 10 percent of electricity to gas		
Mt CO_2 (electricity and gas)	1,739	74
Net dollars	—	6.8 billion
Net CC CO_2 ($/t)	—	−92
TOTAL Savings from Electricity/Fuel Efficiency and Fuel Switching		
Mt CO_2	1,739	890
Net dollars	170 billion	56 billion
Net CC CO_2 ($/t)	—	−63

NOTE: Growth in building stock (additions minus demolitions) is ignored.

BARRIERS TO IMPLEMENTATION

Past experience in attempting to implement energy efficiency programs has demonstrated that a number of obstacles may inhibit the achievement of optimal electricity efficiency in the residential and commercial sectors.

After the precipitous drop in oil prices in late 1985, efficiency trends in primary energy began to decline. As shown in Figure 21.4, energy use in the residential and commercial buildings sector grew at more than 3 percent per year from 1986 to 1989; Figure 21.3 shows that total primary energy use once again escalated at nearly the same rate as GNP between 1986 and 1988, with energy consumption leveling off slightly in 1989. From 1973 to 1988, GNP grew 46 percent, and energy use 7 percent. Virtually all of this 7 percent increase from 1973 to 1988 occurred during the last 4 years (U.S. Department of Energy, 1989c; Rosenfeld et al., 1991; Figure 21.3). Although they have produced some gains, it is clear that market forces have not achieved optimal efficiency in this area (Hirst, 1989b). As a result, it is useful to expand upon the institutional and economic restrictions that appear to inhibit the translation of efficiency potential into electricity savings. Recent research highlights the variety of barriers that exist (Hirst and Brown, 1990):

• Perhaps most important is the empirical observation that most businesses and homeowners will not invest in large-scale energy-saving improvements unless the investment can be recovered almost immediately—typically in no more than 2 years (see Figure 21.11) (Putnam, Hayes and Bartlett, 1987; Plunkett, 1988; Wiel, 1989; Hirst and Brown, 1990).

• Information about the cost, reliability, and performance of efficiency technologies is not widely diffused, particularly among consumers (Putnam, Hayes, and Bartlett, 1987; Hirst and Brown, 1990).

• Rental and speculative buildings are subject to the problem of split incentives. Landlords have little reason to invest in efficiency measures when the energy bill is passed on to tenants, whereas tenants rarely make such investments because their tenure in the building is typically uncertain. Likewise, given far-from-perfect information among consumers, speculative builders are less likely to invest up front in premium-cost, high-efficiency measures because they will not pay for energy use in the building after its purchase (Putnam, Hayes, and Bartlett, 1987; Hirst and Brown, 1990).

• Another barrier to adoption of more efficient technology is aesthetic. Objects lighted by fluorescent lamps sometimes do not look natural to consumers. Problems of color rendition have been mitigated to a considerable extent by reformulation of phosphors, and many new high-efficiency bulbs can fit into conventional sockets, permitting consumers to use existing lamps and fixtures. Nonetheless, additional data on consumer acceptance of efficiency measures are needed; they are expected to be developed as part of the continuing, large-scale efficiency efforts discussed below.

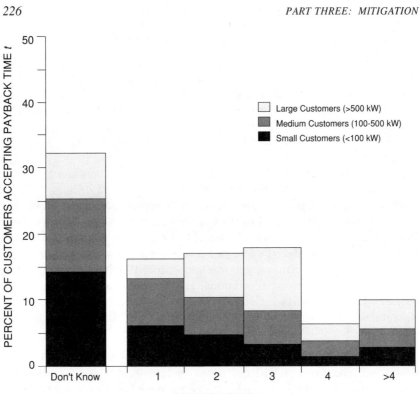

FIGURE 21.11   Maximum tolerable payback time for investments in energy efficiency.

SOURCE: Barker et al. (1986).

These obstacles—combined with others, such as the perceived risk of energy efficiency investments, constraints on the infrastructure of energy efficiency vendors and suppliers, and uncertainty about future fuel prices—provide formidable resistance to the realization of technical efficiency potential (Hirst and Brown, 1990). It is also possible that regulation has kept the price of electricity below its marginal cost. If this is the case, reform of utility ratemaking could raise the price of electricity and lead consumers to invest more in energy conservation. A final barrier should be mentioned: lack of national data on energy efficiency. Since the early 1980s, DOE has greatly restricted its role in collecting such information, and state governments and utilities have made only limited efforts to do so. As a result, relatively few rigorous data exist on the performance and cost-effectiveness of energy efficiency programs (Hirst, 1989b).

POLICY OPTIONS

Several options are available for implementing an energy efficiency program:

• Regulatory reform designed to make energy efficiency the most profitable resource option for electric and natural gas utilities
• Stronger appliance efficiency standards and energy-efficient building codes
• Direct subsidies in the form of tax credits, loans (including low-interest loans), and grants to encourage energy efficiency benefits—including revenue-neutral tax measures such as variable hookup fees for buildings
• Direct government control requiring all electric utilities to develop and implement broad-based, comprehensive energy efficiency programs
• Public education

Each of these options is discussed below.

Direct Investment in Efficiency by Utilities

Experience suggests that, as a matter of policy, the potential for large, cost-effective efficiency savings may not be realized unless the economic and organizational burden of such a program is placed on those who will directly receive its benefits—electric utilities and their customers. Utilities are in the best position among society's institutions and economic actors to overcome the barriers described above—particularly those relating to technical knowledge, access to information, ability to develop programs suited to a particular region's efficiency potential and supply mix, need for a delivery mechanism, and expectations regarding rate of return and, more generally, profits. In addition, utilities are in the best position to respond to economic (although not necessarily regulatory) forces that make it desirable to deliver energy services at the lowest possible cost.

As noted, consumers generally require no more than a 2-year payback on efficiency investments (a 33 to 100 percent internal rate of return). Conversely, collective social investment in power generation (e.g., by electric utilities) rarely repays utility shareholders or ratepayers in less than a decade. As a result, many efficiency investments rejected by consumers would appear favorable to a utility (Hirst and Brown, 1990).

At least since the first OPEC oil price shock, numerous observers have suggested that this market disconnection be remedied by placing the purchase of both demand and supply options under the unified control of the utility (Lovins, 1977; Roe, 1984). Beginning in the late 1970s, electric utilities—often guided by federal mandate—began to experiment with energy efficiency by funding residential energy audits and informational campaigns. However, other than by promoting load management programs (shifting the time of use of electricity without necessarily decreasing total electrical demand), utilities rarely attempted to realize the benefits of energy efficiency by making extensive direct capital investments in customer facilities (Investor Responsibility Research Center, 1987; Vermont Public Service Board, 1991). Indeed, as discussed below, the regulatory regime in virtually every state has inhibited such efforts (Moskovitz, 1989), because it in effect penalizes a utility that seeks to provide energy services through efficiency.

Although much has been accomplished to convince a number of utilities to begin undertaking aggressive direct investments in efficiency, most analysts agree that continued progress in the case of privately owned utilities (which supply 83 percent of the nation's retail electricity (Cambridge Energy Research Associates and Arthur Andersen and Company, 1989)) depends on changing the economic rules under which these firms operate.

Under the current rate regulation system, nearly every unit of electricity sold contributes profit to the utility's shareholders; conversely, every unit of electricity not sold due to efficiency improvements deprives the utility of profit (Kahn, 1988). Under these rules, an electric company responsible to its shareholders is likely to undertake efficiency investments only to the extent that they are absolutely required to avoid rate disallowances or other regulatory sanctions (DeCotis, 1989; Hirst, 1989a; Moskovitz, 1989; Wiel, 1989).

Incentives in Practice

Recently, a variety of proposals have been put forward to align the privately owned utility's profit motive with the public interest in promoting electrical efficiency. All of them involve a mechanism by which an electric company can profit as much or more from making its customers energy efficient as from maintaining or increasing electric sales (Hirst, 1989a; Moskovitz, 1989). This is consistent with recent action by the National Association of Regulatory Utility Commissioners—a nationwide group representing the state agencies that regulate most utilities—endorsing the concept that a utility's "least-cost" plan should represent its most profitable course of action (National Association of Regulatory Utility Commissioners, 1989).

One such approach, recently adopted by utility regulators in Rhode Island, Massachusetts, and New Hampshire, allows utility shareholders to recover through the rate structure the direct costs of efficiency programs and to keep as profit a portion of the total economic savings created by these investments (Massachusetts Department of Public Utilities, 1990; New Hampshire Public Utilities Commission, 1990; Rhode Island Public Utilities Commission, 1990). Under this approach, the largest retail utility in

Massachusetts, Massachusetts Electric Co., will boost its 1990 net earnings by at least $5.3 million—or 8.5 percent—by implementing an aggressive efficiency investment program. Although large, this incentive payment represents less than one-tenth of the net savings ($56 million) that will accrue to the utility's customers through lower energy use (Massachusetts Department of Public Utilities, 1990); nonetheless, to the utility it represents an attractive investment—23 percent of 1989 net income (New England Electric System, 1990b). Highlights of other incentives are as follows:

• In Rhode Island, Narragansett Electric Co. received approval for a $1.7 million incentive payment on net customer savings of $17 million. The incentive represents 10 percent of after-tax 1989 income (New England Electric System, 1990b).

• The New Hampshire Public Utilities Commission recently approved an incentive of up to $400,000 on a $1.7 million efficiency program, expected to produce customer savings of $2 million. After taxes, the incentive is 50 percent of 1989 income (New England Electric System, 1990b).

National Demonstration Projects

Two major programs in the United States have helped to demonstrate, under real-world conditions, that energy efficiency programs directed by utilities are a primary option among policy alternatives that may be selected to mitigate greenhouse warming. These programs were developed in the Pacific Northwest and New England. A third program was initiated in California in 1990.

Pacific Northwest The Pacific Northwest was the first region in the United States to undertake a major utility-driven program to improve electrical energy efficiency. Under the Pacific Northwest Electric Power Planning and Conservation Act of 1980, Congress authorized the creation of a multistate electric planning agency—the Northwest Power Planning Council—covering Oregon, Washington, Idaho, and western Montana. The council was charged with developing a plan that would require the region's utilities to invest in efficiency improvements rather than new electric supply, whenever the former cost less.

Over 8 years (1981 to 1989), the region's major electric utility—the federal Bonneville Power Administration (BPA)—invested more than $600 million to enhance efficiency in residential and commercial buildings and in industrial facilities. As a result, BPA saved nearly 300 MW in generating capacity, at a cost of approximately 2 cents/kWh (Bonneville Power Administration, 1990)—less than half the cost of obtaining the equivalent supply from new coal-fired generation (Northwest Power Planning Council, 1989). From 1978 to 1988, expenditures on energy efficiency savings in areas served by Pacific Northwest utilities, including the BPA, totaled approximately $1.3 billion (Lee, 1989). In addition, two pilot projects conducted in the region illustrate the effectiveness of direct capital investment in customer facilities:

• In the Hood River Conservation Project, the utility analyzed, supervised, and completely paid for full weatherization of electrically heated homes in a single county; the program achieved a participation rate of 85 percent (Hirst, 1987). Per-home weighted average savings were 2600 kWh/yr at a per-home cost of $4400, annualized at 7.1 cents/kWh. Although this average is high, Hood River was designed to explore the limits of cost-effective conservation.

• In the other program, called Energy Edge, the utility provided comprehensive design assistance and paid the full cost of increasing energy efficiency in new commercial buildings above the level required by a model building code. Initial estimates project that Energy Edge will increase efficiency in treated buildings 30 percent above the levels that would have been achieved through application of the already energy-efficient building code effective in the region. Program cost is about 2.1 cents/kWh, half that of the cheapest supply option (Anderson et al., 1988; Benner, 1988).

Notwithstanding the findings of these pilot programs, the region drastically reduced its efficiency investment activity in the mid-1980s, when demand slowed in response to a lagging regional economy (Northwest Power Planning Council, 1987; Collette, 1989); currently, efficiency budgets are again on the rise as the region moves out of a power deficit condition.

New England   In 1988, New England became the site of a program designed to test the real-world feasibility of large-scale efficiency projects implemented by electric utilities.

Rapid economic growth in the Northeast, combined with the region's aging stock of electricity-generating plants and the regulatory and political difficulty of siting new ones, led to predictions of severe electric capacity shortages in New England as early as the late 1980s (Russell, 1989). In 1987 the Conservation Law Foundation, Inc., a Boston-based environmental organization, led a consumer and environmental coalition in extensive administrative litigation before the region's state utility regulators. It proposed that, prior to constructing substantial new power facilities, utilities should be required to undertake extensive, direct investments in energy efficiency at customer sites (Collette, 1989; Russell, 1989; Flavin, 1990).

By mid-1990, as a result of favorable agency action and voluntary settlements, 15 retail electric power companies in New England and New York had agreed to cooperate with state regulators and public interest groups to design, implement, monitor, and refine programs for large-scale direct efficiency investments to reduce customer electricity use (Cohen, 1990). Under these programs, the utilities analyze customer homes and commercial facilities for potential efficiency improvements costing less than equivalent power generation; arrange and supervise installation of the measures; and, in most cases, pay the full installation and labor costs associated with each project (New England Electric System and Conservation Law Foundation, Inc., 1989). Eleven of these utilities have together committed to spending at least $1.2 billion on efficiency during the next 5 years, equal to 2.4 to 8.2 percent of their annual (1987) revenues. The largest utility in Massachusetts projects that it will save 10 percent of its 1987 peak load capacity by the fifth year of its program and 28.2 percent by the twentieth year (Chernick, 1990).

Ultimately, firm conclusions concerning the energy yield of these efficiency efforts must await the results of their specific measurement and evaluation protocols. The New England utilities currently have not developed detailed estimates of long-term savings because programs have been in the field for only 2 years at most. However, it is conservatively projected that they will eliminate between one-third and one-half of the otherwise-realized demand growth (Wald, 1988; Destribats et al., 1990). In addition, a technical potential study suggests that the region's total electricity generation requirements would remain constant (at 96,000 GWh) from 1985 to 2005 if all cost-effective, commercially available efficiency measures were implemented and that the requirements could be reduced by 33 percent if the measures encompass expected technological developments (New England Energy Power Council, 1987). It is also estimated that, if all cost-effective efficiency improvements were implemented, by the year 2004 New England electric utilities could reduce CO_2, SO_2, and NO_2 emissions by 38.9 Mt/yr, 169,000 t/yr, and 133,000 t/yr, respectively (Banwell et al., 1990).

In the field, early data suggest that a comprehensive, utility-driven and ratepayer-funded approach may be an effective means of implementing investment in electrical efficiency:

• In one program in Rhode Island that involved direct installation of, and full payment for, high-efficiency lighting in small commercial buildings, a participation rate of more than 90 percent was achieved among customers contacted. Anticipated savings for the current version of this program are 10 to 15 percent of total kilowatt-hours used by participating customers. More than 600 buildings were treated in 6 months (M. Miller, New England Electric System, personal communication to Robert H. Russell, Conservation Law Foundation, Inc., May 23, 1990; New England Electric System, 1990a; Liz Hicks, New England Electric System, personal communication to Robert H. Russell, Conservation Law Foundation, Inc., August 22, 1990).

• In a residential program mounted by the same utility, which provides high-efficiency lighting and hot water conservation measures to low-income neighborhoods, the utility achieved a penetration rate of more than 50 percent in the targeted areas (Liz Hicks, New England Electric System, personal communication to Robert H. Russell, Conservation Law Foundation, Inc., August 22, 1990).

• In its first 18 months of operation, a Northeast Utilities program involving Connecticut Light and Power and Western Massachusetts Electric Company has treated with a package of efficiency measures approximately 24 percent of all projected new floor space in its service territory and estimates savings to be at least 20 percent above baseline practice (Connecticut Light and Power Company, 1990). The program pays for the full cost of improving electrical efficiency in new buildings and industrial plants. As of August 1990 the retail utilities had entered into contracts that offered $5.5 million in incentives and would create an estimated 24,357 MWh of annual electricity savings—at a cost per kilowatt-hour saved of approximately 3 cents (Frederick F. Wajcs, Jr., Northeast Utilities, personal communication to Armond Cohen, Conservation Law Foundation, Inc., August 22, 1990).

• Recently, a large New England utility estimated that one of its least-expensive future supply options, a combined cycle plant, would cost nearly twice as much (8.3 cents/kWh) as each of three efficiency programs it is in the process of implementing—a commercial and industrial building retrofit program (4.3 cents/kWh), a program to improve the efficiency of new commercial buildings and industrial facilities (5.2 cents/kWh), and a residential new construction program (4.4 cents/kWh) (New England Electric System, personal communication to Conservation Law Foundation, Inc., June 7, 1990).

California Following New England's lead, the four largest electric and natural gas utilities in California recently announced stepped-up investment plans aimed at doubling their 1988 efficiency investments (collectively about $150 million per year (A&C Enercom et al., 1990)) within 2 years—an additional aggregate annual expenditure of nearly $150 million (Collette, 1990). Thus they are expected to approach the investment level of the early 1980s, approximately $320 million per year, or 2 percent of revenues (A&C Enercom et al., 1990).

Under the California "collaborative process," the four utilities have negotiated with regulators and public interest groups to implement new investor incentives designed to make efficient energy savings more profitable than selling additional kilowatt-hours of electricity or units of natural gas. Each utility has negotiated a different investor incentive. Pacific Gas and Electric, California's largest utility, has been the most aggressive and has developed a program where savings generated can be shared between ratepayers and the utility's investors in the ratio of 85:15. One example of the earnings that are expected to be achieved involves plans by Pacific Gas and Electric to give compact fluorescent lamps to its customers. The wholesale cost of each lamp is about $10, with advertising and delivery adding another $2. The utility recovers this $12 promptly from its ratepayers through adjustments in the utility rates that customers pay. During its life, the lamp will avoid about $42 of electric bills; so the net savings is $30, assuming an undifferentiated rate structure. The utility's investors are permitted to retain 15 percent of these savings, or $4.50. This is paid out over 3 years, producing a highly favorable internal rate of return.

Pacific Gas and Electric has implemented a $100-million-per-year shared savings program that is expected to yield 1990 earnings of $30 million to $40 million, a 4 to 5 percent increase over typical profits of $800 million (D. Schultz, California Public Utilities Commission, private communication to Arthur M. Rosenfeld, Lawrence Berkeley Laboratory, May 1990). Other utilities have proposed more modest incentives, such as a premium rate of return on investments on demand-side measures.

Appliance Efficiency Standards and Building Codes

One mechanism that has been used to increase efficiency is the imposition of efficiency standards—for example, forthcoming standards under the U.S. National Appliance Efficiency Act, fluorescent ballast standards, and efficiency-oriented building codes. Although useful, direct government regulation of building and equipment efficiency may not realize optimal efficiency investment.

National standards usually will be set to the level that is cost-effective for national average energy costs. Avoided energy costs vary between utilities and regions (Cambridge Energy Research Associates and Arthur Andersen and Company, 1989). Higher efficiencies will be cost-effective in some areas, and lower efficiencies will be cost-effective in others. For example, the U.S. National Appliance Energy Conservation Act mandates only those efficiency improvements that carry a 3-year payback or less (Rosenfeld, 1988). Moreover, the electric efficiency levels of the most advanced state building codes can be cost-effectively exceeded by more than 30 percent (Benner, 1988). Statewide standards are more likely to reflect local cost conditions; unfortunately, costs vary widely even within states, and many states do not have the bureaucratic infrastructure to support efficiency standard setting (Paul Chernick, Resource Insights, Inc., personal communication to the Conservation Law Foundation, Inc., May 31, 1990).

In addition, standards generally must take into account, on a national level, the practical limits that manufacturers face in producing the new efficient equipment. Thus utility programs that are phased in over time may afford a more practical approach to the development of necessary markets (P. Chernick, personal communication to the Conservation Law Foundation, Inc., May 31, 1990).

Government Subsidies and Tax Policy

Tax credits, loans (including low-interest loans), and grants represent an alternative policy option that all levels of government, but particularly the federal government, have used to promote efficiency investments by individuals and firms.

However, this approach has many of the same drawbacks as do standards (P. Chernick, personal communication to the Conservation Law Foundation, Inc., May 31, 1990). In addition, direct subsidy does not necessarily encourage investment in cost-effective, comprehensive energy efficiency. The market barriers outlined above—particularly those relating to information costs, risk aversion, split incentives, and need for rapid payback of investment—will continue to operate unless programs underwrite much of the cost of proven efficiency measures (Plunkett and Chernick, 1988).

If government funding is provided by direct subsidy, this will not only require additional layers of management but also transfer payments from taxpayers to electricity users. Such transfers may not drastically redistribute wealth, but they will have to be authorized by a legislature that has shown little interest in obtaining energy efficiency by regulation at this scale.

One concept that attempts to combine features of a taxation system with direct regulation may hold more promise. This is a so-called "fee-bate" revenue-neutral system—currently only at the stage of proposed legislation—that sets a target peak demand or target energy consumption (or both) per square foot for particular building types. Buildings that exceed the target pay into a fund, and those using less than the target energy collect a rebate from the fund. The target would be adjusted to provide the desired incentive, and the fee and rebate levels would be calibrated so that one cancels the other (Rosenfeld, 1988).

Like standards, this system of fees and rebates tied to building efficiency involves a lower degree of governmental intervention and cost, but, unlike standards, it offers an incentive to exceed the target. In addition, by using baseline standards and by setting rewards and penalties that may increase with distance from the target, the system can encourage efficiency in proportion to its added social value.

Direct Governmental Control

The government might consider the creation of a comprehensive efficiency assessment and delivery structure to identify and implement all cost-effective efficiency measures. To avoid unfair burdens on taxpayers with low electric usage and limited opportunities to participate, the cost of the program could be recovered through assessments on electric utilities and other energy providers.

The advantages of this type of approach include the ability to cover all energy uses (electricity, natural gas, and oil) and geographic comprehensiveness. Disadvantages include the duplication of existing utility relationships with customers, the creation of an additional governmental bureaucracy, the overhead costs of public accountability, the possibility that a market-based incentive system would achieve the same result at a lower cost to society, and the risk that if the program failed its failure would be total, representing a nationwide setback for energy efficiency. Perhaps most important, the establishment of such a governmental structure for delivery of efficiency services does not seem to be as politically feasible as the creation of a regulatory environment that encourages utilities to provide these services (P. Chernick, personal communication to the Conservation Law Foundation, Inc., May 31, 1990).

Public Education

Although policymakers are increasingly recognizing energy efficiency's considerable potential, members of the public and many of their representatives do not appear to be aware of the large costs involved in failing to take efficiency measures. Corrective educational efforts are particularly important in view of the earlier discussion concerning implied discount rates and the fact that in many cases the consumer, rather than the technology or the law, will have the final say on whether to adopt a given efficiency measure. Such efforts could focus on the individual economic benefits of increased efficiency, its relative lack of disadvantages, and the environmental cost (particularly the portion that will be assessed to future generations who are not currently represented in the political process) of unnecessary deployment of central generation plants. Indeed, given the extent to which policy changes must be made before theoretical efficiencies can be realized, no large-scale efficiency initiative, however structured, may be feasible without a fundamental alteration in public attitude. This is an area in which federal education could help to overcome transaction costs, although it should be noted that energy prices continue to exercise an important influence on consumer knowledge and choice. The development of clear and informative consumer energy bills, properly corrected for price and weather, is one area in which federal research funding could promote the refinement of what is essentially a price-driven mechanism (Kempton and Montgomery, 1982; Kempton, 1989; Kempton and Layne, 1989).

International Implications

The industrial nations, including the United States, have realized major efficiency gains during the past 15 years. This trend can be accelerated and, with U.S. assistance and leadership, even replicated in other nations. In many cases, efficiency investments that approach avoided cost in this country can be implemented at a far lower cost elsewhere (U.S. Agency for International Development, 1988, 1990).[10]

Growth in electric demand in the developing world is proceeding at a rate that is nearly 3 times higher than that forecast for the United States—between 6.6 and 7 percent annually (Munasinghe et al., 1988; Moore and Smith, 1990). Less-developed nations in Asia plan to more than double their installed capacities between 1989 and 1999 (Moore and Smith, 1990). Other nations predicting rapid growth, such as Brazil, forecast expansion of electricity production by as much as 150 percent during the next 15 years (Geller, 1986). As a consequence, during the next three to five decades, the United States and other Organization for Economic Cooperation and Development (OECD) nations are expected to account for a declining share of greenhouse gas emissions, whereas rapidly industrializing developing nations will contribute a far greater share (U.S. Agency for International Development, 1990).

A recent World Bank study of 70 less-developed countries (LDCs) concludes that these nations have plans to increase coal-fired generation during the 1989-1999 decade from 907 BkWh—44.7 percent of the total supply of electricity for these nations—to 1793 BkWh—46.6 percent of the total supply 10 years later; this represents a 98 percent increase in the use of coal in one decade. China, one of the nations in the study, anticipates an increase in its coal-fired generating capacity of 64,000 to 90,000 MW by the year 2000 (World Bank, 1985; Moore and Smith, 1990). For a variety of economic, logistical, and safety reasons (particularly in the wake of Chernobyl), as well as matters relating to public perception, nuclear power is not expected to make a substantial additional contribution in the next two decades (Flavin, 1987b; Keepin, 1988; Moore and Smith, 1990).

Deployment of fossil fuel capacity on this scale carries with it major economic consequences that may strain national economies. The less-developed nations already spend $50 billion to $100 billion per year, a quarter of their public debt, on power supply expansion and improvement (India, China, and Brazil account for about one-half of the total); approximately one-fifth of all funding from the World Bank and regional development banks is applied to power supply development (Heron, 1985; Flavin, 1987a; Churchill and Saunders, 1989). By 2008, in the absence of substantial efficiency improvements, it is estimated that 1500 GW of additional generating capacity will be needed in the developing world, at a cost of approximately $2.6 trillion, equal to more than $125 billion per year (U.S. Agency for International Development, 1988); by contrast, in 1988, total installed generating capacity in the United States was 658 GW (Cambridge Energy Research Associates and Arthur Andersen and Company, 1989).

A recent analysis of the developing world concluded that efficiency improvements could reduce total generating capacity needs by more than half, with annual savings of $15 billion to $50 billion (U.S. Agency for International Development, 1988). The buildings sector efficiency measures described in this chapter may be particularly important in view of the fact that, throughout the 1980s, electricity consumption in residential and commercial buildings significantly outpaced growth in total electricity consumption in many developing countries; this trend is expected to intensify (U.S. Agency for International Development, 1990). Two major efficiency opportunities are lighting, which accounts for 20 percent of U.S. electricity consumption and nearly that in many developing nations (e.g., 17 percent in India), and large commercial buildings, which consume large amounts of electricity and do not significantly vary in design worldwide.

Despite the apparent existence of promising energy efficiency opportunities in the developing world, major sources of seed capital have yet to make a significant commitment to this potential. The World Bank, for example, continues to support major power supply projects at the expense of energy efficiency. In 1990, it was estimated that a mere 1 percent of the bank's energy loans were conservation-related.

In one of the few practical attempts to apply the concepts described earlier in this chapter to conditions in a developing nation, the Conservation Law Foundation, Inc., a Boston-based environmental organization, is currently working with the Jamaica Public Service Company, that island nation's government-owned utility, to design and implement comprehensive energy efficiency measures of the type now in place in New England. A recent study performed in Jamaica reaches the following conclusions:

1. For less than the avoided cost of producing power, Jamaica could save more than 20 percent of projected system load during the next 10 to 15 years; long-term savings could reach 40 percent of projected demand. The cost during the next 15 years would be about $80 million (1990 net present value dollars discounted at 10 percent).

2. The project would reduce the cost of providing power by about $277 million, reduce imports by about $188 million, and avoid environmental damage valued at about $476 million (Conservation Law Foundation, Inc., 1990).

OTHER BENEFITS AND COSTS

Although not included in the cost-benefit calculations that appear in this report, other significant positive effects may result from the efficiency strategy described in this chapter. These are in addition to the benefits realized from mitigation of greenhouse warming and may not be taken into account in the direct price of energy or its inputs. Nonetheless, they are real and should be considered during the process of designing an optimal policy "mix" directed at reducing carbon emissions. They include the following:

• *Power costs and reliability:* The cost of stretching existing supplies by investing in efficiency averages half (or less than half) the cost of building new power plants. This means that an energy-efficient economy will produce more competitive products, increase disposable consumer income, and reduce capital outflows for expensive plant construction and imported fuel (an especially important advantage for developing countries). End-use efficiency also makes power systems more reliable by dampening the demand swings that can be caused by extreme weather and economic cycles, and it makes utility planning less volatile by allowing incremental investments rather than massive power additions.

• *Other environmental benefits:* Greenhouse warming is far from the only major environmental threat posed by electricity production. Fossil fuel power plants in the United States account for about two-thirds of the major acid rain precursor—SO_2; one-third of the major smog precursor—NO_2; and a variety of toxic pollutants. Large-scale hydroelectric projects can destroy precious plant and animal habitat, displace native populations, and dramatically degrade water quality. Nuclear power plants generate substantial quantities of high-level radioactive waste, whose disposal to date has proved technically debatable and politically intractable. In addition, land use problems can be avoided because of the reduced need to site new energy generation and disposal facilities. All of these impacts are mitigated to the extent efficiency displaces supply.

• *Local economic development:* Efficiency investments are highly labor intensive and typically employ labor that is available locally. The materials required for large-scale efficiency programs also can often be produced locally.

• *Energy independence:* Recent events in the Persian Gulf have again emphasized the importance of this factor. In addition, energy independence would avoid the domestic economic cost of price shocks such as those that occurred during the 1973 OPEC embargo.

RESEARCH AND DEVELOPMENT NEEDS

Existing technology is capable of producing major efficiency gains. However, it is apparent that large additional savings could be obtained by perfecting and introducing experimental technologies, backed by further research. The government should consider substantially increasing research and development funding, particularly for research designed to overcome engineering barriers that inhibit the commercial availability of promising new technologies.

Specific research activities identified by the National Research Council's Alternative Energy Research and Development Committee (1990) include the following:

- develop advanced insulation materials for building walls, windows, and roofs;
- develop nongreenhouse-gas foams and evacuated-panel technology;
- develop controls, expert systems, diagnostics, and feedback systems to minimize energy use in the construction, commissioning, and operation of buildings; and
- implement existing technologies with carefully planned and monitored demonstrations and research on energy-related motivation and decision making.

For most of the 1980s the federal government, through DOE, played only a limited role in supporting research and development of energy-efficient technologies and approaches. Of the $2.8 billion national energy technology research and development budget in 1988, 9 percent was devoted to energy efficiency, and 53 percent to more capital-intensive fossil fuel, fusion, and nuclear research (Hirst, 1989b). Between 1974 and 1988, DOE spent $4 billion on energy efficiency research and development, whereas between 1954 and 1968, the federal Atomic Energy Commission spent $22 billion on nuclear reactor research and development (Hirst, 1989b; Hirst and Brown, 1990). It is important to recognize, however, that different types of energy require different levels of capital investment.

In addition, more information is needed on the effectiveness of different energy efficiency policy measures. Here, also, the federal government has greatly restricted its activities and support. Yet one of the major barriers to the implementation of comprehensive electricity efficiency programs is lack of knowledge about their design, implementation, and effectiveness.

CONCLUSIONS

Policies designed to substitute broad-based, comprehensive energy efficiency programs for large-scale central generation of power and use of fossil fuels serve two goals: reduction of greenhouse gases, particularly CO_2, and economic efficiency. Overall, the means chosen to overcome the substantial market barriers that inhibit realization of these goals depend on considerations of policy and political reality. Nonetheless, one policy option holds considerable merit: regulatory reform designed to give utilities an incentive to conserve energy.

Specific conclusions include the following:[11]

- If all technically feasible electricity efficiency measures were applied to building end uses in the commercial and residential sectors, U.S. carbon emissions from the generation of electricity could be reduced by nearly half, to about 500 Mt CO_2/yr. This reduction could be achieved at an average cost of –$57/t CO_2.

• Electricity efficiency measures applied to commercial and residential buildings in the United States currently have the potential to save about 50 percent of the electricity used by this sector. More than half of these savings can be achieved at a cost of 2.5 cents/kWh or less, and all of the savings can be obtained at negative "avoided" cost—that is, for less than 7.5 cents/kWh, which is the average price of U.S. electricity supplied to the buildings sector. The average net cost of these savings is –5 cents/kWh.

• The technology to realize these reductions is either commercially available or has been developed and tested. However, market imperfections and in some cases consumer resistance greatly impede the implementation of efficiency measures and, consequently, the realization of more than a fraction of the potential monetary and environmental savings. Specifically, commercial and residential electricity users demand short-payback periods for their investments in efficiency measures—typically no more than 2 years. However, electric utilities accept payback periods that are considerably longer.

• Through regulatory reform, particularly at the state level, government can provide utilities with a strong incentive to develop effective, broad-based energy efficiency programs. This can be done by ensuring, through the rate-making system, that purchase by a utility of all cost-effective energy efficiency from its customers represents the most financially attractive option.

• Other policy options that attempt to overcome market barriers and realize available cost-effective savings include direct governmental programs, governmental subsidies for efficiency investment, appliance efficiency standards, more stringent building codes, and revenue-neutral tax measures such as variable hookup fees for buildings.

• In addition to electricity savings of 500 Mt CO_2, a combination of fossil fuel efficiency programs and fuel switching from electricity to natural gas or fuel oil could produce further savings of 374 Mt CO_2/yr at a cost of –70/t CO_2 equivalent for fuel savings and –$92/t CO_2 equivalent for fuel switching. These savings, summarized on Table 21.7, could be brought about through the same policy options applicable to electric utilities. Additional research is necessary to realize the full scope of the savings that may be available.

To summarize, the total potential savings from this combination of electricity and fuel efficiency measured in the commercial and residential sector is 890 Mt CO_2/yr at an average cost of –$63/t CO_2. This chapter has illustrated the policy options and research needed to achieve these savings.

NOTES

1. One exajoule (10^{18} joules of primary energy) equals 1/1.054 quadrillion (10^{15}) Btu which also equals 85 BkWh of electricity. One exajoule (EJ) or 1 quadrillion Btu is often referred to as 1 quad.

2. Avoided cost or avoided price of electricity is the cost (usually expressed as an average or marginal cost in cents per kilowatt-hour) of the electricity rendered unnecessary by implementation of one or more energy efficiency measures.

3. It should be noted that the base load capacity represented by this price is coal-fired, the most damaging from an environmental standpoint. If environmental externalities were to be internalized, the price could more than double.

4. Throughout this report, tons (t) are metric; 1 Mt = 1 megaton = 1 million tons; and 1 Gt = 1 gigaton = 1 billion tons.

5. A natural question is whether lighter surfaces are a significant disadvantage in winter. In fact, they make relatively little difference in the temperature because daily solar radiation is much reduced. Thus on a clear December day in New York, solar gain is only 25 percent of its June daily value, and cloudier average weather reduces this by one-fourth to one-eighth. There is indeed the inconvenience that on a clear winter day in New York, thin patches of ice melt more slowly on a lighter-colored roadway, but this is more than offset by the summer reduction of smog. Dark surfaces contribute about two-thirds of summer heat islands, which in turn cook smog faster. In Los Angeles, the heat island is responsible for about one-third of the smog episodes.

6. See Table 21.2 for similar data, developed by Rosenfeld et al. (1991).

7. This is based on the assumption that natural gas contains 14.5 kg C/MBtu and that oil contains 20.3 kg C/MBtu (Edmonds et al., 1989).

8. It is estimated that if 33 percent of its hot water heating customers and 80 percent of its space heating customers were to convert to alternative, on-site fuels (oil, natural gas, and propane), Central Vermont Public Service, Vermont's largest utility (410-MW total system capacity in 1989), would be required to generate 3,000,000 MWh fewer over a 20-year period, an annual savings of 150,000 MWh (5.2 percent of total generation) (A. Shapiro, Vermont Energy Investment Corporation, Burlington, Vermont, memorandum, September 12, 1990).

9. In New England, fuel switching measures tend to displace electricity generated by oil, so fuel security is an important consideration.

10. Such efforts must also include correction of major market imperfections and other barriers to efficiency. For example, in India, a compact fluorescent lamp subject to import fees would retail for $35; thus CFLs are virtually unavailable there. Nonetheless, CFL plants are about 100 times less expensive than the power plants they replace. Data developed as part of the BELLE (Bombay Efficiency Lighting Large-scale Experiment)—a collaboration between the U.S. Agency for International Development (AID), Lawrence Berkeley Laboratory, and the Bombay utility—show that an Indian CFL plant, which would cost $7.5 million to build, could be expected to produce about 2 million 16-W CFLs per year and after 6 years to save 1000 MW of capacity and avoid about 1 BkWh/yr—worth about $100 million per year (enough to purchase another CFL plant every month) (Gadgil and Rosenfeld, 1990).

A second example involves coal in China, which (like electricity in many less-developed countries) is heavily subsidized by the government. However, building insulation is not. As a result, new homes in Peking—a city with a mean temperature lower than Boston's—are not insulated. Nonetheless, insulation measures with a payback period of 6 years could be installed at a cost of conserved coal of 50 cents/MBtu, 66 percent lower than the $1.50/MBtu price of coal on international markets (Huang et al., 1984).

11. All calculations use a 6 percent discount rate.

REFERENCES

A&C Enercom, Association of California Water Agencies, California Department of General Services, California Energy Coalition, California Energy Commission, California Large Energy Consumers Association, California/Nevada Community Action Association, California Public Utilities Commission Division of Ratepayer Advocates, Independent Energy Producers Association, Natural Resources Defense Council, Pacific Gas and Electric Company, San Diego Gas and Electric Company, Southern California Edison Company, Southern California Gas Company, and Toward Utility Rate Normalization. 1990. An Energy Efficiency Blueprint for California: Report of the Statewide Collaborative Process. Available from California Public Utilities Commission, San Francisco, Calif.

Akbari, H., J. Huang, P. Martien, L. Rainer, A. Rosenfeld, and H. Taha. 1988. The impact of summer heat islands on cooling energy consumption and global CO_2 concentration. In Proceedings of the ACEEE 1988 Summer Study on Energy Efficiency in Buildings, 5:11023. Washington, D.C.: American Council for an Energy-Efficient Economy.

Akbari, H., K. Garbesi, and P. Martien. 1989. Controlling Summer Heat Islands: Proceedings of the Workshop on Saving Energy and Reducing Atmospheric Pollution by Controlling Summer Heat Islands. Berkeley, Calif.: Lawrence Berkeley Laboratory.

Akbari, H., A. Rosenfeld, and H. Taha. 1990. Summer heat islands, urban trees, and white surfaces. ASHRAE Transactions: 90-24-1: January.

American Council for an Energy-Efficient Economy (ACEEE). 1986. Residential Conservation Power Plant Study, Phase I, Technical Potential. Report prepared for Pacific Gas and Electric. Washington, D.C.: American Council for an Energy-Efficient Economy.

American Council for an Energy-Efficient Economy (ACEEE). 1989. The Potential for Electricity Conservation in New York State. Final Report prepared for New York State Energy Research and Development Authority et al. Energy Authority Report No. 89-12. Washington, D.C.: American Council for an Energy-Efficient Economy.

Anderson, K., N. Benner, and E. Copeland. 1988. The energy edge project: Energy efficiency in new commercial buildings. Paper presented at Solar Energy Division Conference, American Society of Mechanical Engineers, Denver, April 10-14, 1988.

Banwell, P., C. Wake, and R. Harris. 1990. Trace Gas Emissions from Electric Utilities in New England: Potential Effects of Demand-Side Management. May

17, 1990. Durham: Institute for the Study of Earth, Oceans and Space, University of New Hampshire.

Barker, B. S., S. H. Galginaitis, E. Rosenthal, and Gikas International, Inc. 1986. Summary Report: Commercial Energy Management and Decision-making in the District of Columbia. Washington, D.C.: Potomac Electric Power Company.

Benner, N. 1988. Investigation into the pricing and ratemaking treatment to be afforded new electric generating facilities which are not qualifying facilities. Testimony before the Massachusetts Department of Public Utilities, Docket No. 86-36, May 2, 1988. Massachusetts Department of Public Utilities, Boston.

Bevington, R., and A. Rosenfeld. 1990. Energy for buildings and homes. Scientific American 263(3):76-86.

Bonneville Power Administration. 1990. Backgrounder. March.

Cambridge Energy Research Associates (CERA) and Arthur Andersen and Company. 1989. Electric Power Trends. Cambridge, Mass.: Cambridge Energy Research Associates.

Chernick, P. 1990. Proceeding to adopt an electrical energy plan for Commonwealth Edison Company. Testimony before the Illinois Commerce Commission, Docket No. 90-0038, May 25, 1990. Illinois Commerce Commission, Chicago.

Churchill, A., and R. Saunders. 1989. Financing of the Energy Sector in Developing Countries. World Bank Industry and Energy Department working paper, Energy Series Paper No. 14. Washington, D.C.: World Bank.

Cohen, A. 1990. "Least-cost doing": The New England collaborative experience. In Proceedings of the 1990 ACEEE Summer Study on Energy Efficiency in Buildings. Washington, D.C.: American Council for an Energy-Efficient Economy.

Collette, C. 1989. Back east to the future. Northwest Energy News 8(5):18-22.

Collette, C. 1990. California re-enters the conservation challenge. Northwest Energy News 9(3):25-29.

Connecticut Light and Power Company (CL&P). 1990. Energy Alliance: Conservation and Load Management Programs Annual Report. Berlin, Conn.: Connecticut Light and Power Company.

Conservation Law Foundation, Inc. (CLF). 1990. Power by Efficiency: An Assessment of Improving Electrical Efficiency to Meet Jamaica's Power Needs. Boston, Mass.: Conservation Law Foundation, Inc.

DeCotis, P. 1989. Balancing shareholder and customer interests in incentive ratemaking. The Electricity Journal 2(10):16.

Destribats, A., J. Lowell, and D. White. 1990. Dispatches from the front: New concepts in integrated planning. Paper presented at EPRI Innovations in Pricing and Planning Conference, Milwaukee, Wis., May 3, 1990.

Edmonds, J., W. Ashton, H. Cheng, M. Steinberg. 1989. A Preliminary Analysis of U.S. CO_2 Emissions Reduction Potential from Energy Conservation and the Substitution of Natural Gas for Coal in the Period to 2010. Report DOE/NBB-0085. Washington, D.C.: Office of Energy Research, U.S. Department of Energy.

Electric Power Research Institute (EPRI). 1990. Efficient Electricity Use: Estimates of Maximum Energy Savings. Final Report CU-6746. Research Project 2788. Palo Alto, Calif.: Electric Power Research Institute.

Energy Information Administration (EIA). 1987. Residential Energy Consumption Survey: Consumption and Expenditures: April 1984 through March 1985. Report DOE/EIA-0321/1(84). Washington, D.C.: Energy Information Administration, U.S. Department of Energy.

Energy Information Administration (EIA). 1988. Energy Conservation Indicators: 1986. Report DOE/EIA-0441(86). Washington, D.C.: Energy Information Administration, U.S. Department of Energy.

Flavin, C. 1987a. Electrifying the third world. In State of the World, 1987, L. Brown, ed. New York: W. W. Norton.

Flavin, C. 1987b. Reassessing nuclear power. In State of the World, 1987, L. Brown, ed. New York: W. W. Norton.

Flavin, C. 1990. Yankee utilities learn to love efficiency. WorldWatch 3(2):5-6.

Gadgil, A., and A. Rosenfeld. 1990. Conserving Energy with Compact Fluorescent Lamps. Berkeley, Calif.: Center for Building Science, Lawrence Berkeley Laboratory.

Geller, H. 1986. Electricity Conservation Potential in Brazil. Washington, D.C.: American Council for an Energy-Efficient Economy.

Heron, A. 1985. Financing electric power in developing countries. IAEA Bulletin (Winter), No. 4, 27:44(6).

Hirst, E. 1987. Cooperation and Community Conservation. Final Report DOE/BP-11287-18. Portland, Oreg.: Hood River Conservation Project.

Hirst, E. 1989a. Electric-Utility Energy-Efficiency and Load-Management Programs: Resources for the 1990s. Contract No. DE-AC05-84OR21400. Oak Ridge, Tenn.: Oak Ridge National Laboratory.

Hirst, E. 1989b. Federal Roles to Realize National Energy-Efficiency Opportunities in the 1990s. Contract No. DE-AC05-84OR21400. Oak Ridge, Tenn.: Oak Ridge National Laboratory.

Hirst, E., and M. Brown. 1990. Closing the Efficiency Gap: Barriers to the Efficient Use of Energy. Contract No. DE-AC05-84OR21400. Oak Ridge, Tenn.: Oak Ridge National Laboratory.

Huang, Y., A. Rosenfeld, A. Canha de Piedade, and D. Tseng. 1984. Energy efficiency in Chinese apartment buildings: Parametric analysis with the DOE-2.1A computer program. Energy 9(11-12):979-994.

Investor Responsibility Research Center (IRRC). 1987. Generating Energy Alternatives at America's Electric Utilities. Washington, D.C.: Investor Responsibility Research Center.

Kahn, E. 1988. Electric Utility Planning and Regulation. Washington, D.C.: American Council for an Energy-Efficient Economy.

Keepin, W. 1988. Greenhouse warming: Efficient solution or nuclear nemesis? Testimony before House Subcommittee on Natural Resources, Agricultural Resources, and the Environment and Subcommittee on Science, Research and Technology. Snowmass, Colo.: Rocky Mountain Institute. June, 29, 1988.

Kempton, W. 1989. Cost-Effective Energy Conservation Feedback: Program Design and Evaluation of Behavioral Response, Volume II. Princeton University, Center for Energy and Environmental Studies. September.

Kempton, W., and L. Layne. 1989. The Consumer's Energy Information Environment. Princeton University, Center for Energy and Environmental Studies. November.

Kempton, W., and L. Montgomery. 1982. Folk Quantification of Energy. Energy 7(10):817-827.

Krause, F., J. Brown, D. Connell, P. DuPont, K. Greely, M. Meal, A. Meier, E. Mills, and B. Nordman. 1988. End-Use Studies, Volume III: Analysis of Michigan's Demand-Side Electricity Resources in the Residential Sector. Report LBL-23026. April. Berkeley, Calif.: Lawrence Berkeley Laboratory.

Lawrence Berkeley Laboratory (LBL). 1990. Compact Fluorescent Lamps. Energy Efficiency Note No. 2. Berkeley, Calif.: Center for Building Science, Lawrence Berkeley Laboratory.

Lee, G. 1989. Conservation: The Northwest's north slope. Northwest Energy News 8(4):9-12.

Lovins, A. 1977. Soft Energy Paths: Toward a Durable Peace. Washington, D.C.: Friends of the Earth.

Lovins, A. 1986. Advanced Electricity-Saving Technology and the South Texas Project. Snowmass, Colo.: Rocky Mountain Institute.

Lovins, A., and H. R. Heede. 1990. Electricity-Saving Office Equipment. Snowmass, Colo.: Rocky Mountain Institute.

Massachusetts Department of Public Utilities. 1990. Order in Docket No. 89-194/-195, In re: Massachusetts Electric Company, Boston, March 30.

Meier, A., J. Wright, and A. Rosenfeld. 1983. Supplying Energy Through Greater Efficiency: The Potential for Conservation in California's Residential Sector. Berkeley, Calif.: University of California Press.

Miller, P., J. Eto, and H. Geller. 1989. The Potential for Electricity Conservation in New York State. Washington, D.C.: American Council for an Energy-Efficient Economy.

Moore, E., and G. Smith. 1990. Capital Expenditures for Electric Power in the Developing Countries in the 1990s. World Bank Industry and Energy Department working paper, Energy Series Paper No. 21. Washington, D.C.: Industry and Energy Department, World Bank.

Moskovitz, D. 1989. Profits and Progress Through Least-Cost Planning. Washington, D.C.: National Association of Regulatory Utility Commissioners.

Munasinghe, M., J. Gilling, and M. Mason. 1988. A Review of World Bank Lending for Electric Power. World Bank Industry and Energy Department working paper, Energy Series Paper No. 2. Washington, D.C.: Industry and Energy Department, World Bank.

National Association of Home Builders Research Foundation, Inc. 1985. Final Report on an Assessment of Energy Consumption in New Homes. Rockville, Md.: National Association of Home Builders Research Foundation, Inc.

National Association of Regulatory Utility Commissioners (NARUC). 1989. Resolution adopted by the annual meeting, Boston, November 15, 1988.

National Research Council. 1990. Confronting Climate Change: Strategies for Energy Research and Development. Washington, D.C.: National Academy Press.

New England Electric System (NEES). 1990a. Conservation and load management annual report. Filed with Massachusetts Department of Public Utilities, Docket No. 86-36, May 1, 1990. Massachusetts Department of Public Utilities, Boston.

New England Electric System (NEES). 1990b. 1990 Conservation and load management incentive summary. On file at the Conservation Law Foundation, Inc., Boston.

New England Electric System (NEES) and Conservation Law Foundation, Inc. 1989.

Power by Design: A New Approach to Investing in Energy Efficiency, Volumes I and II. Westboro, Mass.: NEES.

New England Energy Policy Council (NEEPC). 1987. Power to Spare: A Plan for Increasing New England's Competitiveness through Energy Efficiency. Boston: New England Energy Policy Council.

New Hampshire Public Utilities Commission. 1990. Generic investigation of financial incentives for conservation and load management. Order in Docket No. DE89-187, August 7, 1990. Concord: New Hampshire Public Utilities Commission.

Northwest Power Planning Council (NPPC). 1987. A Review of Conservation Costs and Benefits: Five Years of Experience Under the Northwest Power Act. Portland, Oreg.: Northwest Power Planning Council.

Northwest Power Planning Council (NPPC). 1989. Assessment of Regional Progress toward Conservation Capability Building. Issue Paper 89-8. Portland, Oreg.: Northwest Power Planning Council.

Pacific Northwest Laboratory. 1983. Recommendations for Energy Conservation Standards and Guidelines for New Commercial Buildings, Volume IV-C: Documentation of Test Results: Large Office Building, prepared for DOE under contract DE-AC06-76RLO 1830. Richland, Wash.: Pacific Northwest Laboratory.

Plunkett, J. 1988. Investigation into the pricing and ratemaking treatment to be afforded new electric generating facilities which are not qualifying facilities. Testimony before the Massachusetts Department of Public Utilities, Docket No. 86-36, May 4, 1988. Massachusetts Department of Public Utilities, Boston.

Plunkett, J., and P. Chernick. 1988. The role of revenue losses in evaluating demand-side resources: An economic re-appraisal. In the Proceedings of the 1988 ACEEE Summer Study on Energy Efficiency in Buildings. Washington, D.C.: American Council for an Energy-Efficient Economy.

Putnam, Hayes, and Bartlett, Inc. 1987. Supporting documents on conservation and load management. Prepared for the Boston Edison Review Panel. March. Cambridge, Mass.

Rhode Island Public Utilities Commission. 1990. In re: Narragansett Electric Company conservation and load management adjustment provision. Report and Order in Docket No. 1939, May 16, 1990. Rhode Island Public Utilities Commission, Providence.

Roe, D. 1984. Dynamos and Virgins. New York: Random House.

Rosenfeld, A. 1988. Energy efficiency versus "draining America." Testimony before Subcommittee on Fisheries and Wildlife Conservation and the Environment, U.S. House of Representatives, Oversight Hearing on Oil Development in ANWR and National Energy Policy, March 31, 1988. Washington, D.C.

Rosenfeld, A., C. Atkinson, J. Koomey, A. Meier, R. Mowris, and L. Price. 1991. A Compilation of Supply Curves of Conserved Energy. LBL #31700. Berkeley, Calif.: Center for Building Science, Lawrence Berkeley Laboratory.

Russell, D. 1989. The power brokers. The Amicus Journal (Winter):31-35.

Solar Energy Research Institute (SERI). 1981. A New Prosperity: Building a Sustainable Energy Future. Andover, Mass.: Brickhouse Publishing.

U.S. Agency for International Development (U.S. AID). 1988. Power Shortages in

Developing Countries: Magnitude, Impacts, Solutions, and the Role of the Private Sector. A Report to Congress. Washington, D.C.: U.S. Agency for International Development.

U.S. Agency for International Development (U.S. AID). 1990. Greenhouse Gas Emissions and the Developing Countries: Strategic Options and the U.S. A.I.D. Response. A Report to Congress. Washington, D.C.: U.S. Agency for International Development.

U.S. Department of Energy (DOE). 1989a. Analysis and Technology Transfer Annual Report, 1988. Buildings and Community Systems. Report DOE/CH-00016-H2. Washington, D.C.: U.S. Department of Energy.

U.S. Department of Energy (DOE). 1989b. A Compendium of Options for Government Policy to Encourage Private Sector Responses to Potential Climate Change. Report DOE/EH-0103. Washington, D.C.: U.S. Department of Energy.

U.S. Department of Energy (DOE). 1989c. Monthly Energy Review. Report DOE/EIA-0035(89/12). Washington, D.C.: Energy Information Administration, U.S. Department of Energy.

U.S. Department of Energy (DOE). 1989d. State Energy and Price Expenditure Report 1987. Report DOE/EIA-0376(87). Washington, D.C.: Energy Information Administration, U.S. Department of Energy.

U.S. Department of Energy (DOE). 1989e. Technical Support Document: Energy Conservation Standards for Consumer Products: Refrigerators and Furnaces. Report DOE/CE-2077. Washington, D.C.: U.S. Department of Energy.

U.S. Department of Energy (DOE). 1989f. State Energy Data Report: Consumption Estimates 1960-1987. Report DOE/EIA-0214(87). Washington, D.C.: Energy Information Administration, U.S. Department of Energy. April.

U.S. Department of Energy (DOE). 1989g. Energy Conservation Trends: Understanding the Factors That Affect Conservation Gains in the U.S. Economy. Report DOE/PE-0092. Washington, D.C.: U.S. Department of Energy.

Usibelli, A., B. Gardiner, W. Luhren, and A. Meier. 1983. A Residential Conservation Database for the Pacific Northwest. Berkeley: University of California at Berkeley and Buildings Energy Data Group for Bonneville Power Administration, Lawrence Berkeley Laboratory.

Vermont Public Service Board. 1991. Investigation into least-cost investments, energy efficiency conservation and management of demand for energy. Order in Docket No. 5270-CV-1, Order entered March 19, 1991, Vermont Public Service Board, Montpelier.

Wald, M. 1988. Utility sets plan to cut power use. The New York Times, May 26:D1.

Wiel, S. 1989. Making electric efficiency profitable. Public Utilities Fortnightly. July 6.

World Bank. 1985. China: The Energy Sector. Washington, D.C.: World Bank.

22

Industrial Energy Management

The industrial sector is made up of a wide variety of manufacturing and other industries that use energy to extract, refine, and process raw materials to produce a variety of goods. The nomenclature used to define industrial categories varies from country to country. In the United States, the Standard Industrial Classification (SIC) system is used to designate industry groups at different levels of aggregation. Table 22.1 shows the major elements of the U.S. industrial sector. The heterogeneity of this sector makes an analysis of energy use and potential savings substantially more difficult than for other sectors of the economy contributing to greenhouse gas emissions.

Table 22.1 also shows the direct consumption of energy by the U.S. industrial sector (classified by SIC code) for 1986 which amounts to 21.7 quads.[1] Adding the 6.4 quads lost in the generation and distribution of electricity brings the total sector share to 28.1 quads of total primary energy use. This total consumption amounts to 36 percent of all primary energy used in the United States (Oak Ridge National Laboratory, 1989). Six industry groups account for more than 70 percent of total primary industrial energy use. These major groups, and their corresponding percentage of total industrial energy consumption, are chemicals (21 percent); petroleum refining (19 percent); primary metals (14 percent); pulp and paper (8 percent); stone, clay, and glass (4 percent); and food and kindred products (4 percent). Purchased fuel oil and natural gas each account for roughly one-third of the total direct energy used by industry. Electricity, coal, and other energy sources (primarily wood) account for the remainder.

International studies show that the industrial sector accounts for the largest component of most nations' energy use, averaging nearly 43 percent of total primary energy consumed in the Organization for Economic Coopera-

TABLE 22.1 End-Use Industrial Energy Consumption in 1986 (quads)

Industry Group	SIC Code[a]	Electricity[b]	Natural Gas	Fuel Oil	Coal	Other Sources	Total[c]
Chemicals	28	0.52	1.86	1.74	0.33	0.21	4.67
Petroleum refining	29	0.12	2.28	2.59	0.00	0.10	5.18
Primary metals	33	0.50	0.66	0.15	1.41	0.14	2.85
Pulp and paper	26	0.28	0.36	0.28	0.23	0.47	1.62
Stone, glass, clay	32	0.10	0.40	0.04	0.30	0.17	1.03
Food	20	0.15	0.40	0.08	0.11	0.14	0.89
Textile mills	22	0.08	0.07	0.03	0.03	0.06	0.27
Fabricated metals	34	0.08	0.14	0.02	0.00	0.09	0.33
Machinery	35	0.12	0.12	0.02	0.02	0.08	0.36
Transportation equipment	37	0.11	0.11	0.03	0.05	0.05	0.35
Other manufacturing industries[d]		0.34	0.23	0.09	0.07	0.13	0.86
Nonmanufacturing industries[e]		0.39	0.05	2.82	0.06	0.05	3.41
TOTAL		2.79	6.69	7.90	2.63	1.70	21.71

[a]SIC Code = Standard Industrial Classification.
[b]Direct electricity consumption represents 30 percent of the total primary energy associated with electric energy use. Losses in the generation and transmission of electricity are approximately 2.3 times the direct use. Total losses for the industrial sector are 6.41 quads.
[c]To obtain primary energy consumption, add electrical losses (see footnote b).
[d]Includes all remaining SICs between 20 and 39.
[e]Includes agriculture, construction, and mining.

SOURCE: Oak Ridge National Laboratory (1989).

tion and Development (OECD) countries in 1985. The percentage is even higher in developing countries, where industrial energy use accounts for nearly 60 percent of all energy consumption. Reported values for the former Soviet Union are slightly under 50 percent (Lashof and Tirpak, 1991).

RECENT TRENDS

Several recent studies have documented dramatic decreases in the energy intensity of the U.S. manufacturing sector (Ross, 1989a; U.S. Department of Energy, 1989a; Schipper et al., 1990). Figure 22.1 shows the long-term (27-year) trend in the aggregate energy intensity of U.S. manufacturing (i.e., the ratio of energy used per unit of production as defined by the Bureau of Labor Statistics). In the last 20 years, the average energy intensity of U.S. manufacturing (which does not including the mining, agriculture, and construction industries) has decreased by nearly 40 percent. Most of this decline was due to decreased direct use of fossil fuels, whose intensity fell by 50 percent between 1971 and 1985 (Figure 22.2). Electricity intensity, on the other hand, declined only slightly during that same period. The total levels of manufacturing energy use from 1958 to 1985 are shown in Figure 22.3.[2]

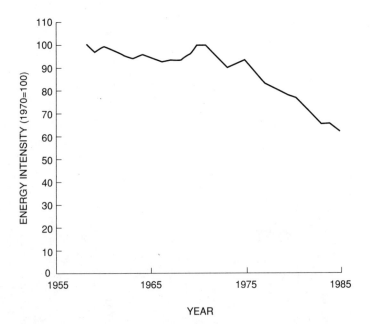

FIGURE 22.1   The aggregate energy intensity of U.S. manufacturing (relative to 1970).

SOURCE: Ross (1989a).

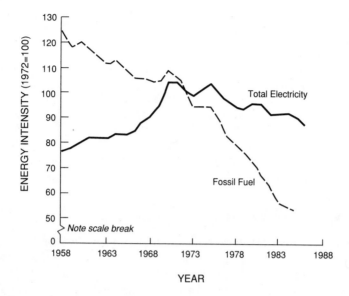

FIGURE 22.2   The aggregate electricity and fossil fuel intensities of U.S. manufacturing (relative to 1972).

SOURCE: Ross (1989a).

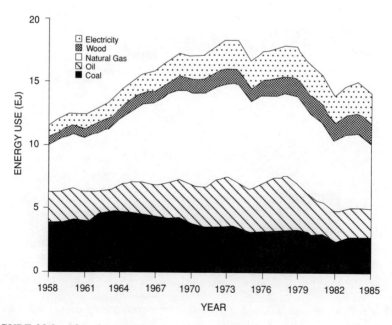

FIGURE 22.3   Manufacturing energy use by fuel type.

SOURCE: Schipper et al. (1990).

   Two major factors contributed to the trends shown in Figures 22.1 through
22.3. One was a structural shift in the economy, resulting in lower demands
for energy-intensive products such as steel, aluminum, and paper. The
other factor was improvements in the efficiency of manufacturing processes,
resulting in less energy needed per unit of production (Boyd et al., 1987).
The relative importance of structural changes and energy efficiency improvements has been analyzed by the U.S. Department of Energy (1989a),
which attributes two-thirds of the overall change since 1970 to energy efficiency improvements. A more recent study by Schipper et al. (1990) draws
similar conclusions using other measures of industrial production to examine the effects of structural and efficiency changes.

Effects of Structural Changes

   Figure 22.4 shows the impact of structural changes alone on manufacturing energy use (i.e., the energy use that would have occurred if the products
and energy intensities of each industry group had remained constant at their
1973 levels while the proportion of manufacturing sector output produced

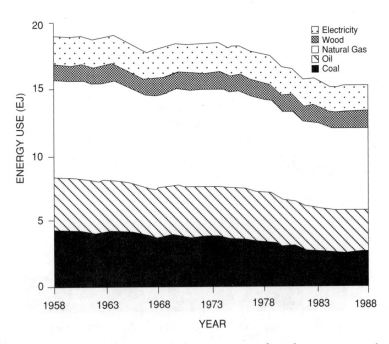

FIGURE 22.4 Impacts of structural changes on manufacturing energy use (activity and intensity fixed at 1973 levels).

SOURCE: Schipper et al. (1990).

by each industry group followed its actual historical pattern). By this measure, energy use between 1973 and 1985 would have declined by 18 percent due to structural changes alone. This analysis found that the largest contributor to the structural change was a decline in output from coal-intensive industries, particularly iron and steel (Schipper et al., 1990). The longevity of structural changes in industrial output remains somewhat more speculative. Several studies suggest a decline in the per capita consumption of energy-intensive products as industrial countries attain higher levels of affluence (e.g., Williams et al., 1987; Lashof and Tirpak, 1991). This "saturation" phenomenon implies a long-term reduction in the demand for energy-intensive materials, which could (if sustained) have important implications for future industrial energy demand.

Other factors believed to have contributed to the changing structure of U.S. manufacturing include higher oil prices and economic policies that affect the competitiveness of U.S. goods. The extent to which structural changes will continue to affect the total demand for energy in the industrial sector depends also on the absolute growth rate of manufactured products. There is some controversy over whether manufacturing represents a constant or declining share of real U.S. gross national product (GNP). To the extent that manufacturing output is coupled to GNP, decreases in energy intensity due to structural shifts may be offset at least partially by a higher total demand for manufactured goods as GNP continues to rise. Recent studies performed for DOE, however, assume a decline in the future manufacturing share of GNP (Ross, 1989b).

Effects of Efficiency Improvements

Recent improvements in energy efficiency for the U.S. manufacturing sector have been analyzed by DOE for the period from 1980 to 1985 (U.S. Department of Energy, 1990) and by Schipper et al. (1990) for the 29-year period from 1958 to 1987. The latter study attempted to develop an indicator of aggregate energy efficiency improvements independent of the structural changes noted earlier. The output of each industry group was assumed to remain constant at its 1973 value, whereas its energy intensity followed the actual historical path. By this measure, the structure-adjusted energy intensity of the manufacturing sector as a whole declined by 2.5 percent per year from 1958 to 1973 and by 2.7 percent per year from 1973 to 1985. The aggregate changes for 1958 to 1985 (Figure 22.5) were 15, 37, and 44 percent for coal, gas, and oil, respectively, and 6 percent each for wood and electricity intensity. For the period from 1985 to 1987, aggregate energy intensity continued to fall by roughly 2 percent per year. Overall, the structure-adjusted reduction in energy intensity between 1973 and 1987 was estimated at approximately 33 percent, due primarily to a reduction in direct fossil fuel use (Schipper et al., 1990).

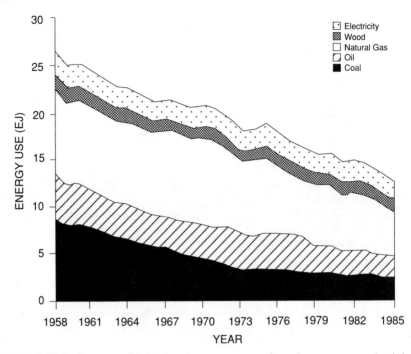

FIGURE 22.5   Impacts of intensity changes on manufacturing energy use (activity and structure fixed at 1973 levels).

Source: Schipper et al. (1990).

A DOE industry-by-industry analysis for 1980 through 1985 supports the conclusion of a continuing trend toward greater energy efficiency in the industrial sector (Table 22.2).   Although the energy price shocks of the 1970s undoubtedly contributed to improvements in energy efficiency, the more significant driving force for energy improvements in the industrial sector appears to have been the long-term changes in basic process technology, which reduce overall production costs as well as energy costs.   Thus, even at the relatively low energy prices prior to 1973 and since 1980, manufacturing processes have become increasingly energy efficient.   Although energy prices certainly have affected the fuel mix in the industrial sector (e.g., oil and gas use fell significantly in response to price increases of the 1970s), the sustained improvements in energy efficiency indicate that the industrial sector is not merely substituting one fuel for another (e.g., electricity for oil and gas).   Rather, real reductions in energy intensity are being achieved through conservation measures and process technology innovations.   The outlook is that this trend will be sustained through the turn of the century.

TABLE 22.2 Energy Efficiency Changes in Manufacturing Industry
Groups, 1980 through 1985

SIC	Industry Group	Energy Efficiency Ratios[a] 1980	1985	Energy Efficiency Change[b,c](%)
20	Food and kindred products	3.5	2.7	22.9
21	Tobacco manufactures	Q	Q	Q
22	Textile mill products	5.7	4.8	16.3
23	Apparel and other textile products	NA	NA	NA
24	Lumber and wood products	Q	Q	Q
25	Furniture and fixtures	1.9	1.6	17.4
26	Paper and allied products	16.0	13.9	13.0
27	Printing and publishing	1.1	0.9	15.2
28	Chemicals and allied products	15.1	12.4	17.6
29	Petroleum and coal products	5.4	4.4	19.8
30	Rubber and miscellaneous plastic products	4.3	3.1	27.8
31	Leather and leather products	Q	Q	Q
32	Stone, clay, and glass products	21.6	16.6	23.0
33	Primary metal industries	16.4	14.6	11.0
34	Fabricated metal products	2.8	2.3	16.4
35	Machinery, except electrical	1.7	0.9	43.6
36	Electrical and electronic equipment	1.7	1.2	26.4
37	Transportation equipment	1.5	1.1	25.0
38	Instruments and related products	1.7	1.2	29.3
39	Miscellaneous manufacturing industries	1.8	1.4	23.9
—	All manufacturing	5.8	4.4	25.1

NOTE: Q = Withheld because relative standard error is greater than or equal to 50
percent; NA = not available.

[a]Thousand British thermal units per constant (1980) dollar of value of shipments.
[b]A decrease in energy efficiency ratios from 1980 to 1985 indicates an improvement
in energy efficiency and thus a positive value for "energy efficiency change."
[c]Estimates of energy efficiency change are calculated from unrounded energy efficiency ratios and may differ from changes calculated from the rounded ratios in
columns 1 and 2.

SOURCE: U.S. Department of Energy (1990).

EMISSION CONTROL METHODS

Carbon dioxide emissions from the industrial sector are due primarily to the combustion of fossil fuels for heat and power: CO_2 is formed from the primary fuels used in boilers and process heaters and from the use of fuel by-products such as coke, petroleum plant gas, and coke oven gas. Additional emissions occur from industrial processes such as calcining and cement manufacture, which give off CO_2 when raw minerals (e.g., limestone) are heated.

The use of purchased electricity contributes to CO_2 emissions indirectly from the combustion of fossil fuels at power plants. Thus the magnitude of electricity-related CO_2 emissions depends on the utility fuel mix in a particular region. Because many energy-intensive industries tend to be located in regions of (historically) cheap electricity (e.g., hydroelectric power), the national average fuel mix may not necessarily be a good indicator of potential CO_2 emission reductions from reduced electricity demand.

Because of the extraordinary heterogeneity of the industrial sector, this chapter makes no attempt to discuss specific technological measures for reducing energy use in each of the major industries. Excellent summaries of energy use technologies on an industry-by-industry basis are available elsewhere (e.g., Decision Analysis Corporation, 1990). The intent here is to outline more generally the *categories* of methods available to industry and to estimate—insofar as possible—the magnitude of CO_2 emission reductions achievable using current technology. Toward this end, 11 general mechanisms for reducing CO_2 emissions in the manufacturing sector have been identified by Ross (1990a), who estimated qualitatively their overall potential and limitations (Table 22.3). These measures can be aggregated into four general categories: (1) fuel and energy switching, (2) energy conservation measures, (3) process design changes (including recycling), and (4) macroeconomic structural changes.

Fuel and Energy Switching

Fuel and energy switching measures reduce CO_2 emissions by substituting fuels with less carbon per unit of energy for those fuel and energy forms currently in use. For example, switching from coal to natural gas reduces CO_2 emissions by approximately 40 percent (for the same energy use), and substituting oil for coal lowers CO_2 by roughly 20 percent. The potential for fuel substitution is limited by the technical and economic circumstances of different industries. For example, the largest use of coal occurs in the iron and steel industry for the production of coke, which is used in blast furnaces to produce iron. This use of coal cannot be eliminated by simple fuel substitution. Similarly, when fuel such as coal and oil are used in

TABLE 22.3 The CO_2 Reduction Mechanisms in Manufacturing—Technological Opportunities and Constraints

CO_2 Reduction Mechanisms	Overall Reduction Potential[a]	Physical Limitations	Capital Limitations	Need for New Technology
Conservation	High	Mod	Mod	Mod
Housekeeping	Low	Imp	—	—
Process change	High?	Mod	Imp	Imp
Energy switching				
Other fuels to natural gas	High	Imp	—	—
Fuels to electricity	High	Imp	Imp	Imp
Co-generation	High?	Imp	Mod	Mod
Fossil to biomass	Low	Imp	Mod	Mod
Recycle	High	Mod	Mod	Imp
Materials substitution	Low?	Imp	Mod	Mod
Sectoral shift	Low	Imp	Mod	Mod
Manufacturing share	Low	Imp	Imp	Mod

NOTE: Imp = important, Mod = moderately important, and — = relatively little importance.

[a]Judged by size of opportunity and potential degree of public policy impact.

SOURCE: Ross (1990a).

remote locations, such as in the forest products industry, substitution of natural gas (requiring a pipeline) is unlikely to be feasible.

The principal opportunities for fuel substitution lie in industrial boiler applications, particularly in industries that switched more heavily to coal during the 1970s in response to fuel price and regulatory pressures. The price, availability, and reliability of alternate fuel supplies are the key issues in all circumstances.

The technical potential for short-term fuel substitution at existing facilities has been estimated by DOE on the basis of a recent survey of manufacturers (U.S. Department of Energy, 1988). Results are shown in Figure 22.6, which displays the maximum, minimum, and actual 1985 fuel usage for the manufacturing sector. Actual 1985 coal use is seen to be near its maximum technical potential, whereas distillate and residual oil use were near their technical minima. A rough estimate of the potential reduction in CO_2 emissions from fuel switching at existing facilities can be obtained by assuming that 0.6 quad of current coal use (the difference between actual and minimum use) is displaced by either oil or natural gas. Based on the average carbon content of fossil fuels, this would yield a CO_2 reduction of

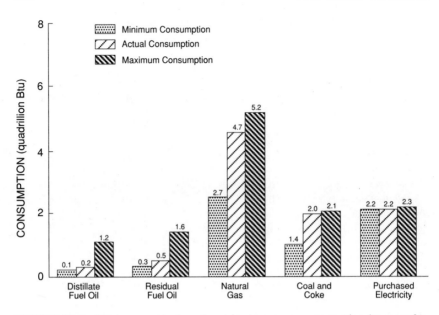

FIGURE 22.6   Minimum, actual, and maximum energy consumption by manufacturers for 1985.

SOURCE: U.S. Department of Energy (1988).

24 Mt using gas or 13 Mt using oil.[3] The cost-effectiveness of this reduction would depend on oil and gas prices relative to coal prices. Figure 22.7 shows that for recent price premiums of about $1.5 to $2/MBtu for oil and about $1.5/MBtu for gas, the reduction in CO_2 would cost about $40 to $80/t CO_2.

The longer-term technical potential for fuel switching is, of course, much greater than the short-term estimates based on facilities currently in place. The magnitude of such changes, however, is dependent on future changes in fuel prices, process technology, and the turnover of capital stock. Uncertainty over the long-term availability and price of gas and oil can be expected to inhibit fuel conversions, even where technologically feasible.

Emission reduction measures can also include switching from fossil fuels to electricity, which already is occurring to some degree. This may or may not reduce CO_2 emissions, depending on (1) the fuels used for power generation, (2) the fuel for which electricity is being substituted, and (3) the relative efficiencies of the current and substitute processes. Because substituting electricity for fossil fuels entails new capital costs, the much higher price of electricity relative to fossil fuels requires that the electricity-based process be roughly 3 times more efficient than the fossil fuel system to be competitive. Such opportunities, however, do exist (Ross, 1989b).

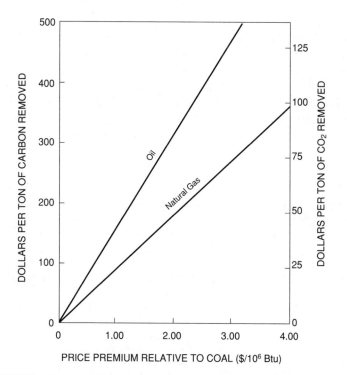

FIGURE 22.7   Cost of CO_2 reduction for fuel switching from coal to oil or gas.

Switching from fossil fuels to biomass fuels (i.e., waste or by-products from the food processing and forest products industries) is another option that is technically feasible and has already been implemented in certain industries, particularly paper manufacturing. The remaining opportunities appear to be relatively small, barring more aggressive programs to utilize existing forest and field residues, to increase crop production for fuel use, or to improve the current efficiency of biomass combustion (Ross, 1990a).

Energy Conservation Measures

Energy conservation and efficiency measures reduce the CO_2 emissions associated with the fuel or energy source that is conserved. Opportunities here range from "housekeeping" improvements, which conserve relatively small amounts of energy at low to negligible cost, to more substantial measures requiring much higher capital investments but with potentially larger energy cost savings. A number of recent studies have addressed potential energy conservation measures for the industrial sector (e.g., Oak Ridge National Laboratory, 1989; Ayres, 1990; Decision Analysis Corporation, 1990).

Although many conservation measures tend to be industry- or process-specific, a number of "generic" measures, including more efficient lighting, the use of more efficient variable-speed motors, and the more efficient recovery of waste heat, also have been identified. Table 22.4 shows one example from a European study of how energy efficiency can be improved in the use of electricity for motive power, the largest use of electricity in industry (International Energy Agency, 1989). The opportunity for energy efficiency improvements lies principally in single-phase and three-phase

TABLE 22.4 Breakdown of Electricity Consumption for Motive Power and Possible Efficiency Improvements (example: Germany)

100% electricity consumption			
69% for motive power			31% for process heat, lighting, and other
37% for three-phase AC motors		32% for DC motors, one-phase AC motors, and small-scale motors	
All three-phase motors			
For 60%, electronic control already exists or is not recommended	For 40%, electronic control is possible		
22.2% of total	14.8% of total	32% of total	
Motors already optimized	Motors that can be influenced 46.8% of total electricity used for motive power		
	Electronic control Savings: 25%	Correct size, high-efficiency motors Savings: 10%	

SOURCE: International Energy Agency (1989).

AC motors and associated drive trains. The inability of AC drives to operate at the variable speeds required by many industrial processes (in applications such as fans, pumps, blowers, and conveyors) can result in energy losses of 40 to 80 percent using conventional means of speed control. New electronic control systems, coupled with improved motor efficiencies (from higher quality magnetic materials and other loss-reducing measures), and more attention to correct motor sizing, can yield significant improvements in overall energy efficiency.

In principle, a conservation supply curve (CSC) could be developed on a process-by-process or industry-by-industry basis showing the amount of energy savings obtainable at different energy prices (analogous to supply curves for primary fuels). The functional and sectoral categories of information needed for constructing CSCs needed for the manufacturing sector are indicated in Table 22.5 (Ross, 1990b). However, the present ability to quantify energy conservation potential in this matter remains extremely limited.

Unlike the buildings and transportation sectors, where energy use is concentrated in a relatively small number of processes that have been extensively studied, the enormous diversity and variability of industrial processes remain to be characterized to a similar extent. In particular, there is little publicly available information on the *costs* of energy conservation measures in the industrial sector. In part this is due to the often proprietary nature of such information. Difficulties also are encountered in ascribing costs to many of the energy savings that accrue from large-scale changes in production methods or plant operation (e.g., converting from ingot casting to continuous casting in steel manufacturing). The "bottom line" is that the types of conservation curves outlined in Table 22.5 are simply not available today to quantify energy and CO_2 reduction potential in a manner analogous to the residential, commercial, and transportation sector analyses. Rather, the estimates presented in this chapter derive from a limited number of studies of key U.S. industries.

Electricity Savings

The most widely studied area in the industrial sector has been the potential for conserving electricity use. For the United States, Ross (1990a,b) has developed a conservation supply curve for electricity use in the U.S. manufacturing sector based on an aggregation of results from several key process industries. Details are described in Appendix D. Figure 22.8 is an electricity conservation supply curve showing that with current technology, a reduction in energy intensity of up to 30 percent could be achieved in the use of electricity by the manufacturing sector, yielding a savings of about 200 billion kilowatt-hours (BkWh) of electricity based on current energy use. The corresponding reduction in CO_2 emissions would be about 140

TABLE 22.5 Categories for Constructing Conservation Supply Curves
for Manufacturing

Function	Sector (SIC)
Movement of material	Fabrication and assembly (all SICs 20-39,
Liquid pumping	except those listed below)
Air handling	Pulp and paper mills (261, 262, 263, 266)
Solids conveying	Industrial inorganic chemicals (281, 287
	except 2879)
Mechanical process (other than above)	Industrial organic chemicals (282, 286)
Crushing	Petroleum refining (29)
Compressing (gases)	Glass (321, 322)
Cutting/etching	Cement (324)
Assembling	Iron and steel (331, 332, 339)
Extruding	Nonferrous metals (333, 334, 335, 336)

Heating
  Space heating
  Water heating
  Cooking
  Process heating
  Storage

Cooling
  Space cooling
  Process cooling
  Storage

Physical/chemical transformation
  Melting
  Extruding
  Separating
  Drying
  Curing
  Welding
  Coating
  Chemical synthesis
  Cleaning

Lighting, commercial/industrial

Information handling
  Energy management systems
  Office equipment

SOURCE: Ross (1989a).

Mt/yr based on the current national average utility fuel mix. Comparable maximum technical savings, in the range of 24 to 38 percent, have been estimated by the Electric Power Research Institute (EPRI) for the year 2000 (Barakat and Chamberlin, Inc., 1990; Electric Power Research Institute, 1990). Details of the EPRI analysis are shown in Appendix D. Note that in both the EPRI and the Ross studies the bulk of the savings comes from the use of more efficient motors, electrical drive systems, and lighting, which constitute the primary uses of electricity in industry.

Empirical evidence suggests that for the industrial sector, discount rates of 20 to 30 percent or more, corresponding to payback periods of less than 3 years, are required to stimulate investments in energy efficiency improvements (Ayres, 1990; Ross, 1989a, 1990b). Figure 22.8 shows that for such criteria, electricity prices would have to triple to induce a 30 percent savings in overall electricity use. On the other hand, lower real discount rates typical of public funding projects and large-scale utility investments (i.e., 3 to 10 percent) would substantially lower the annualized cost of conservation investments. As is discussed in Appendix D, at these lower discount rates, electricity conservation investments would yield a net cost savings analogous to those seen earlier for the buildings sector (Chapter 21). For a 6 percent real discount rate, for example, the net cost of conservation (i.e., the investment cost less the electricity savings) for a maximum savings of 200 BkWh is about –$20/t CO_2, compared to $100/t for a 30 percent discount

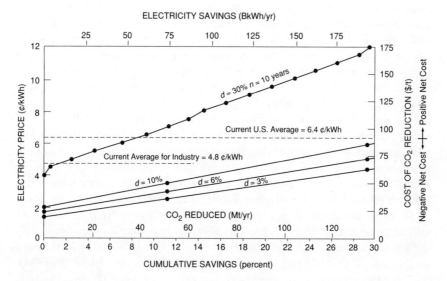

FIGURE 22.8   Electricity conservation supply curve for manufacturing (d = real discount rate).

rate. The costs shown in Figure 22.8 are similar to those reported by EPRI for a comparable rate of return (see Appendix D). Policy measures for stimulating investments in energy conservation are discussed later in this chapter and again in Chapter 29.

Co-generation

Another energy-conserving measure applicable to the industrial sector is the use of co-generation to produce heat and power simultaneously. Applications of co-generation to industrial processes have been practiced for many years and are discussed extensively in the literature. Economical applications of this technology require fairly steady heat loads, which are not available in many industrial processes that operate in a more cyclical fashion. Thus co-generation tends to be found primarily in the chemicals, paper, and petroleum refining industries. Nevertheless, opportunities do exist to utilize co-generation more extensively, for example, by using newer gas turbine technology that better matches typical industrial energy demands and provides larger overall fuel savings (Williams et al., 1987).

New financial incentives for co-generation also now exist as a result of the 1978 Public Utility Regulatory Policies Act (PURPA), which requires utilities to purchase independently generated electricity that is available below the utility's own avoided cost. However, studies of the chemical and paper industries, where co-generation is most prevalent, suggest that the absolute price of purchased electricity, rather than the potential revenue from sales of the electricity generated through co-generation, is the primary driving force for this technology (Ross, 1989b).

Largely as a result of PURPA, co-generation capacity has expanded rapidly in the past decade, principally in California and Texas. It is expected that this trend will continue. The California Energy Commission (CEC) and the Northwest Power Planning Council are among the leading regulatory agencies who have analyzed the potential for increased co-generation on a regional basis (Bonneville Power Administration, 1989; California Energy Commission, 1990; Northwest Power Planning Council, 1990). The CEC, for example, estimates that co-generation capacity in California could more than double over the next 10 years (California Energy Commission, 1990). A national estimate of future industrial co-generation potential has been developed by RCG/Hagler, Bailly, Inc. (1991), as shown in Table 22.6. Here, too, a doubling of current industrial capacity from 22 GW to 47 GW is projected in the next decade. This result is roughly consistent with the amount of new co-generation capacity estimated by DOE in 1984 based on the replacement of aging industrial boilers (Department of Energy, 1984).

The CO_2 implication of increased industrial co-generation principally is a reduction in emissions from the combustion of natural gas, which is the

TABLE 22.6   Projected Industrial Co-generation Market Development

	Cumulative Capacity (MW) at Year End		
	1990	2000	2010
By industry			
Food	1,560	6,310	9,400
Pulp and paper	4,940	9,400	12,180
Chemicals	9,240	17,800	22,550
Petroleum refining	3,100	5,175	6,500
Primary metals	1,060	1,660	2,030
All others	2,175	6,840	11,350
TOTAL	22,075	47,185	64,010
By type of system			
Boiler/steam turbines	9,750	19,740	27,460
Gas turbines	2,825	5,960	8,450
Combined cycles	9,500	21,485	28,100

SOURCE: RCG/Hagler, Bailly, Inc. (1991), based on data from the RCG/Hagler, Bailly Independent Power Data Base.

fuel of choice for such installations (which range in size from a few mega-watts to over 100 MW). Co-generation units typically employ either a boiler/steam turbine, combined cycle, or gas turbine to achieve higher over-all energy efficiency in comparison with to the separate generation of steam and electricity (Larsen and Williams, 1985). Where co-generation displaces electricity purchased from a utility, the CO_2 implications depend on the fuel mix that obtains. In many cases, industrial demand is met by peak load electricity also generated by natural gas. For purposes of this study, a rough estimate of the CO_2 reduction potential of co-generation assumes that natural gas used by industry and utilities to generate steam and electricity is instead utilized in co-generation facilities to supply energy demands more efficiently. Based on recent studies of future co-generation potential, an additional 25 GW of industrial capacity is assumed. These savings will be available only as long as the substitution of natural gas for other energy sources is possible. Appendix D summarizes the performance and eco-nomic assumptions employed.

The result is an estimated 45 Mt/yr of CO_2 that could be reduced using current technology at a net cost of roughly –$20 to –$5/t CO_2. This 45 Mt CO_2 reduction amounts to 4 percent of current industrial sector emissions (Edmonds and Ashton, 1989). This figure is similar to an independent estimate by Ross (1990a) of a 5 percent reduction in fuel CO_2 from wider use of co-generation in the next two decades. The net negative cost reflects the same societal perspective used throughout this report, i.e., a 6 percent real discount rate to annualize the investment cost of energy savings (in this case, an estimated \$1000/kW for a co-generation installation saving natural gas). In practice, of course, the economics of co-generation depends strongly on the selling price of electricity, the local tariffs for natural gas, and the actual discount rates of industrial investors. Such factors have been considered in the capacity expansion estimates of California Energy Commission (1990) and others cited earlier in this report.

Other Conservation Measures

A wide variety of other energy-saving measures have been identified in industry-specific studies that focus on the details of industrial processing. Such measures range from improved waste heat recovery at chemical plants to soaking pit enhancements in steel mills to boiler efficiency improvements in the food processing industry, and so on. As noted earlier, however, a major limitation of most studies is the absence of information on the costs of energy savings. Current analyses by DOE, for example, rely heavily on regression models of energy use versus fuel price, plus independent judgments of "autonomous" energy efficiency improvements in forecasting future industrial energy demands and their environmental implications (e.g., AES Corporation, 1990; Energy Information Administration, 1990). At the present time, the limited amount of engineering costs data compared with that available for the residential and transportation sectors precludes a rigorous analysis of the cost-effectiveness of CO_2 mitigation measures for the industrial sector.

For purposes of the present study, rough estimates of the magnitude and cost of additional fuel conservation measures have been derived from a few published studies of specific industrial plants. For example, Figure 22.9 shows cost versus energy reduction curves for a petroleum refinery and an integrated steel mill (Ross, 1987; Larsen, 1990). Overall energy savings of up to nearly 30 percent are represented. To the extent these results are generally applicable to the industrial sector, CO_2 reductions of up to about 350 Mt/yr may be achievable at little or no net cost using the societal discount rates assumed in this report (see Appendix D for details of this estimate).

Other recent reports also document the potential for continued energy savings in the industrial sector. For example, Nelson (1989) reports the results of an energy conservation contest held at one division of the Dow Chemical Company since 1982. To date, over 500 different projects have been identified and undertaken. As shown in Table 22.7, the average return on investment of the winning projects was nearly 200 percent, correspond-

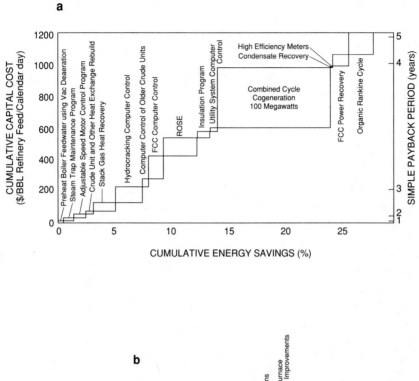

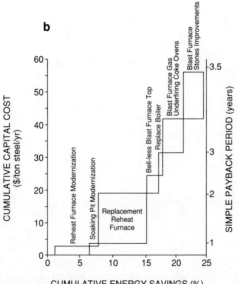

FIGURE 22.9   Energy conservation supply curves for (a) a petroleum refinery and (b) an integrated steel mill.

SOURCE: (a) Larsen (1990); (b) Ross (1987).

TABLE 22.7 Summary of Energy Conservation Projects of Less Than $2 Million Each in the Annual Dow Chemical Company Louisiana Division Contest

Item	1982	1983	1984	1985	1986	1987	1988	1989	1990
Number of winning projects	27	32	38	59	60	90	94[a]	69[a]	133[a]
Capital and expenses, $M	1,708	2,197	4,038	7,120	7,113	10,619	9,329	7,486	13,130
Savings, $M/yr									
Fuel gas[b]	1,783	4,590	4,635	5,557	6,832	7,110	4,965	3,519	5,114
Yield	83	-63	1,506	2,498	798	2,550	10,790	18,460	8,656
Capacity						1,197	2,578	13,275	
Maintenance	10	45	-59	187	357	2,206	583	1,121	1,675
Miscellaneous						19	-98	154	2,130
TOTAL return on investment,	1,876	4,572	6,082	8,242	7,987	13,082	18,818	36,529	17,575
percent	99	197	139	105	102	112	191	477	122

[a]Includes some waste reduction projects with a return on investment of greater than 30 percent.
[b]Dollar savings and returns on investment are calculated using fuel gas valued at $2.25/MBtu.

SOURCE: Nelson (1989) and personal communication from K. Nelson to E. Rubin, 1991.

ing to payback periods of much less than a year. (The minimum return on investment established by Dow was 30 percent.) While the total fraction of energy saved from these projects is proprietary information, it is nonetheless reported to be considerable (K. Nelson, Louisiana Division, Dow Chemical USA, Plaquemine, Louisiana, personal communication to E. Rubin, Carnegie-Mellon University, Pittsburgh, Pennsylvania, January 1991). More importantly, data for very recent years show that energy savings continue to be available at attractive rates of return. Anecdotal information, however, suggests that the type of contest run by Dow at this division is not widespread within the industry. More aggressive attention to energy-saving measures in the industrial sector undoubtedly could yield national energy and CO_2 reductions at costs competitive with other investment opportunities.

Changes in Process Design

To the extent that new industrial process technology continues to reduce the energy intensity of manufacturing, CO_2 emissions will decline. As seen earlier, this method of energy reduction appears to be one of the most significant long-term mechanisms for reducing energy use and consequent emissions. Two types of measures are discussed here: recycling and fundamental process changes.

The principal opportunities for reducing energy use and CO_2 emissions through increased recycling lie in the primary metals, pulp and paper, organic chemicals, and petroleum refining industries (Ross, 1990a). Recycled materials substitute for raw materials whose processing and refining typically are the most energy-intensive phases of manufacturing. Thus significant energy savings can be achieved when the demand for raw materials is reduced. Because of impurities typically associated with recycled material, some process modifications or preprocessing steps often are necessary to utilize recycled materials. In some cases, impurities preclude a material's being reused for its original purpose (e.g., printers ink in recycled newspaper). Thus other applications of recycled material may be sought (e.g., wastepaper for insulation materials rather than newsprint). Major limitations to increased recycling at the present time include the creation of markets for postconsumer recycled material in the manufacture of higher-quality products than heretofore and the reliable and clean collection of a high fraction of selected postconsumer materials (Ross, 1989b).

More fundamental changes in process technology hold theoretically large potential for energy intensity reductions (Ross, 1987) but need to be quantified through more detailed industry-specific studies, including costs. Although the energy savings actually achievable through process innovations cannot be quantified readily, a number of potentially attractive opportuni-

TABLE 22.8 Estimates of Energy Efficiency Potential
by Industry, 1990 through 2020

Industry	Average Energy Intensity Reduction, percent/yr
Steel	1.0
Aluminum	0.5
Chemicals	1.5
Pulp and paper	2.2
Glass	1.0
Fabrication and assembly	1.5
Petroleum	0.5

SOURCE: National Research Council (1990).

ties have been identified in industry-specific studies (e.g., Oak Ridge National Laboratory, 1989; Decision Analysis Corporation, 1990). Historical trends, however, indicate that the time scales for introducing new technology are relatively long (i.e., on the order of a decade or more). The role of research and development in accelerating the pace of process innovation is discussed in the section "Research and Development Needs" below. In the long run, it is clear that technology innovation holds the key for sustainable and significant reductions in greenhouse gas emissions from the industrial sector. Table 22.8 summarizes one set of judgments on energy-efficiency potential from experts in several major industries (National Research Council, 1990). A sustained improvement of 1.5 percent per year in energy efficiency through new process technology would yield a 25 percent decrease in overall industrial energy demand shortly after the turn of the century. The corresponding CO_2 reduction would be on the order of 300 Mt/yr, based on current energy use.

Macroeconomic Structural Changes

The measures discussed above reduce greenhouse gas emissions by lowering the energy requirements of a particular industrial process. In turn, the mix of processes and industries that constitutes the overall industrial sector determines the total magnitude of greenhouse gas emissions at the national level. Three mechanisms contribute to structural changes. One is materials substitution, which alters the demand for various industrial products (e.g., the substitution of plastics for metals in automobiles or the use of ceramics in engines). Changing demands for industrial products contribute in part to the historical sector shifts shown earlier for the United States. The impact of materials substitution on greenhouse gas emissions is complex and remains largely unstudied. Policy measures such as increased emphasis on recycling could induce further changes in materials substitution patterns.

Another structural factor has been a shift in activity away from primary manufacturing of materials such as steel and aluminum toward downstream processes such as fabrication and assembly (Ross, 1989b). In terms of greenhouse gas emissions, this trend implies a reduction in CO_2 emissions as a result of a shift toward less-energy-intensive processes. To some extent, however, such emission reductions may be offset by increased manufacturing and processing of raw materials in other parts of the world.

BARRIERS TO IMPLEMENTATION

The most significant barriers to achieving more rapid reductions in energy intensity and CO_2 emissions in the industrial sector are (1) the relatively short payback period demanded by industrial decision makers for investments in energy conservation technology and (2) the relatively long time required to replace existing capital equipment with newer processes that are more energy efficient. Because the most energy-intensive manufacturing processes are also extremely capital-intensive (e.g., chemicals, primary metals, and paper), the rate of capital turnover is typically measured in decades. Policy measures that can hasten the rate of capital turnover and the introduction of more-energy-efficient process technology can therefore speed the long-term trend in energy efficiency improvements indicated earlier. Related to this, regulatory requirements for process operating permits (i.e., as required by air and water pollution control agencies) may pose an additional barrier to the introduction of new technology. Changes in permitting procedures to minimize the "hassle" and delays in bringing new or modified processes on-line may significantly affect industrial willingness to implement process improvements.

Similarly, measures that directly or indirectly affect the payback period or discount rate used to evaluate investments in energy conservation can also influence the pace of CO_2 emission reductions. Relative to other industrial nations, investment in energy conservation measures by the U.S. industrial sector is still low. Although this difference is due at least in part to lower real energy prices, the emphasis on short-term profitability that characterizes much of the U.S. industrial sector also plays a fundamental role.

The total level of production also significantly influences the industrial sector's contribution to greenhouse gas emissions. To some extent, sectoral shifts and the total demand for products can be influenced by government policies either directly or through indirect effects on international competitiveness and the overall costs of doing business. While it is beyond the scope of this study to assess the complex interactions between market forces and public policy initiatives, their existence certainly must be recognized in considering policy measures that affect U.S. industry.

POLICY OPTIONS

A number of policy measures that can accelerate the reduction in CO_2 emissions from the industrial sector are summarized in Table 22.9. These measures include various forms of regulation, fiscal incentives, and information programs (U.S. Department of Energy, 1989b). In considering these options, it must be recognized that manufacturing processes tend to vary significantly both within and across industries and are typically proprietary in some or all of their designs. Thus direct government regulation of industrial energy use would be much less effective than price as a means of inducing energy efficiency and other measures that reduce CO_2 emissions. Policy instruments likely to be most useful in managing CO_2 emissions in industry thus include fuel taxes, regulatory changes to encourage co-generation and other conservation measures, and tax credits or other incentives to induce investments in research, recycling, and new process technology that uses energy more efficiently.

Fuel Taxes

Fiscal measures such as a fossil fuel use tax or a carbon tax can provide a flexible and general incentive for reducing fossil fuel consumption and encourage wider use of lower-emission fuels. However, fuel taxes do not directly address the high discount rates implicit in industrial decision-making and could also cause serious dislocations in international trade unless similar taxes are adopted by other countries. Tradeable emission permits, analogous to current Clean Air Act allowances for SO_2 emissions, could offer similar CO_2 reduction benefits, although implementation and allocation procedures could prove much more cumbersome than for SO_2. Fuel use fees or a carbon tax are preferred over direct regulation of energy use because industries differ greatly in their energy needs (U.S. Department of Energy, 1989b).

A related concept that has been proposed is to incorporate externality costs into the prices of fuel and/or raw materials. Such externalities might include the environmental damages from mining through end use. For example, any increase in virgin materials price due to externality costs would increase the attractiveness of recycled materials. The effect on net energy consumption would depend on the magnitude of the price changes. However, actual implementation of this policy measure could be very difficult. Not only would externality costs be very difficult to determine, but the adoption of different policies in different countries could lead to widespread disruption in international trade absent any new and enforceable international accords imposing similar externality costs.

Efficiency Incentives

As noted earlier, the Public Utility Regulatory Policies Act (PURPA) encourages the development of electricity co-generation, i.e., the combined production of electricity and process heat. For many manufacturing processes, co-generation saves fuel and produces excess electricity that can be sold to a utility. Although some industries (e.g., petroleum refining and petrochemicals) have taken advantage of these savings, others (e.g., cement) have not. Industries that do not use co-generation could be encouraged to do so through regulatory incentives, although more information is needed to first determine why existing incentives are insufficient (U.S. Department of Energy, 1989b).

Significant potential also exists for electric utility companies to provide energy services to industry, much like the residential and commercial sector opportunities that are now receiving attention in some parts of the country (see Chapter 21). Such programs effectively lower the applicable discount rate for investments in new equipment. As discussed in Chapter 21, pioneer programs in California and Massachusetts are now providing financial incentives to electric utilities to invest in end-use technologies that are more cost-effective than building new plant capacity. Extension of such programs to other states, and to the industrial sector, could be accomplished through regulatory changes at the state level. Model programs and legislation could help guide the introduction of such changes. Indeed, cooperative efforts between utilities and industrial firms may constitute one of the most promising policies for achieving more rapid energy and CO_2 reductions in the industrial sector. In principle, such arrangements could be extended to other utilities, such as regulated gas companies, where fuel savings opportunities could be targeted.

Investment Tax Credits

Another method of reducing energy consumption is to change the corporate tax code to encourage quicker capital turnover and investment in more fuel-efficient production processes. This policy would encourage the many industries with old capital equipment and low rates of capital turnover (e.g.,

TABLE 22.9 Policies for the Manufacturing Sector

Policy/Activity	Fossil Fuel Combustion for Process Heat	Electricity Use for Process Heat or Electrolysis	Electricity Use for Motors and Motive Force	Disposing of Greenhouse Gas By-products
REGULATION				
Controls	Provide federal incentives (e.g., contingent state aid) and model legislation for states and municipalities to implement recycling of fossil-fuel-intensive materials	Provide incentives and model legislation for state public utility commissions to encourage utilities to invest in cost-effective end-use technologies similar to programs for the residential and commercial sectors now emerging in some states[a]		
Standards	Require bio-offsets for industrial fossil fuel combustion to promote switching away from fossil fuel and to compensate for fossil fuel combustion		Exempt co-generation fuels and remarketed electricity from any special fees or restrictions placed on fossil fuel combustion elsewhere	
Licensing and Certification				

FISCAL INCENTIVES
Prices

Fossil fuel use fee, tradeable fossil fuel use rights, or a carbon deposit-refund scheme to encourage energy conservation through process redesign, improved energy management, and combustion efficiency	Promote electricity conservation in process heat applications Consider fossil fuel use fee, tradable fossil fuel use rights or deposit-refund to promote switch from fossil-fuel-based electricity	Encourage process changes in industries that release CO_2, provide financial incentives for industrial investments that limit CO_2 release through emission fees, tax credits, or subsidies
Impose a fossil fuel use fee or tradeable co-use permits on all industry to promote switching away from coal to fuels with lower emissions	Promote more efficient use of electricity by motors	
Encourage recovery and recycling of fossil-fuel-intensive manufactured materials to reduce energy use, consider deposit-refund systems on all glass and aluminum beverage containers, automobiles, and major appliances		
Provide fiscal incentives to induce substitution from some fossil-fuel-intensive manufactured goods		

(Table 22.9 continues)

TABLE 22.9 *(continued)*

Policy/Activity	Fossil Fuel Combustion for Process Heat	Electricity Use for Process Heat or Electrolysis	Electricity Use for Motors and Motive Force	Disposing of Greenhouse Gas By-products
FISCAL INCENTIVES— *continued*				
Taxation	Alter the corporate tax code to provide incentives for investment in fossil-fuel-efficient production processes and to speed capital turnover in heavy industry		Encourage self and co-generation by manufacturers, provide corporate income tax credits to encourage the necessary capital investment for co-generation	Offer tax credits to firms investing in technology to control noncombustion (by-product) CO_2
Subsidies	Support investment in scrap processing equipment			
Direct Expenditures				
INFORMATION/ ADVERTISING				
Advertising			Engage in marketing-oriented advertising programs to help commercialize new electric drive technology and substitute processes, add necessary positive financial inducements	

276

Education	Conduct or support informational workshops or energy audits to describe practical waste heat recovery methods and improved energy management, specific to individual industries	
Moral Suasion		Explore foreign trade initiatives that minimize competitive disadvantage to U.S. industries from greenhouse gas prevention regulations, fees, and restrictions
RESEARCH, DEVELOPMENT, AND DEMONSTRATION		
Public invention support programs	Promote industrial research and development on basic manufacturing processes that conserve energy	Encourage research and development on CO_2 capture from noncombustion processes in the cement and aluminum industries

277

(Table 22.9 continues)

TABLE 22.9 (*continued*)

Policy/Activity	Fossil Fuel Combustion for Process Heat	Electricity Use for Process Heat or Electrolysis	Electricity Use for Motors and Motive Force	Disposing of Greenhouse Gas By-products
RESEARCH, DEVELOPMENT, AND DEMONSTRATION— *continued*				
Commercialization Education				Encourage research and development to develop biotechnology for calcium carbonate production
Provision of specialized information				
Demonstrations				

*a*This option was added by the current study and did not appear in the original source.

SOURCE: Department of Energy (1989b).

278

steel and paper) to invest in more efficient processes. Past experience shows that encouraging investment through the tax code can have a large and rapid effect on industry investment, although there is some disagreement over the benefits of the 1981 corporate tax revisions (Hall and Jorgenson, 1967; Bosworth, 1985; Summers, 1985). While it appears that some past efforts to encourage energy conservation through federal tax credits for specific qualifying equipment did not succeed in significantly influencing investment behavior (Alliance to Save Energy, 1983), larger tax credits and more broadly defined qualifying criteria likely would get a strong response. An investment tax credit also provides certainty of a payback when firms are risk averse due to uncertainty about future energy prices, as well as a justification for investment when financial market imperfections restrict the availability of funds (U.S. Department of Energy, 1989b). The windfall implications of investment tax credits, however, also must be considered in evaluating this option.

RESEARCH AND DEVELOPMENT NEEDS

Increased research and development holds the potential to accelerate the application of new process technologies that reduce industrial energy requirements, with a corresponding reduction in CO_2 emissions. A number of recent studies (e.g., Oak Ridge National Laboratory, 1989; Decision Analysis Corporation, 1990) have identified research and development opportunities for specific industries (e.g., chemicals, petroleum refining, steelmaking, cement, and paper), as well as general technological developments that would provide benefits across the industrial sector (e.g., improved waste heat recovery). Table 22.10 summarizes the results of one comprehensive study that evaluated some promising research and development options for reducing energy consumption (Oak Ridge National Laboratory, 1989) and also attempted to estimate some of the ancillary benefits of research and development in addition to energy-saving potential (e.g., economic competitiveness, secondary environmental impacts, energy security, social feasibility, and technology transfer to developing countries). In general, these ancillary benefits are positive.

CONCLUSIONS

The major conclusions that emerge with regard to CO_2 mitigation measures for the industrial sector are the following:

• The industrial sector typically imposes the greatest demand for primary energy, making it (in most cases) the largest contributor to greenhouse gas emissions associated with the use of energy. For developing countries,

TABLE 22.10 Evaluation of Promising Research and Development
Options for Energy End Use

	Energy Significance	
Technological Opportunities	Near Term[a]	Long Term[b]
INDUSTRIAL GROUPS		
Chemicals	H	H
Catalyst	M	M
Electroprocessing	L	L
Separations		
Membrane	M	M
Supercritical fluid extraction	L	L
Continuous freeze concentration	M	M
Heat flow optimization	M	M
Combustion heater optimization	M	M
Sensors and computer control	M	M
Refining	L	L
New hydrocarbon conversion	L	L
Waste heat recovery	L	L
Separations	L	L
Improved catalysts	L	L
Sensors	L	L
Energy management systems	L	L
Aluminum	L	L
Carbothermic reduction of ore	L	L
Carbothermic reduction of alumina	L	L
Aluminum sulfide electrolysis	L	L
Alcoa process	L	L
Permanent anode	L	L
Wetted cathode	L	L
Steel	M	L
Scrap benefication	L	L
Advanced ironmaking processes	M	L
Advanced ore to steel processes	L	L
Advanced scrap to steel processes	M	L
Advanced casting	M	L
Sensors and controls	L	L
Advanced refractories	M	L

TABLE 22.10 *(continued)*

	Energy Significance	
Technological Opportunities	Near Term[a]	Long Term[b]
Paper	M	M
Chemical pulping	M	L
Paper/fiber recycle	L	L
Mechanical pulping	L	L
Papermaking	M	L
Advanced pulping technologies	M	L
Agriculture	M	M
Increased fertilizer productivity	L	L
Improved tillage	L	L
Improved irrigation	L	L
Animal biotechnology	L	L
Plant biotechnology	L	L
TECHNOLOGICAL AREAS		
Reject Heat Recovery	H	M
Industrial Combustion	H	H
Fuel flexible furnaces	H	L
Atmospheric fluidized-bed combustion	H	H
Pressurized fluidized-bed combustion	L	H
Circulating fluidized-bed combustion	M	M
Hot gas cleanup	L	H
Flue gas desulfurization	H	H
Recycle of wastes	M	M

[a]Does this technology have the potential for making a major near-term (by the year 2000) contribution to our energy system (if the economics prove reasonable)?

   H = 1 quad/yr equivalent
   M = at least 0.2 quad/yr
   L = less than 0.2 quad/yr

[b]Does this technology have the potential for making a major longer-term (by 2040) contribution?

   H = 4 quads/yr equivalent
   M = 1 quad/yr
   L = less than 1 quad/yr

SOURCE: Oak Ridge National Laboratory (1989).

the industrial sector accounts for up to 60 percent of the primary energy demand, compared to about 40 percent for developed countries.

• In the United States the energy intensity of the industrial sector (i.e., the amount of energy per unit of production) has been declining steadily over the past three decades. Analyses of the manufacturing sector suggest that improvements in energy efficiency account for most (on the order of two-thirds) of the changes observed to date. The remainder are due to structural shifts that have resulted in less demand for energy-intensive products such as steel, aluminum, and paper. This trend in energy intensity reduction is expected to continue, exerting downward pressure on CO_2 emission growth.

• A major factor in the long-term improvement in energy efficiency has been innovations in process technology that appear to be independent of changes in energy prices. Although the cost of energy is certainly a factor in decisions regarding fuel choice and energy consumption levels, other factors related to industrial productivity generally dominate energy considerations.

• While the potential for further energy savings in the industrial sector has been widely studied, there is relatively little information on the costs of energy reduction measures. Further study of costs is needed to analyze more rigorously the relationships between industrial energy use and greenhouse gas mitigation measures.

• Estimates of the energy savings from energy conservation investments that reduce the use of electricity for manufacturing (via more efficient motors, drives, process technology, and so on) indicate that savings up to about 25 to 30 percent are achievable with current technology. The reduction in CO_2 emissions for these savings would be roughly 140 Mt/yr. However, electricity prices would have to increase by a factor of 2 to 3 at the implicit rates of return now prevalent in the industrial sector (i.e., payback periods of 3 years or less). On the other hand, for lower rates of return, typical of public sector and utility investments, significant energy savings appear achievable at a net negative cost based on current electricity prices.

• Expanded use of co-generation and other existing measures to improve fuel use efficiency at industrial plants was estimated to achieve an overall energy savings of roughly 30 to 35 percent, producing a reduction in CO_2 emissions of nearly 400 Mt/yr. As with the estimated electricity savings, the implicit rates of return required to achieve these savings would have to be substantially lower than those now prevalent in the industrial sector. However, for a social discount rate of 6 percent, substantial CO_2 reductions appear achievable at a net negative cost.

• Given the long-term trend in energy efficiency improvements through process technology innovation, policies that stimulate research and development, and encourage more rapid capital turnover, may offer some of the best long-term strategies for mitigating CO_2 emissions from the industrial sector.

• Government policy measures or incentives that effectively lower the rate of return (increase the project payback period) could accelerate investments in energy conservation. State-level incentives by public utility commissions to encourage utilities to invest in cost-effective measures at industrial facilities, similar to programs now emerging for the residential and commercial customers, may constitute one of the most promising means of addressing the industrial sector.

NOTES

1. 1 quad = 1 quadrillion (10^{15}) British thermal units (Btu).
2. Values are in exajoules (EJ); 1 EJ = 10^{18} J = 1/1.054 quad = 85 bkWh of electricity.
3. Throughout this report, tons (t) are metric; 1 Mt = 1 megaton = 1 million tons; and 1 Gt = 1 gigaton = 1 billion tons.

REFERENCES

AES Corporation. 1990. An Overview of the Fossil2 Model. Prepared for the U.S. Department of Energy. Arlington, Va.: AES Corporation, July 1990.

Alliance to Save Energy. 1983. Industrial Investment in Energy Efficiency: Opportunities, Management Practices, and Tax Incentives. Washington, D.C.: Alliance to Save Energy.

Ayres, R. U. 1990. Energy conservation in the industrial sector. In Energy and the Environment in the 21st Century. Cambridge, Mass.: MIT Press.

Barakat and Chamberlin, Inc. 1990. Efficient Electricity Use: Estimates of Maximum Energy Savings. Report No. EPRI CU-6746. Palo Alto, Calif.: Electric Power Research Institute.

Bonneville Power Administration. 1989. Assessment of Commercial and Industrial Cogeneration Potential in the Pacific Northwest, prepared by Tech Plan Associates, Inc., for Bonneville Power Administration, Portland, Oreg., March 1989.

Bosworth, B. 1985. Taxes and the investment recovery. Pp. 1-45 in Brookings Papers in Economic Activity. Washington, D.C.: The Brookings Institution.

Boyd, G., J. F. McDonald, M. Ross, and D. A. Hanson. 1987. Separating the changing composition of U.S. manufacturing production from energy efficiency improvements: A divisia index approach. The Energy Journal 8(2):77-96.

California Energy Commission. 1990. Staff Testimony on qualifying Facilities/Self-Generation Forecast. Docket No. 88-ER-8. Sacramento, Calif.: California Energy Commission.

Decision Analysis Corporation. 1990. Energy Consumption Patterns in the Manufacturing Sector. Report on Subtask 7B prepared for U.S. Department of Energy, Washington, D.C. Vienna, Va.: Decision Analysis Corporation.

Edmonds, J., and W. Ashton. 1989. A Preliminary Analysis of U.S. CO_2 Emissions Reduction Potential from Energy Conservation and the Substitution of Natural

Gas for Coal in the Period to 2010. Report DOE/NBB-0085. Washington, D.C.: Office of Energy Research, U.S. Department of Energy.

Electric Power Research Institute. 1990. New push for energy efficiency. EPRI Journal 15(3):4-17.

Energy Information Administration. 1990. PC-AEO Forecasting Model for the Annual Energy Outlook. Model Documentation. Report DOE/EIA-M036(90). Washington, D.C.: Energy Information Administration, U.S. Department of Energy.

Hall, R. E., and D. W. Jorgenson. 1967. Tax policy and investment behavior. American Economic Review 57:391-414.

International Energy Agency. 1989. Improving the Efficiency of Electricity End-Use. Paris: International Energy Agency, Organization for Economic Cooperation and Development.

Lashof, D. A., and D. A. Tirpak, eds. 1991. Policy Options for Stabilizing Global Climate. Washington, D.C.: U.S. Environmental Protection Agency.

Larsen, E. D., and R. H. Williams. 1985. A Primer on the Thermodynamics and Economics of Steam-Injected Gas Turbine Cogeneration. Report PU/CEES 192. Princeton, N.J.: Princeton University.

Larsen, W. G. 1990. Energy Conservation in Petroleum Refining. Ph.D. dissertation. University of Michigan, Ann Arbor.

National Research Council. 1990. Confronting Climate Change: Strategies for Energy Research and Development. Washington, D.C.: National Academy Press.

Nelson, K. C. 1989. Are there any energy savings left? Chemical Processing (January).

Northwest Power Planning Council. 1990. Draft 1991 Northwest Conservation and Electric Power Plan, Volume II. Portland, Oreg.: Northwest Power Planning Council.

Oak Ridge National Laboratory. 1989. Energy Technology R&D: What Could Make a Difference? Report ORNL-6541/V2/P1. Oak Ridge, Tenn.: Oak Ridge National Laboratory.

RCG/Hagler, Bailly, Inc. 1991. Industrial Cogeneration Markets. RCG/Hagler, Bailly, Inc., Washington, D.C. January 29. Memorandum to E. Rubin, Carnegie-Mellon University.

Ross, M. 1987. Industrial energy conservation and the steel industry of the United States. Energy 12(10/11):1135-1152.

Ross, M. 1989a. Improving the efficiency of electricity use in manufacturing. Science 244:311-317.

Ross, M. 1989b. Energy and transportation in the United States. Annual Review of Energy 14:131-171.

Ross, M. 1990a. Modeling the energy intensity and carbon dioxide emissions in U.S. manufacturing. In Energy and the Environment in the 21st Century: Proceedings of a Conference at Massachusetts Institute of Technology. Cambridge, Mass.: MIT Press.

Ross, M. 1990b. Conservation supply curves for manufacturing. In Proceedings of the 25th Intersociety Energy Conversion Engineering Conference. New York: American Institute of Chemical Engineers.

Schipper, L., R. B. Howard, and H. Geller. 1990. United States energy use from

1973 to 1975: The impacts of improved efficiency. Annual Review of Energy 15:455-504.

Summers, L. H. 1985. Comments and discussion. Brookings Papers on Economic Activity 1:42-44.

U.S. Department of Energy. 1984. Industrial Cogeneration Potential (1980-2000) for Application of Four Commercially Available Prime Movers at the Plant Site. Report DOE/CS/40403-1. Washington, D.C.: U.S. Department of Energy.

U.S. Department of Energy. 1988. Manufacturing Energy Consumption Survey: Fuel Switching 1985. Report DOE/EIA-0515(85). Washington, D.C.: U.S. Department of Energy.

U.S. Department of Energy. 1989a. Energy Conservation Trends, Understanding the Factors That Affect Conservation Gains in the U.S. Economy. Report DOE/PPPE-0092. Washington, D.C.: U.S. Department of Energy.

U.S. Department of Energy. 1989b. A Compendium of Options for Government Policy to Encourage Private Sector Responses to Potential Climate Change. Report DOE/EH-0103. Washington, D.C.: U.S. Department of Energy.

U.S. Department of Energy. 1990. Manufacturing Energy Consumption Survey: Changes in Energy Efficiency 1980-1985. Report DOE/EIA/0516(85). Washington, D.C.: U.S. Department of Energy.

Williams, R. H., E. D. Larsen, and M. H. Ross. 1987. Materials, affluence, and industrial energy use. Annual Review of Energy 12:99-144.

23

Transportation Energy Management

The transportation sector accounts for 28 percent of the fossil fuel and 63 percent of the petroleum consumed in the United States, resulting in the emission of a number of greenhouse gases, including 30 percent of U.S. CO_2 emissions (International Energy Agency, 1984; European Economic Community, 1988; Lyman, 1990). Petroleum-fueled personal passenger vehicles (both automobiles and light trucks) account for 58 percent of all transportation energy use (Ross, 1989) and thus the majority of transportation-related CO_2 emissions.

In reviewing methods of reducing greenhouse gas emissions from the transportation sector, the panel focused on three areas: vehicle efficiency, alternative transportation fuels, and transportation system management.

In the short run, transportation energy consumption can change rapidly as consumers adjust their demands concerning when and how to travel. On a slightly longer time scale, higher vehicle and fuel prices, along with shifts in vehicle and transportation demand, will lead to changes in the types of vehicles in use. On a significantly longer time scale, investments can be made in alternative transportation fuels, construction of new mass transit facilities and high-occupancy-vehicle (HOV) lanes, land use planning and jobs/housing balance, research and development, and tooling for technological improvements.

VEHICLE EFFICIENCY

The oil embargoes of the 1970s heightened concern for the efficient use of energy in the transportation sector. In the 1980s, however, declining oil costs led to reduced vehicle operating costs, and the concern for energy efficiency diminished. More recently, oil prices have begun to rise again, and that, combined with a growing concern about greenhouse warming and the role of CO_2 as a greenhouse gas, has once again focused attention on the efficient use of transportation fuel. Vehicle efficiency involves technological improvements in fuel economy—improving the miles per gallon of vehicles. The more efficient a vehicle is, the less fuel it burns to travel a given distance. The less fuel it burns, the lower are the amounts of CO_2 emitted. These methods of emission reduction and their cost-effectiveness are evaluated in the following sections for light-duty vehicles, heavy-duty trucks, and domestic air carriers. The emphasis is on light-duty vehicles because they represent the largest and most thoroughly studied sector. Table 23.1 shows the amount of fuel used by each type of vehicle for different modes of operation. The information presented here indicates that light-duty vehicles consume the largest quantity of transportation fuel, with heavy-duty trucks second and aircraft third.

Recent Trends

The recent trend in fuel economy from 1975 to 1989 for the new U.S. passenger car fleet is presented in Figure 23.1a (Amann, 1989). Figure 23.1b shows the fuel economy index (FEI) for the period from 1930 to 1990. The FEI is an index of powertrain efficiency including weight and performance. Studies by Leone and Parkinson (1990) and by Greene (1989) indicate that the trend in the period from 1975 to 1982 was a response to increased fuel prices and fuel economy regulations. As discussed below in the "Barriers to Implementation" section, there is some disagreement on the relative impact of fuel prices and regulations on the supply of fuel-efficient vehicles. The vehicles manufactured during that period were, on the average, 450 kg (1000 pounds) lighter within each market segment, were degraded in performance and other attributes, and incorporated various fuel-efficient technologies. Figure 23.2 indicates how consumer preferences for vehicles changed from 1972 to 1986. As shown, some consumers accepted the smaller vehicles offered to improve energy efficiency, while others resisted the change in performance and either did not buy cars or shifted to light-duty trucks and vans.

Because market conditions and fuel prices cause consumer preferences for fuel-efficient vehicles to change over time, one should distinguish between the trends in overall vehicle fuel economy and powertrain efficiency. Therefore it is important to look not only at miles per gallon but also at the FEI. The FEI is used to control for other vehicle changes, as shown in Figure 23.1b for the period from 1930 to 1990. This parameter, used to judge passenger cars for many decades, provides a better indicator of powertrain efficiency than does fuel economy alone by controlling for both weight and performance.

TABLE 23.1 Transportation Energy Use by Mode, 1987

	Energy Use (trillion Btu)	Thousand Barrels per Day Crude Oil Equivalent[a]	Percentage of Total
Highway[b]	16,213.5	7,658.1	73.6
Automobiles	8,862.9	4,186.2	40.3
Motorcycles	24.6	11.6	0.1
Buses	156.8	74.1	0.7
Transit	74.3	35.1	0.3
Intercity	21.6	10.2	—[c]
School	60.9	28.8	0.3
Trucks	7,169.2	3,386.2	32.6
Light trucks[d]	4,031.9	1,904.4	18.3
Other trucks	3,137.3	1,481.8	14.2
Off-Highway[b] (heavy duty)[e]	665.2	314.2	3.0
Construction	209.9	99.1	1.0
Farming	455.3	215.1	2.1
Nonhighway[b]	4,490.6	2,121.0	20.4
Air	1,893.9	894.5	8.6
General aviation[f]	139.1	65.7	0.6
Domestic air carriers	1,564.2	738.8	7.1
International air carriers	190.6[g]	90.0	0.9
Water	1,326.0	626.3	6.0
Freight	1,095.7	517.5	5.0
Domestic trade	370.7	175.1	1.7
Foreign trade	725.0	342.4	3.3
Recreational boats	230.3	108.8	1.0
Pipeline	775.0	366.1	3.5
Natural gas	562.9	265.9	2.6
Crude petroleum	91.0	43.0	0.4
Petroleum product	67.4	31.8	0.3
Coal slurry	3.7	1.7	—[c]
Water	50.0	23.6	0.2

(Table 23.1 continues)

An envelope of currently "acceptable trades" in the United States is shown in Figure 23.3 in a schematic calculated by Amann (1989). The envelope represents measured performance and fuel economy data for 50 different models of cars produced in 1985 and 1986, all equipped with automatic transmissions. The y-axis in Figure 23.3 represents FEI, the product of vehicle mass and fuel economy. The weight class averages are from 1979, 1984, and 1989. The weight is defined as the test-weight class and the fuel economy is measured by the Federal Test Procedure, both as

TABLE 23.1   *(continued)*

	Energy Use (trillion Btu)	Thousand Barrels per Day Crude Oil Equivalent[a]	Percentage of Total
Nonhighway—continued			
Rail	495.7	234.1	2.2
Freight[h]	471.9	197.4	1.9
Passenger	77.8	36.7	0.3
Transit	41.0	19.4	0.2
Commuter rail	21.4	10.1	—[c]
Intercity	15.4	7.3	—[c]
Military Operations	647.3	305.7	2.9
TOTAL[i]	22,016.6	10,399.0	100.0

[a]Based on Btu content of a barrel of crude oil.
[b]Civilian consumption only; military consumption shown separately.
[c]Negligible.
[d]Two-axle, four-tire trucks.
[e]1985 data.
[f]All aircraft in the U.S. civil air fleet except those operated under CFR parts 121 and 127 (i.e., air carriers larger than 30 seats or a payload capacity of more than 7500 pounds). General aviation includes air taxies, commuter air carriers, and air travel clubs.
[g]This figure represents an estimate of the energy purchase in the United States for international air carrier consumption.
[h]Includes Class 1, 2, and 3 railroads.
[i]Totals may not include all possible uses of fuels for transportation (e.g., snowmobiles).

SOURCE: Davis et al. (1989).

defined by the Environmental Protection Agency (EPA). The performance index on the *x*-axis is the time (in seconds) required to accelerate from 0 to 60 mph. Though subject to abuse, performance is an attribute desired for freeway merging, highway passing, hill climbing, and towing. The negative slope of this parallelogram quantifies the inherent trade-off between fuel economy and performance for a car of given mass and level of powertrain technology.

Emission Control Methods

The efficiency of transportation vehicles can be increased in a number of ways, including improving the engine and transmission efficiency, reducing

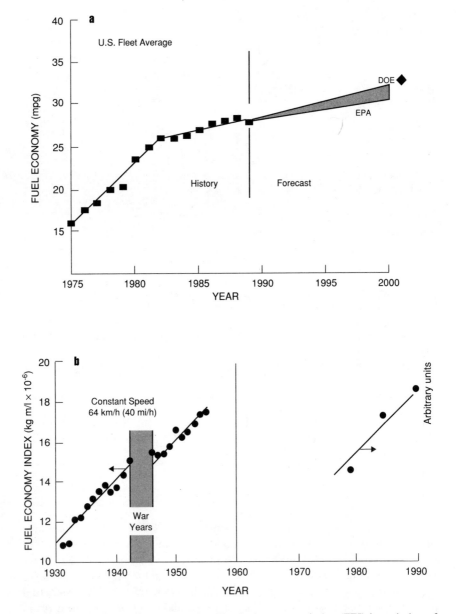

FIGURE 23.1   Fuel economy trends. The fuel economy index (FEI) is an index of powertrain efficiency, the product of vehicle mass and fuel economy.

SOURCE: Data are from Amann (1989).

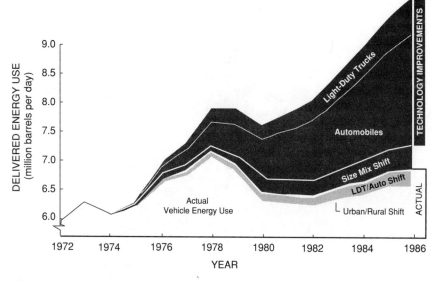

FIGURE 23.2   Components of change in light-duty vehicles.

Source: U.S. Department of Energy (1989).

weight, improving vehicle aerodynamics, and reducing the tire-rolling resistance. Each of these methods and their cost are discussed below.

Technological Improvements in Light-Duty and Heavy-Duty Vehicles

Efforts to improve conventional gasoline engines focus on obtaining the optimal engine operation possible through methods such as improving part-load operations (power required at less than peak efficiency) and combustion characteristics, reducing engine warm-up time, increasing compression ratios, reducing frictional losses, and extending the operating regime of engines (Bleviss, 1988).

Another method of improving vehicle efficiency is to increase transmission efficiency. The focus here is on reducing the losses associated with either automatic or manual transmissions through design changes. Automatic transmissions provide shifting at the optimal moment (unlike manual transmissions, which depend on the driver) so that the vehicle can remain at full load, but they have pumping and frictional losses. Manual transmissions do not have these losses. However, drivers do not generally operate manual transmissions at maximum efficiency by shifting at the optimal moment. A number of methods for increasing transmission efficiency have

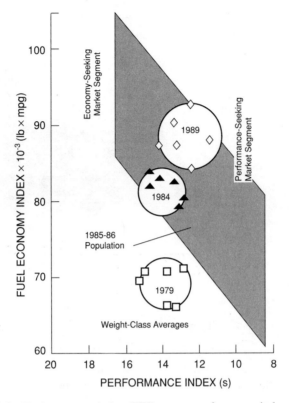

FIGURE 23.3   Fuel economy index (FEI) versus performance index. Envelope of fuel economy and performance measures for a 50-car population of 1985-1986 vehicles with automatic transmissions. Circles contain averages for the six EPA weight classes in 1979. Performance index is defined as the time (in seconds) required to accelerate from 0 to 60 mph. The lower the performance index, the better the performance.

SOURCE: Amann (1989).

been suggested, including designs that include the continuously variable transmission (CVT).

Reducing a vehicle's weight can yield major improvements in fuel economy. By reducing the weight of a vehicle 10 percent, city fuel economy can be improved 7 to 8 percent, and highway fuel economy 4 to 5 percent. The weight of the vehicle is reduced by substituting advanced materials for the steel and cast iron that were used in the past. New materials that can reduce vehicle weight include high-strength low-alloy (HSLA) steel, aluminum, magnesium, and plastics (Bleviss, 1988).

Improving the aerodynamics of a vehicle involves changing the exterior structure through changes in areas such as wheel openings, windshield wiper location, glass location, and underbody. A 10 percent decrease in aerodynamic drag will result in a 5 to 6 percent (highway) and 2 to 3 percent (city) reduction in fuel consumption (Bleviss, 1988).

Another method of improving fuel economy is to reduce tire-rolling resistance. In the 1970s the introduction of radial and P-metric tires improved average fuel economy by 5 to 9 percent relative to the previously used bias-ply tires. Currently, a 10 percent improvement in tire-rolling resistance improves vehicle fuel economy by 3 to 4 percent (Bleviss, 1988).

Additional fuel economy improvements can be made by improving the efficiency of vehicle accessories such as the air conditioner, alternator, power steering, water pump and fan, oil pump, and lights (Bleviss, 1988).

Approximately 20 percent of the fuel expended on the U.S. highway system is utilized by heavy trucks and other heavy-duty vehicles. The opportunities to conserve fuel and minimize emissions parallel those for light-duty vehicles and light-duty trucks.

Technological Improvements in Aircraft

The third most significant component of transportation energy use is that of domestic airlines. The most advanced new jet aircraft are far more efficient than older aircraft still in service. Carlsmith et al. (1990) estimate that on a 1000-mile trip, aircraft produced in the 1960s are capable of between 40 and 50 seat-mpg, while the new Boeing 757 and 767 now in service have a fuel efficiency of 70 seat-mpg. Improvements now being introduced arise from a combination of higher-bypass-ratio engines, increased compressor and turbine efficiencies, and more energy-efficient flight planning and operations. Like highway vehicles, aircraft can also benefit from weight reduction and better aerodynamics. Efficiencies approaching 130 to 150 seat-mpg are estimated for planned vehicles utilizing improved fanjets along with other new technologies. A 20 percent gain for some existing vehicles in the fleet can be achieved via improved fanjet technology alone.

Cost Estimates for Vehicles and Air Carriers

Costs for achieving higher fuel economy for light- and heavy-duty vehicles have been derived from data produced in three studies. Data from the Mellon Institute study (Shackson and Leach, 1980) and from two Department of Energy (DOE) studies (Ledbetter and Ross, 1989; Difiglio et al., 1990) were assembled (see Appendix E) to calculate the three different curves in Figures 23.4 (6 percent discount rate) and 23.5 (30 percent discount rate). These curves show the cost in dollars per gallon relative to the improvement in on-road fuel economy. Values from the average new car

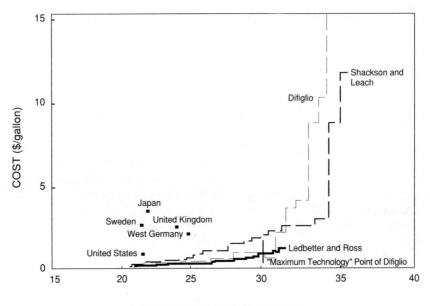

FIGURE 23.4   Cost of gasoline and efficiency (6 percent discount rate).

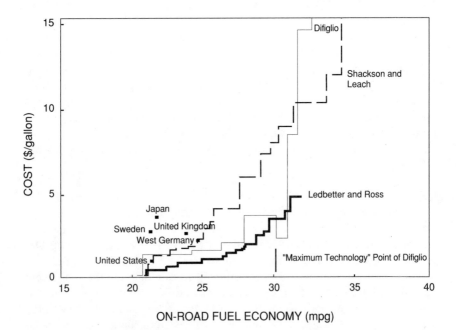

FIGURE 23.5   Cost of gasoline and efficiency (30 percent discount rate).

fleet efficiencies along with the average fuel prices for Japan, Sweden, United Kingdom, United States, and West Germany have been plotted as squares on the same figures. Cost-effectiveness values are highly uncertain and vary significantly from technology to technology. Although some cost-effective technologies create a net savings to the consumer, less efficient technologies generate costs exceeding \$10/t CO_2 equivalent (at 6 percent discount rate) for those not involving life-style adjustments and more than \$700/t CO_2 (at 6 percent discount rate) for those that involve changes in life-style.[1] The costs are much higher when a discount rate of 30 percent is used—the rate of return consumers generally desire for investing in vehicle efficiency. Overall cost estimates depend on a variety of assumptions involving the costs, effectiveness, and interactions of technology combinations as well as consumer preferences and market behavior. Further complications arise from variations in the cost structures of different manufacturers, variations across market segments, cost differences due to exchange rates, and international differences in driving behavior and vehicle use patterns.

The discontinuity in the slope of the Difiglio curve at approximately 31 mpg (on-road fuel economy) is the arbitrary point at which sales shifts in the vehicle mix are required to gain higher average fuel economy levels. Difiglio has labeled this point the "maximum technology" point for the year 2000.[2] In the region beyond this arbitrarily defined point, downsizing of the fleet or development of expensive technology will be required to achieve future efficiency improvements. Efficiency gains beyond this point are achieved by downsizing (which reduces passenger and carrying capacity) and by compromising other attributes such as performance, comfort, and safety.

The average cost-effectiveness values, as distinct from marginal cost-effectiveness values, which increase substantially as one moves past 25 mpg, are summarized in Table 23.2 as a function of discount rate for all three cost curves (see Appendix E). This table shows the net implementation cost and potential emission reduction for light-duty vehicles, heavy-duty trucks, and aircraft. Both the more accurate full-cycle emission accounting and an accounting including only the emissions generated during consumption are shown. Cost and emission reductions for light-duty vehicles are shown for the three analyses available for that sector. The net implementation cost—which subtracts the fuel saved from the implementation cost—is presented for four different interest rates (3, 6, 10, and 30 percent). Beyond the "maximum technology" point, the amount of CO_2 reduction and the corresponding cost-effectiveness values are summarized in Table 23.3, which repeats the analysis in Table 23.2 for improvements that involve life-style adjustment—the "maximum technology" point on the Difiglio supply curve shown in Figures 23.4 and 23.5. The net implementation cost and potential emission reduction are shown in Table 23.3 for light-duty vehicles, both with the more accurate full-cycle emission accounting

TABLE 23.2 Implementation Cost of Vehicle Efficiency Improvements with No Change in Fleet Mix

	Net Implementation Cost ($/t CO$_2$ equivalent)				Emission Reduction (Mt CO$_2$ equivalent/yr)
	$d = 3\%$	$d = 6\%$	$d = 10\%$	$d = 30\%$	
Full-Cycle Emission Accounting					
Light vehicle, Ledbetter and Ross	-52	-50	-46	-2	379
Light vehicle, Shackson and Leach	-10	-1	+10	+191	389
Light vehicle, Difiglio	-26	-22	-13	+128	397
Heavy truck	-42	-38	-32	+45	61
Aircraft retrofit			+230		13
Consumption Emission Accounting					
Light vehicle, Ledbetter and Ross	-81	-78	-71	-3	245
Light vehicle, Shackson and Leach	-16	-2	+16	+296	251
Light vehicle, Difiglio	-40	-34	-20	+198	256
Heavy truck	-65	-59	-50	+70	39
Aircraft retrofit			+357		8

TABLE 23.3 Implementation Cost of Vehicle Efficiency Improvements with Change in Fleet Mix

	Net Implementation Cost ($/t CO$_2$ equivalent)				Emission Reduction (Mt CO$_2$ equivalent/yr)
	$d = 3\%$	$d = 6\%$	$d = 10\%$	$d = 30\%$	
Full-Cycle Emission Accounting					
Light vehicle, Ledbetter and Ross	+13	+25	+41	+293	35
Light vehicle, Shackson and Leach	+306	+356	+427	+1,609	108
Light vehicle, Difiglio	+527	+657	+777	+2,820	129
Consumption Emission Accounting					
Light vehicle, Ledbetter and Ross	+20	+39	+64	+454	23
Light vehicle, Shackson and Leach	+474	+552	+663	+2,494	70
Light vehicle, Difiglio	+887	+1,018	+1,204	+4,370	83

(i.e., the emissions generated from production to consumption of the fuel), and the consumption emission accounting. The full-cycle costs are the most appropriate for determination of the cost of vehicle efficiency. Even so, the costs and emission reductions in the consumption accounting section have to be used for comparison with the other options in this report—which, unfortunately, are not full cycle—because information on the full-cycle emissions is not currently available. As illustrated here, the difference between full-cycle emission accounting and consumption emission accounting is quite large and could make a difference in comparing different emission reduction options. Note also that the CO_2 emissions determined in these analyses are multiplied by 1.55 to obtain CO_2 equivalents and thus account for non-CO_2 greenhouse gas emissions equivalence for both the cost-effectiveness and the emission reduction numbers. Because the technologies save fuel, the cost-effectiveness values were credited with $1.00/gallon for the social discount rates of 3, 6, and 10 percent and $1.25/gallon for the 30 percent discount rate.

The cost estimate for heavy-duty vehicle improvements is more difficult than that for light vehicles because of the meager data base. However, on the basis of this limited information, it is possible to determine some cost data, as summarized in Table 23.2.

Cost calculations for domestic air carriers are also shown in Table 23.2. This estimate is based on retrofitting half of the 4000 transportation vehicles in the fleet with the improvement in fanjet technology mentioned above.

Barriers to Implementation

Until now, the industry has offered each market segment an amount of fuel-saving technology commensurate with the perceived value of fuel savings to the consumer. Of course, as the price of fuel varies, the offerings to the consumer must vary. In principle, the consumer has no preference in a choice between buying a technology and buying fuel when they are perceived as equal. The equality is dependent on the baseline fuel economy, the gain from the technology, the technology price, the fuel price, and discount rates, as well as expectations involving amount of driving, vehicle life, vehicle retention, and future fuel prices. Because of variations in these parameters, many analyses using the same data can differ dramatically. Therefore there is disagreement among social scientists as to the relative impact of fuel prices and mandated fuel economy levels on the supply of fuel-efficient vehicles. For example, comparisons of the results of econometric analyses by Godek (1990), Greene (1989), and Leone and Parkinson (1990) reveal differences on the relative importance of command-and-control mechanisms.

If it is assumed that market mechanisms are effective incentives for introducing new technologies when a sufficient number of competitors are present, a look at the real-world data in Figures 23.4 and 23.5 can guide the discussion. As fuel prices increase, many technologies become cost-effective, and manufacturers supplying these technologies gain a competitive advantage.

As indicated in Figures 23.4 and 23.5, fuel prices in many nations are sufficiently high to justify the introduction of more-efficient technologies. Inappropriate assumptions, however, involving driving habits, vehicle use patterns, scrappage rates, price expectations, industry cost structure, or cost of capital limit the applicability of this information to the United States. It is also possible that inappropriate exchange rates distort these international comparisons.

Although, as shown in Figure 23.4, a number of efficiency measures are cost-effective at a social discount rate of 6 percent, studies indicate that the average consumer often evaluates efficiency investments (as discussed in Chapter 21 and shown in Figure 21.11) at a discount rate of 30 percent. The perspective in Figure 23.5 is that of a consumer expecting a 10-year benefit stream from a 30 percent discount rate on future benefits. If consumers in these five nations had no preference in a choice between purchasing fuel economy technology and purchasing gasoline, they would choose a set of technologies on one of the three curves. If, on the other hand, consumers valued other attributes in their vehicles that are sacrificed by fuel economy technologies, they would choose a level of fuel economy lower (i.e., to the left) of the curves in Figure 23.5.

There are a number of explanations of why the actual data points generally show consumers buying less fuel economy than they might in a perfect market. First, the cost curves assume perfect markets, but the real-world data points may reflect a variety of market imperfections. Second, because Figure 23.5 is based on a consumer's personal discount rate of 30 percent, the Mellon curve may represent the real supply curve; in this case, the figures demonstrate that consumers are using a high discount rate. Third, consumers may value attributes in their vehicles that are degraded as fuel economy increases; in this case, the reason for the disparity is that the value of these lost attributes is not captured by the supply curves. Finally, since government regulation that alters free-market consumer choice can increase consumer costs, the cost curves may be too low because they do not reflect the costs of regulatory measures used by different countries to promote increased fuel economy.

Difiglio et al. (1990) calculate that fuel economy achieved by significant mix shifting has a potential consumer loss equivalent to $24 billion per year—$3500 per car in their scenario, wherein only 8 of the original 40 car lines remain. The simulation model of Kleit (1988) indicates that mix shifting to achieve a 2.5-mpg increase beyond the point at which technologies are cost-effective will impose an average consumer cost of over $800 per car sold. These costs are equivalent to $8.4 billion per year in the United States or $4.61/gallon above the cost of gasoline (Kleit, 1988).

Manufacturers produce vehicles with the attributes that they believe consumers will purchase. Based on past experience and current market conditions, producers apparently do not believe there is a market for a high-attribute, high-fuel-economy vehicle. Although some consumers have expressed a desire for high-attribute vehicles, with gas mileage of 50+ mpg (as is available in small, low-attribute vehicles), this does not currently constitute a market in the eyes of both large- and small-volume producers. Therefore a consumer cannot purchase a high-attribute vehicle with gas mileage at the 50+ mpg range. Until these producers believe that a market for such a vehicle is available, they are unlikely to produce one—especially as it would involve a potentially risky investment in light of their available information.

The information provided here has been designed to emphasize the importance of both fuel economy and other consumer-driven attributes at reasonable cost in all sectors of the automotive market. As Atkinson and Halvorsen (1984, 1990) have made clear, consumers recognize the trade-offs between these and other attributes in exercising their choices in the market. It is also clear that some levels of fuel economy require technologies that are not cost-effective when compared to other societal options (Bleviss, 1988). Furthermore, with regard to specific technologies, there are significant differences between the efficiency gains estimated by DOE and those estimated by engineers in the industry.

To summarize, there are a number of barriers to improving vehicle efficiency:

- *Uncertainty in technology availability:* Whether a technology will ever be available that can produce desired efficiency gains at a cost lower than the lifetime fuel savings from the technology is uncertain. There is some chance that this barrier can be overcome by increased spending on research and development, particularly the development and testing of prototypes.
- *Consumer resistance:* Some consumers resist buying efficient vehicles at the expense of other desired attributes (e.g., perceived safety and performance).
- *Consumer perception:* Some consumers often do not perceive the financial benefit from buying a more fuel-efficient vehicle because they look only at the capital cost of the vehicle they are paying at that time instead of the financial savings due to lower fuel consumption over the life of the vehicle.

These barriers imply that (at current fuel prices) changes in current consumer perceptions and behavior would be needed for *significant* reductions in transportation fuel consumption—and the resulting greenhouse gas emissions. These consumer perceptions and behavior affect the actions taken by producers of vehicles.

Policy Options

One problem with achieving vehicle efficiency improvements is that it will take years for their full effect to be felt. Long lead times are required to meet and reach the emission reductions necessary. Cars must be designed, manufacturing equipment must be retooled, emission standards must be met, and the cars must eventually be sold as consumers decide to purchase new vehicles (U.S. Department of Energy, 1989). A new vehicle takes 4 to 5 years in the United States to go from prototype to new product (Altshuler et al., 1984), and commercial aircraft take even longer (U.S. Department of Energy, 1989). Passenger car turnover rates are also slow, on the order of 7 to 8 years (Holcomb et al., 1987), and rates for other types of vehicles such as heavy trucks are even slower (12 to 15 years) (U.S. Department of Energy, 1989). If the selection of large vehicles is constrained, consumers may choose to retain less-efficient vehicles, and scrappage rates may be reduced. The following policy options could be used to encourage vehicle efficiency improvements.

Corporate Average Fuel Economy (CAFE) Standards

The most common method used to increase fuel economy in the past has been the Corporate Average Fuel Economy (CAFE) standards. The 1975 Energy Policy and Conservation Act required manufacturers to increase the sales-weighted fuel economy of their products from 14.2 mpg in 1973 to 18 mpg in 1978; this mechanism has continued to be used and reached 27.5 mpg by 1985 (U.S. Department of Energy, 1989). The purpose of the CAFE standards is to stimulate technological improvement and reduce fuel consumption. In particular, CAFE standards may have played a role during the middle to late 1980s, when fuel economy increased despite declining oil and gasoline prices.

Because CAFE may affect manufacturers' prices for large and small cars, the weight and horsepower of these cars, the share of imports, the rate at which new cars replace old cars on the road and the number of miles driven, and because consumers adjust their travel patterns as fuel prices change, CAFE increases cannot translate directly into changes in petroleum use. There is therefore no consensus in the scientific community on the net reduction in fuel use attributable to CAFE.

Studies of the effects of CAFE reach very different conclusions. Greene (1989) argues that the behavior of manufacturers in the 1980s proves that CAFE is far more effective in improving new car efficiency than are higher gasoline prices. Greene and Liu (1988) find that the engineering changes undertaken by domestic manufacturers between 1978 and 1985 to increase average fuel efficiency from 18.7 to 25.8 mpg cost only $200 to $500 per car ($0.22 to $0.55/gallon over the vehicle's lifetime assuming 10,000 miles per year at a discount rate of 10 percent). This is far less than the cost of fuel saved over the vehicle's lifetime. An earlier engineering study by the Congressional Budget Office (1980) estimated that the engineering cost of improving the current 27.5 mpg standard by 18 to 27 percent would be $560 to $620 (in 1980 dollars) per car.

Economists studying the vehicle manufacturers' and consumers' reactions to CAFE have argued that size mix changes, postponement of new car purchases, and increases in miles traveled offset a large share of the apparent gains from CAFE. Leone and Parkinson (1990) constructed a simulation model of the full effects of CAFE and concluded that past CAFE increases cost between $0.52 and $0.79/gallon saved above the cost of the gasoline and that such gains could have been achieved more efficiently with an $0.08/gallon tax on gasoline. Kwoka (1983) argues that under certain circumstances CAFE could actually increase gasoline consumption due to mix and sales volume changes. Kleit (1990) estimates that increasing CAFE could initially increase fuel consumption and that further increases would reduce consumption at a cost of about $10/gallon saved.

Many of the differences between the technological costing and energy modeling studies arise because the technological costing studies do not examine feedback effects of design changes on consumer demand, vehicle safety, or vehicle miles traveled. The energy modeling studies attempt to account for such effects, but must do so using a series of assumptions that may be difficult to verify or controversial. In its present state the literature does not provide a conclusive estimate of the implementation costs of past CAFE regulations nor an estimate of how much fuel has been saved.*

CAFE standards have some advantages as a mechanism for improving fuel economy. Because CAFE standards have been in place in the past, both the government and automakers have experience in implementing them. Past experience would also indicate that they can work selectively, having

---

*Robert Crandall, a member of the Mitigation Panel, believes that "the panel's conclusions on the cost of energy conservation through improvements in vehicle efficiency are excessively optimistic and likely to be misinterpreted as reflecting the cost of further extensions of CAFE. Any estimate of the full costs of a policy designed to improve the fuel efficiency of new vehicles must include all such costs, including the feedback effects on vehicle mix, average vehicle age, and as some analyses indicate, on highway fatalities."

been responsible for some of the increase in automobile efficiency. A schedule of CAFE standards focuses automotive design decisions as product lines are planned. Fuel standards can also be set for vehicles other than automobiles, including light and heavy trucks as well as commercial aircraft, with potentially significant improvements (Greene et al., 1988; U.S. Department of Energy, 1989).

Carbon or Gasoline Taxes

Carbon (or gasoline) taxes constitute another mechanism for increasing vehicle efficiency. They could affect purchasing behavior by driving up the cost of operating inefficient vehicles. Owners of inefficient vehicles would thus have an incentive to replace their vehicles sooner. Although owners of more efficient vehicles would not be paying enough to induce them to trade in their cars, they would tend to drive fewer miles and thus lower CO_2 emissions. Heavy truck and airline owners would be more likely than automobile owners to replace inefficient vehicles, due to the higher number of miles traveled by these vehicles (U.S. Department of Energy, 1989).

Fuel pricing alone, however, may not be capable of achieving potential vehicle efficiency improvements. Other industrialized countries with gasoline prices 2 to 3 times higher than those in the United States nevertheless have new vehicle fleet efficiencies only slightly higher than those in the United States. Also, as vehicles become more fuel efficient, the percentage of operating costs attributable to fuel falls off rapidly. At fuel economies of 30 mpg and above, even doubling or tripling fuel costs barely increases total automobile operating costs (Ross, 1989). However, as discussed later in the transportation system management section, increasing fuel efficiency does appear to affect the frequency of vehicle trips (Pucher, 1988).

The impact of a high fuel tax may cause inequities—especially for those who make their living from travel or live in areas where a great deal of travel is necessary. These inequities have been exhibited in congressional debates on fuel taxes—residents in the far-reaching western United States oppose such taxes because they would affect their states more than states in the East.

Tax/Rebate Vehicle Packages

Another alternative for reducing greenhouse gas emissions is a "guzzler/sipper" tax. In this case, the consumer can be encouraged to purchase a fuel-efficient ("sipper") vehicle through sales tax reductions, income tax credits, rebates, and so on. The lost income could be made up by the purchaser of an inefficient vehicle ("guzzler"), who would have to pay a higher sales tax.

Such packages have a number of desirable features. Because the guzzler tax applies only to new cars, low-income persons will be largely unaffected. Because such taxes involve a large penalty imposed at the point of purchase, they may have a stronger effect on purchasing decisions than the desire to avoid higher fuel costs over a long period of time.

The disadvantage of this method is that it would create a large used-vehicle market that might make it difficult for new car purchasers to sell their old cars and as a result nullify the price incentive. In addition, if the cars were sold overseas, greenhouse gas emissions might increase there. Another disadvantage of this method is the question of its effectiveness. A gas guzzler tax is currently in effect for new automobiles that get fewer than 22 mpg, but the tax has been found to have relatively little effect on consumer behavior because for the mostly imported, high-performance, expensive vehicles affected, this tax is small in relation to purchase price (U.S. Department of Energy, 1989). The tax may, however, have had the effect of increasing the fuel economy of the least-efficient vehicles offered to consumers.

ALTERNATIVE TRANSPORTATION FUELS

Although alternative transportation fuels have not made major inroads in the United States, they have in several other countries, including Canada, New Zealand, and Brazil. California does have a fledgling program in which a move to the alternative transportation fuel methanol is being considered. In each of these cases, the motive is to improve either energy security or air quality (Sathaye et al., 1988; U.S. Department of Energy, 1989).

Despite major programs in each of these countries, only Brazil has achieved success. In Brazil a program costing the government approximately $3.7 billion, and industry $2.7 billion, over 10 years has resulted in approximately 20 percent of the light vehicle fleet using ethanol (Sperling, 1988). However, although the New Zealand and Canadian programs (costing $25 million) have been in effect for 5 years, less than 1 percent of the Canadian and approximately 11 percent of the New Zealand light vehicle fleets use alternative fuels. Each country is employing a package of policy options to encourage fuel switching. The experience of these countries indicates that a sustained and costly effort is needed for successful substitution of alternative fuels for gasoline (U.S. Department of Energy, 1989).

Emission Control Methods

Three studies (DeLuchi et al., 1988; California Energy Commission, 1989; Ho and Renner, 1990) have examined the impact of using alternative motor vehicle fuels on greenhouse gas emissions. These are summarized in Table 23.4. Note that one must consider not only the type of fuel but also the

TABLE 23.4 Summary of the Relative Greenhouse Gas Emissions from Various Fuels

Fuel	DeLuchi et al. (1988)	CEC Low (1989)	CEC High (1989)	Ho and Renner (1990)	This Report[a]
Gasoline	100	100	100	100	100
Diesel	81	76	76		84
Clean gasoline[b]					87
Reformulated gasoline					99
Natural gas	81	78	88	86	83
Liquefied natural gas from natural gas					85
Methanol from natural gas	97	91	101	95	96
Methanol from coal	198	167	192	180	
Methanol from wood	0				4
Ethanol from biomass	0			115	4
Hydrogen from nonfossil sources	0				
Electricity from nonfossil sources	0				
Electricity from natural gas	82				
Electricity from current mix	99				
Electricity from coal	126				

[a]Based on average values in California Energy Commission (1989) with an average N_2O emission rate of 0.04 g/mi rather than the 0.12 g/mi used in that report.
[b]Contains 25 percent ether derived from biomass.

source of that fuel, illustrating the need for full-cycle emission accounting. For example, methanol from wood generates low greenhouse gas emissions, while methanol from coal generates almost twice that from gasoline. In addition, Table 23.4 contains some estimates that were derived by using what the panel considers to be more realistic estimates of vehicular N_2O emissions (column 5). All of the estimates in Table 23.4 include the contributions of CO_2, N_2O, and CH_4 not only from the exhaust, but also from losses associated with production of the fuel and emissions associated with transport and distribution of the fuel.

Although the emissions of CH_4 and N_2O are small in comparison with CO_2 emissions, their much greater infrared absorption efficiencies make their contributions to vehicular greenhouse gas emissions measurable. For example, in the California Energy Commission (1989) "low estimate," the assumed exhaust emissions from a gasoline-powered vehicle are CO_2 = 311 g/mi, CH_4 = 0.04 g/mi, and N_2O = 0.12 g/mi. When these are converted to CO_2 equivalents, the rates become 1.1 to 3.3 g/mi for CH_4 and 36 g/mi for N_2O, which when combined represent 11 percent of the total greenhouse gas exhaust emissions. When the production losses of CH_4 are included, the total CH_4 emissions represent 6 to 15 percent of the greenhouse gas emissions, and the sum of the N_2O and CH_4 emissions accounts for 14 to 23 percent. The large range associated with the CH_4 contribution occurs because of different assumptions regarding the relative greenhouse gas efficiency of CH_4. The larger values do not take into consideration the lifetime of CH_4, which is relatively short in comparison with that of CO_2. As a result, calculations that have not considered lifetimes may erroneously inflate the CH_4 contributions. Consequently, the numbers in Table 23.4 are based only on those calculations that considered the CH_4 lifetime and used a CH_4/CO_2 greenhouse gas efficiency of 10 to 11 on a molar basis. The difference between 10 and 11 is negligible for the purposes of this discussion.

Other differences in the numbers reported in Table 23.4 are due to different estimates of production losses and of transportation and distribution emissions and to slightly different N_2O, CH_4, and CO_2 exhaust emission estimates. In any case, these differing assumptions have a negligible effect on the conclusions that will be made from these data. There is one exception, however: the estimate for ethanol from biomass made by Ho and Renner (1990) assumes that the fuel used to produce, transport, and distribute the ethanol is not derived from biomass, whereas the same calculation done by DeLuchi et al. (1988), and by the panel (column 5), assumes that biomass-derived ethanol is used as the fuel. This one assumption has a dramatic effect on the viability of using ethanol as a fuel. In the "more reasonable" N_2O emission scenario, the panel used an N_2O emission rate of 0.04 g/mi (Science and Policy Associates, Inc., 1990) rather than the 0.12 g/mi used in the California Energy Commission (1989) report. Concerning the data in Table 23.4, note that the greenhouse gas emissions are expressed relative to present-day gasoline, which is assigned a value of 100. For those fuels that have two or more estimates, the agreement is generally within a few percent (ethanol, an exception, is discussed above). The fuels can be divided conveniently into three categories: those that will reduce greenhouse gas emissions by less than 25 percent, those that will increase greenhouse gas emissions, and those that will completely or nearly eliminate greenhouse gas emissions. Those that will reduce the emissions by less than 25 percent relative to gasoline include the following:

- diesel fuel;
- natural gas;
- liquefied natural gas (LNG) from natural gas;
- methanol from natural gas;
- clean gasoline (spiked with 25 percent biomass-derived ether);
- electricity from new natural gas power plants;
- electricity from current power plant mix; and
- reformulated gasoline.

The "clean gasoline" contains 25 percent ether derived from biomass. The benefit from burning this is not lower CO_2 emissions, but the use of a renewable biomass fuel. The "reformulated gasolines" are those being evaluated to see if they can produce lower emissions of volatile organic compounds, which react to produce photochemical smog. The amount of CO_2 emitted during the combustion of gasoline is a function of the carbon/hydrogen ratio in the fuel. In the reformulated fuels program, this ratio is altered slightly by changing the relative amounts of aromatics and olefins in the fuels. The mean carbon/hydrogen ratio of commercially available gasoline is about 0.55. The lowest carbon/hydrogen ratio of a fuel being used in the Auto/Oil Reformulated Gasoline Program is about 0.52. This ratio would result in a maximum CO_2 emission reduction in vehicle exhaust of about 1.7 percent. Consequently, reformulated gasoline will have a negligible impact on greenhouse gas emissions.

Fuels that could result in increased greenhouse gas emissions include the following:

- methanol from coal;
- electricity from new coal-fired power plants; and
- ethanol from biomass, but produced and transported using fossil fuel.

The fuels that eliminate or nearly eliminate greenhouse gas emissions include the following:

- methanol from wood using biomass fuel to produce and transport the fuel;

- ethanol from biomass using biomass fuel to produce and transport the fuel;
- hydrogen from nonfossil-fuel-generated electricity; and
- electricity from nonfossil fuels.

If fuel from biomass is going to ameliorate greenhouse warming, biomass fuel must also be used to produce and transport it. According to Ho and Renner's (1990) calculation, this may not be possible because it appears that the energy available from ethanol is less than the energy required to produce ethanol from corn. However, there is some disagreement as to the magnitude of the energy required, which may or may not be greater than the energy provided by ethanol (Ho and Renner, 1990; Marland and Turnhollow, 1990). In one scheme, where ethanol is produced from woody biomass employing an enzymatic hydrolysis process, no external energy is required (Bergeron and Hinman, 1990); however, this process is only in the research stage. At present, we lack both the production systems and the infrastructure needed for biomass fuels to replace gasoline. The environmental impacts of converting sufficient additional land to grow corn (the preferred ethanol feedstock) or fast-growing trees (the preferred methanol feedstock) need to be considered.

For hydrogen, several problems must be dealt with before it is a viable option. The primary options are compressed hydrogen (3000 psi), hydrides (Mg_2Ni or FeTi), and cryogenic liquid (20 K). These three options have respective fuel storage volumes of 15, 4, and 4 times that for gasoline, and respective fuel storage weights of 25, 17, and 1.5 times that for gasoline. Cryogenic storage, the most practical based on volume and weight considerations, has the disadvantage of evaporative loss of hydrogen, a safety and fuel economy concern. A second major problem is the lack of an economical production system. Currently, most of the hydrogen in the United States is produced by steam reforming of CH_4 (from natural gas), which produces H_2 and CO_2. Consequently, when the energy required to produce the steam is considered, this process produces more CO_2 than if the natural gas was used directly as a vehicle fuel. In order to produce hydrogen from a nonfossil fuel source, it must be produced electrolytically using non-fossil-fuel-generated power. The cost per unit energy of electrolytically produced hydrogen has been estimated to be 3 to 5 times that of gasoline. There are also some combustion-related problems. Electric vehicles (EVs) are a viable option only if the electricity is produced from nonfossil fuels. However, further technological advances, particularly with batteries, but probably also involving the electrical charging infrastructure, are needed to produce electric vehicles that will be as convenient to use as today's fossil-fuel powered vehicles. For nearly a century, battery limitations have prevented the EV from satisfying personal transportation demands on a widespread basis. The principal problem is the batteries' low (compared to liquid fuel) specific energy, i.e., energy per unit mass. This is manifested in the short range (distance traveled before recharging is necessary) of the vehicle. Even when the thermal efficiency of the internal combustion engine is taken into account, the specific energy storage of gasoline is nearly an order of magnitude greater than that of the best contemporary battery (Amann, 1990). The specific power is also low in comparison with that provided by the combustion of liquid fuel. This manifests itself as inferior vehicle performance and long times required to recharge the batteries (hours compared to minutes to fill a gasoline tank). However, it appears that progress is being made in some of these areas. General Motors claims its "Impact" EV can accelerate from rest to 60 mph in 8 s and has a cruising range of about 190 km between charges. Nevertheless, a concerted effort has been mounted by the major auto companies and the U.S. government to explore alternative battery technology that will produce improvements in the areas cited above.

The panel attempted to determine the cost-effectiveness of these alternative transportation fuels, but found the task to be too formidable because of the numerous assumptions involved, more than for any other mitigation option discussed in this report. To properly calculate the gasoline-equivalent cost-effectiveness for alternative transportation fuels, assumptions need to be made as to the feedstock costs, production costs, capital charges, long-distance shipping costs, distribution costs, retail markup, and fuel/gasoline energy conversion rate. The cost of each of these is affected by such factors as vehicle design, available subsidies, location of markets, technological development and trade-offs, timing, magnitude of development, and many other factors. A change in any one of these can make tremendous differences in determining the cost-effectiveness. Therefore the panel decided that development of a single cost-effectiveness number would be inaccurate and that to develop one for the range of possibilities was not possible in the time available in this study and also would involve forecasts the panel was unwilling to make. This was also the conclusion of a recent (and concurrent) Office of Technology Assessment study (U.S. Congress, 1990) on this issue. Chapter 21 of that report discusses these difficulties for the case of substituting methanol for gasoline (which has more information available for it than the three fuels mentioned above).

Barriers to Implementation

Increased use of any of the alternative fuels will require the resolution of a "chicken and egg" problem: the automobile industry is reluctant to produce vehicles capable of running on alternative fuels if motorists cannot easily purchase such fuels, and the fuel industry is reluctant to create a new infrastructure for the distribution of alternative fuels if few vehicles can use them. If alternative fuel vehicles are used first in centrally fueled fleets, however, the initial distribution infrastructure could be smaller.

Policy Options

One option to encourage the use of alternative fuels is a carbon tax. The impact of such a tax is likely to be immediate and to encourage the development and use of alternative fuels. The research and development of alternative fuels would be encouraged even more if the revenues of the carbon tax were used to subsidize alternative fuel development. The tax could also be used to subsidize the reduction of alternative fuel costs (U.S. Department of Energy, 1989). Past experience indicates that if an alternative fuel is not priced within a few cents of gasoline, it is unlikely to gain acceptance (Greene, 1989).

TRANSPORTATION SYSTEM MANAGEMENT

Transportation system management involves activities such as the construction of new mass transit facilities and high-occupancy-vehicle (HOV) lanes, land use planning, and development of a jobs/housing "balance" that can potentially reduce the energy consumed in transportation.

Recent Trends

Cars and light trucks drove more than 1.7 trillion miles in the United States in 1987—double the amount driven in 1965 (Motor Vehicle Manufacturers Association, 1989). The number of vehicle miles traveled (VMT) grew at a rate of 3.5 percent per year during the early 1980s, but the annual increase should slow to 2.4 percent annually as the growth in newly licensed drivers levels off due to the end of the baby boom and the saturation of women entering the labor force and becoming drivers (Ross, 1989). Nevertheless, even at this lower projected growth rate, VMT would double again by 2020.

One particularly noticeable trend is the growth in sales of, and energy use by, light trucks, a category that includes pickups, vans, and utility vehicles. Since 1982, light truck sales have increased at an average annual rate of 12 percent; they now account for nearly one-third of the light-duty vehicle market (Davis et al., 1989). Reasons for the shift to using pickup trucks as passenger vehicles may include the decreasing number of passengers in typical trips, the longer lifetime of light trucks, and the fact that they are less regulated with respect to fuel economy, emissions, and safety than cars (Ross, 1989).

Because light trucks stay on the road longer and are less fuel efficient than automobiles, they account for about half of the fuel consumed for personal transportation (Bleviss and Walzer, 1990). Surveys indicate that approximately three-quarters of light trucks are being used essentially as cars—for commuting, passenger travel, and errands (as opposed to hauling or other activities requiring a truck's special features). The U.S. motor vehicle gasoline consumption would have been 39 percent lower in 1987—a savings of nearly 50 billion gallons of gasoline—if more-fuel-efficient automobiles had been used for the approximately 312 billion VMT by light trucks in situations where automobiles could perform the same task (Motor Vehicle Manufacturers Association, 1989; Ross, 1989).

Increases in VMT by both automobiles and light trucks have significantly outpaced highway construction. The number of new highway miles rose 9 percent from 1960 to 1987, a period during which VMT increased 168 percent (U.S. General Accounting Office, 1989). By 1987, nearly two-thirds of peak-hour travelers on urban interstate highways experienced delays (U.S. Department of Transportation, 1990). Even if roadway capacity is expanded by 20 percent, urban freeway congestion is projected to increase by 300 percent by 2005 (U.S. General Accounting Office, 1989). Congestion in turn will lower fuel economy, which can decline by 30 percent when an automobile is traveling at 15 mph in heavy traffic rather than at 55 mph on the open road (Davis et al., 1989).

Both demand-side and supply-side approaches are being used to deal with the growth in VMT and traffic congestion. Interest has grown in transportation demand management as a means of slowing VMT growth and reducing congestion. A growing number of governmental and private sector programs are using public information, financial incentives, parking restrictions, and provision of transportation alternatives such as carpools and vanpools to reduce peak-hour vehicle trips. On the supply side, traditional highway construction and expansion programs are being supplemented by construction of exclusive HOV lanes, park-and-ride lots, and new mass transit capacity. The most ambitious such plan has been established in southern California, where a combination of aggressive transportation demand management (to create 1.6 million new ridesharing trips and 1.4 million new mass transit trips) and construction of more than 1200 miles of HOV lanes is projected to reduce base-case VMT growth by 24 percent and hours of traffic delay by 90 percent by 2010 (Southern California Association of Governments, 1989). Evaluation of these programs and enforcement of their provisions are, of course, still in the infancy stage.

Emission Control Methods

Transportation system management uses both demand-side and supply-side measures to create a least-cost system for meeting mobility needs.

Generally, management measures are designed to divert automobile drivers—especially solo commuters—into high-occupancy vehicles (buses, vanpools, and carpools) or onto mass transit (Suhrbier and Deakin, 1988; Hillsman and Southworth, 1990).

Transportation system management is useful in a CO_2 emission reduction strategy for several reasons. First, shifting automobile and light truck users, particularly solo commuters, to other transportation modes can reduce energy use and thus CO_2 emissions. Second, without control measures, growth in VMT could completely offset the CO_2 reduction effects of improved fuel economy. Third, reducing travel demand and commuting distances can make alternative fuels more practicable by reducing the amount of fuel needed and shortening the required range of alternative fuel vehicles.

During the 1980s, substantial increases in vehicle fuel economy were more than offset by increases in vehicle use, producing net increases in transportation sector fuel use and CO_2 emissions. The VMT increase of 56 million miles of automobile travel and 27 million miles of light (two-axle, four-wheel) truck travel that occurred from 1987 to 1988 (Motor Vehicle Manufacturers Association, 1989) produced nearly 40,000 t CO_2 emissions. The amount by which these emissions could have been reduced depends on the alternative transportation modes the drivers would have chosen. In general, however, alternatives are less energy intensive than the automobile. Table 23.5 presents information on the different amounts of energy and vehicle occupancy for different modes of travel. As shown here, a commuter automobile carries, on average, 1.15 occupants and uses 50 to 60 percent more energy per passenger-mile than bus or rail transit.

Barriers to Implementation

A number of structural barriers, regulatory hurdles, and market imperfections must be overcome before substantial changes will occur in transportation demand, fuel use, and CO_2 emissions. Among the most significant barriers to efficient transportation management are the inaccuracy of price signals in reflecting the full social cost and the lack of more-efficient transportation alternatives.

Americans seldom see the full costs of their transportation choices (whether automobile or transit) and virtually never pay these costs as transportation user charges. Instead of user fees, public and private funds pay for a substantial part of the infrastructure needed to extract and distribute gasoline, to construct and operate highways and transit systems, and to provide parking. With respect to the automobile, these hidden costs include the following:

• *Highway construction and maintenance:* User charges and earmarked taxes at all levels of government financed only 46 percent of highway ex-

TABLE 23.5 Energy Intensities for Passenger Travel by Mode and for Peak Travel Time

	Average Vehicle Occupancy	Btu per Vehicle-Mile	Btu per Passenger-Mile[a]
Automobile			
All travel[b]	1.70	6,530	3,841
Commuting	1.15[c]	8,333[d]	7,246
Transit bus			
All travel[b]	10.2	38,557	3,761
Commuting	20.0[e]	42,413[f]	2,121
Transit rail			
All travel[b]	22.8	80,550	3,534
Commuting	50.0[e]	89,500[f]	1,790
Commuter rail			
All travel[b]	36.1	113,228	3,138
Commuting	65.0[e]	125,809[f]	1,935
Vanpool			
Commuting	10.9[g]	9,615[h]	882
Carpool			
Commuting	2.2[c]	8,333[d]	3,788

[a]Btu per passenger-mile were calculated by dividing Btu per vehicle-mile by the average vehicle occupancy rate.

[b]Davis et al., 1989, Table 2.13.

[c]Pisarski, 1987.

[d]Assumes an average passenger car fuel efficiency of 15 mpg rather than 19 mpg during commuting periods due to decreased efficiency from reduced vehicle speeds.

[e]Assumes that load factors during peak periods are approximately double average load factors.

[f]Assumes that fuel efficiency decreases 10 percent due to heavier loads and increased idling time.

[g]Calculated from Table 2.13 (vanpools) in DOT/UMTA (1989b).

[h]Assumes an average passenger van (light truck) fuel efficiency of 13 mpg (MVMA, 1989).

penditures in the United States in 1987; the remaining $36 billion came from general tax revenues (U.S. Department of Transportation, 1989). This situation is reversed in Western Europe, where revenues from taxes on gasoline and automobile ownership far exceed government expenditures for highways (Pucher, 1988).

• *Parking:* Seventy-five percent of all commuters in the United States park in "free" employer-provided parking spaces that actually cost employers $1,000 to $15,000 per space to construct (plus annual maintenance and operation costs). Tax policy encourages these expenditures by treating free parking as a tax-free benefit for employees and a tax-deductible expense for the businesses that provide it (Pucher, 1988; Institute of Transportation Engineers, 1989).

• *Foregone tax revenue:* Close to half of the land in a typical American city is devoted to the infrastructure needed to support the automobile. More than 60,000 square miles of the United States—2 percent of the total surface area of the country and the equivalent of 10 percent of all arable land—is paved. Much of this land has been removed from the tax rolls and is thus indirectly subsidized by local municipalities (Ketcham and Pinkwas, 1980; Renner, 1988).

Americans have no way of knowing that they are indirectly paying these costs to support their driving habits. Indeed, the out-of-pocket costs of driving have fallen substantially in recent years. Americans paid only $0.96/ gallon for gasoline in 1988, less (in real dollars) than they paid at any time during the previous decade and perhaps the lowest price ever. The cost of operating an automobile has fallen to $0.32/mi (1987 dollars), with the costs of fueling the vehicle dropping 8.4 percent annually from 1985 to 1988 (Davis et al., 1989). It is not surprising that American drivers responded to these declining out-of-pocket costs by driving more. When apparent automobile operating costs are low, Americans have no good economic reason to purchase dual- or alternative-fuel cars, to worry about the fuel efficiency of their automobiles, or to use mass transit.

Another barrier to effective transportation system management is the lack of safe, convenient, and cost-effective mass transit services in most areas of the country. Although U.S. mass transit programs served almost 9 billion riders in 1988, ridership was concentrated in a few large markets. Americans averaged only 36 transit trips per capita in 1987 (American Public Transit Association, 1989; Davis et al., 1989), one-fourth to one-half as many as citizens of other industrialized countries (Pucher, 1988).

The inadequacies of the U.S. mass transit system reflect the low priority the federal government has given these transportation modes relative to the private automobile. This priority is also reflected in the amount of public money spent to subsidize these modes. Mass transit systems, for example, received only $10.5 billion in local, state, and federal capital and operating assistance in 1988, less than one-third of the $36 billion spent on highways in 1987 (U.S. Department of Transportation, 1989; U.S. Department of Transportation, Urban Mass Transit Administration, 1989b).

Policy Options

A number of transportation system management options can be used to reduce greenhouse gas emissions. These include altering demand through more accurate pricing mechanisms, through parking and transportation demand management, and by increasing the supply of HOV lanes and mass transit.

Pricing Strategies

Behavioral studies indicate that out-of-pocket transportation costs—such as gasoline, parking, tolls, and transit fares—are explicitly considered in daily travel decision making and that changes in such costs strongly influence travel choices (Wachs, 1989). Pricing strategies can also be used to make drivers, particularly solo commuters, responsible for more of the out-of-pocket and social costs imposed by their automobile use. The policy objective would be to ensure that each class of transportation system user pays the full marginal social costs they impose on the system. At least three types of pricing strategies are available: increasing the cost of gasoline through taxation, increasing the cost of driving through higher tolls and roadway pricing, and increasing the cost of purchasing automobiles through taxes and higher registration fees (Deakin, 1990). (Increased parking costs are treated below as a parking management measure.)

Gasoline prices in the United States have always been low in comparison with those of other countries, and they dropped drastically during the 1980s. A gallon of gasoline cost less in 1989 in real terms (corrected for inflation) than it did in 1979. In 1986, gasoline and motor oil accounted for only 15 percent of total car operating costs per mile in the United States, down from 26 percent in 1975 (Davis et al., 1989). Taxation policies strongly affect the cost of gasoline. Federal, state, and local fuel taxes in the United States total only $0.20/gallon (U.S. Department of Transportation, 1989). Per-gallon taxes on gasoline are 3 to 7 times higher in European countries, and the difference is overwhelmingly due to deliberate taxation policies, not to differences in the cost of petroleum. This price differential is, in part, responsible for the fact that cars are used for only 50 percent of trips in most Western European countries and less than 40 percent of trips in Switzerland, Sweden, Italy, and Austria, but are used for 80 percent of all U.S. trips (Pucher, 1988), although it does not appear large enough to increase incentives for vehicle efficiency improvements (Ross, 1989).

Higher gasoline prices may help reduce vehicle usage because they are the type of out-of-pocket cost consumers weigh when making travel decisions. There are, however, limits to reducing VMT through gasoline pricing, especially for owners of fuel-efficient cars for which gasoline costs are a small proportion of total operating costs. Even with gasoline priced at $2.00/gallon, the owner of a car with in-use fuel economy of 30 mpg will save only $28 per month in fuel charges by eliminating a daily one-way commute of 10 miles.

A variety of proposals have been advanced for increasing the cost of vehicle use through roadway pricing mechanisms such as tolls and congestion charges. Graduated fee schedules could be used to encourage multioccupant and off-peak travel. One roadway pricing approach is currently being applied in the Singapore central business district (Southern California Association of Governments, 1989). Research and empirical experience in other settings are needed to determine elasticities and project drivers' responses to roadway pricing changes so that the potential emission reductions and cost-effectiveness can be calculated.

Pricing strategies that increase the cost of purchasing automobiles, such as sales taxes or registration fees, may be used to modify both the type (size and/or fuel economy) and the number of vehicles purchased. One reason for VMT growth is growth in the number of vehicles in operation in the United States. The number of vehicles per household increased from 1.55 in 1970 to 1.87 in 1987; there have been more vehicles than licensed drivers in the United States since 1985 (Davis et al., 1989). Reductions in the number of vehicles purchased due to higher sales taxes and registration fees may account, in part, for the smaller share of travel by automobile in Western European countries, which generally charge a higher sales tax on new cars than the United States does. Sales taxes in the United States average only 5 percent, while those in Europe range from 33 percent in France to 47 percent in the Netherlands to 186 percent in Denmark (Pucher, 1988).

Parking and Transportation Demand Management

Parking availability is a crucial element in the calculus of commuting: a worker who cannot inexpensively park his or her car in close proximity to work is less likely to commute alone on a daily basis. Parking for U.S. workers is frequently subsidized by employers and therefore inexpensive. Approximately 75 percent of all commuters park in free employer-provided parking spaces, and another 11 percent use free off-street parking (Pucher, 1988). Case studies representing large and small employers, from both suburban and urban areas in all parts of the United States and Canada, indicate that the provision of free parking leads to more solo commuting. When parking fees are imposed, the percentage of employees driving to work alone falls as the price of parking rises (Willson et al., 1989). Indeed, making parking very costly may work better than raising fuel prices to discourage single-occupant vehicle use.

Increasing parking costs, limiting parking, and providing incentives to carpoolers and transit users can encourage the use of mass transit and HOV modes such as carpooling and vanpooling. The removal of parking subsidies or the introduction of parking fees can reduce the mode share of solo driving by as much as 30 percent. Two recent U.S. Department of Transportation surveys have concluded that parking management is an essential element of any broader transportation demand management program (U.S.

Department of Transportation, Urban Mass Transit Administration, 1989b; U.S. Department of Transportation, Federal Highway Administration, 1990).

A variety of parking management strategies have been identified. These include the following:

- establishing a surcharge on parking for single-occupant vehicles and/ or a discount for multioccupant vehicles;
- requiring preferential parking for ridesharers;
- eliminating peak-period on-street parking and/or free employer-provided parking; and
- capping the number of parking spaces permitted in a zone or for a particular project (Southern California Association of Governments, 1989).

Strategies that eliminate parking carry a negative cost for employers and developers: they save $1,000 to $15,000 for each parking space they do not provide (Institute of Transportation Engineers, 1989). Alternately, converting free or subsidized parking into paid parking provides a revenue stream for the employer, developer, or local government (if a parking tax or surcharge is used).

One possible parking management strategy would use public and private measures to reduce the amount of, and impose user charges on the remainder of, all currently "free" employer-provided parking in U.S. metropolitan areas by 1995. The 48 million workers in U.S. metropolitan areas (Pisarski, 1987) are provided approximately 36 million free parking spaces by their employers. Under the parking management program described in Appendix F, 25 percent, or 9 million, of these spaces would be eliminated. The remaining 36 million spaces would be priced (through a combination of fees, taxes, and surcharges) at a level designed to reduce the solo commuting share by 15 percent, from 65 to 50 percent. Such a parking management program would produce a cumulative CO_2 reduction of 49 Mt annually at a cost of -$4.75 billion to $2.6 billion, for a cost-effectiveness value of -$97/t CO_2 to $53/t CO_2.*

The term "transportation demand management" (TDM) encompasses a variety of actions whose purpose is to alleviate traffic and congestion prob-

---

*Panel members Robert Crandall and Douglas Foy have further views on the practicality of this option. Crandall believes that the existing economic literature on modal choice in transportation indicates reason for skepticism. He notes the panel's failure to measure, through existing modal-choice models, the magnitude of the fees, taxes, and surcharges that would be required to shift 9 million commuters from private automobiles to various collectivized transit modes, many of which are already heavily subsidized. Were such an analysis done, he believes that the results would show extremely large costs, not cost savings. Foy believes that there is ample empirical evidence that commuters' modal choice can be varied through relatively low cost policies affecting variables such as parking pricing and availability. He also notes that the high occupancy vehicle and transit modes to which automobile commuters switch are often publicly subsidized, but no more (and probably less) than automobile commuting.

lems through improved management of demand for vehicle trips. These TDM measures may be designed to eliminate trips (through telecommuting), shift automobile trips to other modes, move trips to off-peak periods, or decrease the length of trips (through jobs/housing balance mechanisms).

Transportation demand management efforts have generally been targeted at reducing traffic during peak commuting hours, when congestion is at its worst, and vehicle occupancy at its lowest. The target of most peak-hour TDM efforts is single-occupant commuting vehicles, which account for up to 60 percent of trips during these times (Pisarski, 1987; Davis et al., 1989). Reductions in such trips are relatively easy to achieve (because the occupant is traveling between the same two points at the same time daily) and are desirable because the commuting takes place during the most congested time of day (U.S. Department of Transportation, Federal Highway Administration, 1990). Shifting such trips onto transit or increasing vehicle occupancy are more productive approaches than simply moving the trips to off-peak periods.

Transportation demand management strategies now in use by public and private sector organizations include the following:

• creating a transportation management organization at the work site, with a coordinator to provide information and services to employees;
• promoting carpooling through preferential parking for carpools and computerized matching services;
• promoting vanpooling by providing vanpools (both subsidized and self-supporting);
• encouraging use of mass transit with incentives such as free or subsidized passes or shuttle buses from nearby transit stations;
• encouraging use of bicycles through provision of secure storage areas and shower facilities;
• providing a guaranteed ride home for mass transit, carpool, and vanpool users in emergency situations; and
• eliminating commuting through work-at-home and telecommuting programs (U.S. Department of Transportation, Urban Mass Transit Administration, 1989a; Southern California Association of Governments, 1989; Deakin, 1990; U.S. Department of Transportation, Federal Highway Administration, 1990).

Intensive automobile use in the United States has been driven in part by land-use and tax policies that encourage construction of low-density communities of single-family homes. Because travel demand is heavily influenced by such development patterns, reshaping land use and growth to support a variety of commuting alternatives may be critical to the success of travel demand management efforts. Land use and growth management TDM techniques are, however, future-oriented and cannot always address existing traffic system problems (Deakin, 1990).

Land use planning strategies that local governments and planners can use to manage travel demand include requiring land use plans and zoning to be consistent with transportation capacity, planning future development densities to accommodate present and future transportation capacity, and restricting uses that generate excessive numbers of trips (Deakin, 1989). Another set of regulatory approaches focuses on reducing trips associated with new developments by requiring developers to meet certain site design criteria, provide for transportation and other infrastructure, and comply with trip reduction ordinances (Suhrbier and Deakin, 1988). The Southern California Association of Governments (SCAG) has proposed one of the most far-reaching land-use-oriented TDM programs—the redistribution of some population growth into job-rich areas and some jobs growth into housing-rich areas in order to promote jobs/housing balance (Southern California Association of Governments, 1989).

Employer-based TDM programs have successfully changed commuting behavior and reduced the use of single-occupant vehicles. A recent survey by the Federal Highway Administration concluded that TDM programs, especially when undertaken in conjunction with parking management programs, should normally be able to achieve trip reductions in the range of 20 to 40 percent (U.S. Department of Transportation, Federal Highway Administration, 1990). TDM programs can be even more effective if they address some of the reasons commuters prefer to drive (e.g., the need to leave children at day care and concern that the car may be needed during the day for emergencies) through methods such as provision of day care at the work site and guaranteed ride home programs for emergencies (U.S. Department of Transportation, Urban Mass Transportation Administration, 1989a; U.S. Department of Transportation, Federal Highway Administration, 1990).

The cost of TDM programs varies widely depending on the measures used, the size of the employer, and other factors. Costs are frequently in the range of $15 to $55 per employee, but may be as high as $100 per employee per year (Municipality of Metropolitan Seattle, Service Development Division, 1989; U.S. Department of Transportation, Urban Mass Transit Administration, 1989a).

Using TDM to increase average vehicle occupancy could be a cost-effective way of reducing CO_2 emissions. In the United States the average occupancy level of commuter vehicles is only 1.1 persons per vehicle. If this could be increased to 2.1 persons per vehicle, 30 to 40 million gallons of gasoline would be saved daily (American Public Transit Association, 1989). While increasing the peak-hour vehicle occupancy rate to 2.1 persons per vehicle would be a daunting (some would say impossible) task, achieving this long-term goal would result in an annual CO_2 reduction of 98 to 131 Mt. Even if the TDM costs needed to achieve this goal are as high as $100 per employee per year for each of the 96.7 million workers in the United States (Pisarski, 1987), the offsetting gasoline savings of $10.95 billion per year ($1/gallon for 30 million gallons/day) would eliminate 98 Mt of CO_2 emissions at a cost of −$13/t.

High-Occupancy-Vehicle Lanes

Pricing measures, parking management, and transportation demand management are all designed at least in part to increase average vehicle occupancy during peak commuting hours. One way of accommodating the increased number of multioccupant vehicles would be to increase the supply of specially designated high-occupancy-vehicle (HOV) lanes. Such lanes are built for the exclusive use of buses, vanpools, and (sometimes) carpools carrying three or more persons.

In recent years, construction of HOV lanes has gained acceptance as an effective means of reducing commuting time, encouraging ridesharing, and increasing vehicle occupancy rates (Southern California Association of Governments, 1989). HOV lanes can reduce commuting time on congested highways by 45 to 50 percent and also reduce the total VMT (Davis et al., 1989; Institute of Transportation Engineers, 1988). The Institute of Transportation Engineers has concluded that HOV lanes are often the lowest-cost type of fixed transit facility, with benefit-cost ratios in excess of 6 (Institute of Transportation Engineers, 1988, 1989). Despite these advantages, HOV lanes—especially when converted from existing general-purposes lanes—have met with political opposition from drivers upset by the sight of seemingly unused capacity in the more free-flowing HOV lanes.

High-occupancy-vehicle lanes often cost far less than equal amounts of new highway capacity because each HOV lane (both at and well before the point at which the incentive to drive in the lane reaches zero) carries more persons than a regular highway lane. Costs generally range from $30,000 to $2 million per lane-mile when existing lanes are converted to HOV lanes and from $4 to $8 million per lane-mile when HOV facilities are constructed in existing or separate rights of way (Turnbull and Hanks, 1990).

OTHER BENEFITS AND COSTS

By reducing fuel use, vehicle use, and traffic congestion, transportation system management measures produce a variety of benefits in addition to CO_2 emission reductions. These include reducing dependence on imported oil, lowering emissions of conventional and toxic air pollutants, and avoiding productivity losses from delays in the movement of goods and people. These benefits may total tens of billions of dollars. At the same time, there are costs—including potential consumer welfare losses from required lifestyle changes—incurred in adopting transportation demand measures.

Reducing transportation energy use could significantly improve the U.S. balance of trade and energy security position. The transportation sector accounts for approximately two-thirds of all U.S. oil use, an amount greater than that produced domestically (Davis et al., 1989). The direct costs of importing petroleum products account for nearly 40 percent of the U.S. trade deficit. The United States incurs other costs because of this dependence on imported oil, including those related to using the military to protect strategic supply regions, maintaining the Strategic Petroleum Reserve, and living with the risk of supply disruptions. These costs have been estimated at between $21 billion and $125 billion annually (Greene et al., 1988), or $7 to $40 for each of the 8.3 million barrels of oil imported daily during the first four months of 1990.

Reducing VMT will reduce emissions of air pollutants, for which permissible standards are set in terms of grams of pollutant emitted per mile. The transportation sector, particularly light trucks and automobiles, is responsible for a large proportion of U.S. air pollution, particularly in urban areas. Motor vehicles emit five of the six "criteria" pollutants regulated under the Clean Air Act, including fine particulates and

- 70 percent of CO;
- 40 percent of volatile organic compounds, which are precursors to the formation of ozone, the primary component of urban smog;
- 40 percent of NO_x, regulated pollutants that are precursors to both acid rain and photochemical air pollution; and
- 35 percent of lead, a potent neurotoxin particularly dangerous to young children (MacKenzie, 1988; U.S. Office of Technology Assessment, 1989). Motor vehicles are also responsible for a variety of toxic emissions (especially benzene and formaldehyde) from exhaust and gasoline vapors, all of which also could be reduced by greenhouse gas mitigation measures.

Air pollution adversely affects human health and the environment. Estimates of the total societal cost of pollutant emissions from refineries, fueling stations, and motor vehicles range from $11 billion to $187 billion annually, depending on assumptions about both the numbers of deaths and illnesses and the monetary value assigned to the loss of life (Greene et al., 1988).

Another benefit of transportation system management is that measures limiting the number of VMT or reducing the degree of congestion encountered while traveling avoid substantial productivity losses from delays in the movement of goods and people. National estimates of delay on urban highways and resulting productivity losses have been prepared by the Federal Highway Administration and reviewed by the General Accounting Office. In 1987, highway delays cost motorists $7.8 billion in wasted time. By 2005 the cost of delays is projected to increase to $29 billion to $43 billion. Another type of lost productivity is the cost of delaying trucks carrying goods. The Federal Highway Administration has estimated that the total annual cost of truck delay on highways alone is $4.2 billion to $7.6 billion; additional trucking productivity losses from congestion on urban streets would add $19.4 billion to $22.9 billion to this total (U.S. General Accounting Office, 1989).

These estimates of $52.6 billion to $73.5 billion in annual productivity losses at current congestion levels do not include delays faced by commuters on local streets or the costs of tardiness to employers. When surveyed, employers frequently cite reductions in tardiness and absenteeism as reasons for sponsoring ridesharing programs. One survey of 20 such programs found that 18 of 20[a] ridesharing programs had cost-benefit ratios greater than 1 when the benefits of reduced tardiness, absenteeism, and need to construct parking facilities were calculated; cost-benefit ratios were frequently in excess of 10 (Wegmann, 1989).

Despite these benefits, there are costs—primarily in the form of consumer welfare losses—that will likely occur due to efforts to reduce solo commuting and vehicle usage. For many workers, commuting could take longer and result in lost productivity. A typical mass transit commute in the United States averages 13 to 14 mph, whereas commuters driving alone or in a carpool travel at 31.5 to 33.5 mph while covering a comparable distance (Pisarski, 1987). (Although such losses cannot be quantified, commuters and other drivers will also suffer "consumer welfare" losses from real or perceived reductions in personal mobility and freedom.)

These consumer welfare losses can, however, be minimized by focusing transportation system management efforts on reducing commuters' travel time. Transit can be made more convenient and faster; HOV lanes can be used to reduce travel time for buses, vanpools, and carpools. Differences in commuting time between automobiles and other modes will also narrow if congestion increases automobile travel times: average vehicle speeds in southern California are projected to fall to 19 mph in the absence of transportation system management (Southern California Association of Governments, 1989). In addition, behavioral studies indicate that commuters are more concerned about travel time reliability than total elapsed travel time (Wachs, 1989); thus minimizing variations in travel time on mass transit and in the use of HOV lanes should reduce consumer welfare losses.

RESEARCH AND DEVELOPMENT NEEDS

The research and development needs for each of the three primary mitigation options described above are listed in this section. Recently, the National Research Council's (1990) alternative energy research and development study made the following recommendations:

• Improve batteries for vehicle propulsion to achieve higher performance and durability and to reduce costs.
• Adapt alternative fuels (e.g., alcohols) to engines and vehicles.
• Reduce emissions from efficient power plants such as the diesel.

- Evaluate vehicle systems to ensure the safety of smaller cars built with lightweight structural materials.
- Investigate innovative electric transportation systems.

The Mitigation Panel would also include hydrogen in the list of alternative fuels that need to be adapted to current engines and vehicles and would note that the focus of these alternative fuel efforts should be generation of fuels (such as methanol) from sources such as biomass and nonfossil electricity that do not increase greenhouse gas emissions. Since the method by which primary energy is generated is such an important factor in alternative transportation fuels, a number of research and development recommendations in the energy supply sector (see Chapter 24) are also applicable here.

Transportation system management has, to date, been a largely empirical exercise—governments and private employers put measures into effect and only subsequently evaluate which work or why. Surveys, pilot programs, and other research tools should be used to predict and evaluate which methods are most effective in altering transportation behavior. In particular, the relative efficacy of different pricing mechanisms—gasoline taxes, parking fees, tolls, sales taxes, and registration fees—should be evaluated (Deakin, 1990; Hillsman and Southworth, 1990).

CONCLUSIONS

The transportation sector accounts for 30 percent of CO_2 emissions. Changes in transportation over the next several decades could substantially affect the nation's contributions to greenhouse warming. Moreover, such changes are likely to influence practices elsewhere as well. For these reasons, a focus on transportation is an important component of policy.

Of the three different types of methods for reducing greenhouse gas emissions from the transportation sector, vehicle efficiency has the greatest potential. However, implementation of vehicle efficiency measures will be slow because of the low turnover of vehicles in the marketplace and the time delay between design and production of vehicles.

Each of the alternative transportation fuels has problems. Biomass fuels require production systems and infrastructures not currently available. In addition, there is concern about the ability to convert sufficient land to grow corn for ethanol or woody biomass for methanol or ethanol.

For hydrogen, the production systems and infrastructure would have to be created. There are storage and safety concerns to be resolved for vehicles having on-board reservoirs of hydrogen. If hydrogen is to be used to reduce greenhouse gas emissions, it must be made by using nonfossil-fuel-generated energy.

Electric vehicles are a viable option only if the electricity is produced from nonfossil fuels. Further technological advances, particularly with batteries, but probably also involving the electrical charging infrastructure, are needed to produce electric vehicles that will be as convenient to use as today's fossil-fuel-powered vehicles.

If alternative fuels are to serve as a significant alternative to gasoline in the next century, the federal government will have to both increase funds for research and development programs and tax gasoline to reflect its full social costs and make alternative fuels cost-competitive. In the interim, alternative fuels should not be used if the switch from gasoline increases life-cycle carbon emissions.

In the area of transportation system management, supply-side measures such as providing HOV lanes and increasing mass transit capacity—and demand-side measures involving pricing, parking availability, and transportation demand management—can cost-effectively and substantially reduce vehicle miles traveled, traffic congestion, fuel use, and CO_2 emissions. One particularly attractive feature of transportation demand management is that CO_2 emission reductions could occur during the period when fuel economy changes are being phased in; these measures will also protect fuel economy improvements in the longer term. To gain these benefits, barriers such as inappropriate transportation pricing and lack of alternatives must be overcome. In addition, steps must be taken to reduce potential consumer welfare losses due to increases in commuting time and reductions in personal freedom. Transportation system management has the potential, however, to be a cost-effective CO_2 reduction strategy for small amounts of CO_2 reduction while fulfilling its primary goal of providing mobility for people at the least total cost to society.

Major uncertainties stand in the way of large-scale reductions in greenhouse gas emissions from transportation. Several are discussed here because they are especially important to U.S. national policy:

• Uncertainty over the degree of willingness of vehicle owners (households and firms) to purchase smaller, more fuel-efficient vehicles when fuel prices are low poses a significant barrier to the adoption of more fuel-efficient vehicles. Ways of overcoming this barrier while preserving the dynamics of competition in the U.S. vehicle market will have to be identified, evaluated, and implemented.

• Policies aimed at altering vehicle use, including fuel pricing, transportation demand management, and changes in urban design, also face large uncertainties. Promising attempts are beginning in southern California, motivated by concern over air quality. Careful monitoring and deliberate experimentation in this and other metropolitan areas could yield important findings over the next decade.

Perhaps the largest uncertainty is the degree to which consumers and voters will be willing to respond to changing price and policy signals by buying more fuel-efficient cars, changing commuting patterns, and otherwise altering their life-style. One should bear in mind that the emergence of current vehicle use patterns in industrialized societies occurred over the last half-century, a time span comparable with that in which greenhouse warming may occur.

NOTES

1. Throughout this report, tons (t) are metric; 1 Mt = 1 megaton = 1 million tons; and 1 Gt = 1 gigaton = 1 billion tons.

2. Subsequent to the preparation of these results, K. G. Duleep (co-author with Difiglio and Greene) has refined the estimate of the "maximum technology" point. Duleep estimates that in 1996 all available technologies could produce a CAFE mpg of 29.3 (22.5 on-road) and in 2001 all available technologies could produce a CAFE mpg of 36.0 (27.7 on-road) (Plotkin, 1991).

REFERENCES

Altshuler, A., M. Anderson, D. Jones, R. Roos, and J. Womack. 1984. The Future of the Automobile. Cambridge, Mass.: MIT Press.

Amann, C. A. 1989. The automotive spark-ignition engine—An historical perspective. In History of the Internal Combustion Engine, ICE, Volume 8, Book No. 100294-1989, E. F. C. Somerscales and A. A. Zagotta, eds. New York: American Society of Mechanical Engineers.

Amann, C. A. 1990. Technical options for energy conservation and controlling environmental impact in highway vehicles. Paper GMR-6942 presented at the Energy and the Environment in the 21st Century Conference, Massachusetts Institute of Technology, Cambridge, Mass., March 26-28, 1990.

American Public Transit Association. 1989. Transit Fact Book. Washington, D.C.: American Public Transit Association.

Atkinson, S. E., and R. Halvorsen. 1984. A new hedonic technique for estimating attribute demand: An application to the demand for automobile fuel efficiency. Review of Economics and Statistics 66(3):416-426.

Atkinson, S. E., and R. Halvorsen. 1990. Valuation of risks to life: Evidence from the markets for automobiles. Review of Economics and Statistics 72(1):137-142.

Bergeron, T. W., and N. D. Hinman. 1990. Fuel Ethanol Usage and Environmental Carbon Dioxide Production. Golden, Colo.: Solar Energy Research Institute. January.

Bleviss, D. 1988. The New Oil Crisis and Fuel Economy Technologies. New York: Quorum Books.

Bleviss, D., and P. Walzer. 1990. Energy for motor vehicles. Scientific American 263(Sept.):103-109.

California Energy Commission (CEC). 1989. Comparing the Impacts of Different Transportation Fuels on the Greenhouse Effect. Sacramento: California Energy Commission.

Carlsmith, R. S., W. U. Chandler, J. E. McMahon, and D. J. Santini. 1990. Energy

Efficiency: How Far Can We Go? Report ORNL/TM-11441. Prepared for the Office of Policy, Planning and Analysis, U.S. Department of Energy. Washington, D.C.: U.S. Department of Energy.

Congressional Budget Office. 1980. Fuel Economy Standards for New Passenger Cars After 1985. Washington, D.C.: U.S. Congress.

Davis, S. C., D. B. Shonka, G. J. Anderson-Batiste, and P. S. Hu. 1989. Transportation Energy Data Book: Edition 10. Report ORNL-6565 (Edition 10 of ORNL-5198). Prepared for the U.S. Department of Energy. Washington, D.C.: U.S. Department of Energy.

Deakin, E. A. 1989. Land use and transportation planning in response to congestion problems: A review and critique. Pp. 77-86 in Congestion, Land Use, and Transportation Planning. Transportation Research Record No. 1237. Washington, D.C.: Transportation Research Board, National Research Council.

Deakin, E. A. 1990. Suburban Traffic Congestion, Land Use and Transportation Planning Issues: Public Policy Options in Traffic Congestion and Suburban Activity Centers. Transportation Research Circular No. 359. Washington, D.C.: Transportation Research Board, National Research Council.

DeLuchi, M. A., R. A. Johnston, and D. Sperling. 1988. Transportation fuels and the greenhouse effect. Transportation Research Record 1175:33-44.

Difiglio, C., K. G. Duleep, and D. L. Greene. 1990. Cost effectiveness of future fuel economy improvements. The Energy Journal 11(1):65-86.

European Economic Community (EEC). 1988. Energy analysis of the transport sector: Determining factors and forecasts. In Energy in Europe: Energy Policies and Trends in the European Community. Brussels: Directorate General for Energy, European Economic Community.

Godek, P. E. 1990. The Corporate Average Fuel Economy Standard 1978-1990. Working Paper, October.

Greene, D. L. 1989. CAFE or Price?: An Analysis of the Effects of Federal Fuel Economy Regulations and Gasoline Price on New Car MPG, 1978-89. The Energy Journal 11(3):37-58.

Greene, D. L., and J-T. Liu. 1988. Automotive fuel economy improvements and consumers' surplus. Transportation Research 22A:203-218.

Greene, D. L., D. Sperling, and B. McNutt. 1988. Transportation energy to the year 2020. In A Look Ahead: Year 2020. Washington, D.C.: Transportation Research Board, National Research Council.

Hillsman, E. L., and F. Southworth. 1990. Factors that may influence responses of the U.S. transportation sector to policies for reducing greenhouse gas emissions. Pp. 1-11 in Global Warming: Transportation and Energy Considerations 1990. Transportation Research Record No. 1267. Washington, D.C.: Transportation Research Board, National Research Council.

Ho, S. P., and T. A. Renner. 1990. The global warming impact of attainment strategies using alternate fuels. Paper presented at the Air and Waste Management Association Conference on Tropospheric Ozone, Los Angeles, Calif., March 19-22, 1990.

Holcomb, M. C., S. D. Floud, and S. L. Cagle. 1987. Transportation Energy Date Book: Edition 9. Report ORNL-6325. Prepared for the U.S. Department of Energy. Oak Ridge, Tenn.: Oak Ridge National Laboratory.

Institute of Transportation Engineers. 1988. The Effectiveness of High-Occupancy Vehicle Facilities. Washington, D.C.: Institute of Transportation Engineers.

Institute of Transportation Engineers. 1989. A Toolbox for Alleviating Traffic Congestion. Washington, D.C.: Institute of Transportation Engineers.

International Energy Agency (IEA). 1984. Fuel Efficiency of Passenger Cars. Paris: International Energy Agency, Organization for Economic Cooperation and Development.

Ketcham, B., and S. Pinkwas. 1980. Beyond autocracy: The public's role in regulating the auto. In Technology, Government and the Future of the Automobile, D. Ginsburg and W. Abernathy, eds. Cambridge, Mass.: Harvard Graduate School of Business Administration.

Kleit, A. N. 1988. The impact of automobile fuel economy standards. Working Paper 160. February 1988. Bureau of Economics, Federal Trade Commission, Washington, D.C.

Kleit, A. N. 1990. The effect of annual changes in fuel economy standards. Journal of Regulatory Economics 2(2):151-172.

Kwoka, J. E., Jr. 1983. The limits of market-oriented regulatory techniques: The case of automotive fuel economy. Quarterly Journal of Economics 97:695-704.

Ledbetter, M., and M. Ross. 1989. Supply curves of conserved energy for automobiles. Draft paper prepared for Lawrence Berkeley Laboratory by the American Council for an Energy-Efficient Economy, Washington, D.C.

Leone, R. A., and T. W. Parkinson. 1990. Conserving energy: Is there a better way? May 1990. Paper prepared for the Association of International Automobile Manufacturers, Arlington, Va.

Lyman, F. 1990. The Greenhouse Trap. Boston: Beacon Press.

MacKenzie, J. J. 1988. Breathing Easier: Taking Action on Climate Change and Energy Insecurity. Washington, D.C.: World Resources Institute.

Marland, G., and A. Turnhollow. 1990. CO_2 Emissions from production and combustion of fuel ethanol from corn. Report ORNL/TM-11180. Oak Ridge, Tenn.: Oak Ridge National Laboratory.

Motor Vehicle Manufacturers Association. 1989. MVMA Motor Vehicle Facts and Figures '89. Detroit, Mich.: Motor Vehicle Manufacturers Association.

Municipality of Metropolitan Seattle, Service Development Division. 1989. Transportation Demand Management Strategy Cost Estimates. Seattle: Service Development Division, Municipality of Metropolitan Seattle.

National Research Council. 1990. Confronting Climate Change: Strategies for Energy Research and Development. Washington, D.C.: National Academy Press.

Pisarski, A. 1987. Commuting in America: A National Report on Commuting Patterns and Trends. Westport, Conn.: Eno Foundation for Transportation, Inc.

Plotkin, S. E. 1991. Testimony before Senate Committee on Energy and Natural Resources. Washington, D.C.: Office of Technology Assessment. March 20, 1991.

Pucher, J. 1988. Urban travel behavior as the outcome of public policy: The example of modal split in Western Europe and North America. The Journal of American Planners Association 54(4):509-520.

Renner, M. 1988. Rethinking the Role of the Automobile. Washington, D.C.: Worldwatch Institute, 1988.

Ross, M. 1989. Energy and transportation in the United States. Annual Review of Energy 14:131-171.

Sathaye, J., B. Atkinson, and S. Meyers. 1988. Alternative Fuels Assessment: The International Experience. Report LBL-24736. Berkeley, Calif.: Lawrence Berkeley Laboratory.

Science and Policy Associates, Inc. 1990. The Greenhouse Effect and Motor Vehicle Emissions of Greenhouse Gases. Washington, D.C.: Science and Policy Associates, Inc.

Shackson, R. H., and H. J. Leach. 1980. Using Fuel Economy and Synthetic Fuels to Compete with OPEC Oil. Pittsburgh, Pa.: Carnegie-Mellon University Press.

Southern California Association of Governments. 1989. Regional Mobility Plan. Los Angeles: Southern California Association of Governments.

Sperling, D. 1988. New Transportation Fuels: A Strategic Approach to Technological Change. Berkeley: University of California Press.

Suhrbier, J. H., and E. A. Deakin. 1988. Environmental Considerations in a 2020 Transportation Plan: Constraints or Opportunities. Proceedings of the Conference on Long-Range Trends and Requirements for the Nation's Highway and Public Transit Systems. Washington, D.C.: Transportation Research Board, National Research Council.

Turnbull, K., and J. Hanks. 1990. A Description of High-Occupancy Vehicle Facilities in North America. College Station, Tex.: Texas Transportation Institute.

U.S. Congress, Office of Technology Assessment. 1990. Replacing Gasoline: Alternative Fuels for Light-Duty Vehicles. OTA-E-364. Washington, D.C.: U.S. Government Printing Office.

U.S. Department of Energy (DOE). 1989. A Compendium of Options for Government Policy to Encourage Private Sector Responses to Potential Climate Change. Report DOE/EH-0103. Washington, D.C.: U.S. Department of Energy.

U.S. Department of Transportation. 1989. National Transportation Statistics. Washington, D.C.: U.S. Department of Transportation.

U.S. Department of Transportation. 1990. Moving America: New Directions, New Opportunities. Washington, D.C.: U.S. Department of Transportation.

U.S. Department of Transportation, Federal Highway Administration. 1990. Evaluation of Travel Demand Management Measures to Relieve Congestion. Washington, D.C.: U.S. Department of Transportation.

U.S. Department of Transportation, Urban Mass Transportation Administration. 1989a. An Assessment of Travel Demand Approaches at Suburban Activity Centers. Washington, D.C.: U.S. Department of Transportation.

U.S. Department of Transportation, Urban Mass Transportation Administration. 1989b. National Urban Mass Transportation Statistics, 1988, Section 15, Annual Report. Washington, D.C.: U.S. Department of Transportation.

U.S. General Accounting Office (GAO). 1989. Traffic Congestion: Trends, Measures and Effects. Washington, D.C.: U.S. General Accounting Office.

U.S. Office of Technology Assessment. 1989. Traffic Congestion: Trends, Measures, and Effects. Report GAO/PEMD-90-1. Washington, D.C.: U.S. Office of Technology Assessment.

Wachs, M. 1989. Transportation demand management: Policy implications of recent behavioral research. Paper presented at the Symposium on Transportation Demand Management, Los Angeles, October 12-13, 1989.

Wegmann, F. 1989. Cost-effectiveness of private employer ridesharing programs: An employer's assessment. Transportation Research Record 1212:88-100.

Willson, R., D. Shoup, and M. Wachs. 1989. Parking Subsidies and Commuter Mode Choice: Assessing the Evidence. Los Angeles: Southern California Association of Governments.

24

Energy Supply Systems

Energy supply can come from a wide variety of systems. Since most of them are discussed extensively in the technical literature, the panel does not attempt here to provide a comprehensive review. Rather, the panel indicates the range of possible energy supply systems in the United States and their implications for greenhouse gas emissions at the current time. The panel leaves to more specialized analyses the detailed consideration of system design and selection. Projections as to the cost and path of technological development of various energy supply systems in the future are not attempted, but are discussed generally in terms of their relevance to greenhouse warming.

Our energy supply is currently obtained in basically three ways: (1) combustion of fossil fuels such as oil, natural gas, and coal; (2) nuclear fission; and (3) other nonfossil-fuel-based sources such as biomass and hydroelectric power. The level at which we use each of these primary energy sources has a major impact on greenhouse gas emissions, primarily because of the differing levels of CO_2 that these sources introduce into the atmosphere.

It is particularly relevant to examine how fossil fuels are used since they are currently our principal source of energy. One estimate of the carbon contained in fossil fuels, and hence of the potential for mankind to alter the CO_2 concentration of the atmosphere, is given in Table 24.1 (Fulkerson et al., 1989). The atmosphere currently contains about 750 Gt of carbon as CO_2.[1] Figure 24.1 documents the course of fossil fuel burning over the last 30 years and the simultaneous increase in the mass of atmospheric CO_2.

The mass of carbon in the recoverable resources of conventional oil and natural gas (250 Gt C, see Table 24.1) is notably smaller than the mass of carbon in the atmosphere (750 Gt C, where 1 ppmv of CO_2 in the atmosphere is equal to 2.13 Gt C). Consequently, the CO_2 doubling so often

TABLE 24.1 Estimated Remaining Recoverable World Resources of Fossil Fuels and Their Potential Effect on Atmospheric CO_2

Fuel	Quantity	Energy Content (10^{18} Btu)	Carbon Content (Gt)	CO_2 Concentration Increase (ppmv)		
				$f=0.4$	$f=0.55$	$f=0.7$
Oil	1.25×10^{12} barrels (0.2×10^{12} m^3)	7	130	24	34	43
Natural Gas	8,200 TCF (232×10^{12} m^3)	8	120	23	31	39
Coal	5,500 Gt	153	3,850	723	994	1,265
TOTAL (rounded off)		168	4,100	770	1,060	1,350

NOTE: Abbreviations: ppmv = parts per million by volume, TCF = trillion cubic feet, and f = fraction of CO_2 retained in the atmosphere. In addition to these amounts of carbon, comparable or larger amounts may be available in other fossil resources such as heavy oils, oil shale, tar sand, and lower grades of coal. Thus the quantity of carbon ultimately released to the atmosphere as CO_2 could conceivably be 1.5 to 2 times the total shown in the table.

SOURCE: Fulkerson et al. (1989).

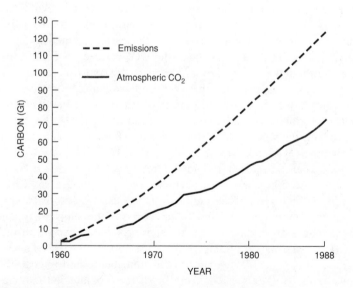

FIGURE 24.1 Cumulative emissions of CO_2 from fossil fuel burning since 1959 and observed increases in the atmosphere at Mauna Loa.

SOURCES: Data are from Keeling et al. (1989); Marland (1990).

examined in climate models could not be accomplished even if all of the conventional oil and gas were burned. The world recoverable resources of coal, on the other hand, are very large. Over the long term, if mankind is to produce perturbations of atmospheric CO_2 up to and beyond a doubling, it will be because of the oxidation of large quantities of coal and low-grade, unconventional fuels such as oil shale. Estimates of ultimately recoverable resources are, of course, very uncertain. As currently understood, world recoverable resources of coal are heavily concentrated in three large northern hemisphere nations: the United States, the former USSR, and the People's Republic of China. These three nations contain an estimated 87 percent of world recoverable resources of coal.

As primary sources of usable energy, fossil fuels release heat through the exothermic reaction of atmospheric oxygen with the carbon and hydrogen of fuel. The consequent release of CO_2 is fundamentally different from many traditional pollutant releases in which a low grade (e.g., trace metal) or otherwise unintended (e.g., CO or SO_2) by-product is released to the environment or a purposeful product reaches beyond its intended application (e.g., pesticides). The emission of CO_2 is an essential consequence of burning fossil fuels.

Largely because the carbon to hydrogen ratios of fossil fuels differ, their rate of CO_2 production per unit of useful energy differs. Natural gas is principally CH_4, with a 1:4 ratio of carbon to hydrogen, and it releases 13.8 kg C per gigajoule (GJ). Although coal has a wide range of chemical compositions, it contains less hydrogen than natural gas, and to a first approximation the heating value varies with the carbon content. The value 24.1 kg C/GJ can be used to estimate the CO_2 release on combustion for most coals, although for very low grade coals this ratio increases slightly. Liquid petroleum products fall somewhere in between natural gas and coal. The CO_2 release for average world crude oil (and hence the average for a mixture for all products) can be taken at about 19.9 kg C/GJ. For a discrete refined product, the value differs: for example, 18.5 is appropriate for automotive gasoline (Marland, 1983).

While CO_2 can be intimately and accurately related to fossil fuel combustion, there are other, less well characterized, greenhouse gas emissions from the fossil fuel cycle. The production, processing, and distribution of natural gas inevitably allow some CH_4 to escape to the atmosphere, and the natural gas that is associated with petroleum production can result in venting (as CH_4) or flaring (to produce CO_2). Methane also exists dispersed in coal seams and is generally released to the atmosphere during coal mining.

Nitrous oxide (N_2O) emissions from fossil fuel combustion may be very small. Recent studies (Muzio et al., 1989) have cast doubt on all earlier measurements, and it is not now clear how much N_2O is released during combustion processes. (Note that N_2O is different from the more common oxides of nitrogen (NO_x)—NO and NO_2—associated with fuel combustion.)

RECENT TRENDS

An initial step in looking at recent trends is to review the sources of the U.S. energy supply, and these are shown in Figure 24.2. Oil is the largest source of energy supply at 41 percent, and coal is second at 23 percent. Renewables account for 8 percent, with hydropower providing almost half

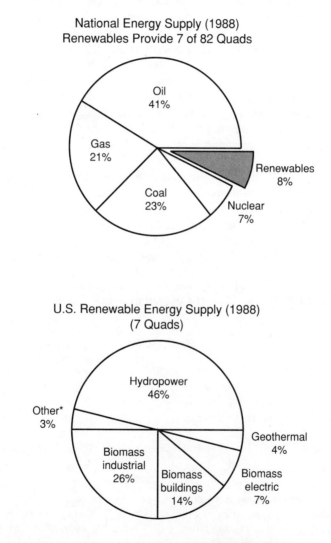

* Other: wind, alcohol fuels, solar thermal, and solar photovoltaics.

FIGURE 24.2   National energy supplies and the renewable contributions.

Source: Solar Energy Research Institute (1990).

of that. Biomass used in the industrial, buildings, and electricity sectors provides roughly the same amount of energy as hydropower. Very little energy currently comes from solar, wind, geothermal, or other sources of renewable energy (Solar Energy Research Institute, 1990).

Table 24.2 shows electricity generation and the carbon emissions from generation in the United States in 1988. Coal is the largest generation source of U.S. electricity at 57 percent, with nuclear second at 19.5 percent. Renewables represent only a small portion of U.S. electric power generation. Electricity generation in the United States is responsible for approximately 35 percent of U.S. CO_2 emissions and 8 percent of worldwide anthropogenic CO_2 emissions (Edmonds et al., 1989).

To contrast the various energy systems and their greenhouse gas implications, it is necessary to inventory full fuel cycle costs. For a gasoline-powered automobile, for example, CO_2 emissions are not simply those discharged from the engine but also those CO_2 (and other trace gas) emissions discharged during petroleum exploration, production, refining, and product distribution.

Although there are many difficulties in detail with using a CO_2 accounting, in theory comparisons can be made. One estimate is that for every direct use of liquid fuel, CO_2 emissions equivalent to those that would result from the use of an additional 11.8 percent of petroleum products are produced in activities upstream from the final products at the refinery. Under this accounting system, these greenhouse gas emissions should be charged

TABLE 24.2 Electric Power Generation in the United States, 1988

Fuel	Carbon Emissions (Million tons)[a]	Generation (BkWh)[b]	Percentage of Generation
Coal (758×10^6 short tons)	398 (85%)	1,538	57.0
Oil (248×10^6 barrels)	31 (7%)	149	5.5
Gas (2634 billion ft^3)	39 (8%)	252	9.3
Nuclear	—	526	19.5
Hydroelectric	—	223	8.3
Renewables	Negligible	12	0.4
TOTAL	468	2,700	100.0

[a]These are net emissions at the point of power generation and do not include emissions related to system capital or other portions of the fuel cycle. The assumption is made that biomass fuels are raised in a sustainable manner so that combustion releases are balanced by photosynthetic capture. Tons are metric.
[b]BkWh = billion kilowatt-hours.

SOURCE: National Research Council (1990).

at the point of product use. Similar values for natural gas and coal are less well established but have been estimated at 18.8 percent for gas delivered to the customer and 2.2 percent for coal at the minehead (Marland, 1983).

In the 1987 global economy, 95 percent of total commercial energy (energy that is traded in commercial markets but not including "traditional fuels" such as wood) was produced from fossil fuels. This varied from virtually 100 percent in some resource-poor countries largely dependent on imported petroleum, to 62 percent for France (where 77 percent of electricity is from nuclear plants) and 29 percent for Norway (where hydroelectric plants contribute a large fraction of the total energy). The value was 89 percent in the United States. (These fractions are based on numbers from the United Nations, but they count nuclear power and hydroelectricity at their conventional fuel equivalents by assuming fuels could be converted to electricity at a 33 percent net plant conversion efficiency.)

On the global scale, petroleum contributes the largest share (44 percent) of the energy from fossil fuels, with coal (32 percent) and natural gas (24 percent) following, but coal is the dominant fuel in a number of countries (China, India, and the former German Democratic Republic). In the United States, 83 percent of coal is used in electric power plants and another 5 percent is used in the iron and steel industry (Organization for Economic Cooperation and Development, 1987). The transportation sector is the largest user of petroleum in the United States (62 percent), with the remainder spread over many applications, including nonfuel applications (some of which do not emit greenhouse gases). Twenty-five percent of U.S. natural gas is used in residences, with another 17 percent used for electric power generation and the remainder scattered throughout the commercial and industrial sectors (U.S. Department of Energy, 1988).

EMISSION CONTROL METHODS

A number of alternatives are available for reducing net greenhouse gas emissions from the production of energy. In this chapter, the discussion is divided into two major topics. Energy supply systems purely for electricity generation are discussed first. Then energy supply systems on a broader basis are examined. Some examples of existing efficient energy systems are given, and a concept called integrated energy systems is discussed. The relevance of new fuel supply and conversion options is treated in this context. Following the descriptions of the technical options, a separate section illustrates how the cost-effectiveness of different options can be compared. Because of the number and complexity of options available, it is not possible to make this discussion comprehensive and all-inclusive. Rather the attempt here is to convey a picture of the technological options available and the methodology employed.

Electricity Generation

Electricity can be generated from coal, oil, natural gas, nuclear energy, and a variety of renewable forms of energy including hydraulic resources, wind, geothermal, solar thermal, and solar photovoltaic energy. With the exception of oil, each is discussed below. Although oil historically has been used for power generation in some regions of the United States (principally in the Northeast), its use has declined dramatically in the past decade and no significant increase is foreseen. The primary use of oil for electricity and steam generation in the United States is in the industrial sector, which is discussed in Chapter 22. The power generation technology options discussed below for coal and natural gas also are applicable to oil in many instances.

Coal

Coal is the most abundant fossil fuel resource in the United States and is the principal fuel powering the economies of several other nations including China and the former USSR. Coal is used primarily for electric power generation, but also for industrial process heat and, in some cases (mostly in developing countries), domestic heating and cooking. Barring severe environmental repercussions, coal is likely to continue to be a major energy source for power generation and other energy needs well into the twenty-first century.

From the point of view of greenhouse gas emissions, the principal issues are the quantities of coal that will be used and the efficiency of coal combustion and energy conversion. Conventional pulverized-coal-fired power plants now being built are capable of overall thermal efficiencies (the efficiency with which coal is converted to electricity) of about 38 percent without scrubbers (the SO_2 removal systems that reduce emissions of acid rain precursors but also reduce net power plant efficiency). The average for all coal-fired power plants now in place in the United States, however, is about 33 percent (U.S. Department of Energy, 1989).

Several technological developments hold promise for continued improvement in coal-based electric power generation (Rubin, 1989). Table 24.3 summarizes performance estimates by the Electric Power Research Institute (EPRI) for several power generation options, which range from improvements in current technology to newer systems not yet commercially demonstrated (Electric Power Research Institute, 1986).

Overall, efficiency improvements on the order of 10 percent or more are expected from technological advances over the next decade. The most promising near-term options include integrated gasification combined cycle (IGCC) systems and pressurized fluidized-bed combustion (PFBC) systems. The latter technology is planned for demonstration in the United States

TABLE 24.3 Efficiency of Coal-Based Power Generation Systems

Technology	Heat Rate (Btu/kWh)[a]
Conventional coal-steam with wet limestone flue gas desulfurization:	
Supercritical boiler	9,660
Subcritical boiler	10,060
Advanced pulverized coal-steam with flue gas desulfurization	8,830
Atmospheric fluidized-bed	10,000
Pressurized fluidized-bed combined cycle	8,980
Coal gasification combined cycle:	
Current turbine	9,775
Advanced turbine	9,280
Gasification fuel cell combined cycle	7,130
Gasification combined cycle methanol co-product	12,875

[a]The annual average heat rate, which is a reciprocal of efficiency, is the performance measure most commonly used for utility systems. Data are for an Illinois bituminous coal and a plant size of approximately 500 MW.

SOURCE: EPRI (1986).

under the Department of Energy's (DOE's) Clean Coal Technology Program, and other PFBC demonstration plants are being constructed in Europe.

Integrated gasification combined cycle technology has been demonstrated at the 100-MW scale at the Cool Water Facility operated by Southern California Edison. Although a number of U.S. utilities are studying the feasibility of building additional IGCC capacity, that technology in most cases is not yet economically competitive with conventional pulverized coal combustion. Advanced IGCC designs employing the concept of "hot gas cleanup" (i.e., removing pollutants without having first to cool the flue gas) hold promise of greater efficiency gains and lower cost (Bajura, 1989). Such technologies are currently under development.

In the near term, boiler repowering, in which an older existing unit is replaced with a more efficient new one, is another method by which the overall efficiency of coal utilization can be improved. In this type of application, atmospheric fluidized-bed combustion (AFBC) units may be attractive because of their compact size and fuel versatility. Several repowering projects are now under way in the United States using AFBC boilers.

As mentioned above, a negative impact on CO_2 emissions can result from the flue gas desulfurization (FGD) systems, or "scrubbers," used to remove SO_2. Because the energy needed to operate the scrubber reduces overall power plant efficiency, CO_2 emissions per unit of useful electricity increase proportionately. Modern FGD systems require only 1 to 2 percent of the power plant output for operation, down by a factor of 2 from systems built in the early 1980s. This improvement has resulted from more efficient scrubber designs and the elimination of stack gas reheat systems.

Fluidized-bed combustion systems have a comparable loss of thermal energy when limestone is used for SO_2 control. The SO_2 removal systems using lime or limestone reagents (whether in scrubbers or fluidized beds) release additional CO_2 directly through the chemistry of sulfur removal. This additional CO_2 stream is small, however, in comparison with the CO_2 emissions from coal combustion.

There are small differences in CO_2 emissions due to differences in coal quality. In general, coals with higher sulfur content emit less CO_2 per unit of energy, complicating any policy designed to reduce both CO_2 and SO_2 emissions. High-rank bituminous coals produce 5 to 10 percent less CO_2 than do lower-rank subbituminous and lignite coals (Winschel, 1990); however, most coals actually burned at the present time fall within a narrower range of 2 to 3 percent. Thus the differences in CO_2 emissions resulting from the combustion of different coal types are roughly the same order of magnitude as the reductions anticipated from near-term combustion efficiency improvements.

For the immediate future, perhaps the most cost-effective means of CO_2 reduction from existing coal-fired power plants lies in heat rate (efficiency) improvements achievable by improved plant maintenance and operation. EPRI estimates that such measures could result in a 2 to 4 percent reduction in current CO_2 emissions at a very small cost (Gluckman, 1990). The resulting efficiency improvements have the potential for saving roughly 2 to 4 percent in fuel consumption, offsetting the small costs that are incurred (and perhaps even generating net additional revenues and thus yielding a net negative cost of CO_2 abatement). Heat rate improvements are actively being pursued by many utilities today.

Finally, future developments for coal-fired power plants conceivably could include control technology for the removal of CO_2 from flue gases. This option, which could apply generally to fossil fuels, is discussed later in this chapter.

Natural Gas

As pointed out previously, the combustion of natural gas emits less CO_2 than the combustion of coal because of the higher ratio of hydrogen to carbon. There are a number of ways natural gas can be used in place of coal for electricity generation.

Combined Cycle Systems   In a gas turbine combined cycle (GTCC) system, the exhaust from a gas turbine is fed into a residual heat boiler that generates steam for a bottoming steam turbine cycle. If natural gas is used to fuel the gas turbine, the overall efficiency of the system can be slightly more than 50 percent. The capital cost of such a system is about $500/kW. Combined cycle systems have not been considered a serious option in the planning of future power generation until very recently, largely because of the uncertainty in the availability of natural gas and the poor reliability of GTCC systems in the past. The latter was not due to inherent technical barriers but to a lack of attention from the industry.

Two recent events changed the situation. First, EPRI, in cooperation with Southern California Edison and Texaco, proposed the organization of a consortium to develop a $300 million IGCC system—the Cool Water project. For the first time, the issue of the reliability of combined cycle systems received serious attention. Second, Japan, in an effort to diversify energy sources, ordered several gigawatts of combined cycle systems to use liquefied natural gas.

Further, as discussed in a number of reports (e.g., Tabors and Flagg, 1986), GTCC is competitive economically with alternative forms of energy supply. The attractiveness of GTCCs, therefore, has been broadly recognized both in its economics and in its potential contribution to the reduction of greenhouse gases.

Other Natural Gas Options   One of the most difficult issues in the global greenhouse warming problem is how developing nations can participate in mitigation efforts without damaging their economic development. Some of these nations might require options with capital costs even lower than those of GTCC. Steam injection in aircraft-type gas turbines might be an option to consider, even though the efficiency may be slightly lower (Williams, 1989). For small plants, El-Masri (1988) has proposed a regenerative system that is attractive from the viewpoints of both cost and efficiency. This system has not yet been tried, but the technical and economic basis is sufficiently sound to warrant consideration. In addition, the Kalina cycle, a type of steam cycle used in conjunction with a natural gas turbine, can have an efficiency of more than 55 percent with today's commercial gas turbines (Exergy Inc., 1989).

Nuclear Energy

Apart from the CO_2 emitted in the exploration, production, and enrichment of uranium, nuclear plants do not emit CO_2. Reactors based on nuclear fission have operated for many years and provide a significant contribution to the production of electric power in many countries of the world—19 percent in the United States.

In the United States, however, the nuclear reactor market is, for all practical purposes, moribund, in spite of industry's efforts to reactivate it. There are five concerns:

- safety,
- economics,
- waste disposal,
- proliferation, and
- resources.

The lack of acceptance of nuclear power in the United States is a complex issue. Utilities are no longer willing to order new nuclear plants, principally because of economics and perceived financial risk. The unattractive economics of nuclear energy is due to a host of problems. Another concern is the current lack of radioactive waste disposal facilities in the United States.

Utility companies argue that the present generation of reactors is safe enough and can be improved further by the ongoing development work on advanced light water reactors both in and outside the United States. Nonetheless, passively safe reactors have been proposed by others as alternatives. By definition, a passively safe reactor requires no action by any component or subsystem to prevent an accident. This is different from the "defense in depth" concept of present reactors, in which, if there is a malfunction, other systems will intervene. However, whether any specific reactor technology is passively safe is often a subject for debate.

Appendix G provides a description of some of the proposed new technologies. These descriptions are not intended to be a comprehensive and critical analysis of the technological options for future development of nuclear power nor an endorsement of particular technologies. Such an analysis will be provided in a forthcoming report by a committee of the National Research Council's Energy Engineering Board.

Proliferation may be the ultimate problem of nuclear energy. There will always be the fear that an irresponsible party may develop a nuclear weapon capability with the help of plutonium from recycled power reactor fuel. Proliferation is an international issue. Whether greenhouse warming will stimulate a new international cooperative effort on proliferation, only time will tell.

A long-term commitment to nuclear power would also confront the resource issue. Is there enough uranium for nuclear energy to have a significant impact? To give some perspective on this issue, Weinberg (1989) proposed the following assumptions:

- In the year 2040 the world will require 500 quads of energy (the current figure is 300 quads);[2]

- If the present trend of retaining only half of the CO_2 emitted in the atmosphere continues, the CO_2 concentration in the atmosphere can be stabilized if the emission is limited to 3 Gt C/yr (the total emission is currently about 6 Gt C/yr). (This is a controversial "if.")
- All nonfission, nonfossil sources will supply 50 quads/yr by 2040.

Weinberg raised the question of whether there is enough uranium to supply 300 quads of primary energy with nuclear energy (limiting the fossil supply to 150 quads). This would mean 5000 reactors, or 10 times the number of nuclear reactors now in existence worldwide. Weinberg estimated that at $130/kg, there may be 31×10^6 tons of uranium if one includes the speculative resources (Organization for Economic Cooperation and Development, IEA, 1983). With that much uranium, the 5000 reactors could be sustained for about 40 years without recycle, 80 years with recycle, and 2000 years with breeders.

Weinberg also raised the question of the importance, at this scale, of the energy needed in the production of uranium, in particular the CO_2 emitted from fossil fuels used for uranium mining and processing. The analysis of Rotty et al. (1976) showed that this is a small fraction of the CO_2 from a comparable coal-fired plant.

Each of these nuclear fission issues—safety, economics, waste disposal, proliferation, and resources—is currently being addressed by the Energy Engineering Board committee. The committee's report, projected for release in 1992, will discuss what is needed to preserve nuclear power as an option. It should shed more light on the complex problem of nuclear power acceptance.

An alternative nuclear option that has been under development since the 1950s is nuclear fusion. The theoretical attractiveness of this concept is why the efforts in many countries have continued. It has the potential to solve many of the safety and environmental concerns of nuclear fission, but the technical and economic feasibility have yet to be proven. Considering the advances needed, fusion cannot be considered an energy option at this time. Research and development should continue, however. A brief description of the state of the art can be found in Appendix G.

In summary, acceptance of nuclear energy as a principal source of energy supply would change in important respects the prospects of greatly reducing the discharge of CO_2 into the atmosphere. Whether this is feasible is a complex question that goes beyond the charge of this panel, which here limits itself to observing nuclear energy's close connection with the problem of greenhouse warming.

Renewable Energy

In addition to energy supply systems that rely on the extraction, consumption, and ultimate depletion of resources, there are others that rely on natural energy flows and, hence, are renewable if not inexhaustible. These range from the large and virtually inexhaustible flow of energy from the sun, to the smaller but still inexhaustible flow of water from high elevation, to the comparatively small and probably exhaustible flow of steam or hot water in wet geothermal systems.

For the application of each of these energy sources, one needs to inquire into the magnitude of the flow that can be tapped, the cost of doing so, and the ecological repercussions of altering or harnessing the natural flows. A series of new questions involving factors such as regional distribution and energy storage must also be confronted. Each of these energy supply systems is presumably sustainable at some level with little or no net CO_2 release other than from fossil fuel investments in plant capital and fossil fuel supplements to system operation. In the latter case, especially, it is apparent that CO_2 emissions are a function of energy supply system design and are not inherent in system utilization (as is the case with fossil fuel burning). As an example, ethanol fuels could theoretically be derived from a sustainable corn crop with all of the carbon recycled and no net CO_2 emissions to the atmosphere.

On the other hand, the current ethanol production system uses diesel fuel to plant and harvest corn, natural gas to produce nitrogen fertilizers, and coal to generate power and heat for grinding and processing. The result is that total energy supply system CO_2 emissions from ethanol use in the United States are nearly as high (80 percent) (Marland and Turnhollow, 1990) as those from the direct utilization of gasoline as a motor fuel. This need not be the case, however, because the system could operate with ethanol fuels for farm machinery and nuclear electricity for corn processing.

In general, it is useful to keep in mind both how each energy supply system currently operates at the margin of the U.S. or world economy and how it could operate in a closed economy or if it were a dominant component of the energy supply.

The list of technologies in this class includes hydroelectric, wind, geothermal, solar photovoltaic, and solar thermal electric.

Hydroelectric Power   Conventional hydroelectric generation currently represents 12 percent of the total U.S. electricity supply, with an installed capacity of approximately 69,000 MW and an identifiable potential for another 46,000 MW of capacity (Fulkerson et al., 1989). However, the real potential for future development is undoubtedly less than this because of competing demands on water and other resources. Fulkerson et al. (1989) estimate that hydroelectric systems could produce an additional 125 millon kilowatt hours (MkWh) of electricity annually in the United States, from a base of 231 MkWh, but the Solar Energy Research Institute (1990) estimates the increased capacity by 2030 will be less than one-fifth of Fulkerson's potential 46,000 MW.

Wind Energy   More than 660 MW of installed capacity of wind-generated electric power exists in the United States (Fulkerson et al., 1989). Substantial additional resources exist, but a precise estimate is hard to achieve because of the importance of site-specific characteristics that include the temporal variability of the wind. Wind power is on the threshold of economic viability, and advances in technology, economics, and resource analysis can be expected. The Solar Energy Research Institute (1990) maintains that "wind has the potential to make meaningful contributions in virtually all areas of the country."

Geothermal Energy   Potentially usable geothermal energy exists at steam vents, in deep hot waters, in hot, dry rocks, and in near-surface magmas. According to the U.S. Geological Survey (USGS), approximately 23,000 MW of electrical power will be available over the next 30 years with current geothermal technology. The CO_2 emissions are less than 5 percent of those from coal, and the cost of the 2,800 MW of geothermal electricity currently in production is $0.04 to $0.06/kWh. In California, for example, geothermal resources are currently providing 7 percent of the state's electric power and are displacing 1,700 MW (thermal) of fossil fuels in heating and industrial applications at a cost savings of 25 to 35 percent (Solar Energy Research Institute, 1990). The currently exploited high-quality resource in California is, however, relatively rare.

There are a number of constraints on the development of geothermal energy. First, the majority of present geothermal plants are relatively small, between 1 to 5 MW and 25 to 60 MW, with a few at 110 MW, resulting in a lack of acceptance by utilities. Second, most usable sites are at locations where concerns for scenic values, wildlife issues, or other environmental problems make it difficult to develop the geothermal power. A number of technological constraints limit the development of geothermal energy, including the risk associated with the discovery of the resource, verification of the well size, projection of long-term reservoir performance, well integrity, operational uncertainties, and energy conversion (Solar Energy Research Institute, 1990).

In sum, geothermal energy will probably continue to contribute to the U.S. energy mix, but resource constraints will limit its role in minimizing greenhouse gas emissions.

Solar Photovoltaics   Photoelectric technology has experienced considerable progress over the last decade (Hubbard, 1989). Efficiencies of more than 22 percent have been achieved for the conversion of solar to electrical energy under ordinary sunlight. Atlantic Richfield and Pacific Gas and Electric have completed a 6.5-MW power plant, and "tens of thousands of PV [photovoltaic] systems are already providing power for a variety of applications" (Hubbard, 1989), mostly in remote areas. Photovoltaic modules are now expected to last 20 to 30 years. Hubbard believes that photovoltaic power systems should be competitive for generating central station peaking power by the late 1990s.

Because of the intermittent character of the solar resource, solar power cannot be expected to grow beyond some fraction of total electric power demand unless some form of energy storage can be devised. Displacement of baseline power production for daytime usage plus peaking power accounts for about 17 percent of today's installed capacity, and one study suggests that reliance on photovoltaics for more than 13 percent of power—without storage capability—could lead to serious problems (Hubbard, 1989).

The potential for photovoltaics to avoid fossil fuel burning—and CO_2 emissions—is high if costs continue to drop as forecasted and some appropriate scheme can be devised for energy storage. Although solar photovoltaics are relatively expensive at this time, some analysts suggest that continuing developments could reduce the cost by 70 percent (Hubbard, 1989). Further, a viable storage system would increase system potential, albeit at some cost. A more detailed discussion of photovoltaics can be found in Appendix H.

Solar Thermal Electric Systems In California, parabolic trough solar thermal electric systems of 194 MW have been installed. In these systems a parabolic trough concentrator with a highly reflective surface focuses solar energy on a heat-collecting pipe, called the receiver. A fluid, either water or some other heat transfer material, circulates in the pipe, collecting the solar energy and transferring it to the power block of the plant to generate electricity. The design has evolved to a hybrid form in which natural gas is used to extend the operation of the plant during periods of the day when solar energy is unavailable.

With additional development, the cost of electricity from this type of system is expected to improve. Again, the environmental benefits may improve the economic outlook further if externalities are internalized (California Energy Resources, Conservation and Development Commission, 1989). Cost-effectiveness is discussed in Appendix J.

Integrated Energy Systems

Different technologies can be thought of as elements of "integrated energy systems" (IESs). As technologies evolve and externalities are internalized, the economic attractiveness of different energy supply options changes. To the degree that this may occur, the energy supply structure can change to accommodate different ways of supplying energy and of reducing emissions from the generation of that energy. Therefore it is useful to examine some technologies as elements in an energy system instead of viewing electricity production alone. Integrated energy systems themselves are discussed first, followed by five technologies that are potential elements in the system: biomass to produce ethanol and methanol; solar energy to produce hydrogen fuels; fuel cells; superconducting cables; and collection and disposal of CO_2 in the deep ocean or in natural gas wells.

In integrated energy systems, supply and demand are not treated separately but are considered elements of a system. A number of papers have been written on IESs (e.g., Hafele et al., 1986; Lee et al., 1990). The concept is not new. The oil refinery/petrochemical complex and the steel mill, which have been in existence for years, are two good examples of IESs, even though they are never referred to as such. In an oil refinery/petrochemical complex, there is no clear distinction between product streams and energy streams. Crude oil, liquefied petroleum gas, natural gas, and other industrial gases are the primary materials used, but each is used for many purposes. For example, natural gas is used as fuel in heaters, as a feedstock, or as fuel for the unit making hydrogen. The entire steam cycle is integrated: high-quality steam for turbines and low-quality steam for preheaters. The result is a robust, flexible system, highly efficient and economically sound.

In a steel mill the primary raw materials are coal and iron ore. Despite the mill's huge need for energy, it does not burn coal but uses it as a chemical raw material. The coal is coked. By using the gas released as a fuel, the coal is heated to remove all chemicals, which are recovered. The associated fuel gas is used in both coke ovens and open hearth furnaces. The coke is used as the chemical reducing agent for iron oxide in the blast furnaces.

By extending this experience to energy systems in general, one can formulate the general concept of an IES as shown in Figures 24.3 and 24.4. Although Figure 24.3 contains a number of boxes, representing technological steps, the boxes represent options, not required components. There are five aspects to the system: (1) energy sources, including sunshine, fuels, air, and water; (2) transformation processes (incoming fuels are transformed to

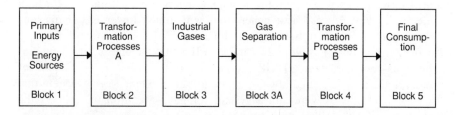

FIGURE 24.3 Simplified representation of an integrated energy system.

SOURCE: Lee (1989).

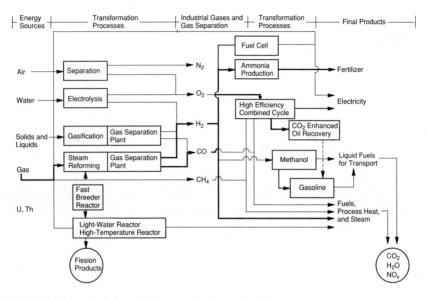

FIGURE 24.4   Functional diagram of an integrated energy system.

SOURCE: Lee (1989).

industrial gases); (3) industrial gases and gas separation; (4) second transformation processes to change industrial gases to more useful energy forms
(electricity or chemicals); and (5) product to final consumption. One useful
feature of this concept with regard to environmental protection should be
noted. At present, all parties in the energy production chain share responsibility for environmental protection. In an IES, the responsibility can be
focused on the upstream process (the left-hand portions of Figures 24.3 and
24.4). This should make the job of environmental protection easier.

   One of the simplest IESs, the co-generation system using natural gas to
generate both electricity and heat, can be traced, for example, from gas to
combined cycle to electricity, process heat, and steam. Another system can
utilize two primary energy sources, nuclear energy and natural gas, for both
electricity and process heat generation, with much lower CO_2 emissions
than would result from burning gas alone.

   The heavy lines in Figure 24.4 trace an IES that includes a high-temperature gas-cooled reactor (HTGR), a steam reformer (for the conversion of
natural gas to hydrogen and CO), a gas turbine combined cycle system that
utilizes CO and oxygen, and a system for gas separation that allows the
recovery of CO_2 either as a by-product or for disposal. The system is
designed to have nuclear fuels, natural gas, and air as inputs and to have
electricity, hydrogen, and CO_2 as outputs. The economics of such a system

can no longer be assessed as easily as the traditional cents per kilowatt hour calculation. For example, the cost of electricity now depends on the price of hydrogen and CO_2. If an end use can be found for the CO_2, such as enhanced oil recovery, and hydrogen can be sold at today's market price, the electricity generated can be competitive with that produced by a GTCC system. On the other hand, if hydrogen can be sold at its heating value only, and there is no end use for the CO_2, then the cost of electricity is much higher. Under these conditions, one might want to resort to the conventional air-fired gas turbine combined cycle system and also eliminate the gas separation system for the synthesis gas. The CO_2 must then be removed downstream. It should be noted that, per kilowatt hour, this system generates much less CO_2 because only part of the primary energy is from fossil fuel, the remainder being from nuclear energy. The synthesis gas behaves as the carrier of nuclear energy.

An important feature of the IES concept is the ability to accept and adopt new technologies when they are developed. Systems can be designed with combinations of existing technologies and can be modified to accept new technologies, be they solar photovoltaic or superconducting transmission lines.

Two questions need to be addressed:

1. If IESs are so good, why are they not being used today?
2. What is the role of government if more IESs are to become a reality in the energy economy?

There are two answers to the first question. First, IESs are not the practice today largely because our current economic and business system is not horizontally integrated, but vertically integrated in the energy and chemical sector. (Vertically integrated systems for coal, for example, involve integration from mining to transport to electricity generation. Horizontal integration involves electricity generation, steel mills, and coal gasification for production of synthesis gas.) In spite of that, steel mills and refineries do exist. Second, many of the social costs of energy systems are not internalized. As the emphasis on environmental protection intensifies, some of the social costs may become the responsibility of the polluters in the future. The economics of IESs will then change. One study (Organization for Economic Cooperation and Development, 1981) showed that the costs of SO_2 scrubbers can be justified by the social costs of the effects of SO_2. Another study (Styrikovich and Chizhov, 1988) showed that the social costs of coal combustion can be higher than the current market price of coal.

Legal, informational, and institutional barriers do exist. The second question is really the other side of the first one. Probably the most critical role of the government is to ensure that viable, horizontally integrated alternatives will not be overlooked because of institutional barriers.

Biomass

Fuels from wood, grain, herbaceous crops, and urban waste are considered under the collective heading of biomass fuels. Biomass fuels, mostly wood but including animal dung and crop residues, supplied a large fraction of man's energy needs until very recent times, and moving from these traditional fuels to commercial fossil fuels is still often perceived as representing social progress and economic development. This progression may represent environmental progress as well because traditional fuels are often used in very inefficient ways, with large atmospheric effluent streams, and are not produced in a sustainable manner. The challenge for biomass in the future is to ensure a sustainable harvest, possibly from energy plantations, and to develop efficient and nonpolluting systems for fuel conversion and use. Among the attractive features of biomass fuels are that they avoid the storage problems of the intermittent flows of solar energy and that they can be used to provide both central station fuels and liquid transportation fuels.

Great strides are being achieved in the area of biomass yield and conversion efficiency, and Fulkerson et al. (1989) estimate that biomass could supply 14.6 exajoules (EJ) per year of liquid fuels in the United States (31.0 EJ of gross biomass) if all of the options were aggressively pursued.[3] At 14.6 EJ/yr, biomass would provide about 40 percent of total U.S. liquid fuel consumption. Current biomass use in the United States is about 3 EJ/yr. The total cost of biomass fuels is strongly influenced by handling and transportation costs, and successful systems are likely to be of modest size so as to rely on short haul distances. Costs would vary considerably from place to place, depending on plantation productivity and handling and transportation costs.

For energy plantations there remain a variety of questions beyond achievable yield. These include the net effect of sequestering carbon (e.g., in soils), the influence on other environmental issues (e.g., low maintenance intensity should lead to less soil erosion than occurs with agricultural crops), the effect on other greenhouse gas emissions (e.g., fertilization could increase N_2O emissions), the vulnerability of large monocultural plantations (e.g., to pests and pathogens), the effect on wildlife species (e.g., plantations may provide a limited habitat but could reduce pressures on natural habitats), and competition for space with agricultural crops. The relatively higher productivities of warmer climates suggest that biomass may play a more important role in some areas than others.

Fulkerson et al. (1989) suggest that the most desired biomass sources, "in order of importance, desirability, and usage are: (1) already collected wastes and residues, (2) commercial forest wood, (3) new terrestrial energy crops, (4) existing agriculture crops devoted to food and feed, and (5) new aquatic crops" (Fulkerson et al., 1989, p. 94). Already-collected waste and residues are broadly used now for energy purposes, especially in the paper industry, and more thorough and efficient utilization of other waste makes increasing sense, especially in the face of increasing problems and costs associated with waste disposal and landfills. The emphasis here is on biomass harvested specifically for its energy content, and the case of wood from energy plantations is used for illustrative purposes (see Appendix I). Economic analysis of the fuel supply is complicated by the many possible combinations of yield, fertilization, weed control, spacing, and harvest; studies are currently under way to discover optimal combinations.

There are also a variety of possible ways in which the fuel is used, such as direct burning, gasification, or conversion to alcohol. Ostlie (1988) suggests that some savings can be achieved from direct burning of wood in place of coal for electric power generation. There is no need, for example, for SO_2 removal and handling. Williams (1989) sees an increase in net conversion efficiency with respect to current power plants, through the use of advanced gas turbine technology. Conversion to liquid fuels will involve a cost increase because of the low efficiency of the conversion process in comparison with that of crude oil refining. The most straightforward case for early implementation focuses on the availability and cost of delivered fuel for electric power generation, although the future holds more opportunities as technologies for gasification and liquefaction are developed and demonstrated. Advances in biotechnology could be useful in altering either the biomass yield or the structure of the plant. It has been suggested that displacement of fossil fuels for electric power generation could be accomplished with little or no difference in the cost of electricity other than the difference in delivered cost of fuel (see, for example, Wright and Ehrenshaft, 1990).

Although productivity, harvest costs, and land costs are highly variable, data from which one can derive a useful estimate for the delivered cost of wood chips are provided in Appendix I. This may turn out to be a high estimate of fuel cost if whole trees can be used, thereby avoiding the cost of chipping the wood (Ostlie, 1988). The numbers used in this analysis are based on short-rotation hardwood crops, with a 6-year rotation on marginal cropland in the U.S. Midwest. The assumed yield is 11 t per hectare of dry biomass, with 15 percent of the material lost or consumed for plantation operation. Wright and Ehrenshaft (1990) assume that 28 million hectares could be available for plantations in the United States, with comparable or lower cost and higher yield, by 2010, if energy crop research proceeds.

Solar Hydrogen

Another potential source of fuel supply is the combination of photovoltaic solar power with the generation of hydrogen. In a solar hydrogen economy, hydrogen would be produced by the electrolysis of water. At the other end of the pipeline, hydrogen would be supplied to power stations, to industry, and eventually to residences for space and water heating. Stored in metal hydrides, hydrogen could also lend itself as a fuel for transportation, replacing gasoline and diesel oil in automobiles, buses, and trucks. Hydrogen could be an important part of an integrated energy system.

Due to the cost and inefficiency of the transmission of electrical power over great distances, solar power by itself might be practical only in regions of high sunshine. For the United States, that would mean the Southwest. To supply power to areas remote from solar energy collecting fields, one would look for a nonpolluting means of energy transport. For this purpose, the transmission of hydrogen gas by pipelines offers many advantages (Ogden and Williams, 1989).

A hydrogen-based power economy is attractive in terms of its impact on the environment but carries with it two concerns (in addition to economic competitiveness)—storage and safety. Appendix H has additional details.

Fuel Cells

Fuel cells utilize hydrogen and oxygen and generate electricity via electrochemical reactions. Since the 1960s, substantial efforts have been made to adapt fuel cells to large-scale applications because of the obvious advantages:

- only water is emitted,
- they are quiet, and
- they can be close to the site where energy is needed.

Most of the work on fuel cells has concentrated on the use of phosphoric acid fuel cells (PAFC). The impediment to this technology has been cost. The cost of fuel cells today is about \$2500/kW, a significant part of which is the cost of the reformer to produce hydrogen. If fuel cells could be used as an element in an integrated energy system, where hydrogen is supplied by other means, the overall economics could change.

Another technology under development utilizes a mixture of alkaline carbonates and promises to have even higher efficiencies: 55 percent compared to 44 percent for PAFC.

Superconducting Cables

Transmission of energy is a critical issue. One reason that oil is attractive is the ease with which it can be transported. Natural gas suffers in this respect, which is why so much research and development is devoted to liquefied natural gas, pipeline, and direct conversion technologies. Electrical energy suffers from the large losses inherent in transmission lines. For this reason, superconducting cables have been of great interest. Studies have been made on the feasibility of operating superconducting cables at liquid helium temperatures. The general conclusion has been that for this technology to be economically attractive, the power transmitted in the cable must be of the order of tens of gigawatts. How to integrate such a cable into a power system from the viewpoint of operations reliability has not been seriously studied. Successful development of high-temperature super-conducting materials may significantly alter the economics of electrical power generation and transmission, but the time scale is highly uncertain.

Carbon Dioxide Collection and Disposal

Another possible way of reducing CO_2 emissions from fossil fuel systems is the collection and subsequent disposal of CO_2 from large concentrated sources. First suggested by Marchetti (1975), and explored further by Baes et al. (1980), CO_2 collection and disposal has been elaborated on by Steinberg et al. (1984). Additional studies are under way now. Since Steinberg (1983) demonstrated that it is not feasible to extract CO_2 from the ambient atmosphere, and because it does not appear practical to collect CO_2 at small or dispersed sources, this possibility focuses on large, concentrated sources such as electric power plants. In 1985, nearly 40 percent of global fossil-fuel-related CO_2 emissions came from electric power plants, and it is this approximately 7 Gt of CO_2 that might be collected.

In a recent summary of CO_2 collection schemes for pulverized coal boilers, Golomb et al. (1989) conclude that the least-energy-intensive system is one that relies on an air separation plant so that combustion takes place in an oxygen-enriched gas stream and the full emission stream is carried to disposal. This scheme has the further advantage that SO_2 and NO_x are disposed of with the CO_2. Table 24.4, from Golomb et al. (1989), compares the energy requirements for several methods of collecting CO_2. The analysis includes compression to 150 atmospheres but does not include CO_2 transport or disposal. The analysis of Golomb et al. suggests that some schemes could actually result in a net increase in CO_2 emissions because CO_2 collection is less than 100 percent efficient and the energy demands of the collection process require an increase in coal burning to yield the same power output. The costs of such a collection scheme (based on recent estimates from the Netherlands) would be in the range of $32/t CO_2. Most studies assume that disposal will be by injection into the deep ocean.

The consensus to date has been that a regenerable amine scrubber is the most likely candidate for such a collection scheme, although other methods have been explored for smaller systems, such as submarines and space craft cabins, and still others might have application here. A variety of commer-

352

TABLE 24.4 Energy Requirement Comparison for CO_2 Scrubbing at Electric Power Plants

Process	Energy Requirement % of Combustion Energy	Thermal Efficiency (%)	Coal Requirement kg of Coal per kWh	Relative to Base Case	Net CO_2 Emissions kg of CO_2 per kWh	% of Base Case	Recovered CO_2 CO_2 Recovery (%)	CO_2 Purity (%)
Base case—no CO_2 removal	0	35	0.35	1	0.88	100	0	—
Air separation/fluidized gas recycling	26–31	24–26	0.48–0.51	1.35–1.45	0	0	100	90
Amine scrubbing	47–79	7–19	0.66–1.68	1.89–4.76	0.17–0.42	19–48	90	99+
Cryogenic fractionation	55–95	2–16	0.78–7.04	2.22–20	0.20–1.76	22–200	90	97
Membrane separation	50–75	9–18	0.71–1.41	2.00–4	0.35–0.70	40–80	80	90

NOTES: Based on a 500-MW plant. Does not include CO_2 transport and disposal.

SOURCE: Golomb et al. (1989).

cial-scale plants have been operated for acid gas processing, and data are available on at least four plants that successfully scrubbed CO_2 from flue gases. All four of the later used monoethanolamine as the working solvent. Gagliardi et al. (1989) provide a description of a modern CO_2 removal system and discuss some of the system parameters.

Ongoing analysis in the Netherlands has examined the possibility of CO_2 collection from an integrated coal gasifier and combined cycle power plant. Efficiency gains associated with the IGCC technology would offset efficiency losses associated with CO_2 collection, and the total cost of CO_2 collection is about $13/t CO_2. The process envisions using a shift reactor to convert synthesis gas to hydrogen and CO_2, and then removing the CO_2 via physical absorption in a solution. An 88 percent reduction in CO_2 emissions results in a 12 percent loss in net power output. With CO_2 disposal in nearby gas wells (an especially feasible option for the Netherlands), the impact on electricity cost is about 30 percent (Blok et al., 1990; Hendriks et al., 1990; K. Blok, personal communication, 1990).

Carbon dioxide streams have been collected and transported on a large scale for enhanced oil recovery projects, and the gas handling technology is well established. The questions with respect to collecting large quantities of CO_2 at electric generating plants involve the cost of collection and what would be done with the CO_2 once it has been collected. The amount of CO_2 generated at power plants dwarfs market demand, and the general assumption is that these large quantities of CO_2 could be injected into the deep ocean. The ecological consequences of such disposal have not been evaluated seriously. Both Baes et al. (1980) and Steinberg et al. (1984) discuss the prospect of placing at least some of the CO_2 in depleted oil and gas fields.

There has also been some discussion of processing fuels so that full fuel oxidation does not occur, and the carbon-bearing product is something other than CO_2. Steinberg (1989), for example, discusses the possibility of processing coal so that the final products are carbon black and water. This process extracts from coal only the energy available from hydrogen oxidation, but it yields a solid carbon product that should be easier to store than gaseous or dissolved CO_2. Steinberg's estimate is that 19 percent of the energy value of coal would be available in such a scheme with no oxidation of fuel carbon, and the fraction would be higher for liquid and gaseous fuels with higher hydrogen content.

Cost-Effectiveness

The method used in determining the cost-effectiveness of energy supply options is described in Appendix J. As mentioned in Chapter 20, it is important to note that the Mitigation Panel's analysis of energy supply options assumes a constant cost. This cost could change for any number of reasons. For example, implementation of the energy efficiency options described in Chapters 21, 22, and 23 could decrease demand and therefore the cost of electricity. The cost impact could also go the other way. As the price of natural gas or electricity changes, so would the cost-effectiveness calculations in Chapters 21, 22, and 23. Further, a change in the availability of a particular commodity could affect price. For example, since natural gas reserves may be limited, a major increase in the demand for natural gas may cause demand to exceed the supply available, and thus the price of natural gas may increase. On the other hand, a new major source of natural gas may be found. A sensitivity analysis conducted by the panel of the impact of the constant cost assumption on the calculation caused the price of the option in the analysis to range from 3.3 to 4.5 cents/kWh for an assumed escalation in natural gas price of 4 percent per year. In addition, a major crisis or deliberate action of some kind anywhere in the world may reduce the supply of a particular commodity and affect the price. This has been recently observed following the invasion of Kuwait, as well as the OPEC oil embargo during the 1970s. Moreover, technology innovation may substantially reduce the price of a particular technology. For example, the price of energy from solar photovoltaics has constantly been decreasing and may continue to do so.

It is for this reason that the panel made a deliberate decision to avoid projections of price or of the potential of a particular technology to replace fossil fuels. Accordingly, the panel assumed a constant cost for existing technology, even though in doing so a number of potentially important variables are neglected. In addition, the panel has not tried to develop a capital replacement scenario but has examined current costs of replacing a fully depreciated facility.

Therefore to estimate the cost of reducing CO_2 and the potential magnitude of reductions from electric power generation, the panel has considered the prospect of replacing the existing fossil-fuel-fired plants with other options once those plants have been totally written off and are to be replaced. The replacement process would likely take 30 to 40 years.

Assumptions from the Electric Power Research Institute's Technical Assessment Guide (Electric Power Research Institute, 1989) were used whenever appropriate to estimate the cost and performance of various power generation systems; however, in a few cases, the panel felt that different assumptions were needed. For example, in the case of nuclear power plants, it was felt that the EPRI values did not reflect the full range of costs of bringing a plant to full operation in the different regions of the United States, and a range of capital costs between the EPRI value and twice that figure was evaluated. For natural gas combined cycle, a higher efficiency (representing advanced technology) was combined with a zero fuel escalation rate to obtain a lower bound on cost.

Although four real discount rates (3, 6, 10, and 30 percent) were used to evaluate energy demand, only one (6 percent) was used in the power generation calculations. This value is representative of current utility economics in a regulated environment. A more in-depth discussion of the assumptions and calculation methods used is provided in Appendix J. The results of this analysis are presented in Figure 24.5 and Table 24.5.

Figure 24.5 illustrates the relative cost-effectiveness of different forms of energy supply. Costs should be reviewed in relation to the current price of the U.S. energy mix, which includes coal, oil, natural gas, nuclear power, and renewable sources. As shown here, a fully depreciated coal-fired plant is the least expensive option but generates the most CO_2. Nuclear and renewables (solar photovoltaics, wind, geothermal, and biomass) are the most expensive but generate no CO_2. Natural gas is roughly the midpoint between depreciated coal plants and the nuclear/renewables options. For new plants, natural gas is much more attractive than new pulverized coal-fired plants. The slope of the line from the high estimate of nuclear to the U.S. mix is equivalent to the CO_2 tax that would be needed to make nuclear energy competitive with the current U.S. energy supply (approximately \$51/t CO_2).

Table 24.5 compares the cost-effectiveness and potential CO_2 abatement for different forms of energy supply. Although some forms of energy, such

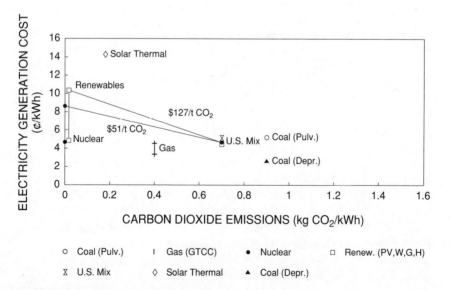

FIGURE 24.5 Cost-effectiveness of electricity supply options.

SOURCES: Electric Power Research Institute (1989); Solar Energy Research Institute (1990); Wright and Ehrenshaft (1990).

TABLE 24.5 Cost-Effectiveness of CO_2 Reduction for Different Sources of Electricity Supply

Energy Source	Cost[a] (¢/kWh)	Emissions (kg CO_2/kWh)	CO_2 Tax Needed for Indifference with U.S. Fuel Mix[b] ($/t CO_2)
U.S. mix	5	0.7	0
Coal, advanced pulverized	5.1	0.86	NA
Coal, running cost of depreciated plant	2.0–3.5[c]	0.9	NA
Gas, combined cycle	3.3–4.5[d]	0.41	NA
Nuclear	4.7–8.6[e]	0	NA to 51
Hydroelectric	5.6	0	9
Geothermal	4.9	0	NA
Solar photovoltaic	10.3	0	76
Solar thermal/gas hybrid	14.3	0.18	177
Wind	5.1–13.9	0	1 to 127
Biomass	4.8–6.0	0[f]	NA to 14

NOTE: NA = Not applicable (i.e., cost less than U.S. mix).

[a]Based on assumptions from EPRI (1989), SERI (1990), and Wright and Ehrenshaft (1990).
[b]$/t CO_2 = (Option Cost – U.S. Mix Cost) ($/100¢)(1000 kg/ton).
[c]Assumed by Mitigation Panel.
[d]Assumes 50 percent thermal efficiency and no gas price escalation for low-cost and EPRI efficiency plus 4 percent annual fuel escalation for high-cost estimates.
[e]High estimate assumes capital cost twice EPRI value.
[f]Biomass sequestered CO_2 before it was burned, so the net carbon emission is zero.

as hydroelectric and biomass, are limited in their potential, others, such as nuclear and coal, have no comparable limit.

For the rest of the world, estimates of energy cost are much more difficult because we do not know the capital cost, capital structure, accounting procedures, fuel costs, and so on. However, a rough estimate of the potential costs can be made. To a first approximation, U.S. electricity consumption is about 45 percent of consumption by the Organization for Economic Cooperation and Development (OECD) countries. The fraction that comes from coal is about the same, around 56 percent of the total. For non-OECD countries, coal is responsible for almost 70 percent of the total. Also, demand outside OECD has grown faster. In 1971, non-OECD electricity consumption was 47 percent of the sum of OECD countries. In 1987, it grew to 69 percent. Thus, to a first approximation, the potential emission reduction in CO_2 is 1.2 times that of the United States in the rest of the OECD and 2 times that of the United States in non-OECD countries (International Energy Agency, 1989).

While the panel makes no attempt to evaluate potential CO_2 savings from energy supply systems outside the United States, the potential is very large because in many areas the efficiency of current electric power and other conversion facilities is markedly lower than in the United States and other developed countries such as Japan.

BARRIERS TO IMPLEMENTATION

There are varied and complex barriers to changing the way electricity is generated. Some of these barriers were identified in a recent U.S. Department of Energy (1989) report:

• Although the utility industry is concentrated, it has many varied actors including the utility itself, the Federal Energy Regulatory Commission (FERC), the Nuclear Regulatory Commission (NRC), the financial community, state and federal environmental regulators, equipment vendors, architectural and engineering firms, ratepayers, and independent power producers. There is a complex decision making system. The varied actors are often contentious and have different objectives and time frames, which slows decision making.

• The utilities themselves are of differing size and complexity, ranging from large private holding companies with multiple operating entities in some cases to large private utilities to small publicly run distributors. In some cases, they may provide just one of the three services—power generation, transmission, or distribution—or they may be vertically integrated and provide all three.

• Utilities are reluctant to commit to additional power due to past problems with public utility commissions' (PUCs) not allowing in the rate base the costs of new plants. This is because of optimistic forecasts of demand growth as well as Public Utility Regulatory Policies Act (PURPA) requirements that they purchase power from independent power producers (IPPs). Therefore utilities have little incentive to purchase new sources of power to replace the coal they currently use.

• The previous problems result in a low capital turnover rate as utilities extend the physical lifetime (40+ years) of their plants beyond their financial life (30 years). Figure 24.6 shows the age distribution of fossil fuel plants still operating in 1986.

• The use of gas to replace coal with either conventional plants or combined cycle technologies is perceived as limited by domestic supplies of natural gas.

• In addition, projected domestic supplies of natural gas (as estimated by DOE) will increase from 16.6 quads (1988) to 17.5 quads (1995) but then decline to 13.5 quads (2010) and continue to decline until conventional reserves are depleted. Therefore, the conclusion is that natural gas could replace coal in the short term, but imported natural gas or the discovery of additional reserves is needed for long-term replacement of coal with natural gas.

Because of these and other circumstances, it will take many decades to replace existing coal-fired plants. For renewable sources, both economics and resource limitations present further barriers to implementation.

The resource limitation issue for natural gas is a controversial issue. While Fulkerson et al. (1989) pointed out that the recoverable resources of conventional natural gas are about 35 times the current annual usage, a paper one year later (Fisher, 1990) gave an estimate of 50 times. The situation is also similar worldwide. The annual world reserves estimates as published by the *Oil and Gas Journal* from 1977 to 1989 showed an increase of almost 60 percent. The reasonable conclusion is that our knowl-

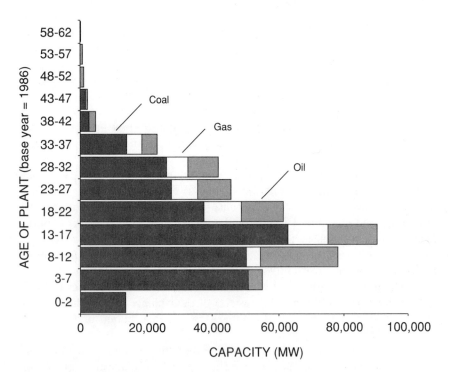

FIGURE 24.6   Megawatts of capacity by age of fossil plants and fuel type.
Sources: U.S. Department of Energy (1989).

edge of gas reserves is not reliable.   But as long as the perception of resource limitation is there for some, it is a constraint on accelerated substitution of gas for coal.

A recent white paper, developed by a committee representing several national laboratories, identified the barriers to increased use of renewable sources of energy (Solar Energy Research Institute, 1990). A summary of its judgment is illustrated in Figure 24.7 and expanded more fully, to include potential methods for removing these barriers, in Table 24.6.   The basis of the committee's judgment, as summarized below, divides the barriers into four categories: regulatory, financial, infrastructural, and perceptual:

Regulatory
• Transmission access rulings may constrain grid connection of remote renewable technology installations.
• Utility ownership of qualifying facilities (co-generation and renewable generation facility) is limited by the Public Utility Regulatory Policies Act (PURPA).

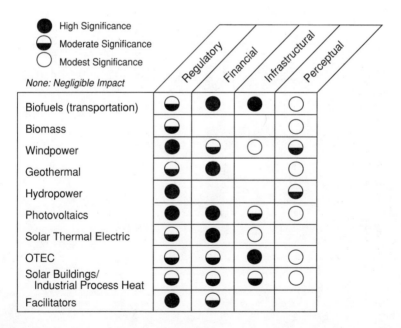

FIGURE 24.7   The significance of institutional factors for renewable energy options.

SOURCE: Solar Energy Research Institute (1990).

TABLE 24.6 Institutional Constraints for Renewable Energy

Sector/Technology	Category	Constraint	Opportunity
Dispatchable Electric			
Hydropower	Regulatory	Electric Consumer Protection Act regulations	Develop valid methodology for evaluating comparative impacts; technical support for relicensing and mitigation
	Perceptual	Perception that federal agencies are pursuing significant research, development and demonstration (RD&D) activities	Education
		Accounting for pumped storage	Develop valid reporting methods
Geothermal	Regulatory/ perceptual	Utility understanding or acceptance	Tax credits or other incentives
		Scenic and wildlife management issues	Education
		Geothermal perceived as limited to base load	Demonstration projects

360

	Type	Barrier	Recommendation
	Financial	Uncertain reservoir life	Improve definition of reservoir characteristics
	Financial	High front-end costs	Tax credits or other investment incentives
	Infrastructural	Lack of transmission paths for hydrothermal	Facilitate construction/use of transmission
	Regulatory	Environmental issues on resource procurement, transport, emissions from combustion and waste disposal	Develop control technologies; internalize environmental costs of landfills
Biomass electric	Perceptual/regulatory	Consistent accounting practices to account for use of resources to displace conventional fuels	Develop adequate tools and procedures
		Municipal solid waste siting difficult near load centers	Continue Public Utility Regulatory Policies Act (PURPA) preferences; discourage land disposal of municipal solid waste
	Infrastructural/regulatory	Biomass resources may not be located near electric load centers	Policy changes to encourage small generating facilities and to encourage biomass farm to supply larger facilities

(Table 24.6 continues)

361

TABLE 24.6 *(continued)*

Sector/Technology	Category	Constraint	Opportunity
Solar thermal	Regulatory/ infrastructural	PURPA gas use (25%) restrictions; size restriction (80 MW)	Policy decision to encourage use
	Financial	High front-end costs	Tax credits or other investment incentives
	Infrastructual	Operational constraints related to high levels of penetration	Federal RD&D to provide analysis
Sector/Technology	Category	Constraint	Opportunity
Ocean thermal energy conversion	Regulatory/ financial	Environmental impacts	Federal tests and demonstrations
		High front-end costs	Tax credits or other investment incentives
	Infrastructural	No industry developed	Aid development of U.S. industry

362

Intermittent Electric			
Wind	Perceptual	Applicable only to tropical band locations	Supporting incentives for these areas
		Utility acceptance or risk and reliability	Long-term demonstrations
	Perceptual/ regulatory	Utility acceptance, dispatch-ability costs	Technology transfer demonstrations, tax or other incentives
	Infrastructural	U.S. industry capability to compete in U.S. market against government-financed foreign corporations	Utility involvement, loan guarantees
Photovoltaic	Perceptual/ regulatory	Utility acceptance	Assess risks of front-end versus fuel escalation costing
	Regulatory	Environmental issues during manufacture	Define and assess impacts
		Land use issues	Define different systems such as rooftop systems
	Financial/ infrastructural	Cost of capital to add manufacturing capability	Federal support of RD&D
		High front-end costs	Loan guarantees to utilities to buy photovoltaics

(Table 24.6 continues)

TABLE 24.6 *(continued)*

Sector/Technology	Category	Constraint	Opportunity
Transportation			
Biofuels	Regulatory	Alcohol subsidy/farm commodity	Subsidy phase-out
		Farm programs that dictate land use	Modify programs to encourage energy crops
		Biotechnology regulation	Facilitate licensing
	Financial	Risk of new technology	Cost-shared demonstrations
	Infrastructural	Demands for fuel	Need further analysis leading to policy formulations
		Vehicle market structure	Promote cleaner burning fuels
	Regulatory/ infrastructural	Land use issues	Policy decisions to encourage use
Stationary			
Solar buildings, industrial process heat	Financial	High initial costs	Assess value of front-end versus fuel escalation costing; federal assistance on loans

	Infrastructural	Integration of bio-derived gas into existing gas delivery systems	Demonstration and tax credits
		Lack of developer/architect interest	Design guides and technical transfer
	Perceptual/ infrastructural	Lack of awareness (public or developers)	Technical transfer
	Perceptual	Consumer preferences and aesthetics	Education, technical transfer
Facilitators			
Storage	Regulatory	Difficulty in siting or developing hydro storage	Same as for hydropower
	Financial	Long lead time developments mean high risk	Develop improved tools for licensing
Transmission	Infrastructural/ perceptual	Need access to transmission and distribution systems	Policy decisions regarding access; development and technical transfer of tools and procedures; education
Wind	Regulatory	Capacity value	Analyses to develop equitable approaches

(Table 24.6 continues)

TABLE 24.6 *(continued)*

Sector/Technology	Category	Constraint	Opportunity
Wind—*cont'd*		Land use issues	Public education
	Financial	High front-end costs	Financial incentives on energy supply
	Infrastructural/regulatory	Lack of utility participation	Allow utility ownership under PURPA

SOURCE: SERI (1990).

• Hydropower facilities are licensed and relicensed under the Energy Policy and Conservation Act.

• Siting of waste-to-energy facilities in municipalities is problematic.

Financial

• Capital markets generally perceive the deployment of emerging technologies as involving more risk than established technologies. The higher the perceived risk, the higher is the rate of return demanded on the capital.

• The perceived length and difficulty of the permitting process are an additional determinant of risk.

• The high front-end financing requirements of many renewable technologies often present additional cost-recovery risks for which capital markets demand a premium.

Infrastructural

• Fragmentation and lack of standardization in the building construction industry can hinder the adoption of many cost-effective solar buildings technologies.

• The existing automobile production and gasoline marketing and delivery infrastructure may retard development and integration of biomass-derived alternative fuels.

• The longer-term biofuels contribution may be limited if sufficient land and resources are not devoted to appropriate biomass production, unless the production of biofuels becomes attractive to farmers.

Perceptual

• Aesthetic problems exist, such as the visual impact of a large "farm," or array of wind turbines, or residential active solar heating systems.

• Environmental issues, such as the damming of wild rivers and streams for hydropower development or effluents from waste-to-energy plants, are problematic.

Also listed in Table 24.6 are opportunities for overcoming these barriers.

POLICY OPTIONS

In Chapter 21, one potential supply-side option, least-cost utility planning (LCUP), was discussed as a policy option for conservation. Additional supply-side options that should be evaluated include

• regulatory and economic incentives to increase the capital turnover rate,

• carbon or greenhouse gas taxes, and

• technology or emission standards (U.S. Department of Energy, 1989).

The capital turnover rate can be increased through a number of actions, including allowing accelerated depreciation for investments in new generating equipment; revising rate-of-return regulations to change the risk distribution for investing in generating capacity; and expedited siting, permitting, and certification procedures. Economic incentives such as accelerated depreciation reduce the present value of capital costs and encourage investment in new capital. The actions would likely reduce federal revenue. An alternative would be to change present rate-of-return regulations to reduce the present risk burden to utility shareholders. The question here, however, is how to guard ratepayers from opportunistic exploitation by shareholders. Another regulatory improvement change might be to streamline the permitting process (U.S. Department of Energy, 1989).

A carbon or greenhouse gas emission tax is a direct and flexible market incentive. A disadvantage is that setting an appropriate emission tax rate is not a simple task, and there are many problems with unilateral adoption of such taxes. There is little practical experience with emission taxes in the United States, and they have been unpopular politically because some view them as "licenses to pollute" and their effectiveness is uncertain. A disadvantage of applying the tax to the utility is related to who pays the tax. If the tax is paid by the ratepayers, there may be a stimulus to reduce energy consumption, but it might have no effect on the utility's incentive to switch fuels, improve efficiency, or invest in technologies with lower emissions (and vice versa). If a tax were targeted toward electricity only, other forms of energy (with potentially equivalent greenhouse gas emissions) might be encouraged to fill the gap (U.S. Department of Energy, 1989). This option is discussed more fully in Chapter 21.

Technology or emission standards are a third alternative. Although emission and technology standards for SO_2 and NO_x are in place today, CO_2 technology standards beyond efficiency requirements are much harder to envision (U.S. Department of Energy, 1989). Standards or limits may be based on unrealistic expectations of the potential of these technologies. If a commercial-scale experiment began immediately, it would probably still take 10 to 15 years to set the standards or limits, and it would take even longer for these regulations to have any impact on greenhouse gas emissions. The advantage of this method is that standards are a simple and direct method of reaching emission goals if they can be monitored and enforced (U.S. Department of Energy, 1989). However, standards can become obsolete because of technological changes, and the slowness in changing standards can impede progress.

OTHER BENEFITS AND COSTS

Although there are many costs associated with changing the energy supply strategy of the nation, there are a variety of benefits. First, with the

United States continuing to increase the amount of energy it imports, development of alternative domestic sources of energy would improve energy security. Second, actions to change to alternative sources of energy may help other environmental problems such as air and water pollution. Third, if renewable sources can be tapped, their capacity is very large and may resolve future problems of diminishing worldwide supplies of oil and gas.

One concern with the analysis presented here is that the cost and benefits calculated are not "full cycle"; that is, it does not include the costs and benefits from production to consumption of the energy. For example, there are important questions even within the greenhouse gas discussion. Methane leakage could increase if natural gas consumption increased. The rate of this leakage is very uncertain, and better information on the leakage rate in existing natural gas systems is needed. Methane emissions from coal mining also constitute a factor to be considered.

The costs beyond actual implementation costs in the energy sector are tremendous and difficult to enumerate. For example, a massive reduction in coal consumption could create major economic dislocations in coal mining areas and the rail transport sector. Past experience with attempts to reduce SO_2 emissions under the Clean Air Act illustrates the potential distributional costs of such an effort.

RESEARCH AND DEVELOPMENT NEEDS

A recent study by the Alternative Energy Committee of the National Research Council's Energy Engineering Board entitled *Confronting Climate Change: Strategies for Energy Research and Development* offers a number of recommendations as to where energy research and development funds should be spent (National Research Council, 1990). A number of actions recommended by the Alternative Energy Committee under its "focused research and development strategy" are summarized below:

Fossil Energy
• Increase the efficiency of fossil generating equipment by using currently available, high-efficiency options such as the gas turbine/steam turbine combined cycle.
• Develop substantial improvements in the combined cycle and other advanced gas-turbine-based technologies for firing with natural gas or a gaseous fuel derived from biomass.
• Achieve economic recovery of gas from known domestic reserves.
• Improve reservoir characterization through basic geoscience research to enable future resource recovery.
• Define greenhouse gas emissions as one criterion in evaluating new approaches to coal combustion.

Nuclear Energy
- Determine through social science research the conditions under which nuclear options would be publicly acceptable in the United States.
- Conduct an international study to establish criteria for globally acceptable nuclear reactors.

Conservation and Renewable Energy

UTILITY SYSTEMS
- Provide research, development, and demonstration support to new and improved technology for electric storage, and for alternating current and direct current system components.
- Develop an efficient, flexible, and reliable network to operate the electric power system in the most environmentally acceptable way.

PHOTOVOLTAICS
- Accelerate research and development on materials and module manufacturing to increase efficiency and reduce costs of photovoltaic systems.

BIOMASS AND BIOFUEL SYSTEMS
- Expand through basic research the understanding of the mechanisms of photosynthesis and genetic factors that influence plant growth.
- Perform systems analyses to define and prioritize infrastructure requirements with expanded use of biomass-derived fuels.
- Assess the potential environmental impacts of biomass production (e.g., through silviculture), including impacts on biodiversity and the availability of water resources.

The Alternative Energy Committee believes that these research and development activities would need to be supplemented by government actions to stimulate the adoption of these technologies and processes.

The Alternative Energy Committee also discusses an "insurance strategy" to pursue research and development in energy systems that would be viable only in the presence of concerns about global climate change. These technologies, according to the committee, are not cost-competitive today and may never be feasible without federal support of research and development and market intervention. These strategies include the following:

Fossil Fuel
- Fund an exploratory study to ascertain if there are viable approaches (economically and environmentally) for removing and sequestering CO_2.

Nuclear Energy
- On the strength of public acceptability and global reactor studies performed under the focused research and development strategy, fund an industry-led or industry-managed program to develop and demonstrate an advanced reactor.

Conservation and Renewable Energy
• Stimulate production (at the rate of about 10 MW/yr each) of the three to five most promising photovoltaic technologies; the same should be done in the areas of solar thermal and wind energy conversion.
• Demonstrate "new" projected storage systems such as compressed gas, battery arrays, and superconducting magnets.
• Develop approaches for federal cost-sharing and utility procurements of renewable energy technologies or of electricity generated by them. Such financing mechanisms should enable manufacturers to compete in niche markets (both domestic and export) to sustain production at levels sufficient to determine the ultimate potential of the technologies.
• Develop and demonstrate photovoltaic electricity resources for buildings, including lighting and water heating.

Biomass and Biofuels System
• Develop and demonstrate promising biomass-to-fuel conversion processes, particularly for cellulose and hemicellulose.
• Select and demonstrate on a large scale the use of improved plant species to enhance biomass production.
• Develop strategies to mitigate the environmental impacts of large-scale use of biomass.

Although one might argue about these details, they are beyond the scope of this inquiry and the panel finds general accord with these earlier National Research Council recommendations. In addition, as mentioned earlier, another report, forthcoming from the National Research Council, will focus on nuclear energy. The challenge is to develop a range of options for providing energy with maximum efficiency and minimum greenhouse gas emissions so that society can respond as it evaluates the threat of greenhouse warming.

CONCLUSIONS

After reviewing the various methods by which energy can be supplied and the interaction of the entire energy system, the Mitigation Panel has come to the following conclusions:

• Coal is likely to remain a major source of energy for many years. Therefore efforts to improve the efficiency with which coal is burned (as well as improving end-use efficiency, as described in Chapter 21) should be pursued. This includes the development of more efficient combined cycle systems.
• Natural gas can potentially replace some coal use in the near term, but concerns for availability of the supply remain.
• Nuclear fission can potentially replace some coal use. However, con-

cerns about safety, economics, waste disposal, proliferation, and resources have resulted in a lack of acceptance. To what extent the concern about greenhouse warming will induce a fresh look at the possibilities of developing "passively safe" nuclear plants and eliminating long-lived radioactive waste is not clear at this time. What is clear, however, is that research and development efforts on alternative reactor concepts should continue. Although nuclear fusion is still far in the future, research and development should proceed.

• Hydroelectric, wind, and geothermal energy represent a limited potential energy supply because of resource constraints.

• Solar photovoltaics constitute another potential source of energy. A number of advances need to be made before the cost of photovoltaics is close to present energy prices, and storage problems still remain to be solved. To the extent that these problems are solved, solar energy can usefully replace a portion of the U.S. energy supply.

• Fuels from other solar energy technologies (including direct heat) and biomass offer potential, but advances—both technical and economic—must still be made.

• Carbon dioxide sequestration is a potentially viable option, but CO_2 disposal is problematic. Further inquiry seems appropriate.

• The many actors involved in energy supply, the low capital turnover rate, and the long lead times are major barriers to the implementation of new energy supply options.

• Social and economic costs of energy systems that are not internalized should become more important considerations in evaluating future energy supply systems.

NOTES

1. Throughout this report, tons (t) are metric; 1 Mt = 1 megaton = 1 million tons; and 1 Gt = 1 gigaton = 1 billion tons.
2. 1 quad = 1 quadrillion (10^{15}) British thermal units (Btu).
3. 1 EJ = 1 exajoule = 10^{18} joules.

REFERENCES

Baes, C. F., Jr., S. E. Beall, D. W. Lee, and G. Marland. 1980. Options for the Collection and Disposal of Carbon Dioxide. Report ORNL-5657. Oak Ridge, Tenn.: Oak Ridge National Laboratory.

Bajura, R. A. 1989. Gasification and gas stream cleanup overview. In Proceedings of the Ninth Annual Contractors Review Meeting. Report DOE/METC-89/6107, Volume 1. Washington, D.C.: U.S. Department of Energy.

Blok, K., C. A. Hendriks, and W. C. Turkenburg. 1990. The role of carbon dioxide removal in the reduction of the greenhouse effect. In Proceedings of an Experts'

Seminar on Energy Technologies for Reducing Emissions of Greenhouse Gases, April 13-14, 1990. Paris: Organization for Economic Cooperation and Development.

California Energy Resources, Conservation and Development Commission. 1989. Technology characterizations. Docket 88-ER-8, Staff Issue Paper 7R, Final Report. October 11, 1989. California Energy Resources, Conservation and Development Commission, Sacramento.

Edmonds, J. A., W. B. Ashton, H. C. Cheng, and M. Steinberg. 1989. A Preliminary Analysis of U.S. CO_2 Emissions Reduction Potential from Energy Conservation and the Substitution of Natural Gas for Coal in the Period to 2010. Report TR 045 DOE/NBB 0085. Washington, D.C.: U.S. Department of Energy.

El-Masri, M. 1988. Gas Turbine Cycle Incorporating Simultaneous, Parallel, Dual Mode Heat Recovery (U.S. Patent No. 4,753,068). Wayland, Mass.

Electric Power Research Institute. 1986. Technical Assessment Guide, Electricity Supply. Report EPRI P-4463-SR. Palo Alto, Calif.: Electric Power Research Institute, December.

Electric Power Research Institute. 1989. EPRI 1989 Technical Assessment Guide, Electricity Supply. Report EPRI P-6587-L. Palo Alto, Calif.: Electric Power Research Institute.

Exergy Inc. 1989. The Kalina Power Cycles, A Progress Report. Haywood, Calif. June 1989.

Fisher, W. L. 1990. Recent Trends in Domestic Natural Gas: The Case for Optimism Natural Gas Symposium. Houston, Tex. Sept. 27, 1990.

Fistedis, S. H., ed. 1989. Experimental Breeder Reactor-II Inherent Safety Demonstration EBR-II Division. Argonne, Ill.: Argonne National Laboratory.

Fulkerson, W. (study leader). 1989. 1989 Energy Technology R&D: What Could Make a Difference? Report ORNL 6541, 3 Vols. Oak Ridge, Tenn.: Oak Ridge National Laboratory.

Gagliardi, C. R., D. D. Smith, and S. I. Wang. 1989. Strategies to improve MEA CO_2-removal detailed at Louisiana ammonia plant. Oil and Gas Journal 87(10):44-49.

Gluckman, M. 1990. CO_2 emission reduction cost analysis. Palo Alto, Calif.: Electric Power Research Institute.

Golomb, D., H. Herzog, J. Tester, D. White, and S. Zemba. 1989. Feasibility, Modeling and Economics of Sequestering Power Plant CO_2 Emissions in the Deep Ocean. Report MIT-EL-89-003. Cambridge: Massachusetts Institute of Technology Energy Laboratory.

Hafele, W., H. Barnert, S. Messnr, M. Strubegger, and L. Anderer. 1986. Novel integrated energy systems: The case of zero emissions. In The Sustainable Development of the Biosphere, W. C. Clark and R. E. Munn, eds. New York: Cambridge University Press.

Hendriks, C., K. Blok, and W. Turkenburg. 1990. Technology and Cost of Recovering and Storing Carbon Dioxide from an Integrated Combined Cycle. Utrecht, The Netherlands: Department of Science, Technology and Society, University of Utrecht.

Hubbard, H. M. 1989. Photovoltaics today and tomorrow. Science 244:297-304.

International Energy Agency. 1989. IEA Statistics, World Energy Statistics and Balances, 1971-1987. Paris: International Energy Agency, Organization for Economic Cooperation and Development.

Keeling, C. D., R. B. Bacastow, A. F. Carter, S. C. Piper, T. P. Whorf, M. Heimann, W. G. Mook, and H. Roeloffzen. 1989. A three dimensional model of atmosphere CO_2 transport based on observed winds. 1. Analysis of observational data. In Aspects of Climate Variability in the Pacific and the Western Americas, D. H. Peterson, ed. Geophysical Monograph 55. Washington, D.C.: American Geophysical Union.

Lee, T. H. 1989. Making models matter—Lessons from experience. European Journal of Operational Research 38:290-300.

Lee, T. H., B. C. Ball, and R. D. Tabors. 1990. Energy Aftermath. Cambridge, Mass.: Harvard Business School Press.

Marchetti, C. 1975. On Geoengineering and the CO_2 Problem. Laxenburg, Austria: International Institute for Applied Systems Analysis.

Marland, G. 1983. Carbon dioxide emission rates for conventional and synthetic fuels. Energy 8:981-992.

Marland, G. 1990. Carbon dioxide emission estimates: United States. In TRENDS '90: A Compendium of Data on Global Change, T. A. Borden, P. Kanciruk, and M. P. Farrell, eds. Report ORNL/CDIAC-36. Oak Ridge, Tenn.: Carbon Dioxide Information Analysis Center, Oak Ridge National Laboratory.

Marland, G., and A. Turnhollow. 1990. CO_2 Emissions from production and combustion of fuel ethanol from corn. Report ORNL/TM-11180. Oak Ridge, Tenn.: Oak Ridge National Laboratory.

Muzio, L. J., M. E. Teague, J. C. Kramlich, J. A. Cole, J. M. McCarthy, and R. K. Lyon. 1989. Errors in grab sample measurements of N_2O from combustion sources. Journal of the Air Pollution Control Association 39:287-293.

National Research Council. 1990. Confronting Climate Change: Strategies for Energy Research and Development. Washington, D.C.: National Academy Press.

Ogden, J. M., and R. H. Williams. 1989. Solar Hydrogen: Moving Beyond Fossil Fuels. Washington, D.C.: World Resources Institute.

Ostlie, L. D. 1988. The whole tree burner, a new technology in power generation. Biologue (December/January):7-9.

Organization for Economic Cooperation and Development Report (OECD). 1981. The Costs and Benefits of Sulphur Oxide Control. Paris: Organization for Economic Cooperation and Development.

Organization for Economic Cooperation and Development (OECD). 1987. Energy Balances of OECD Countries. Paris: International Energy Agency, Organization for Economic Cooperation and Development.

Organization for Economic Cooperation and Development/International Energy Agency. 1983. Uranium Resources, Production and Demand. Paris: Organization for Economic Cooperation and Development.

Purucker, S. L., and J. H. Reed. 1989. Power Plant Life Extension and Pollution Emissions. ORNL/TM-10942. Oak Ridge, Tenn.: Oak Ridge National Laboratory.

Rotty, R. M., A. M. Perry, and D. B. Reister. 1976. Net Energy from Nuclear Power. Report FEA/B-76/702. Oak Ridge Associated Universities, Oak Ridge,

Tenn. (Available from National Technical Information Service, Springfield, Va., as publication PB-254-059.)

Rubin, E. S. 1989. Implications of future environmental regulations of coal-based electric power. Annual Review of Energy 14:19-45.

Solar Energy Research Institute. 1990. The Potential of Renewable Energy: An Interlaboratory White Paper. Report SERI/TP-260-3674. Golden, Colo.: Solar Energy Research Institute.

Steinberg, M. 1983. An Analysis of Concepts for Controlling Atmospheric Carbon Dioxide. Report DOE/CH/00016-1. Washington, D.C.: U.S. Department of Energy.

Steinberg, M. 1989. An Option for the Coal Industry in Utilizing Fossil Fuel Resources with Reduced CO_2 Emissions. BNL-42228. Upton, N.Y.: Brookhaven National Laboratory.

Steinberg, M., H. C. Cheng, and F. Horn. 1984. A Systems Study for the Removal, Recovery, and Disposal of Carbon Dioxide from Fossil Fuel Power Plants in the U.S. Report DOE/CH/00016-2. Washington, D.C.: U.S. Department of Energy.

Styrikovich, M., and N. Chizhov. 1988. Ecological advantages of natural gas over other fossil fuels. In The Methane Age, Thomas Lee et al., eds. Boston, Mass.: Kluwer Academic Publishers.

Tabors, R. D., and D. P. Flagg. 1986. Natural gas fired combined cycle generators: Dominant solutions in capacity planning. IEEE Transactions on Power Systems PWRS 1(2):122-127.

U.S. Department of Energy. 1988. Annual Energy Review 1987. Report DOE/EIA-0384(87). Washington, D.C.: U.S. Department of Energy.

U.S. Department of Energy. 1989. Monthly Energy Review 1989. Report DOE/EIA-0035(89/01). Washington, D.C.: U.S. Department of Energy.

Weinberg, A. M. 1989. Nuclear energy and the greenhouse effect. Paper presented at the Midwest Energy Consortium Symposium, Chicago, November 6, 1989.

Williams, R. H. 1989. Biomass gasifier/gas turbine power and the greenhouse warming. In Energy Technologies for Reducing Emissions of Greenhouse Gasses. Proceedings of an Expert Seminar, Volume 2. Paris: International Energy Agency, Organization for Economic Cooperation and Development.

Winschel, R. A. 1990. The relationship of carbon dioxide emissions with coal rank and sulfur content. Journal of the Air and Waste Management Association 40(6):861-865.

Wright, L. L., and A. R. Ehrenshaft. 1990. Short Rotation Woody Crops Program: Annual Progress Report for 1989. Report ORNL-6625. Oak Ridge, Tenn.: Oak Ridge National Laboratory.

25

Nonenergy Emission Reduction

Nonenergy-related sources of greenhouse gases include manufactured halocarbons, methane and nitrous oxide from agriculture, and methane from landfills.

HALOCARBONS

"Halocarbon" is the general label applied to chemicals such as chlorofluorocarbons (CFCs), hydrochlorofluorocarbons (HCFCs), hydrofluorocarbons (HFCs), halons, and chlorocarbons (CCs). Halocarbons have the largest radiative impact per molecule of any of the greenhouse gases. However, halocarbon emission volumes are much lower than CO_2 emission volumes, so that the total halocarbon contribution to global warming is less than that of CO_2 from other sources. The CFCs also threaten the stratospheric ozone layer. Emissions of CFCs are scheduled to be eliminated under the Montreal Protocol, an international treaty signed in 1987 and strengthened in 1990, that commits nations to act to preserve the ozone layer. Positive action under the Protocol—including bringing additional nations under its umbrella—continues to be a visible demonstration of the possibility of global action on environmental questions.

Recent Trends

More than 1 Mt of CFCs and halons were produced and consumed on a worldwide basis in 1986.1 Figure 25.1 shows that the United States is the largest consumer of CFCs in the world (approximately one-third). Other developed countries also consume large amounts of CFCs. During the 1970s, scientists became concerned about the potential impact of CFCs on the

376

ozone layer (Rowland and Molina, 1974). Concern continued, and in 1985 scientists detected unexpected seasonal losses in the stratospheric ozone layer above Antarctica (Farman et al., 1985). In 1987, these concerns resulted in the Montreal Protocol—an international agreement to reduce by 1998 the production and use of CFCs, in developed countries, to 50 percent of their 1986 levels and to freeze halon production at 1986 levels by 1993. By 1988, research had shown that chlorine from man-made sources, primarily CFCs and CCs, contributed to the temporary early spring ozone losses above Antarctica. The Montreal Protocol was amended in 1990 to require a total phaseout of CFCs, halons, and carbon tetrachloride by the year 2000 in developed countries (2010 in developing countries). Not all countries have agreed to sign the Montreal Protocol, however, and this fact, along with the possibility that some countries may not comply with the agreement, has caused concern. More than 100 countries with over 67 percent of the global population and about 10 percent of current CFC use—India and China included—have not yet signed the agreement.

The United States has signed the Montreal Protocol. In addition, the 1990 amendment to the Clean Air Act will further regulate halocarbons in the United States. Figure 25.2 illustrates how CFC consumption will decline between now and 2010 because of the new Clean Air Act amendment.

Besides having a role in ozone depletion, CFCs are also greenhouse gases. Unlike the other greenhouse gases, which began to increase during the Industrial Revolution (1850), CFCs were not introduced until the early

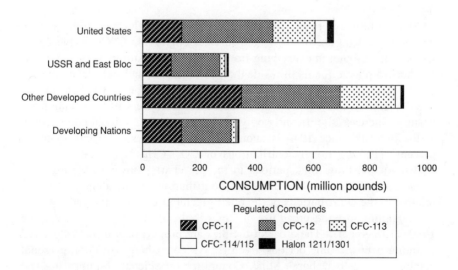

FIGURE 25.1   CFC and halon consumption by geographic region, 1985.
SOURCE: Cogan (1988).

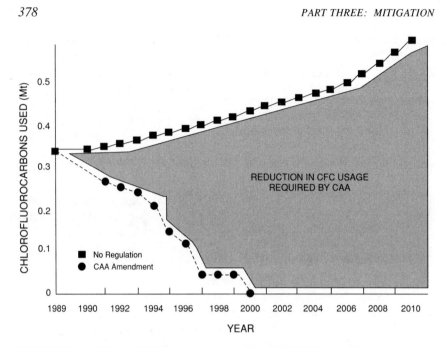

FIGURE 25.2   Effect of Clean Air Act Amendment of 1990 on CFC usage.

SOURCE: Data are from F. A. Vogelsberg, Du Pont, personal communication to Deborah Stine, National Academy of Sciences, 1990.

1930s. Future use rates, and hence emissions, of fluorocarbons will be driven by societal use of goods and services employing CFCs (Table 25.1), which can be found in everything from mobile air conditioners to fire extinguishers to plastic foams in residential, commercial, and industrial applications. Over the last decade, the fractional contribution of CFCs to greenhouse warming has been about 20 percent. Because CFC concentrations began to increase significantly only after 1960, their fractional contribution to the increase since 1940 is about 15 percent, and since 1850 about 10 percent. The fractional contributions of CO_2, CH_4, N_2O, and CFCs are shown for the three time periods in the pie charts shown in Figure 25.3. These charts illustrate how the CFC contribution to greenhouse warming relative to the contributions of the other greenhouse gases changed between the beginning of widespread use of CFCs in the 1940s (14 percent) and the 1980s (19 percent). The areas of the pies are proportional to the calculated warming over the time periods given (F. A. Vogelsberg, Du Pont, personal communication to Deborah Stine, Committee on Science, Engineering and Public Policy, 1990).

TABLE 25.1 Primary Uses of CFCs and Halons

Application	Primary Compound(s) Used in United States in 1986 (million pounds)	Where or How Used
Stationary air conditioning and refrigeration	CFC-12 (68.5) CFC-11 (14.5) CFC-115 (9.9) CFC-114 (2.2)	45 million homes and most commercial buildings 100 million refrigerators 30 million freezers 180,000 refrigerated trucks 27,000 refrigerated rail cars 250,000 restaurants 40,000 supermarkets 160,000 other food stores
Mobile air conditioning	CFC-12 (120.0)	90 million cars and light-duty trucks
Plastic foams	CFC-11 (150.7) CFC-12 (48.2) CFC-114 (6.6)	Rigid insulation for homes, buildings, and refrigerators; flexible foam cushioning, food trays, and packaging
Solvents	CFC-113 (150.7)	Microelectronic circuitry; computer and high-performance air- and space-craft, dry cleaning
Sterilants	CFC-12 (26.4)	Medical instruments and pharmaceutical supplies
Aerosols	CFC-12 (15.6) CFC-11 (9.9)	Essential uses in solvents, medicines, and pesticides
Miscellaneous	CFC-12 (22.0)	Food freezants for shrimp, fish, fruit, and vegetables
Fire extinguishing	Halon 1301 (7.7) Halon 1211 (6.2)	Computer rooms, telephone exchanges, storage vaults

SOURCE: Cogan (1988).

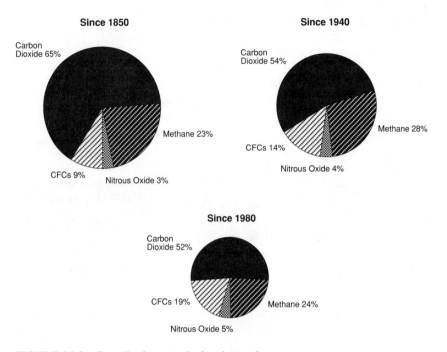

FIGURE 25.3   Contribution to calculated warming.

SOURCE: Data are from Du Pont (1989).

The goal of minimizing contributions to global warming should be considered in the context of other goals, including minimizing the potential for
ozone depletion, maintaining safety standards for chemicals (low toxicity
and low flammability), maintaining energy efficiency, and continuing to
realize the substantial economic and societal benefits of CFC-using technologies while making the transition from CFCs to alternatives.

Several alternatives are being evaluated in an attempt to balance these
goals. As a group, the HCFCs and HFCs under evaluation have about one-
tenth the global warming potential of CFCs, and less than one-twentieth the
ozone depletion potential of CFCs, because the hydrogen in these two alternatives destabilizes these chemicals and lowers their residence time in the
atmosphere and thus their potential to contribute to greenhouse warming
and ozone depletion. Furthermore, because HFCs contain no chlorine, they
cannot contribute to ozone depletion (see Table 25.2). Thus, even with
emission rates comparable to those of CFCs, the contributions to calculated
global warming and ozone depletion would be significantly reduced, as
shown in Figure 25.4.

TABLE 25.2 Global Warming Potentials of CFCs

Trace Gas	Lifetime[a] (years)	Ozone Depletion Potential[b]	Global Warming Potential[c]	ΔF for ΔC per Molecule Relative to CO_2[d]	Rate of Increase in 1986 (ppb/yr)[e]
Carbon dioxide	120	NA	1	1	1.2×10^{-3}
Methane	10	NA	21	58	13
Nitrous oxide	150	NA	260	206	0.7
CFC-11	60	1	2,000	12,400	9×10^{-3}
CFC-12	130	1	6,200	15,800	1.7×10^{-2}
CFC-113	90	0.8	2,800	15,800	4×10^{-3}
CFC-114	200	0.7	7,900	18,300	
CFC-115	400	0.4	14,000	14,500	
HCFC-22	15	0.05	680	10,700	7×10^{-3}
HCFC-123	2	0.02	38	9,940	
HCFC-124	7	0.02	190	10,800	
HCFC-141b	8	0.1	190	7,710	
HCFC-142b	19	0.06	710	10,200	
HFC-125	28	0	1,100	13,400	
HFC-134a	16	0	550	9,570	
HFC-152a	2	0	62	6,590	
HFC-143a	41	0	1,400	7,830	
Carbon tetrachloride	50	1.1	680	5,720	2×10^{-3}
Methyl chloroform	6	0.15	45	2,730	6×10^{-3}

[a]From Intergovernmental Panel on Climate Change (1990), Table 2.8.
[b]Average of values in World Meteorological Organization (1989), Table 4.3-3.
[c]Calculated from lifetimes and change in radiative forcing (ΔF) for a change in molar concentration relative to CO_2.
[d]From Intergovernmental Panel on Climate Change (1990), Table 2.3 (Table 19.4 of this report). ΔF = change in radiative forcing; ΔC = change in temperature.
[e]From National Aeronautics and Space Administration (1988), Table C-8.1.

Table 25.2 shows the atmospheric lifetimes, ozone-depleting potentials, global warming potentials, calculated equilibrium warming, and rate of increase of atmospheric concentration for CO_2, CH_4, N_2O, fluorocarbons, and chlorocarbons. The global warming potentials are calculated on a mass basis relative to a global warming potential of 1.0 for CO_2. These global warming potentials are estimates of the total cumulative (over time) calculated warming due to emission of 1 kg of a compound relative to the total cumulative calculated warming due to emission of 1 kg CO_2. All of the

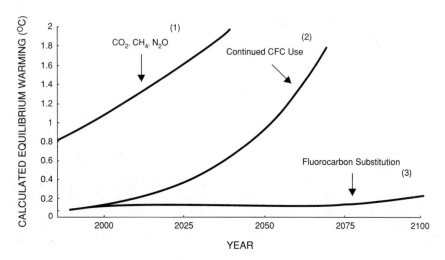

FIGURE 25.4 Calculated global warming contributions: (1) based on emission scenario in World Meteorological Organization (1985); (2) assumes unregulated use of CFCs with continued growth in worldwide demand; (3) assumes global compliance with a phaseout of CFCs by 2000 (2010 in developing countries), a phaseout of HCFC substitutes over the period from 2030 to 2070, and continued growth in demand for HFC substitutes throughout the next century. The curve represents the contribution of residual CFCs plus HCFCs plus HFCs.

SOURCE: Data are from Du Pont (1989).

compounds have large global warming potentials compared to that of CO_2, but this fact can be misleading because it does not account for relative emission rates. This method of calculating global warming potentials differs slightly from that used by the Intergovernmental Panel on Climate Change (1990). They computed relative effects over the first 20, 100, and 500 years after instantaneous injections of 1 kg of each of the compounds into the atmosphere to derive the values in Table 2.8 of IPCC (Intergovernmental Panel on Climate Change, 1990). The values in Table 25.2 of this report are based on the same atmospheric lifetimes and values for radiative forcing as used in the IPCC report, but relative effects are computed from total integrated forcing by assuming a CO_2 lifetime of 120 years.

The last two columns of Table 25.2 can be used to estimate current contributions to calculated warming. Multiplying the values in these columns yields the 1986 contribution to global warming. Dividing the individual contributions by the sum of all the contributions yields an estimate of the relative contribution of each gas. This shows that although the global warming potential and calculated equilibrium warming for CO_2 are small per unit of CO_2, it nevertheless contributed about 55 percent of the total calculated warming in 1986.

Figure 25.4 shows the projected calculated warming from fluorocarbon substitutes based on options for meeting a growing demand for goods and services that currently rely on CFCs. A comparison of the curve for continued use of CFCs with the lower curve demonstrates the effects of the decreased demand for fluorocarbons due to conservation and replacement by nonfluorocarbon alternatives, and also the lower global warming potentials of the HCFCs and HFCs targeted to replace CFCs. Global compliance with a CFC phaseout by 2000 (2010 in developing countries) and an HCFC phaseout from 2030 to 2060 (not yet required by treaty, but in a nonbinding agreement) would stabilize the contribution of fluorocarbons to global warming even though the demand for goods and services they provide is projected to increase at about 3.5 percent per year.

Emission Control Methods

Production and use of CFCs will probably be eliminated over the next 10 years (20 years in developing countries) because of concerns about ozone depletion. A variety of options can be used to meet growing demands for the goods and services as CFCs are eliminated:

• increased conservation of CFCs in the short term and of their replacements over the longer term,

• nonfluorocarbon alternative compounds for technologies not requiring a gas, and

• substitution of other compounds in the fluorocarbon family—HCFCs and HFCs.

Figure 25.5 illustrates how the demand for services now provided by CFCs could be satisfied in the year 2000 (deadline for phaseout under the amended Montreal Protocol). Conservation and recycling measures can reduce worldwide demand for CFC production by 30 percent and provide environmental benefits by reducing the need for virgin CFC production. Replacement of certain applications, primarily aerosols in Europe, with nonhalocarbon substitutes ("not-in-kind" options) can reduce CFC demand by an additional 30 percent. Fluorocarbon alternatives can replace CFCs in the remaining 40 percent of applications (Du Pont, 1989). However, some of the substitute chemicals—developed to avoid reaction with ozone in the upper atmosphere—may have radiative properties that would result in significant contributions to greenhouse warming (Shine, 1990).

Increased conservation and recycling of CFCs and their fluorocarbon replacements are initiatives that can provide benefits to consumers, industry, and the environment. United States tax legislation has more than doubled

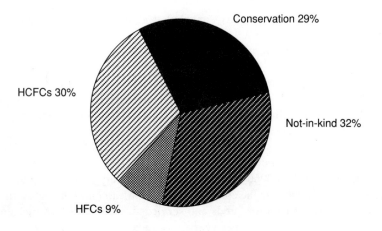

FIGURE 25.5   How CFC demand is satisfied in 2000.

SOURCE: Adapted from Du Pont (1989).

the price of CFCs since January 1, 1990. Escalating tax rates will raise the price of CFCs by approximately 500 percent in the next 10 years. These price increases are exclusive of additional increases from producers due to mandated production cuts and higher fixed costs, increased raw materials costs, and the need for revenue to invest in alternatives. In addition, fluoro-carbon alternatives are expected to cost up to 5 times as much as present (untaxed) CFCs. Clearly, economic incentives for conservation and recy-cling will grow rapidly with these price increases.

A review of the different industries that use CFCs illustrates the feasibil-ity of each of the substitution options. The foam plastics industry uses CFC blowing agents in the insulation it produces. Conservation measures are difficult for this industry to implement because about 80 percent of the CFC blowing agent ends up in the bubbles of rigid foam insulation. The industry currently recovers 50 percent of the fugitive emissions that occur during manufacture (Aulisio, 1988). The best options for this industry are CFC substitutes such as HCFCs 22, 123, 141b, and 142b, which will become available in increasing quantities in 1994 and 1995, when the market could be fully supported by HCFC alternatives. Higher prices may cause consum-ers to choose not-in-kind substitutes such as fiberglass and fiberboard insu-lation. Because these substitutes are less energy efficient, the net contribu-tion to global warming may be adverse, a possibility that should be taken into account.

Appliance manufacturers put insulating foam in refrigerators to increase their energy efficiency as required by statute. Manufacturers will be able to use some CFC substitutes such as HCFC-123. However, until these products are widely available, manufacturers will have to balance the need for energy efficiency with the availability of substitutes. Whirlpool has estimated that refrigerators with the new CFCs would cost about $100 more per unit to produce. CFCs are also used in refrigerators as refrigerants. Used refrigerant is currently being recycled, and manufacturers of commercial refrigeration and air conditioning equipment are working to reduce fugitive emission losses in the field (Cogan, 1988).

Mobile air conditioning is the largest market for CFC consumption in the United States; however, because new automobiles account for only 20 to 25 percent of the CFCs used in this sector, phaseout of CFCs by automobile producers will afford only a small reduction initially. Seventy-five percent of the consumption is in servicing the existing 125 million automobile air conditioners after the refrigeration fluid has leaked to the atmosphere (Putnam, Hayes, and Bartlett, 1987). Of the 120 million pounds used for replacement, 30 million pounds replaced fluid lost through normal operation, and 40 million pounds replaced fluids flushed out during servicing and repairs (Radian Corp., 1987). Therefore conservation and recycling of these CFCs are critical to reduce emissions from this industry.

The automobile industry has examined numerous alternative refrigerants. After independent analysis, mobile air conditioner manufacturers have agreed that HFC-134a is the best replacement for CFC-12. Significant technical issues need to be solved before HFC-134a can be used in new mobile air conditioning systems, most notably the development of a new system lubricant, hardware and elastomer modifications, toxicological testing of HFC-134a, and development of feasible chemical HFC-134a synthetics. Excellent progress has been made in all areas, such that domestic automobile manufacturers plan to switch to HFC-134a over a several-year period, with conversion expected to be complete by 1996. However, HFC-134a is not a drop-in replacement for CFC-12 in mobile air conditioning systems, and it is not expected to be a retrofit option. The automobile industry is making serious efforts to minimize the release of CFC-12 from these air conditioning systems; for example, one major domestic producer (General Motors) is requiring that all of its dealerships use refrigerant recovery and recycling equipment by October 1990. Conversion from CFC-12 to HFC-134a will reduce the greenhouse impact of mobile air conditioners by more than 90 percent. Serious efforts at refrigerant recovery and recycling in the mobile air conditioning industry can further reduce this greenhouse contribution to less than 5 percent of its present level.

No nonfluorocarbon alternative air conditioning technology is currently suitable for this mobile market. The alternative technology most frequently considered is the Stirling gas refrigeration cycle (using helium or nitrogen), but there has been no demonstration of a high cooling capacity, energy efficient, reasonably priced Stirling air conditioning system suitable for vehicle applications.

The electronics industry accounts for roughly one-fourth of CFC demand in the United States. This industry currently uses CFC-113 solvent to clean semiconductors and circuit boards. Recovery and recycling technology is available, and equipment is already in place for an estimated 50 percent of the applications; implementation of the best available equipment technology in the remaining 50 percent could reduce emissions by 25 percent or more. Water-based solvents are alternative cleaning agents used by a number of companies (ICF, 1987). These systems afford a trade-off of longer-lived CFCs for shorter-lived volatile organic carbon (VOC) emissions and increased waste-water treatment loads for municipal and industrial waste treatment facilities.

Halons are used to extinguish fires and are mainly contained within fire extinguishers, tanks, and so on, until released during testing or actual use. Seventy-five percent of halon emissions occurred during testing prior to the Montreal Protocol. Currently, the industry has ceased using halons as a requirement in the test. Not-in-kind substitutes are not yet available for these compounds (Cogan, 1988). Recently, two U.S. companies (Great Lakes Chemical Corporation and Du Pont) announced potential halocarbon substitutes for these halons. Large-scale demonstration of these substitutes has yet to be accomplished.

Carbon tetrachloride (CCl_4) and methyl chloroform (CH_3CCl_3) emissions are controlled in the amended Montreal Protocol because of their potential contributions to ozone depletion. The use of CCl_4 will be eliminated by 2000, and the use of CH_3CCl_3 by 2005. As can be seen from Table 25.2, both compounds are relatively small contributors to calculated global warming (<1 percent in 1986).

The primary use of CCl_4 is as a feedstock to produce CFCs 11 and 12. Only very small amounts (less than 1 percent of the quantity consumed) are emitted to the atmosphere during CFC production. However, based on atmospheric measurements of the concentrations of CCl_4 and its model-calculated lifetime, atmospheric emissions of CCl_4 are estimated at about 10 percent of the amount used for CFC production. This indicates that significant emissions occur from other uses. Carbon tetrachloride was used extensively as a solvent. However, in the United States and most other developed countries, CCl_4 is currently used as a solvent in only very specialized applications with tight control on atmospheric emissions due to concerns about toxicity. Thus it appears unlikely that the United States, Japan, and Western Europe are major sources of CCl_4 emissions. Based on analysis of measurements of CCl_4 and CFCs on the coast of Ireland, Prather (1985) concluded that Europe and, in particular, Eastern Europe might constitute a significant source of CCl_4 emissions; however, uncertainties in the results prevent a definitive assessment (Prather, 1985). Further work is needed to determine the sources of CCl_4 emissions.

The primary use of CH_3CCl_3 is in industrial cleaning. It contributes only a small fraction of the calculated warming, but restrictions on CH_3CCl_3 could increase future contributions to global warming by decreasing energy efficiency. Producers of CH_3CCl_3 have stated that aqueous cleaning methods require more energy to dry the cleaned materials. The impact of CH_3CCl_3 regulations on energy use should be evaluated.

The analysis presented in this section deals only with the direct effect of CFCs on the chemical and radiative properties of the atmosphere. A more complete approach, beyond the scope of this analysis, would require an evaluation of the net change in contribution to global warming resulting from the use of different systems to meet a given societal need. For example, fluorocarbons are used in some applications because of their contributions to energy efficiency. In those cases, the energy saved, and hence the CO_2 emissions prevented, may reduce the contribution to global warming by an amount that is greater than the direct contribution from emission of the fluorocarbon.

Chlorofluorocarbons will be replaced in most countries because of concerns over their potential contribution to ozone depletion. Costs of the transition will probably be high but are difficult to estimate. A recent study by the Department of Energy (Energy Information Administration, 1989) estimates the cost of one aspect of the CFC phaseout—the cost of capital obsolescence in the United States over the next decade was estimated to be between $19 billion and $34 billion.

Appendix K attempts to estimate the additional cost for replacement of CFCs, both in the United States and throughout the world, with the options discussed earlier. Those options include meeting CFC demand by increased conservation and by use of not-in-kind or fluorocarbon substitutes. The costs reflect changes only in the cost for new equipment and new substitutes, and not in costs due to capital obsolescence. As determined in the calculation described in Appendix K, costs of the CFC phaseout are calculated to be approximately $2 billion per year in the United States and $6.3 billion per year throughout the world (in constant 1990 dollars at 6 percent). Cost estimates at other interest rates are also shown in Appendix K. Table 25.3 summarizes the cost of phasing out CFCs in the United States and the CO_2-equivalent reduction of those CFCs. Figure 25.6 summarizes the abatement cost for each policy option.

These costs will be incurred regardless of global warming concerns; implementing the options that reduce contributions to global warming should constitute only a small incremental cost. Companies involved in research on substitutes are evaluating the potential contribution of these compounds to greenhouse warming in an attempt to obtain optimal solutions that take

TABLE 25.3 Cost Impact of CFC Phaseout in the United States

CFC Phaseout Policy Option	CFC Reduction (Mt/yr)	CO_2 Equivalent Reduction (Mt/yr)	Total Cost (3%) (M$/yr)	Abatement Cost (3%) ($/t CO_2 Equivalent)
Not-in-kind substitution for cleaning agents and blowing agents, aerosols, and refrigerants	0.086	302	3	0.01
Conservation and recycle	0.098	509	16	0.03
Fluorocarbon substitution for cleaning agents, blowing agents, and refrigerants	0.074	248	167	0.67
Fluorocarbon substitution for refrigerants				
Chillers	0.023	88	206	2.35
Mobile air conditioning	0.030	170	721	4.25
Appliances	0.002	11	98	8.67
Other	0.010	67	221	3.32
Fluorocarbon substitution for appliance insulation	0.007	14	329	23.59
TOTAL	0.33	1,409	1,761	

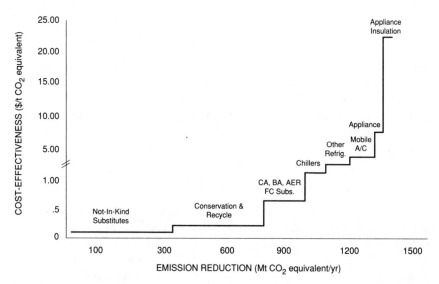

FIGURE 25.6   Cost and greenhouse warming benefit of CFC phaseout policy options in the United States.

into account all safety and environmental concerns. Companies that will use the substitutes in their products are working to maximize energy efficiency and thus minimize potential contributions to global warming. Therefore most of the costs incurred due to global warming concerns will be hidden in the total transition costs. Initiation by government agencies such as the National Institute of Standards and Technology (NIST) and DOE of the type of systems analysis discussed in the preceding section would assist industry in obtaining optimal solutions.

Barriers to Implementation

Consumers are likely to be largely indifferent to the use of CFC substitutes, as long as substitutes do not raise prices significantly or suddenly, and as long as the technical capabilities of the substitutes match reasonably well those of the CFCs they displace. Both criteria may be satisfied, although some CFC substitutes will cost substantially more to produce and distribute.

Alternatives to CFCs constitute a significant market for chemical manufacturers, although several large firms are also likely to see their earnings erode as CFCs are phased out. A significant cost of phaseout is the replacement of equipment rendered obsolete by the elimination of CFCs.

According to estimates, future emissions of CFCs are dominated by contributions from industrializing economies of the Third World. It is as yet unclear whether, and under what circumstances, large developing countries such as China would join any framework agreement on greenhouse warming. A significant inducement to joining a global management regime could be technology transfers financed by contributions from industrial nations, similar to recent provisions added to the Montreal Protocol for ozone depletion control (DeCanio and Lee, 1991). However, the cost of implementing new technology will be an important factor for any nation considering a CFC phaseout.

Policy Options

Within the United States, there have been embryonic discussions regarding a proposal for a global emissions tax, based on global warming potentials, to reduce carbon emissions. Currently, there is an excise tax on the Montreal Protocol CFCs, based on ozone depletion potential, applied at the production stage. Since CFCs are produced by a limited number of manufacturers, implementation of such a tax in the case of ozone depletion is not very difficult. However, actual application of a similar tax based on global warming potentials would be much more difficult because of the numerous methods by which greenhouse gases are generated.

For example, suppose the common denominator was equivalent CO_2, and a tax was in place. If HFC-134a were used as a propellant, and there was no additional energy effect, it would be a simple matter to tax the compound based on its global warming potential relative to CO_2. However, if the same compound, HFC-134a, was used as a coolant in a refrigerator, and HFC-134a had greater energy efficiency than an alternative refrigerant, the HFC-134a would result in less CO_2 emissions from a power plant, due to lower energy consumption, and lower power usage in the refrigerator's 20-year life. How would that energy reduction be accounted for in a tax based on HCF-134a alone? Such questions and many more would need to be addressed in regulations, a considerable task because not only the production but also the consumption of products that generate greenhouse gases is involved.

To encourage world compliance, international policy should continue to be negotiated through processes, such as the Montreal Protocol, that recognize the differences in time tables for implementing these options in developed and developing countries. National policies should encourage an examination of available resources, an assessment of priorities, and implementation of the options within the Montreal Protocol framework in the most timely manner possible.

As mentioned above, the signatory nations of the Montreal Protocol have recently negotiated a new, more restrictive agreement, which will effect a phaseout of CFC and halon production by 2000 for developed nations and by 2010 for developing nations. These nations have also issued a declaration of intent to phase out HCFCs by 2040. Global compliance with such an agreement would reduce atmospheric concentration of chlorine-containing compounds to pre-1978 levels by the end of the twenty-first century. At the same time, the agreement would have the effect of stabilizing the contribution of halocarbons to global warming.

The Montreal Protocol requires that parties establish mechanisms to ensure that developing nations (allowed 10-year delays in meeting all Protocol deadlines) obtain the financial and technological assistance necessary to facilitate compliance with the Protocol.

Technology transfer to developing nations can be divided into two areas: "in-use" technology and manufacturing technology. In-use technology refers to application, equipment maintenance, service, and so on. This is anticipated to be the more important technology, and the more difficult to transfer, as it requires expertise in several applications. Changeover in developed countries, however, will facilitate the transition of technology to developing countries, as lessons will have been only recently learned (Du Pont, 1989).

Manufacturing technology will be transferred once economic incentives are created, and financing will come from the private sector. It is important to realize the role that creating economic incentives will play in the creation of indigenous demand for such technology. There will be no natural economic incentive for buying equipment using HCFCs or HFCs, because equipment intended for new compounds will be more expensive than equipment designed for CFC use. (Several decades of product optimization, fixed cost depreciation and write-off, and expertise cannot be matched in a few short years.) Economic incentives therefore must come from other sources, and several mechanisms can be employed at the national and international levels to help create them. Most promising among these are marketable emissions permit systems and a price structure that reflects environmental impacts. International environmental and trade agreements are logical vehicles for introducing these mechanisms (U.S. Environmental Protection Agency, 1990b).

Finally, financial aid from the developed countries will be a necessary part of technology transfer. It is anticipated that the need for a coordinated worldwide approach for ozone protection will enable mechanisms to form naturally as a function of that worldwide cooperation. Additionally, much of the incentive for cooperative effort in providing financial aid will come from the strong desire for developing countries not to undermine the efforts of developed countries (United Nations Environment Programme, 1989).

The subject of financial aid is still being addressed on a world scale. The Economic Panel Report on the Montreal Protocol and Substances That Deplete the Ozone Layer (United Nations Environment Programme, 1989) makes no recommendation as to the amount or the sources of the funds that might be made available for this purpose. It does, however, make some recommendations as to where the funding for technology transfer could be generated:

- Industrial nations could set aside a percentage of the national product.
- Industrial nations could set aside a fixed amount of money.
- Governments could implement a tax on CFC and halon use, and use those tax revenues for technology transfer.

Such monies generated could be regulated and managed by the World Bank, which is set up for such a purpose.

Other Benefits and Costs

The obvious benefit of moving to CFC alternatives is a reduction in stratospheric ozone depletion. However, although nonfluorocarbon alternatives provide an important option to meet CFC demands, care must be taken that such options provide adequate safety and environmental acceptability as well. For example, conversion of aerosol applications to hydrocarbons may lead to an increase in the formation of local photochemical smog.

Research and Development

Significant research and development programs will be required to implement "third-generation" heat pump, refrigeration, and insulation technology in support of a phaseout of HCFCs as early as 2015 to 2020 (the dates specified in the Clean Air Act, agreed to by the House/Senate Conference Committee). A "systems" approach should be employed to ensure that third-generation technologies do not lead to a net increase in calculated warming. Unless the energy efficiency of the third-generation technology is at least as great as that of the HCFC technology it would replace, the added contribution from increased CO_2 emissions due to increased energy consumption could offset the decreases due to elimination of HCFCs.

Finding and implementing suitable third-generation technology could prove to be a significant challenge, and it is currently unclear what that technology might be. Producers and users of CFCs are evaluating alternatives that would minimize environmental effects while maintaining the safety and performance standards of CFCs. The atmospheric lifetime of a gas chosen to replace CFCs is a major factor in determining its potential environmental effects. If its lifetime is less than 6 months, some of the gas can decompose near the point at which it escapes to the atmosphere, possibly contributing to local environmental problems (such as smog). Many gases with short atmospheric lifetimes are also flammable or toxic, and thus worker and consumer safety concerns are associated with their use.

If the lifetime of a gas is longer than about a year, the gas will disperse before significant decomposition occurs; however, if emission rates are large enough, the compound's global concentrations can build to the point at which it has the potential to contribute to global environmental concerns. If the gas contains chlorine, it may potentially contribute to ozone depletion; if it absorbs infrared radiation, it may contribute to greenhouse warming.

The HCFCs and HFCs have been chosen to replace CFCs because of their shorter atmospheric lifetimes. To date, no one has identified an alternative that meets the safety and performance standards of CFCs and also has no potential to contribute to either local or global environmental concerns. The HCFCs and HFCs provide a near-term option to balance societal needs, environmental concerns, consumer and worker safety, and efficiency and performance standards.

Conclusions

Global compliance with the 1990 revisions to the 1987 Montreal Protocol would stabilize the contribution of CFCs to calculated global warming by the end of the twenty-first century. Reducing CFCs as required by the Protocol will be achieved most effectively by a combination of increased conservation and recycling; replacement of CFCs with not-in-kind substitutes (e.g., replacement of CFCs in aerosol products by lower-cost, but flammable, hydrocarbons); and switching some 40 percent of existing essential uses of CFCs (e.g., refrigeration, air conditioning, and medical) to HCFCs and HFCs, which have lower global warming effects because of their shorter atmospheric lifetimes. The Montreal Protocol provides a mechanism to monitor and manage this result to ensure protection of the stratospheric ozone shield. Policymakers must provide incentives to encourage and support global compliance.

AGRICULTURE

The agricultural sector is relevant to greenhouse gas emissions in five contexts:

1. The agricultural sector includes two major worldwide sources of CH_4 gas: decomposition in rice paddies and digestion in ruminants in livestock production.

2. Agriculture uses nitrogenous fertilizer and is thus a source of N_2O emissions.

3. Agricultural production decisions alter land use, which in turn affects greenhouse gas emissions.

4. Agricultural production uses fossil fuel energy sources and provides potential for reduced energy-related emissions.

5. Agriculture offers biomass fuel potential.

The agricultural sector is responsible for only a small portion of green-house gas emissions in the United States. Therefore reduction of green-house gas emissions from the agricultural sector in the United States is unlikely to have a major impact on greenhouse warming. On a global basis, however, agriculture contributes a substantial portion of global greenhouse gases. Thus, although the reduction of greenhouse gases from the agricul-tural sector may be relatively small within the United States, these reduc-tions may represent a large portion of the global greenhouse gas emissions.

Contexts 1, 2, and 3 are discussed in this section. Land use changes (context 3) are also discussed in the context of deforestation policies in Chapter 27 and Appendix O. Energy efficiency (context 4) is extensively treated in Chapters 21, 22, and 23, and Appendixes C, D, and E. Context 5 is discussed in Chapter 24.

Agricultural emissions can be reduced by using a variety of methods. In the case of livestock production, methods include proper handling of ma-nure to reduce CH_4, eliminating overproduction of livestock and feed, re-ducing energy and agrochemical use, and improving the conversion of feed to milk and meat through breeding, hormones, and vaccines to reduce feed requirements. Agricultural practices can also be improved through reducing biomass burning, conserving tillage and using advanced machinery to re-duce use of energy and agrochemicals, and increasing the use of on-farm sources of nitrogen fertilizers through better manure management and nitro-gen-fixing plants to reduce the need for commercial nitrogen fertilizers (U.S. Department of Energy, 1989).

However, in looking at the agricultural sector from a technical perspec-tive, it is difficult to say that a particular practice will work in all types of agriculture. Many promising technologies do not work in practice or do not work everywhere. Therefore, rather than focusing on the potential of par-ticular technologies as in previous chapters, this analysis attempts to deter-mine the impact of various taxes and subsidies on agricultural practices. In that way, each agricultural source of greenhouse gas can reduce emissions in the way that is most technically acceptable in any particular part of the country, and according to consumer desire for a particular product. The analysis in this chapter reviews both the potential of reducing emissions during production and the desire of the consumer for agricultural goods that generate greenhouse gas emissions.

Methane

The primary agricultural sources of CH_4 in the United States are paddy rice and ruminants. Information on reducing emissions from both of these sources is discussed in this section.

Recent Trends

The United States contributes a relatively small share of the global CH_4 emissions from paddy rice (Barker and Herdt, 1985). Most paddy rice is produced in Asia, with China and India contributing half the world's total and Asian countries accounting for almost 90 percent (Crutzen et al., 1986). Ruminants (e.g., cattle, buffalo, horses, and sheep) are also major contributors of CH_4 and constitute the largest source of U.S. agricultural CH_4 emissions. Ruminants are used as work animals in parts of Asia and Africa, with some use in Latin America, but are used for food, leather, and wool in high-income countries. Biomass burning is another agricultural source of CH_4 (and N_2O—see the "Nitrous Oxide" section below).

Table 25.4 shows emission reduction parameters on a per-hectare or per-head basis for paddy rice, draft animals, and other ruminants. For purposes of assessing the relative impacts of U.S. emission controls and controls in other countries, the range of emission reduction (million tons of carbon) from a 10 percent reduction in rice production or ruminant production in different regions is shown. Here it can be seen that the United States is a minor contributor of CH_4 from rice paddies and contributes virtually nothing from work animals. It is an important source of CH_4 from other ruminant animals (as are other industrialized countries).

Emission Control Methods

Methods for controlling CH_4 emissions include the following:

1. Improving the biological efficiency of rice plants and of ruminant animals.
2. Improving waste and residue management.
3. Changing agricultural practices.
4. Reducing consumption and production of paddy rice and ruminant animals.

The biological efficiency of both rice and ruminant animals can be improved. For example, the biological efficiency of paddy rice has improved in recent decades. Most of the world's irrigated and shallow-water-rainfed rice area is currently planted to the more-efficient modern varieties. However, further progress, while possible, is not likely to be dramatic. In the case of ruminant animals, agricultural scientists and farmers themselves have achieved improvements in animal efficiency through selective breeding. This work has resulted in improved animals that convert grains and roughage into meat, milk, and other products more efficiently. In this case, there is considerable scope for further improvement.

TABLE 25.4 Methane Mitigation Policy Options in Agriculture

Rice Paddy Options	Carbon per Hectare	Area Affected (million hectares)	Carbon Mitigated Mt C as CH$_4$	$/t C as CH$_4$
Price policy reforms				
United States (reduce supports)	2	0.3	0.6	Negative
Other countries	1	Little	—	—
Production tax: 50 percent				
United States	2	0.75	1.5	45–90
Other countries	1	70	70?	45–90
Regulatory quotas: 50 percent				
United States	2	0.75	1.5	45–90
Other countries	1	70	70?	45–90
Buyout (annual)				
United States (all rice products)	2	1.5	3	100–50
United States (50% production)	2	0.75	1.5	25–10
Other countries (20%)	1	Infeasible?	28	25–10
Buyout (permanent)				
United States (all rice land)	2	1.5	3	100–50
Other countries (10%)	1	Infeasible? 14	14	100–50

	Emissions (t C as CH$_4$/animal)	Animals Affected (millions)	Carbon Mitigated	
Ruminant Options			Mt C as CH$_4$	$/t C as CH$_4$
Price policy reform				
United States	0.05–0.12	150	Increase	
Other	0.05–0.12	750	Increase	
Ruminant tax (25%) or quota				
United States	0.05–0.12	375	19–45	150–30
Other developed countries	0.05–0.12	125	6.3–15	150–30
Less developed countries	0.05–0.12	62.5	3.1–7.5	150–30
Buyout option	Ineffective	Infeasible		

	Emissions (t C as CH$_4$/animal)	Animals Affected (millions)	Carbon Mitigated	
Work Animal Options			Mt C as CH$_4$	$/t C as CH$_4$
Machine subsidy				
United States	Ineffective			
Less developed countries	Ineffective			

Waste management in some livestock systems could be improved through regulations, and some animal wastes could be converted to biogas use. For many livestock systems, these options are not feasible, however. Improved residue straw management in rice paddies offers some scope for CH_4 reduction, but this is limited because rice straw provides nutrients to soils that would otherwise come from fertilizer, which itself entails N_2O emissions.

Agricultural practices can also be changed so that greenhouse gas emissions are reduced. Since work animals provide a considerable part of the world's energy for agriculture, the development of improved tractors and implements could bring about a reduction in work animals. This would reduce CH_4 emissions, but at the cost of increased CO_2 emissions. A number of logging and agricultural practices include the burning of crop residues, grasses, or shrubs, increasing the emissions of a number of greenhouse gases. Alternatives to biomass burning can be encouraged through information dissemination campaigns. Regulations and taxes can be used to discourage biomass burning.

Both suppliers and consumers can be discouraged from producing or consuming products that increase greenhouse gas emissions. Alternatively, substitutes for these products can be encouraged. For example, consumption of paddy rice and ruminant products can be reduced either by enhancing the supply of substitute products or by making paddy rice and ruminant products more costly than substitutes to consumers (through taxes and other price-increasing practices). Methods for enhancing the supply of substitutes for paddy rice include the improvement of upland (nonpaddy) rice production as well as the improvement of other cereal grain production. For ruminant products the methods include the development of cereal substitutes for meats. Methods for inducing consumers to consume less rice and ruminant products require that the prices of these commodities rise relative to prices of substitute commodities. This can be achieved through taxes, quotas, and regulations or "buyouts" of production reserves. Consumer education programs may also affect meat and egg consumption.

Barriers to Implementation

The barriers to improving the biological efficiency of rice plants and of animals are technological. Virtually every country in the world has an active program of agricultural research to achieve these goals. A system of International Agricultural Research Centers support these efforts.

Regulation of residue and waste management requires an efficient regulatory system, and such systems do not exist in most developing countries. This is also the case for regulation of biomass burning. For developed countries, the necessary systems are in place.

Enhancing the supply of substitute products is the object of a number of research programs and initiatives in many countries. As with the in., ment of biological efficiency, the limitations are technological. The question is whether upland rice is likely to replace paddy rice. Since technological improvements in paddy rice have been achieved at a more rapid pace than for upland rice, it is unlikely that upland rice will displace paddy rice.

Programs to intervene in markets to raise the price of rice and ruminant products will generally be in conflict with welfare concerns. This is particularly likely to be the case for rice, the staple food for most of the world's poor. These programs may be in conflict with or in harmony with current U.S. farm policies with objectives (i.e., incentives to reduce production) related to greenhouse gas concerns. In general, most developed countries, including the United States, intervene in markets to raise prices to the consumer for the purpose of raising producer incomes. They are thus amenable to raising the prices of agricultural goods, but not necessarily to raising the *relative* prices of rice and ruminant products. Most developing countries, by contrast, resist raising prices to consumers—especially for staple commodities such as rice.

Policy Options

Consumption and production of paddy rice and ruminant products could be reduced by increasing the price of these goods. When prices to consumers increase, it is well established that consumption shifts to substitute products. Price increases to consumers can be achieved through (1) elimination of subsidies to consumers, (2) taxes on the product, and (3) reduced supply of the product. The first option is generally limited to low-income farm countries, where rice consumption may be subsidized. Most low-income countries seek to provide urban consumers with low-priced staple foods. In many cases, imports of rice are subsidized. Removal of these subsidies would curtail consumption and reduce imports. However, a nongreenhouse-gas-producing food crop would need to be developed to replace the rice.

All developed market economies, in contrast, have policies in place that are designed to raise net incomes to farmers. These policies are designed to raise both producer and consumer prices above normal market levels. Taxes on production or sales are not used because these would result in lower producer prices. Importing countries typically impose import tariffs or quotas to reduce supplies, and this causes higher domestic producer and consumer prices. Japan, for example, limits rice imports to such a degree that domestic prices are more than 5 times world prices. South Korea and Taiwan and most European economies also protect domestic producers through import controls. These same countries pursue similar policies with respect to beef and milk production. These policies have a cost to the economy

because they cause resources to be inefficiently allocated. The value that consumers place on the protected products (as measured by the prices consumers pay) exceeds the real cost to the economy (as measured by world prices).

Thus most food-importing countries are already limiting rice and ruminant product consumption, and this generally means less production and CH_4 emissions. They bear costs in doing so, but the motives for doing so are not to reduce CH_4 emissions. Further CH_4 emission reduction could be achieved by increased protection at a cost of $16 to $20/t CH_4 mitigated for rice and $50/t CH_4 mitigated for ruminant products (see Appendix L for calculations).

For countries that are exporters of rice and ruminant products, the policy options are different. Thailand is the only low-income rice-exporting country, and Thailand has actually used a rice tax on producers to raise government revenue. This tax reduces production and income and CH_4 emissions at a cost of $20/t CH_4 mitigated. Thailand has lowered this tax in recent years, however.

High-income rice-exporting countries—the United States is the chief example—seek to protect the incomes of rice producers. They can do this by subsidizing exports or by making direct payments to producers. In recent years in the United States, producer prices have been maintained at roughly 30 percent above world export prices. Indirect export subsidization and direct payments to producers are made. Irrigation water is heavily subsidized in California. The direct payment schemes do require acreage restrictions. The net effect of this mix of policies is that total rice production is probably higher than it would be in the absence of the policies. Thus some CH_4 mitigation could be achievable if these policies were eliminated, but they exist for reasons having little to do with CH_4 emissions, and direct CH_4 policies would require either more acreage restrictions—compensated by direct payment—or land buyouts. The costs per ton CH_4 mitigated through further acreage restrictions are probably in the range of $10 to $200. The buyout options range in cost from $50 to $150 (see Appendix L).

Buyout programs could be pursued in developing countries as well. International agencies could seek to buy paddy rice land out of production by making payments to farmers. This policy would have two complications and is probably not very feasible. First, if the buyouts were substantial, rice prices would rise, and this would affect the welfare of rice consumers. Second, the rise in rice prices would induce the farmers who had not been bought out to plant more rice unless a system of controls was in place (as is feasible in the United States). Thus buyout programs are likely to be quite costly.

For ruminant products, the agricultural policies of developed exporting countries are more complex than for rice. For products that can be stored at low cost (e.g., dry milk), most OECD countries attempt to reduce supply to achieve higher prices. Supply reduction programs are often ineffective and produce surpluses. Some reduction in CH_4 emissions is probably achieved for dairy products. For beef cattle the costs of carrying surpluses are sufficiently high that few direct programs are attempted.

A ruminant tax could be imposed on ruminant products to achieve reduced consumption and production. The imposition of the tax would create an adjustment problem, but once the adjustment was made the implications for producers would not be great. The cost of attaining CH_4 mitigation via a ruminant tax in the United States would be approximately \$100/t CH_4 (see Appendix L).

Waste and residue management in the United States can be improved by reviewing current waste regulations. For many systems, tightened regulations may be in order. For other countries, this will not be feasible in the short term, but increased awareness of CH_4 problems is likely to produce long-term gains. Further experiments with biogas systems in livestock production systems and selective subsidies to achieve more experience with such systems could be productive.

Biomass burning in the United States could be reduced by tightening burning regulations. Taxes might be used in some instances. The costs will vary greatly from case to case and should be carefully considered in drawing up new regulations. For developing countries, educational programs and technical assistance from developed countries could be helpful. In some cases, subsidies from international agencies could be used to achieve reduced burning. Such programs need to be sensitive to each situation.

Table 25.4 summarizes CH_4 mitigation policy options in agriculture. For each option, the effect per hectare (or animal) and the total ton of carbon mitigated are estimated, along with an estimated range for dollars per ton of carbon mitigated. More information on the way in which these estimates were calculated is given in Appendix L.

Price policy reforms would probably have no real effect on greenhouse gas emissions except in U.S. rice production. Taxes or regulatory quotas by the United States and other countries would reduce greenhouse gas emissions at moderate costs. The lowest costs per ton of carbon mitigated are for limited annual buyouts of rice producers. These options affect production very little. Permanent buyouts are more costly. Ruminant product options are generally more costly than rice options. They, too, are limited in terms of total reductions but do offer some scope for U.S. policies.

None of these calculations considers the distributional consequences of these options. Because these policy options lead to higher rice, meat, and milk prices and because low-income households spend a higher proportion of their incomes on these goods than do high-income households, these policies have undesirable distributional consequences.

Nitrous Oxide

Soil cultivation (tillage and fertilizing) in conventional agriculture leads to the release of N_2O as well as CO_2. N_2O is also released in land clearing (Wuebbles and Edmonds, 1988).

Recent Trends

The major biogenic source of atmospheric N_2O growth is the use of nitrogenous fertilizer to increase crop yields: 34 percent of anthropogenic N_2O emissions by one estimate (Krause et al., 1989). Although the accuracy of these values is questionable due to lack of worldwide information on biogenic sources, they do indicate the importance of the contribution to N_2O emissions from fertilizer application in relation to that from fossil fuels. The IPCC estimates that N_2O was responsible for approximately 5 percent of the greenhouse gas contribution during the 1980s (see Chapter 19 for more details; Intergovernmental Panel on Climate Change, 1990). The U.S. N_2O emissions from nitrogenous fertilizers can be estimated at approximately 0.9 teragrams (Tg) of nitrogen per year by taking the total world N_2O emissions and dividing by the land area of the United States.

Available data (see, for example, Eicher, 1990) show that the magnitude of N_2O emissions varies greatly with the form in which nitrogen fertilizer is applied and suggest that magnitudes may also depend on agricultural practices, biogenic processes, soil properties, and climate. The form of, and application method for, nitrogen are factors that could be managed if further analysis were to confirm that they are important variables in N_2O control.

Emission Control Options

There apparently is some scope for changing N_2O emissions by choosing different fertilizers and by altering fertilizer and other chemical application practices. There are currently many types of chemical fertilizer, and more may be developed. Researchers may develop improvements, but as with energy and other activities, costs will be a factor. If the lowest-cost fertilizer is the heaviest emitter, then a tax or regulation would be required to limit its use (which is costly). Scientists have been working on nitrogen-fixing crops for many years, but additional progress is possible and needs to be made.

Therefore reduction of fertilizer use is probably the least costly method for significantly lowering the growth of agricultural sources of atmospheric N_2O emissions. There are many approaches, including altering planting and tillage practices, to reduce the amount of fertilizer application required. One of the most attractive is crop rotation, interspersing legumes (which are efficient extractors of atmospheric nitrogen) with grains. More organic waste recycling would also be helpful, and its use could be effectively increased. An alternative mitigation approach is the application of additional chemicals that reduce N_2O emissions from soils.

A summary of possible mitigation techniques includes the following:

- controlling erosion,
- improving crop varieties,
- matching available nitrogen to crop needs,
- using the lowest-emitting nitrogen fertilizers whenever suitable,
- adding nitrification inhibitors to fertilizers,
- limiting fertilizer use, and
- extending no-tillage or low-tillage farming using nitrogen-fixing plants.

Barriers to Implementation

Fertilizer use has long been essential to efficient agricultural production. Many improvements in crop varieties have depended on an enhanced responsiveness to fertilizers to achieve greater productivity. For many less-developed countries a reduction in nitrogen fertilizer use would be seen as a strong and direct threat to their capacity to produce food. Many countries have been actively seeking to increase fertilizer use (Barker and Herdt, 1985; Hayami and Ruttan, 1985).

In developed countries where there is an interest in controlling production of commodities as part of farm programs designed to achieve higher prices, a nitrogen tax, provided it applied to all farmers for all uses, would probably be politically feasible. The political feasibility of such programs is discussed in the section on "Methane" above.

Policy Options

Nitrogen fertilizer use is widespread, being heaviest in Europe. Some crops in some countries use little fertilizer (cassava and legumes), but cotton, paddy rice, and maize rely heavily on nitrogen fertilizer. A ban on nitrogen fertilizer would have a major impact on the production of these crops. Thus a tax to reduce N_2O emissions could be quite costly. In most developing countries, extension advisors to farmers usually recommend more nitrogen fertilizer use than farmers actually apply. In general, the value of the increase in crops produced by nitrogen fertilizer—the "marginal product"—is higher than the price of the fertilizer applied (Hayami and Ruttan, 1985).

Several studies of fertilizer demand estimate that a 10 percent increase in price (from a tax) would decrease use by roughly 5 percent (Gardner, 1987).

If such a tax were applied on all nitrogen fertilizer in the United States, it would have a cost of $25 million and would reduce N_2O emission by 50,000 t N/yr at a cost of $500/t N.

Research and Development

Biological efficiency can be improved by supporting and strengthening agricultural research programs. CH_4 reduction objectives can be incorporated directly into research programs. Specific programs for animal improvement can be implemented. Past experience with agricultural research programs indicates that most programs have been highly productive (Evenson, 1990). Expanded support for CH_4 concerns is likely to be effective. Paddy rice production and consumption can be reduced by enhancing substitutes such as upland rice. The production of such rice could be improved through research programs. It should be recognized, however, that the substitute crops for upland rice are other upland crops, not paddy rice. More upland rice production will increase rice supplies and lower rice prices generally, however, thus having a small discouragement effect on paddy rice production.

Ruminant products could be replaced with cereal-based substitutes with additional development. Given that substantial research and development activities directed toward this objective are in place, it is unlikely that a specific subsidy to such research and development would speed up the process significantly. Subsidies to substitutions for rice and ruminant products would reduce CH_4 but could be more costly than other policies (see below).

Naturally produced or fixed nitrogen by plants is quite important and may be enhanced by further research. Legumes (e.g., beans, soybeans, and lentils) fix nitrogen. The Azolla fern is used in parts of Asia to fix nitrogen in rice fields, but its use is limited by high labor requirements and temperature sensitivity.

Conclusions

The agricultural sector constitutes a major sink for sequestering of carbon, and because this carbon is constantly recycled, the sink is a long-term one. The sector is a major source of CH_4 and N_2O, and to the extent that agricultural production uses fossil fuels it is also a small source of CO_2. Land use change also leads to direct emission of CO_2.

The political climate for policies (e.g., taxes, subsidies, and buyouts) to reduce CH_4 and N_2O emissions through reductions in supply of ruminant products and rice in the United States is favorable because farm interest groups seek higher prices; however, there is some concern regarding the efficiency and effectiveness of such mechanisms. For other industrialized countries, the political situation is similar and would likely not constitute a major barrier to the implementation of greenhouse gas emission control options.

Developing countries, on the other hand, offer quite a large scope for potential greenhouse gas mitigation. Political and distributional concerns are barriers to mitigation options in these countries because they often reduce production and consumption of vital goods. International mechanisms for sharing costs would be required to realize mitigation in many developing economies.

Finally, although there are few impending breakthroughs in technology, the potential for improved technology from research and development in both food and biomass fuel production is good in the long run.

LANDFILL METHANE

On a worldwide basis, municipal landfills are a relatively small but increasing source of CH_4 emissions to the atmosphere. The EPA estimates that worldwide landfill emissions account for approximately 3 percent of total global CH_4, but that this would increase to roughly 7 to 9 percent by 2025 in the absence of new abatement measures (Lashof and Tirpak, 1990). For the United States, however, landfills are the largest source of CH_4 emissions, as seen in Chapter 19.

Landfill CH_4 is produced primarily by the decomposition of municipal and industrial solid wastes under anaerobic conditions (i.e., a lack of oxygen). The quantity and rate of CH_4 production depend on a number of factors, including composition of the waste; age, moisture and oxygen content, temperature, and acidity (pH); and the presence of nutrients or biological inhibitors that either stimulate or repress the activity of bacteria responsible for decomposition. Biological decomposition in landfills is typically accompanied by other chemical reactions and by vaporization of some landfill constituents. Thus "landfill gas" includes not only CH_4, but CO_2, nitrogen, and a variety of non-CH_4 organic compounds. The average composition of waste at active U.S. landfills is shown in Table 25.5. Household waste at approximately 72 percent (by weight) is the largest contribution by far.

Figure 25.7 depicts the typical evolution of landfill gas constituents, illustrating the dominant biochemical processes over time (U.S. Environmental Protection Agency, 1990a). Actual elapsed time is measured in decades and depends on landfill composition. As a rough approximation, most studies assume that landfill gas is 50 percent CH_4 and 50 percent CO_2 by volume, with trace amounts of other constituents.

The time required for significant production of CH_4 can vary from 10 to 100 years or more, depending on the landfill properties noted above. The

TABLE 25.5   Average Composition of Waste in Active
Municipal Waste Landfills

Waste Type	Mean Waste Composition (wt %)
Household waste	71.97
Commercial waste	17.19
Household hazardous waste	0.08
Asbestos-containing waste material	0.16
Construction/demolition waste	5.83
Industrial process waste	2.73
Infectious waste	0.05
Municipal incinerator ash	0.08
Other incinerator ash	0.22
Sewage sludge	0.51
Other waste	1.19

SOURCE: U.S. Environmental Protection Agency (1990b).

EPA estimates typical rates of CH_4 production at 1000 to 7000 cubic feet per ton of municipal solid waste deposited (Lashof and Tirpak, 1990).

Recent Trends

Estimates of landfill CH_4 and CO_2 generally are based on population estimates for a particular region, together with assumptions about the quantity and composition of refuse associated with that population. Table 25.6 summarizes the assumptions employed by Barnes and Edmonds (1990) in a study for DOE. These estimates are based on the work of Bingemer and Crutzen (1987), who estimate current landfill CH_4 emissions at approximately 30 to 70 Mt/yr worldwide. Note that the model described by Barnes and Edmonds (Table 25.6) does not include a time lag between waste generation and landfill gas emissions.

In the United States, more detailed estimates of CH_4 generation rates have recently been developed by EPA as part of a proposal for controlling air emissions from municipal solid waste (MSW) landfills (U.S. Environmental Protection Agency, 1990a,c). Table 25.7 summarizes EPA estimates of CH_4 and non-CH_4 organic compound emissions for new and existing landfills in 1997 in the absence of any regulatory action. A simple two-parameter model is used to estimate CH_4 generation rates as a function of the landfill opening and closing dates and of the annual average refuse acceptance. The two chemical parameters in the model reflect the type of

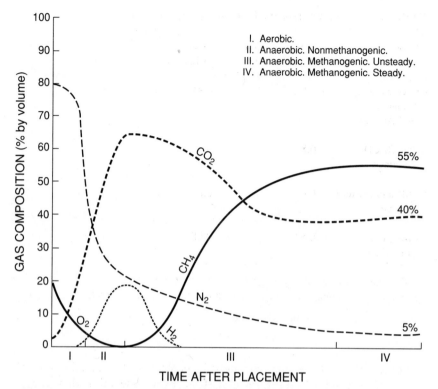

FIGURE 25.7 Evolution of typical landfill gas composition.

SOURCE: U.S. Environmental Protection Agency (1990a).

refuse in each landfill and the various dependency factors (temperature, moisture, and so on) listed earlier.

As noted earlier, CO_2 emissions are roughly comparable in magnitude to CH_4 emissions on a volume basis. Adjusting for the differences in molecular weight, CO_2 mass emissions thus are approximately 2.75 times greater than the CH_4 values in Table 25.7.

Emission Control Methods

Reduction of CH_4 from active or inactive landfills requires that the gas first be collected and then utilized in an energy recovery system or simply burned (flared). Either alternative produces CO_2 and water vapor, but a net benefit in terms of greenhouse effects still results because CH_4 contributes more radiative forcing than CO_2 (see Chapter 19, Table 19.4) and because with CH_4 as an energy source, some use of an alternative fuel has been displaced.

TABLE 25.6 Parameters for Estimating Landfill Gas Emission Rates

Region	Waste Generated (kg/person/day)	Fraction of Waste to Landfill	Organic Carbon Fraction in Waste[a]
United States, Canada, and Australia	1.8	0.91	0.22
Other OECD countries	0.8	0.71	0.19
USSR and Eastern Europe	0.6	0.85	0.175
Developing countries	0.5[b]	0.08	0.15

[a]Half of this is assumed to produce CH_4 and half CO_2.
[b]Based on urban population only, assumed to be 22 percent of total.

SOURCE: Barnes and Edmonds (1990).

In the United States, approximately 17 percent of the operating municipal landfills employ some form of CH_4 recovery and mitigation system, although less than 2 percent of the sites recover CH_4 for energy use (Lashof and Tirpak, 1990). Recently, however, EPA announced its intent to require the collection and control of landfill gases under Section 111 of the Clean Air Act (which pertains to new sources). The EPA standards (for new sources) and guidelines (for existing sources) currently being drafted would apply to all municipal landfills emitting more than 100 t/yr of non-CH_4 organic compounds (U.S. Environmental Protection Agency, 1990c). Such facilities would be required to design and install gas collection systems and then combust the captured landfill gases (with or without energy recovery). The combustion control device would have to be capable of reducing non-CH_4 organic compounds in the collected gas by at least 98 percent.

As background to its draft regulatory proposal, EPA analyzed three regulatory options for new and existing landfills. The three alternatives were based on cutoff sizes of 25, 100, and 250 t/yr of non-CH_4 organic compounds from a given landfill. The lowest cutoff level would influence the greatest number of facilities. For each regulatory alternative, engineering and economic models were used to estimate the overall emission reductions and costs of landfill gas mitigation. The assumed control technology was an active gas collection system coupled with either a flare or an energy

TABLE 25.7 National Baseline CH_4 and Non-CH_4 Organic Compound Emission Estimates, 1997

Landfill Category	Number of Landfills	Methane Emissions (t CH_4/yr)	Nonmethane Organic Compound Emissions (t CH_4/yr)
Existing municipal solid waste landfills (active and closed)	7,480	1.8×10^7	510,000
New municipal solid waste landfills	928	5.3×10^5	10,000
All affected landfills	8,408	1.8×10^7	520,000

SOURCE: U.S. Environmental Protection Agency (1990b).

recovery system for gas combustion. Because the latter option entails higher capital costs, its economical viability depends on the site-specific nature of by-product energy use or markets, which EPA was not able to evaluate. Thus the costs reported by EPA are based on application of active gas collection systems and flares to all landfills above the specified emission level cutoffs (U.S. Environmental Protection Agency, 1990c).

The control cost results for new and existing landfills are presented in Table 25.8. The average CH_4 emission reduction encompassed by the three regulatory alternatives ranges from 39 to 82 percent at costs of $9 to $29/t CH_4 removed. The current EPA draft proposal calls for implementing "regulatory

TABLE 25.8 Landfill CH_4 Reduction Control Costs

Regulatory Alternative	New Landfills		Existing Landfills	
	CH_4 Reduction (%)	Cost[a] ($/t CH_4)	CH_4 Reduction (%)	Cost[a] ($/t CH_4)
1	82	28	81	29
2[b]	65	22	60	23
3	43	9	39	20

[a]Methane control costs shown were derived from figures reported by EPA normalized on non-CH_4 organic compound emissions. Those costs were adjusted by using the reported ratios of non-CH_4 organic compounds to CH_4 for each regulatory alternative. All costs are based on a 1992 reference year.

[b]As calculated in Appendix M, the cost for this regulatory alternative is approximately $1/t CO_2 equivalent.

SOURCE: U.S. Environmental Protection Agency (1990c).

alternative No. 2," which would reduce CH_4 emissions by 60 to 65 percent over the life of U.S. landfills.

Because emissions, as well as capital and operating costs, vary significantly over the life of a facility, EPA's analysis employs a two-stage discounting procedure to calculate cost-effectiveness. First, capital costs are annualized over the useful life of the equipment by using a 10 percent rate of return. Then, the annual capital costs, operating costs, and emission reduction are brought back to a reference year (1992) by using a 3 percent social discount rate. Cost-effectiveness is calculated by dividing the total annualized cost by the total annualized emission reduction. Landfill lifetimes employed in the calculation range from 64 to 119 years, depending on the type of facility and the regulatory stringency. Although this calculation procedure differs from one used earlier in this report for CO_2 reduction measures (where emissions do not vary from year to year), the discount rate assumptions employed by EPA are similar to those employed in earlier chapters. Note, however, that 1992 (the effective date for regulation) rather than 1990 is used as the basis for EPA's cost results.

The panel's analysis of landfill gas cost-effectiveness in terms of CO_2 equivalence, which is based on the EPA results in Table 25.8, is presented in Appendix M.

Barriers to Implementation

Of primary interest here are barriers to the utilization of landfill gas as an energy resource. The economic viability of this option is hampered both by the quantity of gas available and by the fact that the energy content of landfill gas is only about half that of natural gas. Thus, under present conditions, landfill gas is economically viable as a fuel only if used close to the landfill site (e.g., within 2 to 3 miles). One such option could involve coupling directly to an electricity grid via a co-generation plant. Landfill operators have not traditionally been concerned with by-product recovery and utilization, however. Most landfills also tend to be in relatively remote locations. Another significant impediment to energy recovery is that some existing state regulations establish unlimited liability for any potential contamination problems at landfill resource recovery projects (Lashof and Tirpak, 1990).

Policy Options

As discussed above, EPA already plans to require collection and combustion of landfill gas from large facilities. This policy will reduce the emissions of greenhouse gases. The magnitude of the reduction will depend on a final determination of the size of facilities affected.

In the long term, landfill gas emissions can be reduced through increased recycling so that less waste is available for decomposition. Alternative methods of waste disposal also could be promoted. For example, an analysis could be conducted that evaluated the relative greenhouse gas benefits of incineration versus landfill disposal. Policy incentives to encourage wider use of energy recovery systems could also be devised and implemented.

Other Benefits and Costs

The U.S. Environmental Protection Agency (1990a,c) lists four major health and welfare effects that motivate the regulation of landfill gas emissions: (1) human health and vegetation effects caused by tropospheric ozone, which is formed from non-CH_4 organic compound emissions; (2) carcinogenicity and other health effects associated with air emissions of toxic species; (3) global warming effects of CH_4; and (4) gas explosion hazards. Additional consequences cited by EPA are odor nuisance and hazardous effects on soil and vegetation (U.S. Environmental Protection Agency, 1990a). Policies that reduce waste generation would also help communities that are running out of landfill space.

Research and Development

One important focus for research and development is to explore and improve techniques for enhancing CH_4 gas production yield from landfills. Methods such as the controlled addition of nutrients and moisture, control of landfill acidity, and bacterial seeding could help improve the economic viability of landfill gas recovery as an alternative to flaring (Lashof and Tirpak, 1990).

Conclusions

Major conclusions emerging from the above discussion on the potential mitigation of landfill gas are the following:

• Municipal landfills account for a small but growing fraction of CH_4 emitted from the decomposition of organic materials in refuse worldwide.
• In the United States, EPA is about to promulgate new measures that would require the collection and combustion of landfill gas from larger facilities, thus reducing overall emissions from new and existing landfill sites.
• The utilization of landfill gas as an energy resource is currently quite low. Increased research and development could enhance the economic feasibility of this energy option.

NOTE

1. Throughout this report, tons (t) are metric; 1 Mt = 1 megaton = 1 million tons; 1 Gt = 1 gigaton = 1 billion tons.

REFERENCES

Aulisio, L. 1988. Presentation at International Conference on CFC and Halon Alternatives, Washington, D.C., January 14, 1988.

Barker, R., and R. Herdt. 1985. The Rice Economy of Asia. Washington, D.C.: Resources for the Future.

Barnes, D. W., and J. A. Edmonds. 1990. An Evaluation of the Relationship Between the Production and Use of Energy and Atmospheric Methane Emissions. Report DOE/NBB-0088P. Washington, D.C.: U.S. Department of Energy.

Bingemer, H. G., and P. A. Crutzen. 1987. The production of methane from solid wastes. Journal of Geophysical Research 92:2181-2187.

Cogan, D. G. 1988. Stones in a Glass House. Washington, D.C.: Investor Responsibility Research Center.

Crutzen, P. J., et al. 1986. Methane production by domestic animals, world ruminants, other herbivorous fauna and humans. Tellus 38B:184-271.

DeCanio, S. J., and K. N. Lee. 1991. Doing well by doing good: Technology transfer to protect the ozone layer. Policy Studies Journal 19(2):140-151.

Du Pont. 1989. An Industry Perspective on Technology Transfer and Assistance to Help Less Developed Countries (LDCs) Phaseout of Chlorofluorocarbons (CFCs). Wilmington, Del.: E.I. du Pont de Nemours and Company.

Energy Information Administration. 1989. Potential Cost of Restricting Chlorofluorocarbon Use. Service Report SR/ESD/89-01. Washington, D.C.: Energy Information Administration, U.S. Department of Energy.

Eicher, C. K. 1990. Building scientific capacity for agricultural development. Agricultural Economics 4:117-143.

Evenson, R. E. 1990. Human capital and agricultural productivity change. In Agriculture and Government in an Interdependent World, A. Maunder, ed. Alderahot, England: Dartmouth Publishing Co.

Farman, J. C., B. G. Gardiner, and J. D. Shanklin. 1985. Large losses of total ozone in Antarctica reveal seasonal ClO_x/NO_x interaction. Nature 315:207-210.

Gardner, B. 1987. The Economics of Agricultural Policies. New York: Macmillan.

Hayami, Y., and V. W. Ruttan. 1985. Agricultural Development, An International Perspective. Baltimore: John Hopkins Press.

ICF. 1987. Regulatory Impact Analysis: Protection of Stratospheric Ozone. Volume III, Part 7, Solvents. Prepared by ICF, Inc., for the Office of Air and Radiation, U.S. Environmental Protection Agency.

Intergovernmental Panel on Climate Change. 1990. Climate Change: The IPCC Scientific Assessment, J. T. Houghton, G. J. Jenkins, and J. J Ephraums, eds. New York: Cambridge University Press.

Krause, F., W. Bach, and J. Koomey. 1989. Energy Policy in the Greenhouse, Volume 1. El Cerrito, Calif.: International Project for Sustainable Energy Paths.

Lashof, D. A., and D. A. Tirpak, eds. 1990. Policy Options for Stabilizing Global Climate. Washington, D.C.: U.S. Environmental Protection Agency.

National Aeronautics and Space Administration. 1988. Publication 1208. Washington, D.C.: National Aeronautics and Space Administration.

Prather, M. J. 1985. Continental sources of halocarbons and nitrous oxides. Nature 317:221-225.

Putnam, Hayes, and Bartlett, Inc. 1987. Economic Implications of Potential Chlorofluorocarbon Restrictions: Final Report. Washington, D.C.: Putnam, Hayes, and Bartlett, Inc.

Radian Corp. 1987. Regulatory Impact Analysis: Protection of Stratospheric Ozone. Volume III, Part 3, Mobile Air Conditioning. Prepared by Radian Corp. for the Office of Air and Radiation, U.S. Environmental Protection Agency. Research Triangle Park, N.C.: Radian Corp.

Rowland, F. S., and M. J. Molina. 1974. Stratospheric sink for chlorofluoromethanes: Chlorine atom-catalysed destruction of ozone. Nature 249:810-812.

Shine, K. 1990. Effects of CFC substitutes. Nature 344:492-493.

United Nations Environment Programme. 1989. Economic Panel Report: Montreal Protocol and Substances That Deplete the Ozone Layer. Nairobi, Kenya: United Nations Environment Programme.

U.S. Department of Energy (DOE). 1989. A Compendium of Options for Government Policy to Encourage Private Sector Responses to Potential Climate Change. Report DOE/EH-0103. Washington, D.C.: U.S. Department of Energy.

U.S. Environmental Protection Agency. 1990a. Air Emissions from Municipal Solid Waste Landfills—Background Information for Proposed Standards and Guidelines. Draft. March 1990. Research Triangle Park, N.C.: U.S. Environmental Protection Agency.

U.S. Environmental Protection Agency. 1990b. Final Report to the Administrator of the U.S. Environmental Protection Agency from the International Environmental Technology Transfer Advisory Board. Washington, D.C.: U.S. Environmental Protection Agency.

U.S. Environmental Protection Agency. 1990c. Standards of Performance for New Stationary Sources and Guidelines for Control of Existing Sources: Municipal Solid Waste and Landfills. Draft Federal Register Notice. March 1990. Research Triangle Park, N.C.: U.S. Environmental Protection Agency.

World Meteorological Organization (WMO). 1985. Global Ozone Research and Monitoring Project. Report 16. Geneva: World Meteorological Organization.

World Meteorological Organization (WMO). 1989. Scientific Assessment of Stratospheric Ozone. Report 20. Geneva: World Meteorological Organization.

Wuebbles, D. J., and J. Edmonds. 1988. A Primer on Greenhouse Gases. Washington, D.C.: U.S. Department of Energy.

26

Population

Despite recent declines in population growth rates, the world's population today is 5.2 billion (International Institute for Environment and Development and World Resources Institute, 1987) and is expected to continue to grow rapidly. This increasing population is one of the factors affecting trends in greenhouse gas emissions. The more people there are in the world, the greater is the demand put on resources to provide food, energy, clothing, and shelter for them. All these activities necessarily involve emissions of greenhouse gases.

Income growth also affects greenhouse gas emissions. As income per capita grows, the demand for goods also grows, particularly for such goods as health and education services, transportation, and housing.

Most nations in the world have policies to reduce population growth rates, and all seek to achieve rapid growth in income per capita (and other development objectives such as improvements in health). The interests of greenhouse gas emission policy are well served by the first objective but would appear to be in conflict with the second. This chapter explores the greenhouse gas implications of slowing population growth and the nature of this apparent conflict of objectives.

RECENT TRENDS

Both the global population and the population growth rate have been increasing rapidly over the past few centuries. The world population of 0.25 billion in A.D. 1 doubled by 1650. Two hundred years later, in 1850, it had doubled again to about 1.1 billion. By 1930, world population stood at 2 billion; it reached 4 billion by 1975 and is 5.2 billion today. Despite recent declines in the growth rate (International Institute for Environment and Development and World Resources Institute, 1987), world population is expected to continue to increase rapidly. According to the United Nations, the population at the end of this century will be about 6.25 billion, and by 2025 about 8.5 billion. United Nations estimates indicate that population will stabilize at 10 billion perhaps a century from now.

The U.N. Population Fund considers this projection optimistic, because the projection assumes that fertility rates in the developing world will decrease by one-third in the next 30 to 40 years. This, in turn, assumes that the number of women using family planning in the developing countries will increase from its present level of 45 percent to 58 percent by 2000 and to 71 percent (the current level in industrialized countries) by 2025; it also assumes that contraceptive effectiveness will be as high as it is today in developed countries. If this decrease in fertility rates does not occur, U.N. estimates show population approaching 10 billion by 2025 and eventually stabilizing at 14 billion (Sadik, 1989).

Current World Bank estimates put the world population at 10 billion by 2025, stabilizing at approximately 11.5 billion early in the twenty-first century (Bulatao et al., 1989a,b,c,d).

As the population increases, the distribution of the world's population also changes. Africa is growing much faster than the rest of the world, at over 3 percent annually, as opposed to only 1.9 percent for Asia. Although Africa trails Asia, Europe, the former USSR, and the Americas in population today, by the year 2000 it will be second in size only to Asia. This growth is occurring in spite of the fact that population growth in Africa is affected disproportionately by the AIDS epidemic. In addition, many family planning programs in Africa have been established later than similar programs in Asia. Today, Asia contains 58.3 percent of the world's population; Europe and the former USSR contain 15.9 percent; the Americas contain 13.8 percent; Africa contains 11.5 percent; and Oceania, 0.5 percent. By 2020, World Bank estimates show Asia at 58.2 percent, Africa at 18.9 percent, the Americas at 12.4 percent, Europe and the former USSR at 10.1 percent, and Oceania at 0.5 percent (Bulatao et al., 1989a,b,c,d).

Current emission patterns show that industrialized countries are emitting much higher quantities of greenhouse gases per capita (and in total) than less developed countries (LDCs). As LDCs become more industrialized, their per capita emissions are expected to increase. Furthermore, according to current population projections, LDCs will account for an ever-increasing share of the world's population. At present, 77 percent of the world's population lives in the LDCs. Bulatao et al. (1989a,b,c,d) project that LDCs will make up 84 percent of the world's population by 2025 and 88 percent by 2100. According to the U.N. Population Fund, if current rates of growth in energy consumption and population continue, LDCs will be emitting four times as much greenhouse gas in 2025 as industrialized countries.

POPULATION PROGRAMS AS AN
EMISSION CONTROL METHOD

There appears to be a general consensus that the only feasible and ethically acceptable way to reduce population growth is to achieve reduced fertility rates (Lapham and Simmons, 1987). Reducing fertility rates, however, is complex and depends on a number of factors. Fertility rates tend to slow as more education is provided for girls and as the status of women in the society improves. As noted by Repetto (1985),

> New aspirations and alternatives for women are especially important. There is overwhelming evidence that increased education, increased participation in the economy outside the home, increased control over finances, and increased status within the home are all associated with lower fertility, because they either delay marriage or lower marital fertility or both. No other change exerts a more powerful and predictable influence over the pace of fertility decline.

Provision of health services may also be key to slowing population growth. Urbanization and industrialization have also been linked to decreased fertility rates (Johnson and Lee, 1987; National Research Council, 1987; Gillespie et al., 1989).

The provision of family planning services is another important policy variable in achieving reduced fertility. "Most countries that have experienced rapid fertility declines have made vigorous efforts to bring modern means of birth control within reach of the entire population and have brought social and economic change and opportunities to the large majority of the population," notes Repetto (1985).

Lapham and Mauldin (1987) reviewed literature on factors effecting a lowering of fertility. They conclude that socioeconomic status and family planning program efforts work together. Countries that rank high on both generally have higher contraceptive prevalence and greater fertility decrease than countries that rank well on just one or the other. Nevertheless, the existence of family planning programs, which increase the availability of contraceptives, results in greater contraceptive use.

Perhaps the most relevant (although most aggregate) evidence in support of the proposition that the "demographic transition" (from high to low fertility rates) is closely related to economic and social development is to be gleaned from the experience of the past 30 years. Virtually all of the countries in the world today that have not achieved a significant reduction of population growth rates over the past 30 years also cannot be said to have achieved a development transition to modern economic growth. Conversely, almost all countries that have achieved some degree of demographic transition in the past 30 years have also achieved rapid economic growth. The highly successful cases of economic development have attained relatively complete demographic transitions in a very short period of time. Several other economies in Latin America (Colombia, Brazil, Mexico, and Costa Rica) and Southeast Asia (Thailand, Indonesia, and Malaysia) have also achieved significant demographic transitions while attaining development objectives.

In contrast, the economies in southern Asia (e.g., India, Bangladesh, and Pakistan) have not fully achieved large reductions in fertility rates, despite substantial family planning program investments. Countries in sub-Saharan Africa have achieved some reductions in fertility from the extraordinarily high levels of a few years ago, but fertility rates remain high.

Microstudies of population program effectiveness generally support these aggregate observations. Women in very low income economies usually express a desire for large families and thus have little interest in contraception. When education levels and employment opportunities for women improve, women demand contraceptive services, including sterilization. The effectiveness of contraceptive use increases as well (Schultz, 1988).

In those countries where the demographic transition is not under way, family planning programs generally reach only a small proportion of the population. They do serve an educational role, and they do reduce births. However, without the associated economic change they cannot achieve large impacts on fertility rates.

Family planning services are often provided both by public health systems and by private suppliers. When the development-based demand conditions for contraception improve, public and private suppliers of contraceptives and contraceptive information find expanded markets. There is also a related demand for better health care and nutrition, and programs providing these services become highly effective. (These programs are also effective in countries not yet entering the demographic transition.)

Thus population control options exist in countries not achieving economic growth development, but they probably cannot produce large changes and initiate a large demographic transition unless economic development takes place. When development does occur, the demographic transition can be very rapid, as demonstrated by Taiwan, Singapore, Hong Kong, and South Korea.

This interaction or complementarity between economic and social change and the demand for and effectiveness of population programs has two implications for greenhouse gas policy. The first is that the effectiveness of a population program is itself limited by economic and social conditions. The second is that this interaction effectively removes much of the apparent conflict between the objectives of reduced population growth and increased per capita income. It is not a practical option to achieve a major reduction in population growth without some increase in per capita income. Indeed, there is some evidence not only that population programs are more effective when incomes grow but also that such programs themselves induce income growth.

The analysis of population programs as a mitigation option has two parts. The first, as discussed above, is an examination of the apparent conflict between greenhouse gas concerns and income growth. The second is a calculation of the greenhouse gas emission reduction associated with a reduction in births.

This attempt to determine the actual impact of population policies on greenhouse gas emissions begins with a question. Would a country that failed to achieve a demographic transition and also failed to achieve economic growth emit more greenhouse gases over the next century than a country that achieved a demographic transition and economic growth as well?

To address this question, the panel has chosen to analyze the actual experiences of developing economies over the past 25 to 30 years.

The World Bank's annual World Development Report (World Bank, 1989) classifies developing countries as low income (excluding China and India), lower-middle income, and upper-middle income. The newly industrialized economics (NIEs) are middle-income (South Korea, Brazil) or high-income (Singapore, Hong Kong) countries.

By utilizing these categories of actual economic growth experience and projected population growth rates, the scenarios for population, per capita income, CO_2 emissions, and the family planning effect are computed and reported in Table 26.1. Each group of countries is indexed to 1.00 in 1990. Thus numbers reported for the years 2020, 2050, and 2100 are multiples of the 1990 base. For a more detailed explanation of the procedures used to derive Table 26.1, see Appendix N.

According to this analysis, the apparent conflict between economic development programs and greenhouse gas concerns is not an actual conflict. Countries that are able to achieve rapid economic growth (NIEs) also achieve earlier and more rapid population declines. After a century, these countries will not have emitted substantially more greenhouse gases than countries that remain poor. Thus support of both population and economic development programs is not self-defeating from a greenhouse gas mitigation standpoint. However, it is important to note that countries experiencing rapid economic growth will need greenhouse gas mitigation programs similar to those needed for developed countries.

BARRIERS TO IMPLEMENTATION

The experience of demographic change in the twentieth century indicates that large-scale economic, institutional, and social changes accompany— and may cause—declining birth rates. The institutional changes include

TABLE 26.1 Relationship Between Population and Greenhouse Gas
Emissions

	Low-Income Economies	Lower-Middle-Income Economies	Upper-Middle-Income Economies	Newly Industrialized Economies
Population	(2.6)	(2.1)	(1.7)	(0.8)
1990	1.0	1.0	1.0	1.0
2020	2.16	1.87	1.66	1.27
2050	4.03	3.10	2.10	1.61
2100	9.36	4.62	3.12	1.61
Per capita income	(1.5)	(2.2)	(2.9)	(6.2)
1990	1.0	1.0	1.0	1.0
2020	1.56	1.92	2.35	6.07
2050	2.43	3.69	5.54	14.31
2100	5.11	10.95	23.14	59.75
CO_2 emissions, annual				
1990	1.0	1.0	1.0	1.0
2020	3.37	3.59	3.90	6.17
2050	9.79	11.44	11.63	16.12
2100	47.83	40.47	67.06	57.71
CO_2 emissions, cumulated				
1990	1.0	1.0	1.0	1.0
2020	65.5	68.8	73.5	107.5
2050	262.9	294.3	306.4	441.3
2100	1,703.4	1,591	2,271	2,286
Family planning effect (base = CO_2 emission, cumulated)				
1990				
2020	0.20	0.56	0.49	1.34
2050	2.94	3.43	6.54	7.01
2100	58.71	51.90	34.65	89.09

social insurance, so that parents need not rely on their descendants for material support in old age. Changes in the status of women also appear to be influential in the decisions of women to limit family size. Government policies to guarantee the material support of the elderly connect to a wide range of fundamental policy issues, including the evolution of the macro-economy and the labor force. For matters of this scale, political will is an indispensable element of policy formulation. Similarly, the reverberations of changes in family size and the status of women are too large to be set aside in policy design. These matters of national interest are central to the international discussion of population.

Accordingly, although specific policy alternatives abound in areas such as tax treatment of children and provision for the costs of child-rearing, including education and health care, uncertainties remain as to the nature of the most successful strategies for population policy. Within the United States, the controversy surrounding abortion as a means of controlling family size has complicated discussions of a national population policy and the demographic components of U.S. foreign policy.

POLICY OPTIONS

A National Research Council (1987) study noted that those countries that have had unusually effective family planning programs have put significant personnel and resources into them. Availability of resources appears to be a necessary precondition for family planning program effectiveness. Yet less than 1.5 percent of the total international development assistance goes into population programs. The United States provided about $227.1 million in population assistance in 1988, that is, about 2.2 percent of the total U.S. development assistance that year (Population Crisis Committee, 1990).

Survey data have shown that a substantial demand for limiting and spacing births remains unmet by current family planning programs (Gillespie et al., 1989; Repetto, 1985). It would appear that the current annual world-wide expenditure of $3.2 billion for contraceptives is insufficient to meet demand in the LDCs. Gillespie et al. (1989) estimate that at least an additional $250 million each year over the next 20 years will be required to meet minimum LDC demand. The Population Crisis Committee (1990) estimates that expenditures must reach $10 billion per year by 2000 to slow population growth substantially.

Increasing availability of contraceptives where they are demanded and the concomitant reduction in fertility rates could help to hold down overall greenhouse gas emissions at a relatively inexpensive cost per ton of CO_2. It would be prudent for the United States to consider increasing funding for voluntary family planning services for LDCs requesting such assistance. For example, U.S. funding for the U.N. Population Fund could be restored, or U.S. Agency for International Development (AID) funds for population programs could be increased.

OTHER BENEFITS AND COSTS

Slowing population growth may well lead to less stress on the environment. In reviewing research on population growth and economic development, a National Research Council (1986) report concluded that slower population growth is likely to lead to a reduced rate of degradation of renewable common-property resources such as air, water, forests, land, and species of plants and animals. As discussed above, it should also be noted that population reduction programs may themselves have income consequences.

RESEARCH AND DEVELOPMENT

The links between population growth and greenhouse gas emissions are not fully understood. While some researchers indicate that increased population growth will result in increased greenhouse gas emissions, others feel that a reduction in population will result in increased greenhouse gas emissions as the per capita income of the population increases. A better understanding of the links among population growth, economic growth, and greenhouse gas emissions would aid decision makers in their determination of whether family planning is a worthwhile policy to pursue with regard to greenhouse warming.

CONCLUSIONS

The world population is growing rapidly. If there is not a significant reduction in fertility rates, the population may reach 14 billion before stabilizing.

The National Research Council (1986) report noted that reducing fertility would produce at every subsequent point slower population growth and smaller population size. Both World Bank and U.N. population projections show that the sooner fertility rates are reduced, the smaller the world population will be at stabilization.

The links between population growth and greenhouse emissions are complex and not well understood. However, at any given rate of greenhouse gas emissions per capita, a smaller population will mean less total emissions, as well as less stress on the environment in general. For example, at any given level of per capita emissions in 2025, the U.N. low population projection would involve 11 percent less total emissions than the medium projection, and 24 percent less than the high population projection (Sadik, 1990).

Greenhouse gas mitigation is thus well served by well-designed family planning, health, and education programs. It is furthered by broader economic development programs if they complement population reduction programs and enable earlier and more complete demographic transition.

REFERENCES

Bulatao, R. A., E. Bos, P. W. Stephens, and M. T. Vu. 1989a. Africa Region Population Projections: 1989-90 Edition. World Bank Staff Working Paper WPS 330. Washington, D.C.: World Bank.

Bulatao, R. A., E. Bos, P. W. Stephens, and M. T. Vu. 1989b. Asia Region Population Projections: 1989-90 Edition. World Bank Staff Working Paper WPS 331. Washington, D.C.: World Bank.

Bulatao, R. A., E. Bos, P. W. Stephens, and M. T. Vu. 1989c. Europe, Middle East, and Africa (EMN) Region Population Projections: 1989-90 Edition. World Bank Staff Working Paper WPS 328. Washington, D.C.: World Bank.

Bulatao, R. A., E. Bos, P. W. Stephens, and M. T. Vu. 1989d. Latin America and the Caribbean (LAC) Region Population Projections: 1989-90 Edition. World Bank Staff Working Paper WPS 329. Washington, D.C.: World Bank.

Gillespie, D. G., H. E. Cross, J. G. Crowley, and S. R. Radloff. 1989. Financing the delivery of contraceptives: The challenge of the next twenty years. In The Demographic and Programmatic Consequences of Contraceptive Innovation, S. Segal, A. Tsui, and S. Rogers, eds. New York: Plenum.

International Institute for Environment and Development and World Resources Institute. 1987. World Resources 1987. New York: Basic Books.

Johnson, D. G., and R. D. Lee, eds. 1987. Population Growth and Economic Development: Issues and Evidence. Madison: University of Wisconsin Press.

Lapham, R. J., and W. P. Mauldin. 1987. The effects of family planning on fertility: Research findings. In Organizing for Effective Family Planning Programs, R. J. Lapham and G. B. Simmons, eds. Washington, D.C.: National Academy Press.

Lapham, R. J., and G. B. Simmons. 1987. Overview and framework. In Organizing for Effective Family Planning Programs, R. J. Lapham and G. B. Simmons, eds. Washington, D.C.: National Academy Press.

National Research Council. 1986. Population Growth and Economic Development: Policy Questions. Washington, D.C.: National Academy Press.

National Research Council. 1987. Organizing for Effective Family Planning Programs. Washington, D.C.: National Academy Press.

Population Crisis Committee. 1990. 1990 Report on Progress Towards Population Stabilization. Washington, D.C.: Population Crisis Committee.

Repetto, R. 1985. Population, resource pressures, and poverty. In The Global Possible, R. Repetto, ed. New Haven, Conn.: Yale University Press.

Sadik, N. 1989. The State of World Population 1989. New York: United Nations Population Fund.

Sadik, N. 1990. The State of World Population 1990. New York: United Nations Population Fund.

Schultz, T. P. 1988. Population programs: Measuring their impact on fertility. Journal of Policy Modeling 10:1.

World Bank. 1989. 1989 World Development Report. Washington, D.C.: World Bank.

27

Deforestation

Deforestation through logging, burning, and clearing for cultivation and pasturing (Smithsonian Institution/International Hardwood Products Association, 1990) is occurring rapidly in the tropics and involves heavy social and ecological costs, especially where the forests are cleared by burning, which releases CO_2, CH_4, and other greenhouse gases. Deforestation rates for the 1980s are uncertain: rates change rapidly, satellite coverage is spotty, and substantial (and expensive) verification is required. The best available analyses suggest many reasons for trying to limit the rate of deforestation, one of them being that deforestation accounts for 20 percent of the worldwide anthropogenic contribution to greenhouse warming (World Resources Institute, 1990). Where forests must be used, the goal is to practice what is called "sustainable forestry," in which harvesting practices maintain the forests and protect soil, water, wildlife, and future resources.

RECENT TRENDS

Figure 27.1 illustrates how emissions of carbon to the atmosphere due to deforestation and changing land use have varied over time on the major continents (Dale et al., 1991). The estimates are based on recent calculations by Houghton and Skole (1990) and Houghton (1991). Forests are cut for a number of reasons, including to provide land for agriculture and wood for wood products and fuel. Although the rate of deforestation in temperate areas is currently low, the deforestation of tropical countries is continuing. At one time, Europe and North America were experiencing net deforestation, but today this is negligible due to a number of factors, including resource depletion and sustainable management of what remains. A factor that has reduced pressure on remaining forests has been the movement of

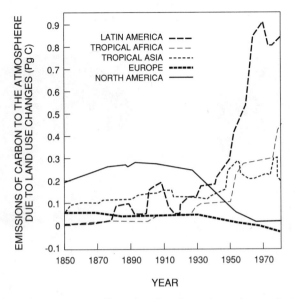

FIGURE 27.1   The annual net flux of carbon from the major continental areas.
SOURCE: Dale et al. (1991).

population from rural to urban areas due to overall economic growth and the expansion of nonagricultural jobs. It should be noted, however, that because of industrialization, acid rain and other air pollutants are a serious threat to forests in some temperate areas (World Resources Institute, 1985).

On the other hand, deforestation in many developing countries is believed to be increasing. As shown in Figure 27.2, recent estimates of tropical deforestation are larger than the 1981 to 1985 projection of the U.N. Food and Agriculture Organization. As indicated in both this figure and Figure 27.1, deforestation estimates vary tremendously; it is not clear whether estimation techniques have changed or the rate of deforestation has increased. Table 27.1 shows the rate of deforestation for a number of developing tropical countries (World Resources Institute, 1990).

EMISSION CONTROL METHODS

Recently, a number of tropical forestry experts met to discuss the causes of tropical deforestation and what could be done to slow deforestation. They arrived at a number of conclusions, some of which are summarized below (Smithsonian Institution/International Hardwood Products Association, 1990):

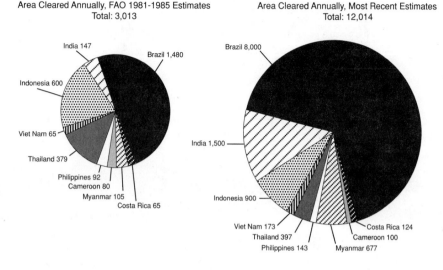

FIGURE 27.2   Area of closed forests cleared annually in *selected* tropical Countries, 1980s (in thousand hectares).   (See Table 27.1 for the total of all tropical forest clearing.)

SOURCE: World Resources Institute (1990).

• Tropical forests will be preserved only if they are accorded economic value.

• Blanket bans and embargoes (in contrast to selective ones) on tropical hardwood will tend to depress the value of these hardwoods and the forests that contain them. Such constraints generally diminish the economic incentives to conserve and manage these forests in the face of alternative land uses that lead to their destruction.

• In areas where prices received for timber do not fully cover the cost of forest management, there is a lack of incentive and commitment to forest management.

• Funds obtained from products of the tropical forests must be rechanneled into managing and regenerating those forests.

• The international tropical timber industry should encourage the continued establishment of conservation areas solely dedicated to forest preservation.

It is a challenge to understand the costs of limiting tropical deforestation and to finance such efforts.

The Conservation Foundation (CF), World Wildlife Fund (WWF), and Fundacion Neotropica (FN) have proposed development of a "forestry fund" through the use of conservation endowments (Conservation Foundation, World Wildlife Fund, and Fundacion Neotropica, 1988). A conservation endow-

TABLE 27.1 Deforestation of Closed Tropical Forests in Selected Countries

Country	FAO Annual Estimate 1961-1985 (thousand hectares)	Annual Rate of Loss Based on FAO Estimate (%)	WRI Estimate 1987 (thousand hectares)	Annual Rate of Loss Based on WRI Estimate (%)
Brazil	1,480	0.4	4,500[a]	2.2
Cameroon	80	0.4	100	0.6
Costa Rica	65	4.0	124	7.6
India	147	0.3	1,500	4.1
Indonesia	600	0.5	900	0.8
Myanmar (Burma)	105	0.3	677	2.1
Philippines	92	1.0	143	1.5
Thailand	379	2.4	397	2.5
Viet Nam	65	0.7	173	2.0
TOTAL	3,013	1.8	12,914	2.6
Total, all tropical countries	11,400		20,400	

NOTE: Closed forests have trees covering a high proportion of the ground and grass does not form a continuous layer on the forest floor. Open forests have trees interspersed with grazing land. One thousand hectares (ha) is 10 km^2.

[a]The World Resources Institute's original estimate of 8000 was based on 1987, which exhibited extremely anomalous conditions. Subsidies were scheduled for removal in 1988, driving up clearing, and a drought contributed to unusually high loss to fires. The total deforestation for the period from 1979 to 1989 has been estimated at 25 million hectares. The greatest deforestation occurred in 1987, and the rate in the latter half of the 1980s is probably closer to 4 million hectares per year. The actual deforestation is probably between 4 and 5 million hectares per year. No precise numbers are available.

SOURCE: World Resources Institute (1990, p. 103).

ment would provide a stable source of funding for long-term technical assistance and would support efforts to manage existing forest resources and to reforest degraded areas. Of particular interest here are the portions of the plan that would attempt to (1) stop deforestation of currently protected areas such as parks and reserves through improved protection and management and (2) slow logging and clearcutting on private lands by providing technical assistance and incentives for both farmers and the commercial sector to practice sustainable forestry (Conservation Foundation, World Wildlife Fund, and Fundacion Neotropica, 1988).

The endowment would be created by placing $200 per hectare in a financial institution. The interest from that endowment would be used as a financial incentive for people living near the tropical forest to practice sustainable forestry. These people would maintain claim to both public lands and interest from the endowment as long as they practiced sustainable forestry. If they did not, funding would be withdrawn. The purpose of the endowment would be to compensate people for the additional income they would have received if they had continued to use current agricultural techniques (Conservation Foundation, World Wildlife Fund, and Fundacion Neotropica, 1988).

A conservation endowment is being attempted in Costa Rica. The WWF has estimated that management and protection of the Golfo Dulce Forest Reserve and Corcovado National Park would save 8.7 Mt of carbon over the 10 years of the project.[1] These measures and others would provide a total carbon savings from the Costa Rican project of at least 21.8 Mt over 40 years (Conservation Foundation, World Wildlife Fund, and Fundacion Neotropica, 1988).

The cost and carbon sequestration figures from WWF's estimates are extrapolated for the present rate of deforestation in Appendix O. Although these figures are obviously rough, they should provide some idea of the cost of implementing such an option. The results of this analysis indicate that at the present rate of deforestation the release of approximately 7000 Mt CO_2 equivalent per year could be avoided. The cost of such a program would be approximately $0.40/t CO_2 avoided.

BARRIERS TO IMPLEMENTATION

Determining the cost and capacity of different methods for preventing deforestation is very difficult. It is one of the least certain of the various options examined in this report. The primary reason is that preventing deforestation involves changing the behavior of individuals in many developing countries. It is not something that the United States can pursue unilaterally, but rather will require careful attention to the needs and desires of a wide variety of people and cultures. It is important to realize that the pressures behind deforestation differ widely among the many tropical countries involved. There is no common cause, no common cure.

Furthermore, government policies that tend to put low value on the benefits of intact natural forests, and high value on the benefits from forest exploitation and conversion, lead to deforestation without a full understanding of the biological impact. Some countries have exploited their tropical forest resources to solve fiscal, economic, social, and political problems elsewhere in society (Repetto, 1988). The United States can act to prevent further degradation of its own forests, but in terms of affecting potential climate change, there are greater opportunities to be had in helping developing tropical countries to limit deforestation.

POLICY OPTIONS

Integrating concern for the long-term sustainability of tropical forests into international economic development and U.S. foreign policy would help to advance forest protection. The economic development of tropical nations intersects in important ways with those nations' management of their forestlands. Tropical forests also hold a major share of the world's species. Until recently, exploitation of tropical forests has been regarded as a means for developing nations to obtain income from forested lands and space for expanded settlement. Increasing interest in the sustainable uses of forests, both to produce commodities such as rubber and to promote services such as ecotourism, reflects a growing appreciation of nondepleting use patterns as being valuable in their own right and as ways of attracting international assistance and investment. It should be noted, however, that exploitive uses such as logging provide near-term economic returns in an already well-established business setting and that the pressures of expanding populations are real. Both forest products firms—most of which are located in developed nations—and tropical nations are understandably reluctant to disturb activities that are profitable in the near term.

Multilateral aid and technology transfer are likely to be necessary for forest protection for some time to come, because the costs of nonexploitive uses of forest resources are uncertain and high in some cases. This involvement tends to increase developing nations' concern that developed nations' environmental interest in the Third World may intrude on the developing nations' autonomy.

A constructive step in this circumstance is to focus on concrete projects, in which the gains and risks to all participants can be gauged. Policies that focus on bilateral or multilateral efforts to develop ecotourism, for example, can be carried out without resorting to abstract principles of international equity. Similarly, review and revision of the tropical forest action plans advanced by the U.N. Environment Programme can stress the concrete over the abstract.

Although it is uncertain at this time whether U.S. forests are a net source or a net sink for CO_2, it appears that they are near equilibrium. Therefore, although deforestation is not a source of greenhouse gas emissions in the United States, forestry policy related to greenhouse could be enhanced by consideration of the global environmental impacts. These impacts have not been a component of U.S. forest management thinking, and the inclusion of such considerations might not only enhance the role of U.S. forests in reducing greenhouse gas emissions, but also provide leadership for other nations.

OTHER BENEFITS AND COSTS

Tropical forests hold a major share of the world's species. Reducing deforestation can help maintain biodiversity. To put it simply, for the Amazon ecosystem to operate, it must maintain its wildlife and tree diversity. In addition, tropical forests provide soil protection, hydrological cycle balance, and products such as resins, essential and edible oils, fruits and nuts, natural fibers, and pharmaceuticals (Salati et al., 1989).

The destruction of tropical forests is due to growing population, growing infrastructure, and the economic activities associated with certain occupations. Unless people who work in cattle ranching, timber extraction, farming, charcoal production, and gold or oil exploration can find an alternative source of revenue compatible with their skills, their income will drop and their country's subsequent economic development will suffer. Further, growing populations maintain pressures for homesteads, farmland, traditional fuel resources, and other land-based resources.

RESEARCH AND DEVELOPMENT

After studying deforestation in the Amazon, Salati et al. (1989) indicated the following problems:

> The lack of knowledge of the basic functioning mechanism of the Amazonian ecosystem and of the most suitable methods of sustainable development of the region are the main reasons for the failure of many of the agricultural and cattle ranging projects. In addition, institutional problems are serious. The lack of research funds is impairing the continuity of many research programs and also the implementation of technical recommendations and enforcement of legal exigencies.

Their recommendations (Salati et al., 1989) include the following areas of research, which they believe are needed to adequately respond to deforestation:

• An expansion of international support to research groups and institutions dedicated to the study of the basic functioning mechanisms of the ecosystem, especially those with programs under way for a considerable time.

• The design of integrated interdisciplinary regional programs to study factors affecting the steady state equilibrium of the entire ecosystem.

• The design of programs to reclaim already degraded areas, particularly through reforestation.

• The implementation of anthropology research programs designed to acquire better knowledge of the forest management practices of native peoples. We should not forget that they have been living in the forest and from the forest for thousands of years.

• The stimulation of extractive activities for natural products, apart from logging, that have already proved to be economically profitable and cause no harm to forest integrity.

In a broader geographic sense, it is important to understand both the variety of factors leading to deforestation throughout the tropics and the way in which countries such as the United States can contribute to solutions without challenging national sovereignty and sensibilities.

CONCLUSION

The causes of deforestation are many and varied and relate largely to population and economic pressures in developing tropical nations. To prevent deforestation over the long term, there will have to be alternative solutions for a variety of social and economic problems. Developed countries such as the United States may be able to help by providing a suitable financial setting, but they will have to be cognizant of the varying national needs, aspirations, and sensitivities.

NOTE

1. Throughout this report, tons (t) are metric; 1 Mt = 1 megaton = 1 million tons; 1 Gt = 1 gigaton = 1 billion tons.

REFERENCES

Conservation Foundation (CF), World Wildlife Fund (WWF), and Fundacion Neotropica (FN). 1988. The Forestry Fund: An Endowment for Forest Protection, Management, and Reforestation in Costa Rica. Washington, D.C.: World Wildlife Fund.

Dale, V. H., R. A. Houghton, and C. A. S. Hall. 1991. Estimating the effects of land-use change on global atmospheric CO_2 concentrations. Canadian Journal of Forestry Research 21:87-90.

Houghton, R. A. 1991. Release of carbon to the atmosphere from degradation of forest in tropical Asia. Canadian Journal of Forestry Research 21:132-142.

Houghton, R. A., and D. L. Skole. 1990. Changes in the global carbon cycle between 1700 and 1985. In The Earth Transformed by Human Action, B. L. Turner, ed. New York: Cambridge University Press.

Repetto, R. 1988. The Forest for the Trees?: Government Policies and the Misuse of the Forest Resource. Washington, D.C.: World Resources Institute.

Salati, E., R. L. Victoria, L. A. Martinelli, and J. E. Richey. 1989. Deforestation and its role in possible changes in the Brazilian Amazon. In Global Change and

Our Common Future, R. S. DeFries and T. F. Malone, eds. Washington, D.C.: National Academy Press.

Smithsonian Institution/International Hardwood Products Association (IHPA). 1990. Tropical Forestry Workshop: Consensus Statement on Commercial Forestry Sustained Yield Management and Tropical Forests. Alexandria, Va.: International Hardwood Products Association.

World Resources Institute (WRI). 1985. World Resources 1986. New York: Basic Books.

World Resources Institute (WRI). 1990. World Resources 1990-91. New York: Oxford University Press.

28

Geoengineering

In this chapter a number of "geoengineering" options are considered. These are options that would involve large-scale engineering of our environment in order to combat or counteract the effects of changes in atmospheric chemistry. Most of these options have to do with the possibility of compensating for a rise in global temperature, caused by an increase in greenhouse gases, by reflecting or scattering back a fraction of the incoming sunlight. Other geoengineering possibilities include reforesting the United States to increase the storage of carbon in vegetation, stimulating an increase in oceanic biomass as a means of increasing the storage and natural sequestering of carbon in the ocean, decreasing CO_2 by direct absorption, and decreasing atmospheric halocarbons by direct destruction. It is important to recognize that we are at present involved in a large project of inadvertent "geoengineering" by altering atmospheric chemistry, and it does not seem inappropriate to inquire if there are countermeasures that might be implemented to address the adverse impacts.

Our current inadvertent project in "geoengineering" involves great uncertainty and great risk. Engineered countermeasures need to be evaluated but should not be implemented without broad understanding of the direct effects and the potential side effects, the ethical issues, and the risks. Some do have the merit of being within the range of current short-term experience, and others could be "turned off" if unintended effects occur.

Most of these ideas have been proposed before, and the relevant references are cited in the text. The panel here provides sketches of possible systems and rough estimates of the costs of implementing them.

The analyses in this chapter should be thought of as explorations of plausibility in the sense of providing preliminary answers to two questions and encouraging scrutiny of a third:

1. Does it appear feasible that engineered systems could actually mitigate the effects of greenhouse gases?

2. Does it appear that the proposed systems might be carried out by feasible technical means at reasonable costs?

3. Do the proposed systems have effects, besides the sought-after effects, that might be adverse, and can these be accepted or dealt with?

An exhaustive literature search and analysis has not been completed, but it has been possible to find useful material in the literature and to make first-order estimates that suggest positive answers to these first two questions. This being the case, it seems appropriate to continue consideration of the range of geoengineering possibilities and to pursue answers to question 3 above. In virtually all cases, there are significant missing pieces of scientific understanding.

Carrying the examination further would first require more detailed understanding, theoretical modeling, and simulation analyses of the physics, chemistry, and biology in the light of what is known about the geophysical, geochemical, climate, and ecological systems. If these further analyses suggest that the answers to the questions continue to be positive, experiments could then be carried out. These would not be full-scale climate mitigation experiments, but rather experiments intended to answer questions that might still remain after theoretical analysis, e.g., questions concerning optical effects and properties of various kinds of dust or aerosols, lifetimes and cloud stimulation properties of tropospheric sulfate aerosol, and so on. There is also a need for more detailed design, development, and cost analysis of the proposed deployment systems, perhaps including experimentation with specific hardware for deployment. Such work would give much more information with which to decide whether such systems could be deployed at a reasonable cost, and whether they would be likely to work as suggested by the preliminary evaluations included below.

If the theoretical analyses, experiments, and development work show that these mitigation ideas continue to have promise, the possibility of actual deployment would raise additional issues. The global climate and geophysical, geochemical, and biological systems under examination are all highly nonlinear systems involving the interaction of many complicated feedback systems. Such systems are likely to exhibit various forms of instability, including dynamic chaos, as well as various unintended side effects. These possibilities must be seriously considered before deployment of any mitigation system, and the risks involved weighed against alternatives to the proposed system.

Would attempts to mitigate greenhouse warming using one of these geoengineering systems result in putting a global system into some unintended and undesired state? Effects that have been suggested as possible results of greenhouse warming itself, and which might result from attempts to mitigate it, include a shift to a glacial state and major shifts in ocean currents.

Our current models and understanding of geophysical systems do not allow us to predict such effects. Our understanding and modeling have so far not even permitted us to make a map of the possible states of the system. We might require a different modeling approach even to be able to do so.

It can be argued that, in the face of such uncertainty, we should not consider "tinkering" with the only earth we have. However, we are not entirely without understanding of this matter. The principal characteristic of chaos instability, for example, is that the behavior of states with only slightly different initial conditions may be totally different. This is frequently expressed by the statement that "the alighting of a butterfly may change the future of the earth." However, in the sense that we know something of the effects of various kinds of events on parts of the geophysical system, we do know a good deal about this.

For example, we know something of the effect of the dust and aerosols resulting from volcanic eruptions on the climate system and on atmospheric chemistry, and we know something of the effect of industrial sulfur emissions on the climate system. It seems reasonable to assume that mitigation systems that put dust or aerosols into the atmosphere at altitudes and in quantities that are within the bounds of the natural experiments or of previous experiments would not produce instabilities or effects that had not been produced before. This expectation could provide one criterion for use of a geoengineering option: the activity must be within the natural variability of the geophysical system. We could use natural variability, or what are effectively previous experiments, as tests of the stability of the geophysical system and as opportunities to search for possible side effects. However, we must also consider that the chemistry of the atmosphere is changing, particularly from the injection of chlorofluorocarbons (CFCs) and from the increased injection of other greenhouse gases, so past chemistry will be an incomplete guide to the future. We can use the past and our understanding of the nature of the physics and chemistry to guide us in looking for new effects as natural events occur: the next significant volcanic eruption, for example, can be used as an opportunity to extend our understanding of the effects of dust, sulfuric acid aerosol, and chemicals produced by volcanic eruptions on stratospheric chemistry and the climate system.

The possibility would have to be taken into account that a natural event occurring during a mitigation activity could push the system beyond its normal bounds. For example, a large volcanic eruption occurring while artificial volcanic dust was in place might result in a dust loading beyond that previously experienced. Given some knowledge of the statistics and occurrence of eruptions (but noting their current unpredictability in detail) and of the lifetime aloft of the dust or aerosol in question, it should be possible to make a reasonably prudent statistical design for such a mitigation system and to compare its risks with other alternatives.

In many simple nonlinear systems the phenomenon of hysteresis is observed. In these cases, as some physical variable is changed, the system changes its state in a particular way, but if the same physical variable is then returned to its initial value, the system does not retrace the path; it changes state along a different path. Thus attempting mitigation by decreasing the quantity of greenhouse gases in the atmosphere could, in principle, lead the system into a region of instability even though increasing them had not done so. The problem we face is that, given that the climate system is nonlinear and that we do not understand its state space, all actions can potentially lead to instability, and even a small-scale action is not necessarily less likely to do so than a large-scale action. Because of the possible sensitivity of geophysical systems to chaotic instability, we must proceed with caution in any geoengineering effort. We have to compare the nature and size of proposed actions with what we know about what has already been observed to occur in the system as a result of similar stimuli to it. This gives us a way of testing proposed actions. We can also try to learn the structure of the state space of the geophysical system by theoretical, modeling, and simulation analysis combined with observation of the system and its history, perhaps using small stimulus experiments that we believe to be safe to add to our understanding. While geological history provides evidence of what appear to be major changes in state, there is a great deal of observed variation in the system and in stimuli to the system that do not appear to result in changes of state.

Improving our understanding of these matters in this way may enable us to make rational decisions on what risks to take if we desire to use geoengineering or other means of mitigation to counter any greenhouse warming produced by greenhouse gas increases. Particular caution must be exercised because although changing atmospheric chemistry and changing global reflectivity may both have an impact on global mean temperature, the relevant physics for each is very different. The geographic distribution of effects may also be very important.

The kinds of steps that may be taken include the following:

• Theoretical modeling and simulation analyses of the physics, chemistry, and biology of the relevant geophysical, geochemical, climate, and ecological systems.
• Study of the potential for induced instability and chaos.
• Small-scale mitigation experiments to determine physical, chemical, and biological properties where these are unknown.
• Detailed design, development, and cost analysis of proposed deployment systems.

- Study of related natural events to understand their relevant properties, including the statistics of their occurrence.
- Study of possible ecological, geophysical, geochemical, and atmospheric side effects, including considerations of reversibility.

REFORESTATION

Reforestation is one possible method of slowing the buildup of CO_2 in the atmosphere. While some countries are a source of emissions because of deforestation (as discussed in Chapter 27), most temperate countries (such as the United States) are a net sink of emissions in that new growth at least compensates for trees harvested. This analysis focuses on the opportunities for rural reforestation in the United States. Urban reforestation is discussed in Chapter 21. It should be noted that uncertainties regarding land availability and cost make extrapolation from the few available figures difficult.

Reforestation efforts are relevant to the mitigation of greenhouse gas emissions because during photosynthesis green plants take in CO_2 and release oxygen. The carbon "fixed" during photosynthesis in excess of that released during respiration is stored in plant tissue. For perennial species such as trees, the amount of stored carbon can accumulate for decades. Therefore reforestation could potentially take in (or sequester) some of the CO_2 the United States generates from energy sources.

Recent Trends

Forests cover about one-third of the earth's land surface, stretching from evergreen forests in the moist tropics to vast boreal forests in the subarctic. Terrestrial biota and soils are an important part of the carbon cycle. They store 2,280,000 Mt (2,280 petagrams) of carbon compared to the 750,000 Mt (750 petagrams) of carbon in the atmosphere (World Resources Institute, 1990).[1] Although it should be noted that the amount of carbon stored in the ocean and lithosphere is much larger than that in either the atmosphere or the land, the time scales over which they equilibrate with the atmosphere are very large.

The land area of the United States has lost close to 25 percent of its forest cover since settlement of the North American continent began, and forest cover continues to decline. This is notwithstanding the planting of more and more trees over time (Figure 28.1). The 1989 decrease in tree planting is due to a decline in planting under the Conservation Reserve Program (CRP). In 1989, tree planting increased on National Forest and other federal lands, but decreased on private, state, and nonfederal public lands. A breakdown of total planting and seeding by ownership category in 1989 is given in Table 28.1; private sources planted 85 percent of the trees

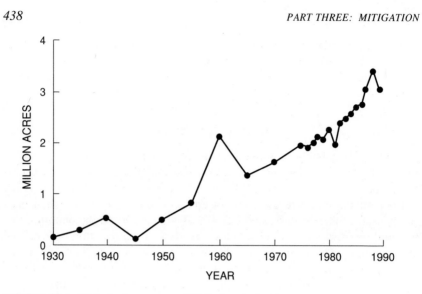

FIGURE 28.1 Historical summary of U.S. forest planting.

SOURCE: U.S. Forest Service (1990).

TABLE 28.1 Total Planting and Seeding by Ownership Category in FY 1989

	Acres	Percent of All Planting
Federal government		
National forests	307,138	10.2
Department of the Interior	52,006	1.7
Other federal agencies	9,257	0.3
TOTAL	368,401	12.2
Nonfederal public		
State forests	57,133	1.9
Other state agencies	6,013	0.2
Other public agencies	13,515	0.4
TOTAL	76,661	2.5
Private		
Forest industries	1,248,565	41.3
Other industry	22,225	0.8
Nonindustrial owners	1,306,096	43.2
TOTAL	2,576,886	85.3
GRAND TOTAL	3,021,948	100.0

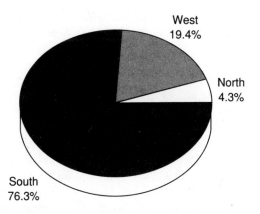

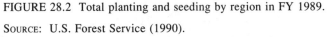

FIGURE 28.2 Total planting and seeding by region in FY 1989.

SOURCE: U.S. Forest Service (1990).

in the United States in that year. Figure 28.2 shows that the great majority of planting (76.3 percent) is in the southern United States (U.S. Forest Service, 1990).

Storing Carbon in Trees

Forests take up carbon fastest during their early years of rapid growth (which may be up to 80 years for some species). As trees age, their growth rates decline and the rate at which they sequester carbon also declines. As a result, stands of young trees, on a net basis, actively increase stores of carbon (per unit area) more rapidly than mature forests, where photosynthesis is more closely balanced by respiration and death. On the other hand, a mature forest generally contains more stored carbon overall than a younger forest does.

The ability of a particular type of tree to store carbon depends on a number of factors, including its intrinsic growth rate as well as site and stand attributes. Carbon is stored in stemwood, branches, and roots, and in the soil around the tree. Carbon incorporated in leaves is recycled rapidly, often on an annual basis, and thus is less important from a carbon storage standpoint.

Researchers have documented drastic improvements in the present net productivity (carbon uptake) of several species of trees. Heilman and Stettler (1985) managed short rotations of hybrid cottonwoods on fertilized, irrigated plots in western Washington and achieved nearly 14 t of carbon uptake per hectare (ha) per year of total production. A study by Steinbeck and Brown (1976) of intensely managed American sycamores on a 4-year rotation in Georgia yielded a carbon uptake of 6.5 t C/ha/yr. On the average, however, Marland (1988) estimates that U.S. commercial forests have an uptake of roughly 0.82 t C/ha/yr. If they were fully stocked, the average forest's productivity could increase to 1.35 t C/ha/yr. In sum, both the species of tree and the management practices are important considerations in reforestation policy, as are the kinds of land on which the trees are planted and the climatic zones in which planting occurs. Therefore a reforestation strategy for sequestering carbon might theoretically involve the use of fast-growing species with advanced silviculture techniques on optimal sites. However, there is a trade-off between maximum carbon storage and maximum rate of carbon uptake. For example, in the sycamore experiment mentioned, trees were harvested every 4 years to maintain the high growth rates of young vigorous plants. These data on short-rotation forestry demonstrate that rates of carbon uptake can be dramatically increased by forest management strategies. For net U.S. carbon emissions to be reduced, trees must be either protected from oxidizing to CO_2 or used to replace fossil fuel burning. In general, more intensive management requires more energy inputs, and these must be compensated to determine net carbon benefit.

The most comprehensive analysis of the potential for sequestering carbon in trees in the United States is that undertaken by Moulton and Richards (1990) of the U.S. Forest Service. This is a detailed analysis of the land available in the United States that could support trees, the carbon uptake that might be expected, and actual costs for each type of land to be managed. According to Moulton and Richards, it is possible to sequester up to 720 Mt C on economically marginal and environmentally sensitive pasture and croplands and nonfederal forestlands. After analyzing the potential carbon uptake and cost per ton in 70 region and land-type classes, Moulton and Richards arrange these in order by cost per ton and assemble a supply curve for carbon sequestering. The analysis concludes that up to 56.4 percent of U.S. CO_2 emissions could be sequestered in domestic trees at costs ranging from $5.80 to $47.75/t C.

Recognizing that the Moulton and Richards analysis suggests that 56.4 percent of U.S. CO_2 emissions could perhaps be offset with a massive commitment to a reforestation program, the Mitigation Panel takes a very conservative approach in estimating the carbon offset that might be envisioned. As discussed in Appendix P, the Mitigation Panel's analysis accepts that the 10 percent objective described by Moulton and Richards is a reasonable initial target and that reforestation of economically marginal or environmentally sensitive pasturelands and croplands and nonfederal forestlands to a total of 28.7 Mha could take place at costs as described in their analysis.

Several factors in the Moulton and Richards analysis, however, heavily influence the numeric results and are likely to elicit some discussion as to the magnitude and cost of reforestation. Their analysis has a 40-year time horizon, so it does not confront the consequences of declining growth rates as trees approach maturity or of the long-term possibilities for tree maintenance or harvest. In addition, land rental rates and the ratio between carbon uptake in marketable timber and total ecosystem carbon uptake are somewhat uncertain. Taking these factors into account, the Mitigation Panel's analysis suggests that 240 Mt CO_2 equivalent per year could be sequestered at costs between \$3 and \$10 per ton of CO_2 (average cost is \$7.20/t CO_2). Demonstration projects could verify the lower costs and higher targets for total sequestration suggested by Moulton and Richards.

Obstacles to Implementation

There are several constraints on implementing a reforestation policy. First, there are land use commitments. For reforestation to be pursued on a large scale, planting would have to take place on marginal agricultural lands. This represents a long-term commitment to nonagricultural uses.

Second, there may be resource constraints (e.g., water). Great care and understanding would be required to select tree species, species mixes, and management strategies to maximize the potential of sites with widely different available resources.

Policy Options

Public policy decisions to increase carbon storage through reforestation involve such silviculture issues as replanting, selection of species to be planted, and land management practices such as fertilization. To implement these reforestation options, however, someone must pay for the reforestation itself and for the cost of maintaining land in forest cover. Landowners face a variety of alternative opportunities and liabilities. Policies to increase and maintain forests to store carbon must therefore address questions of economics as well as silviculture.

The cost of sequestration, considered apart from the value to be recaptured by sales of timber, ranges upward from zero. The economic cost—which can, of course, be negative if the investment in sequestration is less than the return from the sale of harvested products and other benefits—is determined both by the value of forest products and by the value of alternative land uses. Because forests have a biological time scale on the order of decades, significant uncertainty is the norm in economic analyses. Public policies can affect management choices by changing, for example, the taxes levied on timber harvest, the regulations that govern forest practices, or real estate taxes.

To ensure long-term sequestering of wood on private lands, governments may need to purchase title or limited property rights.

Other Benefits and Costs

Reforestation can have many other positive benefits, including enhanced biodiversity, wildlife, air and water quality, aesthetics, forest products, and recreational opportunities. Reforestation can also raise environmental concerns, and there is some apprehension about the implications if planting were to occur as broad expanses of monocultural plantations.

Research and Development

A recent National Research Council (1990) report entitled *Forestry Research: A Mandate for Change* provides a number of research recommendations relative to societal concerns regarding the relationship of forests and climate, biological diversity loss, forest product demand, "pristine" forest area demand, sustainable wood production in conjunction with environmental protection, and maintenance of forest health. The NRC Forestry Research Committee (1990) recommends

- improving understanding of the basic biology and ecology of forests,
- developing information to sustain productivity of forests as well as to protect their inherent biological diversity, and
- understanding the economic and policymaking processes that affect the fate of forests.

Conclusions

Reforestation has the potential to offset a large amount of CO_2 emissions but at a cost that increases as the amount of offset increases. This analysis recognizes the large land resource required and adopts a conservative approach with respect to the U.S. Forest Service analysis of the amount of carbon that might be sequestered. It also recognizes that forests will mature and that reforestation is thus an interim approach to the long-term concerns of greenhouse warming. In addition, if a forest is harvested, the only true CO_2 offset is the amount of carbon stored in soil, roots, and as lumber or other long-lived products. Furthermore, there is some apprehension about the implications for biodiversity if planting were to occur as broad expanses of monocultural plantations. Overall, however, reforestation seems to provide a method of storing carbon with little adverse societal impact and a number of benefits.

INCREASING OCEAN ABSORPTION OF CARBON DIOXIDE

The Approach

The oceans already play an enormous role in establishing planetary climate, both through the transport of heat and supply of water vapor and through the absorption of a large fraction of fossil fuel CO_2. Estimates of the net ocean sink for CO_2 range from the traditionally accepted value of some 40 percent of fossil fuel CO_2 emissions (through reaction of CO_2 gas with carbonate ion over the entire ocean surface, and based upon models derived from Oeschger et al. (1975)), which today gives close to 3 Gt C/yr, to the much lower value of 0.6 Gt C/yr recently reported by Tans et al. (1990). No realistic model of earth's climate can escape simulation of the oceans in some form.

While the oceanic role in moderating the present-day fossil fuel increase depends almost totally on the rate of mixing and the alkalinity, the potential future role of ocean biota cannot be neglected. The potential amount of total carbon that could be utilized by oceanic photosynthesis has been estimated to be 35 Gt/yr. However, this figure represents the gross fixation of carbon in the ocean; the net effect on the atmosphere will depend on the return flow from decomposition and will eventually reach steady state. Ice core records (Neftel et al., 1982; Barnola et al., 1987) show that in the past, the atmospheric CO_2 level has fluctuated independently of the activities of man, with ice age CO_2 concentrations some 30 percent lower than the most recent preindustrial value. A key question is thus, Can this state be achieved today?

In 1984, three independent research groups published hypotheses on this phenomenon (Knox and McElroy, 1984; Sarmiento and Toggweiler, 1984; Siegenthaler and Wenk, 1984). Each reached the conclusion that the key lay in the surface nutrient concentrations in polar ocean regions. In areas such as the far North Pacific and the antarctic circumpolar ocean, high concentrations of nitrate and phosphate (the key ingredients for plant growth) are unused. The problem did not seem to be insufficient light, or bitter cold, but some other variables not yet recognized. The 1984 models showed that if these nutrients were assimilated, the conversion of CO_2 to organic carbon could readily account for the ice age signal. These nutrients can be regarded as an important unused chemical capacity of the ocean, one of a scale to significantly affect the global carbon balance. A radical solution to this ice age CO_2 puzzle has been proposed by Martin and co-workers (Martin and Fitzwater, 1988; Martin and Gordon, 1988; Martin, 1990; Martin et al., 1990). These scientists achieved the first reliable measurements of "dissolved" iron, at the nanomolar level, in ocean waters through stringent avoidance of the all-pervasive contamination problem. They further showed that addition of trace amounts of iron to natural populations of phytoplankton stimulated photosynthesis, and they hypothesized that iron limited the phytoplankton growth in these areas. Thus trace inputs from atmospheric dust events could trigger blooms of the plankton and ultimately lower atmospheric CO_2. Finally, the ice core record shows that glacial times, with dry and dusty continents, are characterized by strong dust input to oceans.

The route to contemporary utilization of this unused oceanic potential is therefore direct: the addition of trace amounts of iron to vast areas of the ocean surface to stimulate phytoplankton growth has recently received widespread publicity. The tenuous nature of the hypothesis, the presence of other limiting factors, the discrepancy between the total ocean surface area involved in natural reaction with the atmosphere and the relatively small area (approximately 16 percent) of the ocean surface available for active manipulation of the iron concentration—all call for caution in expectations for this class of phenomena. Return flow of the products of decomposition of the fixed carbon negates the possibility of a one-time fix. However, this concept usefully raises issues of what must be considered in any discussion of active intervention in the oceanic carbon cycle. It was in this spirit that iron fertilization, along with the potential use of macroalgae to assimilate large quantities of CO_2, was examined in a recent National Research Council (NRC) workshop on Marine Algal Productivity and Carbon Dioxide Assimilation (October 31, 1990).

Phytoplankton specialists at the NRC workshop agreed that it is conceptually feasible to slow the increase in atmospheric CO_2 levels through enhanced new primary production in oceans, resulting in enhanced net transport of CO_2 from the atmosphere to the oceans. From existing models, they estimated that an additional 2 Gt C/yr can be removed from the atmosphere if new primary production is enhanced and most unused nutrients are assimilated. Because iron is required at concentrations in the nanomolar range, they projected the cost of iron fertilization to be low.

Cost Estimates

There are two bases for the cost of iron fertilization; one based on the work of Martin, and the other based on the NRC workshop mentioned above.

The work of Martin would indicate that fertilization of the entire southern ocean could be accomplished with only 0.43 Mt of iron (Fe) per year, the amount required to support the removal of 2 to 3 Gt C/yr (Martin, 1990). Martin gives no number for the area of ocean to be fertilized and suggests no specific chemical form for the iron.

The NRC workshop suggests that iron fertilization might remove an average of 1.8 Gt C/yr over a 100-year period. The workshop suggests an application of 1 to 5 Mt Fe/yr in the form of a solution of ferrous chloride ($FeCl_2$), "or perhaps in some other form," and gives the area to be fertilized as "approximately 18 million square miles."

A cost estimate will be composed of the cost of ships and ship operations, and the cost of the chemicals, with some allowance for overall system operations.

For estimating purposes a 1-million-square-nautical-mile area divided into lanes 1 mile wide will be considered. This gives 1 million miles of steaming required each year.[2] Fifteen ships, each steaming 240 miles per day (at 10 knots) for 300 days per year, would travel 1 million miles. When replenishment time, and so on, is considered, we can specify 20 ships, each of 10,000-ton capacity, each replenished every 2 months.

If we assume $100 million per ship, with each ship having a $10,000 per day operating cost, we get a cost for the fleet of $2 billion, giving an annual capital cost (amortized over 20 years) of $0.10 billion and an annual operating cost of $73 million. This gives a total annual operating cost for 1 million square miles of coverage of $173 million. For 18 million square miles the system must be increased in size by a factor of 18, giving about $3 billion per year. In the antarctic ocean we must give a generous allowance for weather contingencies; let us use a factor of 3, giving an estimate of $9 billion per year for ship costs and operations. To this we may add $1 billion per year for general system operations, giving an operations total of $10 billion per year.

To the operations estimate we must add the cost of the iron fertilizer. The form of iron usually absorbed easily by living organisms is the ferrous form. The cheapest bulk ferrous iron compound easily available is ferrous sulfate. Martin's 0.43 Mt of iron is equivalent to about 1.2 Mt of ferrous sulfate, which can be purchased in bulk for $10 to $15/t (Chemical Marketing Reporter, 1991), for a total of $12 to $18 million per year.

Ferrous chloride, mentioned by the NRC workshop, is much more expensive than ferrous sulfate. It can be bought in bulk for $220/t Fe in the chemical (Alfred M. Tenney, Eaglebrook, Inc., private communication to Lynn Lewis, G.M. Research, April 11, 1991). The NRC workshop requirement for 1 to 5 Mt Fe gives a ferrous chloride cost of $0.22 to $1.1 billion per year.

Thus the range of chemical cost may be between $0.012 and $1.1 billion per year. However, both ferrous sulfate and ferrous chloride are relatively cheap because they are the waste product of steel "pickling" with acid. The current North American availability of ferrous chloride is estimated to be about 150,000 tons of iron equivalent, and the world amount may be a million tons (Alfred M. Tenney, Eaglebrook, Inc., private communication to Lynn Lewis, G.M. Research, April 11, 1991). Thus it is not clear what the price of ferrous chloride might be in million- to multimillion-ton quantities per year. If we assume that the price will be less than 100 times the current price of ferrous chloride, we get a total range of cost for iron fertilizer of $0.010 to $100 billion per year.

Adding the operations cost to the fertilizer cost, we get a cost range of $10 to $110 billion per year. This will mitigate 1.8 to 3 Gt C (using the range from both Martin and the NRC workshop), equivalent to the mitigation of about 7 to 11 Gt CO_2/yr. This gives a final range of about $1 to $15/t CO_2/yr.

Further thought is likely to lead to simpler, more automatic, and cheaper means for the distribution of iron fertilizer.

Some Problems

Peng and Broecker (1991) argue that on dynamic considerations the scheme of fertilization by iron is unlikely to succeed as a continuing full-scale pump of CO_2 from the atmosphere into the ocean. They argue that vertical transport in the antarctic is sufficiently sluggish that the flow of CO_2 into the ocean from the atmosphere would rapidly saturate the surface waters with CO_2, and, since the circulation would not carry the saturated water away fast enough, the transfer of CO_2 from the atmosphere into the ocean would stop. This presumably would leave the storage of CO_2 (as carbon) represented by the standing crop of algae in place as long as the fertilization were to continue. They estimate that 100 years of fertilization would result in a lowering of the atmospheric CO_2 content by 30 ± 15 ppm. It is possible that small-scale experiments might be devised to test this by fertilizing a limited area for a period of time and studying the results. Recently reported observations by De Baar et al. (1990) suggest that iron may not be the sole limiting factor in antarctic phytoplankton growth.

In addition to using microalgae to assimilate CO_2, use of macroalgae (seaweed) has also been proposed. Advantages of macroalgae include a faster rate of sedimentation, as well as their value as a biomass fuel and a source of chemicals and feeds. Their use, however, would require an engineered system of production to achieve large areas of cultivation.

There are numerous questions to be answered pertaining to the use of both microalgae and macroalgae for CO_2 assimilation before better estimates of costs of carbon removal can be made for either system. Key aspects associated with cost projections include productivity rates in open oceans, nutrient recycle, micronutrient (especially iron) limitations, and the detailed design of a system for the controlled delivery of millions of tons of iron over large areas of open oceans.

As with other mitigation options, important environmental questions raised by the use of algae to assimilate CO_2 include those concerning food chain effects, the introduction and proliferation of nonindigenous species (especially for macroalgae), anaerobic decomposition of algae to CH_4, and the possible formation of large amounts of haloforms and dimethyl sulfide. As noted in the discussion of cloud stimulation below, the natural organisms whose growth would be stimulated by the addition of iron might be expected to produce dimethyl sulfide, which would form cloud condensation nuclei. At times and places of little cloudiness, the area fertilized might be expected to become more cloudy, which, might in turn have a further cooling effect. There is also concern about the possibility of creating an anoxic layer in the shallow subsurface.

SCREENING OUT SOME SUNLIGHT

Another option for mitigating a global warming would be to try to control the global radiation balance by limiting the amount of incoming radiation from the sun. This could be done by increasing the reflectivity of the earth, i.e., the albedo. Proposals for increasing the whiteness of roofs and surface features would have some effect, but only a fraction of incident solar radiation reaches the earth's surface and a purposeful change in albedo would have more impact if done high in the atmosphere. According to Ramanathan (1988), an increase in planetary albedo of just 0.5 percent is sufficient to halve the effect of a CO_2 doubling. Placing a screen in the atmosphere or low earth orbit could take several forms: it could involve changing the quantity or character of cloud cover, it could take the form of a continuous sheet, or it could be divided into many "mirrors" or a cloud of dust. Preliminary characterizations of some of the possibilities that might be considered are provided below.

Estimating Screen Parameters

The calculation here assumes the screen is a continuous sheet. Note that if the dust particles are of a size comparable to the wavelength of light, scattering effects will have to be taken into account.

Given the equatorial radius of the earth and a nominal low orbit of 222 km, the radius of the sphere in which the sheet, or parasol, is to be located is 6.6×10^3 km. Then the area of the sphere to completely wrap the earth is 5.5×10^{14} m^2. To compensate completely for the greenhouse warming from a doubling in the concentration of CO_2 in the atmosphere,[3,4] the parasol must cover 1 percent of the area, or 5.5×10^{12} m^2.

If this parasol must be 1 micron (μm) thick, 5.5×10^6 m^3 of material is required. At a density of 1 g/cm^3, 5.5×10^9 kg would have to be lifted into low earth orbit. The cost of establishing such a project is dominated by the cost of putting the parasol into orbit. At an optimistic cost of $1,000/kg, the cost of lifting the material into orbit would be $5.5 trillion.[5] Such a parasol would mitigate about 1000 Gt of carbon emissions, for a cost of about $5.5/t C mitigated or about $1.5/t CO_2 (rounding the number). At current launch costs of $10,000/kg, the cost would be $55/t C mitigated or about $15/t CO_2.

The assumption that a 1 percent decrease in sunlight is equivalent to mitigating the greenhouse effect of 1000 Gt of carbon (or 4000 Gt CO_2) is key for all of the estimates that follow.[6] Ramanathan's increase of 0.5 percent in planetary albedo quoted above as sufficient to halve the effect of a CO_2 doubling is used here and below as a 1 percent screening effect for estimating purposes. Using Figures 3.1 and 3.2 of the report of the Synthesis Panel (Part One), we see that the total change in greenhouse gases since before the Industrial Revolution until 2030 may be equivalent to about 3.3 W/m^2, or slightly less than 1 percent of the 349 W/m^2 of solar insolation.

Space Mirrors

A single mirror would be unmanageable and would probably create problems in the regions where its shadow fell as it moved around the earth. However, a set of smaller mirrors might be considered, each maneuvered as a solar sail in earth orbit. By changing its angle to the sun (and hence the solar radiation pressure forces on it), the orbit of each sail could be controlled.

If each sail is 10^8 m^2 in area (a large sail to manage), 55,000 such sails would be required. This appears to be a very difficult, if not unmanageable, control problem. However, if the requirement is for the mitigation of 8 Gt CO_2 equivalent (the 1988 U.S. emission of greenhouse gases), a parasol 500 times smaller in area, equivalent to 110 such solar sails, would be required. At the previous $1.5/t CO_2 mitigated, the cost would be $12 billion; at current launch costs, the cost would be $120 billion.

The question of how often (because of damage to the sails resulting from debris collisions) sail replacement would be required has not yet been examined. If replacement of all of the sails were required each year, the figures above would be annual costs; the 40-year cost would be 40 times larger, and similarly for other replenishment rates. With this possibility in mind, by using previous costs of $1.5 to $15/t CO_2, costs may be estimated as in the range of $0.1 to $15/t CO_2/yr.[7]

Space Dust

The space parasol could be designed as an orbiting dust cloud. To minimize launch costs, very small dust particles are required. However, because of solar radiation pressure, small dust is driven out of orbit or into the earth's atmosphere in very short times; the particles are barely orbital (Mueller and Kessler, 1985). Peale (1966), quoted by Mueller and Kessler (1985), gives 1500 cm^2/g, or the equivalent of aluminum oxide particles 3 μm in size, as the limit below which this sweeping effect gives dust a short lifetime. A reflecting cloud of fine dust in orbit does not appear to be practical, and the launch costs for large dust particles appear to be too high to be practical.

Stratospheric Dust

Although the space dust option does not appear to be sensible, computations of the residence times of 0.2-μm dust above 20 to 40 km are of the order of 1 to 3 years (Hunten, 1975). It seems to be generally accepted that volcanic aerosols remain in the stratosphere for several years (Kellogg and Schneider, 1974; Ramaswamy and Kiehl, 1985). A screen could be created in the stratosphere by adding more dust to the natural stratospheric dust to increase its net reflection of sunlight.

An alternative to dust is sulfuric acid aerosol, the other principal natural component of stratospheric haze. Dust seems a better choice because it is similar to dust from natural soil and so should have no noticeable effect on the ground as it gradually falls into the troposphere and rains out. (Other possible effects are referred to below.) However, Budyko (1982) suggests the use of sulfuric acid aerosol, to be created by the burning of sulfur in situ, resulting in sulfur dioxide (SO_2), which will automatically absorb atmospheric water to result in droplets of sulfuric acid solution. He gives the required tonnage of sulfuric acid to reduce the total radiation by 1 percent as 600,000 t. As we will see, this is less than one-tenth of the amount we estimate is required as dust. Budyko goes on to point out that the amount of sulfur required to be burnt in the stratosphere to produce the aerosol is 200,000 t, or possibly even as little as 40 percent of this, depending on the amount of water that might be absorbed from the air. Thus the lift requirements might be only one-seventh to one-third of that estimated for sulfuric acid itself. He also assumes 2 years as the lifetime of the aerosol in the stratosphere. In any case, Budyko's maximum requirement is much less than we use below to estimate the cost of the material and lift requirements. (Sulfur costs are about $0.05/pound, and we assume less than $0.25/pound for dust.) The costs to do the screening using sulfuric acid aerosol in the stratosphere would be less than those which are estimated below for dust, if we use the estimates of Budyko.

The amount of dust emitted into the atmosphere from natural and manmade (mostly natural) sources is noted (from material quoted by Toon and Pollack, 1976) to be about 1 to 3 Gt/yr, or 1 to 3×10^{12} kg/yr.[8] This is about 100 to 300 times the amount proposed below to be added to the atmosphere.

Mass Estimates

Ramaswamy and Kiehl (1985) estimate that an aerosol dust loading of 0.2 g/m^2 for dust with a radius of about 0.26 μm increases the planetary albedo by 12 percent, resulting in a 15 percent decrease of solar flux reaching the surface. Since an approximately 1 percent change in solar flux is required, and their Figures 13 and 15 suggest that, at these loadings, the dust effects may reasonably be extrapolated downward linearly, estimates will be made by using a dust loading of 0.02 g/m^2 with a particle radius of 0.26 μm.

Ramaswamy (private communication) points out that their model does not contain clouds. At high loadings of dust, this probably is not too important because the optical thickness of the dust is high. When extrapolating downward in loading by an order of magnitude, the increased albedo due to clouds could be important. A factor of 2 might possibly be used, but careful computations should be done. It seems clear that the required density of dust is distinctly lower than the 0.2 g/m^2 in Ramaswamy and Kiehl's computation, which produces a decrease of 15 percent in radiative forcing. The required loading may be somewhat greater than the 0.02 g/m^2 used below to obtain a 1 percent change in radiative forcing. This effect can presumably be studied by using global climate models. This will broaden the uncertainty band of the system costs, but it seems likely that the costs are between the minimum computed by the panel and 10 times that minimum.

By using 0.02 g/m^2, the mass of dust required to mitigate 1000 Gt C (4000 Gt CO_2) is 10^{10} kg. Thus a kilogram of dust in the stratosphere mitigates the greenhouse effect of about 100 t C in the atmosphere as CO_2.[9] To mitigate the 1989 U.S. input of CO_2-equivalent greenhouse gases (8 × 10^9 t), 2 × 10^7 kg of dust would be required.[10]

The dust in Ramaswamy and Kiehl's model is distributed between 10 and 30 km in the stratosphere, uniformly over the globe. The actual effect on radiative forcing of a global distribution of additional dust would be somewhat greater at low than at high latitudes because more of the sunlight is effective there for geometric reasons. This would decrease slightly the equator-to-pole temperature gradients and might have some effect on weather intensity. Presumably, this effect can also be studied with global climate models.

Possible Side Effects

This dust heats the stratosphere, and the effect of such heating is included in the computation of Ramaswamy and Kiehl (1985). One possible effect of this heating might be to change the atmospheric chemistry to augment or destroy stratospheric ozone. Additional stratospheric dust could provide additional surface area on which chlorine compounds could be adsorbed, thus possibly increasing the rate of destruction of stratospheric ozone. In the antarctic stratosphere during the winter darkness, chemical reactions involving chlorine compounds derived from the breakup of CFCs take place on the surfaces of ice crystals. These reactions, which do not occur without the presence of the surfaces, produce other chlorine compounds, which, when released and photolyzed (broken up by the action of light) by spring and summer sunshine, produce chemical species that destroy ozone.

Laboratory experiments at stratospheric temperatures appear to show that similar reactions occur on the surface of sulfuric acid solutions (and presumably would occur on the surfaces of sulfuric acid and dust particles), but are 100 to 1000 times slower (Tolbert et al., 1988). Given the rapid alternation of light and dark at mid-latitudes compared to the 6-month cycling at the poles, these reactions are estimated to account for a ≤ 1 percent depletion of ozone at present. However, in the presence of enhanced concentrations of sulfuric acid (or, presumably, dust) in the stratosphere, the reactions could become much more important.

The El Chichon volcanic eruption in 1982 is estimated to have released 1.2×10^{10} kg of sulfur compounds, compared to the release of 10^{10} kg of dust or aerosol discussed above, leading to a concentration of 0.03 g/m^2, compared to the target of 0.02 g/m^2 discussed above, about 10 times the background concentration of 0.002 g/m^2. After this eruption the ozone concentration within the eruption plume in the stratosphere decreased by amounts up to 20 percent. However, since the volcano also emitted enormous quantities of hydrochloric acid (HCl) (equivalent to 9 percent of the existing HCl in the entire stratosphere), it is not clear how much of the depletion was caused by reactions involving the dust and aerosol, and how much was due to the increased Cl from the HCl (Hoffman and Solomon, 1989).

It appears that destruction of stratospheric ozone due to chemical reactions on the surface of added dust or aerosol in the stratosphere is a possible side effect that must be considered and understood before this possible mitigation option can be considered for use.

A National Research Council (1985) report cites papers by Cadle et al. (1976) and Mossop (1963, 1965) that give the amount of silicate particles from the 1963 Mount Agung eruption with sizes between 0.2 and 2.0 µm as 1×10^{10} kg, about the loading the panel assumed would have to be added. The half-life of this dust is not given, but the life of a sulfate aerosol with a size of 0.2 to 0.45 µm and a column height of 23 km is given as roughly 1 year, consonant with the panel's lower estimate.

Note that the dust can be expected to produce visible optical effects, such as spectacular sunsets, as in the case of volcanic dust.

Delivery Scenarios

Naval Rifles A 16-inch naval rifle fired vertically could put a shell weighing about 1 t up to an altitude of 20 km. With larger propellant loadings, some sacrifice in payload, or the use of sabots (a device fixed to the shell so that it will fit properly in the rifle barrel), higher altitudes could be achieved. Note that any launch technology could be used, but so much less is known about items such as rail guns that system and cost estimates based on existing launch technologies seemed the best choice.

The economics of keeping 10^{10} kg of dust in the stratosphere is determined by the lifetime of the dust aloft and the means used to put the material there. A dust lifetime in the stratosphere of 2 years is assumed, requiring that 10^{10} kg be placed in the stratosphere 20 times during the 40 years until 2030.

The panel has estimated the cost of such a naval rifle system, and some details of the estimates follow. Full details of the cost estimate are contained in Appendix Q.[11]

The project is designed to mitigate 10^{12} t C continuously, equivalent to 4 $\times 10^{12}$ t CO_2; the undiscounted 40-year cost is \$5/t C or $\approx$\$1/t CO_2 mitigated. The undiscounted annual cost is \$0.125/t C/yr, or \$0.03/t CO_2/yr. If a 1-year lifetime is assumed (Hunten's (1975) estimate for the 20-km altitude is 1.25 years), the annual cost will double to \$0.25/t C/yr, or \$0.06/t CO_2/yr. If the amount of dust required is 10 times the amount used for the estimate, the cost might be as high as \$3/t C/yr, or \$0.75/t CO_2/yr. If the quantity to be mitigated is the amount of the 1989 U.S. emissions, the scale of the project can be divided by 500, to give an annual cost of about \$0.25 billion to \$0.50 billion.[12]

To summarize this naval rifle scenario, the system lifts dust to the stratosphere at a rounded cost of about \$10 to \$30/kg of dust. Each kilogram of dust in the stratosphere mitigates about 100 t C. The system mitigates carbon at an undiscounted rounded cost of \$0.1 to \$0.3/t C or \$0.03 to \$0.06/t CO_2. Uncertainty regarding clouds and the required dust density for a 1 percent effect on radiative forcing suggests that it is reasonable, and even conservative, to put these costs in the range \$0.03 to \$1.0/t CO_2 mitigated.

Rockets   At the present time, the cost of sounding rocket launches (using available surplus rockets such as the Nike Orion, which cost about \$25,000 and carry a payload of 500 pounds) is about \$100/kg of dust lifted, 5 times the estimated cost of firing the material aloft with large guns. These figures are for launches to 70 km; thus the achievable efficiency should be higher, and costs for a new rocket system might be closer to those estimated for guns.

Balloons   Current scientific payload helium balloons lift about 5000 pounds at a cost of \$200,000 per flight, giving a cost of \$80/kg of dust lifted, or about 4 times the cost with naval rifles. Hydrogen balloons might be cheaper. The cost of lifting the dust with hydrogen balloons is estimated in Appendix Q and appears to be in the same range as that estimated for 16-inch naval rifles. Hot-air balloons do not appear to be as cost-effective as hydrogen balloons. The design and cost of such balloons are also discussed in detail in Appendix Q.[13]

Aircraft Exhaust   Penner et al. (1984) suggested that emissions of 1 percent of the fuel mass of the commercial aviation fleet as particulates, between 40,000- and 100,000-foot (12- to 30-km) altitude for a 10-year period, would change the planetary albedo sufficiently to neutralize the effects of an equivalent doubling of CO_2. They proposed that retuning the engine combustion systems to burn rich during the high-altitude portion of commercial flights could be done with negligible efficiency loss. Using Reck's estimates of extinction coefficients for particulates (Reck, 1979a, 1984), they estimated a requirement of about 1.168×10^{10} kg of particulates, compared with the panel's estimate of 10^{10} kg, based upon Ramaswamy and Kiehl (1985). They then estimated that if 1 percent of the fuel of aircraft flying above 30,000 feet is emitted as soot, over a 10-year period the required mass of particulate material would be emitted.

However, current commercial aircraft fleets seldom operate above 40,000 feet (12 km), and the lifetimes of particles at the operating altitudes will be much shorter than 10 years. An estimate (National Research Council, 1985) for the half-life of smoke is 1.4×10^{-7}/s.[14] This gives a half-life of 83 days, or a little less than one-quarter of a year. Thus the amount of fuel to be turned into soot continuously for complete mitigation (10^{12} t C) is closer to 40 percent than to 1 percent. That seems impractical. However, if the amount of mitigation required is equivalent to the 1989 U.S. emissions of greenhouse gases equivalent to CO_2 (8×10^9 t CO_2), the amount of soot required would be 500 times smaller, and the required soot corresponds to less than 0.1 percent of the fuel burned. If 1 percent of the fuel were used, about 25×10^9 t CO_2/yr could be mitigated.

In 1987, 16 percent of the cash operating expenses of airlines were spent on fuel (U.S. Bureau of the Census, 1988). Because the operating revenue in that year was $45,339 million, the approximate cost of the particulate emissions from jet engines for mitigation of the 1989 U.S. CO_2 equivalent emissions would be about $7 million, or about $0.001/t CO_2/yr plus the capital costs of adjusting the aircraft engines.

This provides a cost range of $0.001 to $0.1/t CO_2/yr. An alternate possibility is simply to lease commercial aircraft to carry dust to their maximum flight altitude, where they would distribute it. To make a cost estimate, a simple assumption is made that the same amount of dust assumed above for the stratosphere would work for the tropopause (the boundary between the troposphere and the stratosphere). The results can be scaled for other amounts. The comments made above about the possible effect of dust on stratospheric ozone apply as well to ozone in the low stratosphere, but not in the troposphere. The altitude of the tropopause varies with latitude and season of the year.

In 1987, domestic airlines flew 4,339 million ton-miles of freight and express, for a total express and freight operating revenue of $4,904 million

(U.S. Bureau of the Census, 1988). This gives a cost of slightly more than $1 per ton-mile for freight. If a dust distribution mission requires the equivalent of a 500-mile flight (about 1.5 hours), the delivery cost for dust is $500/t, and ignoring the difference between English and metric tons, a cost of $0.50/kg of dust. If 10^{10} kg must be delivered each 83 days, (provided dust falls out at the same rate as soot), 5 times more than the 1987 total ton-miles will be required. The question of whether dedicated aircraft could fly longer distances at the same effective rate should be investigated. However, if the requirement is to mitigate the 1989 U.S. emissions of CO_2, 500 times less dust is needed, the cost is about $10 million per year, and implementation would require about 1 percent of the ton-miles flown in 1987. If 10 percent of the ton-miles flown in 1987 were used, the system could mitigate 80 Gt CO_2. These costs should probably be increased by the cost of delivered dust (say, $0.50/kg) and of delivery systems in the aircraft, but better-than-average freight rates could probably be arranged. Thus the costs appear to be about $0.0025/t CO_2.

Clearly, the amount of dust required could be greater by a factor of 10, and the cost would be $0.025/t CO_2. This provides a cost estimate in the range of $0.003 to $0.03/t CO_2.

Multiple Balloon Screen

A screen can be created by putting a vast number of aluminized, hydrogen-filled balloons at a high enough altitude that they do not interfere with air traffic. They would provide a reflection screen. The properties of such a system are examined in Appendix Q.

The multiple balloon parasol system requiring billions of 1- to 6-m-diameter balloons would appear to cost about 20 times as much as distributing dust in the stratosphere. The large number of balloons, and the trash problem posed by their fall, make the system somewhat unattractive.

Changing Cloud Abundance

A more detailed discussion of the possibility of changing cloud abundance appears as Appendix Q.

The Approach

Independent studies estimated that an approximately 4 percent increase in the coverage of marine stratocumulus clouds would be sufficient to offset CO_2 doubling (Reck, 1978; Randall et al., 1984). Albrecht (1989) suggests that the average low-cloud reflectivity could be increased if the abundance of cloud condensation nuclei (CCN) increased due to emissions of SO_2. It is proposed that CCN emissions should be released over the oceans, that the release should produce an increase in the stratocumulus cloud albedo only, and that the clouds should remain at the same latitudes over the ocean where the surface albedo is relatively constant and small.

Albrecht (1989) estimates that a roughly 30 percent increase in CCN would be necessary to increase the fractional cloudiness or albedo of marine stratocumulus clouds by 4 percent. Albrecht's idealized stratocumulus cloud, which he argues is typical, has a thickness of 375 m, a drizzle rate of 1 mm per day, and a mean droplet radius of 100 μm, and he assumes that each droplet is formed by the coalescence of 1000 smaller droplets. The rate at which the CCN are depleted by his model is $1000/cm^3$ per day. Consequently, about $300/cm^3$ per day (30 percent of 1000) of additional CCN would have to be discharged per day at the base of the cloud to maintain a 4 percent increase in cloudiness. This assumes that the perturbed atmosphere would also remain sufficiently close to saturation in the vicinity of the CCN that additional cloud cover would be formed every time the number of CCN increased.

Mass Estimates of Cloud Condensation Nuclei

With Albrecht's assumption in mind that cloudiness in a typical ocean region is limited by the small number of CCN, we now extrapolate to the entire globe. On the average, 31.2 percent of the globe is covered by marine stratiform clouds (Charlson et al., 1987). If no high-level clouds are present, the number n of CCN that need to be added per day is 1.8×10^{25} CCN/day. The mass of a CCN is equal to $4/3\pi r^3 \times$ density, and it is assumed that the mean radius r is equal to 0.07×10^{-4} cm (Charlson et al., 1987). Because the density of sulfuric acid (H_2SO_4) is 1.841 g/cm^3, the CCN mass is 2.7×10^{-15} g. The total weight of H_2SO_4 to be added per day is 31×10^3 t per day SO_2 if all SO_2 is converted to H_2SO_4 CCN.

To put this number in perspective, a medium-sized coal-fired U.S. power plant emits about this much SO_2 in a year. Consequently, the equivalent emissions of 365 U.S. coal-burning power plants, distributed homogeneously, would be needed to produce sufficient CCN.

To estimate the value of the sulfur directly, the total weight of SO_2 to be added per day would equal 32×10^3 t, or about 16×10^3 t of sulfur (S) per day, which is equivalent to about 6×10^6 t S/yr. If the average market price of sulfur delivered at the mine or plant is taken as \$96.60/t for the years 1983 to 1987, the cost would be about \$580 million per year. Equating this yearly cost to the 300 parts per million by volume (ppmv) of CO_2 necessary for full compensation gives \$580 $\times 10^6$/yr/(3890 $\times 10^6$ t C/ppmv $CO_2 \times 300$ ppmv CO_2), or about a fraction of 1 cent/t CO_2. To obtain an equivalence to conserved carbon, known emissions of carbon in 1978, 1979, and 1980 have been compared with the total measured increase of CO_2 to obtain the equivalence: 3890×10^6 t C $\cong$ 1 ppmv CO_2. A 4 percent increase in cloudiness was then equated to a 300-ppmv CO_2 decrease, which translates into a reduction of 1200 Gt C or 4400 Gt CO_2.

Cost Estimates

The primary cost of this process involves the mechanism for distributing SO_2 in the atmosphere at the correct location. Assume a fleet of ships, each carrying sulfur and a suitable incinerator. The ships are dedicated to roaming the subtropical Pacific and Atlantic oceans far upwind of land while they burn sulfur. They are vectored on paths to cloud-covered areas by a control center that uses weather satellite data to plan the campaign. In addition to choosing areas that contain clouds, it would be important to distribute the ships and their burning pattern so as not to create major regional changes, or the kind of change with a time or space pattern likely to force unwanted wave patterns. These restrictions (which perhaps cannot now be defined) could present a difficult problem for such a system to solve.

From the above, 16×10^3 t per day or 6×10^6 t/yr would be needed. If we allocate 10^2 t per ship per day, and a ship stays out 300 days each year, roughly 200 ships of 10,000-t capacity (one reprovisioning stop every 100 days) are required. At a cost of $100 million per ship (surely generous), the capital cost of the fleet is $20 billion. Amortized over 20 years, the annual capital cost is $1 billion. Sulfur will cost another $0.6 billion per year, and $2 million per ship per year for operating costs (this is $10,000 per operating day), giving a total cost of $2 billion per year. Over 40 years (until 2030), this gives a cost of $80 billion, or approximately $100 billion. This continuously mitigates 10^3 Gt, for a cost of $0.10/t C/yr, or $0.025/t CO_2/yr. This provides a cost estimate in the range of $0.03 to $1/t CO_2. Of course, this continues to be a yearly cost of $2 billion per year.

The SO_2 could also be emitted from power plants. These plants could be built out in the ocean near the equator (the Pacific gives more room than the Atlantic) and could furnish power for nearby locations (e.g., South America). Transmission or use of the power in the form of refined materials, or possibly by the use of superconducting power transmission systems, could be considered. It would likely require eight large power plants using "spiked" coal (with 4 times the normal amount of sulfur), at a cost of $2 to $2.5 billion per plant. Most of the cost might be borne by those buying the power; so imagining a cost of, at most, 10 percent per year (the interest on the investment), total cost would be $2 billion per year (with the above conversion, $2 \times 10^9/3890 \times 10^6 \times 300 \approx \$0.0005/t$ CO_2).

Possible Acid Deposition

One must consider whether the injection of this much additional SO_2 into the atmosphere would cause an acid deposition problem. It must be kept in mind that the principal component of naturally occurring CCN is sulfate from marine algae. Schwartz (1988) quotes estimates of 16 to 40×10^{12} g/yr or perhaps about 25×10^9 kg/yr emitted from this source. The addition of about 6×10^9 kg/yr, one-quarter of the total natural amount, is being considered, although locally much more would be added to the amount naturally present. The oceans have an enormous buffering capacity (Stumm and Morgan, 1970), so that the additional rainout of sulfate (especially after dilution through cloud dispersal and droplet coalescence) seems unlikely to have any effect, even locally, although there is clear disagreement on this point. The principal concern would be to avoid additional sulfate deposition over land. With a 30 percent rainout per day, this could be ensured to a 90 percent level by operating about a week upwind of land. Such a constraint would have to be added to the others stated above.

Another possible way of dealing with the problem of acid rain would be to introduce sulfate in the form of ammonium sulfate or bisulfate, both of which are neutral salts. This would avoid the acid question from the start. These salts are frequently used as fertilizers and, in the dilutions to be seen here, would have a mild fertilizing effect locally. These salts can be made by reacting ammonia with sulfuric acid. The price of ammonia is about $100/t, so the cost of the CCN might double, and there would be an additional cost for equipment to run the reaction at sea. These additional costs might increase the total by as much as 50 percent, to $0.15/t C mitigated per year or $0.04/t CO_2.

It may also be sensible to consider using ships that pump a seawater aerosol into the air above the ocean, thus increasing the density of sea salt aerosol crystals, which can act as CCN (Latham and Smith, 1990).

ATMOSPHERIC CHLOROFLUOROCARBON REMOVAL

Another option for mitigating greenhouse warming could be to remove chlorofluorocarbons (CFCs) from their principal reservoir, the lower atmosphere or troposphere. The expected tropospheric residence time for CFCs exceeds 65 years (cf. Table 19.2); evidently these highly inert gases disappear only by very slow loss to the stratosphere, where ultraviolet rays from the sun cause molecular decomposition. A reasonable query is whether this natural process of CFC depletion can be significantly enhanced by large-scale technical means.

It has been suggested that extremely powerful lasers might be used to break up tropospheric CFCs (Stix, 1989). Vast arrays of pulsed lasers at mountain altitudes would launch intense infrared beams into the atmosphere. The laser beams would then selectively destroy chlorofluorocarbon molecules in the atmosphere through the process of multiphoton dissociation. Due to the low atmospheric concentration of the CFCs (less than one part per billion by volume), any process to remove them must be highly selective. That is, the process cannot afford to waste energy in reactions involving any of the far more abundant non-CFC molecules in the atmosphere. The suggested laser scheme then depends first upon finding bands of strong laser-light absorption by CFC molecules. Second, within these bands, one must find "spectral windows" where absorption of the laser light by non-CFC molecules in the atmosphere is virtually absent. Computer calculations making use of an extensive atmospheric-gas infrared cross-section data base suggest that 90 percent transmission over 50-km paths would be possible through dry atmospheres.

Nevertheless, a large number of questions remain unexplored, among them laser and optical technology, electro-optical conversion efficiency, anomalous or unexpected laser-light absorption channels including excited-state processes and stimulated rotational Raman scattering, infrared band-pass mirrors, adequate laser selectivity, pulse shaping benefits, wind velocity and atmospheric humidity patterns, site availabilities, and safety and ecology. Even making very optimistic assumptions about the resolution of these and other questions, the expense associated with the installation and operation of the elaborate and extensive laser facilities would be prohibitive: to remove 10 percent of the atmospheric CFCs per year, the electric power bill alone is estimated to exceed $10 billion. Nevertheless, if technological breakthroughs were to introduce a factor of 10 to 20 improvement in overall efficiency, the cost of such processing of the atmosphere, although very large indeed, might be worth evaluating.

In conclusion, the panel does not believe that the use of lasers to remove CFCs from the atmosphere is currently feasible.

CONCLUSIONS

Several of the geoengineering possibilities discussed in this chapter, including atmospheric CFC removal, space mirrors, and the multiple balloon stratospheric screen, appear, with current technology or that expected to be available soon, to be either impractical, too cumbersome to manage, or too expensive. These ideas might merit some further study to be certain of this conclusion but do not now seem worth great effort. They should be kept in mind, however, because technological changes may make them more attractive.

Reforestation is a low-cost, ecologically attractive option that could be adopted rapidly as an expanded program. It is, however, limited in its low-cost form by the easy availability of appropriate land. Therefore the panel hesitates to look beyond its initial potential mitigation of 240 Mt CO_2/yr. In addition, a number of years would be required to build reforestation to its full mitigation potential.

Stimulation of ocean biomass with iron may be feasible and would be a relatively low-cost option. Its application appears to be limited at most to the mitigation of about 7 Gt CO_2 equivalent per year (about 1.5 times U.S. annual CO_2 emissions). The biological, ecological, and ocean chemical and physical dynamics of this possibility are not well understood and should be investigated further, both theoretically and experimentally. There continue to be questions as to whether iron is the limiting nutrient. Furthermore, the circulation dynamics of the antarctic ocean might severely limit the effect. If feasible, the mitigation potential of the possibility—storage of CO_2 in a standing crop and as dissolved CO_2 with slow sequestering of carbon to the ocean bottom—could probably be established over several years. If applications of iron were stopped, the standing crop would be expected to die within days or weeks, thus ending the mitigation effect.

Cloud stimulation by provision of cloud condensation nuclei appears to be a feasible and low-cost option capable of being used to mitigate any quantity of CO_2 equivalent per year. Details of the cloud physics, verification of the amount of CCN to be added for a particular degree of mitigation, and the possible acid rain or other effects of adding CCN over the oceans need to be investigated before such a system is put to use. Once a decision has been made, the system could be mobilized and begin to operate in a year or so, and mitigation effects would be immediate. If the system were stopped, the mitigation effect would presumably cease very rapidly, within days or weeks, as extra CCN were removed by rain and drizzle.

Several schemes depend on the effect of additional dust (or possibly soot) in the stratosphere or very low stratosphere screening out sunlight. Such dust might be delivered to the stratosphere by various means, including being fired with large rifles or rockets or being lifted by hydrogen or hot-air balloons. These possibilities appear feasible, economical, and capable of mitigating the effect of as much CO_2 equivalent per year as we care to pay for. (Lifting dust, or soot, to the tropopause or the low stratosphere with aircraft may be limited, at low cost, to the mitigation of 8 to 80 Gt CO_2 equivalent per year.) Such systems could probably be put into full effect within a year or two of a decision to do so, and mitigation effects would begin immediately. Because dust falls out naturally, if the delivery of dust were stopped, mitigation effects would cease within about 6 months for dust (or soot) delivered to the tropopause and within a couple of years for dust delivered to the midstratosphere.

Such dust would have a visible effect, particularly on sunsets and sunrises, and would heat the stratosphere at the altitude of the dust. The heating would have an effect on the chemistry of the stratospheric ozone layer, and this possibility must be considered before major use of such a mitigation system. The amount of dust to be added is within the range of that added from time to time by volcanic eruption, so the effects on climate would not be expected to go beyond those experienced naturally. However, either the natural or the artificial effects on the chemistry might be very serious under conditions of increased CFC chlorine in the stratosphere, and the result of having these effects continuously must be considered, so the option might not be usable. Better specification of dust characteristics and size for best effect and better data on the fallout rate of dust from various altitudes as well as on chlorine chemistry are needed. It will be important to observe the effects on stratospheric chemistry of any volcanic eruptions that occur, with special attention to separating the effects of dust, aerosol, and hydrochloric acid.

Of these systems to alter the planetary albedo, the increase of low-level marine clouds by increasing CCN and the delivery of dust to the stratosphere by using large rifles seem the most promising. The rifle system appears to be inexpensive, to be relatively easily managed, and to require few launch sites. However, the possible effect of the additional stratospheric dust on ozone chemistry may be a serious problem, and the noise of the rifles would have to be managed. Balloons also appear to be a good possibility, but the return of the balloons to ground level would require management.

Sunlight screening systems would not have to be put into practice until shortly before they were needed for mitigation, although research to understand their effects, as well as design and engineering work, should be done now so that it will be known whether these technologies are available if wanted.

Perhaps one of the surprises of this analysis is the relatively low costs at which some of the geoengineering options might be implemented. If, however, further analyses support the preliminary conclusions, it will bear further inquiry to decide if they can produce the targeted responses without unacceptable additional effects. The level at which we are currently able to evaluate the cost-effectiveness of engineering the global mean radiation balance leaves great uncertainty in both technical feasibility and environmental consequences. This analysis does suggest that further inquiry is appropriate.

NOTES

1. Throughout this report, tons (t) are metric; 1 Mt = 1 megaton = 1 million tons; 1 Gt = 1 gigaton = 1 billion tons.

2. The ships can distribute material across the lane by towing hoses spread away from the ship with paravanes, a well-known minesweeping technology.

3. $4\pi(6.6)^2 \times 10^6$ km$^2 \times (10^3$ m/km)$^2 = 547 \times 10^{12}$ m$^2 \cong 5 \times 10^{14}$ m^2. The screening only requires covering the illuminated disk, or πr^2, but in many of the cases treated it will not be possible to maneuver the screening material so as to remain only above the sunlit side of the disk, therefore $4\pi r^2$ is used.

4. The correct parasol coverage area may be 1.4 percent because the Ramanathan computation is for 1 percent increase in the 30 percent albedo, but this change will have slight effect on the estimates. See also Penner et al. (1984), who estimate a dust requirement of 1.168×10^{10} kg.

5. The current space transportation system costs about \$5200/kg; \$130 million per launch with a capacity of 55,000 pounds to 160 nautical miles at 28.5 degrees. A Delta rocket costs \$45 million per launch for 11,000 pounds to 100 nautical miles, or \$9000/kg. Even at \$100/kg, the cost of the material would be only 2 percent of the cost of putting the material into orbit.

6. If the correct equivalence is 1 percent to 1200 Gt, for example, all material quantities, etc., are smaller by a factor of 10/12; if the equivalence is 800 Gt, the numbers are larger by a factor of 10/8, etc. For costs per ton of CO_2, all costs per ton of carbon should be divided by $44/12 \cong 4$.

7. In this connection, see also Early (1989). Estimates range between \$1/t CO2/ yr for the lower launch cost and long-lived mirrors and \$10/t CO_2/yr for the higher cost and annual replenishment.

8. From Toon and Pollack (1976), one can make a crude estimate of the mass of lower stratospheric dust by noting that they give the density at 20 km as about 1 mg/ m3. The "all sizes" curve in their Figure 9 suggests a reasonably constant concentration in the 8 km from 12 to 20 km. So the mass can be taken to be roughly 5×10^{14} m$^2 \times 8 \times 10^3$ m $\times 10^{-6}$ g/m$^3 = 40 \times 10^{11}$ g $= 4 \times 10^{12}$ g $= 4 \times 10^9$ kg, or roughly half the amount to be injected to form the screen.

9. It is interesting that this is the same mass as that computed above for the space mirror, given an assumed density of 2 g/cm^3 for dust instead of the 1 g/cm^3 used previously (clay has a density of 1.8 to 2.6, alumina of 4, basaltic lava of 2.8 to 3.0).

10. Another suggestion is to shape the dust into highly conductive needles about 0.1 m in radius by 0.5 m long, the scattering at an optical wavelength of 1 m would be dipole scattering with an effective scattering cross section 100 times greater than for spheres, thus requiring 100 times less material. Mack and Reiffen (1964) computed these effects in connection with the West Ford project. The maximum cross section expected for a perfectly conducting half-wave resonant dipole is 0.86λ. In the case of a dipole such as that specified above, which has an area of $1/2 \times 1/5$ λ a scattering cross section enhancement of $0.86 \times 10 = 8.6$ is obtained. This enhancement would be decreased by averaging over all angles of the dipole to the incoming radiation. Mack and Reiffen compute this effect to be about 0.1 for backscattering for several polarizations of the incoming light. In addition, highly conducting dipoles would have Q values too large to cover the necessary optical bandwidth effectively. It appears that assuming Mie scattering of dust with a size spectrum optimized to the scattering of the visible part of the solar spectrum, roughly comparable to the estimate of Ramaswamy and Kiehl (1985), is fairly efficient.

11. Material from staff at Naval Surface Weapons Center, Dahlgren, Virginia, was furnished to John I. Connally, Jr., vice president of Scientific Applications

International Corporation, and by him in a letter to Lee Hunt, executive director, Naval Studies Board, National Research Council.

12. The cost factors will scale proportionately except for any economies of scale, which have not been considered.

13. Data for Nike Orion and scientific balloons from Ray Pless (Wallops Island, NASA, private communication, 1990).

14. This estimate uses the value given in Table 7.2 of National Research Council (1985) for the column (Turco et al., 1983) at 11 to 13 km.

REFERENCES

Albrecht, B. A. 1989. Aerosols, cloud microphysics, and fractional cloudiness. Science 245:1227-1230.

Barnola, J. M., D. Raynaud, Y. S. Korotkevich, and C. Lorius. 1987. Vostock ice core provides 160,000 year record of atmospheric CO_2. Nature 329:408-414.

Budyko, M. I. 1982. The Earth's Climate: Past and Future. New York: Academic Press.

Cadle, R. D., C. S. Kiang, and J-F. Louis. 1976. The global scale dispersion of the eruption clouds from major volcanic eruptions. Journal of Geophysical Research 81(18):3125-3132.

Charlson, R. J., J. E. Lovelock, M. O. Andreae, and S. G. Warren. 1987. Oceanic phytoplankton, atmospheric sulphur, cloud albedo and climate. Nature 326:655-661.

Chemical Marketing Reporter. 1991. Chemical prices for week ending March 29, 1991. (April 11):35.

De Baar, H. J. W., A. G. J. Buma, R. F. Nolting, G. C. Cadee, G. Jacques, and P. J. Treguer. 1990. On iron limitations of the southern ocean: Experimental observations in the Weddell and Scotia seas. Marine Ecology Progress Series 65:105-122.

Early, J. T. 1989. Space-based solar shield to offset greenhouse effect. Journal of the British Interplanetary Society 42:567-569.

Heilman, P. E., and R. F. Stettler. 1985. Genetic variation and productivity of Populas Trichocarpa T and G and its hybrids. II. Biomass production in a 4-year plantation. Canadian Journal of Forest Research 15:384-388.

Hoffman, D. J., and S. Solomon. 1989. Ozone destruction through heterogeneous chemistry following the eruption of El Chichon. Journal of Geophysical Research D4 94:5029-5041.

Hunten, D. M. 1975. Residence times of aerosols and gases in the stratosphere. Geophysical Research Letters 2(1):26-27.

Kellogg, W. W., and S. H. Schneider. 1974. Climate stabilization: For better worse? Science 186:1163-1172.

Knox, F., and M. B. McElroy. 1984. Changes in atmospheric CO_2: Influence of the marine biota at high latitude. Journal of Geophysical Research 89:4629-4637.

Latham, J., and M. H. Smith. 1990. Effect on global warming of wind-dependent aerosol generation at the ocean surface. Nature 347:372-373.

Mack, C. L., Jr., and B. Reiffen. 1964. RF characteristics of thin dipoles. Proceedings of the IEEE 52:533-542.

Marland, G. 1988. The Prospect of Solving the CO_2 Problem Through Global Reforestation. Report DOE/NBB-0082. Oak Ridge, Tenn.: Oak Ridge National Laboratory.

Martin, J. H. 1990. Glacial-interglacial CO_2 change: The iron hypothesis. Paleooceanography 5:1-13.

Martin, J. H., and S. E. Fitzwater. 1988. Iron deficiency limits phytoplankton growth in the northeast Pacific subarctic. Nature 331:341-343.

Martin, J. H., and R. M. Gordon. 1988. Northeast Pacific iron distribution in relation to phytoplankton productivity. Deep-Sea Research 35:177-196.

Martin, J. H., R. M. Gordon, and S. E. Fitzwater. 1990. Iron in antarctic waters. Nature 345:156-159.

Mossop, S. C. 1963. Stratospheric particles at 20 km. Nature 199:325-326.

Mossop, S. C. 1965. Stratospheric particles at 20 km altitude. Geochimica et Cosmochimica Acta 29:201-207.

Moulton, R. J., and K. R. Richards. 1990. Costs of Sequestering Carbon Through Tree Planting and Forest Management in the United States. General Technical Report WO-58. Washington, D.C.: Forest Service, U.S. Department of Agriculture.

Mueller, A. C., and D. J. Kessler. 1985. The effects of particulates from solid rocket motors fired in space. Advances in Space Research 5(2):77-86.

National Research Council. 1985. The Effects on the Atmosphere of a Major Nuclear Exchange. Washington, D.C.: National Academy Press.

National Research Council. 1990. Forestry Research: A Mandate for Change. Washington, D.C.: National Academy Press.

Neftel, A., H. Oeschger, J. Schwander, B. Stauffer, and R. Zumbrunn. 1982. Ice core sample measurements give atmospheric CO_2 content during the past 40,000 yrs. Nature 295:220-223.

Oeschger, H., U. Siegenthaler, U. Schatterer, and A. Gugelmann. 1975. Box diffusion-model to study carbon dioxide exchange in nature. Tellus 27:168-192.

Peale, S. J. 1966. Dust belt of the earth. Journal of Geophysical Research 71(3):911-932.

Peng, T. H., and W. S. Broecker. 1991. Dynamical limitations on the antarctic iron fertilization strategy. Nature 349:227-229.

Penner, S. S., A. M. Schneider, and E. M. Kennedy. 1984. Active measures for reducing the global climatic impacts of escalating CO_2 concentrations. Acta Astronautica 11(6):345-348.

Ramanathan, V. 1988. The greenhouse theory of climate change: A test by an inadvertent experiment. Science 243:293-299.

Ramaswamy, V., and J. T. Kiehl. 1985. Sensitivities of the radiative forcing due to large loadings of smoke and dust aerosols. Journal of Geophysical Research 90(D3):5597-5613.

Randall, D. A., J. A. Coakley, Jr., C. W. Fairall, R. A. Kropfli, and D. H. Lenschow. 1984. Outlook for research on subtropical marine stratiform clouds. American Meteorological Society Bulletin 65(12):1290-1301.

Reck, R. A. 1978. Thermal Effects of Cloud Parameter Variations in the Manabe-Wetherald Radiative-Convective Atmospheric Model. Report GMR-2820. Warren, Mich.: General Motors Research Laboratories, and paper presented at the Conference on the Parameterization of Extended Clouds and Radiation for Climate Models, sponsored by the International Council of Scientific Unions and organized by the Joint Organizing Council of the Global Atmospheric Research Program of the United Nations, Oxford, England, September 1978.

Reck, R. A. 1979a. Comparison of fixed cloud-top temperature and fixed cloud-top altitude approximations in the Manabe-Wetherald radiative-convective atmospheric model. Tellus 31:400-405.

Reck, R. A. 1979b. Carbon dioxide and climate: Comparison of one- and three-dimensional models. Environment International 2:387-391.

Reck, R. A. 1984. Climatic Impact of Jet Engine Distribution of Alumina (Al_2O_3): Theoretical Evidence for Moderation of Carbon Dioxide (CO_2) Effects. Report GMR-4740. Warren, Mich.: General Motors Research Laboratories, and paper presented to the American Geophysical Union, San Francisco, Calif., December 1984.

Sarmiento, J., and J. R. Toggweiler. 1984. A new model for the role of the oceans in determining atmospheric pCO_2. Nature 308:621-624.

Schwartz, S. E. 1988. Are global cloud albedo and climate controlled by marine phytoplankton? Nature 336:441-445.

Siegenthaler, U., and T. Wenk. 1984. Rapid atmospheric CO_2 variations and ocean circulation. Nature 308:624-626.

Steinbeck, K., and C. L. Brown. 1976. Yield and Utilization of Hardwood Fiber Grown on Short Rotations. Applied Polymer Symposium, 28:393-401. New York: Wiley & Sons.

Stix, T. H. 1989. Removal of chlorofluorocarbons from the atmosphere. Journal of Applied Physics 66:5622-5626.

Stumm, W., and J. J. Morgan. 1970. Aquatic Chemistry. New York: Wiley-Interscience.

Tans, P. P., I. Y. Fung, and T. Takahashi. 1990. Observational constraints on the global atmospheric carbon dioxide budget. Science 247:1431-1438.

Tolbert, M. A., M. J. Rossi, and D. M. Golden. 1988. Heterogeneous interactions of chlorine nitrate, hydrogen chloride, and nitric acid with sulfuric acid surfaces at stratospheric temperatures. Geophysical Research Letters 8(15):847-850.

Toon, O. B., and J. B. Pollack. 1976. A global average model of atmospheric aerosols for radiative transfer calculations. Journal of Applied Meteorology 15:225-246.

Turco, R. P., O. B. Toon, T. Ackerman, J. B. Pollack, and C. Sagan. 1983. Nuclear winter: Global consequences of multiple nuclear explosions. Science 222:1283-1293.

U.S. Bureau of the Census. 1988. Statistical Abstract of the United States: 1989, 109th edition. Washington, D.C.: Government Printing Office.

U.S. Forest Service. 1990. FY 1989 U.S. Forest Planting Report. Washington, D.C.: U.S. Forest Service, U.S. Department of Agriculture.

World Resources Institute. 1990. World Resources Report 1990-91. New York: Oxford University Press.

29

Findings and Recommendations

In the previous chapters, the Mitigation Panel has discussed various options for responding to the emission of greenhouse gases to the atmosphere. Here the panel has organized that material within the framework of the charge it received to evaluate the effectiveness of various policies that could potentially mitigate greenhouse warming. No attempt has been made to judge *whether* action to mitigate greenhouse warming should be taken. If through the political process, however, the United States decides to attempt to mitigate greenhouse warming, it should do so as efficiently as possible, with a broad appreciation of the alternatives available, their potential effectiveness, and the implications of their implementation. This means (1) taking a global perspective with respect to possible actions, (2) assembling the best information available about the cost per ton of CO_2-equivalent reductions, and (3) evaluating other costs and benefits of prospective actions.

The panel again emphasizes that substantial uncertainties cloud *all* the numerical estimates summarized in this chapter. The degree of uncertainty varies greatly, but in many important instances such as the large-scale "geoengineering" alternatives, it is so large that even relative judgments must be made tentatively. More generally, the assembly of information in this report should be regarded as useful primarily for comparing large families of options, and not as specific recommendations of steps to be taken without additional analysis, research, or empirical study.

U.S. MITIGATION POLICY

United States policy toward greenhouse gas mitigation is important for a number of reasons. First, the United States is currently the largest emitter of greenhouse gases. As such, should greenhouse warming require active intervention, the United States has a responsibility to do its part to reduce greenhouse emissions, and unilateral action could contribute significantly to a reduction in the rate of emission growth. However, the U.S. role in greenhouse warming, although large (approximately 20 percent of world-wide CO_2-equivalent emissions), is not so large that unilateral action could stabilize global climate. At least a 60 percent reduction in current world-wide CO_2-equivalent emissions would be needed for stabilization, according to the Intergovernmental Panel on Climate Change (Intergovernmental Panel on Climate Change, 1991). As discussed in Chapter 28, geoengineering options may be able to reduce the amount of reduction required, but international agreement and participation in such actions would be necessary in order to undertake such action on a planetary scale.

Second, U.S. policy and technology will affect the inclination and capability of other nations to respond to greenhouse warming. The U.S. policy is of instrumental importance, both in meeting our potential national responsibilities within the world community and in leading constructive change in that community. The large magnitude and long time scale of potential adjustments imply that any response will require a coherent and sustained commitment on a global scale. What is needed is not a single national policy, but a long-term strategic perspective on greenhouse warming and its implications for the world economy.

Third, developing countries are unlikely to be able to respond to the potential threat of greenhouse warming at the same level as industrialized countries. The United States should not focus exclusively on interventions within its own boundaries because greenhouse warming is a global issue and emission reduction in one country could be as beneficial as in another. It may be appropriate for the United States and other industrial economies to seek low-cost opportunities for reducing greenhouse gas emissions in developing countries, or to provide economic and technological support, through the political process, should these countries decide that such actions are warranted.

Three basic premises are central to the panel's comparison of different mitigation policy options.

• First, possible *responses to greenhouse warming should be regarded as investments in the future of the nation and the planet.* That is, the actions needed would have to be implemented over a long time. They should be evaluated as investments, in comparison with other claims on the nation's resources, bearing in mind their often widespread implications for the economy.

• Second, *cost-effectiveness is an essential guideline.* The changes in energy, industrial practice, land use, agriculture, and forestry that might be implemented to limit greenhouse gas emissions, or the use of geoengineering options, imply an investment effort lasting several generations and large enough to affect the macroeconomic profile of the country. Costs of climate policy therefore need to be considered as a central element. A sensible guideline is cost-effectiveness: obtaining the largest reductions in greenhouse gas emissions at the lowest cost to society. Positive or negative effects of any mitigation option on societal factors not related to greenhouse warming must also be taken into account.

• Third, a *mixed strategy is essential.* The magnitude of the economic changes at stake, together with the need to pursue a cost-effective approach, implies that a mixed strategy, employing a variety of measures, would be required. This simple observation complicates the task of analysis and policy design, however, because a mixed strategy that is cost-effective can be designed and implemented only through comparisons of activities in different sectors of the economy.

CATEGORIES OF MITIGATION OPTIONS

A brief description of the mitigation options analyzed by the Mitigation Panel is shown in Table 29.1. In its comparison of different options, the panel examined several factors. The first of these was cost-effectiveness—how much reduction the United States can get in greenhouse warming for each dollar spent. By using the index of dollars per ton of CO_2 equivalent, the panel was able to contrast not only the mitigation options that affect CO_2 emissions, but also those that address emissions of halocarbons, N_2O, and CH_4.[1] As noted in Chapter 20, cost-effectiveness was evaluated using four different discount rates: 3, 6, 10, and 30 percent. Options that do not involve emission reductions, but would seek to reduce the level of greenhouse gases already in the atmosphere or to compensate for their climatic effects, were also reviewed. These "geoengineering options" have been converted to CO_2 emission reduction equivalence so that they can be compared with emission reduction options. The comparison is made by using the objective of *climate stabilization* rather than emission reduction per se. In the case of the geoengineering options, the cost-effectiveness was annualized for comparison purposes but was not discounted. This is because the panel felt that these options were so futuristic in nature that discounting would provide these "back of the envelope" cost estimates a degree of accuracy not available at the current time.

Assessment of the anticipated magnitude of climatic effects and appraisal of their impact on society have been the work of the Effects and Adaptation Panels (Parts Two and Four). That work builds a basis for informed judgments of the appropriate magnitude and rate of mitigation.

Barriers to implementing these mitigation options are also a major concern. Although it may be technically possible to achieve emission reduc-

TABLE 29.1 Brief Descriptions of Mitigation Options Considered in This Study for the United States

---

RESIDENTIAL AND COMMERCIAL ENERGY MANAGEMENT (CHAPTER 21)

Electricity efficiency measures

White surfaces/vegetation	Reduce air conditioning use and the urban heat island effect by 25% through planting vegetation and painting roofs white at 50% of U.S. residences.
Residential lighting	Reduce lighting energy consumption by 50% in all U.S. residences through replacement of incandescent lighting (2.5 inside and 1 outside light bulb per residence) with compact fluorescents.
Residential water heating	Improve efficiency by 40 to 70% through efficient tanks, increased insulation, low-flow devices, and alternative water heating systems.
Commercial water heating	Improve efficiency by 40 to 60% through residential measures mentioned above, heat pumps, and heat recovery systems.
Commercial lighting	Reduce lighting energy consumption by 30 to 60% by replacing 100% of commercial light fixtures with compact fluorescent lighting, reflectors, occupancy sensors, and daylighting.
Commercial cooking	Use additional insulation, seals, improved heating elements, reflective pans, and other measures to increase efficiency 20 to 30%.
Commercial cooling	Use improved heat pumps, chillers, window treatments, and other measures to reduce commercial cooling energy use by 30 to 70%.
Commercial refrigeration	Improve efficiency 20 to 40% through improved compressors, air barriers and food case enclosures, and other measures.
Residential appliances	Improve efficiency of refrigeration and dishwashers by 10 to 30% through implementation of new appliance standards for refrigeration, and use of no-heat drying cycles in dishwashers.
Residential space heating	Reduce energy consumption by 40 to 60% through improved and increased insulation, window glazing, and weather stripping along with increased use of heat pumps and solar heating.
Commercial and industrial Space heating	Reduce energy consumption by 20 to 30% using measures similar to that for the residential sector.
Commercial ventilation	Improve efficiency 30 to 50% through improved distribution systems, energy-efficient motors, and various other measures.

TABLE 29.1

Oil and gas efficiency	Reduce residential and commercial building fossil fuel energy use by 50% through improved efficiency measures similar to the ones listed under electricity efficiency.
Fuel switching	Improve overall efficiency by 60 to 70% through switching 10% of building electricity use from electric resistance heat to natural gas heating.

INDUSTRIAL ENERGY MANAGEMENT (CHAPTER 22)

Co-generation	Replace existing industrial energy systems with an additional 25,000 MW of co-generation plants to produce heat and power simultaneously.
Electricity efficiency	Improve electricity efficiency up to 30% through use of more efficient motors, electrical drive systems, lighting, and industrial process modifications.
Fuel efficiency	Reduce fuel consumption up to 30% by improving energy management, waste heat recovery, boiler modifications, and other industrial process enhancements.
Fuel switching	Switch 0.6 quads[a] of current coal consumption in industrial plants to natural gas or oil.
New process technology	Increase recycling and reduce energy consumption primarily in the primary metals, pulp and paper, chemicals, and petroleum refining industries through new, less energy intensive process innovations.

TRANSPORTATION ENERGY MANAGEMENT (CHAPTER 23)

Vehicle efficiency	
Light vehicles	Use technology to improve on-road fuel economy to 25 mpg (32.5 mpg in CAFE[b] terms) with no changes in the existing fleet.
	Improve on-road fuel economy to 36 mpg (46.8 mpg CAFE) with measures that require changes in the existing fleet such as downsizing.
Heavy trucks	Use measures similar to that for light vehicles to improve heavy truck efficiency up to 14 mpg (18.2 mpg CAFE).
Aircraft	Implement improved fanjet and other technologies to improve fuel efficiency by 20% to 130 to 140 seat-miles per gallon.

(Table 29.1 continues)

TABLE 29.1   *(continued)*

Alternative fuels

Methanol from biomass	Replace all existing gasoline vehicles with those that use methanol produced from biomass.
Hydrogen from nonfossil fuels	Replace gasoline with hydrogen created from electricity generated from nonfossil fuel sources.
Electricity from nonfossil fuels	Use electricity from nonfossil fuel sources such as nuclear and solar energy directly in transportation vehicles.
Transportation demand management	Reduce solo commuting by eliminating 25% of the employer-provided parking spaces and placing a tax on the remaining spaces to reduce solo commuting by an additional 15%.

ELECTRICITY AND FUEL SUPPLY (CHAPTER 24)

Heat rate improvements	Improve heat rates (efficiency) of existing plants by up to 4% through improved plant operation and maintenance.
Advanced coal	Improve overall thermal efficiency of coal plants by 10% through use of integrated gasification combined cycle, pressurized fluidized-bed, and advanced pulverized coal combustion systems.
Natural gas	Replace all existing fossil-fuel-fired plants with gas turbine combined cycle systems to both improve thermal efficiency of current natural gas combustion systems and replace fossil fuels such as coal and oil that generate more CO_2 than natural gas.
Nuclear	Replace all existing fossil-fuel-fired plants with nuclear power plants such as advanced light-water reactors.
Hydroelectric	Replace fossil-fuel-fired plants with remaining hydroelectric generation capability of 2 quads.
Geothermal	Replace fossil-fuel-fired plants with remaining geothermal generation potential of 3.5 quads.
Biomass	Replace fossil-fuel-fired plants with biomass generation potential of 2.4 quads.
Solar photovoltaics	Replace fossil-fuel-fired plants with solar photovoltaics generation potential of 2.5 quads.
Solar thermal	Replace fossil-fuel-fired plants with solar thermal generation potential of 2.6 quads.

TABLE 29.1

Wind	Replace fossil-fuel-fired plants with wind generation potential of 5.3 quads.
CO_2 disposal	Collect and dispose of all CO_2 generated by fossil-fuel-fired plants into the deep ocean or depleted gas and oil fields.

NONENERGY EMISSION REDUCTION (CHAPTER 25)

Halocarbons

Not-in-kind	Modify or replace existing equipment to use non-CFC materials as cleaning and blowing agents, aerosols, and refrigerants.
Conservation	Upgrade equipment and retrain personnel to improve conservation and recycling of CFC materials.
HCFC/HFC-aerosols, etc.	Substitute cleaning and blowing agents and aerosols with fluorocarbon substitutes.
HFC-chillers	Retrofit or replace existing chillers to use fluorocarbon substitutes.
HFC-auto air conditioning	Replace existing automobile air conditioners with equipment that utilizes fluorocarbon substitutes.
HFC-appliance	Replace all domestic refrigerators with those using fluorocarbon substitutes.
HCFC-other refrigeration	Replace commercial refrigeration equipment such as that used in supermarkets and transportation with that using fluorocarbon substitutes.
HCFC/HFC-appliance insulation	Replace domestic refrigerator insulation with fluorocarbon substitutes.

Agriculture (domestic)

Paddy rice	Eliminate all paddy rice production.
Ruminant animals	Reduce ruminant animal production by 25%.
Nitrogenous fertilizers	Reduce nitrogenous fertilizer use by 5%.
Landfill gas collection	Reduce landfill gas generation by 60 to 65% by collecting and burning in a flare or energy recovery system.

GEOENGINEERING (CHAPTER 28)

Reforestation	Reforest 28.7 Mha of economically or environmentally marginal crop and pasture lands and nonfederal forest lands to sequester 10% of U.S. CO_2 emissions.

(Table 29.1 continues)

TABLE 29.1   *(continued)*

Sunlight screening

Space mirrors	Place 50,000 100-km² mirrors in the earth's orbit to reflect incoming sunlight.
Stratospheric dust[c]	Use guns or balloons to maintain a dust cloud in the stratosphere to increase the sunlight reflection.
Stratospheric bubbles	Place billions of aluminized, hydrogen-filled balloons in the stratosphere to provide a reflective screen.
Low stratospheric dust[c]	Use aircraft to maintain a cloud of dust in the low stratosphere to reflect sunlight.
Low stratospheric soot[c]	Decrease efficiency of burning in engines of aircraft flying in the low stratosphere to maintain a thin cloud of soot to intercept sunlight.
Cloud stimulation[c]	Burn sulfur in ships or power plants to form sulfate aerosol in order to stimulate additional low marine clouds to reflect sunlight.
Ocean biomass stimulation	Place iron in the oceans to stimulate generation of CO_2-absorbing phytoplankton.
Atmospheric CFC removal	Use lasers to break up CFCs in the atmosphere.

[a]1 quad = 1 quadrillion Btu = 10^{15} Btu.
[b]Corporate average fuel economy.
[c]These options cause or alter chemical reactions in the atmosphere and should not be implemented without careful assessment of their direct and indirect consequences.

tion to a given level, the necessary actions might not be taken for any number of social, economic, or political reasons. For example, some actions that are economically sensible will not be undertaken by households and firms because they involve up-front costs and the households or firms face liquidity constraints that make them unwilling or unable to undertake the investment. In these cases, it could be desirable to find some institutional mechanism to overcome the constraints. In the case of energy efficiency, for example, the natural focus for such changes is builders, manufacturers, and utilities (i.e., the providers of electric power and natural gas). They are, in principle, in a position to make credit available, directly or indirectly, to purchasers who are constrained in their decisions by inadequate liquidity. Yet institutions may also face obstacles to moving to best practice or encouraging their customers to do so. Thus building codes are typically out of date and may limit local builders from incorporating the latest proven energy-saving materials in construction. In most states, public utility pricing formulas reward public utilities for building new power plants, but not for investments that conserve energy. Examples exist in many areas. It should be remembered, however, that some of these "constraints" serve other social objectives. For example, there are many reasons people drive their cars to work instead of taking mass transit, and many reasons they select large, less-efficient vehicles. The reasons may lie in time saved, safety, or personal flexibility, but in each case energy conservation is not the only social objective that enters into the decision process. Altering long-standing practices is rarely easy—even if such changes may bring economic as well as potential climatic benefits.

Many of the potential climate interventions, of course, have effects other than merely reducing atmospheric CO_2 or its equivalent. Some of these effects will be positive, others negative, and some will have different effects on different parts of society. It is also important to remember that these inquiries occur on a planet where the population is still increasing and most of the inhabitants aspire to a higher standard of living. Therefore another important factor in analyzing various mitigation policies involves the costs and benefits (beyond implementation) that are likely to occur should the mitigation action be taken. Thus some low-cost options will be unattractive on other grounds, while some high-cost actions will provide additional benefits.

In the present study the Mitigation Panel has barely touched on issues such as the barriers to implementation and the social, environmental, and economic implications of the strategies investigated. The panel hopes that the mention of these issues in this analysis through the use of the categories described below will contribute to their visibility and raise them to a higher level of consideration in more detailed studies later. The panel has tried to be qualitatively sensitive to these issues and to discourage direct dollar comparisons of options with widely different external implications. These three factors—cost-effectiveness, implementation obstacles, and other costs and benefits—suggested the categories for analysis.

The three categories of options are as follows:

• *Category 1 options:* "Best-practice" mitigation options available at little or no net cost that are not fully implemented due to various implementation obstacles.

• *Category 2 options:* Mitigation options that are either relatively costly or face implementation obstacles not fully represented in the implementation cost. They may also have other benefits and costs not fully represented.

• *Category 3 options:* Mitigation options that appear to be feasible with the current, limited state of knowledge. They may, with additional investigation, research, and development, provide the ability to change atmospheric concentrations of greenhouse gases, or radiative forcing, and the ultimate impact of greenhouse warming on a substantial scale.

In none of the categories have full institutional costs been estimated. This is important because most Category 1 options, particularly the ones estimated to produce net savings, require institutional changes before they become available to buyers and sellers of goods and services that release greenhouse gases. The costs of changing these institutional barriers are unknown. Without an appraisal of institutional costs, any comparison is incomplete; such an appraisal has not been done in this report. The panel believes it has provided a framework within which these appraisals can be made in future studies. A major rationale for discussing options under three categories is that the panel does not believe the full range of options should be compared on a simple monetary scale.

In Tables 29.2 to 29.7 the panel summarizes the mitigation strategies that have been reviewed using the three categories. Although the menu of options reviewed is not intended to provide an inventory of all possibilities, it seeks to identify the most promising options. The panel hopes that it provides the beginnings of a structure and a process for identifying those strategies that could appropriately respond to the prospect of greenhouse warming.

Category 1 Options

Every progressive society finds its economic activities on average falling short of best practice in most areas. This is because new practices are being contrived continually and it takes time for them to diffuse throughout the economy. Thus every progressive society enjoys opportunities for improving its overall situation by reducing the gap between average practice and best practice. Obstacles to more rapid diffusion of better practice include lack of information, lack of opportunity (e.g., if stores do not stock the improved products), political resistance, capital investment, risk aversion, and simple human inertia. Cost of replacement is also an obstacle, but one that disappears as old equipment wears out and renewal becomes necessary. Within organizations, better practices may not be introduced because of divisions in responsibility, for example, if those making the decisions to go ahead do not get credit for the benefits that flow from the new practice (e.g., "maintenance" pays for the light bulbs, but "operations" pays the electric bills).

Thus there are typically many improvements that "ought" to be undertaken, and most of them will be undertaken, eventually, because they are in the interests of those undertaking them. These decisions can be hastened by providing information and opportunity. Heightened awareness will encourage stores to stock improved products, top management to review the division of responsibilities within their firms, and so on.

The general proposition that economic activities fall short of best practice applies to every area of the economy. Many opportunities for reducing greenhouse gas emissions will also improve economic well-being, because they are more efficient than prevailing practices, judged in conventional terms. These "no-regrets" actions show up in Table 29.2 as measures with a net savings or very low cost. This negative cost does not imply that no expenditure is required to implement these actions, but rather that the real rate of return to the initial investment in making the change exceeds the common societal discount rates. However, as discussed in Chapters 21 and 22, households and firms do not have perfect information, and they are often observed to behave as if a 30 percent rate of return were needed to invest in one of these options. Therefore a column with a 30 percent discount rate has been added to illustrate what some households or firms seek in the marketplace prior to investment. As shown here, even at a 30 percent discount rate (well above their rate of return for other investment opportunities), firms and households will still receive a benefit for investment in many of these options. In other words, these "movement to best practice" actions involve attractive rates of return and would be undertaken voluntarily in many cases. However, as discussed in Chapters 21, 22, and 23, the timing can be accelerated if information, technical assistance, and financing can be provided.

Category 2 Options

As shown in Table 29.3, there are actions to reduce greenhouse gas emissions, or compensate for their climatic effects, that are either economically costly in the sense that the nation or the world must reduce its future income to reduce the potential for climate change, must face implementation obstacles, or will encounter additional benefits and costs not fully reflected in the implementation cost. The panel has tried to make rough estimates of the costs of reducing carbon in the atmosphere through various actions. The range of costs is wide, varying from well under $1/t CO_2 equivalent reduction to over $500/t.

As discussed in Chapter 25, reduction in CFC consumption can also help reduce stratospheric ozone depletion. In another case of issues beyond current cost, the information in Chapter 24 indicates that solar energy is relatively costly now, but anticipated technological developments may lower the price substantially—perhaps making it a cost-effective option. Nuclear power faces not only cost obstacles, but also implementation obstacles because of public concerns about nuclear plant safety and management of radioactive waste. The replacement of coal power plants with natural gas also faces implementation obstacles as utilities concerned about an uncertain natural gas supply resist investment in plants with a 30-year lifetime. Chapter 24 discusses each of the energy options in more depth.

TABLE 29.2 Category 1 Mitigation Options by Source

Mitigation Option	Net Implementation Cost ($/t CO$_2$ equivalent)				Potential Emission Reduction (Mt CO$_2$ equivalent/yr)	
	$d = 3\%$	$d = 6\%$	$d = 10\%$	$d = 30\%$	Option	Cumulative Sector[a]
RESIDENTIAL AND COMMERCIAL ENERGY MANAGEMENT						890
Electricity efficiency measures						
White surfaces/vegetation	−85	−84	−83	−74	32	
Residential lighting	−81	−79	−77	−61	39	
Residential water heating	−76	−74	−70	−49	27	
Commercial water heating	−75	−72	−68	−45	7	
Commercial lighting	−74	−71	−67	−42	117	
Commercial cooking	−73	−70	−66	−40	4	
Commercial cooling	−68	−64	−59	−26	81	
Commercial refrigeration	−65	−60	−54	−17	15	
Residential appliances	−51	−44	−35	22	72	
Residential space heating	−47	−39	−29	33	74	
Commercial and industry space heating	−43	−35	−24	43	15	
Commercial ventilation	−8	1	25	141	32	
Oil and gas efficiency	−71	−62	−53		300	
Fuel switching		−90			74	
INDUSTRIAL ENERGY MANAGEMENT						527
Co-generation		−30 to −5			45	
Electricity efficiency measures						
10% Reduction	−57	−51	−44	29	46	

476

20% Reduction	-44	-36	-26	67	91
30% Reduction	-30	-20	-7	106	137
Other energy efficiency measures					
15% Reduction	-26	-24	-20	3	173
30% Reduction	-5	1	9	60	345

TRANSPORTATION ENERGY MANAGEMENT 290

Vehicle efficiency					
Light vehicles (no fleet change)	-81 to -16	-78 to -2	-71 to 16	-3 to 296	245 to 256
Heavy trucks	-65	-59	-50	70	39

ELECTRICITY AND FUEL SUPPLY 47

Heat rate improvements (existing plants)	≈0	47

NONENERGY EMISSION REDUCTION 220

Landfill gas		
Gas collection systems	0.4 to 1	220

NOTE: The options that the Mitigation Panel has classified as Category 1 are listed by source category. Category 1 options are "best practice" options available at little or no net cost that are not fully implemented due to various implementation obstacles. The cost-effectiveness analysis is based on 1990 cost estimates presented for three different discount rates—3, 6, and 10 percent—plus 30 percent for the efficiency options. The potential emission reduction assumes 100 percent penetration of the current market. This table summarizes information presented throughout Part Three.

[a]Cumulative sector emission reductions are computed by adding the emission reduction from each mitigation option in that sector. If the emission reduction is a range, the arithmetic mean is used to compute the cumulative emission reduction.

TABLE 29.3 Category 2 Mitigation Options by Source

Mitigation Option	Net Implementation Cost ($/t CO$_2$ equivalent)				Potential Emission Reduction (Mt CO$_2$ equivalent/yr)		Other Factors[b]
	$d = 3\%$	$d = 6\%$	$d = 10\%$	$d = 30\%$	Option	Cumulative Sector[a]	
INDUSTRIAL ENERGY MANAGEMENT						324	
Fuel switching (coal to gas)	≈60				24		Fuel availability
New process technology (including recycling)	?				300		Technical advancement needed
TRANSPORTATION ENERGY MANAGEMENT						1130	
Vehicle efficiency							
Light vehicles (change fleet mix)	20–887	39–1018	64–1204	454–4370	23–83		Life-style change
Aircraft retrofit	357				13		
Alternative fuels							
Methanol from biomass	?				1130		Resource availability
Hydrogen from nonfossil energy	?				1130		Technical advancement needed
Electric from nonfossil energy	?				1130		Technical advancement needed
Transportation system management	−22				49		Life-style change

ELECTRICITY AND FUEL SUPPLY[c]   0–177   1700

Technology	Value	Concern
Advanced coal	200	Natural gas supply
Natural gas (combined cycle)	1000	Safety and other concerns
Nuclear	1700	Resource availability
Hydroelectric	30	Resource availability
Biomass	130	Technical advancement needed
Solar photovoltaics	400	Technical advancement needed
Solar thermal	540	
Wind	30	
CO_2 disposal	1700	

NONENERGY EMISSION REDUCTION   1409   Stratospheric ozone depletion

Halocarbons[d]				
Non-HCFC substitution	0.01	0.02	0.04	302
Conservation	0.03	0.04	0.04	509
HCFC/HFC aerosols, etc.	0.6	0.6	0.6	248
HFC chillers	2	3	4	88
HFC auto air conditioning	4	5	6	170
HFC appliance	8	11	13	11
HCFC other refrigeration	3	4	4	67
HCFC/HFC appliance insulation	23	28	36	14

(Table 29.3 continues)

TABLE 29.3 (continued)

Mitigation Option	Net Implementation Cost ($/t CO$_2$ equivalent)				Potential Emission Reduction (Mt CO$_2$ equivalent/yr)		
	$d = 3\%$	$d = 6\%$	$d = 10\%$	$d = 30\%$	Option	Cumulative Sector[a]	Other Factors[b]
Agriculture						223	Life-style change
Paddy rice		0–4			84		
Ruminant animals		0–5			126		
Nitrogenous fertilizers		0–1			23		
GEOENGINEERING						242	
Reforestation		3–10					Agricultural land loss

NOTE: The options that the Mitigation Panel has classified as Category 2 are listed by source category. Category 2 options are those that are either relatively costly or face implementation obstacles not fully represented in the implementation cost. They may also have other benefits and costs not fully represented. The cost-effectiveness analysis is based on 1990 cost estimates presented for 3 different discount rates—3, 6, and 10 percent—plus 30 percent for the efficiency options. The potential emission reduction assumes 100 percent penetration of the current market. This table summarizes information presented throughout Part Three.

[a]Cumulative sector emission reductions are computed by adding the emission reduction from each mitigation option in that sector. If the emission reduction is a range, the arithmetic mean is used to compute the cumulative emission reduction.

[b]Factors other than implementation cost that affect mitigation policy decision-making.

[c]Costs reflect indifference to the present energy mix as discussed in Chapter 24. Emission reduction is potential available for each option alone.

[d]HCFC = hydrochlorofluorocarbon; HFC = hydrofluorocarbon.

The point of Category 2 is that the relative attractiveness of the various options is not adequately captured in the simple index of cost per ton of CO_2 equivalent. The relative appeal of Category 2 options is greatly affected by other social, environmental, and economic externalities.

Category 3 Options

Category 3 options (Table 29.4), mainly geoengineering options, are those that appear to be feasible with the limited information now available, which may—with additional investigation, research, and development—provide the ability to change atmospheric concentrations, or radiative forcing, and the ultimate impact of greenhouse warming on a substantial scale. By and large, they deal with the symptoms rather than the causes. Some of these actions could be initiated after a deleterious climate change was clearly identifiable, if research and development had been completed earlier. Near-term research of the Category 3 options as a "backstop" measure is likely to be beneficial and relatively inexpensive. In the end, as discussed in Chapter 28, some of these options could be inexpensive, safe, and reversible.

Many of the Category 3 options appear relatively inexpensive from an implementation standpoint but have large unknowns as to their environmental or carbon cycle side effects should they be implemented. For example, increasing phytoplankton growth through addition of iron to the oceans may be a feasible mitigation option, but the impact of tinkering with the oceanic balances of iron, carbon, oxygen, and other nutrients is unknown at this time. These options should be investigated further and should be well understood before implementation is considered seriously.

COMPARING THE DIFFERENT MITIGATION OPTIONS

Tables 29.5, 29.6, and 29.7 summarize the information in Tables 29.2, 29.3, and 29.4 by adding up the maximum potential emission reduction available from each sector and placing the net cost of the various options in categories. Categorization of cost numbers helps to illustrate that a great deal of uncertainty is, of course, associated with many of these numbers. Because this is a "first-order" analysis, the Mitigation Panel has used information from many sources, most of which were not intended to be used for comparative cost analysis. Improvement of the cost estimates will undoubtedly modify the priority ordering of options; at this time, therefore, categories are an appropriate way to compare alternatives. In addition, cost categorization allows comparison of costs of different options relative to a wide-ranging policy instrument such as a carbon tax and its impact on fuel prices.

Figure 29.1 illustrates how mitigation options might be ranked both on

TABLE 29.4 Category 3 Mitigation Options by Source

Mitigation Policy	Net Implementation Cost[a] ($/t CO_2 equivalent)	Potential Emission Reduction (Mt CO_2 equivalent/year)
GEOENGINEERING		
Sunlight screening		
Space mirrors[b,c]	0.1–15	+[d]
Stratospheric dust (guns or balloon lift)[e]	0.03–1	+[d]
Stratospheric bubbles (multiple balloons)[f]	0.5–5	+[d]
Low stratospheric dust-aircraft delivery[e]	0.003–1	8×10^3 to 80×10^3
Low stratospheric soot[e,g]	0.003–0.3	8×10^3 to 25×10^3
Cloud stimulated by provision of CCN[h]	0.03–1	+[d]
Stimulation of ocean biomass with iron	0.1–15	7×10^3
Atmospheric CFC removal[i]	?	?

NOTE: The options that the Mitigation Panel has classified as Category 3 are listed by source category. Category 3 options are those that appear to be feasible and may, with additional investigation, research, and development, provide the ability to change atmospheric concentrations, or radiative forcing, and the ultimate impact of greenhouse warming on a substantial scale. They may also have other benefits and costs not fully represented. The cost-effectiveness numbers are undiscounted 1990 cost estimates. This table summarizes information presented throughout Part Three.

[a]Costs have not been discounted.
[b]Replenishment requirements not estimated.
[c]Probably impractical for control management reasons.
[d]The "+" indicates that there is no known physical limit to this method assuming these options work as expected, just a limit on the amount of mitigation for which we are willing to pay (see Chapter 28 for more details).
[e]These options cannot be considered for use until the possible effects of the soot, dust, or aerosol on the destruction of stratospheric ozone are understood.
[f]Probably impractical because of trash problems from bubble fallout.
[g]Slight decrease in aircraft fuel burning efficiency.
[h]CCN = Cloud condensation nuclei.
[i]Probably impractical at reasonable cost with current technology.

TABLE 29.5 Cost-Effectiveness Ordering of Category 1 Mitigation Options

Mitigation Option[a]	Cost[b]	Potential Emission Reduction[c] (Mt CO_2 equivalent/yr)	Potential Emission Reduction in Terms of 1988 U.S. Emissions	
			CO_2 (%)	CO_2 equivalent (%)
Residential and commercial energy efficiency	Savings	850	18	11
Vehicle efficiency (no fleet change)	Savings	290	6	4
Industrial energy efficiency/co-generation	Savings	530	11	7
Power plant heat rate improvements	Savings to Low	50	1	1
Landfill gas collection systems	Low	220	5	3

NOTE: This table summarizes the information by source category and places the options in order of cost-effectiveness for the Category 1 options. Cost-effectiveness estimates are categorized as: Savings (for less than 0), Low (0–$9/t CO_2 equivalent), Medium ($10–99/t CO_2 equivalent), or High (>$100/t CO_2 equivalent). The potential emission savings (assuming 100 percent penetration) are presented as percent reductions in 1988 U.S. CO_2 (4.8 Gt CO_2/yr) and CO_2-equivalent (8 Gt CO_2 equivalent/year) emissions.

[a] Mitigation options are placed in order of cost-effectiveness based on the average (arithmetic mean) of the costs for each option within that category at a social discount rate of 6 percent. Cost ranges are averaged prior to each option addition.

[b] Costs are in ranges shown below:

	$/t CO_2
Savings	<0
Low	0–9
Medium	10–99
High	>100

[c] Cumulative sector emission reductions are computed by adding the emission reduction from each mitigation option in that sector. If the emission reduction is a range, the arithmetic mean is used to compute the cumulative emission reduction. For non-CO_2 emission reductions, the equivalent impact of a CO_2 reduction is computed by multiplying the non-CO_2 reduction by the appropriate range of global warming potential factors given in the IPCC Working Group I report (see Chapter 19).

TABLE 29.6 Cost-Effectiveness Ordering of Category 2 Mitigation Options

Mitigation Option[a]	Cost[b]	Potential Emission Reduction[c] (Mt CO_2 equivalent/yr)	Potential Emission Reduction in Terms of 1988 U.S. Emissions	
			CO_2 (%)	CO_2 equivalent (%)
Transportation system management	Savings	50	1	1
Halocarbons (CFCs, etc.)	Low	1410	29	18
Agriculture (rice, animals, fertilizer)	Low	220	5	3
Reforestation	Low to medium	240	5	3
Industrial fuel switching	Medium	50	1	1
Electricity supply options	Low to high	1700	35	21
Vehicle efficiency (fleet mix change)	High	150	3	2
Alternative transportation fuels	?	1130	24	14
New industrial process technology	?	300[d]	6	4

NOTE: This table summarizes the information by source category and places the options in order of cost-effectiveness for the Category 2 options. Cost-effectiveness estimates are categorized as: Savings (for less than 0), Low (0–$9/t CO_2 equivalent), Medium ($10–99/t CO_2 equivalent), or High (>$100/t CO_2 equivalent). The potential emission savings (assuming 100 percent penetration) are presented as percent reductions in 1988 U.S. CO_2 (4.8 Gt CO_2/yr) and CO_2-equivalent (8 Gt CO_2 equivalent/year) emissions.

[a] Mitigation options are placed in order of cost–effectiveness based on the average (arithmetic mean) of the costs for each option within that category at a social discount rate of 6 percent. Cost ranges are averaged prior to each option addition.

[b] Costs are in ranges as shown below:

	$/t CO_2
Savings	<0
Low	0–9
Medium	10–99
High	>100

[c] Cumulative sector emission reductions are computed by adding the emission reduction from each mitigation option in that sector. If the emission reduction is a range, the arithmetic mean is used to compute the cumulative emission reduction. Options may not be additive because some are mutually exclusive. For example, electricity supply options assume emission reductions are from the same coal-fired power plants. Therefore they are not additive. For non-CO_2 emission reductions, the equivalent impact of a CO_2 reduction is computed by multiplying the non-CO_2 reduction by the appropriate range of global warming potential factors given in the IPCC Working Group I report (see Chapter 19).

[d] Theoretical reductions are several times larger than this.

TABLE 29.7 Cost-Effectiveness Ordering of Category 3 Mitigation Options

Mitigation Option	Cost[a]	Potential Emission Mitigation[b] (Mt CO_2 equivalent/yr)
GEOENGINEERING[c]		
Low stratospheric soot[d]	Low	8×10^3 to 25×10^3
Low stratospheric dust-aircraft delivery[d]	Low	8×10^3 to 80×10^3
Stratospheric dust (guns or balloon lift)[d]	Low	+
Cloud stimulated by provision of CCN[e]	Low	+
Stimulation of ocean biomass with iron[f]	Low to medium	7×10^3
Stratospheric bubbles (multiple balloons)[g]	Low to medium	+
Space mirrors[g]	Low to medium	+

NOTE: This table summarizes the information by source category and places the options in order of cost-effectiveness for the Category 3 options. Cost-effectiveness estimates are categorized as: Savings (for less than 0), Low (0–$9/t CO_2 equivalent), Medium ($10–99/t CO_2 equivalent), or High (>$100/t CO_2 equivalent). The potential emission savings (which in some cases includes not only the annual emissions, but also changes in atmospheric concentrations already in the atmosphere) for the geoengineering options are also shown.

[a]Costs are in ranges shown below:

	$/t CO_2
Savings	<0
Low	0–9
Medium	10–99
High	>100

[b]This number assumes that we not only mitigate the impact of current emissions of CO_2 and other greenhouse gases, but also the stock of those gases. The CO_2-equivalent emission is determined by evaluating the equivalent reduction in radiative forcing (see Appendix Q). These options do not reduce the flow of emissions per se, but rather the impact of greenhouse warming from those emissions. The "+" indicates that there is no known physical limit to this method assuming these options work as expected, just a limit on the amount of mitigation for which we are willing to pay.

[c]Mitigation options are placed in order of cost-effectiveness based on the average (arithmetic mean) of the costs. Cost ranges are averaged prior to each option addition.

[d]These options cannot be considered for use until the possible effects of the soot, dust, or aerosol on the destruction of stratospheric ozone are understood.

[e]Cloud condensation nuclei.

[f]This option cannot be considered for use until the possible effects of large-scale iron additions to the ocean biomass are well understood.

[g]Infeasible options.

their cost-effectiveness and on their potential for reducing emissions. This supply curve is the goal of the analysis discussed in Chapter 20. In Figure 29.1, Category 1 and 2 options are ranked by cost estimates for mitigation measures in that family. Starting with the cheapest option (based on the middle cost estimate) at the left of the graph, the options are added together, so that the incremental cost of implementing the mitigation steps is plotted as a function of the total reduction in CO_2-equivalent emissions.

Figure 29.1 shows three supply curves, one each for the low, middle, and high cost estimates. The middle cost is the average mitigation cost for that option as determined from the information in Tables 29.2 to 29.4. The panel's judgment as to the uncertainty range surrounding the middle cost estimate is then shown as low and high cost.

Note that the order in which options are implemented in the figure is based upon the middle cost estimates, a satisfactory approach for this preliminary analysis with highly uncertain data. In later studies, drawing upon better information, the supply curves should be recalculated for each family of cost estimates to ensure that the lowest-cost alternative remaining is the next one to be selected for implementation.

Several important factors should be noted. First, some options show negative costs, a point discussed above. A second concern is to avoid "double counting" in compiling the supply curve. For example, the nuclear and natural gas mitigation options replace the same coal-fired power plants. Furthermore, improvements in end-use efficiency will also reduce demand for electricity and therefore CO_2-equivalent emissions. This means that some of the options are not additive. Therefore the potential emission reduction for the electricity supply options was determined by subtracting the emission reduction already obtained from end-use and power plant efficiency improvements (which cost less than new power) from the CO_2-equivalent emissions currently generated by power plants.

Further, this method combines the Category 1 and Category 2 options into one figure, which means that the additional considerations identified as "other factors" in Table 29.3 are not considered. Such additional cost and benefits may move these options either up or down on this chart relative to societal preferences.

Another major limitation is that some options with significant potential for reducing CO_2-equivalent emissions have not been included in Figure 29.1 because cost estimates are not readily available (e.g., industrial process technology and efficiency improvements). Many of these options are likely to be more cost-effective than some of those represented in Figure 29.1.

Finally, another important factor to remember is that these reductions include not only CO_2, but also CFCs, CH_4, and N_2O, all of which have a higher impact per molecule on greenhouse warming. Therefore Figure 29.1 shows the reduction of CO_2-equivalent emissions, not just CO_2. In addition, one geoengineering option—reforestation—does not reduce emissions

488

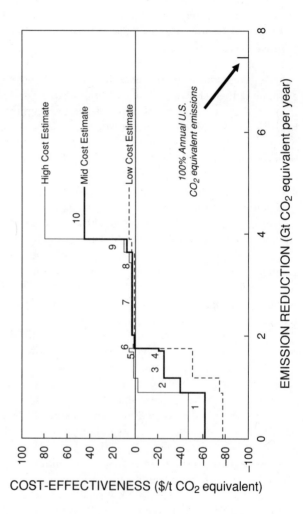

COST-EFFECTIVENESS ($/t CO₂ equivalent)

EMISSION REDUCTION (Gt CO₂ equivalent per year)

	Net Implementation Cost[a] ($/t CO$_2$ equivalent)			Maximum Potential Emission Reduction[b] (Gt CO$_2$ eq./yr.)	Percent Reduction in U.S. Emissions[c]	
	Low	Mid	High		CO$_2$(%)	CO$_2$ eq. (%)
1 Residential & Commercial Energy Efficiency[d]	−78	−62	−47	0.9	18	11
2 Vehicle Efficiency (no fleet change)[d]	−75	−40	−2	0.3	6	4
3 Industrial Electric Efficiency[d]	−51	−25	1	0.5	11	7
4 Transportation System Management[e]	−50	−22	5	0.05	1	1
5 Power Plant Heat Rate Improvements[d]	−2	0	2	0.05	1	1
6 Landfill Gas Collection[d]	0.4	1	1	0.2	5	3
7 Halocarbons[e]	0.9	1	3	1.4	29	18
8 Agriculture[e]	1	3	5	0.2	5	3
9 Reforestation[e]	3	7	10	0.2	5	3
10 Electricity Supply[e]	5	45	80	1.0	21	13

[a]Mitigation options are placed in order of cost-effectiveness based on the average (arithmetic mean) of the costs for each option within that category at a social discount rate of 6 percent. If the cost provided (as shown in Tables 29.2 to 29.4) is a range, the cost range is averaged to determine the options cost. Only a select number of emission reduction methods are included. Those greater than $100/t CO$_2$ eq. or whose cost is unknown are not included.

[b]Cumulative sector emission reductions are computed by adding the emission reduction from each mitigation option in that sector in gigatons per year. If the emission reduction is a range, the arithmetic mean is used to compute the cumulative emission reduction. To remove double-counting, the energy supply emission reduction potential was reduced by the amount of reduction potentially available for the less expensive efficiency options. For non-CO$_2$ emission reductions, the equivalent impact of a CO$_2$ reduction is computed by multiplying the non-CO$_2$ reduction by the 100-yr GWP factors (see Chapter 19).

[c]Percent reduction is in terms of 1988 U.S. CO$_2$ emissions, which are assumed to be approximately 4.8 Gt CO$_2$ per year. Total U.S. greenhouse gas emissions are, of course, larger than this and include emissions of halocarbons, methane, and nitrous oxide. They are assumed to be approximately 7.9 Gt CO$_2$ eq./yr

[d]Category 1 options.
[e]Category 2 options.

FIGURE 29.1 Low-mid-high mitigation cost comparison, assuming 100 percent implementation.

from a source but acts as a sink. Thus this figure should be interpreted with extreme caution; however, the Mitigation Panel believes it provides a useful picture of the way in which many different mitigation options may be compared with one another.

IMPLEMENTING RESPONSE PROGRAMS

Figures 29.2 to 29.5 place Figure 29.1 in the context of other cost estimates and the limitations associated with actually implementing a mitigation response program. To do this, the panel examined the sensitivity to the extent to which these programs are implemented by society. Figure 29.2 displays the Figure 29.1 supply curve for three different levels of implementation of the emission reduction strategies: 25, 50, and 100 percent. As illustrated here, the effectiveness of CO_2-equivalent emission reduction changes greatly as a function of the potential achieved. Figure 29.3 shows the range of technological costing cost estimates. The lower curve is the most optimistic estimate—100 percent implementation of the option as described in Table 29.1, with the lower-cost bound. The upper curve is a more pessimistic estimate—25 percent implementation of the option as described, with the upper-cost bound. Mitigation costs will not be known perfectly; an approach of the kind illustrated in Figure 29.3, which develops bounding cases, can be useful in developing mitigation plans.

Figure 29.4 is a compilation of a number of energy modeling estimates of the cost of CO_2-equivalent reduction. Details on the compilation of this curve are provided in Appendix R. The energy modeling estimates differ in two important characteristics from the technological costing analyses in this report. First, energy modeling estimates are comprehensive energy sector models. That is, they include a consistent accounting of the demand, supply, and resources used in the countries or regions studied. In this respect, they differ from the approach in this report, which looks at the possibilities for greenhouse gas reductions from individual technologies and attempts to make the estimates mutually consistent by manual calculations. One difficulty with the technological costing approach is that calculations are on a constant cost basis; that is, they do not account for how implementation of these measures may affect the cost of the measure. A major surge in the number of natural gas plants, for example, will likely increase demand for and therefore the price of natural gas. This would increase the cost of the mitigation option—perhaps changing its ranking. The same is true for energy efficiency measures: as demand is reduced, the price of electricity would change. This would change the savings available from that energy efficiency measure. The energy modeling approach takes these supply and demand impacts into account, while

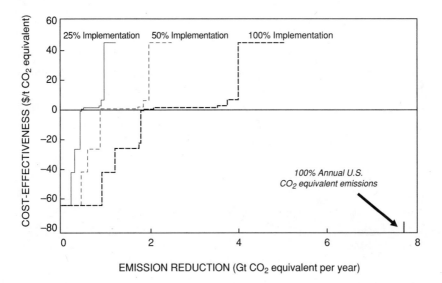

FIGURE 29.2   Mitigation comparison with different levels of implementation.

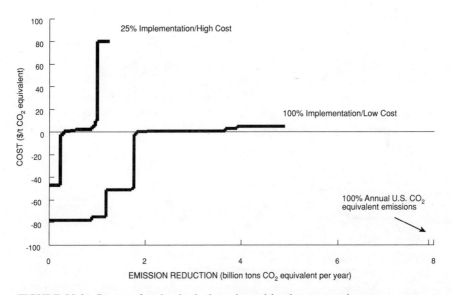

FIGURE 29.3   Range of technological costing mitigation cost estimates.

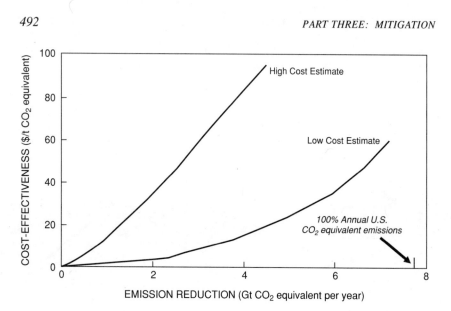

FIGURE 29.4   Range of energy modeling mitigation cost estimates (see Appendix R for more information).

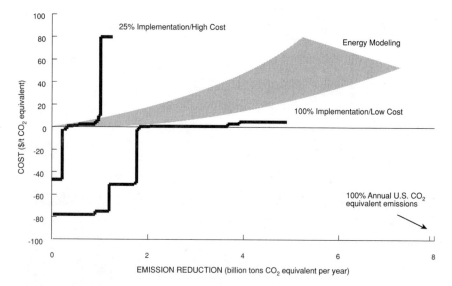

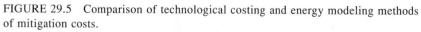

FIGURE 29.5   Comparison of technological costing and energy modeling methods of mitigation costs.

the technological costing approach is based on the margin of the current economy and therefore does not.

A second important difference between the energy modeling approach and the approach taken by the Mitigation Panel is that the models surveyed estimate the cost function for reducing greenhouse gas emissions beginning from the point at which all "negative-cost" options have been employed. In most economic models, the market equilibrium is this point; in one model, where market failures are allowed, the results have been recast so that cost estimates begin from the point at which the market failures have been allowed for. It is important to note then, that the negative-cost part of the cost function, should that exist, is excluded from energy modeling analyses. A full description of the development of this curve is provided in Appendix R.

Finally, Figure 29.5 combines the technological costing mitigation curves in Figure 29.3 and the energy modeling curves in Figure 29.4. The energy modeling curves fall roughly between the bounding estimates of the technological costing approach. The primary difference, as mentioned earlier, is that the energy modeling curves do not include the financial benefits from efficiency measures. At the current limited state of knowledge the panel believes that the actual implementation costs of mitigating greenhouse gas emissions (excluding costs beyond those needed directly for implementation) are likely to fall within the range provided by the technological costing method. It is important to note that while the panel believes that the technological costing approach is better suited to evaluating the comparative advantages and disadvantages of specific mitigation options because current economic models do not have the specificity needed for such an analysis, there are reasons to be skeptical of the degree to which such option-driven assessments can incorporate social responses (including market responses) to alternative courses of action.

A review of Figures 29.2 to 29.5 indicates that it would not be unreasonable to expect that a roughly 25 percent reduction in U.S. greenhouse gas emissions (i.e., 2 Gt CO_2 equivalent) might be achieved at a cost of less than $10/t CO_2 equivalent. This is, in more commonly used terms, roughly an additional $22 per short ton of coal, $4.75 per barrel of oil, $0.60 per million cubic feet of natural gas, $0.11 per gallon of gasoline, or 0.7 cents/kWh for the current U.S. electricity mix.

A wide array of policy instruments is available for implementing mitigation options. Two categories are direct regulation and incentives. Direct regulation instruments mandate action and include controls on consumption (bans, quotas, required product attributes), production (quotas on products or substances), factors in design or production (efficiency, durability, processes), and provision of services (mass transit, land use). Incentive instruments are designed to influence decisions by individuals and organizations, and include taxes and subsidies on production factors (carbon tax, fuel tax), taxes on products and other outputs (emission taxes, product taxes), financial inducements (tax credits, subsidies), and transferrable emission rights (tradeable emission reductions, tradeable credits). The choice of policy instrument depends on the objective to be served.

Interventions at all levels of human aggregation could effectively reduce greenhouse warming. For example, individuals could reduce energy consumption, recycle goods, and reduce consumption of deleterious materials. Local governments could control emissions from buildings, transport fleets, waste processing plants, and landfill dumps. State governments could restructure electric and gas utility pricing structures and stimulate a variety of efficiency incentives. National governments could pursue action in most of the policy areas of relevance. International organizations could coordinate programs in various parts of the world, manage transfers of resources and technologies, and facilitate exchange of monitoring and other relevant data.

Although the analysis of mitigation options in this report does not include all possibilities, the Mitigation Panel is hopeful that it does identify the most promising options considered here. The panel feels confident that it provides the beginnings of a structure and a process for identifying those strategies that could appropriately mitigate the prospect of greenhouse warming.

INTERNATIONAL CONSIDERATIONS

Whatever policies the United States follows in order to truly address greenhouse warming, it will eventually be necessary to achieve broader international consensus in action. Many of the cost-effective options appropriate for the United States are also applicable in other countries, including developing nations. A range of other measures are also relevant, such as removing or reducing market-distorting subsidies that encourage greenhouse gas emissions. Effective participation of developing countries in the reduction of emissions will require political actions by those nations, as well as international negotiations that deal with the availability of financial and technical resources and with competing requirements for current economic growth.

As discussed in Chapter 26, population growth, largely taking place in developing countries, is a basic contributor to the increase in greenhouse gas emissions. This will become even more relevant in the future, as those countries improve their economies with accompanying increased energy consumption. Limiting growth in population is central to limiting future energy consumption and, therefore, to future stabilization of greenhouse gas emissions. Limiting population growth may not be financially costly, but it is beset with political, social, and ideological obstacles. Similarly, as discussed in Chapter 27, reducing or reversing net deforestation as a means of reducing greenhouse gases raises a host of nontechnical issues that are not evident from a financial standpoint.

The international negotiations on greenhouse issues that will be required to lead to common action on these and related matters, and to avoid "free riders" (where one nation benefits from the costly actions of others), will be difficult and will necessarily involve matters of great political and economic concern. International studies and analyses are currently under way in an impressive number of settings, with the recent experience of the Montreal Protocol and Law-of-the-Sea negotiations as guides to approaches that are useful and those that should be avoided. Hard choices remain in the future, however, because negotiations will be more difficult than any of the predecessors in the environmental area. However, the necessarily deliberative nature of those negotiations should not obscure the conclusion that unilateral actions by the United States, or common actions by currently large greenhouse gas emitters among industrialized countries, can be useful on their own. They can reduce emissions below their expected levels in the short term, delay the onset of warming (if warming materializes), and create a precedent that could help lead to coordinated international action.

FINAL THOUGHTS

The Mitigation Panel has attempted to outline a perspective that should be pursued relative to mitigation policy. First, the United States needs to realize that although unilateral actions can contribute significantly to the reduction of greenhouse gases, the greenhouse warming phenomenon is global, and national efforts alone would not be sufficient to eliminate the problem. This means that the nation should take a global perspective with respect to possible actions. Second, cost-effectiveness should be a primary guide in making greenhouse warming mitigation policy as efficient as possible.

Therefore the Mitigation Panel has tried to bring together informed judgments of the cost of greenhouse gas reduction, as well as other costs and benefits of prospective actions. It should be emphasized that the analysis the panel conducted was "cross-sectional" as opposed to a longitudinal analysis of options over time. There was no attempt, for example, to project future levels of economic activity and their implications for greenhouse gas emissions. This study does account, however, for future consequences of current actions. In particular, the direct effects of each option on greenhouse gas emissions are assessed. The panel has not attempted to examine those options under the different overall emission rates that might occur at future times. Its analysis must therefore be seen as an initial assessment of mitigation options in terms of their return on investment under current conditions. A subsequent analysis might consider appropriate strategies under changing conditions. Furthermore, the time required to implement these mitigation options is not considered. Some options, such as those in energy efficiency, can be implemented immediately if the noneconomic obstacles are overcome. Others, such as changes in electricity production, might take considerably longer, on the order of decades. The rates at which these mitigation options are implemented depends on the decision makers in a wide range of firms, households, and governmental units throughout the United States.

Once the cost-effectiveness and mitigation potential of each option were determined, the Mitigation Panel categorized these options. The best-practice (Category 1) options have significant potential for mitigating greenhouse warming at negative or low net implementation cost; however, information and incentive mechanisms are needed to hasten these reductions. Although no firm quantitative estimates of the net contribution of these policies can be given, it is not unreasonable to believe that U.S. greenhouse gas equivalent emissions could be reduced 25 percent from 1990 levels through use of these relatively low cost options alone. The second category of options (Category 2) entails additional costs and benefits not included in the cost-effectiveness estimate. The United States and other countries are already working to reduce CFC emissions—providing a major contribution to the reduction of greenhouse gas emissions at a relatively low cost (in addition to the benefits to the stratospheric ozone layer). Perhaps one of the surprises of this analysis is the relatively low cost at which some of geoengineering options (Category 3) might be implemented. However, it will require further inquiry to decide if geoengineering options can produce the targeted responses without unacceptable additional efforts. The level at which science is currently able to evaluate the cost-effectiveness of engineering the global mean radiation balance leaves great uncertainty in both the areas of technical feasibility and environmental consequences. This analysis does suggest that further inquiry is appropriate.

Finally, greenhouse warming is an international problem that the United States cannot solve alone. Slowing worldwide population growth may be necessary to achieve a significant change in worldwide emissions of greenhouse gases. However, the panel's analysis indicates that reducing population growth alone may not reduce emissions of greenhouse gases if there is continued economic growth. Reduction of deforestation may provide another significant contribution to mitigating greenhouse gas emissions. Due to domestic concerns, however, candidate countries may find these options difficult to implement. The United States can make contributions to international efforts, and such action might significantly slow greenhouse warming at a cost that is less expensive than the cost of options implemented in the United States.

The uncertainties in all of the mitigation alternatives underscore the central role of learning. This is *not* the usual academic call for more research. It is instead a recommendation that policy actions be treated as opportunities to learn and that they be designed and executed so that learning is enhanced. This implies the need for more and better policy analysis. The world being altered by greenhouse warming is one whose geophysical and social character is imperfectly understood. Errors are inevitable. Large errors will be costly and painful. Accordingly, the United States must seek to use small errors as a source of learning, so as to lessen the possibility of serious mistakes.

For example, the time dimension is an important part of formulating a greenhouse warming mitigation strategy. It can have important consequences for determining the optimal timing and quantity of any intervention. This is true if that decision is based on what society gets in the form of lesser global climate change vis-à-vis what it gives up in terms of current satisfaction and the enhanced ability to accommodate future adaptation. In this, fully accounting for all the positive aspects of mitigation—reduced speed of change, reduced total exposure to damage, and final level of global climate change—is important. Each has separate effects on the consequences of societal interest such as rise in sea level, agricultural productivity, and changes in ecological systems. They can also differ in their effects on the distribution of consequences over time and geography. Different instruments may lead to outcomes that diverge from those expected when only tons reduced and costs are considered. Application of the relationships discussed here requires an understanding of the physical relationships among flows, stock, and global climate change that lies beyond current knowledge. It also requires complex judgments about the trade-offs among sometimes competing policy goals.

Political processes will, in the end, determine whether and when these particular mitigation options should be undertaken. The results of this analysis indicate that the United States could make an important contribution to slowing greenhouse warming through adoption of some of these mitigation options. Some options might even provide a net savings to the U.S. economy. Using this analysis and information from the other two panels, the Synthesis Panel judges the extent to which these options should be pursued.

NOTE

1. Throughout this report, tons (t) are metric; 1 Mt = 1 megaton = 1 million tons; and 1 Gt = 1 gigaton = 1 billion tons.

REFERENCE

Intergovernmental Panel on Climate Change. 1991. Climate Change: The IPCC Response Strategies. Covelo, Calif.: Island Press.

Part Four

ADAPTATION

30

Findings

To provide the reader with an overview, this part of the report begins by stating its findings in a few pages. It next states the recommendations that arise from the findings. Then it discusses fully the issues, evidence, and reasoning about impact and adaptation that underlie those findings and recommendations.

CLIMATE CHANGE IS ONE OF MANY CHANGES

The effort and resources that we spend on understanding, predicting, adapting to, and mitigating climate change could be spent on other beneficial acts. Therefore, how much we spend on climate change depends on its projected importance ranked against other problems we face. The rank of climate change as a policy issue during the next century will be influenced by the speed and direction of climate change and the sensitivity of humanity and nature generally to them. Moreover, it is also influenced by the speed and direction of all the other changes, such as changes in population, land use, environment, wealth, and the susceptibilities of humanity and nature to climate and to all the other changes. How much of humanity's limited attention, talent, and money should we concentrate on climate change rather than epidemics and drugs, shelter and food, art and arms? Other things being equal, it is wise to invest more to deal with the changes with the highest rank, provided that those investments can significantly reduce the hazards and risks associated with the changes.

The speed of change of climate and its amount and characteristics are the subject of Part Two, but for estimating the rank of climate change these things must be multiplied by the chance that the changes will happen. Other things being equal, the uncertainty of scenarios reduces the rank of climate change as an issue.

The findings in Part Four about impacts of climate change generally agree with those of other U.S. and international investigations (Smith and Tirpak, 1989; United Nations Environment Programme and The Beijer Institute, 1989; Intergovernmental Panel on Climate Change, 1990). We, however, direct most of our attention to adaptations rather than to impacts.

Enormous uncertainties attend any analysis of climate change and adaptation to it. The present report is necessarily only a statement of present knowledge and is thus a beginning. One of its functions is encouraging further assessments, especially of the indirect costs of adaptation.

An activity that is affected by a change in the weather tomorrow could be insensitive to climate change if it were adaptable and its renewal were faster than the rate of climate change prolonged through decades. If we ignore adaptations, we imagine the climate near the middle of the next century imposed on the people of today, the way they live, and their current natural environment. So, adaptation can change the sensitivity to climate change as time passes and thereby change its rank as a policy issue. The reader will read below that human activities can change fairly rapidly and natural ecosystems more slowly, whereas evolutionary adaptation by genetic changes in populations of organisms is generally even slower.

HUMANITY AND NATURE HAVE
THE POTENTIAL TO ADAPT

Human adaptability is shown by people working in both Riyadh and Barrow and seeking out both Minneapolis and Galveston. Recent American migration has on average been toward warmth.

There are limits on the speed of human responses. These limits make not only the direction but also the rates of climate change crucial. People need time to adapt in situ to a new climate or to move to a region of preferred climate. If they move, they must find places where the other components of the environment, like soil and water, also fit them. Although time is taken to adapt managed things like farming, the historical evidence suggests that American farmers can keep up with gradual climate change of the magnitude the panel assumes.

The capacity of humans to adapt is evident in the rapid technological, economic, and political changes of the past 90 years. The average renewal period for machinery and equipment and the average age of buildings are one to three decades. So, through continuing normal investment, humanity's business activities have the potential to adapt during the next half century to the types of changes upon which our analysis is predicated.

Another factor that may limit adaptation is water. Some activities, like irrigation or cooling, use it in large quantities. Agriculture is highly dependent upon it. Transporting large quantities great distances is possible but expensive and illustrates the environmental costs that adaptations may exact. Therefore, changes in the amount and distribution of precipitation could have serious consequences for human activities in some regions.

Animals and plants live in the Himalayas and in Death Valley, in Manaus and Antarctica. Particular species, however, may not be able to adjust to climate changes rapidly enough to survive in a given location. Again, rate, as well as direction, of climate change is crucial. Under stress, natural systems of plants and animals tend to break up and reformulate in new systems with different species or mixes of species. Thus, the specific mix of plants and animals, that is, an ecosystem suited to a specific arrangement of earth and climate, may disappear from a place if climate changes. Assisting the movement of such ecosystems to suitable new locations may be hard or impossible. Although plants and animals will always be found regardless of climate changes, they may not be the same communities that were there before the changes took place, and some species may become extinct.

A final limit, and a common one, is money. Adaptations like furnaces and air conditioners, sea walls and canals, take money. Resources for such investment require continuing ability to generate wealth.

SOME INDICES MATTER MORE

Global averages are inappropriate as foundations for thinking about impact or adaptation. Because most adaptations are local, their cost cannot be estimated until such factors as water supply and temperature changes can be predicted in specific regions. An analysis of likely effects of climate change suggests several strategic indices about which detailed and extended information is important. The indices are rates and directions of change in:

• First, the flow of water in streams and its supply in soils of a region, including its variation from season to season and year to year. These are important because stream flow integrates many aspects of water availability, and soil moisture is the water actually available to plant roots.

• Second, changes in sea level and height of waves on a shore, because many people are on seashores.

• Third, any major shifts in ocean currents, because changes in those currents could have major climatic implications.

• Fourth, the timing of seasonal events like blooms and migrations, because such changes may signal adjustments in those systems of importance for their functioning.

• Fifth, untoward extremes of heat and cold, because extreme events may evoke the need for adaptation and set the limits on adaptation by people and other organisms.

Because weather is variable, long-term records will be needed to detect changes in climate. Nonetheless, monitoring the local climate, including the water in streams and seasonal events, is crucial over spans of decades and will eventually provide a basis for determining which adaptations are most needed.

SOME ACTIVITIES HAVE LOW SENSITIVITY

Just as an effective strategy requires ranking climate change with all the other changes ahead, it also demands ranking sensitivity and adaptability of human activity and nature into classes of sensitivity and adaptability to climate change alone. Attention can then be concentrated on sensitive areas. Table 30.1 summarizes the ranking the panel made.*

Fortunately, human activities that bulk very large in the national incomes of modern developed countries have low sensitivity to gradual climate change. In addition to having low sensitivity, such activities as industry and the provision of energy are adaptable because machinery and buildings are renewed faster than the projected climate change. So industry should have little trouble adapting.

The climatic changes upon which our analysis is based are within the range that people now experience where they live and to which those who

---

*Panel member Jane Lubchenco believes that "Table 30.1 and the related scheme used in this analysis, though useful as a preliminary organizing framework, are misleading because they imply that the activities and systems are independent and distinct from one another." She points out that "a comprehensive assessment of the feasibility and costs of adaptations must include the interactions and interdependencies among the various activities and systems. For example, the impacts of climate change on economic activities are considered separately, sector by sector (farming, industry, etc.). While this is perhaps understandable given the difficulty of analyzing the interactions, conclusions made without considering them may be faulty. Of particular concern are the indirect costs, such as the environmental costs of various adaptations, which for lack of time and information, the panel did not evaluate.

"The incorporation of environmental costs of adaptations is especially relevant in light of the suspected causes of greenhouse warming. Our current understanding of greenhouse warming supports the conclusion that the predicted climate changes are a result of unforeseen environmental consequences of 'adaptations' to the environment. Examples include the burning of fossil fuels to provide electricity or motive power, or the use of CFCs to cool buildings or automobiles. These are adaptations by one 'activity' (*sensu* Table 30.1) that have serious consequences to other activities or systems. A comprehensive evaluation of adaptation strategies will include a broader view than the system-by-system or activity-by-activity approach adopted in this report. Moreover, divorcing humans from their ecosystems ignores the intimate, if often complex and subtle, dependencies of humans on the natural environment.

"In addition, the observation that there are examples of particular system types currently located in substantially different climatic conditions says little about the ability of a system in a particular location to adjust to changing climate. This is especially relevant for natural ecosystems which, as the report points out, are unlikely to be able to adjust as rapidly as conditions change."

TABLE 30.1 Sensitivity and Adaptability of Human Activities and of Nature to Climate Change Alone (climate is assumed to change gradually by an amount of 1° to 5°C when the planet reaches equilibrium with an equivalent of doubled CO_2)

Subject	Class
Farming	Sensitive but can be adapted at a cost
Managed forests and grasslands	Sensitive but can be adapted at a cost
The natural landscape	Sensitive and adaptation is questionable
Marine ecosystems	Sensitive and adaptation is questionable
Water resources	Sensitive but can be adapted at a cost
Industry and energy	Low sensitivity
Tourism and recreation	Sensitive but can be adapted at a cost
Settlements and coastal structures	Sensitive but can be adapted at a cost
Health	Low sensitivity
Human migration	Sensitive but can be adapted at a cost
Domestic tranquility	Sensitive but can be adapted at a cost

NOTE: In the order of the outline of Chapter 34, the subjects are classified as: Low Sensitivity, Sensitive But Can Be Adapted at a Cost, and Sensitive and Adaptation is Questionable. Since sensitivity is the change in an activity per change in climate, the impact of sensitivity times climate change will be positive or negative according to the climate change. Adaptation modifies sensitivities as, for example, a lessening during the 20th century of the annual cycle of human mortality demonstrates. Given great wealth, a society might move some things from the third class of questionable adaptation to the middle class of sensitive but adaptable at a cost. Or, without the wealth for adaptation, a society would be unable to adapt to things in the second class. Natural and social surprises not analyzed would, of course, alter the classifications. Surprises, for example, could either remove migration and domestic tranquility from the list or overwhelm even costly attempts to adapt. For the climate changes assumed here and for the United States and similar nations, however, the classification is justified.

move usually learn to adapt. The pace of improvements in health from better technology and public measures can and likely will exceed any deterioration from climate change. Epidemics from causes already known, failure to control population growth, and chemical pollution are more serious threats to human health than climate change.

SOME ACTIVITIES ARE SENSITIVE BUT CAN BE ADAPTED AT A COST

As the most valuable outdoor activity, farming would add most to the impact, up or down, of climate change on national income. Experience shows that farming is continually adapted to cope with, even exploit, climate and its stresses and fickleness. Adaptations to climate change will be required in both rich and poor countries and to protect both crops and their foundation of soil and water. Since adaptation will be at a cost, poor nations may adapt painfully. Although less thoroughly managed than farming and while growing a crop with a long life, forestry can also be adapted.

Water supply is vital to all human activities and is sensitive to climate. Fortunately, although its adaptation can be costly in money or inconvenience, experience shows it is possible in many circumstances. Developing better management systems for dealing with present droughts and floods is a vital component of such adaptation.

Should climate warm, most cities will adapt rather than abandon their sites. Although the adaptation may be costly, the costs will be cheaper than moving the city. By far the biggest costs will be in coastal cities if the sea rises, whereas the direct costs from warming will be small. Because the infrastructure of cities is fairly long lived, some adaptations in advance will become profitable if the chance of climate change is high, the wait until the adaptation is needed is short, and the discount rate of money is low.

Since tourism and recreation exploit climatic differences from snow fields to desert oases and although local dislocations will occur, these activities seem adaptable to climate change at little net cost.

Where adaptation is the replacement of one region or activity by another, a small net cost for the nation may be comprised of counteracting winnings and losses. Some regions may win a new activity while it becomes untenable and is lost to another. Also, the same person may have winnings and losses, as by losing skiing and winning swimming or losing barley and gaining corn. Small net differences may result from substantial pluses and minuses.

SOME ACTIVITIES ARE SENSITIVE AND THEIR ADAPTATION OR ADJUSTMENT IS QUESTIONABLE

In the unmanaged systems of plants, animals, and microbes that are much of our landscape and oceans, however, the pace of change of some key processes may be as slow as or slower than climate change, making their future problematic. They have a slower response and hence greater sensitivity to climate change than the managed systems of crops on a farm or timber in a plantation.

Their slow response comes from the long lives of some of their components, like trees in the natural landscape that last longer than the ones planted for timber. It comes from the slow and chancy arrival of seed and birds traveling on the wind, in currents, or along corridors rather than in the trucks of farmers. It comes from plant succession on an acre of wild land or in an estuary taking decades or centuries, and it comes from evolution taking aeons. Climate change will not likely make land barren except at the arid extremes of existing climates. What *is* likely are changes in the composition of ecological communities in favor of those species able to move rapidly and far and the disappearance of some species that move slowly. The impacts of such changes on the functioning of ecological systems, and the consequent impacts on human society, cannot be predicted with confidence.

THE IMPACTS OF SOME CONCEIVABLE CLIMATE CHANGES ARE LARGE BUT CANNOT BE ASSESSED

Although we know of no way to compute the probability of cataclysmic changes on the planet, like the reversal of the ocean current that warms Europe, large changes of climate have happened. New diseases and prolonged wars have caused calamitous centuries. Desperate masses have fled drought in places with marginal farming and growing populations. These disasters were not necessarily related to greenhouse gases, but they could be exacerbated by rapid future climate changes. Clearly, trends of economic and social development have lessened the vulnerability of many societies to climate. At the same time, trends such as increasing populations in river flood plains and low coastal areas have increased the vulnerability of some regions and nations. So, even if the United States could, by and large, adapt to climate change, the misfortunes of others unable to do so could substantially affect the United States and other industrial countries.

Over the next 50 years some nations will probably reduce their vulnerability to climate change, but others may become more vulnerable. Although migration is possible and domestic tranquility can sometimes be maintained, major climate changes could overtax societal capabilities, especially of poor countries. The probability and nature of such unexpected changes are unknown. Therefore, we cannot predict their impacts or devise adaptations to them.

REFERENCES

Intergovernmental Panel on Climate Change. 1990. Climate Change: The IPCC Impacts Assessment, W. J. McG. Tegart, G. W. Sheldon, and D. C. Griffiths, eds. Canberra: Australian Government Publishing Service. Available, in the United States, from International Specialized Book Service, Portland, Oregon.

Smith, J. B., and D. A. Tirpak, eds. 1989. The Potential Effects of Global Climate Change on the United States. Washington, D.C.: U.S. Environmental Protection Agency.

United Nations Environment Programme and The Beijer Institute. 1989. The Full Range of Responses to Anticipated Climatic Change. Nairobi: United Nations Environmental Programme.

31

Recommendations

The recommendations about impacts and adaptations are grouped into three classes. The classes were defined by the panel, and in its judgment the recommendations within the three classes are justified by the assumptions, analyses, and findings stated throughout its report. The first class concerns information and analysis, getting the facts straight and sharing them with people who must decide how hard to try to stop the climate from changing and how to adapt. The second class refers to improving rules and building institutional strength. This is the organizational framework for action. The final class is specific actions requiring investment of hard cash now or soon in ways to reduce future harm and aid adaptation.

IMPROVE INFORMATION AND ANALYSIS

Assess Actual Climatic Impacts

Understanding the impacts of climate now and in the past is the bedrock on which analyses about the future must rest. Every year there are droughts, heat waves, severe storms, and all the other phenomena that are expected to change frequency or location in the future. Understanding how strongly our economy and environment are affected by climate now and how they are changing over time is necessary to help in making decisions about the scale and direction of investments.

Perform Research and Development on
Adaptation for Climate Change

The spectrum of effort from basic research to development needs to be directed at climatic sensitivities, impacts, and adaptation. Both studies of contemporary analogues of future climate changes and studies that are based on scenarios generated by numerical models can be useful. Studies are needed of such subjects as water and ecosystems, and they should be integrated to create a larger, coherent picture. Social, demographic, economic, and ecological data for both the United States and other countries need to be improved to aid impact assessments and adaptations.

Although estimates of impact and suggestions of adaptation abound, many suffer from four shortcomings. First, they may assess, say, the fall in yield of 1990 wheat caused by a 1°C warming in 2030, ignoring the proven adaptability of farmers, who will not behave in 2030 just as they do in 1990 if their environment has changed. Second, the studies may ignore technological changes, such as improved wheat strains. Third, the assessments are usually made without regard for the background of other changes that will affect impacts, for example, how markets for food products are changing and how production is shifting around the world from one region to another because of changes in comparative advantage. Fourth, suggestions of adaptations may fail to anticipate such side effects as salinity from irrigation.

Similar issues arise in impact studies of unmanaged ecosystems, which often study the response of a single species, neglecting the impact of other blows, such as chemical pollution, and amidst the competition and contributions of other species that grow with it. How will one species succeed another as the system adjusts at a place? How will a system of plants and animals migrate if climatic zones shift over half a century?

Many studies of adaptation must be conducted outdoors and in the current climate. The need for specialized research and development concerned with changing climate is moderated by the fact that the climates that may be experienced in 2030 are, for the most part, climates that are today being experienced somewhere, probably nearby. If the climate of Nebraska is going to become like that in Oklahoma today, experiments in Oklahoma fields now help later adaptation in Nebraska. Nevertheless, keeping in mind knowledge from simplified and controlled experiments and searching for global principles rather than catalogs of empiricisms, scientists must learn how disparate, entire systems of species live and reconstitute themselves outside as the environment, especially the concentration of CO_2, changes. Analysis must include so-called pests whose depredations depend on the quality of the host and environment and alter the outcome outdoors. For crop varieties a sound strategy continues to be maintaining diverse strains and adapting them to the weather of the current decade, because the climate of the next decade will not be vastly different, even if climate is changing over a century, and because the useful economic life of a cultivar is only about a decade. It will be useful to demonstrate in the reality of outdoors how to shorten long renewal times so that man-made things can be, and natural things will be, promptly adapted to climate.

Monitor the Climate and Forecast the Weather

Monitoring the current climate and disseminating information about it can aid adaptation. It is useful for people to know if climate is already changing and how. For adaptation, monitoring of the air, streams, and seasonal events in individual localities is what matters. In Chapter 35 we have identified indicators of particular use. Monitoring global and regional climate is also necessary to test predictions of future climate, as discussed by the Effects Panel (Part Two).

Weather forecasts aid adaptation. Improved forecasts on all time scales, from hours to weeks and seasons, help. If warned a few days ahead where and when a hurricane or frost will strike, people can retreat from the shore or buy fuel to warm an orchard. If people know a few weeks ahead whether the season will be dry, they can choose the appropriate crop or store water. Accurate forecasts make all climates safer and more productive.

Since the modern science of meteorology began a century ago, forecasting has gradually improved, and there are reasons to be confident that further improvements can be achieved. In the greenhouse issue, the United States and other nations should find strong, sustained motivation to improve forecasting and the data and research that make the forecasting possible. The quality of weather analyses and forecasts in many poor countries, especially in the tropics, is markedly lower than in industrial countries, particularly in the northern hemisphere. Advances in numerical modeling and extension of technology for monitoring in tropical regions can cause improvements.

IMPROVE INSTITUTIONS

Consider Efforts to Advance Regional Mobility of People, Capital, and Goods

Expanding the territory over which impacts are absorbed and adaptations can occur has historically been a major way to lessen the adverse consequences of climate and weather. For example, food shortage is a greater risk in societies that rely only on local supplies than in those that draw their food from wide areas. Countries vary greatly in their expanse and the range of climates that they encompass, and the ones that are diverse in climate and economic activity are more able to adapt to climate changes.

In general, the questions about opening borders to goods, capital, and people are highly political, raising issues far beyond concerns about future climate change. Nonetheless, we can remind ourselves that larger agglomerations are more robust and able to adapt to climate change than are smaller units. More open and freer trade in goods and capital by themselves will enhance the ability of countries to absorb climate shocks; in a regime of free trade, countries that lose comparative advantage in one climate-sensitive industry (e.g., timber produced in frosty climes) can move to other industries (e.g., fruits produced in warmer climes) and be ensured that markets will be available.

Although freer trade in goods has increased in the last half-century, nations have been increasingly reluctant to allow free migration of people. Countries with roughly the same living standards, however, may find it in their long-run economic interests to consider regional agreements for freer migration. The European Community constitutes an enormous climatic region and during this decade will move to a policy of free internal mobility of its laborers. In the years to come, the major challenge will be to deal with the flows of refugees, and if climate change becomes swift, nations may need to consider how to cope with large numbers of environmental refugees.

Build Effective Government

All adaptive strategies will benefit from administrative capability. In a country like the United States, the establishment and strengthening of agencies like the National Oceanic and Atmospheric Administration, the U.S. Army Corps of Engineers, the Department of Agriculture, the Forest Service, and the Federal Emergency Management Agency have been integral aspects of adaptation to climate. In a rapidly changing climate in the United States, their missions would become even more important. Making such agencies as effective and informed as possible will facilitate adaptation.

While some governments have developed the institutional means to adapt to harvest failures and floods, the governments of countries that are most vulnerable to climate change should take steps now to enhance the capacity of relevant organizations.

Effective government will be useful in the face of climate change not only at the national level but at the local and at the intergovernmental levels as well. Well-administered agencies at the international level in disaster and famine relief, as well as in meteorology and environmental protection, will facilitate adaptation. Thus, we recommend continuing and increasing U.S. support for the World Meteorological Organization, the World Climate Program, the United Nations Environment Program, and other relevant organizations.

Promote Markets

In societies like the United States, most adaptation to changing climate takes place through decentralized individual reactions to social, economic, and political signals. When a war reduces the availability of oil, requiring a reduction in oil consumption, society adjusts primarily as individuals reduce their consumption in the face of higher prices and lower incomes. When changing climate or shifting patterns of comparative advantage shift the relative productivity of different regions, individuals adapt—changing cultivars, occupations, or even residences—primarily in response to signals of prices and incomes. However, where market signals are impeded (such as with price controls or in nonmarket economies), adaptation to changing environments is slowed.

In general, adaptation will be speeded if market signals, primarily prices, reflect changing conditions quickly. Where feasible, governments should work to improve markets, particularly where price signals are missing or misleading.

Outside the United States, particularly in nonmarket economies, the opportunity for market mechanisms to signal climate change is large. Many countries insulate their farm prices from world prices, slowing adjustment and increasing waste.

For the United States, particular concerns are water systems, risk, and environmental externalities. Here and in many other nations, water is allocated largely by water rights. By encouraging water auctions or market-based transfers, while remembering the public and environmental good, governments can prepare to adjust to new climates and water resources. Water markets can allow water to be used where it is most valuable. Also, if runoff changes, the market signals will evoke an efficient adaptation of its use.

Other concerns are risk and environmental externalities. Today, some insurance premiums do not reflect climate risks in areas subject to natural disasters. If premiums did, decisions about where to locate and what to build might be more logical. In addition, improved pricing of environmental externalities could help businesses decide better about adapting to climate change.

IMPROVE INVESTMENTS

Adaptations can be made in anticipation of climate change, simultaneously with it or after it. In these recommendations, we emphasize anticipatory adaptation, since, for the most part, impacts lie some decades in the future. Deciding whether to adapt now or to wait will depend on such factors as the length of time until an adaptation is needed, the probability that it will be needed, the discount rate, and the cost of the adaptation now relative to later.

For example, anticipatory adaptation would be justified in a situation where the effects of climate change would be produced within 50 years, the probability of climate change was at least 0.4, the uninflated discount rate was no more than 3 percent per year, and the cost of future adaptation (retrofit) was at least 10 times the cost of acting now. Possible worthwhile investments in anticipation of climate change are discussed below.

Preserve Biological Diversity

Biological diversity is a natural protection against surprises and shocks, climatic and otherwise. Among diverse species will be some adapted to prosper in a new landscape in new circumstances. In diverse species can be found genes to make crops prosper. So for security, preserving and encouraging biological diversity is recommended. This preservation should include varieties of commercial crops, wild relatives of these crops, and other species that so far lack values in current markets.

The unmanaged systems of plants and animals that are much of our landscape and oceans have a problematic future because of many man-made hazards. The anguish about these hazards arises in part from fears about risky consequences of the transformations and in part from doubting the righteousness of our dominion over living things and the goodness of our stewardship.

To date, most conservation efforts have assumed constant climates. If climate changes, existing reserves may become unsuitable for species currently living there, and landscape fragmentation may make migration more difficult. Therefore, conservation efforts need to give more attention to corridors for movement, to assisting species to surmount barriers, and to maintaining species when their natural environments are threatened. Expenditures for reserving land are an example of an investment that is likely to have a lower cost now than in the future and that keeps options open. At present, the potential for human intervention to ease adaptation in marine ecosystems seems limited.

Cope with Present Variability

Today droughts and floods, cold snaps and heat waves, all take tolls. Whereas justifying costly adaptations now for specified future climates is hard because the climate may never come while we pay interest for decades, the current fickleness of weather is sure and now. We thus recommend investments now to adapt to climate variability through such acts as improved insulation, better disaster management, and control of low coastal areas. Water supply is already sensitive to the variability of today's climate. Diversifying water supply over sources like streams and aquifers, over space and political boundaries by connections, and through time by storage and conservation increases reliability during changing climate.

Remember Long-Lived Facilities and Preservation of Heritage

When long-lived facilities are being planned or infrastructure is being renovated or replaced, investment in anticipatory adaptation is most likely to be justified. The method presented in Chapter 33, the section "Making Decisions in an Uncertain World," illustrates the thinking needed for decisions about incorporating the possibility of climatic change into design. Such methods need to be elaborated.

It is not only functional facilities such as airports and water supply systems that may warrant modification or protection for the contingency of climate change. Every culture treasures buildings, neighborhoods, monuments, and other features of its heritage that may be affected by changing climate or rising seas. These structures in some cases have survived hundreds or thousands of years. Climate change joins a long list of threats to conservation of our physical and cultural heritage. Studies need to be undertaken in this area. It can be expected that investments will be justified to assure the longevity of our cultural heritage in the face of climate change.

Help Others

People in industrial countries with diversified economies are best equipped to cope with the vagaries of climate change. By developing the necessary technology, they have found how to survive and flourish in almost all climates. By contrast, people in poor and small countries often have difficulty in adapting to even minor environmental hazards. Their primary need is for the development of strong and diverse economies when this can be done. But this cannot be achieved quickly. As we share a global interest in adaptation to climate change, we need to help others by finding means and setting conditions in which to transfer resources, knowledge, and technology and to ensure that the recipients can make good use of them.

32

Issues, Assumptions, and Values

Three questions frame the study of climate change: Is it happening? Can we stop it? How can we cope with it? Asking the third question may seem pessimistic. Nevertheless, if during the past two centuries mankind has committed the planet to a new climate, it must be answered. On the other hand, if the planet is not yet committed, balancing the cost of stopping climate change against its result still calls for an answer. And, if humanity is not changing the climate, we need to know how to cope with natural variations in weather and climate. So, against a background of present climatic differences from place to place and changing weather from day to day, the Adaptation Panel here tries to answer for Congress the final "How can humanity cope with climate change?"

DEFINITIONS

Simply put, climate is the average state of the weather. At a deeper level, the climate of a locality is the synthesis of the day-to-day values of the meteorological elements that affect the locality. Synthesis implies more than simple averaging. Various methods represent climate, for example, both average and extreme values, frequencies of values within ranges, and frequencies of weather types. The main climatic elements are precipitation, temperature, humidity, sunshine, wind, and such phenomena as fog and frost. Climatic data are usually stated in terms of an individual month or season (McIntosh, 1972).

The critical matter is that climate is the accustomed seasons, daily cycles, variations, and ties among the factors of weather at a given place. The question is whether the nature and civilization that have evolved in the climate of a place will be greatly affected by or can easily adapt to the future climate. Nature, here, means the natural or unmanaged living things outdoors. Humanity, of course, is part of nature, but we use the word nature to mean the unmanaged environment. In the past the study of the outcome of climate change for nature and humanity dealt largely with the impacts, or blows, themselves. Studies have dealt, for example, with the changes a new climate would cause in the plants of an ecosystem, the yield of a crop, or the safety of a seawall, assuming little or no adaptation. Here the panel integrates projections of impacts into its discussion of how to cope (see Chapter 34).

The most severe challenge in weighing impacts, however, is to compound the outcome of a changing climate with other changes that will occur during the coming decades. These changes range from technological innovations to social changes and from increased numbers of humans to ecological impacts. We can grasp the possible magnitude of some of the kinds of changes that might happen at the same time as a climate change by looking back eight decades. In 1910 the Ottoman, Austro-Hungarian, British, and Russian empires ruled much of the world. In America there were no income taxes, women could not vote, each person commanded 1.5 horsepower, and the major polluters were the 21 million horses (Nordhaus, 1990).

Although the crystal ball for seeing future life and technology is cloudy, the magnitude of the changes of the past 80 years teaches us that we must go beyond computation of the effect of warming of 1° to 5°C on, say, today's corn or coast. We must try to foresee the adjustments in nature and human behavior that will occur in response to changing environmental conditions amidst an army of technological, social, and economic changes. If we ignore these adjustments, which are here termed adaptations, we will write a "dumb people scenario." Imposing the climate near the middle of the next century on the activities of 1990 implicitly assumes that people will dumbly ignore any new environment and circumstances for 80 years and behave as they do today.

Three classes of adaptation by humans can be distinguished (Coppock, 1990). The first might be called adjustments. These are prompt, individual, uncoordinated, and largely spontaneous, such as the changes a farmer makes in crop varieties after a couple of cold years. A second class, which might be called premeditated adaptation, begins with anticipation and information and requires planning, coordinated action, and time. This class is typified by the building of a dam for irrigation. A third class might be called interventions. These actions, typically by governments, manipulate the circumstances of choices and are exemplified by the zoning of wetlands. Here, the word adaptation encompasses all these.

An illustration of a dumb scenario is a vision of the corn varieties and husbandry of 1990 in a changed climate in 2030 and then calculation of the impact of climate change as a change from the 1990 yields. A smarter scenario is a vision of a crop changing for four decades in the future by methods and along a trend somewhat as in the past. Yields, too, would follow a trend, which would be a baseline or reference. With no adaptation to climate, future yields would deviate from that baseline, up if the climate change were favorable and down if it were harmful. Adaptation would change the yields, and, if the climate change were harmful, the adapted yields would lie between the rising baseline of no climate change and the trend of yields not adapted to the changing climate. In the smarter scenario, the impact of climate change would be the net sum in 2030 of the costs of adaptation and the difference between the baseline of yield in an unchanged climate and the yield of the adapted crop in the changed climate.

Ask a farmer who is 70 or 80 years old what is different now compared to when he was a child. He would likely find changing from horses to tractors, from dirt to paved roads and from open pollinated corn to hybrid corn plus the arrival of soybeans and pesticides swamped the assumed climatic warming of a half to whole degree during the 20th century.

Similar illustrations could be drawn from other activities. Figure 4.1 of Part One shows the general case.

Estimating cannot be precise, but the panel realizes or foresees the following:

• The impacts of climate change must be sorted out from other effects caused by simultaneous changes in other factors.

• The baseline or reference of what would happen without climate change will trend up or down.

• The impact of climate change is the net of the cost of adaptation plus or minus the residual change from the baseline that occurs despite adaptation.

• The net impact of climate change can be negative, or, if the residual change is a help greater than the cost of adaptation, the net can be positive.

ASSUMPTIONS

Studies of the impacts of climate change commonly begin with a climate scenario. Will it be 1°C or 5°C warmer? Will 10 percent more or less rain fall? And so forth. But these specifications are shaky at best and only compound the uncertainty already inherent in the complex response to climate.

To some extent, however, the studies of outcome can be independent of the climate scenarios. An activity like farming or forestry will be different in the future than it is today. If climate changes, part of that difference will be the impact of climate change. If the sensitivity to climate of the activity is constant, the impact is simply the climate change times the sensitivity. In that case a student of outcomes can estimate the sensitivity and then leave it to others to calculate the impact of climate change by multiplying the constant sensitivity by any scenario proposed.

More formally, let the rate of change of activity A be dA/dt. Then let the rate of change dA/dt of A equal the sum of products of sensitivities to factors times the rates of change of the factors. Since our subject is climate, the first product is the sensitivity $\delta A/\delta$(climate) of A to climate times the rate of change d(climate)$/dt$. Bringing together all the other factors that affect A, we let the second and remaining product be the sensitivity $\delta A/\delta$(other factors) of A to other things times the rate of change d(other factors)$/dt$. The relative importance of climate change to A depends on its sensitivity to both climate and other factors and on the rates of change of both climate and other factors. Finally, if the sensitivity to climate is unchanged by, say, adaptation or climate, the impact of climate change is simply the constant sensitivity $\delta A/\delta$(climate) times the change in climate, which is the integral of d(climate)$/dt$. In this last case, studies of sensitivity can be separated from scenarios.

Still, there is a limit to the separation of studies of sensitivity from assumptions of climate change. The sensitivity, $\delta A/\delta$(climate), depends on the value of climate. For example, the sensitivity of a tomato per degree is different from 5° to 15°C than at the threshold of 0°C, where it freezes. The sensitivity of a marsh to a sea rising 1 m is not likely to be just 10 times its sensitivity to a rise of 10 cm. The sensitivity of a 1-m wall to 50- and 150-cm rises in sea level is utterly different.

So the panel did not have to assume a precise climate scenario, but it did have to assume the sort and order of climate change. The scenarios that are supportable, the forecasts of climate change, and the warnings about the uncertainties of the forecasts were provided by the Effects Panel. Briefly, they are, in the absence of human efforts to mitigate emissions:

- Greenhouse gases will reach the equivalent of 600 ppm CO_2 near the middle of the 21st century.

- Mathematical models project that this increase of greenhouse gases will warm the planet 1° to 5°C, on average, over the temperature of about 1990. This warming would be achieved if the planet comes to equilibrium with the 600 ppm.

- The warming actually realized during the past century appears to be 0.3° to 0.6°C. Simple logic suggests that lag will make the realized warming by the middle of the 21st century less than the warming at equilibrium with the 600 ppm.

- The projections are plagued by uncertainties about the accumulation of the gases and their absorption and the roles of oceans, clouds, and other environmental elements.

- Projections about the climate of a locality are doubly uncertain. Precipitation may be tens of percent more or less than now.

• A rise in sea level may accompany global warming, possibly in the
range of 0 to 60 cm for the timing and temperature range listed above.
These assumptions about the physical environment are consistent with those
made by others (National Research Council, 1983; Smith and Tirpak, 1989;
Schneider et al., 1990).

The assumed increase of greenhouse gases to 600 ppm near the middle of
the 21st century implicitly assumes that population and economic activity
will increase. The growth of material well-being is relevant, as it partly
determines what adaptations are affordable. In its studies of policy responses, the Environmental Protection Agency (EPA) assumed a world growth
rate of less than 1 percent per year for their slowly changing (low-emission)
world scenario and over 2 percent per year for their rapidly changing (high-
emission) world scenario (Lashof and Tirpak, 1991). The Intergovernmental Panel on Climate Change (IPCC) assumed that annual economic growth
would be 2 to 3 percent in Organization for Economic Cooperation and
Development (OECD) countries and 3 to 5 percent in Eastern Europe and
developing countries during the coming decade and slower thereafter
(Intergovernmental Panel on Climate Change, 1990). The Adaptation Panel
assumed a positive growth of material well-being without specifying it precisely. To assess costs of impacts and adaptations, a further financial assumption on discount rates is required. The Adaptation Panel used discount
rates of 3, 6, and 10 percent in its analysis.[1]

To gauge impacts and foresee adaptations, however, the panel also needed
to go beyond a generality like "1° to 5°C warmer on average" to consider
how the climate affecting a community might be transformed year by year.
Alternatives are depicted in Figure 32.1. The top panel shows a frequency
distribution and no trend for a climate steady in its average and variability.
The second panel shows one sort of change: The frequency distribution is
unchanged in its shape and spread but shifted left because the average falls.
The fall could be either steady or sudden. The third panel shows another
sort of change: The average is unchanged, but the variability is increasing.
It could, of course, have been drawn with decreasing variability. The final
panel shows both the average falling and the variability increasing.

The effects associated with a global cooling of roughly 5°C during the
last ice age 18,000 years ago are known, and a repetition would crush the
upper midwestern United States under ice. No similarly dire outcome has
been found associated with a 5°C warming. None of the projected effects
of the warming would make large areas uninhabitable. So while we com-
plain about the uncertainty of warming by greenhouse gases, we should not
forget that it would make any effects from cooling, which was a subject of
some scientific, public, and congressional concern in the early 1970s, less
likely.

Because computing the average temperature is hard enough, scenarios

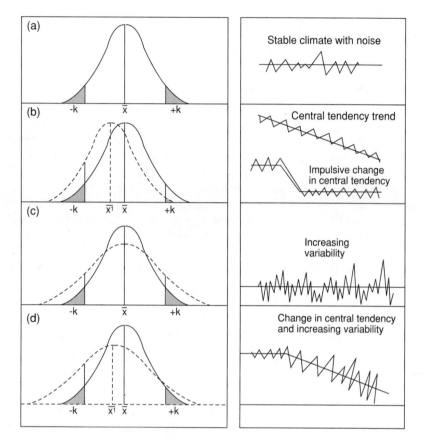

FIGURE 32.1 Several ways climate could change, as illustrated by courses of temperature.

SOURCE: Adapted from Riebsame (1988).

usually give only the average that would be reached at equilibrium for an equivalent CO_2 doubling. Nevertheless, some recent efforts to compute the variability in the new climate foresee a shift in the average temperature without a change in variability (Mearns et al., 1989, 1990; Rind et al., 1989; Smith and Tirpak, 1989). A projection of no great change in variability is not inconsistent with the statement by IPCC Working Group I that neither more nor fewer storms could be predicted for the future climate (Intergovernmental Panel on Climate Change, 1990).

Turning from temperature to precipitation, one encounters fully the need for regional and seasonal predictions of the frequencies of drought and flood. Yet predicting even the change in averages is beyond present skill.

A comparison among the frequency distributions of precipitation today, however, hints at how their interannual variability would usually change if the average changed. If the average falls, the absolute interannual variability, measured by the variance, would fall. The relative variability, measured by the ratio of the standard deviation to the average, however, would increase. Skewness would also increase.[2] Since precipitation cannot be less than zero, future changes in its frequency distributions will generally resemble these differences among its present ones.

A final question concerns the path from the present to future climate. The panel concentrated on a gradual change like the upper trend in the second panel of Figure 32.1. As drawn, the trend might represent a change to less precipitation. If the trend were drawn up, it might represent a change to warmer temperatures. Annual variations around the trend will, of course, continue, and sometimes several years that are above or below the trend will mislead people. A gradual change is not a surprising effect of the gradual increase in greenhouse gases that forces the change, and a gradual change is generally consistent with the computations of models. The panel recognizes that the passage of some threshold or shifting ocean current might cause an abrupt, harmful change. We were unable to evaluate the likelihood of these events, and, while recognizing their potential for significant impacts, we have not analyzed their impacts or adaptations to them. The ability to adapt to every extreme outcome of climate change is, of course, in doubt. This report concentrates on the range of the changes that might occur within the next half century or so and that are stated in the assumptions above. Within that range, moderate changes seem more likely than radical ones. The IPCC stated that business as usual would likely raise the global mean temperature above the present one by about 1°C by 2025 and 3°C before the end of the next century (Intergovernmental Panel on Climate Change, 1990). Furthermore, examining the consequences of, say, a warming of 1°C makes sense even if the eventual warming is greater because the planet would first warm 1°C before warming more. The effects of abrupt and radical changes might well be examined in the future if the physical logic for them becomes convincing. For now, however, the panel concentrated on moderate changes.

In the end the panel considered the sensitivities and adaptations to a gradual change in averages without a great change in variability to climates warmer by a few degrees, where precipitation is tens of percent more or less than at present and the sea is 20 to 30 cm higher by the middle of the next century.

ECONOMIC AND ETHICAL VALUES

In much of the world, certainly in the United States, suppliers signal their willingness by prices and then buyers vote their wishes in markets.

Fundamentally, the economic view is centered on humanity. The activities that are worthwhile in this view are valued by people and expressed in market and political decisions. The economic view is not that nature is without value but that nature's value derives from human values about nature. If people do not care about the landscape, whales, and snails, as shown by their dollars and votes, these things will have no economic worth. On the other hand, in a society that loves the environment, high values and high prices would be placed on parks, wetlands, and open spaces, and these values would carry over to private transactions and legislative mandates.

In a preliminary economic analysis of the impact of climate change, the 1981 national income of $2.4 trillion was divided into 16 sectors. Their sensitivity ranged from the potentially severe impact on farms and forests to the negligible impact on mining and manufacturing. The calculated direct impact of climate change on the national income would be about 1 percent (Nordhaus, 1991). The estimate is only 1 percent because, among other things, the impact on sensitive agriculture may be positive or negative and the impact on the valuable manufacturing and service sectors is negligible. Although the absolute number of dollars may be large, the relative amount of 1 percent is a discouragement for large investments in climate change.

Although the national income accounts capture only the value of marketed goods and services, it is possible to incorporate goods like environmental quality that are not marketed or priced accurately, if at all (Coomber and Biswas, 1973). These environmental intangibles are generally outdoors and so exposed to climate. The incorporation of these nonmarket goods and services might increase the sensitivity of the economy to climate change.

Beyond intangibles that can be assigned a price are ethical values. An appraiser might devise a formula, for example, to give a price for a shade tree, adding it to the value of a home. Beyond that appraisal, however, lies the ethical question of whether it should be cut down, especially if birds are nesting in it.

> If our present evolutionary impetus is an upward one, it is ecologically probable that ethics will eventually be extended to land. The present conservation movement may constitute the beginnings of such an extension. If and when it takes place, it may radically modify what now appear as insuperable economic obstacles to better land use (Leopold, 1933).

All these ways (i.e., economics of marketed goods and services, economics of nonmarket goods and services, and ethical arguments) of measuring human well-being and the quality of our stewardship of the planet need to be taken into account in assessing the seriousness of the impacts of climate change and the potential and appropriateness of adaptations. Taking them into account, of course, requires judgment as well as evidence and computation, and the panel has tried to take these into account fairly in judging findings and eventually recommendations.

NOTES

1. As the exercise in Chapter 33, the section "Making Decisions in an Uncertain World," demonstrates, the assumption of a discount rate is important for adaptation. Rates are crucial for weighing mitigations, which are anticipatory, and rates are discussed at length in Part Three: Mitigation. The rates of 3, 6, and 10 percent are also found in Part One: Synthesis. For growth of incomes see Table 34.1.

2. Among 660 cases of 12 monthly distributions of precipitation at 55 stations, the variance increased as the 1.3 power of the mean. This specifies that both the coefficient of variation and the skewness of the frequency distribution vary as the –0.35 power of the mean (Waggoner, 1989).

REFERENCES

Coomber, N. H., and A. K. Biswas. 1973. Evaluation of Environmental Intangibles. Bronxville, N.Y.: Genera Press.

Coppock, R. 1990. Definitions. Staff paper prepared for the Adaptation Panel of the Panel on Policy Implications of Greenhouse Warming, April 11, 1990.

Intergovernmental Panel on Climate Change. 1990. Climate Change: The IPCC Scientific Assessment, J. T. Houghton, G. J. Jenkins, and J. J. Ephraums, eds. New York: Cambridge University Press.

Lashof, D. A., and D. A. Tirpak. 1991. Policy Options for Stabilizing Global Climate. Washington, D.C.: U.S. Environmental Protection Agency.

Leopold, A. 1933. The conservation ethic. Journal of Forestry 31:634-643.

McIntosh, D. H. 1972. Meteorological Glossary. New York: Chemical Publishing Company.

Mearns, L. O., S. H. Schneider, S. L. Thompson, and L. R. McDaniel. 1989. Analysis of climate variability in general circulation models: Comparison with observations and changes in variability in $2 \times CO_2$ experiments. In The Potential Effects of Global Climate Change on the United States, Appendix I, J. B. Smith and D. A. Tirpak, eds. Washington, D.C.: U.S. Environmental Protection Agency.

Mearns, L. O., P. H. Gleick, and S. H. Schneider. 1990. Climate forecasting. In Climate Change and U.S. Water Resources, P. E. Waggoner, ed. New York: John Wiley & Sons.

National Research Council. 1983. Changing Climate. Washington, D.C.: National Academy Press.

Nordhaus, W. D. 1990. Adaptation: The role of government. Working paper prepared for the Adaptation Panel of the Panel on Policy Implications of Greenhouse Warming, February 12, 1990.

Nordhaus, W. D. 1991. To slow or not to slow: The economics of the greenhouse effect. Economic Journal 101(407):920-937.

Riebsame, W. E. 1988. Assessing the Social Implications of Climate Fluctuations: A Guide to Impact Studies. Nairobi: United Nations Environment Programme.

Rind, D., R. Goldberg, and R. Ruedy. 1989. Change in climate variability in the 21st century. Climatic Change 14:5-38.

Schneider, S. H., P. H. Gleick, and L. O. Mearns. 1990. Prospects for climate change. In Climate Change and U.S. Water Resources, P. E. Waggoner, ed. New York: John Wiley & Sons.

Smith, J. B., and D. A. Tirpak, eds. 1989. The Potential Effects of Global Climate Change on the United States. Washington, D.C.: U.S. Environmental Protection Agency.

Waggoner, P. E. 1989. Anticipating the frequency distribution of precipitation if climate change alters its mean. Agricultural and Forest Meteorology 47:321-337.

33

Methods and Tools

METHODS OF ADAPTATION

Although one cannot be sure how nature and humanity would cope with a new climate, past hazards of weather and changes of climate and the seasons and climates on the planet today give hints of impacts and adaptations.

Adjustment by Nature

Nature on a given tract of land is a system, or ecosystem, of plants, animals, and microbes. If circumstances do not change in a very old forest, for example, the system may cycle with little change in composition in the manner shown by the circle on the left of Figure 33.1. If circumstances change, however, the system adjusts to an alternate composition through a succession as some species grow less numerous while others flourish because they are better suited to the new circumstances. Because flowering, fruiting, and germinating of seed are sensitive to climate, the first adjustment in a system in response to changing climate would probably be failure of some present species to reproduce. This would be followed by the chancy stage of invasion of new species from outside or expansion of species already on the tract but formerly held in check. An opening, the presence of a seed, and the arrival of a seed are all random events in nature. This stage is depicted on the right of Figure 33.1.

Fossils show that, during a climate change, trees lag in adjustment behind other organisms, because either the dispersal of seeds or the development of soils is slow. Disturbances like fires have accompanied past changes in climate and speeded up the adjustments in vegetation. Trees might persist despite a rapid warming or cooling but then be disturbed by a fire,

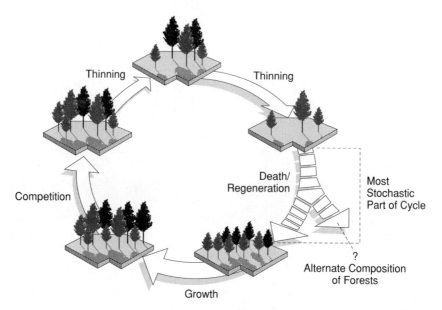

FIGURE 33.1   Growth, thinning by competition, and death of a tract of forest is a cycle.

NOTE: The stage of Death/Regeneration is the "most stochastic" or most uncertain stage. It could lead to "alternate composition" of the forest, that is, a succeeding and different species mix.

SOURCE: Reprinted, by permission, from Shugart et al. (1986). Copyright © 1986 by SCOPE.

storm, or pest. With the death of the persistent trees, the forest would then adjust more rapidly.

Other forces will likely affect the natural system on the tract and its adjustment to climate. People may clear, plant, manage, or abandon the tract; storms could uproot the trees; or fires might blacken the landscape. Their impacts may obscure or modify those of climate change. Or, as explained above, they may hasten the adjustment of the forest to the new climate.

An alternative to thinking of the adjustments on a given tract of land is thinking of the migration of an ecosystem or community from tract to tract in response to climate changes.

Communities are composed of species populations . . . connected by a web of interspecific relationships that have evolved over thousands or millions of years. If entire communities or all the species except for a few minor ones migrate, these community interactions may be preserved. In the highly disturbed and man-influenced global ecosystem, however, it is doubtful that intact *ecosystems* can survive by migration. (Strain and Bazzaz, 1983)

Still another way of thinking of changes in organisms is to think of an individual species. Within a species, under a changed climate, natural selection would favor the combination of genes that was best suited to the new climate and would tend to eliminate other combinations. If no individuals within the species could compete successfully in the changed climate or were not present or could not reach a favorable climate elsewhere, the species could be extinguished.

Instead, if climate changes rapidly, new communities or ecosystems dominated by pioneer rather than climax species are likely to emerge on the margins of zones and populations. There, long-lived things like trees would persist, but if they were ill adapted would fail to reproduce. New kinds of life fitted to the new climate would grow up through the persisting individuals, sometimes hastened by a disturbance. Adapted species already present in a mixture or pioneers from afar could have an advantage in the new climate.

Adaptation by Humanity

The range of climates where people live successfully indicates that societies can cope with wide variations in climate. The main way that people adapt to *changing* climate is by adapting to variability in climate. This is especially true when people are regularly adapting to changes in farming, forestry, construction, and all the other changes that require one to discard old and take up new ways of doing things. Disasters caused by severe weather and degradation of the environment do, nevertheless, illustrate the kinds of large disruptions that could accompany change and adaptation. What lessons can we learn from the adaptations people have made?

The first lesson arises from a survey of the types of responses to hazardous events made in dozens of cases. Although rapid and continuous climate change might eventually outstrip the efficacy of these adjustments that worked for extremes in the past climates, they nevertheless provide a menu of five potential choices: (1) modify the hazard, as by seeding clouds; (2) prevent or limit impacts, as by dikes; (3) move or avoid the loss, as by flood plain zoning; (4) share the loss, as by insurance; and (5) bear the loss, as by rebuilding a house (White, 1974; Burton et al., 1978).

Additional factors affecting this simple menu are whether the adjustment is made before or after an event and whether the adjustment is understood, practical, and affordable. Another factor is the possibility that a climate change might be helpful rather than hazardous. Figure 33.2 separates the adjustments into purposeful and incidental kinds and shows whether they precede or follow an event.

By adjusting to extremes of the current climate, society has already made

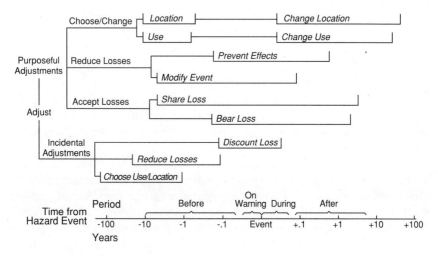

FIGURE 33.2 A choice tree.

NOTE: Adjustment begins with an initial choice of a resource use, livelihood system, and location. For that choice various incidental and purposeful adjustments are available, at somewhat different time scales for initiation. The most radical choice is to change the original use or location.

SOURCE: Reprinted, by permission, from Burton et al. (1978). Copyright © 1978 by Oxford University Press.

investments that would absorb some climate change. The United States has invested $70 billion to $80 billion in local and regional controls for water from storms and floods. Much is invested in heating and air conditioning, coastal protection, and irrigation.

Even in exposed activities like managing water and farming, the capacity to adapt can be high, although the cost may also be high. Past responses are analogs that illuminate how well society might deal with future climate change (Glantz, 1988). One such example was supplied by Indonesia, which set the goal of improving rice growing to make the country self-sufficient during the 1980s. In 1982-1983 a severe drought cut the yield 10 percent or more in some areas, slowing the attainment of self-sufficiency. Farmers, however, planted more off-season crops and increased the yield of second-crop rice through careful cultivation and management of water. So despite the drought, rice production was resilient, production in no province returned to the low levels before 1980, and within 2 years the trend toward self-sufficiency was restored (Malingreau, 1987). While the Indonesian farmers adapted to a drier situation that proved temporary, this example shows the character of adaptation. Moreover, in a world of rapidly and continually changing climate, many adaptations will necessarily have a temporary orientation.

In the United States, water managers have sometimes decreased the annual fluctuations in supply without large construction projects. In California, managers worked with users to reduce peak demand and accommodated annual differences in supply. They explicitly recognized climate instability and built adjustments to extremes of wet and dry into reservoir operations. The new procedures smoothed out the feast and famine caused by the old procedure. In Arizona, a quick and effective adaptation to a series of wet years occurred during the early 1980s (Phillips and Jordon, 1986; Riebsame, 1988).

Adaptation is part of the interaction between society and its environment. Prompt and effective adaptation in that interacting system requires information. It requires that messages be sent and, a rarer thing, that messages be perceived. The clearest lesson from the study of natural hazards is that the key obstacles are not technical but rather involve economics, information, and perception of the threat (Mitchell, 1984).

Messages about a slow change in climate could be misread in two ways, underreading and overreading. Years of experience slant our expectation of the climate of the next decade toward the past one, which is underreading if climate is changing. For example, managers of water systems reported they would keep designing for the climate of the past until they saw a change or heard from a consensus of distinguished authorities that it was changing (Morrisette, 1988; Schwarz and Dillard, 1990), and other professions have a similar expectation of stable climate (Holling, 1986).

If climate is not changing, overreading could be caused by occasional extremes, even though they are only manifesting the variability of the past. In the mid-nineteenth century the myth spread that the climate of the Great Plains was permanently changed for the better and that human settlement itself would improve it further. After farmers flooded into the largely uncultivated margins of the frontier, the forgotten variability of the weather brought drought, and the drought displaced nearly 300,000 Great Plains farmers back to the East and out to the West Coast (Warrick and Bowden, 1981). The hot summer of 1988 cannot be proven to be part of climate change, but many saw it that way, illustrating the potential influence of extreme events on debates over the reality and significance of climate change.

Environmental problems that elicit action are generally those that are serious, soon, certain, and soluble. The last point is key, since experience with the mitigation of natural and technological hazards has shown that people respond less effectively when information about the problem stresses its causes and nature rather than possible solutions. Information about climate must be connected to the experiences of real people and to specific and feasible adjustments or it will be ignored. Because climate change is neither certain nor soon and not easily soluble by a few people, remedies for related, more certain problems like drought should be stressed and linked to climate change where feasible. Examples are suggested below (White, 1988; Ingram et al., 1990; Riebsame, 1990).

Since people feel the events of the moment or year, not the trend line, they will be affected by and adapt to the size or frequency of extremes. We react more strongly to worsened storm surges than to a gradual rise of the sea, more to droughts than to lower average precipitation, and more to heat waves than to gradual warming.

In the United States the history of responses to natural hazards is one of major events calling forth rushes of legislation (May, 1985; National Research Council, 1987). Some of these events have evoked investments that greatly increase our adaptability to climate change. Other investments may delay lasting adaptation, like disaster aid that encourages reconstruction on a flood plain, or the response of the markets and the government to the summer of 1988 that encouraged the expansion of dryland farming in North Dakota (White, 1975; Riebsame et al., 1991), or the planting of citrus trees in freeze-prone sections of Florida (Miller and Glantz, 1988).

Yet another lesson is that the impacts of climate change can be greater at margins of climatic zones and for impoverished people. For example, in the center of the Corn Belt fewer droughts might raise corn yields only a bit, whereas on the belt's dry western margin it could make corn a profitable crop. Where people are poor and food costs much of their income, they may not have the mobility to escape nor the money to import food when drought kills crops. One bad climatic extreme can consume much of the gross national product (GNP) of a small country, as has happened in Tanzania and Nepal (Kates, 1980). Places and people with more resources adapt more easily than those at the margins.

THE TOOLS OF INNOVATION

Much of the interaction between climate and humanity is technological invention of the "hardware" and "software" tools that are at the heart of adaptation (Ausubel, 1991). The hardware includes tractors that can cultivate large tracts in a few days if spring is late and air conditioners that make hot days comfortable. The software is new information, rules, and behaviors such as weather forecasts, insurance restrictions, and repair of leaky faucets. Software is usually indispensable for adopting new hardware. Major breakthroughs like irrigation usually depend on clusters of new social organization and financing as well as new machinery.

Many past innovations in hardware and software have helped people adapt to climate and variable weather: in 1873, preservatives for food in warm weather; in 1879, incandescent bulbs for dark days; in 1885, gasoline-powered automobiles to travel the open road; in 1887, aluminum to resist corrosion; in 1895-1906, refrigeration and air conditioning for heat waves; in 1916, windshield wipers and in 1927, ethylene glycol antifreeze to make travel easy in all weather; in 1930, the first sales of frozen food to span summers; in 1934, radio beam navigation; and in 1960, weather satellites to cope with storms. The technology that allows humans to adapt to long-term climate change will mostly be like that tempering the difference between daytime warmth and nighttime cold, protecting us against storms and heat waves, and helping us live in diverse climates today. No qualitatively new technologies have been proposed to ease adaptation to climate change that may be caused by greenhouse gas emissions.

Experience shows that innovation can be fast in comparison with the climate change envisioned for the next 50 to 100 years. In 1900 dry California had a small crop production, and in 1985 it produced twice as many dollars of crops as second-place Iowa. In 1903 at Kitty Hawk the Wright brothers flew 59 seconds in a favorable wind, and in 1985 in the United States 380 million airplane passengers flew 336 billion miles in all kinds of weather. Penicillin was discovered in 1928, and by 1945 it was saving lives. The microprocessor was introduced in 1971, and in 1990 Americans were using 50 million personal computers (PCs). Both the character and the extent of the impacts of climate change, and adaptation to it, will in large part be a function of the rates of innovation and diffusion of the technologies that continue to transform the human economy.

Even though inventions and their adoption may occur quickly, we must ask whether the broad spectrum of current capital investments could be changed fast enough to match a change in climate in 50 to 100 years. As shown below, this period will comfortably allow the replacement of major technological systems.

In fact, 50 years is enough time to turn over most capital stock. About two-thirds of capital stock is usually in machinery and equipment and one-third in buildings and other structures. In Japan the average renewal period for capital stock in business—the time it takes for machinery and equipment in an industry to be almost entirely replaced—ranges from about 22 years in textiles down to 10 years or less in such fast-moving industries as telecommunications and electrical machinery (Economic Planning Agency, 1989). Renewal is fast in agriculture, too. The estimated life span of the cultivars—varieties that have originated and persisted under cultivation—of five major crops in the United States is less than 10 years, and most experts believe the life span of cultivars will grow shorter (Duvick, 1984).

Figure 33.3 shows the similar youth, compared to greenhouse effects, of the capital stock in the Federal Republic of Germany (FRG) and the USSR for both machinery and such structures as buildings and pipelines. For the FRG in 1985 some 60 percent of the stock of structures was less than 20

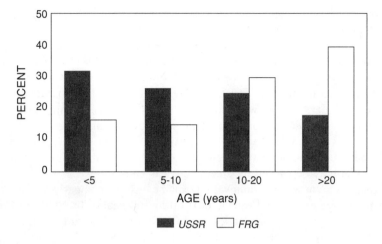

FIGURE 33.3   Age distribution of nonmachinery capital stock in the FRG for 1985 (white bars) and in the USSR as of 1986 (black bars).

SOURCE: Courtesy of Jesse Ausubel.

years old (Statistisches Bundesamt, 1989). In the USSR in 1986 some 80 percent was less than 20 years old (USSR State Committee on Statistics, undated).

   At first such figures may seem surprising. Some of our surprise arises from the justifiable value and thus attention we give to precious monuments and localities like the cathedral of Notre Dame or the city of Venice. Some reflection on the total equipment and buildings we use daily, however, relieves our surprise at seeing Figure 33.3. Consider the office space in a city, whether Hong Kong, Milan, or Denver. Most of the space is in buildings built in the last 20 years. These new buildings are filled with such new equipment as telephone systems. Indeed, even older buildings are filled with modern equipment, such as PCs and FAX machines, that did not even exist 15 or 20 years ago. The same is true for supermarkets, restaurants, and other stores, many of which are less than 20 years old and in any case have modern cash registers and furnishings. A large fraction of residences is similarly young and, in turn, filled with new appliances of all kinds. In fact, if societies grow at 2 to 3 percent per year, as industrialized societies have for the past 150 years, then half of all capital stock will always be less than 30 years old.

   Probably the systems that take the longest to build are infrastructures that provide transport, energy, water, communications, and means of meeting other human needs. Once constructed, many infrastructure systems are (or should be) continuously reconstructed. For example, roads are resurfaced every decade or so, depending on use. The time required for societies to bring forth such systems can be found. They are typically completed in 50 ± 20 years (Grübler, 1990). The 7,000-km canal system of the United States was almost entirely built in about 30 years, between 1820 and 1850. More than 90 percent of the 300,000-mile U.S. railway network was laid in the 65 years between 1855 and 1920. The paving of virtually the entire 6 million-km surface road system of the United States was accomplished between 1920 and 1985. The U.S. interstate highway system was completed, with some localized exceptions, in about 30 years from the time that it was announced by President Eisenhower. It is interesting to consider whether climate change could require any public works on this scale; coastal protection and interbasin water transfer would seem the most likely candidates. Because the siting process for infrastructures can be lengthy, siting is needed early if a decision is anticipated in favor of construction of a major new infrastructure to adapt to changing climate or rising seas.

Because capital stock is continuously turning over on a time scale of a few decades, it will be possible to put in place much technology that is adjusted to a changing climate. This can be done without extraordinary measures given reasonably accurate information about the future. For the shortest lifetimes, even accurate information about the present climate will do. The fact that perhaps 90 percent of the capital stock in place in the year 2040 will have been built after 1990 does not diminish the significance of some long-lived structures. Action may be necessary to protect cities such as Venice, where preservation of historic buildings is the goal. In such cases the fact that much new investment outpaces climate change is not helpful, as processes of replacement are not relevant. However, there is time to do what may be indicated, if the political will and money exist.

Innovation contributes toward making human society less subject to natural phenomena, at least in the short term. With current technology, people can live in virtually any climate that now exists. Heating and cooling, along with medicine and sanitation, have enabled many to inhabit regions that were previously uninhabitable, although reducing vulnerability further may become more difficult and expensive if long-term problems of energy and water availability are not solved. At the same time, it is hard to envision how natural ecosystems could possibly be climate-proofed.

However, it is innovations and technology along with population and economic growth that are currently causing many global changes, not only in climate (increases in CO_2, CH_4, N_2O, and chlorofluorocarbons [CFCs]) but also in depletion of the ozone layer (CFCs), pollution, habitat degradation, etc. Thus, technology and growth, at least in our recent experience, come with prices that were unforeseen, including higher energy consumption. As a result, exclusive reliance on technology to adapt to climate must be viewed with caution.

Just as settlement has become feasible nearly everywhere, production can now proceed continuously, or nearly so, in severe environments. Pumps extract oil 24 hours a day, 365 days a year, in the stormy North Sea. Consumption is also becoming insulated from the environment, not only in Minneapolis and Houston, but also to some extent in New Delhi and Bangkok. Inside shopping malls, only fashions and decorations signal the season. Sports are played increasingly under domes where fans do not know whether it is windy or pouring outside. Where people must be aware of weather, they can prepare for it, because forecasts have become much more accurate in the past two decades, especially in temperate latitudes (World Meteorological Organization, 1988).

Improved technology and social organization seem to have lessened the impacts of climate fluctuations on farming during the past 100 years in the United States (Warrick, 1980). Further evidence for the "lessening hypothesis" is found in a flattening of monthly rates of total mortality in Japan between 1899 and 1973. The flattening is explained in part by the diminution of winter and summer mortality peaks that used to be associated with exposure to cold and heat (Weihe, 1979). That the peak season for vacations in developed countries is late summer—a peak season for labor in agricultural societies—further indicates the transformation that has taken place.

MAKING DECISIONS IN AN UNCERTAIN WORLD

A facile recommendation about adaptation is "factor in climate change." We, however, are and will remain uncertain about climate change and its effect on temperature, moisture, and sea level. We shall be especially uncertain of the specifics for a locality where people are mulling over the construction of a dam, bridge, or seawall. So, what method can factor in climate change?

One method is to postpone decisions until the climate prediction is less uncertain. In an economic analysis, decisions concerning climate change were exemplified by whether or not to build a seawall. The economical course turned out to be to lay the foundation for the wall and wait to learn more before spending more (Yohe, 1990).

Uncertainty is generally lowered by cycles of prediction followed by observation, testing the prediction, and revising it. So long as prior predictions are iffy, however, the revised or posterior predictions later in the cycles will be only a little more certain (Fiering and Matalas, 1990). Given this prospect of continuing uncertainty, a method is needed for decisions about adaptation during the building of things with long lives. Although much equipment and even buildings have lives shorter than the periods thought of for climate change, some urban infrastructure is long lived. The cost of modifying or adapting it later is likely to be large in comparison with the cost of the initial adaptation.

As an example think of building a new bridge over an estuary. Ignore the possibility that the traffic to justify the bridge may not come in 50 years. Imagine that during construction $100,000 today will buy the adaptation of an added meter of height above sea level. Let it happen that after 50 years the sea rises and the bridge without the added clearance needs a $5 million retrofit or adaptation. Discounted at 6 percent per annum, the present value of the $5 million is $271,000. If we are certain the sea will rise, adding the meter for $100,000 makes a benefit of $271,000 minus $100,000. In general, adaptation during construction is economical as long as the ratio of the cost of a present adaptation divided by the present value of the retrofit is less than the probability of higher seas, and other superior investment opportunities are not available. Thus, in the example above, probabilities greater than 100,000/271,000 or 0.37 would justify the added investment.

Let the justified cost be in cents warranted now for a dollar of retrofit later. The probability that the adaptation will be needed, how long the wait before it is needed, and the discount rate set the justified cost, as illustrated in Figure 33.4. The mathematics in the figure's caption shows a percentage rise in the probability that the adaptation will be needed raises the justified cost by the same percentage. Regardless of how long the wait or how great the discount, raising the probability that the bridge must be adapted by 10 percent from, say, 50 to 55 percent raises the justified cost by 10 percent from, say, 20 to 22 cents—10 percent more probable, 10 percent more cost today justified by this calculation.

On the other hand, either raising the discount or lengthening the wait by 1 percent lowers the justified cost by 1 percent times the discount rate times the wait. The percentage rise in the justified cost caused by a percentage fall in discount or wait is their product: discount rate times years. Imagine lowering the product of discount times wait 1 percent from 6 percent times 100 years to either 6 percent times 99 years or 5.94 percent times 100 years. This raises the justified cost by 1 percent times 0.06 times 100, or fully 6 percent. If the justified cost before was 20 cents, it rises to 21.2 cents.

Figure 33.4 shows the justified costs for three combinations of years, discount rate, and probability of need. The center row of bars could be labeled either 50 years at 6 percent or 100 years at 3 percent. Lower discount rate, shorter wait, and higher probability or certainty raise the warranted expenditure. Lifting the justified cost of the present adaptation above 10 cents per dollar retrofit takes probabilities above 0.4 plus discounts below 3 percent and waits shorter than 50 years.

The percentage change in the justified cost always equals a percentage change in probability of need but is the discount rate times the years of wait

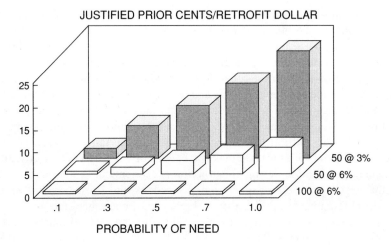

FIGURE 33.4   The justified cost of an adaptation in cents justified now for a dollar of retrofit later.

NOTE: The probability that the adaptation will be needed because, say, sea level rises is shown from left to right. The front row of short bars pertains to a wait of 100 years before the adaptation is needed and a discount rate of 6 percent. The back row of bars rising above 20 cents pertains to a wait of only 50 years and a discount rate of only 3 percent. Since the justified cost is approximately set by the product of discount rate and wait, the middle row, for example, could have been labeled 100 at 3 percent as well as 50 at 6 percent.

A little mathematics illustrates several points about justified costs. Let the ratio ϕ be the cost of a present adaptation relative to the cost of retrofit. It is cents per dollar in the figure. Adaptation during construction is warranted as long as the ratio ϕ of the costs is less than

$$\phi' = P/(1 + i)^n$$

where P is the probability of need, i is the discount rate, and n is the years until adaptation is needed. For commonplace discount rates, the approximation is

$$\log(\phi') \approx \log(P) - (in)$$

The approximation explains why the justified cost is set by the product of the discount rate and the wait. It explains why the middle row in the figure, for example, could have been labeled either 100 years at 3 percent or 50 years at 6 percent.

The approximation is convenient for thinking about such relative changes or elasticities as $(d\phi/\phi')/(dP/P)$. The elasticity of ϕ' for a change in the probability P is simply 1; for a change in (in), it is (in).

Because the elasticity of ϕ' for a change in P is 1, a 10 percent improvement in certainty or P always raises justifiable cost 10 percent. On the other hand, the elasticity for changes in discount times years is (in). The higher i and n, the bigger the percentage change in the ratio ϕ' for a percentage change in (in). The justifiable cost rises from left to right by the same percentage as the probability, but it rises more between the middle and rear rows than between the front and middle rows.

SOURCE: Figure courtesy of Jon Liebman.

times the percentage change in rate or wait. So for rates times waits like 0.06 times 100, foretelling rates and waits has more leverage than raising the probability of need.

Choosing a discount rate is clearly exactly as important as forecasting the length of wait. In Chapter 32, the section "Assumptions," the panel set rates of 3, 6, and 10 percent.

So in the face of this uncertainty, rational people will start work on more adaptations than they complete. They will make more adaptations as their certainty grows. And they will pay special attention to how high the discount rate and how long the wait.

PARTIAL JUSTIFICATIONS AND MULTIPLE GOALS

Many of the ways used and proposed for adaptation to climate change are justified only partly on the basis of climate change. For example, farmers build irrigation systems to increase current yields and to diminish the effects of variable weather. The prospect of climate change provides an additional justification for investment in irrigation. In almost all cases discussed in this report, climate change provides only a partial justification for particular actions or investments. For example, stricter zoning of shorelines could serve not only to minimize the impacts of sea level rise but also to lessen habitat destruction. Planting trees in urban areas would provide shade and comfort if the climate became hotter and would also make a small contribution to retaining carbon in the biosphere. Several actions that are proposed to lower greenhouse gas emissions, like reduction in coal usage, are similarly proposed because they serve multiple goals.

One adaptation has the virtue of shortening the wait for benefits: thorough adaptation to the present variability of weather. For example, Gleick (1990) found that among five indicators a small storage capacity relative to supply was the one that most frequently indicated vulnerability of water systems in the eastern United States. If more storage capacity were built to adapt to present variability, it would also be an adaptation to a change to a drier climate.

Thus, we must ask whether a set of partial justifications, including climate change, adds up to a full justification. From efficiency of water and energy use to coastal zone management, one could argue that these are things that societies already ought to be doing anyway. Does climate change then put certain projects over the investment hurdle? If not, how impressive are these remedies and what are the obstacles to them? Like suitors, solutions court problems; the problem of climatic change is used to justify numerous solutions. One must ask why these solutions have not yet been accepted. Gaining acceptance may well require removing a fundamental obstacle like cost, convenience, or ignorance rather than merely adding another justification.

CRITERIA FOR USING THE TOOLS OF GOVERNMENT

Government can speed adaptation with many tools. One is to provide timely information, like weather forecasts. Another is to support fundamental research, which is primarily sponsored by governments. To go beyond these unexceptionable actions to regulation or investment, however, one must examine the criteria for using government tools.

Although the most important and by far the greater number of adaptations are made by private agents like consumers and enterprises, governments can ensure that the legal and economic structure encourages adaptation. Changing incomes, prices, and environment cause more or less automatic adaptations. These include migration of capital and labor along with technology evoked by changing conditions. Buildings will be built above an advancing sea, people escape unpleasant climates, and agricultural and industrial capital leave lands that lose their advantage.

But governments can ensure that climatic impacts are translated into signals of price and income that spur private adaptation. This may be hard because many impacts of climate change are improperly priced. For example, climate change will probably alter runoff. But in the United States and most of the world, water is often not allocated efficiently and may not be when its availability changes (Frederick and Kneese, 1990). So governments can speed adaptation by using such devices as water auctions that dispatch resources to the most valuable uses as shown by the ability to pay.

Now, recur to the fallacy of conceiving a slowly changing climate as a blow on today's world and of ignoring the inevitable evolution during the coming decades. That is, think again of the "dumb people scenario" and the challenge of integrating the outcome of a changing climate with other changes that will occur during the coming decades. During this evolution it is probably unwise to prescribe in detail much adaptation now to smooth the transition to climate change over the next century. Like generals building a Maginot Line in the wrong place, we might bankrupt ourselves building dikes against floods that never come. In addition, the evident speed of innovation and replacement allows us to wait in most cases until we see the whites of the enemies' eyes. Financial markets adjust in minutes, labor moves in a few years, the economic long run is no more than two decades, and only major technologies like highways replacing rails or one school of thought forcing out another take as long as climate change.

Thus, three criteria for government action to promote adaptation can be that (1) the amount of time needed to carry out the adaptation is so long that we must act now, (2) the action is profitable even if climate does not change, and (3) the penalty for waiting a decade or two is great.

REFERENCES

Ausubel, J. H. 1991. Does climate still matter? Nature 350:649-652.

Burton, I., R. W. Kates, and G. F. White. 1978. The Environment as Hazard. New York: Oxford University Press.

Duvick, D. N. 1984. Genetic diversity in major farm crops on the farm and in reserve. Economic Botany 38:161-178.

Economic Planning Agency. 1989. Economic Survey of Japan, 1987-1988. Tokyo: Economic Planning Agency.

Fiering, M. B., and N. C. Matalas. 1990. Decision-making under uncertainty. In Climate Change and U.S. Water Resources, P. E. Waggoner, ed. New York: John Wiley & Sons.

Frederick, K. D., and A. V. Kneese. 1990. Reallocation by markets and prices. In Climate Change and U.S. Water Resources, P. E. Waggoner, ed. New York: John Wiley & Sons.

Glantz, M. H., ed. 1988. Societal Responses to Regional Climate Change: Forecasting by Analogy. Boulder, Colo.: Westview Press.

Gleick, P. H. 1990. Vulnerability of water systems. In Climate Change and U.S. Water Resources, P. E. Waggoner, ed. New York: John Wiley & Sons.

Grübler, A. 1990. The Rise and Fall of Infrastructures: Dynamics of Evolution and Technological Change in Transport. Heidelberg, Germany: Physica.

Holling, C. S. 1986. The resilience of terrestrial ecosystems: Local surprise and global change. In Sustainable Development of the Biosphere, W. C. Clark and T. E. Munn, eds. Cambridge: Cambridge University Press.

Ingram, H. M., H. J. Cortner, and M. K. Landy. 1990. The political agenda. In Climate Change and U.S. Water Resources, P. E. Waggoner, ed. New York: John Wiley & Sons.

Kates, R. W. 1980. Climate and society: Lessons from recent events. Weather 35(1):17-25.

Malingreau, J. P. 1987. The 1982-83 drought in Indonesia: Assessment and monitoring. In The Societal Impacts Associated with the 1982-83 Worldwide Climate Anomalies, M. H. Glantz, R. Katz, and M. Krenz, eds. Boulder, Colo.: National Center for Atmospheric Research.

May, P. J. 1985. Recovery from Catastrophes. Westport, Conn.: Greenwood Press.

Miller, K. A., and M. H. Glantz. 1988. Climate and economic competitiveness: Florida freezes and the global citrus processing industry. Climatic Change 12:135-164.

Mitchell, J. K. 1984. Hazard perception studies: Convergent concerns and divergent approaches during the past decade. In Environmental Perception and Behavior, T. F. Saarinen, D. Seamon, and J. L. Sell, eds. Research Paper No. 209, Department of Geography. Chicago: University of Chicago Press.

Morrisette, P. M. 1988. The stability bias and adjustment to climatic variability: The case of the rising level of the Great Salt Lake. Applied Geography 8:171-198.

National Research Council. 1987. Confronting Natural Disasters. Washington, D.C.: National Academy Press.

Phillips, D. H., and D. Jordon. 1986. The declining role of historical data in reservoir management and operations. In Preprints of the Conference on Climate and Water Management, August 4-7, 1986. Boston: American Meteorological Society.

Riebsame, W. E. 1988. Adjusting water resources management to climate change. Climatic Change 12:69-97.

Riebsame, W. E. 1990. Anthropogenic climate change and a new paradigm of natural resources management. Professional Geographer 42:1-12.

Riebsame, W. E., S. A. Changnon, and T. R. Karl. 1991. Drought and Natural Resources Management in the United States. Boulder, Colo.: Westview Press.

Schwarz, H. E., and L. A. Dillard. 1990. Urban water. In Climate Change and U.S. Water Resources, P. E. Waggoner, ed. New York: John Wiley & Sons.

Shugart, H. H., M. Ya. Antonovsky, P. G. Jarvis, and A. P. Sandford. 1986. CO_2, Climatic change and forest ecosystems: Assessing the response of global forests to the direct effects of increasing CO_2 and climatic change. In SCOPE 29, The Greenhouse Effect, Climatic Change and Ecosystems, B. Bolin, B. R. Döös, J. Jäger, and R. A. Warrick, eds. Chichester, United Kingdom: John Wiley & Sons.

Statistisches Bundesamt. 1989. Wirtschaft und Statistik. Stuttgart: Metzler-Poeschl.

Strain, B. R., and F. A. Bazzaz. 1983. Terrestrial plant communities. In CO_2 and Plants, E. R. Lemon, ed. Boulder, Colo.: Westview Press.

USSR State Committee on Statistics. Undated. Statistics on Social Indicators and Capital Vintage Structure in Industry. Institute for Social and Economic Statistics, Moscow. Memorandum, courtesy of A. Grübler, Laxenburg, Austria.

Warrick, R. A. 1980. Drought in the Great Plains: A case study of research on climate and society in the USA. In Climatic Constraints and Human Activities, J. Ausubel and A. K. Biswas, eds. Oxford: Pergamon Press.

Warrick, R. A., and M. J. Bowden. 1981. The changing impacts of drought in the Great Plains. In The Great Plains: Perspectives and Prospects, M. P. Lawson and M. E. Baker, eds. Lincoln: University of Nebraska Press.

Weihe, W. H. 1979. Climate, health and disease. In Proceedings of the World Climate Conference, World Meteorological Organization. Geneva, Switzerland: World Meteorological Organization.

White, G. F., ed. 1974. Natural Hazards: Local, National, Global. New York: Oxford University Press.

White, G. F. 1975. Flood hazard in the United States: A research assessment. Monograph No. 6., Natural Hazards Center. Boulder: University of Colorado at Boulder.

White, G. F. 1988. Global warming: Uncertainty and action. Environment 30(6):i.

World Meteorological Organization (WMO). 1988. The World Weather Watch. WMO Report No. 709. Geneva: World Meteorological Organization.

Yohe, G. 1990. Uncertainty, global climate and the economic value of information: An economic analysis of policy options, timing and information under long term uncertainty. Paper presented at the Annual Meeting of the American Association for the Advancement of Science, New Orleans, La., February 15-20, 1990.

34

Sensitivities, Impacts, and Adaptations

In Chapter 32 we wrote that the impact of a climate change on some activity is the integral during the change of the sensitivity times the rate of change of the climate. The hope, of course, is that adaptation can modify the sensitivity, ameliorating bad and increasing good impacts of a given climate change. In the sections that follow, the sensitivities, impacts, and adaptations of activities are examined. Because this is a U.S. report, much of the examination is of U.S. activities. The scenarios of change are generally within the ranges stated in our Assumptions, and they are given precisely in the cited publications.

Estimating the cost of impacts or adaptations is fraught with uncertainties. Uncertainties range from those about climate scenarios to ones about sensitivities and future technology. We do not know whether people will choose to adapt more or suffer more from harmful climate changes and benefit less from helpful climate changes. So, national let alone planetary estimates are difficult and may be misleading. Nevertheless, the scale or order of things must be judged. Accordingly, Table 34.1 gives some illustrative costs of impacts and adaptations.

The footnotes show that the cost estimates are drawn from diverse sources. Their accuracy ranges from the precision of the budget of the U.S. Weather Service to the imprecise multiplication of an assumed cost of a house by the number of houses that newspapers report that a storm destroyed. Few of the estimates, if any, include, for example, personal suffering, the advantages of a renewed home, or a construction boom after a flood. The accuracy of each cost can be judged from the cited sources.

These costs illustrate those of adapting and those that might be suffered more or less frequently if climate changed. For example, if hurricanes became more frequent and no one adapted, costs like the $5 billion for

TABLE 34.1 Illustrative Costs of Impacts and Adaptations in Current Dollars. An impact may help, as when a warmer climate reduces snow removal, or harm, as when a drier climate makes droughts more frequent. Adaptations may temper the harm or exploit the benefit of a new climate, as when a new and adapted wheat variety is created or forest planted. Some entries, like the U.S. gross national product (GNP) or the changing GNP per capita in the world, give a scale for judging the costs of impacts and adaptations. The numbers included for scale are in italics.

Class	Description	Dollars	Per
GNP	*1985 total U.S.*[a]	*4,015 billion*	
	1985 average U.S.[a]	*17 thousand*	*capita*
	1985 global average[b]	*3 thousand*	*capita*
	2100 global average projected[b]	*7-36 thousand*	*capita*
	2100 average U.S.[c]	*150 thousand*	*capita*
Climate hazards[d]	1980 U.S. heat wave[e]	20 billion	
	1988 U.S. drought[f]	39 billion	
	1983 Utah heavy snow, floods, and landslide[g]	300 million	
	1985 Ohio and Pennsylvania tornados[h]	500 million	
	1985 West Virginia floods[i]	700 million	
	1989 Hurricane Hugo[j]	5 billion	
Recent annual average U.S. losses[k]	Hurricanes[l]	800-1,800 million	
	Floods[m]	3 billion	
	Tornados and thunderstorms[n]	300-2,000 million	
	Winter storms and snows[o]	3 billion	
	Drought[p]	800-1,000 million	
	1988 budget U.S. Weather Service[q]	*323 million*	

542

Farming	**Comment:** In an extremely adverse year, climate hazards may cost $40 billion or 1 percent of the $4,000 billion U.S. GNP, which is about $160 per capita.		
	Create successful wheat variety[r] Kansas Agricultural Research Experiment Station[s]	1 million	
	U.S. and state agricultural research[t]	33 million	
	1974-1977 drought, federal expenditures[u]	2.3 billion	
	1986 U.S. farm GNP[v]	7 billion	
		76 billion	
	Comment: During the drought of the 1970s, annual federal expenditures on drought relief averaged about 3 to 4 percent of farm GNP.		
Forestry[w]	Prepare and plant	130	acre
	Treat with herbicide	41	acre
	Fertilize	36	acre
	Thin	55	acre
	Protect from fire for 1 year	1.36	acre
	1983 fire protection on state and private forests[x]	245 million	
	1986 U.S. forestry and fishery GNP[y]	*17 billion*	
	Comment: Increasing expenditures to $1.36 per acre on all forest land would cost about a half billion dollars or 3 percent of forest and fishery GNP.		

(Table 34.1 continues)

543

TABLE 34.1 *(continued)*

Class	Description	Dollars	Per
Natural landscape	Preserve seed accession in a gene bank[z]	20	year
	Preserve a plant in botanical garden[aa]	500	year
	Purchase an acre in a large reserve[bb]	50–5,000	acre
	Preserve a large mammal in zoo[cc]	1,500–3,000	year
	Preserve a large bird in zoo[dd]	100–1,000	year
	Recover peregrine falcon[ee]	3 million	1970–1990
	Recover all endangered birds of prey[ff]	5 million	year
	1985 expenditure on wildlife-related recreation, including hunting and fishing[gg]	*55.4 billion*	
	Budget of National Park Service[hh]	*1 billion*	*year*
	Comment: The cost of recovering all endangered birds of prey is 1 ten-thousandth and the cost of the National Park Service is 2 percent of the annual expenditures on wildlife associated recreation.		
Water	Delaware River above Philadelphia[ii]	51	acrefoot
	Sacramento Delta[jj]	137	acrefoot
	High flow skimming, Hudson River[kk]	555	acrefoot
	Desalting[ll]	2,200–5,400	acrefoot
	Present national average[mm]	*533*	*acrefoot*

544

	Present irrigation water in California[nn]	*15*	*acrefoot*
	Annual water bill for domestic use[oo]	*60*	*capita*
	Annual cost of water for irrigation[pp]	*45*	*acre*
	Value of an acre of tomatoes[qq]	*4,000*	*acre*

Comment: Doubling the cost of domestic water would cost a person $60/$17,000 or a third of a percent of per capita GNP in the United States. Raising the cost of irrigation water from the present $15 per acrefoot to the $137 per acrefoot for the prospective water from the Sacramento Delta would cost 2 percent of the value of the tomatoes on an acre.

Industry	Raise offshore drilling platform 1 m[rr]	16 million	
	1986 U.S. manufacturing GNP[ss]	*824 billion*	

Comment: The cost of raising an offshore drilling platform 1 m is less than 1 percent of its total cost.

Settlement	Raise a Bangladesh embankment 3 m[tt]	800	m length
	Raise a Dutch dike 1 m[uu]	3 thousand	m length
	Build seawall, Charleston, South Carolina[vv]	6 thousand	m length
	Nourish beach for 1 year, Florida[ww]	35–200	m length
	Nourish beach for 1 year, Charleston, South Carolina[xx]	300	m length
	Hurricane evacuation[yy]	35–50	person

(Table 34.1 continues)

545

TABLE 34.1 *(continued)*

Class	Description	Dollars	Per
Settlement—*cont'd*	Strengthen coastal property for 100-mph wind[zz]	30-90 billion	U.S. coast
	Floodproof by raising house 3 ft[aaa]	10-40 thousand	house
	Move house from floodplain[bbb]	20-70 thousand	house
	Levees, berms, and pumps[ccc]	17 thousand	1/4 acre
	1986 U.S. state and local services[ddd]	*331 billion*	
	Comment: Strengthening coastal properties for 100 mph wind would cost between a tenth and a third of current state and local service budgets for the entire United States. The cost of moving a house would be one to four times the present U.S. per capita GNP and a tenth to a half of that of 2100.		
Migration	Resettle a refugee in 1989, federal contribution[eee]	7 thousand	person
	Move contents of 450 ft^2 apartment about 400 miles to a 4°C cooler climate[fff]	1,500	

[a]National income in 1985 was $3,222 billion. U.S. Bureau of the Census (1987, Table 670).

[b]Lashof and Tirpak (1990). The range for 2100 is from their slowly changing world scenario to their rapidly changing world scenario.

[c]Assumes 1.9% growth per year, which is the annual average growth rate for U.S. GNP from 1800 to 1985. U.S. Bureau of the Census (1987) and U.S. Department of Commerce (1975).

[d]Climate hazard figures represent estimates of total losses, including both private losses and government expenditures.

546

[e]Riebsame et al. (1986).

[f]Riebsame et al. (1991).

[g]National Hazards Research and Applications Information Center (NHRAIC), University of Colorado, Boulder. NHRAIC maintains an unreferenced data base on national hazards. Numbers referenced as NHRAIC are from their data base.

[h]These tornados also caused 85 deaths. NHRAIC data base.

[i]These floods also caused 47 deaths. NHRAIC data base.

[j]Hurricane Hugo also caused 20 deaths. NHRAIC data base.

[k]Dollar figures for average annual U.S. losses are estimates of total losses, including both private losses and government expenditures.

[l]Riebsame et al. (1986).

[m]Personal communication from Office of Hydrology, National Weather Service, Silver Spring, Maryland, to W. Riebsame, NHRAIC, Boulder, Colorado, 1990.

[n]Kessler and White (1983).

[o]Gordon (1982).

[p]Riebsame et al. (1986).

[q]The actual expenditure in 1988 for the U.S. National Weather Service was $322,913,000. U.S. Office of Management and Budget (1989, p. I-F14).

[r]Newlin (1990).

[s]U.S. Department of Agriculture (1989b).

[t]U.S. Department of Agriculture (1989b).

[u]Wilhite (1983).

[v]U.S. Bureau of the Census (1987, Table 670).

[w]Forestry numbers are from Straka et al. (1989) unless otherwise noted.

[x]The 1983 expenditures on about a half billion acres of State and private forest land was $0.50 per acre. The difference between this $0.50 and $1.36 times 736 million acres of total forest land is about a half billion dollars. U.S. Department of Agriculture (1986, Tables 661, 667, and 668).

[y]U.S. Bureau of the Census (1987, Table 670). Agriculture, etc., less farming.

[z]National Plant Germplasm System, ARS, USDA operating costs only for regeneration, storage, and distribution. Personal communication

(Table 34.1 continues)

547

TABLE 34.1 *(continued)*

from S. Eberhart, National Seed Storage Laboratory, Fort Collins, Colorado, to P. Waggoner, Connecticut Agricultural Experiment Station, May 13, 1991.

[aa]$500 per year is the amount of the subsidy from the Center for Plant Conservation to member gardens for maintaining a sample. Personal communication from V. Heywood, Center for Plant Conservation, to P. Waggoner, Connecticut Agricultural Experiment Station, New Haven, Connecticut, July 4, 1990.

[bb]Range is $50-$500 per acre for land far from cities; $300-$5,000 per acre for land near cities. Personal communication from J. Ball, Woodland Park Zoo, Seattle, Washington, to G. Orians, University of Washington, Seattle, Washington, April 1990.

[cc]Costs for food and labor only. Personal communication from J. Ball, Woodland Park Zoo, Seattle, Washington, to G. Orians, University of Washington, Seattle, Washington, April 1990.

[dd]Costs for food and labor only. Personal communication from J. Ball, Woodland Park Zoo, Seattle, Washington, to G. Orians, University of Washington, Seattle, Washington, April 1990.

[ee]Personal communication from J. Ball, Woodland Park Zoo, Seattle, Washington, to G. Orians, University of Washington, Seattle, Washington, April 1990.

[ff]Cade (1988).

[gg]U.S. Bureau of the Census (1987, Table 380).

[hh]U.S. Bureau of the Census (1988, Table 371).

[ii]Cost for raw water from modifications to F. E. Walter Reservoir. Personal communication from R. Tratoriano, Delaware River Basin Commission, to D. Sheer, Water Resources Management, Columbia, Maryland, 1990.

[jj]New Bureau of Reclamation, Central Valley Project. Cost for raw water at the plant. Does not include costs for delivery facilities to point of use. These figures are for construction costs of Auburn Dam allocated to water supply only—23% of total construction costs. Other costs allocated to flood control, instream flow, hydropower, and recreation. Personal communication from J. Denny, U.S. Bureau of Reclamation, Sacramento, to D. Sheer, Water Resources Management, Columbia, Maryland, 1990.

[kk]Includes cost of treatment and delivery facilities. R. Alpern, New York City Department of Environmental Conservation, First Intergovernmental Task Force Report.

[ll]Costs for desalting run from $2,000-$5,000/acrefoot/yr capital costs, plus operating costs of $2,000-$4,000/acrefoot (mainly energy costs). This equates very approximately to $2,200-$5,400/acrefoot.

548

[mm]National average water rates for water delivered to the end user were on the order of $533 per acrefoot for small users, less for large users. Arthur Young Water and Wastewater Survey (1988).

[nn]Maximum of new contracts of U.S. Department of the Interior, Southern California. Personal communication from K. Frederick, U.S. Department of the Interior, to P. Waggoner, Connecticut Agricultural Experiment Station, February, 1991.

[oo]Use of 105 gallons per day (Solley et al., 1989) at $533 per acrefoot costs $63 per year.

[pp]At $15 per acrefoot, the 3 ft evaporating in a year would cost $45 per acre.

[qq]27,000 acres in California produced 7,453 cwt of tomatoes valued at $18.30 per cwt. U.S. Department of Agriculture (1986).

[rr]New York Times, December 19, 1989.

[ss]U.S. Bureau of the Census (1987, Table 670).

[tt]Raising an embankment from 12 to 15 ft high to 18 to 25 ft high to protect from major cyclones and to fortify them with concrete or boulders would cost about $25,000 per 100 ft (New York Times, May 12, 1991).

[uu]Goemans (1986).

[vv]Gibbs (1986).

[ww]National Research Council (1987).

[xx]Gibbs (1986).

[yy]NHRAIC data base.

[zz]Unnewehr (1989).

[aaa]Illinois Department of Transportation (1986).

[bbb]Illinois Department of Transportation (1986).

[ccc]Federal Insurance Administration (1984).

[ddd]U.S. Bureau of the Census (1987, Table 670).

[eee]Kritz (1990).

[fff]From Washington, D.C., to Oak Bluffs, Massachusetts. Personal communication from J. Ausubel, The Rockefeller University, to P. Waggoner, Connecticut Agricultural Experiment Station, May 10, 1991.

Hurricane Hugo would become more frequent. On the other hand, the cost of adaptation would include more frequent expenditures of $35 to $50 per person to evacuate or $30 billion to $90 billion to strengthen coastal buildings for stronger winds. In another example, a warmer and drier climate and no adaptation could raise the $800 million to $1,000 million per year for drought and cut the $3 billion for floods and $3 billion for winter storms and snows. Or, climate warming could raise the cost of floods by causing more rain and less snow in the spring. Adaptations would include costs for air conditioning and irrigation. They might include $1 million for an adapted wheat variety and some portion of the $33 million per year for the agricultural experiment station of a state in the Grain Belt. The residual impact would be the net of a new arrangement of production, comparative advantages, and prices.

Some entries in the table provide scale. For example, the U.S. gross national product (GNP) in 1986 of $4,235 billion is a standard for judging the $30 billion to $90 billion for strengthening coastal buildings for 100-mph winds. The projected change from a global average income of $3.0 thousand in 1985 to $7.1 to $35.6 thousand in 2100 suggests the future wealth for adaptation.

Again, these costs of impacts and adaptations are uncertain. Combining them with uncertain climate scenarios compounds the uncertainty. Nevertheless, the table illustrates the scale or order.

Before beginning these examinations of sensitivities, impacts and adaptations, we raise eight questions to keep in mind throughout the examination (Ausubel, 1991). They are familiar ones. Stating them at the outset makes our examination more exact. After the examination of activities, we will revisit these questions.

1. Is faster change worse than slow?
2. Will waiting to make policy and act drive up costs?
3. Are there only losers from climate change?
4. Will the most important impacts be on farming and from the rise of sea level?
5. Will changes in extreme climatic conditions be more important than changes in average conditions?
6. Are the changes unprecedented from the perspective of adaptation?
7. Will impacts be harder on less developed countries than on developed countries?
8. Are some hedges clearly economical?

Raising these questions at the outset provides a backdrop for our examinations. After examination of activities, we will see how these questions should be revised.

PRIMARY PRODUCTION OF ORGANIC MATTER

Why This Subject

Investigation of sensitivity, impact, and adaptation to climate change begins with a paradox. The chief greenhouse gas, CO_2, is feared for its effect on climate, but at the same time it is the key building material of all living things. Green plants are the eventual source of essentially all foods used by living organisms, whether plant or animal. They manufacture the food from CO_2 and water in their green leaves, which are essentially all outdoors and hence subject to climate.

The vital role of plants for food, the peculiar effect of CO_2 on them, and their exposure to climate cause us to examine farming, forestry, and the natural landscape early in this chapter. First, however, we examine commonalities among all three: photosynthesis, the pores that funnel CO_2 in and water out of leaves, and the limits on experiments with systems of plants outdoors.

Photosynthesis

Using the energy from sunlight, plants convert CO_2 from the air and water from the soil into food and oxygen. Since CO_2 is the raw material for photosynthesis, one expects that enriching the air with CO_2 will deliver more raw material and speed the formation of food. Although bottlenecks or limiting factors in the photosynthetic factory of a plant can restrict the speedup enabled by the delivery of more raw material, Figure 34.1 shows that the expected can happen. In a controlled atmosphere in a laboratory, raising CO_2 from about 300 to 600 ppm speeds photosynthesis in corn by about 20 percent. In wheat it speeds photosynthesis more, by about 60 percent. Corn exemplifies plants called C4 whose photosynthesis is fast and yield is high today. Wheat typifies a more common sort of plant called C3 whose photosynthesis is slower than the other class today. Most plants in natural landscapes fall into the slower class.

Leaf Pores

CO_2 arrives at the site of photosynthesis inside leaves through minute pores in the leaves. Since the interior of leaves is moist, water escapes through the pores. So much escapes that evaporation from an acre of foliage is about the same as from an acre of a lake. Not surprisingly, most plants have pores that close at night when photosynthesis stops. They also narrow when CO_2 is abundant. The closing or narrowing saves water.

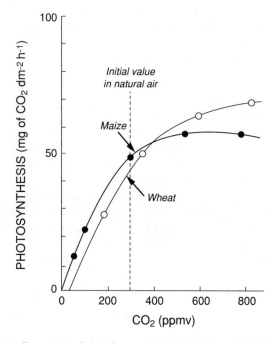

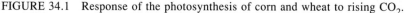

FIGURE 34.1   Response of the photosynthesis of corn and wheat to rising CO_2.

NOTE: Wheat exemplifies the many species of plants called C3 whose photosynthesis responds more to rising CO_2 than does that of C4 plants, which are exemplified by corn.

SOURCE: Reprinted, by permission, from Waggoner (1983). Copyright © 1983 by the National Academy of Sciences.

Some Initial Reasoning

Simple, direct argument from the physiological principles of the preceding paragraphs could lead to several broad conclusions about plants outdoors. At present concentrations of CO_2 in the air, corn should yield more than wheat. Enriching the atmosphere to 600 ppm CO_2 should increase all yields, especially plants with a photosynthesis like wheat that responds sharply to more CO_2. It should close the gap between wheat and corn. It should especially favor the many plants in the natural landscape that have a responsive photosynthesis like wheat. Where ones with responsive photosynthesis compete with ones with unresponsive photosynthesis, the enrichment with CO_2 should make the former more competitive. It should slow evaporation and save water. By speeding photosynthesis and slowing evaporation, CO_2 should increase the efficiency of the use of water, the tons of yield per 1000 m^3 of evaporation.

Limiting Factors

Experience supports the first conclusion: The average U.S. yield per acre of grain of corn is two to three times that of wheat. The other conclusions, however, cannot be tested in the same robust way. Instead, the behavior of an entire landscape must be argued or scaled up from laboratory or small controlled experiments. A logical question about scaling up is whether bottlenecks or limiting factors restrict the speedup of photosynthesis and slowing of evaporation.

About 1980 the debate was vigorous whether natural temperature, moisture, and nutrients outdoors would reduce the effects demonstrated in the laboratory. In the years since, experiments in chambers and laboratories have shown that enrichment with CO_2 actually tempers the impacts of heat, drought, and salinity. More CO_2 increases the growth of roots, shoots, and seed, more or less in step (Rogers et al., 1983; Cure, 1985; Oechel and Strain, 1985). Nitrogen deficiency does not bar the help of more CO_2 to white oak seedlings (Norby et al., 1986) but may bar it for corn (Wong, 1979). Whether fertilizer deficiency bars the help of more CO_2 remains ambiguous (Kimball, 1982; Goudriaan and de Ruiter, 1983; Pearcy and Bjorkman, 1983; Acock and Allen, 1985).

The argument about more CO_2 narrowing pores and slowing evaporation shows the difficulties of scaling up. The narrowing of pores and slowing of evaporation can be shown in the laboratory. More CO_2 may even increase photosynthesis of drought-stricken plants (Idso, 1988). The argument is whether the larger leaves encouraged by more CO_2 plus the consequent warming of first the leaf and then the surrounding air will make the slowing minor (Jarvis and McNaughton, 1986). A comprehensive physical model of an unchanged canopy of a grassland, forest, or wheat field in a steady climate shows, however, that although 40 percent more stomatal resistance to evaporation would not cut evaporation 40 percent, it would cut it 12 to 17 percent (Rosenberg et al., 1990). In fact, when stomata were narrowed by a chemical spray, the evaporation from a barley field or a pine plantation slowed by 5 to 20 percent (Waggoner et al., 1964; Waggoner and Bravdo, 1967).

After all complications are tallied, a survey of many species, conditions, and experiments shows a 1/4 to 1/2 percent change in growth for each percentage change in CO_2 (Gates, 1985).[1] In other terms, a rise in CO_2 of half from 350 to 525 ppm would raise growth by 1/8 to 1/4.

The generality of plants with a responsive photosynthesis gaining on others in rising CO_2 has been demonstrated by crops and weeds. The responsive weed, velvet leaf, increased its growth more than the less responsive corn when CO_2 was raised. Further, the weed, itch grass, which has the less responsive sort of photosynthesis, gained less than soybeans, which have the more responsive sort of photosynthesis. Limited nutrients did not nullify the help of CO_2, including greater height and leaf area that will affect competition for light (Patterson and Flint, 1980, 1982).

When four species grew together, the effects of moisture and CO_2 amplified each other. One species with more responsive photosynthesis and that is adapted to wet soil gradually displaced one species with less responsive photosynthesis as CO_2 and moisture were raised. The total weight of the four species rose with rising CO_2, but the proportion produced by the two other species was low and remained low (Bazzaz and Carlson, 1984).

A final consideration is the long term. When the CO_2 in the air above a tract of Alaskan tundra was raised, photosynthesis rose as expected but then declined to that of land exposed to normal air. In a continuing experiment in coastal wetlands near Chesapeake Bay, however, more CO_2 in the air increased the carbon sequestered throughout the first 3 years and continues to increase it (Tissue and Oechel, 1987; Drake, 1989). So far, these contradictory results have not been reconciled.

Limitation on Experiments

Experiments with one or two factors controlled help us understand the effect of more CO_2. Extrapolating or scaling up these brief experiments to the prolonged behavior of entire systems of plants is nonetheless full of uncertainty. In some experiments the light or ventilation in the chamber was unrealistic; the benefit of slower transpiration was not shown; the roots were restricted in pots, but the foliage was not crowded by neighbors; the treatments were not replicated or randomized; or the experiments were too brief to show adaptation, reproduction, or competition (Bazzaz et al., 1985; Eamus and Jarvis, 1989; Rose, 1989). Beyond these limitations of the experiments lie doubts whether unforeseen things like pests would appear and change the results of longer experiments or whether unforeseen interactions would arise in a whole system of plants unlike those in the simple one in a chamber.

Natural ecosystems as well as managed ones have herbivores eating plants and predators eating herbivores. The standing crop of plants on an area is a function not only of the primary production from plants but also of the amount of plant material removed by grazers and pests. Thus, even if increasing CO_2 implies more plant growth, any change in the standing crop is uncertain. On farms plants will be protected by such techniques as integrated pest management and pest resistance in crops. In natural systems, on the other hand, CO_2 fertilization might lower the nitrogen content of plants and thus change insect feeding or change populations of grazers and predators on them.

Similar doubts arise whenever reasoning cannot be tested because experiments are impossible or because size and complication make them impractical. One wise course is to reason critically, rank the importance of the question against others, devote resources according to the rank, and then experiment as large and as long as resources permit. Another wise course is to analyze observations of the outdoors.

Observations Outdoors

In an ideal world, all the living things on the land, in the soil, and in the ocean could be weighed annually and the change in carbon in them assessed just as the changing CO_2 in the air can be seen in the record from Mauna Loa. This is, of course, impractical because things vary from place to place and because one large number would be subtracted from another, nearly equal, one.

The rings in long-lived trees have been examined for evidence of growth changing in step with the CO_2 in the air. The trees were certainly growing faster, but one person interpreted it as evidence of the help of CO_2 and another as the help of more precipitation (LaMarch et al., 1984; Gates, 1985).

Failing in a direct observation of changing growth of living things, one can turn to the CO_2 record itself for evidence. While the average CO_2 during the year is rising, the amplitude of the fluctuation from winter to summer increases about 1/2 percent per year. This is consistent with the CO_2 enrichment of the air increasing growth worldwide. Although even this conclusion is clouded by uncertainties, it appears that the accumulation of biomass on the planet is either increasing or is steady, not decreasing (Revelle and Kohlmaier, 1986).

Summary

Because plants are sensitive to CO_2 in the air, its concentration in the air is one of the things that will modify the change in the primary production of food as climate changes. In experiments more CO_2 increases photosynthesis and slows evaporation. The question is whether these benefits will be large or small compared to the influences of climate and other changes.

Uncertainties attend scaling experiments up to the reality of a whole landscape. Nevertheless, the experiments do suggest that—even where factors like fertilizer or water are short—CO_2 will speed photosynthesis, slow transpiration, and make plants with responsive photosynthesis more competitive. We know that any speeding, slowing, and competing will not be added to or subtracted from activities as they are today, but will modify the outcome of other changes as plants grow and interact in entire systems of plants.

FARMING

Concentrate on Crops

The dimensions of U.S. agriculture can be seen in 1988 marketings in billions of dollars: livestock, 79; food and feed crops, 66; cotton lint and tobacco, 6; and lumber, 4. Although heat waves can kill chickens and blizzards can starve cattle, it will be argued later that animals are less sensitive to climate than crops. Of course, the economics of livestock production are tightly linked to the condition of range and pasture and with the supply of feed grains. A later section will be devoted to forests. So, the impact of climate change and adaptation of agriculture is examined here largely for crops, and this section is called Farming. Despite the riches of food in some places today, human population growth will swell demand during the decades of expected climate change.

Crop Sensitivity to Climate

It is not difficult to demonstrate that crops are directly sensitive to weather and climate. Frost kills citrus, drought shrivels wheat, and hail shreds soybean leaves. Frosts in Florida during the 1970s and 1980s contributed to the loss of much of that state's orange juice industry to Brazil (Miller and Glantz, 1988).

Another example is the 1988 drought in the United States. In North Dakota about the same area was planted in both 1987 and 1988, but in 1988 only 78 percent of the area was harvested and production was only 38 percent of the prior year. In Iowa about the same area was planted and harvested in both years, but only 69 percent as much was produced in dry 1988 as in 1987 (U.S. Department of Agriculture, 1989a).

There is a tendency in discussions of the potential effects of climate change on crops to consider only temperature and precipitation effects. However, changes in solar radiation (through altered cloudiness), humidity, and windiness are equally likely. They affect crops and must be borne in mind lest we think that prediction of climate change effects on crops will be less complex than it really is.

Weather also affects crops indirectly. When dry weather stops the sporulation of a fungus and its infection of grasshoppers, the hoppers swarm onto crops (Capinera and Horton, 1989). In wet weather, on the other hand, certain fungi blight crops (Waggoner, 1960).[2]

A neglected matter is how climate change would alter the organization and resources of soil, water, and the genetic basis for crops that undergirds farming. Muddy roads and washed-out bridges interrupt the supplies farmers need, and they stop farmers from carrying their produce to feed others.

But washed-out bridges can be rebuilt, whereas eroded soils are not so easily repaired and genes from extinct species can neither improve varieties nor make new crops.

Natural Resources

So far, improvements in farming in many places have increased yields from the constant supply of natural resources as fast as human demands have grown or faster. Agricultural research and the farmers who apply its results have been highly successful. The clear question is: If climate changes during several decades, can these same people maintain the foundation of natural resources and raise more food for the escalating demands and numbers of people?

Soil is easily forgotten when new maps of vegetation zones are drawn for new climates. On the one hand, a new climate of wind or rain could erode an old productive soil. On the other hand, if the climate becomes favorable to crops where it was once arctic but the substratum is granite, centuries may pass before the soil becomes as fertile as the climate is favorable (Jenny, 1941; Joffe, 1949).

Moisture to sustain crops depends on amount and timeliness of precipitation and its balance against evaporation. The balance also fixes how much water is left to supply irrigation water by running off into streams and reservoirs and percolating into aquifers.

Only a few plant species among millions that grew at one time or another provided the genes for the crops that feed farm animals and us. Within a crop, genetic uniformity can cause vulnerability, as when Southern corn leaf blight arose and struck the U.S. corn crop in 1970. Fortunately, the genetic diversity of U.S. crops was broader in 1980 than in 1970 (Duvick, 1984). Nevertheless, we should be concerned that a climate change might extinguish wild races of major crops that might furnish valuable genes or even extinguish species that might become crops (Wilson, 1989). The large effort of preserving seeds in banks is described in the section "The Natural Landscape," below.

Estimating Sensitivity

At the outset of estimating impact, one wonders "of what?" If we want to know the impact of climate change on Iowa corn, we must ask: What will the change be in Des Moines? As related in our Assumptions, the future climate in any locality, especially the crucial factor of precipitation, will not soon be predicted confidently. So, we are left to think about sensitivities that can be multiplied by reasonable rates of climate change and integrated into the impact of a climate change.

One way of estimating the sensitivities is from the history of weather and yield. The regressions of Thompson (1988) exemplify the method. His regression coefficients for, say, corn yield on rain and temperature, month by month, are sensitivities. An early use of these sensitivities in assessing the impact of climate change produced such estimates as 11 percent less corn per 1°C warming in summer maximum temperature and 1.5 percent less for each 10 percent less summer rain (Bach, 1979). Later, a shift in the location of the Corn Belt (Blasing and Solomon, 1982; Newman, 1982), the help of CO_2 enrichment, and even adaptation to the new climate were considered by Waggoner (1983).

Regression equations, while instructive, are not generally reliable for extrapolations beyond the range of the data used in their development. Also, they cannot be used to deal with CO_2 enrichment effects. Process models or simulators that simulate plant growth, yield, and water use offer the best alternative to the regression model. Simulators, however, have their own limitations. For example, most simulate plant development by calculating growing degree days or some other index of heat accumulation. Given warmer temperatures, the simulators predict maturity earlier and so curtail the opportunity for production and accumulation of yield. This is reasonable. Plants do mature earlier in hot years. For this reason, however, simulated effects on summer crops may be too severe. Crops sown in the fall, on the other hand, benefit in simulation from the milder winters, break dormancy sooner, and mature before the hot, dry weather sets in. Hence, only moderate losses are often simulated due to even severe warming.

Thus far, most simulators have not dealt effectively with the episodic events that are most critical in determining yield, such as outbreaks of disease or the sterilization of pollen by extreme temperatures at critical times. One distinct advantage of the simulators is their ability to take direct account of CO_2 fertilization. Another distinct advantage is that they can be used to consider adaptations such as different varieties, planting dates, and tillage practices. By submitting several years of weather records to the simulators, either actual or adjusted by some measure of climate change, the frequency distributions of annual yields can be calculated. Changes in frequency of bumper and disaster years may be as important an impact of climate change as changes in mean yields (Waggoner, 1983). A number of specific simulators that have been used in climate impact analysis are mentioned below.

Parry et al. (1988) summarized an ambitious study conducted through the International Institute of Applied Systems Analysis (IIASA) of impacts that concentrated on the cold and semiarid margins of agriculture. Various regressions and simulators were employed, as were other techniques of geography and climatology. Although various scenarios of climate change were considered, the results of one climate scenario from a global circulation model were applied to all the regions. Existing sensitivities of agriculture to climate variability and potential sensitivities to climate change were identified. Preeminent effects were changes in length of the growing season and in growth rates changing the required growing season; changes in mean yield; changes in yield variability and in the certainty of expectable yields; changes in yield quantity; and changes in the sensitivity of plants to fertilizers, pesticides, and herbicides. Spatial shifts in comparative advantage and of crop potential could follow any or all of these. Climate change may also affect water balance and thus irrigation and flood control requirements as well as soil erosion, soil fertility, and pests.

Simulators were important in the Environmental Protection Agency (EPA) assessment of the potential effects of climate change for U.S. agriculture (Smith and Tirpak, 1989). Regions studied included the Great Lakes (Ritchie et al., 1989), the Southeastern United States (Peart et al., 1989), the Great Plains (Rosenzweig, 1989), and California (Dudek, 1989). Various simulators were used, including CERES-maize (i.e., corn) (Peart et al., 1989; Ritchie et al., 1989; Rosenzweig, 1989), CERES-wheat (Rosenzweig, 1989), and SOYGRO (Peart et al., 1989; Ritchie et al., 1989). Fertilization effects of CO_2 and opportunities for adaptation were considered in these modeling exercises. The climate change scenarios produced by general circulation models (GCMs) for doubled greenhouse gases were applied to these models.

The major findings of these studies were that, without the direct effect of CO_2, yields of wheat, soybeans, and corn declined in the Great Lakes, Southeast, and Great Plains regions, except in the northernmost latitudes, where frost-free season was lengthened. Decreases in yield stemmed mostly from the shortened life span of crops caused by higher temperatures. Differences among climate scenarios led to predicted yields ranging from mild gains to severe losses. Location within regions was important. Irrigation moderated yield losses as did higher CO_2, least in the southeast and most in the north. However, significant increases in irrigation requirement were noted, especially with the more severe climate scenario. The adaptations tested, such as longer-season varieties of corn in Illinois, did not fully compensate for the loss of yield (Easterling, 1989).

More recently, the EPIC simulator has been used in a study sponsored by the Department of Energy to evaluate how climate change would affect agriculture in the Missouri-Iowa-Nebraska-Kansas (MINK) region (Easterling et al., 1991; Rosenberg and Crosson, 1991). Yields on some 50 representative farms were simulated by using the actual weather of the hot, dry 1930s as the scenario of climate change. Results varied between and within the four states because of differences in soil, crops, rotations, and other farming practices. Further, during the 1930s, the weather was not uniformly droughty in all portions of the region. In general, though, yields of summer crops were reduced, on average, 18 to 25 percent. Wheat yields were reduced little. Irrigation requirement increased about 28 percent in Nebraska and Kansas. All of these effects were moderated by an increase in atmospheric CO_2 content from 350 to 450 ppm. Such adaptations as altered planting dates, longer-season varieties, and tillage to conserve moisture moderated the yield losses.

Findings from the Parry et al. (1988) and the EPA (Smith and Tirpak, 1989) studies figure prominently in the recent report of the Intergovernmental Panel on Climate Change (IPCC) (1990b) in which estimated impacts are described as changes in productive potential against a baseline of present technology and management. Key findings were:

• It has not yet been demonstrated conclusively whether, on average, global agricultural potential will increase or decrease.

• Severe negative effects are possible in some regions, particularly those of high present-day vulnerability that are least able to adjust technically.

• Two broad sets of regions appear most vulnerable: (1) some semiarid tropical and subtropical regions (possibly western Arabia, the Maghreb, western Africa, Horn of Africa, southern Africa, and eastern Brazil) and (2) some humid tropical and equatorial regions (possibly southeast Asia and central America).

• Changes causing water shortages in regions that are now exporters of grains (southern Europe, southern United States, parts of South America, and western Australia) may lessen their productive potential.

Estimating Impacts

Whether one calculates the change in evaporation, the change in yield of crops in the southeastern United States or Great Plains, or the economic effect, the differing climate scenarios from reputable predictors produce farm impacts even more strikingly different than the scenarios themselves.

Difficult as it is to estimate yield sensitivities to the impacts of climate change, it may be even more difficult to estimate the economic impacts. Analyzing the impact of a climate change on the national income of the United States, Nordhaus (1991) estimated that the largest impact on a sector would be on farming. He estimated it would be +$12 billion to –$12 billion (see Table 34.6).

Adams et al. (1990), using a spatial equilibrium agricultural model of the United States, tabulated results of the EPA assessments mentioned above and found that for one scenario of climate change prices would fall 18 percent and the economic surplus would rise $9.9 billion, but for the other prices would rise 28 percent and the economic surplus would fall $10.5 billion. In the MINK study (Crosson et al., 1991; Rosenberg and Crosson, 1991), with no adjustments and no CO_2 enrichment, a regional input-output model shows that the decline in regional production of corn, sorghum, wheat, hay, and soybeans would be $4.4 billion (1982 dollars) or 1.4 percent of the total regional production to final demand, if all the decline were in exports. If the decline in the feedgrains, corn and sorghum, were to be only in exports, the loss would be $3.1 billion or 1.0 percent, but if the decline falls on animal producers the loss would be as high as $30 billion (or 10 percent of the regional production) because of impacts on meat packing, the largest manufacturing activity in the region. In all cases, higher CO_2 reduces the losses.

When climate change is foreseen, the specter of worse pests usually rises. The relationships between climate and pests are clear; the northward movement of the overwintering range of insect pests, for example, can be calculated for scenarios of climate change on plant-pest interactions (Stinner et al., 1989).

There are, however, all sorts of pests, some favored by cool weather and some by warm, some by wet weather and some by dry. This diversity can be seen in maps of the prevalence of plant disease, such as the one that shows more apple scab in the humid western part of Washington State and less in the arid central part (Weltzien, 1978). The relationship between weather and weed pests led to the drawing of a "pestograph" with axes of temperature and moisture. Purple nutsedge flourishes in warm wet, weather; field bindweed in warm, dry weather; quackgrass in cool, wet weather; and Canada thistle in cool, dry weather (National Research Council, 1976).

Since the outlook is for warming, the opinion of an expert on tropical diseases of plants is relevant: ". . . it would seem that continued successful production of the majority of tropical crops, which are highly homogeneous genetically, belies both the contention of imminent danger from homogeneity as well as the oft-stated maxim that diseases are worse in the tropics because there is no winter. Neither seems to be a valid generality" (Buddenhagen, 1977). In short, the certain outcome of a climate change is not more nor less plant pests, but rather different ones.

Adaptation of Food Production

Adaptation Also Makes Impacts Uncertain

Added to the uncertainty about climate in, say, 2050 is uncertainty about the sensitivity of farming then to any climate. The impact of a temperature change on, say, corn in Missouri is irrelevant if the Corn Belt moves somewhere else. If yield per acre and hence prices change, demand will change, and technology may change the sensitivity to weather.

The economic effects arrayed for the MINK study (summarized by Rosenberg and Crosson, 1991) were calculated on two unlikely assumptions: first, that the climate changes immediately on the world as it is today and, second, that no adjustments to these changes are attempted. In both the MINK study and the earlier EPA and IIASA studies, some simple adaptations to the shortened crop-growing seasons are tested. The simulators show in general that longer-season varieties and earlier planting can help overcome yield losses. Wilks (1988) modeled the response of North American corn and wheat yields to a doubled CO_2 climate change and reached a similar conclusion. He found that by selecting the most appropriate planting dates and cultivars for the changed climate, yield reductions could be minimized. Had he considered the effect of CO_2 fertilization, his results likely would have been even more optimistic. Substitution of more resilient species, such as sorghum for corn, provides other tactical opportunities. In the MINK study, however, sorghum did not improve the farmer's balance sheet because of its lower price. On the other hand, simple changes in tillage to conserve water reduced loss of yield.

Can Farming Adapt?

If truly radical changes occur in climate—for example, a 5°C warming or severely curtailed or even greatly increased precipitation—simple adaptations will not suffice. It is more reasonable to believe that under such stringencies agricultural systems would be radically changed. Tropical savannah or tropical desert might exist where we now grow corn. Nonetheless, there are some indications that adaptations can be effected even to large changes in climate. The first is the adaptation of wheat to both colder and warmer climates (see Figure 34.2).

Hard red winter wheat has cultural and economic advantages over the competing spring wheats. Most important are that it is planted in the fall, which avoids waiting for the soil to thaw in the spring, and it is harvested before the heat and drought of summer can cut its yield. Its adaptation by breeding and other techniques is illustrated by the difference between the former northern boundary of Sidney, Nebraska (Location 1 in Figure 34.2), and the present one near Sidney, Montana (Location 2 in Figure 34.2). Compared to the old boundary, the new one has 20 percent less precipitation, an average temperature that is 4°C colder, a growing season that is 10 days shorter, and an annual amplitude of monthly means that are 6°C greater (Rosenberg, 1982).

Farmers adapt to a lack of rain by irrigating. From 1954 to 1984 the irrigated acreage in the United States rose from about 30 million to 45 million acres. An adaptation to a shortage of water is raising the efficiency of irrigation. Improved irrigation efficiencies during 1950 to 1980 reduced per-acre applications from the Ogallala Aquifer in the High Plains from Texas to Nebraska by a third. Among irrigation methods, efficiency rises

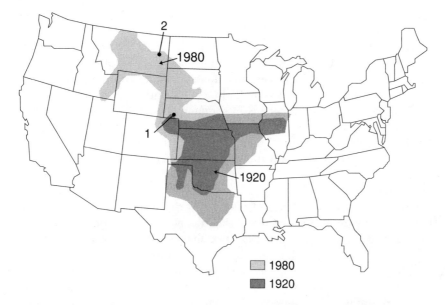

FIGURE 34.2   Adaptation and expansion of hard red winter wheat from 1920 to 1980.

SOURCE: Reprinted, by permission of Kluwer Academic Publishers, from Rosenberg (1982). Copyright © 1982 by Kluwer Academic Press.

from 40 to 50 percent for furrow to 60 to 92 percent for trickle irrigation, but Peterson and Keller (1990) found that improving use of existing technologies was more economical than a change in technology.

An average increased demand for irrigation water of approximately 15 percent (for a mixture of alfalfa, corn, and winter wheat) was found by Allen and Gichuki (1989) for the Great Plains states from Texas to Nebraska in response to two GCM scenarios. Demands may be greater during peak periods, and growing seasons may be lengthened by various adaptations. Similarly, in the MINK study, irrigation demands increase by about 25 percent for corn and sorghum and 10 percent for wheat exposed to the climate of the 1930s. It is important to recognize that, in climate circumstances that create a greater demand for irrigation water, runoff to streams may also be reduced. And of course ground water supplies will not increase, but rather will decline more rapidly. Additionally, as Frederick and Kneese (1990) have shown, demand for limited water supplies for other uses—municipal and industrial, fish and wildlife, recreation and navigation—may make water too expensive for agriculture. This trend is already occurring in the arid West and would likely be accentuated by any climatic change that decreases supplies or increases demand.

Can It Adapt Swiftly and Cheaply?

To adapt successfully to a climate change in a half century or so, adaptations must be quicker than the half-century and they must be economical. The average lifetime of a successful cultivated plant variety shows how fast varieties of a crop can be adapted. In 1981 plant breeders estimated that varieties lasted 7 years in corn, 8 in sorghum and cotton, and 9 in soybean and wheat. They opined that the life spans would grow shorter (Duvick, 1984). In 1990 a commercial seed company testified that a successful new variety of wheat has a useful life of about 6 years and costs $1 million to develop (Newlin, 1990).

Canola illustrates the speed of introduction of a wholly new crop. During World War II a small area of rapeseed was grown in Canada for marine lubricant. Figure 34.3 shows that during the next 30 years or so its production expanded rapidly to a level of more than 3 million tons per year. The expansion required breeding to make the oil edible, changing its name to canola, building processing plants, and organizing markets (Waggoner, 1990).

Irrigation adapts crops to dry climates but requires water and has potential long-term negative consequences that must be taken into account. Dur-

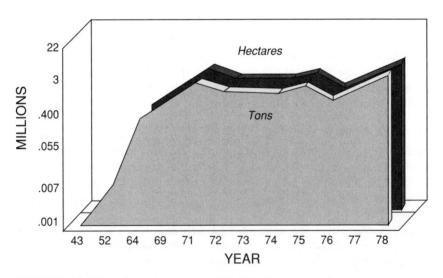

FIGURE 34.3 Rise of canola or rapeseed in Canada.

NOTE: The years are irregularly spaced, and the vertical scale of millions of hectares or tons is logarithmic.

SOURCE: Reprinted, courtesy of Paul Waggoner, from Waggoner (1990).

ing recent decades irrigated area increased by less than 2 percent per year in the West, but by more than 10 percent per year in the East (Peterson and Keller, 1990). These normal life spans and costs of varieties, the introduction of a new crop in about 30 years, and the rates of change of irrigation— all without the spur of changing climate—suggest that adaptation likely can keep ahead of the climate change, as most specialists see it in the next three to five decades, say. But rapid climate change, transient changes such as cooling prior to warming, or major changes in the distribution (variability) of temperature, precipitation, storminess, and so forth, could, of course, challenge this essentially optimistic view of adaptation potentials.

Future Adaptations

Although predictions of future technologies for several decades have erred notoriously by missing large ones altogether, it is worthwhile to describe some strong possibilities. As for varieties, the survey of life spans found, for example, 60,000 corn cultivars and hybrids in preliminary trials in 1980 compared to 454 in commercial use. Future adaptation requires pursuit of such trials and underlying plant breeding by about 1,000 private and public workers, the seed banks, and the natural sources of diversity of crops (Wilkes, 1984). Expansion of irrigation in the West would be hard if the climate grew drier but easy in the East because only a fraction of the supply is consumed today (Peterson and Keller, 1990).

What of the developing world? We have presented a relatively optimistic view in this section of current and future agricultural capability to cope with at least the assumed climate changes. The implicit assumption has been that the research and the farmers in the developed world (more particularly in the United States) will be adequate to the task and that new tools such as biotechnology and computer-guided irrigation will make rapid adaptation easier in the future than it is today. But now we must address the question of means and resources. Can the developing world cope as easily?

There is no reason to believe that the developing countries as a group will be exposed to worse climatic changes than the developed countries. Not everywhere in the developing countries are the climates marginal. What is certain, however, is that their margins of survival are smaller and that the impacts of climatic change might be more immediate and profound where the infrastructure, including research capacity, is smaller. In fact, an Indian agriculturist, Jodha (1989), argues that farmers in developing countries use well-tried techniques in times of stress and that these are an arsenal from which to draw when the evidence of climate change becomes strong enough to convince them and their governments of the need. Jodha provides many examples of these responses, particularly from the Indian experience. In climatically marginal areas, particularly in the semiarid tropics, even a slow, small change toward a worsening climate can, of course, accentuate climatic risks. It is vital to note, however, that the share of gross domestic product from agriculture in less developed countries decreased 50 percent between 1960 and 1980, so that the economic transformation of those countries may be lessening their sensitivity to climate (The South Commission, 1990).

Earlier we pointed out that, to date, impact assessments have tried to answer the question: What would be the impact of a future climate change on the world (nation, region, state) as it behaves today? Insights have surely been gained. However, the really relevant question is: How will a region behave at such time as the climate does change? Impact assessors are obliged to anticipate what agriculture (and all other sectors) will be like when climate changes are finally felt.

The MINK study described above attempts to do this. Starting from an understanding of the region as it is today, its agriculture, forests, water resources, and energy economy are projected to the year 2030. For example, absent climate change, its crops are projected to yield about 75 percent more than they do today. The imposition of the 1930s climate reduces yields by about 25 percent, but the CO_2 enrichment offsets about half of that loss. Adaptations—both autonomous in the sense of being easily accessible and relatively inexpensive to adopt and policy-driven adaptations prompted by the perception or knowledge of certain climate change—bring yields back almost to the level of no climate change.

As in all such studies thus far, the results ought not to be taken as predictions but rather as illustrations of a method that should reveal the potential for adaptations to cope with future climate change.

Summary

If climate changes, crops will be the exposed and sensitive part of agriculture in both rich and poor countries. Their sensitivity is visible as when they prosper after a rain or wither during a drought. The speeding of their photosynthesis by rising CO_2 or encouragement of one of their pests, on the other hand, are invisible. Their sensitivity also lies in the sensitivity of the soil and so forth on which they depend. The direct sensitivity of crops to weather is estimated both from history and experiments. When it comes to estimating the impact of climate change, however, the uncertainties of the scenarios of climate change and the invisible factors and the tempering of exchanges and adaptations cloud the crystal ball. Fortunately, actual experience shows that farmers do adapt promptly. To adapt promptly they need effective research outdoors that applies, among other things, ample biological diversity in breeding. They need incentives and freedom to adapt.

FORESTS AND GRASSLANDS

Concentrate on the Managed Trees

Although the production from the fifth of U.S. land in crops is valuable, forests and rangeland shape much of the landscape. In 1982 forest land was fully 29 percent and pasture of different kinds was another 26 percent of the total land area of the United States (see Figure 34.4a). The forests alone provide a quarter of the industrial raw materials, give millions of people recreation, shed much of the water we use, and shelter countless plants and animals (U.S. Office of Technology Assessment, 1983; Cordell, 1989; Flather and Hoekstra, 1989; Guldin, 1989).

This section will concentrate on the managed forests. The managed pastures may be considered part of farming, dealt with in the preceding section, "Farming." The unmanaged forests and ranges are the subject of the next section, "The Natural Landscape." Figure 34.4b shows, of course, that forests managed for timber and unmanaged ones are not distinct classes. Here, however, the concentration is on managed ones.

Much forest is inaccessible, reserved, or unproductive (Figure 34.4b), removing it from practical management. Unproductive forests yield less

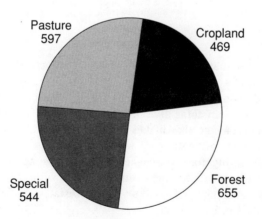

FIGURE 34.4a   Use of land in the United States.

NOTE: Cropland encompasses land used for crops, land that is idle, or land used only for pasture. Pasture is grassland and other nonforest pasture and range. Special land includes urban and transportation areas, government areas for military and primarily for recreation and wildlife, and farmsteads.

SOURCE: U.S. Department of Agriculture (1986).

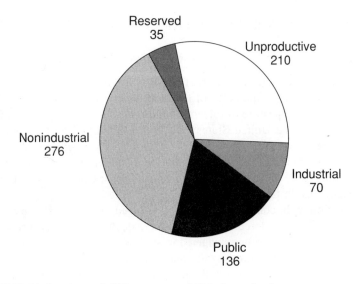

FIGURE 34.4b   Area of different sorts of U.S. forest land.

NOTE: Unproductive forest land is incapable of growing 20 ft^3/A/yr.   Reserved forest land is productive but reserved, as in officially designated wilderness.   Public forest land is held by governments, mostly the U.S. Forest Service.   Nonindustrial private forest land is held by farmers and other private entities who do not own mills.   Industrial forest land is held by companies that also own mills.

SOURCE: Haynes (1989).

than 20 ft^3/A/yr, making their management impractical.   The 10 percent industrial forest is probably the best land and the most managed.   The public and nonindustrial private forests range from intensively managed to ignored.   In sum something like half the forest land is probably managed today.   Climate change that makes more or less land unproductive could change the estimate of "half."

Although planting forests to take in CO_2 from the air is a prominent suggestion when climate change is discussed, the subject here is impact and adaptation to a change.   The topic of reforestation is addressed by the Mitigation Panel in Part Three.

Because trees are long-lived organisms, they are adapted to withstand significant fluctuations in climate.   Although a forester might want to factor climate change into the choice of the species of trees to be planted today, the uncertainty of climate scenarios, particularly at small-scale units that are most useful for forest management, renders prescriptive planning diffi-cult.   For example, storms like hurricanes profoundly affect tall and long-lived trees, but scenarios in such detail are too uncertain for profitable reasoning. We consider only the climate changes considered in Chapter 32, the section "Assumptions."

Just as farming depends on natural resources, forestry does, too. Because forests and ranges are bigger and their yield of money per acre is less than from farms, they may depend more on the natural resources. In all events, soil and its moisture must be right for a new climate to continue to produce lumber and support cattle. And, adapted varieties must be found.

Sensitivities of Forests

As climate changed, the sensitivity of forests to climate changed them. Consider pines in Eastern North America during the 18,000 years since the Ice Age maximum. They started from a block in Georgia and Carolina, nearly disappeared 12,000 years ago, and then spread to occupy one zone from Louisiana to Carolina and another along the northern border of the Canadian prairie (Webb, 1986).

Changes in temperature, precipitation, and atmospheric concentrations of CO_2 may have direct physiological effects on the growth of forest trees. For an individual tree, the impact of a climate change includes the direct effect of CO_2 reported earlier. Although the longer growing seasons of a warmer climate would raise productivity, ill-adapted trees could suffer frost damage during their prolonged growth and others might not be chilled enough to germinate (Cannell and Smith, 1986; Cannell, 1987; Kimmins and Lavender, 1987). The sensitivity of individual trees to moisture is demonstrated by the difference in species from the north to south slopes of many ridges and from the dry, rocky summits to the wet marshes below.

The sensitivity of entire stands of trees has been estimated from tree rings, pollen deposits, and simulations. Although the evidence is equivocal, faster growth of tree rings has been interpreted as evidence of more CO_2 in the air.

Pollen records provide evidence of the past range of various plants. Natural migration rates can be inferred from these data. The rate of migration of temperate forests, as inferred from pollen records, is about 100km per century (Davis, 1981). Isotherms on a map of growing season climate show a gradient of about 2°C per 500 km. So a climate change even in the low end of the assumed range of 1° to 5°C in a century or less would move the isotherms several times as fast as the pollen record shows forests have moved on their own.

More complicated computations by mathematical models generally confirm the rough estimation in the preceding paragraph (Solomon and Tharp, 1985; Solomon and Webb, 1985; Solomon, 1986b; Botkin and Nisbet, 1989; Urban and Shugart, 1989). Model results can be summarized as follows. The response of mature forests depends on the species composition. If the mixture includes some species that are well suited to a warmer climate, the total stand biomass can increase despite the decline or death of some components. The increase may be rather rapid if the responsive species are dominants or can occur more slowly if the responsive species occupy lower canopy positions. If none of the species in the forest are adapted to the warmer climate, total biomass will decline, perhaps rapidly.

Estimating Impacts

As on the farm, climate change—warming, changes in soil moisture, and changes in the composition of the atmosphere—raises the specter of more pests in the forest. If the change itself weakens a tree, it will likely be attacked by some pest. In an analogue, trees weakened by defoliation or air pollution are then attacked by bark beetles or the fungus Armillariella (Smith, 1981). Also, a different climate encourages different pests. As discussed above, however, warmer climates do not today have greater outbreaks and epidemics than cooler ones—just different.

The calculated impact of doubled CO_2 on forests as on farms depends on the climate scenario, region by region. Since that is uncertain, generalities drawn from Figure 34.5 must serve. It is the gist of complex mathematical models and relates growth as a percentage of the maximum for the forest type to a factor of climate, exemplified here by temperature (Botkin et al., 1989; Urban and Shugart, 1989). If the current climate is at the heavy vertical line, spruce fir dominates the forest. If the climate warms to I, both types grow faster and presumably, the growth of the whole forest is faster. If the climate warms on to II, the hardwoods have an advantage, although they may have to wait until the spruce fir die. If the climate warms all the way to III, both types decline.

After the decline, a new forest may or may not emerge. If the new climate were as hot and dry as western Texas, for example, none would emerge. If it were not so severe, the new forest would depend initially on the supply of adapted species on the spot. In a mixed forest these might well be on the spot. If the adapted species were absent, the new forest would depend on their arrival. Although they could be brought by people, their arrival by natural migration could be slow, as already mentioned.

In Figure 34.5 forests are exemplified by spruce fir and northern hardwoods and climate factors by temperature. The curves are set first by zero growth at the limit of the ranges of the two types of forest. Then the maximum of each curve is set at the same maximum at the climate optimum for each type, making the growth rates relative. While the general pattern is realistic, these models probably overstate the sensitivity of the forest to climate change. The limit of zero growth is set by the edge of the current range of the types, but competition more than inability of an

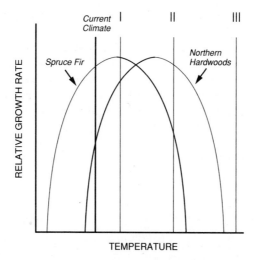

FIGURE 34.5   Gist of models simulating the change in forests.

NOTE: Schematic representation of a JABOWA-type Forest Stand Simulator. Diameter growth of individual trees is simulated as a function of factors such as light, temperature, and soil moisture. Relative growth rate refers to the fraction of the maximum observed for the species in open-growth conditions. Climate warming can either increase the growth of all components in a stand (Case I), increase the growth of one and decrease the growth of another (Case II), or decrease the growth of both (Case III).

SOURCE: Reprinted, courtesy of Clark Binkley, from Binkley (1990).

isolated tree to grow fixes the edge. So, the present forest could persist longer than predicted.

Adaptation

The natural pace of adaptation may be too slow to maintain a particular forest on a particular tract of land. Using climate scenarios like our assumptions, some researchers (Franklin et al., 1989; Urban and Shugart, 1989) estimate that the changes in forests we have discussed will appear in 40 to 70 years. To be effective, adaptive responses must operate within this time frame.

Move Lumbering or Use Less Wood

If climate becomes unfavorable to forests in one region and favorable in another, lumbering can move as it has before. Between the 1700s and today, lumbering moved from colonial New England to the Great Lake states, from there to the South and West, and finally back to the South.

Another adaptation to a changed forest is simply using less timber. If timber becomes scarce, prices will rise and less will be demanded. History shows that actually happens. For example, since 1900 the price of softwood timber in constant dollars rose about 2.5 percent per year, and the consumption of softwood lumber fell from a peak of 530 board feet per capita in 1906 to only 190 today (Binkley, 1988; Binkley and Vincent, 1988; Fedkiw, 1989; Haynes, 1989). Economic adjustments compensate for impacts on the forest, they are felt far from the affected area, and climate change makes winners as well as losers.

Regenerate a Forest

Some forests in the United States—perhaps half of the total—are tended, and on these lands managers can intervene to speed adaptation of forests. The costs of some interventions are given in Table 34.2. If a stand of trees dies, regenerating it with an adapted species is an obvious adaptation. At about $130 per acre based on 1988 costs in the South, it is costly.

To plant a site, foresters already choose trees genetically adapted to it. For example, loblolly pine grows from the wet coastal plains of Virginia and Carolina to dry Oklahoma and Texas. An island of loblolly in central Texas is aptly called the Lost Pines. In Arkansas fast-growing loblolly from North Carolina are planted on most sites, but drought-tolerant local ones are planted on dry sites (Farnum, 1990).

Although knowledge of the genetics of commercially important trees is advanced, the seed of most species of trees in the United States has not been collected and screened. On the other hand, since pines evolved from Mexico and a large number of species of this tree are found there, there is an active program to preserve this genetic material. Expecting warmer climates, foresters should look for candidates in places that are warmer today.

Regeneration is difficult, and a drier climate will make it more difficult. As Smith (1986) noted, "A very crucial race against time which the seedling must make is that of extending its roots downward faster than the loss of water through direct evaporation from the capillary fringe [of the soil] can overtake them." So, success may need first hardy seedlings of a variety adapted to the site and then appropriate control of shade and competitors.

Manage the Forest

Light, nutrients in the soil, and especially moisture govern the growth of a forest. Several ways of enhancing these are shown in Table 34.2. Where

TABLE 34.2 Cost of Forest Management Activities in the
U.S. South, 1988

	Cost ($/acre)	
Activity	Range	Average
Stand establishment		
Site preparation	63.80-158.17	92.66
Planting	34.03-44.28	36.90
Stand management		
Prescribed burning	4.40-10.57	6.52
Herbicide treatment	36.40-52.47	41.25
Fertilization	29.17-41.55	35.84
Fire protection	1.08-1.72	1.36
Precommercial thinning	49.54-63.58	55.58
Genetic screening		
Irrigation		

SOURCE: Adapted from Straka et al. (1989). Copyright © 1989 by
Forest Farmers Association.

moisture is short, removing understory plants increases the productivity as much as 25 percent (Zahner, 1955). In terms of adaptation this could offset a 25 percent decrease in growth by a drier climate. Removing parts of the main canopy and thus the leaf area also saves moisture, prolongs summer growth, and saves some individuals. Cutting less adapted portions of a mixed forest has been estimated to increase productivity by as much as 25 percent (Larson et al., 1989). Although wet forests have been drained, the converse—irrigation—is too expensive to be practical outside nurseries or seed orchards.

If climate grows hotter and drier, controlling fires will be more important and costly, but if the climate grows wetter, it will be less costly. Fire control can be effective. In the early 1900s about 20 million acres burned each year in 40,000 incidents. By the 1960s the area burned declined to only 2 million to 3 million acres annually despite an increase in the number of incidents to 100,000 per year. The recent fires in Yellowstone reflect more a failure to use fire control and management measures than a failure of the measures themselves.

Just as the speed of replacement of capital stock was relevant in the discussion of innovation in Chapter 33, the section "The Tools of Innovation," a shorter rotation from planting to harvesting a forest raises its adaptability. Surprisingly, middle-aged forests are at most risk if climate changes;

young ones can be replaced at comparatively low cost and older ones are valuable to salvage.

The modern practice of replacing the mixture of hardwoods typical of late stages of succession with pure pine typical of the early stages has already shortened rotations. In plantations of southern pine the rotations are 15 to 35 years, and in those of Douglas fir on the Pacific coast they are 35 to 50 years. Although these uniform plantations may lack the diversity of natural forests, the speed of change creates flexibility.

Will the Adaptations Work?

Although adaptations—in the economic system or in the forests—seem technically feasible, will they work in time and on the scale needed? Are they flexible and robust enough for the uncertainty and prolonged wait of climate change? How costly in dollars and in carbon are they?

Because the future climate is uncertain, the most desirable adaptations would be robust, performing well in many climates. And they would be flexible, that is, quick and cheap. Regeneration is neither quick nor cheap. Planting a tree adapted to a climate commits it to that climate for decades. Table 34.2 shows it is not cheap, and eliminating the old stand and replacing it is not quick.

Some management measures rate better, as Table 34.3 shows. The table also shows that two of the measures already are supported by the federal government. Table 34.2 shows the cost of these measures. The costs in carbon must also be estimated lest the management practices we adopt actually worsen the production of greenhouse gases. Shortening rotations will reduce the amount of carbon stored in forests because little carbon is absorbed during regeneration and the small trees grown on short rotations

TABLE 34.3 Flexibility and Robustness of Management

Activity	Flexibility	Robustness	Federal Support
Regenerate	Low	Low	Yes
Weed	Moderate	High	No
Thin	High	Moderate	No
Protect from fire and pests	Low	Moderate	Yes
Cut partially	High	Moderate	No
Shorten rotation	Moderate	Moderate	No

NOTE: The third column shows that two of the measures are supported by a federal program.

produce few products, such as lumber, which store carbon for long periods. A plantation of loblolly pine takes in carbon fastest at age 30, about when it is normally harvested. On the other hand, spruce fir forests take it in fastest at age 95, older than these forests are usually harvested (Birdsey, 1990). The net carbon intake, including subtraction of the fuel used during management from the accumulation of wood in the trees, must be estimated to appraise the effect on greenhouse gases. This comprehensive analysis has not yet been done.

Summary

Forests and pastures each cover more than a quarter of the land in the United States. Because trees live long lives, they are naturally adapted to variations in climate. But their long lives also make them vulnerable to climate change. If plants adapted to the new climate are not on a particular tract of land, they await natural migration or being brought in. Natural migration is too slow to keep up with the anticipated climate change. The needed artificial regeneration of forests will be costly and difficult, and needs adapted species or varieties. The adaptation of valuable forests by management is practical if the methods are robust enough to work in many climates and flexible enough to change quickly and cheaply. Finding the will and way to apply them widely enough to make a difference is a challenge.

THE NATURAL LANDSCAPE

Difference from Farming and Forestry

The natural landscape is made of unmanaged terrestrial ecosystems. It is a goodly portion of the 29 percent of U.S. land that is forest and 26 percent that is pasture. With respect to these natural ecosystems, the goals of adaptation are maintaining species richness, the major types of ecosystems, and the evolution that produces diverse living things adapted to circumstances.

Although they are unmanaged and therefore require no direct expense, the natural ecosystems help humanity in two ways. First, the species of animals, plants, and microorganisms are useful—people harvest them as game, fruit, drugs, and so forth. Also, the systems perform natural services. A growing forest, for example, absorbs CO_2 and stores carbon as wood while emitting O_2. A natural ecosystem can cleanse water while providing a place for exercise and aesthetic pleasure.

The value of these services is hard to quantify, but some attempts have been made. For systems, two values have been estimated. Building a system that would duplicate the treatment of waste water and the spawning of fish in a hectare of Louisiana wetland would cost $205,000. The storage and purification of water, binding of soil, and fertilization by a hectare of streamside vegetation in Georgia is worth $2,000 per year. In carbon monoxide absorbed, the value of a hectare of pasture is 440 kg per year (Wharton, 1970; Gosselink et al., 1973).

No physiological evidence suggests that animals would be affected directly by the projected changes in concentrations of greenhouse gases. The chief effects on animals would be via climate changes induced by CO_2 and by climatically induced changes in the plants that feed and shelter the animals.

Natural ecosystems are more vulnerable to climate change than are managed ones like farms or plantation forests, because, for example, natural ecosystems would not be irrigated nor would their components be replaced to adapt them to a climate change. Our earlier statement that climate was only one among many changes applies especially to natural ecosystems. The total change in an ecosystem depends not only on its sensitivity and the change in climate but also on the system's absolute sensitivity to a variety of other changes influencing soil and water chemistry (e.g., land use, water use, and pollutants) or habitat fragmentation as, say, clearing reduces the acreage of natural vegetation or modifies it.

Sensitivities

Resemblances to Crops and Forests

Experiments showing the advantage of CO_2 enrichment to plants with responsive photosynthesis versus those with less responsive photosynthesis were performed with young, rapidly growing annuals (Bazzaz and Carlson, 1984). Such experiments with a few plants are the basis for computing the sensitivity of entire stands of natural plants (Botkin and Simpson, 1989). The uncertainties of extrapolating or scaling them up to the behavior of entire systems of long-lived plants have already been mentioned, and they are great for the diverse systems of natural landscapes. Looking to the past for analogs of future change is fraught with difficulties because past climates are not known precisely and because what we do know suggests that they differed from those projected for the future. During climate changes since the Ice Age, both individual species and ecosystems appeared, moved, expanded, and disappeared (Spauling and Graumlich, 1986; Davis and Zabinski, 1990). Qualitatively similar changes are likely in the future.

Diversity Is Accompanied by Both Sensitivity and Resistance

The rule that there is security in diversity is an axiom of ecology as well as finance. In a natural landscape many species take in carbon and make food by photosynthesis. The loss of a few species would probably change the photosynthetic rate of the system little. In fact, diseases removed first the chestnut and then the elm from eastern forests, but their photosynthesis was quickly replaced by other species. So, climate change is liable to eliminate species from the natural landscape, but its diversity will protect those functions, such as photosynthesis, that are carried out by many species.

Keystones

Some ecological processes are carried out by only a few species, however, and some species exert strong influences on the functioning of the entire system. For example, only a few species fix nitrogen, and the grazing of a single species of large mammal may alter landscapes. A single parasite infecting a pest like gypsy moth would alter forest dynamics considerably. Seastars and gulls are predators whose activities markedly change the structure of intertidal communities. If climate change removed one of these species or encouraged another, even a diverse landscape could be affected (Paine, 1980).

Calculating Impacts

Some Computed Examples

The way natural landscapes might be affected and even transformed has already been discussed. On a tract, long-lived plants could persist, but not forever, even though their reproduction failed. Formerly suppressed but now better adapted plants could grow up, and new, adapted plants could slowly move in. Therefore, changes in an ecosystem are likely to involve both movement at the margins and reshuffling of the species that formerly defined the system.

Mathematical simulations of natural landscapes have been run that incorporate physiological processes of plants much as GCMs incorporate atmospheric processes. The simulators mimic the present zones of plants in North America. A simulator was fed the climate scenario produced by a GCM for a doubling of greenhouse gases. It produced modest changes in west central Ontario and east central Tennessee. Between the two, however, it resulted in a near disappearance of northern hardwood forest in northwest Michigan. A later quadrupling of greenhouse gases, however, caused a change from one sort of forest to another in Ontario. After four centuries, the mass of plants rose in Ontario, fell in Tennessee, and changed little in Michigan (Solomon, 1986a; Solomon and West, 1986). The simulation using doubled greenhouse gases supports the view that major changes can happen on the margins of zones fed the simulator as well as the validity of the simulator itself.

Another simulation, which assumes summer drought grows more severe, predicts shrinking of forests in central North America eastward and northward as trees die and do not reproduce (Neilson et al., 1989). For crops some scenarios cause more yield and some cause less (Adams et al., 1990), and the same disparity is likely when forests are simulated with other scenarios from other GCMs. Anticipating impacts or designing adaptations is, therefore, difficult.

Animals, Too

Changes in the plants that feed and shelter them would affect animals. For example, one simulation suggests that a warming of 2°C would eliminate the jack pine barrens of central Michigan in a century. Because these barrens are the only breeding ground for Kirtland's warbler, the simulation implies that it, too, would be eliminated unless the management activities currently employed by government agencies to enhance its breeding habitat could be adapted to offset these declines (Botkin et al., 1991).

Adaptation

Some Management of Natural Landscapes Is Justified

Since natural landscapes are, by definition, unmanaged, we logically first examine the responses they make naturally. But a climate change caused by people may require human intervention to protect natural landscapes.

Natural Responses

Although the changes described above were called impacts, they are also the natural responses of landscapes. The question is whether the responses are consistent with the goals we identified—namely, maintaining species, ecosystems, and evolutionary processes.

The simulated landscapes resulting from doubled greenhouse gases support altered communities of plants rather than barrens. Nevertheless, achieving these goals for natural landscapes will be difficult. In the unmanaged systems of plants and animals that are much of our landscape, the ability to change may be much slower than climate change, making their future problematic. The slow pace derives from the long lives of some of their components, such as trees that live longer than the ones planted and cut for timber. It comes from the slow and chancy arrival of seed and migrant animals traveling on the wind, in currents, or along corridors. It comes from the slow rates of succession and from even slower rates of evolution. For the sort of climate change we are assuming, timely adaptation of every species and conservation of the countless cooperators in the natural landscape are highly unlikely.

Intervening in Natural Landscapes

Intervening to maintain species diversity, ecosystem functioning, and evolution can take two broad forms. Components of an area can be saved off the site, which saves some diversity and may permit evolution. The means are gene and seed banks, libraries, gardens, and zoos. Or, the entire landscape can be saved in situ (where it is), which saves systems, diversity and evolution.

Banks or Gene Libraries

Banks for parts, such as tissue, are the most technological and furthest from natural ecosystems. The discovery that genes of a valuable species can be incorporated into a microbe opens the possibility of libraries of genes in test tubes. Going further, genes can be preserved in frozen or freeze-dried form. So far, libraries exist only for a few genes of medical or scientific interest. Although the technique is inexpensive, its extension to the countless species in nature has not begun.

Tissues, like embryos or protoplasts of both plants and animals, can be cultured in a laboratory. Specific cultural methods may be needed for each species. Further, regenerating whole organisms from the tissue may be impossible, or it may be hard or become harder the longer the tissue is cultured. Also, tissue cultures, like gene libraries, need skilled people and laboratories.

Nevertheless, tissue culture is used for plants that are propagated vegetatively or have short-lived seed. It is used for some animals. For example, six replications of 800 cultivars of grapes can be maintained as growing tips in two square meters by transferring them only yearly (Henshaw, 1975; Wilkins and Dodds, 1983).

From a packet of leftover seed saved in a cellar to thousands of collections in the National Seed Storage Laboratory in Fort Collins, seed is the classic way of banking a plant. Special attention is paid to safeguarding the genetic diversity in crops. For example, 60,000 accessions of rice and its relatives are stored at the International Rice Research Institute (International Rice Research Institute, 1983).

Because seed banks have been a reality for decades, we know their problems as well as their promise. Seed does die. Moreover, in the 2 million accessions in banks worldwide, information is lacking about sources in 65 percent, about useful characteristics in 80 percent, and about germination in

95 percent (Peeters and Williams, 1984). The value of seed banks to farming is nonetheless great. The Agricultural Research Service spends $26 million to $28 million annually on germ plasm work, and this does not cover many forms of gene storage (National Research Council, 1990a). Large banks for the diverse seed of natural ecosystems do not, however, exist.

Although generally invisible, microbes are part of the natural landscape. Like seed banks, collections of microbes have been maintained for some time, and about 40,000 species have been collected and are exchanged (U.S. Department of State, 1982). In standard culture, microbes are short lived, they do change, and they must be transferred to new media frequently. To avoid these difficulties, collections are kept cold or dry.

Gardens

A far less technical way of preserving a species is in gardens. Although the managers of botanical gardens or arboreta are more self-conscious of their role, any gardener can help. The wide cultivation of Bougainvillaea and the para rubber tree, for example, protects them from extinction in tropical America. By collecting and breeding novel plants, nurserymen preserve biological diversity. By selling novel plants, they diversify the places the plants are grown and so help preserve them.

The 1,500 botanic gardens and arboreta in the world annually help instill an appreciation of plants in 150 million visitors, and they also conserve biological diversity. A strategy recommended for botanical gardens is concentrating on saving wild species, especially the task of saving those of their locality. They have yet to organize themselves for this work (International Union for Conservation of Nature and Natural Resources, Botanic Gardens Conservation Secretariat, 1989).

Zoos

Zoos are increasing their role in propagating and reintroducing rare and endangered animals. All the zoos in the world, however, now house only about a half million mammals, birds, reptiles, and amphibians. To maintain diversity within a species requires large populations. In the long run, large populations of less than 1,000 species of the more than 20,000 species of these animals can be cared for in zoos. So despite the value of zoos, capturing and reproducing species in them can do little to maintain the diversity of nature (Conway, 1986, 1989).

In Situ

Maintaining the diversity and functioning of species and their systems is like maintaining a chain. It must be steadfast. Once the maintenance and hence the chain or species fails, the prior efforts are lost along with the chain or species.

> Unfortunately, such collections are often dismantled or simply deteriorate after the specialists who built them up are no longer active. . . . Although they are often of great value internationally, [the collections] may if they are not actively utilized come to be viewed as a drain upon . . . the institution where they are housed. Even [with money], it is difficult to provide . . . the meticulous and sustained care that is essential for their survival without the attention of a specialist who is deeply concerned with them. (Raven, 1981)

Because management of banks and gardens is difficult and costly, in situ preservation of species and systems must carry the heaviest burden in programs to adapt to climate change. Methods for in situ preservation include reserving land for samples of representative, rare and endangered ecosystems or habitats. They include increasing the biological diversity in disturbed sites by land management or introduction of species. Finally, helping systems of plants and animals migrate is a method particularly important if climate change moves climate zones faster than plants and animals can follow. All these methods are already being used to maintain biological diversity in the face of harvesting of plants and animals and destruction of their habitats. The possibility of climate change adds a reason and complication for their employment. These methods all require that land be set aside for these purposes. The costs are those of purchase and the other uses of the land that are thereby forfeited.

The importance of maintaining biological diversity is reviewed elsewhere (Wilson, 1988; Western and Pearl, 1989) and need not be examined here. Rather, we concentrate on maintaining it if the system must move. The first method is to pick up a species and move it. The cost of regenerating a simple plantation of trees has already been shown to be high, and moving a whole system of plants and animals would be even more costly. Heavy seeds that are not naturally dispersed far and small animals would most need assistance. Dispersing them in advance of a climate change is not likely to help, especially if we are unsure what new climate they must cope with. Fortunately, they can be carried after climate changed. Although we should watch for species endangered by climate change, we can wait.

Corridors

It may be costly, in terms of both price and lost opportunities, to delay establishing migration corridors for species that are readily stopped by such barriers as freeways, open fields, and suburban sprawl. Determining the best locations for corridors requires examination of maps on which existing migration routes are plotted. This will reveal where the most important barriers lie and their types. With this information, key areas to be acquired and the form of modification of land use that is needed can be identified. Actions may range from simply providing overpasses or underpasses across highways, maintaining native vegetation along railroad rights-of-way, acquiring easements on lands to foreclose uses that would impose barriers to migration, to outright purchase. Other uses of the land compatible with its serving as migration corridors also need to be determined so that total costs of establishing and maintaining corridors can be reduced.

Uncertainty about future climates in a region adds to the reasons for corridors that will allow migration from areas where climates are becoming unsuitable for the organisms living there to areas where climates are more suitable. Even though we do not know how climates may change, a system of corridors connecting natural ecosystems across latitudes and longitudes and elevationally is likely to be useful under many patterns of climate change. It is important to begin a program to establish corridors now because of the long lead times involved in assembling information on locations of existing protected areas, surveying lands, negotiating easements or purchases, developing management plans, and changing existing land use patterns where necessary. Also, land prices are likely to rise, especially in areas where potential corridors are vulnerable to urban development that may also render their future use as corridors impossible.

Summary

From the natural landscape we take valuable plants and animals, and as a system it gives us natural services. Its diversity, functioning as a system and place for evolution, must be maintained despite climate change. Some of its components have long lives. To maintain these systems and their components requires lots of land. Simulations of the impact of climate change show vegetation zones moving slowly, and, as they move, animals are affected. Components of the system and hence diversity and evolution can be helped by preserving them in banks and gardens. The systems, however, are so large and complex that they must surely be preserved outdoors. Adaptation of the natural landscape can be helped by moving species when they are in trouble. To reduce future troubles, corridors along which plants and animals can migrate need to be established.

Because growing numbers of people and their power inevitably press the natural landscape, we must remember that the impacts and adaptations to any climate change will be added to other enormous changes.

THE MARINE AND COASTAL ENVIRONMENT

This section examines the relationship between the postulated effects (global temperature rise is of primary relevance) of greenhouse gas accumulations on the world's oceans and on the coastal ecological zones of the United States.[3]

The Basics

Sea Level

An increase in global surface temperature can increase the volume of water in the world's oceans. Two mechanisms are responsible. First, water itself expands slightly when heated, so heat conveyed from the air to the oceans will increase their volume. Second, higher surface air temperatures can raise the net melting rates of glaciers. There appears to have been considerable variation in sea level in the earth's history. During the last ice age, when global temperatures were some 5°C lower, sea levels are estimated to have been at least 100 m lower than today (National Research Council, 1990b). In the last interglacial period 100,000 years ago, they were over 5 m higher when temperatures were 1° to 2°C higher than today (Smith and Tirpak, 1989).

The Effects Panel (Part Two) estimates that sea level will rise an average of 0 to 60 cm (0 to 2 feet) toward the end of the next century due to warming caused by accumulations of greenhouse gases.[4]

An increase in the volume of seawater does not translate, however, directly to sea level rise as measured at the shoreline. Because some land areas are rising and others are subsiding relative to the earth's center, local changes in measured sea level can vary considerably. For example, the worldwide average sea level rise for the last century is 10 to 15 cm, but the level has risen about eight times that amount in Louisiana and generally about three times that global average on the Atlantic and Gulf coasts of the United States (Smith and Tirpak, 1989). The magnitude of local vulnerability to sea level rise, of course, depends on the local topography, as rising seas will affect more land area in low deltas than where coastal elevation profiles are steep.

Ocean Circulation and Temperature

In addition to sea level, a second important (though not yet very well understood) physical consequence of greenhouse gas emissions is the potential effect on ocean temperatures and currents. Available computer models show that a warming of the lower atmosphere in the range expected for a doubling of CO_2-equivalent emissions is associated with 0.2° to 2.5°C warming in sea surface temperatures (Intergovernmental Panel on Climate Change, 1990b). The models suggest that the maximum warming will occur in the arctic and antarctic regions in their respective winters. Because it would reduce the meridional (north-south) gradient of sea surface temperatures, the relative warming toward the poles could diminish the intensity of ocean currents and trade winds (Mitchell, 1988). However, nearer to land masses, computer simulations show enhanced temperature differences between land and oceans, which could lead to stronger along-shore wind stresses. These types of changes could alter upwelling (Bakun, 1990; Intergovernmental Panel on Climate Change, 1990b). Because there is good correlation between areas of upwelling and very productive fisheries, changes in upwelling could have an impact on those ecosystems.

Some scientists have raised the possibility that a dramatic systematic change in global ocean circulations could be triggered as a result of greenhouse warming (Intergovernmental Panel on Climate Change, 1990b). Broecker and Denton (1990) speculate that altered patterns of rainfall and evaporation, and changes in seasonal intensity may cause the ocean and atmosphere to "flip" into a very different mode of operation. With the flip, ocean circulation is changed, carrying heat around the world differently, resulting in glacial cycles. Although current climate models are insufficient to evaluate the probability of such events, their potential consequences could be immense (Broecker, 1987).

Sensitivities and Impacts for Coastal Habitats

The potential impact on coastal habitats would come mainly as a consequence of warming-induced rising sea level (except in those uncommon areas where there is compensating lift in coastal land masses), which could affect (1) the expanse and productivity of coastal wetlands, (2) shoreline habitats, and (3) barrier islands/reefs. Less well studied, but of growing concern, are (1) the effects of increased sea water temperature (other than thermal expansion); (2) disruption of ocean circulation, possibly resulting in alteration of global weather patterns, shifts in distributions of marine plants and animals, and disruption of upwelling sites; and (3) synergistic effects of rising sea level and increased water temperature.

Wetlands

Concern about coastal swamps and marshlands derives from their special ecological value and the fact that they are already under stress from human development, pollution, etc. Wetlands are among the most biologically productive of natural habitats (Intergovernmental Panel on Climate Change, 1990b), and they serve as nurseries for countless marine and terrestrial species. One measure of their commercial significance is that well over half (one estimate is 80 percent) of all fish caught spend part of their life cycles in coastal wetlands (Intergovernmental Panel on Climate Change,

1990b). In addition, a large proportion of migratory water and shore birds feeds in coastal wetlands as they migrate through the United States (Brown et al., 1990).

In the United States it is estimated that there are 18,000 km^2 of coastal wetlands (U.S. Office of Technology Assessment, 1984). Most are located in the southeastern United States with about 40 percent in Louisiana (Brown et al., 1990). Where local sea levels rise, current wetlands face the risk of flooding, as periods of low tides no longer expose areas to the air. Areas where there are small tidal ranges are particularly sensitive.

Although wetlands have been maintained despite slowly changing sea levels in the past, there are two factors that may limit their responses to the potential effects of greenhouse gases. First, the average rate of change could be (at the upper range) several times faster than it has been in recent times. In the past, through a gradual process of sedimentation and peat buildup near the shore, the biologically productive area of the wetlands has expanded. However, if sea levels rise rapidly, the newly reached tidal areas will not nearly match the areas that have been flooded. Second, human development may restrict a wetland's inland expansion, if a wetland is bounded by a dike or bulkhead constructed to protect agriculture or man-made structures.

Initial attempts have been made to quantify the potential net loss of wetland areas as a function of sea level rise. The EPA estimates that 30 to 70 percent of current U.S. coastal wetlands would be lost with a 1-m rise in sea level, even disregarding the effects of man-made inland barriers. If such barriers are included, the loss is estimated at 50 to 80 percent (Smith and Tirpak, 1989).

The ultimate question is how the potential diminution of coastal wetlands would affect species survival and human activities. Given the complexity of ecological interactions and the incompleteness of our current understanding of the many qualitative and quantitative relationships involved, it is beyond the capacity of current science to provide specific predictions. Nonetheless, substantial reductions in available habitats are certain to reduce populations of many species and are likely to cause extinctions of some of them.

Shoreline Contours

Rising sea levels would amplify the erosion of shorelines that is already occurring. The continental United States has approximately 51,000 km of shoreline, of which about one-half has been classified as erosional by the U.S. Army Corps of Engineers. Currently, only about 1,000 km or 2 percent is protected either by structural or "soft" means (e.g., beach nourishment) (Intergovernmental Panel on Climate Change, 1990b).

Small increases in sea levels can cause relatively large increments in beach erosion. A number of studies show "multipliers" ranging from 50 to many hundreds (Smith and Tirpak, 1989). Thus, beaches that are 50 m wide may well be severely eroded by a 30- or 60-cm rise in sea level. This could affect species (e.g., sea turtles, shorebirds) that nest on beaches or in adjacent dunes.

Shoreline Ecosystems

Coastal or shoreline ecosystems include not only coastal wetlands (such as the salt marshes and estuaries discussed above) but also marine intertidal and subtidal communities. Some of these ecosystems (e.g., kelp forests, coral reefs, and rocky intertidal areas) are among the most productive communities known (Valiela, 1984). Throughout history humans have relied directly and indirectly on these communities for food, medicines, fertilizers, tools, and supplies (Chapman and Chapman, 1980; Tseng, 1984; Santelices, 1989). Artisanal and commercial fisheries depend upon seaweeds, shellfish, and fish harvested directly from these habitats. In addition, commercial nearshore fisheries are often intimately linked to these shoreline ecosystems, either through the habitats or refuges provided to juvenile or adult stages or through dissolved and particulate organic matter transported from these ecosystems to nearshore waters. Because both developed and developing nations rely heavily on products from these shoreline ecosystems, the responses of these ecosystems to greenhouse warming are of great interest.

The often rich assemblages of marine plants and animals that inhabit intertidal and shallow subtidal regions of the world would undoubtedly be altered by the separate and combined effects of rising sea level, increased air temperatures, and warmer water temperatures, all of which may result from greenhouse warming. The consequences of other, less certain, changes (including alterations in the patterns of ocean currents, upwelling, and frequency and intensity of storms and El Niño/Southern Oscillation events) are potentially important but more difficult to evaluate.

The consequences of sea level rise to shoreline ecosystems would vary according to the type of organism and type of community. Shallow subtidal marine ecosystems, such as kelp beds in temperate regions and coral reefs in tropical waters, would probably not be affected much by changes in sea level. Intertidal coral reefs (those exposed to the air during low tides), on the other hand, could either be not affected or killed completely, depending on the rate of sea level rise relative to the rate of growth of the reef. Other intertidal organisms that are attached to the rock substratum (such as seaweeds, barnacles, and mussels) would likely be able to recruit higher on the shore and keep pace with the projected rates of sea level rise, as long as there is sufficient shoreline available.

Support for these predictions is based on evaluations of the consequences of abrupt uplift or depression of the shore following earthquakes. Although earthquake-caused shifts in shoreline height are known to severely disrupt local shoreline plants and animals for a few years (Haven, 1971; Castilla, 1990), recruitment, migration, and subsequent successional events should result in reestablishment of the communities that existed prior to the earthquake.

Increased air temperatures are hypothesized to result in compression of the intertidal zones throughout the world (Lubchenco et al., 1991). Most shores are characterized by horizontal bands or zones of plants and animals. The width of each zone is determined by the complex interaction of physical and biotic factors acting on each species. The upper limits of each zone are usually determined primarily by abiotic factors such as desiccation—species do not live higher on the shore because they would dry out (Connell, 1972; Schoenbeck and Norton, 1978). The lower limits of most species appear to be determined by biotic factors—a superior competitor or a predator precludes a species from living lower on the shore (Lubchenco, 1980). These biotic interactions are generally more intense in the physically more benign lower intertidal and subtidal zones. Warmer air temperatures should result in a more intense desiccation regime on the shore. Species whose upper limits are determined primarily by desiccation would be unable to occupy the upper portions of their current ranges. This would result in compression of the zone occupied by each of those species. The extent of this compression would depend on several factors, including the absolute change in air temperature, the rate of change, and the variance in temperatures. Because each zone is composed of numerous species that interact in a complex fashion, it is not clear whether existing zones would all be compressed equally or whether some zones and/or species would be eliminated. There is insufficient information at present to predict the consequences of this hypothesized compression to the loss of biodiversity, habitat, or productivity of these ecosystems.

Offshore Barriers

Rising seas could also affect the natural protection from the seas afforded by offshore barrier islands. Whether such barriers disintegrate as they are overwashed or are repositioned in such a way to continue to protect coastal habitats is uncertain and may depend crucially on local conditions and the actual rate of sea level rise (Intergovernmental Panel on Climate Change, 1990b). If sea level rises faster than coral reefs are able to grow, their role as a natural barrier in tropical and subtropical regions could be compromised.

Temperature Effects

If ocean temperatures rise, many marine organisms will be confronted with temperatures to which they are not usually exposed. In response to these changes, organisms may migrate, die, adapt, or exhibit no change. Individual organisms will thus respond directly to changes in temperature but will also be affected by changes in other species. For example, the overall response of a species may be strongly influenced by the availability of its prey and interactions with its competitors or with its symbionts. Recent events such as coral reef bleaching and mass mortality of marine populations suggest that even slight increases in temperature may result in severe disruption of ecosystems and loss of habitat diversity, species diversity, and genetic diversity. Particularly susceptible organisms include those currently living close to their thermal maxima, those dependent upon symbiotic interactions with other species, and long-lived species.

Four major widespread coral bleaching and mortality events were reported during the 1980s. These occurred in 1979-1980 and 1982-1983 in the Pacific Ocean and the Caribbean Sea; in 1986-1988 in the Indo-Pacific, Red Sea, and the Caribbean region (including the Flower Garden Banks in the Gulf of Mexico and Bermuda); and in 1989-1990 in the Caribbean (Glynn, 1991). The unprecedented geographic scale and frequency of these bleaching events have attracted considerable attention.

Bleaching results from the loss of symbiotic algae (zooxanthellae) that normally reside inside coral hosts and may supply up to 63 percent of the coral's nutrients (Muscatine et al., 1981). The expulsion of the algae can be triggered by a variety of conditions, including increased or decreased water temperature, increased visible and ultraviolet radiation, desiccation, decreased salinity, high sedimentation, and various pollutants (Glynn, 1991). Although all of these conditions are known to cause stress and result in the expulsion of the algae from corals, the available evidence strongly suggests increased water temperatures as the most likely cause of the recent bleaching events (Glynn, 1991).

The consequences of these bleaching events to coral reef ecosystems are not well known but are undoubtedly related to the intensity and spatial extent of the bleaching. During the unusually strong 1982 to 1983 El Niño/Southern Oscillation (ENSO)[5] event, severe bleaching and mass mortality of corals were reported from Costa Rica (50 percent coral mortality), Panama (75 to 85 percent mortality), and the Galapagos Islands (97 percent mortality). The massive mortality in the Galapagos is being followed by severe bioerosion of the coral reefs. Sea urchins, other grazers, and internal boring animals are eroding the dead coral skeleton (Glynn, 1988a,b). If subsequent recruitment of new corals does not occur on a broad scale, coral reefs may disappear from these locations.

Another possible result of increased oceanic temperatures may be an increase in the incidence of diseases of marine organisms. Recent water temperature increases in the Caribbean were correlated with a massive die-off of the black sea urchin. The mass mortality of black abalone in some California populations was also correlated with increased water temperatures during the 1982-1983 ENSO (Tissot, 1990). Although the causal relationships have not yet been established in these cases, the coincidence of these mass mortality events and increased water temperatures bears further investigation.

Valuable insight into effects of increased water temperatures may be gained by examining the effects of thermal discharge from nuclear power plants on nearby shoreline ecosystems (Lubchenco et al., 1991). Thermal discharge of 4° to 6°C above ambient in the Diablo Canyon Nuclear Power Plant resulted in a dramatic change in the species composition of nearby habitats. Although some of the species changes were predicted (e.g., increases in flora and fauna typical of warmer waters to the south), many others were surprises. The unexpected changes resulted from species influencing one another in addition to the direct responses of each species to the warmer water.

For example, an increase or decrease in the abundance of some species changed the competitive or predator-prey relationships of other species. Because of the complex interactions among species in an ecosystem, these biological interactions must be considered along with the direct effects of changes in abiotic conditions.

Highly mobile marine species would be expected to respond to increases in water temperatures by migrating to cooler waters. Such migration by coastal species could be blocked by natural or man-made barriers, but very little information is available to assess specific impacts on particular species.

Ocean Currents

Many marine plants and animals disperse in ocean currents. This dispersal may be to short or to very long distances, along the shore or across entire oceans. The boundaries of present-day biogeographic regions attest to the importance of oceanic currents in determining species' boundaries and ranges. Alterations in these currents would likely change patterns of species distribution and diversity, but exact predictions are beyond present understanding.

Sensitivities and Impacts for Ocean Habitats

Temperature, light, and nutrients are the suite of factors limiting productivity in the ocean. A modest rise in sea temperatures could, other things being equal, have a positive effect for some species and could enhance photosynthesis and the fixing of CO_2. However, many species of seaweeds achieve maximal production rates during the coolest months of the year (Mann, 1973). Thus, overall effects of increased ocean water temperature cannot be predicted. Moreover, large changes in water temperature could exceed the tolerance levels of tropical species (Smith and Tirpak, 1989).

More important than this is the possibility of changes in the patterns of ocean upwelling, which brings nutrients toward the surface and thus enhances primary organic production. As noted above, there may be compensating changes in ocean currents and winds—intensifying upwellings that are near major land masses and moderating upwellings that are not. Existing information, the IPCC (Intergovernmental Panel on Climate Change, 1990b) judges, does not permit conclusions about which affect might dominate.

Again, the intricate relationships between any species and its physical and ecological setting make specific predictions impossible, as does the lack of knowledge of precise changes in temperature and circulation. Species in the open ocean can adjust to change by moving to more hospitable surroundings, a fact that led the IPCC (Intergovernmental Panel on Climate Change, 1990b) to conclude that the impact on overall biodiversity would be smaller than in coastal communities. However, such shifts in ranges of species could have large impacts (positive or negative) on countries that depend on commercially important marine species in nearby coastal waters.

Although specific predictions are not feasible, the scale and nature of the possible changes can be illustrated by historical experiences. For example, the slight ocean warming that was observed during the first half of this century was associated with the penetration of subtropical fish species into temperate latitudes, but ocean warming in the 1940s and 1950s coincided with both unusually high and low herring populations in two adjacent northern ocean regions (Intergovernmental Panel on Climate Change, 1990b).

During the 1982-1983 ENSO the anchoveta and mackerel catch off the coast of Peru declined, while the catch increased off the coast of Chile (Serra B., 1987).

The impacts of a possible change in the general patterns of ocean circulation cannot be gauged. However, because these patterns profoundly influence ocean habitats and, of course, much more, including large-scale weather and climate far inland, changes in ocean currents are certain to have major effects on distributions and abundances of marine species.

Adaptation

Coastal Environment

With regard to the possible loss of tidal wetlands, one adaptation to rising sea levels could be to prevent future coastal development activities that would impede the inland expansion of intertidal ecological communities. Because development, once begun, is difficult to reverse, there is an understandable argument that near-term action is needed to preserve future options.[6] The state of Maine has already taken such action (Smith and Tirpak, 1989). Indeed, coastal zone management is a very powerful way to both reduce likely property damage if sea levels rise and preserve intertidal habitats and the species that depend upon them.

With ocean (and surface air) warming, marine species will tend to migrate toward the poles. It may turn out that barriers to such migration exist, threatening some species. The "bridging" strategies specified above for terrestrial ecosystems, such as seed banks, artificial reserves, and corridors for migration, are not well suited to the marine environment. For example, seaweeds do not have seeds. While some marine species could be preserved in aquaria, large natural preserves could not be buffered against temperature change. As for providing corridors, present dispersal and migration routes are not known for most marine species.

Ocean Habitats

Prospects for changing ocean habitats—for any species or any region—are so uncertain that it is difficult to contemplate adaptation measures. Some areas may lose their access to significant commercial species, and others may gain. About all that can be said is that the institutions that affect human use of the oceans' resources (e.g., fishery conventions) must consider future flexibility to be a high virtue as they make their rules and agreements. Much needs to be done to provide such flexibility for current variation—flexibility that would have the bonus of helping adapt to global warming.

Summary

Marine and coastal ecosystems are potentially quite vulnerable to climate change. A sea level rise of 1 m could cause a loss of 30 to 70 percent of U.S. coastal wetlands. Compression of the intertidal zone that may also accompany rising sea level and increased air temperatures could result in a significant net loss of primary production to nearshore marine ecosystems. The potential effects on ocean temperature and currents are poorly understood at present, but increased incidence of coral bleaching could have disastrous consequences for tropical marine ecosystems. Alteration of ocean currents could result in altered global weather patterns and changes in upwelling intensity and location. Climate, fisheries, biodiversity, and shoreline would all probably be affected. Predictions of the exact consequences of these changes are difficult. At present, the potential for human intervention to ease adaptation in marine ecosystems seems quite limited.

WATER RESOURCES

The Basics

Among the images that monopolize our thinking about climate change and prompt our decisions, pictures of dusty refugee camps in Africa today and cracked fields in Indiana in 1988 rank high. No question about climate change is more crucial than whether humanity will have reliable, potable, and cheap water. "Resources" are "available means," and so "water resources" are the available water or supply, the difference between precipitation and evaporation in the hydrologic cycle. Because the reservoirs, pumps, and pipes of water systems take a long time to put in place and have long lives, no question demands more foresight. Since cheap water must be collected upstream and run down hill, no question demands more local detail.

We warned that conventional wisdom may sometimes mislead, and the image of drought likely does that about water resources. A tabulation of climate changes affecting water resources shows regional averages for both soil moisture and stream runoff to undergo from a –50 to +50 percent change for an equivalent doubling of CO_2 (Schneider et al., 1990). The regional differences among scenarios that make predictions of farm yields conflict also make opposing predictions of water resources. So, instead of an image of drought alone, we must be prepared for "some regions [to] benefit from changing precipitation patterns, while others . . . experience great losses" (Smith and Tirpak, 1989). And losses might be from excess as well as drought.

General warming provides an exception to the uncertainty engendered by differences among regional predictions. The predictions generally agree that all regions will warm. All else being equal, this will melt snow earlier, increase spring floods, and decrease summer flows and the reliability of storage (Gleick, 1987). The assumption that all else will be equal is, of course, unlikely to prove right.

Sensitivity of Water Resources to Climate

Climate affects first the income of precipitation and the expense of evaporation and then the net of runoff and water resources. From year to year precipitation is variable as the record for 1931-1976 in the Colorado watershed shows (Figure 34.6). For the 48 contiguous states, evaporation consumes two-thirds of the precipitation, and in the Colorado watershed it consumes more than eight-tenths. Runoff is generally a small difference between the larger quantities of precipitation and evaporation and hence fluctuates relatively more. Because the three are plotted on the same logarithmic scale in

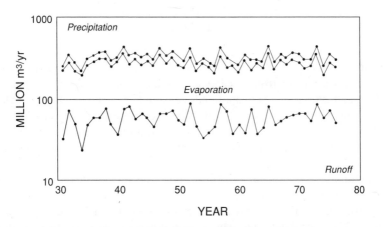

FIGURE 34.6 The relatively greater variability of runoff than of precipitation and evaporation illustrated by 46 years of flow in the Colorado River.

NOTE: The precipitation in millions of cubic meters per year was summed over the watershed. The runoff is the flow near the Utah-Arizona boundary plus (1) the estimated depletions from the river above the point of measurement, (2) evaporation from reservoirs, and (3) change in storage. Evaporation is the difference between precipitation and runoff.

SOURCE: Adapted from Revelle and Waggoner (1983). Copyright © 1983 by the National Academy of Sciences.

Figure 34.6, the vertical swings of the lines are the relative, not absolute, variability. The record of runoff varies relatively more than the records of precipitation and evaporation.

Relative variability is a measure of sensitivity. In watersheds from Carolina and Florida to Kansas and Texas, the elasticity of runoff for a change in precipitation is computed to rise from 2 in the humid eastern part to 4 in the western. For a change in evaporation it is 1 to 2. The classic nomogram relating runoff to precipitation shows similar elasticities, although recent analyses show runoff is somewhat less sensitive to temperature changes than the nomogram showed (Langbein et al., 1949; Karl and Riebsame, 1989; Schaake, 1990).

The great variability of runoff evident in Figure 34.6 hinders the estimation of its sensitivity and obscures evidence of any trends. The practical consequences of such variability are illustrated by the Colorado River compact, which was made during a wet period and anticipated more water than the river can deliver over the long term (Frederick and Kneese, 1990). In an analysis of diverse streams across the United States, Matalas (1990) found little evidence of a trend amidst the year-to-year variability.

Impact

Beyond the sensitivity of runoff to climate, the impact of a climate change depends on whether supply, use, and consumption of water are closely matched. The water withdrawn from streams and wells is said to be "used," and part of the water withdrawn is evaporated, consumed by humans or livestock, or incorporated into products and said to be "consumed" (Solley et al., 1989). The averages for the 48 contiguous states could lull and mislead us because only 24 percent of the supply is withdrawn for use and only 7 percent of the supply is consumed.[7]

Individual water resource regions show the pinch between supply and use. The warning signals in Table 34.4 indicate where consumption, storage, variability, or use of groundwater or hydroelectricity suggest vulnerability. They actually show where supply and use are matched, so that a change would bring significant harm or benefit, depending on which way the climate changed. A climate change would make water resource matters considerably worse or better in the Great Basin, the Missouri, and the California water regions, especially.

The vulnerability of activities can also be appraised. These would surely show the impact of climate change on irrigation. It is most used where precipitation is light, evaporation is high, and the supply is small. It accounts for about half the withdrawals of fresh water and about four-fifths of the consumption. It waters only about an eighth of the crop acreage but produces more than a quarter of the market value. Still, it requires cheap water, and other users already take water from irrigation. So the impact, good or ill, of climate change on irrigation would surely be great. The computed effect on the Eastern states of a warmer and drier climate is an expansion of irrigation. In the Western states, however, a 3°C warming and 10 percent more precipitation would cut irrigated acreage by 15 percent. A 3°C warming and 10 percent less precipitation would cut it by 31 percent (Peterson and Keller, 1990). The impact of less irrigation in the West can be judged by the value of tomatoes from an average acre in California, which was $6,000 to $8,000 in 1989.

Before considering adaptations, one must remember that there are impacts on water supply other than climate change, such as those caused by human use. An example is the depletion of the Colorado River. The average annual depletions in the Upper Colorado River plus diversions and evaporation from reservoirs grew by about a third during each decade from 1952 to 1981, until they reached roughly a quarter of the undepleted flow in 1972-1981 (Kneese and Bonem, 1986). The impact of any climate change will be mixed with the impacts of other factors such as these depletions.

TABLE 34.4 Vulnerability of Water Resource Regions of the United States to Climate Change

Basin	Signal On	D/Q	Q/S	Q_{05}/Q_{95}	H/E	GO/GW
Great Basin	5	*	*	*	*	*
Missouri	4	*		*	*	*
California	4	*	*	*	*	
Arkansas-White-Red	3		*	*		*
Texas-Gulf	3	*		*		*
Rio Grande	3	*		*		*
Lower Colorado	3	*			*	*
Tennessee	2		*		*	
Lower Mississippi	2		*	*		
Upper Colorado	2	*		*		
Pacific Northwest	2		*		*	
Alaska	2		*		*	
Caribbean	2		*	*		
New England	1		*			
Mid-Atlantic	1		*			
South Atlantic-Gulf	1		*			
Great Lakes	1		*			
Ohio	1		*			
Upper Mississippi	1		*			
Souris-Red-Rainy	1			*		
Hawaii	1		*			

NOTE: The vulnerability signaled by an asterisk is a ratio exceeding a threshold set by Gleick (1990). The ratios and characteristics they indicate are D/Q for high consumption, Q/S for little storage, Q_{05}/Q_{95} for high variability, H/E for dependent on hydroelectricity, and GO/GW for groundwater overdraft. The symbols are D, depletion by consumption, etc.; Q, renewable supply; S, storage; Q_{05} and Q_{95}, the stream flows exceed 5 and 95 percent of the time, respectively; H, hydroelectricity; E, all electricity generated; GW, total groundwater; and GO, overdraft of groundwater.

SOURCE: Reprinted, by permission, from Gleick (1990). Copyright © 1990 by John Wiley & Sons.

How Water Can Be Managed

When rain regularly waters crops and the landscape, runs into streams, and fills wells, we need adapt and manage little. The variability illustrated in Figure 34.6 means humanity must usually manage water to get a reliable supply. As the population in a region grows and uses more water, the first signal that they must manage water may be during a drought. The signal could, of course, come during a flood. The subject here, however, is water supply. The signal of a drought would be to begin managing water by controlling use or increasing supply.

Control Use

If water on the surface is used, the sharing between users immediately becomes an issue. Users upstream can capture the water first. Unless everyone accepts a policy for allocating it, trouble may follow. In the humid Eastern United States, the riparian doctrine controls the use of water. Under it an owner of land adjoining a stream has the right to divert as much as he or she wants provided there is no "unreasonable" impact on others downstream. Although what is reasonable is decided by the courts, case by case, the number of cases has been small.

In the dry West the riparian doctrine breaks down because much more water is needed than is available. Determining "reasonability" case by case is unworkable. So most Western states have adopted a system of water rights called the "prior appropriation doctrine." Generally, it gives the right to prevent a newer user upstream from interfering with prior "beneficial" uses. Beneficial is broadly defined.

Although these two allocation policies control the use of water, they have little to do with promoting economically efficient allocation, welfare, or environment. They allocate water without violence, promoting domestic tranquility.

To correct these shortcomings, people put forward new policies and even use some. Environmental regulations protect fish or stop pollution. Most do not balance benefits to the environment against other benefits but pre-empt water to maintain the environment.

Welfare is promoted by conservation measures that limit the right to waste water. Typically, they deal with toilets or showers. Or in an emergency they restrict sprinkling. Prices do affect the use of water (Frederick and Kneese, 1990), and conservation rates penalize using more than is needed for drinking, cooking, cleaning, and sanitation.

Economic efficiency is the goal of water markets. They are much talked about in the West. New users pay old ones to transfer their use to new ones. The transfers are usually limited to ones with no adverse effect on other existing users. When the transfers are between nearby and similar users, they go reasonably well. The lack of adverse effects of wider transfers, however, is often hard to prove, they find their way to court, and they become expensive and slow.

Forecasts of water supply make the control of use more efficient. From generating more hydropower and irrigating more acres to protection against flood, knowing how much water will be available increases its efficient use

(Glantz, 1982). Although all the policies can be used with forecasts to improve efficiency, the policies are usually imposed by different agencies and levels of government, and they are rarely coordinated.

Increase Supply

The supply of water in a place might be made more reliable by long transport between basins, management of the watershed, or even cloud seeding. Generally, however, the supply is made more reliable by storing water in reservoirs, pumping water stored in aquifers, or reclaiming salt and waste water.

The reservoirs on the Colorado River can store water for years, but most reservoirs have only small volumes to smooth the supply for weeks or months. Many aquifers, on the other hand, are large enough to smooth the supply for longer times. The present supply can even be increased by mining ancient or fossil water.

Although salt and waste water can be reclaimed, it is costly in money and energy and only practical for valuable uses in dry places. The cost of desalinization may, of course, fall during a half century (Abelson, 1991). Some benchmark or exemplary costs are shown in Table 34.5. Note that the estimates of the cost of water from the Delaware, Platte, and Sacramento rivers do not include treatment and are only estimates for the present supply. The estimate from the Hudson River includes delivery.

Just as supply can be smoothed by storage that diversifies it over time, it can be smoothed by the diversity of joint operation of water supplies. This has been demonstrated for places as far apart as the Potomac and North Platte rivers and Houston, Texas. Despite its economy and promise, joint operation of independent or even federal systems is rare. The reasons include independent spirits and lack of credible evaluations of the benefits (Sheer, 1985).

How Water Has Been Managed

Water management has become a public, not private, concern because of the wide disruption of floods and droughts, the ubiquitous need for water for health and fighting fires, the need for political support and exercise of eminent domain to acquire strategic sites, and the economies of scale and natural monopoly. Generally, the demand for water grows annually by 1 to 3 percent, until a flood or drought impels governmental action, which increases supply by a leap that delays the need for additional action for years. Although a slowly growing need might have been known for years in advance, a flood or drought causes action. Often, a long-lived canal, dam, or levee is built.

TABLE 34.5 Costs of Present Water and for Securing Reliable
Alternative Supplies

Method	Cost per Acrefoot
Present national average[a]	$533
Delaware River above Philadelphia[b]	
(raw water, modifications to F. E. Walter Reservoir)	$51
High flow skimming Hudson River[c]	
(including treatment and delivery facilities)	$555
South Platte River, Denver, Colorado[d]	
(raw water)	$469
New Bureau of Reclamation, Central Valley Project	
Water at Sacramento Delta[e] (raw water at the plant)	$137
Desalting[f]	$2,200-$5,400

[a]National average water rates for water delivered to the end user were on the order of $533 per acrefoot for small users, less for large users. Arthur Young Water and Wastewater Survey (1988).

[b]Cost for raw water from modifications to F. E. Walter Reservoir. Personal communication from R. Tratoriano, Delaware River Basin Commission, to D. Sheer, Water Resources Management, Columbia, Maryland, 1990.

[c]Includes cost of treatment and delivery facilities. R. Alpern, New York City Department of Environmental Conservation, First Intergovernmental Task Force Report.

[d]Personal communication from D. Little, Denver Water Board, to D. Sheer, Water Resources Management, Columbia, Maryland, 1990.

[e]New Bureau of Reclamation, Central Valley Project. Cost for raw water at the plant. Does not include costs for delivery facilities to point of use. These figures are for construction costs of Auburn Dam allocated to water supply only—23% of total construction costs. Other costs allocated to flood control, instream flow, hydropower, and recreation. Personal communication from J. Denny, U.S. Bureau of Reclamation, Sacramento, to D. Sheer, Water Resources Management, Columbia, Maryland, 1990.

[f]Costs for desalting run from $2,000-$5,000/acrefoot/yr capital costs, plus operating costs of between $2,000-$4,000/acrefoot (mainly energy costs). This equates very approximately to $2,200-$5,400/acrefoot.

The safe yield of a reservoir is figured from the worst drought on record. Using it makes the optimistic assumption that the operator knows when a drought will end. When a new record is set by a worse drought, the safe yield is revised downward, which encourages action after extreme weather. All the forces described in the preceding paragraphs incline officials to view new facilities as insurance against disruptions and restrictions rather than as investments. Recently, growing environmental awareness seems to have made disruptions and restrictions more acceptable.

Summary

Climate change could change the timing of the leaps in strategy or means to adapt to the gradually changing demand for water. Action is generally precipitated by the extremes of flood and drought, and climate change would change the probabilities of these extremes and simply change the frequency of actions to adapt. The response of management will tend to lag behind the impacts of climate change. Unless, however, those changes are adverse and rapid relative to changes in the population-driven demands for water management, the overall impact of climate change is unlikely to be substantially more serious than that of the vagaries of the current climate.

Essentially, the chance of climate change introduces more uncertainty into the already uncertain realm of water management. The better prepared we are to deal with the extremes possible in the present climate, the easier it will be to deal with changes. Climate change makes the following more urgent:

- Improve management of present systems to deal with drought and flood.
- Develop and test methods to deal with more severe ones.
- When investing in new facilities, consider climate change by such a method as described in Chapter 33, the section "Making Decisions in an Uncertain World."
- Monitor to discover any trends.
- Learn the sensitivity and then the direction and size of the impacts of climate change.

INDUSTRY AND ENERGY

Basics

Sensitivity and Income Are Not Congruent

Passing from the farms, forests, water, and natural land and sea scapes into the more man-made things broadly called industry, one encounters a paradox. The former outdoor things get the attention when climate change is considered, but the latter is where most of the money is.

In the national appraisal of effects by the EPA (Smith and Tirpak, 1989), the impacts on agriculture occupy 28 pages and the impacts on forests 21 pages. The only industrial subject, electricity, occupies 11 pages. The contributions to national income, however, of farming and forestry are about 3 percent of the total of all activities (see Table 34.6). The reason for the paradox is the sensitivity of the sectors. Nordhaus (1991) classified farms, forestry, and fisheries as "potentially severely impacted" but all others as "moderate potential impact" or "negligible effect" (see Table 34.6). His

TABLE 34.6 Economic Activities According to Their Sensitivities to Climate Change

Sector	Activity's Percent of Total National Income	Impact for CO_2 Doubling (billions 1981 $)
Severely impacted sectors		
Farms	2.78	
Impact of greenhouse warming and CO_2 fertilization		−10.6 to 9.7
Forestry, fisheries, other	0.32	Small
Total	3.10	
Moderately impacted sectors		
Construction	4.52	Positive
Water transportation	0.26	?
Energy and utilities		
Energy (electric, gas, oil)	1.90	
Electricity demand		−1.7
Nonelectric space heat		1.2
Water and sanitary	0.24	Negative
Real estate-land-rent component	2.12	
Sea level rise damage		
Loss of land		−1.6
Protection of sheltered areas		−0.9
Protection of open coasts		−2.8
Hotels, lodging, recreation	1.05	?
Total	10.09	
Negligible effect		
Mining	1.87	
Manufacturing	24.08	
Other transportation and communication	5.49	
Finance, insurance, and balance real estate	11.38	
Trade	14.47	
Other services	13.47	
Government services	13.96	
Earnings on foreign assets	2.08	
Total	86.81	
TOTAL	100.00	−$6.2

NOTE: A positive number indicates increase in output; a negative number indicates a loss.

SOURCE: Data from Nordhaus (1991).

estimate, in 1981 dollars, of the impact on farming[8] of –$10.6 billion to $9.7 billion far exceeds the second-place estimate of –$2.8 billion for protection of open coasts. It also far exceeds the –$1.7 billion for electricity demand and the $1.2 billion for nonelectric space heat. Completeness requires examining the subjects called industry and electricity here because they make up about 97 percent of the U.S. national income; but we know they are less exposed to climate change.

Sensitivity of Electric Power Generation

According to Jäger (1985), "Relatively few studies have been made of the impact of climate change on energy demand." The Energy Department found that "the state of knowledge regarding the sensitivity of energy systems to climate change is very limited" (U.S. Department of Energy, 1989b). IPCC Working Group II began its summary of energy with threats to biomass and fuelwood rather than with electric power (Intergovernmental Panel on Climate Change, 1990a). Nevertheless, the most directly analyzable impact of warming is on the requirements for electricity for warming and cooling. The above IPCC report cites studies in six nations, and it states that results differ depending on how much energy is related to heating versus cooling.

An American study (Linderer, 1988) estimates the climate change impacts for aggregations of utility systems in the Great Lakes, the Southeast, the Southern Great Plains, California, and the United States as a whole. The most significant result is that for the United States as a whole new capacity requirements deriving from increased temperatures associated with climate change for the year 2066 range from an increase of 12 to 22 percent above the new capacity requirements that electric utilities would face arising from GNP growth and changes in energy intensity.

Whereas this additional capacity is a relatively modest fraction of the total growth in generating capacity that would be needed in any case, the absolute magnitudes involved are significant by many standards. The increase in new generating capacity from climate change would be between 200 and 400 GW and would require utilities to make capital investments of roughly an additional $200 billion to $400 billion in generating capacity from climate change alone. Not surprisingly, the largest increase in additional generating capacity from climate change occurs in the Southeast, where utilities already size their generating capacity based on summer cooling requirements. For the Southeast, utilities would have to add, between now and the year 2055, an additional 35 percent of total generating capacity above and beyond the incremental capacity that would be required because of other factors.

As the IPCC (1990b) Working Group II report states, "By changing water resource availability, climate change may make some present hydro-electric power facilities obsolete and future energy planning more trouble-some, although others may benefit from increased runoff." For the United States, Miller (1990) states that "electric power generation makes greater withdrawals of instream water than any other industry." However, "only a small portion of the water circulating through electric generation plants is actually consumed. Nearly all the currently operating steam power plants in the United States use a water-based cooling system. It is estimated that as of 1980, U.S. withdrawals of fresh water for thermo-electric cooling were equivalent to withdrawals for irrigated agriculture, but while 55 per-cent of irrigation withdrawals were consumptively used, the rate of the consumptive use of thermo-electric cooling was only 2 percent" (Miller, 1990). Electric utilities in the arid sections of the United States have adapted to water scarcity by adopting closed-cooling systems.

The mixture of fuel used for generating electricity would change sensi-tivity to climate change. First, restrictions on carbon emissions to mitigate the greenhouse effect would affect, especially, the burning of coal but not nuclear plants. Then, a climate change could help or hinder generation from water, wind, or solar energy. Finally, a change in the growth of plants would change the amount of biomass for burning.

The quantitative results support the judgment of modest sensitivity of electric power generation to climate change.

Estimating Impacts

Economic

The large income but low sensitivity of industry tempers the statements that the greenhouse effect would disrupt national economies. Examples of such statements are, "This greenhouse effect may by early next century have increased average global temperatures enough to shift agricultural pro-duction areas, raise sea levels to flood coastal cities, and disrupt national economies. . . . A rise [in sea level] in the upper part of this range (25-140 cm) would inundate low lying coastal cities and agricultural areas, and many countries could expect their economic, social and political structures to be severely disrupted" (World Commission on Environment and Devel-opment, 1987).

The effects associated with a global cooling of roughly 5°C experienced during the last ice age 18,000 years ago are documented. They would have had major impact on the world's economy as it exists today. In particular, much of the industrial heartland of this country (the upper Midwest) would have been under an ice sheet. None of the effects in our base scenario (a doubling of CO_2) would make large land areas uninhabitable, and thus the impact would be fundamentally different (and much less severe, as indicated below).

The argument that the impact on the industrial sector would be relatively modest from the climate change in our scenario is put forward convincingly by Schelling (1983). Schelling says that "it is likely that most of the identifiable changes in welfare due to climate change would be, for most parts of the world, swamped by other uncertainties." Schelling goes on to say that one can argue, although not conclusively, that "if the change is slow, the adaptations and replacements, even the migrations, need not be traumatic or even especially noticeable against the ordinary trends of obsolescence, movement and change. The issue is suddenness and unexpectedness." He cautions that "it is wise to be concerned about any prospective change in some major index of climate."

Schelling says further "the only readily identified potential impact of significant magnitude on future living standards is on agriculture. . . . A fair guess seems to be that any likely rate of change of climate due to CO_2 over the coming century would reduce per capita global Gross National Product by a few percentage points below what it would otherwise be. A curve of world per capita income plotted over time would be set back probably less than half a decade." Later, Schelling says "the pure temperature feedback on the use of energy, both as a cost saving (heating) and as an additional cost (cooling) and as a consequent damper or booster to fuel consumption, is of obvious relevance. Such estimates as there are do not indicate that any overall reduction or increase in energy use, due solely to temperature change, would be of major significance, whichever way the net effect goes." An estimate of change in "degree days of heating and cooling yield a result that is not an impressive fraction of the current cost of heating and cooling." Finally, Schelling says that "the most likely possibility emerging from the work done so far in relation to CO_2 is that the impact of climate change on global income and production, and specifically the agriculture component of it, would not be of alarming magnitude."

Barbier (1989) states that the economic impact of any greenhouse effect will most likely be in terms of the rising cost of agricultural displacement and adaptation in the face of climatic instability. He places the impact on agriculture and water supply as a second-order impact and lists the economy (nonagriculture) as a third-order impact.

The one industrial sector that could possibly be an exception to this general conclusion is the forest products industry, since it depends directly on climate, as agriculture does. For this industry the rate of change in climate associated with the greenhouse effect could perhaps exceed the rate at which natural forests could evolve and migrate (U.S. Department of Energy, 1989b). However, analysis by Binkley and Dykstra (1987) indicates that the temperature increase associated with doubling of CO_2 would increase exploitable forest area and forest growth rates and yield a positive economic benefit (precipitation changes and CO_2 fertilization were not addressed). This subject is discussed above in the section "Forests and Grasslands."

Even though there are references to economic disaster resulting from climate change, plausible arguments have been put forth that the impact will be relatively modest.

Relative Economic Power

The large income from industry makes this a logical place to examine the impact of climate change on relative national economic power. Both Schelling (1983) and Nordhaus (1991) conclude that the impact of climate change on global income and production would not be of alarming magnitude. Nordhaus specifically estimates that the upper limit on damage would be around 2 percent of total output (about 1 year's economic growth).

The panel searched for relative impacts on five major regions of the world: the United States, Western Europe, the former Soviet Union, China, and Japan. For agriculture a paper by Tobey et al. (1990) goes beyond change in yields to estimate changes in world prices for agricultural commodities and from that derives estimates of changes in economic value (producer and consumer surpluses) in the various regions of the world. Tobey et al. (1990) developed two cases to bound the likely impact on welfare from a climate change roughly equivalent to our scenario. In the optimistic case, none of the five key regions experience significant economic value changes. The largest change in the optimistic case, in fact, is an increase for the former Soviet Union of 0.3 percent of 1986 gross domestic product (GDP). In the pessimistic scenario, worldwide economic value from agricultural changes decreases by 0.5 percent of 1986 GDP. The changes in all the major regions of the world of concern are slightly less than the worldwide total, with the exception of China, which would experience a 5 percent decrease as a percent of 1986 GDP.

For natural resources the most obvious potential change is in access to Arctic oil reserves. The potentially recoverable reserves from the Arctic region are between 17 billion and 55 billion barrels for the United States and between 50 billion and 80 billion barrels for the former Soviet Union. If all these reserves were proven and recovered, they would extend the life of the oil reserves for the United States by roughly 10 years and the oil reserves for the former Soviet Union by roughly 20 years. Of course, these increases in reserves are small compared to the total proved oil resources in the world of roughly 700 billion barrels, of which about 500 billion are in the Middle East. Specifically, if the additional recoverable Arctic reserves from Canada and Norway are added to those of the United States and the former Soviet Union, the increase in the proved reserves for the world would be only about 20 percent (Gleick, 1989).

Our review of the few reports and judgments strongly suggests that the climate change envisioned cannot affect relative economic power significantly.

Surprises

While accepting the logical arguments about the envisioned climate change, the panel also accepts that surprises do happen. These could arise from nonlinear responses like the passage of a threshold. Two plausible ones are reorganization of the ocean-atmosphere system and changed runoff of water.

Significant reorganizations of the ocean-atmospheric system seem to be the key events that have triggered the advance and retreat of ice sheets for the previous ice ages (Broecker and Denton, 1990). Because our current geophysical fluid dynamics models cannot predict these kinds of nonlinearities (except when they already know what to look for), we need to determine on some scientific basis the confidence levels that current model predictions merit.

The second surprise could be changes in runoff following changes in precipitation. This was discussed in the section "Sensitivity of Water Resources to Climate," above. Even for present predictions from the models, regional variations could be strong for precipitation and the resulting water runoff. If the general distribution and flow of water in a region changed dramatically, the impact could be much more significant than we are predicting for agriculture, industrial distribution, and even the habitability of certain urban areas. Water is cheap, where it is generally available, but where water is not available, it is hard, if not impossible, to provide the quantities needed because of the high cost of its transportation.

Adaptation

In many places in this report the reader encounters the conclusion that if investments have shorter lives than climates adaptation is fairly easy. In Chapter 33, the section "The Tools of Innovation," we showed that many investments do have short lifetimes. The hard adaptations will come in those exceptional cases of long lifetimes.

One example of capability to adapt comes from electric power generation. According to Miller (1990), "It is estimated that by the end of the century, 30 years will be the average age of coal-fired power plants in operation in the United States, and it appears that the average useful service life of power plants may be lengthening as rising real construction costs

induce power companies to refurbish rather than abandon older plants."
Thus, utilities face investment decisions concerning their cooling system
technology with perhaps a 30- to 40-year lead time. As a result, they will
have to factor into such decisions the uncertainty associated with the availability of water for cooling. Technical flexibility can be incorporated in the
design of single power plants to hedge against uncertainty in the availability
of water. Thus, to optimize decision making, utility executives need to
have the best available information about potential changes in the distribution of water availability and the uncertainty in those estimates for a 30- to
40-year period. The adoption during a half century of an efficiency like
superconductivity of transmission lines would, of course, sharply decrease
demand for electricity, and such possibilities add to the uncertainty.

Another example of the ability of industry to adapt to climate warming,
and that the adaptation required is relatively modest, was reported in *The
New York Times* on December 20, 1989. Royal Dutch Shell spent a year
assessing the impact of scenarios involving significant global warming as
one of its major strategic planning initiatives. As a result of this work,
Shell has reviewed its investment decisions that have time horizons that
place the useful life of the investment well into the period of uncertainty
about global climate change. Perhaps Shell's longest-lived investment is its
gas platforms in the North Sea, where the reserves are so large that production from such platforms may go on for up to 70 years. Traditionally, Shell
engineers have sized the platforms a standard 30 m above the water level,
which is the height now thought necessary to stay above the waves that
come in a once-in-a-century storm. As a result of reviewing possible sea
level change from global climate change, Shell engineers have increased the
height of the gas platforms to 31 or 32 m above the ocean. A 1-m increase
will cost an additional $16 million and a 2-m increase, will be roughly
double that. Even the higher cost, however, is only about 1 percent of the
total of the platform, which costs a few billion dollars.

Another piece of evidence that sheds light on the adaptability of the
industrial sector comes from a U.S. Department of Energy (1989a) report
entitled *A Compendium of Options for Government Policy to Encourage
Private Sector Responses to Potential Climate Change*. The report deals
primarily with mitigation but does have some useful information for assessing adaptive capabilities. In particular, the report has some data on the
lifetimes of industries' capital equipment. This report says that the electric
utility sector has capital investments with lifetimes of 30 to 40 years. It
goes on to say that there are other industries where large infrastructure
investments are required, such as steel and paper, that have similar lifetimes
of up to 40 years. A boiler, for instance, lasts about 40 years. Some
papermaking machines are now 70 to 80 years old, although the technology
in the United States is well behind that in Europe, and European machines

are shorter lived because of technological evolution. Such change is likely to come to the paper industry in the United States. In any case, evidence about the lifetime of capital investments in the industrial sector is critical for analyzing the ability of the industrial sector to adapt to climate change.

The evidence to date suggests that the industrial sector can adapt to the changes in global climate by making rather modest changes to the investment plans they would make without climate change. This conclusion seems to hold more clearly for adjustments to temperature change and sea level. As mentioned above, more careful work needs to be done on water runoff and how it may affect the availability of water for industrial use and distribution. The major conclusion, however, of a rather modest impact on the industrial sector does need to be confirmed through careful comparison, industry sector by industry sector, of the investment time horizons and those covered by the models for global climate change. Perhaps most important is a projection of ranges within which industrial managers could assume, with very high confidence, that they would have to operate.

Summary

Fortunately, industrial sectors, including electric power generation, produce much income but are only moderately or negligibly sensitive to climate change. Even though some writers have mentioned economic disasters that might follow from climate change, plausible arguments have been put forth that the impact will be relatively modest. Judgments suggest that the climate change envisioned will not affect relative economic power significantly. Generally, industry can adapt.

TOURISM AND RECREATION

The grand tour that families take one summer to, for example, camp in Yellowstone and the Grand Tetons exemplifies the importance of recreation and how it depends on the climate. The one-third billion visits to national parks and two-thirds billion visits to state parks and recreation areas far exceed, for example, the 48 million attendance at major league baseball games or 36 million at college football.[9] The dependence of tourism and recreation on water is exemplified by swimming and fishing. The section "Water Resources," above, addresses the relationship of water resources to climate.[10] One-third of Americans swim and one-fifth fish. Expenditures on outdoor recreation are substantial. The $55 billion spent in 1985 on wildlife-associated recreation far exceeded the $14 billion spent for books and the $7 billion for new color TVs (U.S. Bureau of the Census, 1987).

Nevertheless, the issue of economic impact and adaptation for tourism and recreation is relatively insignificant since this sector represents about 1 percent of our total GNP. The part of this industry that is likely to be affected by climate change, is of course, the part that is closely associated with nature in one way or another. For this part the simple answer is that the industry will migrate to the new areas of nature that are attractive for tourism and recreation. The assets associated with this industry are primarily roads and lodging places. The useful lifetimes of these investments are on the order of 20 to 30 years. Thus, this industry can wait and see the impact of climate change and then migrate as the attractive areas move. Although such investments may not correspond exactly to the value tourists and sports enthusiasts may attach to particular opportunities, they do give us a first approximation of the likely economic impacts of greenhouse warming.

Skiing is exemplary in two ways. First, it is sensitive to climate. Second, just as popular taste has raised the ski industry during the past half century, a decline in popularity could ruin it in the decades to come, regardless of climate change. A study of recreation in the Great Lakes Basin used a scenario of climate change that shortened the skiing season by a third. Ontario suffered a $50 million loss. This loss would be countered, however, by a camping season about 40 days longer (Wall, 1989). Obviously, this has important consequences for the economies of specific locales. For the nation as a whole, however, such changes are likely to balance out. This probably applies to noneconomic aspects of tourism and recreation as well.

SETTLEMENTS AND COASTAL STRUCTURES

The Basics

Human settlements, including highly developed ones, exist in an amazing range of climatological conditions. Compared to this range, the potential climate change over the next century is small. Thus, it is unlikely that even when climate change exacerbates an already extreme situation (e.g., warming of the currently warmest spot on the planet) the resultant climate would render currently settled areas uninhabitable.

The pertinent questions, then, relate to the extent to which the costs of adapting existing settlements to the new conditions and of maintaining the settlements under the new conditions lead to abandonment or to important modification of the lifestyle or standard of living of the inhabitants.

Sensitivities

Direct climate changes of importance to human settlements are primarily changes in the extremes and seasonal averages of temperature, and changes in the spatial and temporal distribution of rainfall. Though the impacts of these effects may be of importance in some cases, the secondary effects of climate change on the level of water bodies are of much greater significance. Predicted sea level rise will result in a number of major impacts on coastal regions, while the opposite effect—dropping of the level of the Great Lakes due to changes in rainfall patterns—will have different impact on Great Lakes municipalities and facilities. Inland, increased variability may cause the most significant impacts.

Impacts

Sea Level Rise

Major effects of sea level rise are inundation of some areas, shoreline erosion, storm damage, saline intrusion into groundwater and surface water, and groundwater table elevation. Inundation, erosion, and storms all lead directly to property damage, the extent of which depends upon the value of the property, its nearness to the shoreline, and the slope of the shoreline. Although the concentration of Americans along the coast makes these effects important to many, an estimate of the number affected by the wide range of a rise of 0 to 60 cm would lend a misleading sense of precision. Estimates of the inundation of considerable portions of, for example, Egypt and Bangladesh are for scenarios of a 1- to 5-m rise (Intergovernmental Panel on Climate Change, 1990b).

Harbor facilities, bridges, and certain recreational facilities, though suffering no physical damage from sea level rise, will nonetheless be impaired or rendered useless because of their dependence on design distances to the water level.

Sea level rise will cause other water-related difficulties in urban areas besides those that result from inundation, high water level, and erosion. The associated rise in the groundwater table may reduce the ability of the soil to assimilate rainfall and result in larger surface runoff. There will likely be increased seepage into basements, adverse effects on building foundations, and increased corrosion of buried pipelines.

In occasional instances, groundwater may intrude into landfills and waste disposal sites, resulting in leaching of hazardous materials.

A rise in sea level will also change tidal (Gleick and Maurer, 1990) and other currents, causing new patterns of scour and silt deposits in harbor facilities. Ocean outfalls of urban drainage systems and waste treatment facilities may no longer drain properly due to elevation and current changes.

Temperature Rise

The major impact of temperature rise is probably increased electrical demand for cooling in the warmer summers. Though total electric use may not increase significantly (winter use may decrease), peak usage normally occurs in summer, and thus installed generating capacity will have to be increased to accommodate these greater peaks. Compared to the expected baseline no-climate-change required capacity increase, the added requirements are from 20 to 30 percent more in Miami, to 10 to 20 percent in New York City and San Francisco, and 10 percent in Cleveland and most of the Great Plains (Linder et al., 1987; Smith and Tirpak, 1989; Walker et al., 1989).

In some municipalities, warmer temperatures may exacerbate air pollution problems, particularly ozone concentrations.

Walker et al. (1989) imply that problems such as buckling of rails due to heat expansion will become much more common. Asphalt pavement softening may become more frequent in regions where it has been rare before. Some compensation would, of course, come in the form of fewer problems with frost.

Changes in Precipitation Patterns

Flooding difficulties are not limited to communities affected by sea level rise. Global circulation models indicate that in global warming in some communities the month with the highest rainfall could have 50 percent more rainfall than currently. If this additional rainfall is in the form of greater storms, drainage problems in a number of inland cities will require the same sorts of solutions as those in coastal cities (Titus et al., 1987). If, on the other hand, the additional rainfall is more evenly distributed in time, it may result in increased groundwater table levels with associated basement seepage, foundation damage, and subsidence (Walker et al., 1989).

Decreased rainfall, on the other hand, will result in a different set of impacts (in addition to water supply problems, treated elsewhere). Inland rivers used for navigation may no longer be navigable at all or may have reduced capacities. Water pollution problems may be aggravated by the combination of reduced flow and increased water temperature.

Great Lakes Impacts

Urban areas along the Great Lakes constitute a special case as a result of the prediction that levels in the lakes will decrease. Fluctuations in the level of the lakes is, of course, not new. As with sea level rise, this change will adversely affect recreational and harbor facilities that depend on a fixed range of distances from the water level. In addition, sewer and drainage outfalls may no longer have adequate submergence. Some wooden facilities that have been submerged will become vulnerable to dry rot.

Adaptations

Adaptation to Sea Level Rise

The choice facing coastal settlements is between abandoning areas subject to inundation and storm damage and protecting the land or infrastructure from the impacts or modifying it to withstand the impacts. Retreat, which may be economical in areas that are extremely difficult to protect or in low-valued regions, may require the greatest anticipation because it requires zoning measures to prevent growth and development of replacements for abandoned facilities, structures, and land (National Research Council, 1987). Protection by means of levees, dikes, and similar means, though costly, may usually be done in a matter of a few years. Other forms of protection, by modifying facilities to withstand or resist flooding and other impacts, are done more economically if planned in advance, so that the necessary modifications can be designed into new structures over a period of time (Titus and Barth, 1984; National Research Council, 1987).

Retreat and abandonment are not likely to be economical alternatives for major parts of urban areas. Some isolated facilities, particularly those that are obsolete and/or in disrepair, may be abandoned. But in most cases the replacement value of urban areas will make protection or adaptation of one sort or another, though expensive, the best alternative.

Protection against shoreline erosion can be achieved in two fundamental ways. Either the waves that cause the erosion must be intercepted before reaching the surf zone (breakwaters) or the shore profile must be armored or strengthened. Control may also be exerted in some cases, where sand transport along the shore is significant, by reducing the ability of waves to carry sand (groins and other structures) and by increasing the amount of sand available for transport (beach nourishment) (Sorensen et al., 1984).

Protection against inundation is provided by constructing a dike system or by filling in the area and surrounding the fill with a retaining structure. Many areas that already have dike and levee protection will be required to raise these structures, and new structures will be necessary to protect most coastal cities (Sorensen et al., 1984; National Research Council, 1987).

Cost estimates for these alternatives must be determined on a case-by-case basis because both the natural and the economic characteristics of regions are so widely different (National Research Council, 1983). A few estimates, however, can serve to provide a rough cost range. The Committee on Engineering Implications of Changes in Relative Sea Level estimated the annual costs of beach nourishment on the east coast of Florida in a sea level rise situation to be $13 to $82 per foot, amounting to 0.1 to 3.4 percent of the value of beachfront property (National Research Council,

1987). Gibbs (1986) estimated the cost of beach nourishment at Sullivan's Island, Charleston, South Carolina, to be $121 million. Removing $15 million from this estimate for the cost of stabilizing the backside of the island, the remaining cost is approximately $4,000 per foot. Using Gibbs's 3 percent discount rate for an indefinitely long period, this is equivalent to an annual cost of $120 per foot.

Goemans (1986) has estimated the cost in the Netherlands of adapting to a 1-m sea level rise to be $4.4 billion. Of this, 60 percent is for dikes and dunes. Over the 1,000 km of Dutch dikes, this amounts to about $1,000 per foot of existing dike. Gibbs (1986) suggested that the cost of seawall construction to protect Charleston, South Carolina, would be approximately $2,000 per foot of length, amounting to approximately 6 percent of the value of the protected property.

Titus and Greene (1989) synthesized the results of three different studies to estimate the nationwide costs of holding back the sea for various sea level rises. Using a set of plausible and believable assumptions, they calculated the cumulative costs of protecting barrier islands and developed mainland through the year 2100 to be $32 billion to $309 billion (1986 dollars) for sea level rises from 50 to 200 cm. For a 50-cm rise they provided a 95 percent confidence interval of costs from $32 billion to $43 billion.

Gleick and Maurer (1990) evaluated the costs of protecting San Francisco Bay from a 1-m sea level rise, which is more than our assumption. They estimated that building levees, seawalls, and other protective structures to protect the existing infrastructure would cost approximately $1 billion, plus an additional $100 million per year for maintenance. These costs excluded any costs of protecting natural ecosystems and wetlands.

Facilities that depend on fixed distances from water level will require modification. Docking facilities will need to be raised and/or protected against storm and high-tide damage. Some facilities, such as overhead cranes, will have reduced clearances that will diminish their usefulness (National Research Council, 1987). Such facilities may be raised or may simply not be utilized during periods of high tide.

Many bridges that cross bays, estuaries, and the downstream reaches of rivers draining into the sea will either need to be raised or will block marine navigation during high-tide periods (Walker et al., 1989). Other structures, not designed to permit navigation, may need to be raised or strengthened because they will be insufficiently high to protect them from storm damage.

Ocean outfalls of urban drainage systems and waste treatment facilities may, in some cases, need to be moved to permit discharge and/or otherwise protected to prevent damage (Smith and Tirpak, 1989).

Changes in currents within ports and harbors may increase the need for dredging, even though the mean sea level is higher (National Research Council, 1987).

Changes in groundwater levels combined with higher backwaters in river and drainage channels will require major improvements in urban sewage and drainage systems (Walker et al., 1989). Walker et al. (1989) suggest that in the city of Miami the cost of dikes and levees to protect from direct sea level rise will be relatively small, while the upgrading of storm sewers and drainage will be very expensive. In any city in which these problems occur, pipes and drainage channels will have to be increased in size either by replacement or by the addition of supplemental facilities. Systems that have depended upon gravity may need to shift to forced drainage or, in cases within tidal range, to combinations of locks and flap gates that permit drainage during low tides (Titus et al., 1987). Airports in coastal cities, often on landfill in estuaries or bays, may require special attention in this regard (Walker et al., 1989). Highway underpasses will need increased pumping capacity for drainage (National Research Council, 1987).

The elevated groundwater table can require additional adaptations. Increased seepage into basements may require expanded drainage facilities or improved waterproofing (National Research Council, 1987). Building foundations in some locations may be adversely affected and require stabilization to prevent subsidence. However, Walker et al. (1989) point out that in Dade County, Florida, building foundations will probably not be affected because large buildings already have foundations extending into the water table and homes are built on elevated lots. Streets, however, may need to be raised, resulting in additional drainage difficulties for buildings. Groundwater levels rising above buried pipelines will increase corrosion rates, resulting in more frequent leaks and replacement requirements (National Research Council, 1987).

Special problems may occur where the groundwater table rises into landfills and waste disposal sites (National Research Council, 1987). This could result in leaching of hazardous materials into groundwater if the landfill is not adequately sealed against such possibilities. The cost of remediation in such instances may be quite high.

Adaptations similar to many of those listed above will be necessary in inland cities where increased rainfall results in rises in groundwater levels.

Adaptation to Temperature Increase

In addition to increasing their electrical generation capacity, urban areas will need to make only minor adaptations to temperature change. These may include placing additional expansion joints in rails and increasing maintenance on asphalt roadways. However, northern municipalities may be able to build roads with reduced pavement thickness and may have reduced snow removal costs.

Because of the temperature effect on air pollution, even more stringent emission standards will be necessary for automotive exhausts and possibly for stationary combustion plants as well (Smith and Tirpak, 1989).

When to Adapt

Most of the anticipated impacts of global climate change on human settlements are on man-made facilities with relatively long lives (from 20 to 100 years). If these facilities are to be adapted rather than protected or abandoned, it will sometimes be economical to undertake the adaptation at the beginning of the life cycle rather than to retrofit later. One example of the difference in costs between initial design and retrofit is given by LaRoche and Webb (1987), who estimated the increased cost of an anticipated overhaul of a Charleston, South Carolina, drainage system if an 11-in. rise in sea level were included in the design and also the cost of accommodating an 11-in. rise by retrofit if the overhaul were first done for the current sea level. The added cost to accommodate now for the sea level rise was $260,000, 5 percent of the cost of the overhaul; the cost of the later retrofit was $2.4 million. However, anticipatory modification is not always cost effective. Waddell and Blaylock (1987) in a similar study of Ft. Walton Beach, Florida, concluded that the best way to combat sea level rise in this community was by floodproofing the houses. In this case, designing for future rise provided no significant savings over upgrading the floodproofing when the rise occurs.

As with adaptation, abandonment may be most economical when anticipated well in advance. This permits adequate time to provide economic facility replacement and prevents needless upkeep and modernization expenditures on facilities prior to the abandonment. On the other hand, the construction of new facilities, both protective (dikes, levees, etc.) and capacity-increasing (added power generation), can usually be done economically in a relatively short time and therefore can be delayed until needed.

Summary

As information increases, the probability and likely extent of climate change will become better understood. In the interim, as suggested by Titus et al. (1987), public officials must frequently consider whether to include allowances for climate change in current designs. They must view this decision as choosing between leaving future generations with a risk of significant damage or costly retrofits or leaving them with a certainty of added debt repayment for the anticipatory design. These issues are of principal importance when considering long-lived facilities that are difficult or expensive to protect; in such cases, consideration of anticipatory modification of the facility design is warranted.

HEALTH

The Basics

Humans have successfully adjusted to diverse climates. In the course of human evolution, people have advanced into every climatic zone between the equator and the poles and established permanent dwellings in most. Nevertheless, people have evolved with characteristics related to the climate where they have lived for a long time. For example, the short, heavy-set Eskimo is fitted to life in the Arctic, while the long-legged Masai is fitted to life in the savannah. The dense dark pigmentation of humans at low latitudes and its progressive decrease at high latitudes is another example of genetic adaptation to environment.

Birth rates are of the order of 20 per 1,000 population per year, and they are higher in many tropical climates than in some temperate ones. Death rates are of the order of 10 per 1,000 and are not correlated with climate (U.S. Bureau of the Census, 1987, Table 1379).

Besides long-term genetic adaptation, studies show humans are highly adaptable on shorter time scales as well. People routinely adapt to seasonal weather variations. Cold acclimatization provides more tolerance for low temperatures in the winter, while heat acclimatization provides more tolerance for hot summer temperatures. Some researchers suggest that people who move from a cool to a subtropical climate often adapt within 2 weeks (Rotton, 1983).

There are, however, limits to human adaptability. All permanent human settlements are in climates where the maximum temperature is 55°C and the minimum temperature is –60°C. These seem to be the limits of human tolerance. Over two-thirds of the world's settlements are in climates where the temperature ranges from a minimum of –5° to –15°C to a maximum of 30° to 38°C. This is considered the mean comfort zone within which adaptation is easiest (Weihe, 1979).

The principal factor of climate that is biologically influential is temperature. Other factors mainly have importance with respect to temperature. Water vapor pressure gains in influence above 25°C and can be ignored below 10°C, while relative humidity is important at all temperatures. Precipitation is influential through cooling of the air and saturating it with humidity. Wind enforces convection, with a positive effect in the heat and a negative effect in the cold. Several attempts have been made to combine two or more meteorological factors as indices of physical comfort and predictors of habitability (Weihe, 1979).

Climate as a Direct Cause of Disease

Human health would be affected by any climate change because people are directly sensitive to climate and susceptible to diseases whose vectors are sensitive (Weihe, 1979; Kalkstein, 1989; Intergovernmental Panel on Climate Change, 1990a). For all direct impacts of climate, two factors are important: (1) the relative and absolute strength of the stimulus and (2) the exposure time. Injuries and maladjustments caused by climate are summarized in Table 34.7. Probably more important than injury by exposure in a warmer climate are maladjustments from insufficient adaptation to a change in climate. Although these generally occur among newcomers to a climate, they can affect indigenous populations. Although generally treatable, maladjustments such as heat stroke can kill if treatment is not immediate. Maladjustments such as congenital sweat gland deficiency and autoimmune hemolytic anemias render affected individuals permanently incapable of tolerating heat and cold, respectively. Because people can adapt to CO_2 concentrations several times the present one, the projected rise in CO_2 itself presents no particular hazard (Schaefer, 1958; Weihe, 1979).

The relationship between climate, particularly temperature, and mortality has been studied for over a century (Kalkstein, 1989). Generally, mortality peaks in winter, summer, or both. Weihe (1979) concludes that industrialized countries show winter peak mortality mainly from noncommunicable diseases (e.g., cerebrovascular disease). Developing countries, on the other hand, show peak summer mortality rates primarily from infectious diseases. Although mortality increases have been seen during extreme cold waves, several studies found the impact of cold weather on mortality to be less dramatic than that of hot weather (Kalkstein, 1989).

A major question about climate change and human health concerns acclimatization—the ability of people to withstand stress with repeated exposure. It has been postulated that people who survive early heat waves become physiologically and behaviorally acclimatized and therefore deal more effectively with later heat waves (Marmor, 1975).

Kalkstein's (1989) estimation of the change in mortality from a 4° to 6°C warming in the summer underlines a paradox about the present: the cities with the highest weather-induced mortality are in the North rather than in the South. So, a scenario of warmer weather but no acclimatization caused the expected rise in mortality. If the population acclimatized, however, the predicted weather-induced mortality in the summer actually declined in about half the 15 cities examined. For the full sample of 15 cities, a moderate rise of mortality was predicted. On the other hand, Kalkstein noted, "by the [estimation method], the comparatively modest rise in acclimatized mortality (as compared to unacclimatized predictions) parallels the response of people today who reside in southern cities with hot climates. Southern cities represent analogs of expected climate in northern cities, and these

TABLE 34.7 Health Disorders Caused Directly by Climate

	Injuries	Maladjustments
Ultraviolet radiation	Sunburn Sun-blindness (solar retinopathy) Skin cancer	

Heat		Systematic disorders
		  Heat stroke, hyperthermia
		  Circulatory deficiency heat
		    exhaustion
		  Water deficiency heat exhaustion
		  Salt deficiency heat exhaustion
		    (heat cramps)
		  Anhidrotic heat exhaustion
		
		Psychoneurotic disorders
		  Mild heat fatigue
		  Chronic heat fatigue
		
		Skin disorders
		  Prickly heat
		  Anhidrosis
		  Congenital sweat gland
		    deficiency
		  Dermatitis or excema

Cold	Frostbite Chilblains Snow-blindness	Hypothermia Contact dermatitis Cold exhaustion Autoimmune hemolytic anemias (cold agglutinin disease)
Altitude	Anoxia	Acute pulmonary edema Mountain sickness Sickle-cell anemia

SOURCE: Weihe (1979).

warmer cities exhibit . . . fewer weather-induced deaths in summer." Fewer weather-related deaths in the winter were predicted, of course, if the climate warms. To keep the scale of this mortality in mind, remember that the 5 per 100,000 people whose deaths are attributed to summer weather in the surveyed cities is about a quarter the rate from motor vehicle accidents.

Communicable Diseases

Communicable diseases are transmitted from one person to another by actual contact or contagion or by a vector. A person's body is colonized by parasites (e.g., viruses, bacteria, protozoa, and worms). Climate can play a part because parasites require certain climatic conditions for their existence.

Contagious Diseases

Climate plays a minor role in contagious diseases transmitted directly from person to person (Weihe, 1979). Indirectly, weather causes the incidence of contagious diseases to rise in winter when people crowd into dwellings.

Climate affects the survival of viruses outside the host. For example, influenza virus survives longer in low humidity, while higher relative humidity favors the poliomyelitis virus. Viral diseases with seasonal morbidity are common in both temperate and tropical zones. Influenza A, for example, occurs primarily in the winter. Its morbidity is aggravated by sudden cold spells. Several enteroviruses, on the other hand, are most prevalent during the summer. It is not known whether the seasonality of these viral diseases is due to the impact of the climate on the virus, the host, or both. This makes it difficult to predict the impact of climate change on viral diseases. From the evidence about influenza, one would reason that a warmer climate could decrease the incidence of influenza, whereas increased climate variability could increase the incidence.

Vector-borne Diseases

In these diseases, the pathogen is transmitted to a person by another agent, called the vector, such as a tick, flea, or mosquito. Climate can affect these diseases in several ways. It can affect both the infectious agent and the vector directly, or it can affect the vector by influencing the types of vegetation or intermediate hosts of the vector. Although the incidences of tick-borne Lyme disease and Rocky Mountain Spotted Fever are increasing, vector-borne diseases are relatively rare in the United States. Appraisals of the impact of climate change on vector-borne diseases in the United States have been attempted (Haile, 1989; Longstreth and Wiseman, 1989), with varied results. However, they do not incorporate, understandably, such complications as changes in vegetation and habitats for intermediate hosts, less rain versus more puddles of irrigation water, or control measures. As a recent World Heath Organization (1990) report noted, without regional climate projections "any predictions on future vector-borne disease risk can only be speculative."

Other Diseases

Arteriosclerotic heart disease, nonrheumatic chronic endocarditis, and other myocardial degenerations kill fewer people in warm months than in cold months (Rose, 1966; Rosenwaike, 1966). Heat waves are another matter. Hospital admissions for cardiovascular effects seem to rise during heat waves (Sontaniemi et al., 1970; Gill et al., 1988).

Pneumonia, bronchitis, and influenza kill most in cold months (Weihe, 1979). Other respiratory diseases also are related to weather patterns. Currently, 3 to 6 percent of the U.S. population suffers from hay fever and asthma (Smith and Tirpak, 1989). So, changes in climate that change vegetation, and hence pollen, could affect these allergy sufferers.

Because a variety of skin infections are related to temperature and humidity, changes in climate could change them. Relative humidity and rainfall may play a more important role than temperature for some skin diseases. Longstreth and Wiseman (1989) report that in the U.S. Army skin diseases were the greatest single cause of visits by Army personnel to health care facilities in Vietnam. These skin disorders were directly affected by high rainfall and humidity.

Climate and Human Reproduction

Within a country, conception occurs less often during months with hot temperatures (Weihe, 1979), but across countries birth rates are higher in some tropical climates than in temperate ones. So, among the things that affect birth rates, a warmer climate will not likely be a large influence.

The time of maximum fertility affects infant mortality. For example, in the United States, statistically significant increases in preterm births and perinatal mortality during the summer months has been documented (Keller and Nugent, 1983; Cooperstock and Wolfe, 1986). So, a warmer climate could increase this mortality.

Indirect Effects of Climate Change on Human Health

Lack of safe drinking water and adequate sanitation are currently problems in many parts of the world. They bring with them a number of water-borne diseases, such as typhoid and dysentery. If water supplies are changed by climate, as the section "Water Resources," above, discusses, health could change.

Similarly, climate change could change the food supply. So, climate change could affect famine and malnourishment and hence susceptibility to diseases. Warmer climates could cause more food spoilage, exacerbating enterovirus infections, which are already frequent in warm weather. Atmospheric hazards are the most deadly natural hazards in the United States (Riebsame et al., 1986). Floods, lightning, and tornados lead other atmospheric events in causing U.S. fatalities. Changes in the severity and frequency of storms could add to or subtract from these deaths.

Summary

The climatic changes anticipated are within the range now experienced among existing habitats and to which people who move from place to place have generally learned to adapt.

Older people may be at greatest risk of stress from heat waves; but adaptive means should be researched and found.

Arthropod-borne communicable disease may also increase in warmer, more humid climates if precautions are not taken.

Our adaptations are by and large within the present mainstream of medical research and international public health, but the consequences of neglect will be aggravated.

The pace of improvements in health from better technology and its application can and should greatly exceed the deterioration related to climate change. Failure to control global population growth, chemical pollution, and viral epidemics from presently ascertainable causes greatly outstrips the particular health burden from climate change.

MIGRATION

The Basics

How will climate change during the next 50 to 100 years alter where people live within the United States and over the whole planet? Will migrations, internal and international, take on new patterns and with what meaning for the United States? The implications of climate change for population distribution are scarcely treated in either the EPA (Smith and Tirpak, 1989) or IPCC (1990b) assessments. So, demographic and climate indicators in major countries were surveyed, historical responses to climate change were tabulated, and studies of climate and migration were examined.

Unlike subjects like farming or the natural landscape that may be affected by climate change, migration is an impact if people flee a harmful climate and is an adaptation when they arrive in a congenial one. It may be an impact on the destination where they arrive. Nevertheless, as we did for the other subjects, we examine sensitivity, impact, and adaptation for migration.

In the section "Health," above, it was noted that humans live in environments from extreme heat to extreme cold, and from extreme aridity to extreme humidity. Roughly 77 percent of today's population of 5.3 billion people live in developing countries, most in warm climates. Fully 84 percent of the projected 8.2 billion people in 2020 will live in today's developing countries. Growth rates of population are fastest for tropical areas of the globe where temperatures average above 20°C annually, so regardless of climate change, more of the world's population will live in relatively warm climates in the next century (United Nations, 1989b).

Most migrations cover relatively short distances and follow established paths (Lee, 1966). Although international migrations are increasing, most migrations take place within nations and, if international, within regions. Restrictive policies of the industrialized countries are the major constraint on immigration, and, without those policy constraints, levels of international migration would be significantly higher worldwide given the economic and other disparities that exist among nations (Tabbarah, 1988). It is unlikely that international migration would increase significantly as a result of climate change.

Most migration is driven by people's desire to improve their economic and social well-being, but a significant and perhaps growing share is forced or refugee migration. The 1951 United Nations Convention Relating to the Status of Refugees established the definition of "refugee" that is now widely accepted by most countries, including the United States:

> . . . any person who, owing to a well-founded fear of being persecuted for reasons of race, religion, nationality, membership of a particular social group or political opinion is outside the country of his nationality and is unable or, owing to such fear, is unwilling to avail himself of the protection of that country. . . .

By adopting a narrow definition of "refugee," the international community has been able to preclude overwhelming numbers of refugees. The definition leaves, however, a growing number of internationally displaced persons who may be victims of political confrontation although not persecuted themselves, or who may be victims of other forces (such as drought or famine), outside the protection of the United Nations High Commissioner for Refugees (Zolberg, 1989). Although the factors driving refugee migrations are complex, interrelated, and hard to measure, civil strife, war, and government structure seem to account for many and famine and state suppression for fewer (Edmonston and Lee, 1990). Since most of the persons not qualifying as refugees are located in poor neighboring countries in Africa or Asia, the international community needs to consider how refugees and other migrants can be helped in those locations.

Sensitivity

Within the United States

The U.S. population is among the most mobile in the world. About 17 percent of the population changes residence annually and 6 percent changes county of residence. Nonmovers are rare—perhaps no more than 10 to 15 percent of adults have spent their entire lives in their county of birth. In addition to high levels of internal migration, about 1.3 million persons enter the United States annually from abroad. The majority of these are nationals of other countries coming as migrants or refugees to live and work in the United States and the remainder are U.S. citizens returning from residence abroad. No other country in the world accepts as many immigrants as the United States (Bogue, 1985).

Preference for warmer regions has been a key determinant of internal population shifts in the United States and other industrialized countries in the post-World War II era (Figure 34.7). Internal migrations toward the Sunbelt have been eased by science and technology developments that, for

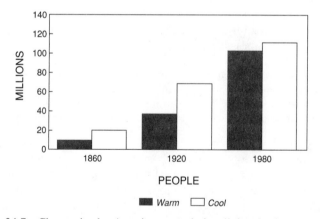

FIGURE 34.7 Change in the American population living in the warm savannah, desert, steppe, mediterranean, and humid subtropical zones of the United States versus the other cooler zones.

SOURCE: Adapted from Schelling (1983). Copyright © 1983 by the National Academy of Sciences.

example, cooled torrid summer air and controlled malaria in the South and along the Gulf coast. Government policies such as social security, differential state and local taxation policies, and siting of military and aerospace industries also contributed to the growth of the southern regions (Renas and Kumar, 1982; Pampel et al., 1984; Carlino and Mills, 1987; Voss et al., 1988).

Variability of climate in the same zone over time has also driven migration. For instance, in the 19th century and the first four decades of the 20th century in the Great Plains region, droughts fueled outmigration of thousands of people (Tannehill, 1947; Parry, 1978). Government policies and private acts can mitigate the effects of drought, as is demonstrated by reduced migration from the Great Plains during drought periods after the 1930s.

Migrations are sensitive even to slight temperature differentials. A study of migration flows within California, the state with the nation's largest elderly population, found a southward shift of population. Though most national studies of migration treat California in its entirety as a Sunbelt state, there exists a clear distinction between its northern and southern portions with respect to the direction migration takes (Ormrod, 1986).

The sensitivity of migration in other wealthy and industrialized societies resembles that in the United States. In nine such countries, for example, migration was triggered by retirement or widowhood—the relatively young and affluent among the elderly tend to move to warmer and more amenable climate zones while the older elderly move to areas where they can obtain care and support from family and friends even if this involves a move back to a colder zone (Serow, 1987).

Global

From Mycenaean drought more than a millennium before Christ to Sahelian droughts in our time, people have responded to climate events (see Table 34.8). However, drought is not the only climate event that has produced a response by people. Floods, cold weather, and even a plant pathogen newly arrived and encouraged by warm and moist seasons have increased outmigration or mortality, the response to dire conditions if the migration response is not available. Generally, places that were almost too cool, too dry, or too something became more so, and people were driven out.

Migration sensitivity to climate change appears to be correlated with three factors: the proportion of population living in regions prone to unstable political situations, the proportion of population that is poor or economically vulnerable, and the proportion living in coastal regions.

Political stability varies considerably across nations. Authoritarian regimes, war, civil strife, ethnic and religious conflicts, and state oppression

TABLE 34.8 Population Response to Climate Change in History

Date/Period	Country/Region	Climate Event	Population Response	Reference
1230–1000 B.C.	Mycenaea	Severe drought and grain shortage induced famine.	Dispersal and outmigration.	Bryson et al. (1974)
1240–1362	North Sea	Flooding of coastal areas.	Death and outmigration; 60 Danish parishes were lost to the sea.	Lamb (1981)
1200–1500	Norse settlement in Greenland	Increased cold and precipitation in winter and summer decreased agricultural production.	Extinction; community turned to spiritual; no adaptation.	McGovern (1981)
1300s to 1600s	Iceland	Increasing cold from volcanic ash led to decline of settled agriculture.	Population shifted southward and from agriculture to fishing.	Thorarinsson (1944)
1587–1601 and 1614–1645	Sweden	Increased cold decreased food supply.	Mass starvation, beggar migrants, slow population growth in the 16th century due to mortality.	Utterstrom (1955)

Period	Location	Climate	Effect	References
1785-1885	Maine	Cool climate with short intervals of warmer weather prevented rational crop selection; growing season was 22 days shorter than period since 1940.	Slow population growth in early part of period and absolute decline due to emigration from 1850 to 1880.	Smith et al. (1981)
1840s to 1850s	Ireland	Warm and moist summers made potato blight fungus spread and caused Irish potato famine.	Emigration of up to 50 percent of population to Britain and United States.	
1890s and 1930s	Great Plains	Drought; low rainfall and cold temperature, as well as bad grazing and plowing caused soil erosion and dust storms.	Population loss of 305,459 from Great Plains in 1930s.	Parry (1978), Tannehill (1947)
1968-1973	Sahel	Drought.	Increased deaths by 100,000 to 200,000; shifted nomads southward.	Campbell (1977), Glantz (1988)

have generated significant numbers of refugees in recent decades (Edmonston and Lee, 1990; U.S. Committee for Refugees, 1990). Most refugees have been produced by a few countries, but several other countries that have not can be considered "prone" to produce them if political conditions worsen. Recognizing that politics and nations' administrative practices affect counts of refugees,[11] one analysis (Edmonston and Lee, 1990) found that there were 8 million refugees in 1986, or slightly over 10 million taking into account 2.1 million Palestinians. By 1990 the generally accepted estimate of worldwide refugees is 15 million (U.S. Committee for Refugees, 1990). Populous countries with large land areas may generate internal migrants who flee one region for another without actually crossing an international border.

Since counts and definitions of refugees are based on political criteria and sensitivities, existing statistics do not identify how many might be considered environmental refugees or persons who moved because climate changes disrupted their livelihood. Environmental refugees are recognized officially only in Africa, where the Organization of African States has adopted a broad definition of refugees that includes persons who have left their homeland due to political, environmental, or other hardships (Zolberg, 1989).

The second source of sensitivity to climate change is the proportion of the population that is poor or economically vulnerable. Levels of economic development correlate strongly with the ability of governments or of people themselves to cope with or reduce the potentially negative effects of climate change on settled populations. Cases such as the stabilization of population in the Great Plains, the building of dikes in the Netherlands, and the Sunbelt shifts of population in the United States and other industrialized countries indicate that levels of economic and technological development mediate climatic effects on population settlements.

In developing countries the governments and most of the people do not have the economic means to use improved technologies to adapt to climate change. As such, larger numbers of people are potentially sensitive to climate shifts, particularly if the latter erodes the sustenance base. Urbanization rates are high in developing countries, and by the year 2020 the United Nations projects that 57.7 percent of the world's population and over half of the developing countries' populations will live in urban areas (United Nations, 1989a). The effects of climate change on rural-to-urban migrations and on the process of urbanization in developing countries are unclear.

The third source of sensitivity to climate change—the proportion of population living at sea level—correlates closely with the other two sources. Developed countries have greater resources and capabilities to respond to sea level rises than do developing countries. Crude estimates suggest that about one quarter of the world's population resides within 100 km of a coast and would therefore be vulnerable to sea level rise. Priority needs to be given to refining these estimates, taking into consideration altitude and development levels.

Impact

The climate change projected for the next 50 years or so might affect internal migration within the United States. For example, it might incline ongoing migration northward and increase migration to cooler mountains. Such a shift would be by many uncoordinated short moves, rather than a mass migration. The aging of the U.S. population and continued early retirement seem bound to increase the seasonal migrations south in winter and north in summer. Climate change could gradually shift the destinations of seasonal migrants, but flows are likely to continue northward or southward along existing migration corridors (e.g., East Coast toward Florida, Great Plains toward the Southwest).

If projections of sea level rise are correct, in the latter part of the 21st century, coastal populations may need to protect their homes or abandon them. Given existing investments in U.S. coastal settlements, people and governments are likely to respond by protecting those investments (see the section "Settlements and Coastal Structures," above). Thus, sea level rise is unlikely to stimulate migration from coastal areas in the United States, but it could in countries where development is too scanty to afford the adaptation of protection.

Large populations are a feature of many low coastal regions such as the Netherlands, Bengal, and Nile deltas. Concentrating on countries that would be hard pressed to build dikes, a 1-m rise in sea level, which is more than our assumption, would cover areas currently accounting for about 7 percent of habitable land and 5 percent of the population in Bangladesh and 12 percent of habitable land and 14 percent of the population in Egypt (Broadus, 1990). Thus, in those two countries alone, a 1-m rise in sea level could displace 14 million people.

Were climate change to displace settled populations in the world's most populous countries, China and India, significant numbers of refugees could be produced. Neither country currently produces a sizeable number of refugees, but even a small rate of refugee emigration from these populous countries would magnify the number of refugees. The impact of such increases would undoubtedly be greatest on neighboring countries in the Asian region.

If climate changes were greater than we have assumed, emigration from the United States could increase. This option would, of course, be limited to the small proportion of the population, largely the wealthy and educated, who would be able to locate jobs in other countries or develop the contacts that would allow such moves to take place (Kritz, 1991).

Adaptation

As pressures for entry increase, developed countries are likely to respond with further restrictions on immigration flows in order to keep the number of immigrants within manageable bounds. The discouragement of illegal migrations to the United States and greater assistance to help Third World refugees in the countries to which they fled rather than resettling them in the United States are also likely policy options. To the extent that climate change is likely to stimulate large inflows, the potential is greatest along existing paths. Examples are from Mexico, the Caribbean, and Central America to the United States, and from North and West Africa to Europe.

Developing countries have less control over their borders than developed countries and therefore are more vulnerable to illegal immigration. Adaptation to migration may thus be especially great at borders like that between Bangladesh and India were sea levels to rise substantially. Droughts in the Sahel region could also stimulate emigration toward coastal and central zones of Africa.

National and international governmental organizations should prepare for the likelihood that climatic change will be an added or complicating factor for migration. Within the United States, regulation of internal migration would be new. Indirect encouragement of migration, on the other hand, is not new and includes development of water supplies and regulation of construction on areas prone to flooding. The decrease in migration from the Dust Bowl and later droughts in the Great Plains illustrate how government policies can stabilize populations or reduce the likelihood of a migration response (Tannehill, 1947; Parry, 1978; Warrick, 1980).

In other countries, adaptations could range from ones that keep people home to others that allow them to settle in neighboring countries that share economic and political ties. Examples of the former include the dikes that make the Zuider Zee into a polder, the air conditioning that makes Texas and Florida attractive, or the climate and jobs that make mountainous regions prosper. Examples of the latter are the European Community, the Economic Commission for West African States, and the Trans-Tasman Agreement, all of which are regional treaties entered into by countries to further their common economic and political objectives and that allow some unrestricted migration of nationals of member states among the treaty signators.

Summary

Historically, people have adapted to a wide range of climates and climate changes. In the United States and other industrialized countries in recent decades, people have migrated toward warmer climates, indicating that they are not averse to hot weather. While migrants adapt by changing location, their impacts on receiving areas increase if they are fleeing refugees. Over the centuries, refugees have fled drought, cold, and flood in addition to political persecution. Today, an array of factors, but especially civil strife, war, and government structure, drive refugees. These factors plus poverty and living at sea level make migration sensitive to climate change. Where nations have these sensitivities, migration could be a large impact of climate change.

DOMESTIC TRANQUILITY

Basics

Most people surely share the goal enshrined in the Preamble to the U.S. Constitution, "to insure domestic Tranquility." While some nations have the economic resources and political institutions that allow them to cope with failing harvests and flooded lands, other nations do not. Moreover, "in no country or city can the rich fortify themselves for long against the poor" (Tickell, 1990). The question is how climate will interact with such strains as terrorism, civil war, bankruptcy, and natural disasters to reduce or enhance the tranquility of nations and then the international condition.

The panel felt that it was important to point to the possibility that the precarious economic and political order in many countries around the world could be weakened further by climate change and to consider the implications for industrial countries. How might domestic and international tranquility be sensitive to climate change?

Sensitivity

Social and technological development probably, on balance, lessens the vulnerability of societies to climate change (Kates et al., 1985), but sensitivity might be of three sorts: brittleness, accumulation of troubles, or overwhelming change.

Brittleness

Societies have developed increasingly elaborate technical and social systems to insulate themselves from recurrent weather fluctuations. These systems have allowed populations to grow in environments that might otherwise be considered "too hot or too cold" or "too wet or too dry" to sustain the livelihood of large numbers of people. Where such developments have occurred, a vulnerability develops if the technical or social systems fail. For example, if the cooling system fails in an extreme heat wave, mortality could increase among those susceptible to high temperatures. If farmers could not get access to credits to purchase fertilizers or equipment that allowed them to grow crops in poor soil, their vulnerability would be increased.

Accumulation of Troubles

The second sort of sensitivity stems from accumulation of troubles in countries already beset by economic and political difficulties. Here, a large or rapid change could trigger further stress. For instance, sea level rises could disrupt populations living in coastal zones and trigger migrations to other poor areas that will have difficulty feeding and housing them. To the extent that these migrations become international ones, political relationships between the sending and receiving countries could be strained.

Overwhelming Change

Extreme climate change (e.g., a 5°C warming and a 1-m rise of sea level in 75 years) could require large-scale food relief and relocation of substantial populations from affected areas. Countries that are small territorially or that lack climatic variability will have difficulty adjusting. Domestic hardships could spill over into neighboring countries as refugees flee harsh conditions at home.

Variation in Sensitivity

Political sensitivity is likely greatest in countries already under population or environmental pressures. For the most part, they are also limited in administrative capacity, and natural disasters often bring a severe breakdown. They are largely more agricultural, less industrialized, and have less technological capacity. Sensitivity is greater where many people live along the world's great rivers (whose flows might change), on low-lying coasts (that might eventually be flooded), or by agriculture that is finely tuned to current climate (e.g., monsoon rains).

Those societies that suffer the greatest economic losses from strategies to control emissions of greenhouse gases would also be sensitive. For example, petroleum or coal exporting nations would be susceptible if they could not find new sources of income, and nations that depend on high consumption of fossil fuels would suffer from draconian cuts.

On the other side of the coin, in parts of the world where climatic changes were economically beneficial, political stability could be enhanced.

Impacts

The first impact could originate from claims that an economic or social goal has not been attained because of climatic change caused by human agency. The greenhouse issue has potential for exacerbating conflict between the poor, and therefore more vulnerable, countries and the industrialized ones that are less vulnerable.

If climate change is greater, the potential political and other effects associated with it will also increase. For instance, substantial reduction of water and buffer stocks of food often leads to increased malnutrition and mortality, especially among infants, and to population shifts internally or internationally. One can see an example in the horn of Africa. Until recently, the United Kingdom supported irrigation projects there. Now, the combination of drought and civil war has made it impossible to continue the projects. Therefore, the financing and experts have been pulled out, and refugees have been generated by both the environmental stress and civil strife (Tickell, 1990).

Adaptation

Within Nations

The paramount adaptation by migration will be within nations and depends on effective government. The most important transfers of money, resources and people will be within nations, but, as sensitivities increase, these could spill over to other countries. Spillover effects could be intensified if climate change alters the relative productive potential of countries.

A proper balance of initiative in the public and private sectors can facilitate adaptation. Governments are increasingly enacting environmental rules, as the example of the United States shows (Figure 34.8), both to prevent environmental damage and to adapt to changing conditions. Not all adaptive policies, however, call for direct government action. Some adaptations call for government to establish incentives and then let market forces signal adaptations. Others only require effective transmission of economic signals. The economic system should send accurate and rapid signals (usually prices) about scarcities of such goods as water. This is true for goods and services that are already exchanged in markets and for those in which mechanisms like markets can be established.

As related in the section "Migration," above, internal and international mobility of labor and other resources can be routes for adaptation. Where there is national diversity in climates and resources, effective governments can facilitate and ease the adaptation.

All adaptive strategies, and hence domestic tranquility, will be helped by effective government. The nations most vulnerable to climatic stress may be those with the weakest governments today. Attributes of effective administration include policy coordination at the highest level of government (heads of government need to pay attention, as they set priorities and allocate budgets); a structure that can turn policy into action; coordination among technical people at the working level; and links between government and nongovernmental organizations and between government and public

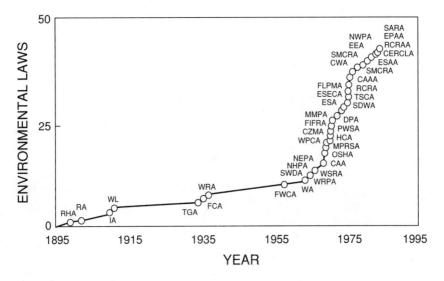

FIGURE 34.8   Growth in the number of U.S. environmental laws.

SOURCE: Reprinted, by permission, from Balzhiser (1989). Copyright © 1983 by the National Academy of Engineering.

opinion (Tickell, 1986, 1990). The establishment of an effective government is likely to be as protracted as climate change.

International

Between nations, migration across frontiers, especially in large numbers, creates problems. Many in the receiving countries feel that the number of people and differences in culture that can be absorbed are limited. Unemployment in the receiving country makes it still harder. Resistance to immigration is popular politics, and more refugees only strengthen the resistance (Tickell, 1990).

Internationally, at least three kinds of actions may lessen the blows of climate change and hence serve as adaptations:

• Assistance for developing countries in building their own indigenous research and assessment. A government is more likely to understand and act if the country has national experts participating fully in the world scientific dialogue on climate change, its causes, its impacts, and adaptations to it.

• Assistance toward rapid, sustainable, balanced growth in per capita income and help in slowing population growth. In both the short and the long run, these are probably the best adaptive strategies. All-round knowledge plus skills and technologies for adapting to climate variation and change should also be provided where they are lacking. Ideally, climate change will fade out as a distinctive problem if climate-oriented policies become part of development policies in general (Meyer-Abich, 1980).

• Disaster reduction and relief. Strengthening both international and national ways to wider and prompter response to natural disasters helps adaptation. Care is needed lest short-term adjustments to climatic hazards do not slow long-term adaptation.

As the negotiations for the Law of the Sea well demonstrated, the process of creating new international law and new international institutions is usually painful and protracted. Furthermore, development assistance is rarely effective except as part of a long-term policy.

Summary

Concern about political tranquility stems from the fear that some governments may not be able to cope with the added stress of climate change. Many countries outside the industrial world may lack the government or resources to manage a continuous environmental crisis, which unfavorable climate change could bring. Difficulties of organizing coordinated, multilateral responses to problems such as hunger are already widely evident. Unfavorable climate change could aggravate present economic, political, and social problems and swamp national governments and international assistance.

Although it is impossible to assess in a scientific manner the contribution that climate change may make to global political tensions, the possibility that climate change will disrupt domestic tranquility cannot be ignored. An analytic base needs to be developed that would allow us to specify the conditions under which this outcome is likely to occur.

QUESTIONS REVISITED

At the beginning of this chapter, we raised questions to keep in mind as we examined sensitivities, impacts, and adaptations. Drawing on our examination, we now comment on several key questions (Ausubel, 1991).

Is Faster Change Worse Than Slow?

Some changes may be beneficial, such as the added rain predicted for some farming regions by some computations. So, the directions of change must be specified before the question is answered. For the answer to matter, the combination of climate change and sensitivity to it must be greater for an activity than other kinds of changes and sensitivities. Also, the usual rate of change and adaptation of the activity must be slow or its forced rate of adaptation must be beyond our means for the answer to matter. Thus, the answer is not universally "yes," although a faster harmful change is clearly worse than a slow one in the same direction for, say, sensitive ecosystems or an impoverished coastal plain. For an activity like planting a new forest, a fast change that is anticipated may matter less than a slow one that is unforeseen. In general, rapid change will be more harmful than slow change, but an anticipated change, even if rapid, may be less harmful than an unforeseen slow one.

Will Waiting to Make Policy and to Act Drive Up Costs?

Sometimes we can calculate the cost of waiting versus acting. Acting now is justified if the cost of acting now relative to that of acting later is lower than a ratio that can be calculated from (1) the probability of the action being required, (2) the discount rate of money, and (3) how long the action can be postponed. The justified ratio is especially sensitive to the discount rate and the possible postponement. In practice these ratios can be computed only, if at all, to a very gross level of approximation. The cost of acting later will be affected by the growth in knowledge, technology, and wealth, which have grown in the past. As the world becomes more crowded, the reservation of sites for infrastructure, for the preservation of precious sites, or for the migration of ecosystems is likely to grow harder. Thus, they might be exempted from the rules of justification.

Are There Only Losers from Climate Change?

Under the assumptions we accepted of gradual warming and redistributed precipitation, there will be a complex and shifting set of winners and losers. Possible losses have frequently been predicted. Some wins may be absolute, for example, an increased crop yield. Some may be relative, as when yields fall less in one place than in another. The argument that there will be more losers than winners arises because we are currently adapted to present climate, and thus any change is likely to require at least some costly adaptation.

Will the Most Important Impacts Be on Farming
and from the Rise of Sea Level?

The adaptability of farming and even the forestry of managed trees is considerable and that of the natural unmanaged landscape or shore is less so. Cities and irrigated farms in dry regions show that water supply can be adapted, and there is room in many areas for further adaptation. Nevertheless, the impact of changes of climate on water supply is relatively large, and the adaptation is likely to be costly. Despite the sensitivity of coasts to the rise of sea level, adaptation will likely preserve valuable sites like cities. So with reasonable adaptation by humanity, it is natural landscapes, shores, and water supply that will be left to suffer more.

Will Changes in Extreme Climatic Conditions Be More Important Than Changes in Average Conditions?

The foundation of this question is a belief that extremes will breach some threshold of sensitivity. Since warming is assumed, the obvious extreme and threshold of frost will be breached less and that of debilitating heat waves more frequently. Because a general increase in variability is not currently predicted, the cause of breaching more thresholds would be a gradual increase in the frequency of warming and in some places drying as their entire frequency distributions crept upward. The answer to the question lies in locating thresholds of sensitivity and predicting shifts in averages and then frequency distributions.

Are the Changes Unprecedented from the Perspective of Adaptation?

Although globally, on average, the assumed climate change for the next century exceeds any for tens of hundreds or thousands of years past, it is much smaller than that from day to night, from summer to winter, or between airports one might leave and reach in an hour. The ways humanity adapts to the present differences are impressive. It is important, therefore, to clarify how the projected climate change will differ from all the climatic variations that humans, the economy, and ecosystems are now accustomed to. Nevertheless, it seems that for impact and adaptation the unprecedented character matters primarily at margins of natural, forestry, or farming zones where the present climate is already close to a threshold of sensitivity.

Will Impacts Be Harder on Less Developed Countries or on Developed Ones?

The impacts are likely to be larger for less developed countries because they derive a greater fraction of income from outdoors and hence sensitive activities like farming, forestry, or fisheries and because they lack wealth to afford adaptation and the infrastructure and technology to accomplish it. A sensitivity that might be forgotten is the effect of striving to mitigate carbon emissions upon a less developed country that depends on the extraction or processing of fossil fuel. In general, the consequences of climate change will likely be consistent with the findings of research about other health and environmental hazards that "richer is safer" (Wildavsky, 1980).

Are Some Hedges Clearly Economical?

Several hedges against gradual climate change are economical and are under way: testing crop varieties, replanting forests with adapted trees, coping with current variability in water supply, improving weather and climate information, clarifying policies for migration, and strengthening programs to reduce the effects of natural disasters. Also, the panel found other potential hedges such as better management of the demand for water and more prudent development of coastal zones. The question must be asked, however, why these apparently prudent actions are not already being pursued more actively. The panel noted the anticipatory investment in a higher offshore oil platform designed for many decades, and offered a simple method for including climate change in the calculus of risks, costs, and benefits of investments. Tools and applications exist for demonstrating more widely the economics of hedging.

NOTES

1. The relative [(change of plant growth)/growth]/[(change of CO_2)/CO_2] is called beta or CO_2 fertilization effect. In models relating the rise in CO_2 in the air to its emission, a standard value of about 0.25 is used, and varying it changes predictions of future CO_2 in the air greatly. See review in National Research Council (1983, p. 20) and Keeling and Bacastow (1977).

2. Damage to crops is figured from weather conditions.

3. This section concentrates on ecological effects and fisheries. Changes in the oceans could also affect tourism, recreation, and coastal structures, subjects covered in the sections "Tourism and Recreation" and "Settlements and Coastal Structures."

4. In the recent past, concerns have been raised about the melting of the West Antarctic ice sheet, which rests on the sea floor. Such melting, it has been estimated, would add over 5 m to the sea level. Current estimates put such large-scale melting at least two centuries into the future.

5. El Niño/Southern Oscillation (ENSO) refers to an anomalous ocean/atmosphere interaction in which sea surface temperatures are warmer than usual in the central and eastern equatorial Pacific, and air pressure is high over the southeastern Pacific and low over the Indian Ocean. Changes in ocean upwelling, sea level, and rainfall accompany ENSO.

6. Note, however, that even without barriers, wetland areas may diminish significantly. Another adaptation strategy would be to develop measures to enhance critically the natural productivity of wetlands, perhaps by augmenting natural sedimentation rates.

7. Publications of the U.S. Geological Survey show 4,200 billion gallons/day (BGD) precipitation and 2,800 BGD evaporation, leaving 1,400 BGD runoff, in the 48 contiguous states. They also show 336 BGD withdrawn for use and 92 BGD consumed in 1985. Use of fresh water rose until 1980 and then declined 11 percent in 5 years because less was used in irrigation and industry.

8. Similar results were obtained by Adams et al. (1990).

9. The 1988 *Statistical Abstract of the United States* has the following relevant facts: 47 million fishermen and 17 million hunters (Table 379); 48 million people in attendance at major league baseball games and 36 million at college football games (Table 372); 345 million visits to national parks (Table 357) and 675 million visits to state parks and recreational areas (Table 362); $55,450 million (1985 dollars) for wildlife-associated recreation (Table 380); $14,072 million for books (Table 366); $7,250 million for purchases of color TVs (Table 371); 34 percent participation of people in swimming and 19 percent in freshwater fishing (Table 374).

10. For a discussion of recreation, wildlife, water, and climate change see Cooper (1990).

11. Some countries, for example, report certain aliens as refugees, but others classify similar migrants as economic or illegal migrants. It is often in the political interest of a government to understate its refugee population or in other cases to inflate the numbers. Some countries admit individuals under classifications other than refugee, and therefore they are not counted in the totals. Finally, asylum seekers, who are growing in number, are not reflected in refugee counts (U.S. Committee for Refugees, 1990).

REFERENCES

Abelson, P. H. 1991. Desalination of brackish and marine waters. Science 251:1289.

Acock, B., and L. H. Allen, Jr. 1985. Crops responses to elevated carbon dioxide concentrations. In Direct Effects of Increasing Carbon Dioxide on Vegetation, B. R. Strain and J. D. Cure, eds. Report DOE/ER-0238. Washington, D.C.: U.S. Department of Energy.

Adams, R. M., C. Rosenzweig, R. M. Peart, J. T. Ritchie, B. A. McCarl, J. D. Glyer, R. B. Curry, J. W. Jones, K. J. Boote, and L. H. Allen, Jr. 1990. Global climate change and U.S. agriculture. Nature 345:219-224.

Allen, R. G., and F. N. Gichuki. 1989. Effects of project CO_2-induced climatic changes on irrigation water requirements in the Great Plains states (Texas, Oklahoma, Kansas, and Nebraska). In The Potential Effects of Global Climate Change in the United States, Appendix C, Agriculture, J. B. Smith and D. A. Tirpak, eds. Washington, D.C.: U.S. Environmental Protection Agency.

Ausubel, J. H. 1991. A second look at the conventional wisdom about the impacts of global climatic change. American Scientist 79(3):210-221.

Bach, W. 1979. The impact of increasing atmospheric CO_2 concentrations on the global climate: Potential consequences and corrective measures. Environment International 2:215-228.

Bakun, A. 1990. Global climate change and intensification of coastal ocean upwelling. Science 247:198.

Balzhiser, R. E. 1989. Meeting the near-term challenge for power plants. In Technology and Environment, J. H. Ausubel and H. E. Sladovich, eds. Washington, D.C.: National Academy Press.

Barbier, E. B. 1989. The global greenhouse effect, economic impacts and policy considerations. Natural Resources Forum (February):20-32.

Bazzaz, F. A., and R. W. Carlson. 1984. Response of plants to elevated CO_2. I. Competition among an assemblage of annuals at different levels of soil moisture. Oecologia 62:196-198.

Bazzaz, F. A., K. Garbutt, and W. E. Williams. 1985. Effect of increased atmospheric carbon dioxide concentration on plant communities. In Direct Effects of Increasing Carbon Dioxide on Vegetation, B. R. Strain and J. D. Cure, eds. Report DOE/ER-0238. Washington, D.C.: U.S. Department of Energy.

Binkley, C. S. 1988. The impact of CO_2-induced climate change on the world's forest sector. In The Impact of Climatic Variations on Agriculture, Volume 1, Assessments in Cool Temperate and Cold Regions, M. Parry, T. Carter, and N. Konijn, eds. Dordrecht, The Netherlands: Kluwer Academic Publishers.

Binkley, C. S. 1990. Climate change and forests. William P. Thompson Memorial Lecture given at Northern Arizona University, Flagstaff, June 5, 1990.

Binkley, C. S., and D. P. Dykstra. 1987. Timber supply. In The Global Forest Sector: An Analytical Perspective, M. Kallio, D. Dykstra, and C. S. Binkley, eds. New York: John Wiley & Sons.

Binkley, C. S., and J. Vincent. 1988. Timber prices in the U.S. South: Past trends and outlook for the future. Southern Journal of Applied Forestry 12:15-18.

Birdsey, R. A. 1990. Estimation of regional carbon yields for forest types in the United States. Unpublished manuscript. U.S. Forest Service, U.S. Department of Agriculture, Washington, D.C.

Blasing, T. J., and A. Solomon. 1982. Response of the North American corn belt to climate warming. Publication 2134. Oak Ridge, Tenn.: Environmental Sciences Division, Oak Ridge National Laboratory.

Bogue, D. J. 1985. The Population of the United States: Historical Trends and Future Projections. New York: The Free Press.

Botkin, D. B., and R. A. Nisbet. 1989. Projecting the effects of climate change on biological diversity in forests. In Consequences of the Greenhouse Effect for Biological Diversity, R. Peters, ed. New Haven, Conn.: Yale University Press.

Botkin, D. B., and L. B. Simpson. 1989. The global carbon cycle and land vegetation. Paper presented at the 198th National Meeting of the American Chemical Society, Miami Beach, Florida, September 10-15, 1989.

Botkin, D. B., R. A. Nisbet, and T. E. Reynales. 1989. Effects of climate change on the forests of the Great Lakes states. In The Potential Effects of Global Climate Change on the United States, Appendix D, Forests, J. B. Smith and D. A. Tirpak, eds. Washington, D.C.: U.S. Environmental Protection Agency.

Botkin, D. B., D. A. Woodby, and R. A. Nisbet. 1991. Kirtland's Warbler habitats: A possible early indicator of climatic warming. Biological Conservation 56: 63-78.

Broadus, J. 1990. Possible impacts of and adjustments to sea level rise: The cases of Bangladesh and Egypt. Contribution No. 7147. Woods Hole, Mass.: Woods Hole Oceanographic Institution.

Broecker, W. S. 1987. Unpleasant surprises in the greenhouse? Nature 328:123-126.

Broecker, W. S., and G. H. Denton. 1990. What drives glacial cycles? Scientific American (January):49-56.

Brown, L. R., A. Burning, C. Flavin, H. French, J. Jacobson, M. Lowe, S. Postel, M. Renner, L. Starke, and J. Young. 1990. State of the World 1990. New York: W. W. Norton.

Bryson, R. A., H. H. Lamb, and D. L. Donley. 1974. Drought and the decline of the Mycenae. Antiquity 48:46-50.

Buddenhagen, I. W. 1977. Resistance and vulnerability of tropical crops in relation to their evolution and breeding. Annals of the New York Academy of Sciences 287:309-326.

Cade, T. J., ed. 1988. Peregrine Falcon Populations, Their Management and Recovery. Boise, Idaho: Peregrine Fund.

Campbell, D. J. 1977. Strategies for Coping with Drought in the Sahel: A Study of Recent Population Movements in the Department of Maradi, Niger. Ph.D. dissertation. Clark University, Worcester, Mass.

Cannell, M. G. R. 1987. Climate warming and spring phenology of trees. In Woody Plant Growth in a Changing Chemical and Physical Environment, D. P. Lavender, ed. Proceedings of the International Union of Forestry Research Organizations Workshop, Vancouver, British Columbia, Canada, July 27-31, 1987. Vienna, Austria: International Union of Forestry Research Organizations.

Cannell, M. G. R., and R. I. Smith. 1986. Climate warming, spring budburst and frost damage on trees. Journal of Applied Ecology 23:177-191.

Capinera, J. L., and D. R. Horton. 1989. Geographic variation in effects of weather on grasshopper infestation. Environmental Entomology 18:8-14.

Carlino, G., and E. Mills. 1987. The determinants of country growth. Journal of Regional Science 27(1):39-54.

Castilla, J. C. 1990. Earthquake-caused coastal uplift and its effects' on rocky intertidal kelp communities. Science 240:440-443.

Chapman, V. J., and D. J. Chapman. 1980. Seaweeds and Their Uses. New York: Chapman and Hall.

Connell, J. H. 1972. Community interactions on marine rocky intertidal shores. Annual Review of Ecology and Systematics 3:169-192.

Conway, W. G. 1986. The practical difficulties and financial implications of endangered species breeding programs. International Zoo Yearbook 24/25:210-219.

Conway, W. G. 1989. The prospects for sustaining species and their evolution. In Conservation for the Twenty-first Century, D. Western and M. Pearl, eds. New York: Oxford University Press.

Cooper, C. F. 1990. Recreation and wildlife. In Climate Change and U.S. Water Resources, P. E. Waggoner, ed. New York: John Wiley & Sons.

Cooperstock, M., and R. A. Wolfe. 1986. Seasonality of preterm birth in the collaborative perinatal project: demographic factors. American Journal of Epidemiology 124:234-241.

Cordell, K. 1989. An analysis of outdoor recreation and wilderness situation in the United States, 1989-2040. Technical document supporting the 1989 Resources Planning Act Assessment. Washington, D.C.: Forest Service, U.S. Department of Agriculture.

Crosson, P.R., L. A. Katz, and J. Wingard. 1991. Agricultural production and

resource use in the MINK region without and with climate change. Working
Paper IIA prepared for U.S. Department of Energy under agreement 041460-A-
K1. Washington, D.C.: U.S. Department of Energy.

Cure, J. D. 1985. Carbon dioxide doubling responses: A crop survey. In Direct
Effects of Increasing Carbon Dioxide on Vegetation, B. R. Strain and J. D. Cure,
eds. Report DOE/ER-0238. Washington, D.C.: U.S. Department of Energy.

Davis, M. 1981. Quaternary history and the stability of forest communities. In
Forest Succession: Concepts and Application, D. C. West, H. H. Shugart, and D.
B. Botkin, eds. New York: Springer-Verlag.

Davis, M. B., and C. Zabinski. 1990. Changes in geographical range resulting from
greenhouse warming: Effects on biodiversity in forests. In Consequences of the
Greenhouse Effect for Biological Diversity. New Haven, Conn.: Yale University Press.

Drake, B. 1989. Elevated Atmospheric CO_2 Concentration Increases Carbon Se-
questering in Coastal Wetlands. Report DE-AC05-OR21400. Oak Ridge, Tenn.:
Carbon Dioxide Information Analysis Center, Environmental Sciences Division,
Oak Ridge National Laboratory.

Dudek, D. J. 1989. Climate change impacts upon agriculture and resources: A case
study of California. In The Potential Effects of Global Climate Change in the
United States, Appendix C, Agriculture, J. B. Smith and D. A. Tirpak, eds.
Washington, D.C.: U.S. Environmental Protection Agency.

Duvick, D. N. 1984. Genetic diversity in major farm crops on the farm and in
reserve. Economic Botany 38:161-178.

Eamus, D., and P. G. Jarvis. 1989. The direct effects of increase in the global
atmospheric CO_2 concentration on natural and commercial temperate trees and
forest. Advances in Ecological Research 19:1-55.

Easterling, W. E. 1989. Farm-level adjustments by Illinois corn producers to
climate change. In The Potential Effects of Global Climate Change in the United
States, Appendix C, Agriculture, J. B. Smith and D. A. Tirpak, eds. Washington,
D.C.: U.S. Environmental Protection Agency.

Easterling, W. E, M. McKenney, N. J. Rosenberg, and K. Lemon. 1991. A Farm-
Level Simulation of the Effects of Climate Change on Crop Productivity in the
MINK Region. Working Paper IIB prepared for U.S. Department of Energy
under agreement 041460-A-K1. Washington, D.C.: U.S. Department of Energy.

Edmonston, B., and S. M. Lee. 1990. Factors affecting refugee emigration. Report
OSC-DPS-UI-3. Washington, D.C: The Urban Institute.

Farnum, P. 1990. Creating new stands: Adapting to the greenhouse effect through
technological preparedness. Paper presented at the U.S. Environmental Protection Agency Conference, Forestry Responses to Climate Change, Washington,
D.C., May 15-17, 1990.

Federal Insurance Administration. 1984. Retrofitting Flood-Prone Residential Structures.
Washington, D.C.: Office of Loss Reduction, Federal Insurance Administration.

Fedkiw, J. 1989. The evolving use and management of the nation's forest, grass-
lands, croplands, and related resources. Technical document supporting the 1989
Resources Planning Act Assessment. Washington, D.C.: U.S. Forest Service,
U.S. Department of Agriculture.

Flather, C. H., and T. W. Hoekstra. 1989. An analysis of the wildlife and fish situation in the United States, 1989-2040. Technical document supporting the 1989 Resources Planning Act Assessment. Washington, D.C.: Forest Service, U.S. Department of Agriculture.

Franklin, J., V. Dale, D. Perry, F. Swanson, M. Harmon, T. Spies, A. McKee, and D. Larson. 1989. Effects of global climatic change on the forests of northwestern North America. In Consequences on the Greenhouse Effect for Biological Diversity. New Haven, Conn.: Yale University Press.

Frederick, K. D., and A. V. Kneese. 1990. Reallocations by markets and prices. In Climate Change and U.S. Water Resources, P. E. Waggoner, ed. New York: John Wiley & Sons.

Gates, D. M. 1985. Global biospheric response to increasing atmospheric carbon dioxide concentration. In Direct Effects of Increasing Carbon Dioxide on Vegetation, B. R. Strain and J. D. Cure, eds. Report DOE/ER-0238. Washington, D.C.: U.S. Department of Energy.

Gibbs, M. 1986. Planning for sea level rise under certainty: A case study of Charleston, South Carolina. In Effects of Changes in Stratospheric Ozone and Global Climate, Volume 4, Sea Level Rise, J. G. Titus, ed. Washington, D.C.: U.S. Environmental Protection Agency.

Gill, J. S., P. Davies, S. K. Gill, and D. G. Beevers. 1988. Wind-chill and the seasonal variation of cerebrovascular disease. Journal of Clinical Epidemiology 41:225-230.

Glantz, M. H. 1982. Consequences and responsibilities in drought forecasting: The case of Yakima, 1977. Water Resources Research 18:3-13.

Glantz, M. H., ed. 1988. Drought and Hunger in Africa. Cambridge: Cambridge University Press.

Gleick, P. H. 1987. Regional hydrologic consequences of increases in atmospheric CO_2 and other trace gases. Climatic Change 10:137-160.

Gleick, P. H. 1989. The implications of climate change for international security. Climatic Change 15:309-325.

Gleick, P. H. 1990. Vulnerability of water systems. In Climate Change and U.S. Water Resources, P. E. Waggoner, eds. New York: John Wiley & Sons.

Gleick, P. H., and E. P. Maurer. 1990. Assessing the Costs of Adapting to Sea Level Rise: A Case Study of San Francisco Bay. Stockholm, Sweden: The Stockholm Environment Institute and Pacific Institute for Studies in Development, Environment, and Security.

Glynn, P. W. 1988a. El Niño-Southern Oscillation 1982-1983: Nearshore population, community, and ecosystem responses. Annual Review of Ecology and Systematics 19:309-345.

Glynn, P. W. 1988b. El Niño warming, coral mortality and reef framework destruction by echinoid bioerosion in the Eastern Pacific. Galaxea 7:129-160.

Glynn, P. W. 1991. Coral reef bleaching in the 1980s and possible connections with global warming. Trends in Ecology and Evolution 6(6):175-179.

Goemans, T. 1986. The sea also rises: The ongoing dialogue of the Dutch with the sea. In Effects of Changes in Stratospheric Ozone and Global Climate, Volume 4, Sea Level Rise, J. G. Titus, ed. Washington, D.C.: U.S. Environmental Protection Agency.

Gordon, P. 1982. Special Statistical Summary: Deaths, Injuries, and Property Loss by Disaster, 1970-1980. Washington, D.C.: Federal Emergency Management Agency.

Gosselink, J. G., E. P. Odum, and R. M. Pope. 1973. The Value of the Tidal Marsh. Baton Rouge: Center for Wetlands Research, Louisiana State University.

Goudriaan, J., and H. E. de Ruiter. 1983. Plant growth in response to CO_2 enrichment, at two levels of nitrogen and phosphorus supply: Dry matter, leaf area and development. Netherlands Journal of Agricultural Science 31:157-169.

Guldin, R. W. 1989. An analysis of the water situation in the United States, 1989-2040. Technical document supporting the 1989 Resources Planning Act Assessment. Washington, D.C.: Forest Service, U.S. Department of Agriculture.

Haile, D. G. 1989. Computer simulation of the effects of changes in weather patterns on vector-borne disease transmission. In The Potential Effects of Global Climate Change on the United States, Appendix G, Health, J. B. Smith and D. A. Tirpak, eds. Washington, D.C.: U.S. Environmental Protection Agency.

Haven, S. B. 1971. Effects of land-level changes on intertidal invertebrates, with discussion of postearthquake ecological succession. In The Great Alaska Earthquake of 1964: Biology, Washington, D.C.: National Academy of Sciences.

Haynes, R. W. 1989. An analysis of the timber situation in the United States, 1989-2040. Technical document supporting the 1989 Resources Planning Act Assessment. Washington, D.C.: Forest Service, U.S. Department of Agriculture.

Henshaw, G. G. 1975. Technical aspects of tissue culture storage for genetic conservation. In Crop Genetic Resources for Today and Tomorrow, O. H. Frankel and J. G. Hawkes, eds. New York: Cambridge University Press.

Idso, S. B. 1988. Three phases of plant responses to atmospheric CO_2 enrichment. Plant Physiology 85:5-7.

Illinois Department of Transportation. 1986. Elevating or Relocating a House to Reduce Flood Damage. Chicago: Illinois Division of Water Resources, Illinois Department of Transportation.

Intergovernmental Panel on Climate Change. 1990a. IPCC: The First Assessment Report, Volume I, Overview and Policymakers' Summaries. Geneva: World Meteorological Organization.

Intergovernmental Panel on Climate Change. 1990b. Climate Change: The IPCC Impacts Assessment, W. J. McG. Tegart, G. W. Sheldon, and D. C. Griffiths, eds. Canberra: Australian Government Publishing Service. (Available from International Specialized Book Service, Portland, Oreg.)

International Rice Research Institute. 1983. Annual Report for 1981. Los Baños, Philippines: International Rice Research Institute.

International Union for Conservation of Nature and Natural Resources, Botanic Gardens Conservation Secretariat. 1989. The Botanic Gardens Conservation Strategy. Kew, Richmond, England: World Wide Fund for Nature and International Union for Conservation of Nature and Natural Resources Botanic Gardens Conservation Secretariat.

Jäger, J. 1985. Energy resources. In Climate Impact Assessment, R. W. Kates, J. H. Ausubel, and M. Berberian, eds. SCOPE 27. New York: John Wiley & Sons.

Jarvis, P. G., and K. B. McNaughton. 1986. Stomatal control of transpiration: Scaling up from leaf to region. Advances in Ecological Research 15:1-49.

Jenny, H. 1941. Factors of Soil Formation. New York: McGraw-Hill.

Jodha, N. S. 1989. Potential strategies for adapting to greenhouse warming: Perspectives from the developing world. In Greenhouse Warming: Abatement and Adaptation, N. J. Rosenberg, W. E. Easterling III, P. R. Crosson, and J. Darmstadter, eds. Washington, D.C.: Resources for the Future.

Joffe, J. S. 1949. Pedology. New Brunswick, N.J.: Pedology Publishing Company.

Kalkstein, L. S. 1989. The impact of CO_2 and trace gas-induced climate changes upon human mortality. In The Potential Effects of Global Climate Change on the United States, Appendix G, Health, J. B. Smith and D. A. Tirpak, eds. Washington, D.C.: U.S. Environmental Protection Agency.

Karl, T. R., and W. E. Riebsame. 1989. The impact of decadal fluctuations in mean precipitation and temperature on runoff: A sensitivity study over the United States. Climatic Change 15(3):423.

Kates, R. W., J. H. Ausubel, and M. Berberian, eds. 1985. Climate Impact Assessment. SCOPE 27. New York: John Wiley & Sons.

Keeling, C. D., and R. B. Bacastow. 1977. Impact of industrial gases on climate. In Energy and Climate, National Research Council. Washington, D.C.: National Academy Press.

Keller, C. A., and R. P. Nugent. 1983. Seasonal patterns in perinatal mortality and preterm delivery. American Journal of Epidemiology 118:689-698.

Kessler, E., and G. F. White. 1983. The thunderstorm in human affairs. In Thunderstorms: A Social, Scientific, and Technological Documentary, E. Kessler, ed. Norman: University of Oklahoma Press.

Kimball, B. A. 1982. Carbon Dioxide and Agricultural Yield: An Assemblage of 430 Prior Observations. WCL Report II. Phoenix, Ariz.: U.S. Water Conservation Laboratory.

Kimmins, J. P., and D. P. Lavender. 1987. Implications of climate change for the distribution of biogeoclimatic zones in British Columbia and for the growth of temperate forest species. In Woody Plant Growth in a Changing Chemical and Physical Environment. Proceedings of the International Union of Forestry Research Organizations Workshop, Vancouver, British Columbia, Canada, July 27-31. Vienna, Austria: International Union of Forestry Research Organizations.

Kneese, A. V., and G. Bonem. 1986. Hypothetical shocks to water allocation institutions in the Colorado Basin. In New Courses for the Colorado River, G. Weatherford and F. L. Brown, eds. Albuquerque: University of New Mexico Press.

Kritz, M. M. 1990. Climate change and migration adaptations. 1990 Working Paper Series, No. 2.16. Ithaca, New York: Population and Development Program, Cornell University.

Kritz, M. M. 1991. International migration systems, processes and policies. In International Migration Systems: A Global Approach, M. M. Kritz, L. L. Lim, and H. Zlotnik, eds. London: Oxford University Press.

LaMarch, V. C., D. A. Greybill, D. A. Fritts, and M. R. Rose. 1984. Increasing atmospheric carbon dioxide: Tree-ring evidence for growth enhancement in natural vegetation. Science 225:1019-1021.

Lamb, H. H. 1981. An approach to the study of development of climate and its impact on human affairs. In Climate and History: Studies in Past Climates and Their Impact on Man, T. M. L. Wigley, M. J. Ingram, and G. Farmer, eds. New York: Cambridge University Press.

Langbein, W. B., et al. 1949. Annual Runoff in the United States. U.S. Geological Survey Circular 5. Washington, D.C.: U.S. Geological Survey.

LaRoche, T. B., and M. K. Webb. 1987. Impact of accelerated sea level rise on drainage systems in Charleston, S.C. In Potential Impacts of Sea Level Rise on Coastal Drainage Systems. Washington, D.C.: U.S. Environmental Protection Agency.

Larson, B., C. Binkley, and S. Winnett. 1989. Simulated effects of climatic warming on the productivity of managed northern hardwood forests. Draft manuscript. School of Forestry and Environmental Studies, Yale University, New Haven, Conn.

Lashof, D. A., and D. A. Tirpak, eds. 1990. Policy Options for Stabilizing Global Climate. Washington, D.C.: U.S. Environmental Protection Agency.

Lee, E. S. 1966. A theory of migration. Demography 3(1):47-57.

Linder, K. P., M. J. Gibbs, and M. R. Inglis. 1987. Potential Impacts of Sea Level Rise on Coastal Drainage Systems. Report 88-2. Albany: New York State Energy Research and Development Authority.

Linderer, K. P. 1988. Regional and national effects of climate change on demands for electricity. In Second North American Conference on Preparing for Climate Change. Washington, D.C.: The Climate Institute.

Longstreth, J., and J. Wiseman. 1989. The potential impact of climate change on patterns of infectious disease in the United States. In The Potential Effects of Global Climate Change on the United States, Appendix G, Health, U.S. Environmental Protection Agency. Washington, D.C.: U.S. Environmental Protection Agency.

Lubchenco, J. 1980. Algal zonation in the New England rocky intertidal community: An experimental analysis. Ecology 61:333-344.

Lubchenco, J., S. A. Navarette, and B. N. Tissot. 1991. Consequences of global warming to shoreline ecosystems along the West Coast of North America. Unpublished manuscript. Department of Zoology, Oregon State University, Corvallis.

Mann, K.H. 1973. Seaweeds: Their productivity and strategy for growth. Science 182:975-981.

Marmor, M. 1975. Heat wave mortality in New York City, 1949 to 1970. Archives of Environmental Health 30:131-136.

Matalas, N. C. 1990. What statistics can tell us. In Climate Change and U.S. Water Resources, P. E. Waggoner, ed. New York: John Wiley & Sons.

McGovern, T. H. 1981. The economics of extinction in Norse Greenland. In Climate and History: Studies in Past Climates and Their Impact on Man, T. M. L. Wigley, M. J. Ingram, and G. Farmer, eds. New York: Cambridge University Press.

Meyer-Abich, K. M. 1980. Chalk on the white wall. In Climatic Constraints and Human Activity, J. H. Ausubel and A. K. Biswas, eds. London: Pergamon Press.

Miller, K. A. 1990. Water, electricity, and institutional innovation. In Climate

Change and U.S. Water Resources, P. E. Waggoner, ed. New York: John Wiley & Sons.

Miller, K. A., and M. H. Glantz. 1988. Climate and economic competitiveness: Florida freezes and the global citrus processing industry. Climatic Change 12:135-164.

Mitchell, J. F. B. 1988. Local effects of greenhouse gases. Nature 332:399-400.

Muscatine, L., L. R. McCloskey, and R. E. Marian. 1981. Estimating the daily contribution of carbon from zooxanthellae to coral animal respiration. Limnology and Oceanography 26:601-611.

National Research Council. 1976. Pest management. In Climate and Food. Washington, D.C.: National Academy of Sciences.

National Research Council. 1983. Changing Climate. Washington, D.C.: National Academy Press.

National Research Council. 1987. Responding to Changes in Sea Level: Engineering Implications. Washington, D.C.: National Academy Press.

National Research Council. 1990a. Managing Global Genetic Resources: The U.S. National Plant Germplasm System. Washington, D.C.: National Academy Press.

National Research Council. 1990b. Sea Level Change. Washington, D.C.: National Academy Press.

Natural Hazards Research and Applications Information Center (NHRAIC). 1990. NHRAIC Data Base. Natural Hazards Research and Applications Information Center, University of Colorado, Boulder.

Neilson, R. P., G. A. King, R. L. DeVelice, J. Lenihan, D. Marks, J. Dolph, B. Campbell, and G. Glick. 1989. Sensitivity of Ecological Landscapes and Regions to Global Climatic Change. Corvallis, Oreg.: U.S. Environmental Protection Agency.

Newlin, O. J. 1990. Testimony regarding amendments to strengthen the Plant Variety Protection Act. Presented to Department Operations, Research and Foreign Agriculture Subcommittee of the House Agriculture Committee, May 1, 1990.

Newman, J. E. 1982. Impacts of rising atmospheric carbon dioxide levels on agricultural growing seasons and crop water use efficiencies. In Environmental and Social Consequences of a Possible CO_2-Induced Climate Change, volume II, Part 8. Washington, D.C.: Carbon Dioxide Research Division, U.S. Department of Energy.

Norby, R. J., J. Pastor, and J. M. Melillo. 1986. Carbon-nitrogen interactions in CO_2 enriched white oak: Physiological and long-term perspectives. Tree Physiology 2:233-241.

Nordhaus, W. D. 1991. To slow or not to slow: The economics of the greenhouse effect. Economic Journal 101(407):920-937.

Oechel, W. C., and B. R. Strain. 1985. Native species responses to increased atmospheric carbon dioxide concentration. In Direct Effects of Increasing Carbon Dioxide on Vegetation, B. R. Strain and J. D. Cure, eds. Report DOE/ER-0238. Washington, D.C.: U.S. Department of Energy.

Ormrod, R. K. 1986. Evidence that California elderly are migrating southward. Sociology and Social Research 70(2):149-151.

Paine, R. T. 1980. Food webs: Linkages, interaction strength and community infrastructure. Journal of Animal Ecology 49:667-686.

Pampel, F. C., I. P. Levin, J. J. Louviere, R. J. Meyer, and G. Ruston. 1984. Retirement migration decision making: The integration of geographic, social and economic preferences. Research on Aging 6(2):139-162.

Parry, M. L. 1978. Climatic Change, Agriculture and Settlement. Folkestone, England: Dawson.

Parry, M. L., T. R. Carter, and N. T. Konijn, eds. 1988. The Impact of Climatic Variations on Agriculture. Dordrecht, The Netherlands: Kluwer Academic Publishers.

Patterson, D. T., and E. P. Flint. 1980. Potential effects of global atmospheric CO_2 enrichment on the growth and competitiveness of C3 and C4 weed and crop plants. Weed Science 28:71-75.

Patterson, D. T., and E. P. Flint. 1982. Interacting effects of CO_2 and nutrient concentration. Weed Science 30:389-394.

Pearcy, R. W., and O. Bjorkman. 1983. Physiological effects. In CO_2 and Plants, E. R. Lemon, ed. American Association for the Advancement of Science Selected Symposium 84. Boulder, Colo.: Westview Press.

Peart, R. M., J. W. Jones, R. B. Curry, K. Boote, and L. H. Allen, Jr. 1989. Impact of climate change on crop yield in the southeastern USA: A simulation study. In The Potential Effects of Global Climate Change in the United States, Appendix C, Agriculture, J. B. Smith and D. A. Tirpak, eds. Washington, D.C.: U.S. Environmental Protection Agency.

Peeters, J. P., and J. T. Williams. 1984. Towards better use of gene-banks with special reference to information. Plant Genetic Resource Newsletter 60:22-32.

Peterson, D. F., and A. A. Keller. 1990. Irrigation. In Climate Change and U.S. Water Resources, P. E. Waggoner, ed. New York: John Wiley & Sons.

Raven, P. H. 1981. Research in botanical gardens. Botanische Jahrbuecher fuer Systematik Pflanzengeschichte und Pflanzengeographie 102:52-72.

Renas, S., and R. Kumar. 1982. Climatic conditions and migration: An econometric inquiry. Annals of Regional Science 17(1):69-78.

Revelle, R., and G. Kohlmaier. 1986. Increasing amplitudes of the seasonal CO_2 cycle. In Climate-Vegetation Interactions, C. Rosenzweig and R. Dickinson, eds. Boulder, Colo.: University Center for Atmospheric Research.

Revelle, R. R., and P. E. Waggoner. 1983. Effects of a carbon dioxide-induced climatic change on water supplies in the western United States. In Changing Climate. Washington, D.C.: National Academy Press.

Riebsame, W. E., H. F. Diaz, T. Moses, and M. Price. 1986. The social burden of weather and climate hazards. Bulletin of the American Meteorological Society 67(11):1378-1388.

Riebsame, W. E., S. A. Changnon, and T. R. Karl. 1991. Drought and Natural Resources Management in the United States. Boulder, Colo.: Westview Press.

Ritchie, J. T., B. D. Baer, and T. Y. Chou. 1989. Effect of global climate change on agriculture: Great Lakes region. In The Potential Effects of Global Climate Change on the United States, Appendix C, Agriculture, J. B. Smith and D. A. Tirpak, eds. Washington, D.C.: U.S. Environmental Protection Agency.

Rogers, H. H., W. W. Heck, and A. S. Heagle. 1983. A field technique for the study of plant responses to elevated carbon dioxide concentration. Journal of the Air Pollution Control Association 33:42-44.

Rose, E. 1989. Introduction. In The Potential Effect of Global Climate Change on the United States, Appendix C, Agriculture, J. B. Smith and D. A. Tirpak, eds. Washington, D.C.: U.S. Environmental Protection Agency.

Rose, G. 1966. Cold weather and ischaemic heart disease. Journal of Preventive and Social Medicine 20:97-100.

Rosenberg, N. J. 1982. The increasing CO_2 concentration in the atmosphere and its implication on agricultural productivity. II. Effects through CO_2-induced climate change. Climatic Change 4:239-254.

Rosenberg, N. J., and P. R. Crosson. 1991. Processes for identifying regional influences of and responses to increasing atmospheric CO_2 and climate change— The MINK Project: An Overview. Draft report prepared for U.S. Department of Energy under agreement 041460-A-K1. Washington, D.C.: U.S. Department of Energy.

Rosenberg, N. J., B. A. Kimball, P. Martin, and C. F. Cooper. 1990. From climate and CO_2 enrichment to evapotranspiration. In Climate Change and U.S. Water Resources, P. E. Waggoner, ed. New York: John Wiley & Sons.

Rosenwaike, I. 1966. Seasonal variation of deaths in the United States, 1951-1960. Journal of the American Statistical Association 61:706-719.

Rosenzweig, C. 1989. Potential effects of climate change on agricultural production in the Great Plains: A simulation study. In The Potential Effects of Global Climate Change in the United States, Appendix C, Agriculture, J. B. Smith and D. A. Tirpak, eds. Washington, D.C.: U.S. Environmental Protection Agency.

Rotton, J. 1983. Angry, sad, happy? Blame the weather. U.S. News and World Report 95:53.

Santelices, B. 1989. Algas Marinas de Chile: Distribucion, Ecologia, Utilizacion y Diversidad. Santiago: Ediciones Universidad Catolica de Chile.

Schaake, J. C. 1990. From climate to flow. In Climate Change and U.S. Water Resources, P. E. Waggoner, ed. New York: John Wiley & Sons.

Schaefer, K. E., ed. 1958. Man's Dependence on the Earthly Atmosphere. New York: Macmillan.

Schelling, T. C. 1983. Climatic change: Implications for welfare and policy. In Changing Climate. Washington, D.C.: National Academy Press.

Schneider, S. H., P. H. Gleick, and L. O. Mearns. 1990. Prospects for climate change. In Climate Change and U.S. Water Resources, P. E. Waggoner, ed. New York: John Wiley & Sons.

Schoenbeck, M., and T. A. Norton. 1978. Factors controlling the upper limits of fucoid algae on the shore. Journal of Experimental Marine Biology and Ecology 31:303-313.

Serow, W. 1987. Why the elderly move: Cross-national comparisons. Research on Aging 9(4):582-597.

Serra B., R. 1987. Impact of the 1982-83 ENSO on southeastern Pacific fisheries, with an emphasis on Chilean fisheries. In Climate Crisis: The Societal Impacts Associated with the 1982-83 Worldwide Climate Anomalies, M. Glantz, R. Katz, and M. Krenz, eds. Boulder, Colo.: National Center for Atmospheric Research.

Sheer, D. P. 1985. Managing water supplies to increase water availability. U.S.G.S. Annual Water Survey 1985:101-112.

Smith, D. C., H. H. Borns, W. R. Baron, and A. E. Bridges. 1981. Climatic stress and Maine agriculture, 1785-1885. In Climate and History: Studies in Past Climates and Their Impact on Man, T. M. L. Wigley, M. J. Ingram, and G. Farmer, eds. New York: Cambridge University Press.

Smith, D. M. 1986. The Practice of Silviculture, 8th ed. New York: John Wiley & Sons.

Smith, J. B., and D. A. Tirpak, eds. 1989. The Potential Effects of Global Climate Change on the United States. Washington, D.C.: U.S. Environmental Protection Agency.

Smith, W. H. 1981. Air Pollution and Forests. New York: Springer-Verlag.

Solley, W. B., C. F. Merk, and R. R. Pierce. 1989. Estimated Use of Water in the United States in 1985. U.S. Geological Survey Circular 1004. Washington, D.C.: U.S. Geological Survey.

Solomon, A. M. 1986a. Linking GCM climate data with data from static and dynamic vegetation models. In Climate-Vegetation Interactions, C. Rosenzweig and R. Dickinson, eds. Report UCAR OIES-2. Boulder, Colo.: University Center for Atmospheric Research.

Solomon, A. M. 1986b. Transient response of forests to CO_2-induced climate change: Simulation modeling experiments in eastern North America. Oecologia 68:567-579.

Solomon, A. M., and M. L. Tharp. 1985. Simulation experiments with late-Quaternary carbon storage in mid-latitude forest communities. Geophysical Monograph 32:235-250.

Solomon, A. M., and T. Webb. 1985. Computer-aided reconstruction of late-Quaternary landscape dynamics. Annual Review of Ecology and Systematics 16:63-84.

Solomon, A. M., and D. C. West. 1986. Simulating forest responses to expected climate change in eastern North America: Applications to decision-making in the forest industry. In Rising Carbon Dioxide and Changing Climate: Forest Risks and Opportunities, W. E. Shands and J. Hoffman, eds. Washington, D.C.: The Conservation Foundation.

Sontaniemi, E., U. Vuopala, E. Huhta, and J. Takkunem. 1970. Effect of temperature on hospital admissions for myocardial infarction in a subarctic area. British Medical Journal 4:150-151.

Sorensen, R. M., R. N. Weisman, and G. P. Lennon. 1984. Control of erosion, inundation, and salinity intrusion caused by sea level rise. In Greenhouse Effect and Sea Level Rise: A Challenge for This Generation, M. C. Barth and J. G. Titus, eds. New York: Van Nostrand Reinhold.

Spauling, W. G., and L. S. Graumlich. 1986. The last pluvial climatic episodes in the deserts of southwestern North America. Nature 320:441-444.

Stinner, B. R., R. A. J. Taylor, R. B. Hammond, F. F. Purrington, and D. A. MacCartney. 1989. Potential effects of climate change on plant-pest infestations. In The Potential Effects of Global Climate Change on the United States, Appendix C, Agriculture, J. B. Smith and D. A. Tirpak, eds. Washington, D.C.: U.S. Environmental Protection Agency.

Straka, T. J., W. F. Watson, and M. Dubois. 1989. Costs and cost trends for forestry practices in the South. Forest Farmer Manual 1989:8-14.

Tabbarah, R. 1988. Prospects for international migration. In International Migration Today, Volume 2, Emerging Issues, C. Stahl, ed. Paris: United Nations Educational, Scientific, and Cultural Organization.

Tannehill, I. R. 1947. Drought, Its Causes and Effects. Princeton, N.J.: Princeton University Press.

The South Commission. 1990. The Challenge to the South. Oxford, United Kingdom: Oxford University Press.

Thompson, L. M. 1988. Effects of changes in climate and weather variability on the yield of corn and soybeans. Journal of Production Agriculture 1:20-27.

Thorarinsson, S. 1944. Tefrokronologiska studier pa isaland. Geografiska Annaler: 1-127.

Tickell, C. 1986. Climatic Change and World Affairs. Lanham, Md.: University Press of America, Inc.

Tickell, C. 1990. Human effects of climate change. Lecture to the Royal Geographic Society, London, England, March 26, 1990.

Tissot, B. 1990. Geographic Variation and Mass Mortality in the Black Abalone; the Roles of Development and Ecology. Ph.D. dissertation. Oregon State University, Corvallis.

Tissue, D. T., and W. C. Oechel. 1987. Response of *Eriophorum vaginatum* to elevated CO_2 in the Alaskan tussock tundra. Ecology 68:401-410.

Titus, J. G., and M. C. Barth. 1984. An overview of the causes and effects of sea level rise. In Greenhouse Effect and Sea Level Rise: A Challenge for This Generation, M. C. Barth and J. G. Titus, eds. New York: Van Nostrand Reinhold.

Titus, J. G., and M. S. Greene. 1989. An overview of the nationwide impacts of sea level rise. In The Potential Effects of Global Climate Change on the United States, Appendix B, Sea Level Rise, J. B. Smith and D. A. Tirpak, eds. Washington, D.C.: U.S. Environmental Protection Agency.

Titus, J. G., C. Y. Kuo, M. J. Gibbs, T. B. LaRoche, M. K. Webb, and J. O. Waddell. 1987. Greenhouse effect, sea level rise, and coastal drainage systems. Journal of Water Resources Planning and Management 113:2.

Tobey, J., J. Reilly, and S. Kane. 1990. An Empirical Study of the Welfare Effects of Climate Change on World Agriculture. Washington, D.C.: Research and Technology Division, Economic Research Service, U.S. Department of Agriculture.

Tseng, C. K., ed. 1984. Common Seaweeds of China. Beijing: Science Press (Kugler Publications bv, Amsterdam).

United Nations. 1989a. Prospects for World Urbanization 1988. New York: Department of International Economic and Social Affairs, United Nations.

United Nations. 1989b. World Population Prospects 1988. New York: Department of International Economic and Social Affairs, United Nations.

Unnewehr, D. L. 1989. Surviving the Storm. Boston, Mass.: All-Industry Research Advisory Council/National Committee on Property Insurance.

Urban, D. L., and H. H. Shugart. 1989. Forest response to climate change: A simulation study for southeastern forests. In The Potential Effects of Global

Climate Change on the United States, Appendix D, Forests, J. B. Smith and D. A. Tirpak, eds. Washington, D.C.: U.S. Environmental Protection Agency.

U.S. Bureau of the Census. 1987. Statistical Abstract of the United States: 1988. 108th ed. Washington, D.C.: Government Printing Office.

U.S. Bureau of the Census. 1988. Statistical Abstract of the United States: 1989. 109th ed. Washington, D.C.: Government Printing Office.

U.S. Committee for Refugees. 1990. World Refugee Survey: 1988 in Review. New York: U.S. Committee for Refugees, American Council for Nationalities Service.

U.S. Department of Agriculture. 1986. Agricultural Statistics, 1986. Washington, D.C.: U.S. Department of Agriculture.

U.S. Department of Agriculture. 1989a. Agricultural Statistics, 1989. Washington, D.C.: U.S. Department of Agriculture.

U.S. Department of Agriculture. 1989b. Inventory of Agricultural Research, Fiscal Year 1988. Washington, D.C.: U.S. Department of Agriculture.

U.S. Department of Commerce. 1975. Historical Statistics of the U.S., Colonial Times to the 1970s. Washington, D.C.: U.S. Department of Commerce.

U.S. Department of Energy. 1989a. A Compendium of Options for Government Policy to Encourage Private Sector Responses to Potential Climate Change. Washington, D.C.: U.S. Department of Energy.

U.S. Department of Energy. 1989b. Energy and Climate Change. Report of the DOE Multi-Laboratory Climate Change Committee, December. Washington, D.C.: U.S. Department of Energy.

U.S. Department of State. 1982. Proceedings of the U.S. Strategy Consensus Conference on Biological Diversity, November 16-18, 1981. Publication 9262, International Organization and Conference Series 300. Washington, D.C.: U.S. Department of State.

U.S. Office of Management and Budget. 1989. Budget of the United States—Fiscal Year 1990. Washington, D.C.: U.S. Government Printing Office.

U.S. Office of Technology Assessment. 1983. Wood Use: U.S. Competitiveness and Technology. Report OTA-ITE-210. Washington, D.C.: U.S. Office of Technology Assessment.

U.S. Office of Technology Assessment. 1984. Wetlands: Their Use and Regulation. Report OTA-0-206. Washington, D.C.: U.S. Office of Technology Assessment.

Utterstrom, G. 1955. Climatic fluctuations and populations problems in early history. Scandinavian Economic History Review III(1):1-47.

Valiela, I. 1984. Marine Ecological Processes. New York: Springer-Verlag.

Voss, P., R. Gunderson, and R. Manchin. 1988. Death taxes and elderly interstate migration. Research on Aging 10(3):420-450.

Waddell, J. O., and R. A. Blaylock. 1987. Impact of Sea Level Rise on Gap Creek Watershed in the Fort Walton Beach, Florida Area. Washington, D.C.: U.S. Environmental Protection Agency.

Waggoner, P. E. 1960. Forecasting epidemics. In Plant Pathology, An Advanced Treatise, Volume 3, J. G. Horsfall and A. E. Dimond, eds. New York: Academic Press.

Waggoner, P. E. 1983. Agriculture and a climate changed by more carbon dioxide. In Changing Climate. Washington, D.C.: National Academy Press.

Waggoner, P. E. 1990. Environmental change in food supply. Proceedings of 23rd Annual Convention of Canola Council of Canada, Ottawa, March 19-21, pp. 63-71.

Waggoner, P. E., and B. Bravdo. 1967. Stomata and the hydrologic cycle. Proceedings of the National Academy of Sciences 57:1096-1102.

Waggoner, P. E., J. L. Monteith, and G. Szeicz. 1964. Decreasing transpiration of field plants by chemical closure of stomata. Nature 201:97-98.

Walker, J. C., T. R. Miller, G. T. Kingsley, and W. A. Hyman. 1989. Impact of global climate change on urban infrastructure. In The Potential Effects of Global Climate Change on the United States, Appendix H, Infrastructure, J. B. Smith and D. A. Tirpak, eds. Washington, D.C.: U.S. Environmental Protection Agency.

Wall, J. 1989. Potential effects on tourism and recreation in Ontario. In First U.S. Canadian Symposium on Impacts of Climate Change on the Great Lakes Basin. Downsview, Ontario: Environment Canada.

Warrick, R. A. 1980. Drought in the Great Plains: A case study of research on climate and society in the USA. In Climatic Constraints and Human Activities, J. H. Ausubel and A. K. Biswas, eds. Oxford: Pergamon Press.

Webb, T. 1986. Vegetation change in Eastern North America from 18,000 to 500 Yr B.P. In Climate-Vegetation Interactions, C. Rosenzweig and R. Dickinson, eds. Report UCAR OIES-2. Boulder, Colo.: University Center for Atmospheric Research.

Weihe, W. H. 1979. Climate, health and disease. In Proceedings of the World Climate Conference. Geneva: World Meteorological Organization.

Weltzien, H. C. 1978. Geophytopathology. In Plant Disease, an Advanced Treatise, J. G. Horsfall and E. C. Cowling, eds. New York: Academic Press.

Western, D., and M. Pearl. 1989. Conservation for the Twenty-First Century. New York: Oxford University Press.

Wharton, C. H. 1970. The Southern River Swamp: A Multiple-Use Environment. Athens: School of Business Administration, Georgia State University.

Wildavsky, A. 1980. Richer is safer. Public Interest 60(Summer):23-39.

Wilhite, D. A. 1983. Government response to drought in the United States: With particular reference to the Great Plains. Journal of Climate and Applied Meteorology 22:40-50.

Wilkes, G. 1984. Germplasm conservation toward the year 2000: Potential for new crops and enhancement of present crops. In Plant Genetic Resources, C. W. Yeatman, D. Kafton, and G. Wilkes, eds. American Association for the Advancement of Science Selected Symposium 87. Washington, D.C.: American Association for the Advancement of Science.

Wilkins, C. P., and J. H. Dodds. 1983. The application of tissue culture techniques to plant genetic conservation. Scientific Progress 68:259-284.

Wilks, D. S. 1988. Estimating the consequences of CO_2-induced climatic change on North American grain agriculture using general circulation model information. Climatic Change 13:19-42.

Wilson, E. O., ed. 1988. Biodiversity. Washington, D.C.: National Academy Press.

Wilson, E. O. 1989. Threats to biodiversity. In Managing Planet Earth, Special Issue. Scientific American 260:108-116.

Wong, S. C. 1979. Elevated atmospheric partial pressure of CO_2 and plant growth. Oecologia 44:68-74.

World Commission on Environment and Development. 1987. Our Common Future. New York: Oxford University Press.

World Health Organization. 1990. Potential Health Effects of Climatic Change. Geneva: World Health Organization.

Zahner, R. 1955. Soil water depletion by pine and hardwood stands during a dry season. Forestry Science 1:258-264.

Zolberg, A. 1989. Escape from Violence: Conflict and the Refugee Crisis in the Developing World. New York: Oxford University Press.

35

Indices

For its work the Adaptation Panel took the available indices of climate change and estimated as best it could the impacts and adaptations to it. An equally logical procedure is to first consider the sensitivities to climate that will cause impacts and evoke adaptations, as has been done in this part, and then, with the sensitivities in mind, ask what indices of climate are relevant.

The investigation of impacts and adaptations produced the following strategic indices of climate change for agencies to monitor and scientists to predict.

The direction and rate of change of:

- First, the flow of water in streams and its supply in soils of a region, including its season and variation from year to year.
- Second, changes in sea level and height of waves on a shore.
- Third, any major shifts in ocean currents.
- Fourth, the timing of seasonal events like blooms and migrations.
- Fifth, untoward extremes of heat and cold.

The argument for the strategic nature of the indices is as follows. Climate is made of many elements, from the sunlight and the pressure of the air to wind and rain. Its effect is in the place where a beach home stands or a corn plant grows. Its effect is at the time of a hurricane or a drought. Thus, a single element like temperature or an average, as over the globe and seasons, will not suffice to estimate impact or adaptation to climate change.

The art of strategy, however, requires selecting a few indices that are most important for estimating the impact. Otherwise, the monitor and predictor of climate are overwhelmed by the demands, and the person studying their result is tangled in a thicket of data. As others have written, "Policy actions either to deal with their effects or to prevent changes require concise information about the nature and timing of the effects at local, regional, and global levels" (Chen and Parry, 1987). The strategic few indices most important for figuring the impacts of climate change have not, however, been chosen, either for agencies to monitor or for scientists to predict. An analysis of likely effects of climate change suggests several indices about which detailed and long-term information would be especially useful.

WATER

The preeminent outdoor business, exposed to climate, is farming. Although frost kills many crops, species from sugarcane in the south to rapeseed in the north all grow food despite the range of temperatures. But they all need water, and they consume it in proportion to their growth (de Wit, 1958). Calculations show that warming would be hard on a crop grown on the northern margin of the Canadian Prairies unless it were balanced by more precipitation (Stewart, 1981). A steady water supply is the critical element for farming. The bare Mojave Desert and dripping Hoh River valley within one nation with an average precipitation of 750 mm (U.S. Geological Survey, 1984) make the point that global, even national, averages over large areas matter little. The water in a specific place matters.

The migration of Americans within the United States since 1960 shows they do not fear warmer climate (National Research Council, 1983). But they need water wherever they go, and their consumption of water in the Southwest now exceeds the average renewable supply (Gleick, 1990). Where the average supply matches demand, storage smooths the variation. The need for storage, however, depends on the variation across years and seasons (Rogers and Fiering, 1990). So, both average and steadiness of the supply of water are crucial for cities and suburbs as well as for farming.

Flow in streams integrates the effects of weather and landscape. The sensitivity of fish to stream flow is evident. Because different vegetation types are associated with particular seasonal patterns of stream flows, changes in flows signal impending vegetation changes. For example, deciduous forests thrive where soils are sufficiently wetted in the winter that trees can tap deep water and grow when the upper soil layers dry out in summer. Reduction in winter precipitation or reduced flows in summer would signal difficulties for that vegetation.

The sensitivity of industry to climate is exemplified by the generation of electricity. The use of water per unit of production by other industries has steadily declined (David, 1984). Water power obviously needs water, and thermoelectric plants are cooled by water, economically (Miller, 1990). So industry is affected by water supply.

SEA LEVEL

Industry and docks in ports, coastal cities, and even sea resorts share sensitivity to sea level. Their sensitivity to waves is obvious. In addition, the shipping in their ports and estuaries and even water supply drawn just upstream are sensitive to the balance between sea level and stream flow (Schwarz and Dillard, 1990).

OCEAN CURRENTS

Choosing currents like the Gulf Stream and oceanic phenomena like the El Niño-Southern Oscillation for indices carries us from climate elements directly affecting humanity and nature to phenomena affected by climate. Nevertheless, their impacts on nations, farm belts, and coasts is profound, as the difference between 51° North in Labrador and England demonstrates. These currents must be named as strategic indices.

SEASONAL EVENTS

Another strategic index of climate change is phenological phenomena, for example, the date that a particular plant species flowers or a particular species of bird migrates to or from a place. Beauty accounts in part for annual celebrations such as the cherry blossom festival at the Tidal Basin in Washington, D.C. The dates that plants flower and seeds ripen, however, are the footings of farming and civilization. This final index is, of course, a biological response to weather. So, a shift in the dates of phenology indicates the kind of farming and natural vegetation that can prosper in a region.[1]

EXTREME TEMPERATURES

Heat and cold waves affect farming, industry, and health. Heat waves have a special impact on the generation of electricity for air conditioning. Winter cold also affects its generation because electricity is used for some heating. It is summer heat waves in several regions, however, that set upper limits on demand on the generators within transmitting distance (Linderer, 1988). Frost kills crops. So the extremes of temperature are crucial.

Lengthening this list would be easy, but it would defeat our goal: a short, strategic list of indices. The five indices listed above are the strategic ones for agencies to monitor and scientists to predict so that the impacts of climate change can be assessed and adaptations can be made.

Although these indices are crucial for estimating impacts and adaptations, they cannot now be computed responsibly. When the menu was presented to the Effects Panel, the members promptly and correctly insisted that there does not exist, nor is it likely that there will soon exist, a predictive capability that could quantify these indices in a useful or credible way. So, we shall not soon have the scenarios required for estimating impacts and adaptations quantitatively. For a long time we must be satisfied with the sort of examples and benchmarks described in this report.

NOTE

1. An agriculturalist book of China written by Fan Sheng-Chih in the first century B.C. begins, "The basic principles of farming are: choose the *right time*, break up the soil, see to its fertility and moisture, hoe early and harvest early" (translated by Shui Sheng-Han, 1982, Science Press, Peking, China).

REFERENCES

Chen, R. S., and M. L. Parry. 1987. Policy-Oriented Impact Assessment of Climatic Variation. Report RR-87-7. Laxenburg, Austria: International Institute for Applied Systems Analysis.

David, E. L. 1984. A quarter century of industrial water use and a decade of discharge controls. Water Research Bulletin 20:409-416.

de Wit, C. T. 1958. Transpiration and crop yields. Verslagen lanbouwkundige Onderzoekingen (Agricultural Research Reports) 64.6. Wageningen, The Netherlands: Pudoc.

Gleick, P. H. 1990. Vulnerability of water systems. In Climate Change and U.S. Water Resources, P. E. Waggoner, ed. New York: John Wiley & Sons.

Linderer, R. P. 1988. Regional and national effects of climate change on demands for electricity. In Second North American Conference on Preparing for Climate Change. Washington, D.C.: The Climate Institute.

Miller, K. A. 1990. Water, electricity, and institutional innovation. In Climate Change and U.S. Water Resources, P. E. Waggoner, ed. New York: John Wiley & Sons.

National Research Council. 1983. Changing Climate. Washington, D.C.: National Academy Press.

Rogers, P. P., and M. B. Fiering. 1990. From flow to storage. In Climate Change and U.S. Water Resources, P. E. Waggoner, ed. New York: John Wiley & Sons.

Schwarz, H. E., and L. A. Dillard. 1990. Urban water. In Climate Change and U.S. Water Resources, P. E. Waggoner, ed. New York: John Wiley & Sons.

Stewart, R. B. 1981. Modeling methodology for assessing crop production potentials in Canada. Technical Bulletin 96. Ottawa: Research Branch, Agriculture Canada.

U.S. Geological Survey (USGS). 1984. National water summary 1983—Hydrologic events and issues. USGS Water Supply Paper 2250. Washington, D.C.: U.S. Geological Survey.

36

Final Words

So far as we can reason from the assumed gradual changes in climate, their impacts will be no more severe, and adapting to them will be no more difficult, than for the range of climates already on earth and no more difficult than for other changes humanity faces. However, because we cannot rule out major changes in ocean currents, atmospheric circulations, or other natural or social surprises, we need to be alert to any substantial probability or signs of such changes that would require responses not considered in our report.

Individual Statement by a Member of the Adaptation Panel

JANE LUBCHENCO

Panel member Jane Lubchenco believes that "the report [of the Adaptation Panel] does not adequately address the potential environmental and global consequences of the different adaptation strategies it recommends, nor does it adequately acknowledge that these consequences must be taken into consideration. The report does address the most obvious and immediate financial costs of some of the adaptations, but does not really consider other costs. Of particular concern are indirect costs, i.e., those emerging as consequences of interactions among the individual sectors considered in the report or as consequences of adaptation measures. The implicit message of the report is that humans can adapt to the predicted climate changes without worrying about these other costs.

"This complacent tone is unwarranted in light of (a) the uncertainties about responses of natural systems to climate change, (b) the reliance of human systems on these natural systems (i.e., interactions among the different sectors considered in the report), (c) the unexamined environmental consequences of recommended adaptations, and (d) the substantial difficulties anticipated for developing nations to adapt to climate change. I concur that the adaptation strategies suggested in the report may be quite reasonable and should possibly be pursued. However, the limitations to and costs of these adaptations must be made explicit. The areas in which adaptations cannot be made, or at least, not easily made (for example those identified in the sections dealing with unmanaged ecosystems), are so fundamentally important to the global system that mitigation—not adaptation—becomes paramount.

"In summary, I disagree with the report's implicit message, that 'we can adapt with little or no problem.' I believe that even the incomplete analysis of the Adaptation Panel supports the recommendations of the Synthesis Panel to adopt effective but inexpensive actions to slow the onset of greenhouse warming."

APPENDIXES

Appendix A

Questions and Answers About Greenhouse Warming

THE GREENHOUSE EFFECT: WHAT IS KNOWN, WHAT CAN BE PREDICTED

1. What is the "greenhouse effect"?

In simplest terms, "greenhouse gases" let sunlight through to the earth's surface while trapping "outbound" radiation. This alters the radiative balance of the earth (see Figure A.1) and results in a warming of the earth's surface. The major greenhouse gases are water vapor, carbon dioxide (CO_2), methane (CH_4), chlorofluorocarbons (CFCs) and hydrogenated chlorofluorocarbons (HCFCs), tropospheric ozone (O_3), and nitrous oxide (N_2O). Without the naturally occurring greenhouse gases (principally water vapor and CO_2), the earth's average temperature would be nearly 35°C (63°F) colder, and the planet would be much less suitable for human life.

2. Why is it called the "greenhouse" effect?

The greenhouse gases in the atmosphere act in much the same way as the glass panels of a greenhouse, which allow sunlight through and trap heat inside.

3. Why have experts become worried about the greenhouse effect now?

Rising atmospheric concentrations of CO_2, CH_4, and CFCs suggest the possibility of additional warming of the global climate. The panel refers to warming due to increased atmospheric concentrations of greenhouse gases as "greenhouse warming." Measurements of atmospheric CO_2 show that the 1990 concentration of 353 parts per million by volume (ppmv) is about one-quarter larger than the concentration before the Industrial Revolution (prior

663

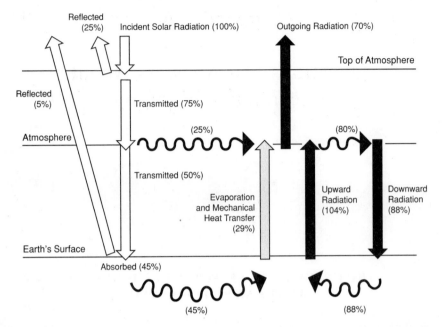

FIGURE A.1 Earth's radiation balance. The solar radiation is set at 100 percent; all other values are in relation to it. About 25 percent of incident solar radiation is reflected back into space by the atmosphere, about 25 percent is absorbed by gases in the atmosphere, and about 5 percent is reflected into space from the earth's surface, leaving 45 percent to be absorbed by the oceans, land, and biotic material (white arrows).

Evaporation and mechanical heat transfer inject energy into the atmosphere equal to about 29 percent of incident radiation (grey arrow). Radiative energy emissions from the earth's surface and from the atmosphere (straight black arrows) are determined by the temperatures of the earth's surface and the atmosphere, respectively. Upward energy radiation from the earth's surface is about 104 percent of incident solar radiation. Atmospheric gases absorb part (25 percent) of the solar radiation penetrating the top of the atmosphere and all of the mechanical heat transferred from the earth's surface and the outbound radiation from the earth's surface. The downward radiation from the atmosphere is about 88 percent and outgoing radiation about 70 percent of incident solar radiation.

Note that the amounts of outgoing and incoming radiation balance at the top of the atmosphere, at 100 percent of incoming solar radiation (which is balanced by 5 percent reflected from the surface, 25 percent reflected from the top of the atmosphere, and 70 percent outgoing radiation), and at the earth's surface, at 133 percent (45 percent absorbed solar radiation plus 88 percent downward radiation from the atmosphere balanced by 29 percent evaporation and mechanical heat transfer and 104 percent upward radiation). Energy transfers into and away from the atmosphere also balance, at the atmosphere line, at 208 percent of incident solar radiation (75 percent transmitted solar radiation plus 29 percent mechanical transfer from the to 1750). Atmospheric CO_2 is increasing at about 0.5 percent per year. The concentration of CH_4 is about 1.72 ppmv, or slightly more than twice that before 1750. It is rising at a rate of 0.9 percent per year. CFCs do not occur naturally, and so they were not found in the atmosphere until production began a few decades ago. Continued increases in atmospheric concentrations of greenhouse gases would affect the earth's radiative balance and could cause a large amount of additional greenhouse warming. Increasing the capture of energy in this fashion is also called "radiative forcing." Other factors, such as variation in incoming solar radiation, could be involved.

4. Has there been greenhouse warming in the recent past?

Best estimates are that the average global temperature rose between 0.3° and 0.6°C over about the last 100 years. However, it is not possible to say with a high degree of confidence whether this is due to increased atmospheric concentrations of greenhouse gases or to other natural or human causes. The temperature record much before 1900 is not reliable for estimates of changes smaller than 1°C (1.8°F).

5. What about CO_2 and temperature in the prehistoric past?

According to best estimates based on analysis of air bubbles trapped in ice sheets, ocean and lake sediments, and other records from the geologic past, there have been three especially "warm" periods in the last 4 million years. The Holocene optimum occurred from 6,000 to 5,000 years ago. During that period, atmospheric concentrations of CO_2 were about 270 to 280 ppmv, and average air temperatures about 1°C (1.8°F) warmer than modern times. The Eemian interglacial period happened with its midpoint about 125,000 years ago. Atmospheric concentrations of CO_2 were 280 to 300 ppmv, and temperatures up to 2°C (3.6°F) warmer than now. The Pliocene climate optimum occurred between 4.3 and 3.3 million years ago. Atmospheric concentrations of CO_2 have been estimated for that period to be about 450 ppmv, with temperatures 3° to 4°C (5.4° to 7.2°F) warmer than modern times. The prehistoric temperature estimates are from evidence dependent

---

surface plus 104 percent upward radiation balanced by 50 percent of incoming solar continuing to the earth's surface, 70 percent outgoing radiation, and 88 percent downward radiation). These different energy transfers are due to the heat-trapping effects of the greenhouse gases in the atmosphere, the reemission of energy absorbed by these gases, and the cycling of energy through the various components in the diagram. The accuracy of the numbers in the diagram is typically ±5.

This diagram pertains to a period during which the climate is steady (or unchanging); that is, there is no net change in heat transfers into earth's surface, no net change in heat transfers into the atmosphere, and no net radiation change into the atmosphere-earth system from beyond the atmosphere.

on conditions during growing seasons and probably are better proxies for summer than winter temperatures. The estimate for the Pliocene period is especially controversial.

6. What natural things affect climate in the long run?

On the geologic time scale, many things affect climate:
- Changes in solar output
- Changes in the earth's orbital path
- Changes in land and ocean distribution (tectonic plate movements and the associated changes in mountain geography, ocean circulation, and sea level)
- Changes in the reflectivity of the earth's surface
- Changes in atmospheric concentrations of trace gases (especially CO_2 and CH_4)
- Changes of a catastrophic nature (such as meteor impacts or extended volcanic eruptions)

7. What is meant by "atmospheric lifetime" and "sinks"?

These concepts can be illustrated by referring to what is called the "carbon cycle." When CO_2 is emitted into the atmosphere, it moves among four main sinks, or pools, of stored carbon: the atmosphere, the oceans, the soil, and the earth's biomass (plants and animals). The movement of CO_2 among these sinks is not well understood. About 45 percent of the total emissions of CO_2 from human activity since preindustrial times is missing in the current accounting of CO_2 in the atmosphere, oceans, soil, and biomass. Three possible sinks for this missing CO_2 have been suggested. First, more CO_2 may have been absorbed into the oceans than was thought. Second, the storage of CO_2 in terrestrial plant life may be greater than estimated. Third, more CO_2 may have been absorbed directly into soil than is thought. However, there is no direct evidence for any of these explanations accounting for all the missing CO_2. CO_2 in the atmosphere is relatively "long-lived" in that it does not easily break down into its constituent parts. CH_4, by contrast, decomposes in the atmosphere in about 10 years. The greenhouse gas with the longest atmospheric lifetime (except for CO_2), CFC-115, has an average atmospheric lifetime of about 400 years. The overall contribution of greenhouse gases to global warming depends on their atmospheric lifetime as well as their ability to trap radiation. Table A.1 shows the relevant characteristics of the principal greenhouse gases.

8. Do all greenhouse gases have the same effect?

Each gas has different radiative properties, atmospheric chemistry, typical atmospheric lifetime, and atmospheric concentration. For example, CFC-12 is roughly 15,800 times more efficient molecule for molecule at trapping heat than CO_2. Because CFC-12 is a large, heavy molecule with many atoms and a

TABLE A.1 Key Greenhouse Gases Influenced by Human Activity

	CO_2	CH_4	CFC-11	CFC-12	N_2O
Preindustrial atmospheric concentration	280 ppmv	0.8 ppmv	0	0	288 ppbv
Current atmospheric concentration (1990)[a]	353 ppmv	1.72 ppmv	280 pptv	484 pptv	310 ppbv
Current rate of annual atmospheric accumulation[b]	1.8 ppmv (0.5%)	0.015 ppmv (0.9%)	9.5 pptv (4%)	17 pptv (4%)	0.8 ppbv (0.25%)
Atmospheric lifetime (years)[c]	(50-200)	10	65	130	150

NOTES: Ozone has not been included in the table because of lack of precise data. Here ppmv = parts per million by volume, ppbv = parts per billion by volume, and pptv = parts per trillion by volume.

[a] The 1990 concentrations have been estimated on the basis of an extrapolation of measurements reported for earlier years, assuming that the recent trends remained approximately constant.

[b] Net annual emissions of CO_2 from the biosphere not affected by human activity, such as volcanic emissions, are assumed to be small. Estimates of human-induced emissions from the biosphere are controversial.

[c] For each gas in the table, except CO_2, the "lifetime" is defined as the ratio of the atmospheric concentration to the total rate of removal. This time scale also characterizes the rate of adjustment of the atmospheric concentrations if the emission rates are changed abruptly. CO_2 is a special case because it is merely circulated among various reservoirs (atmosphere, ocean, biota). The "lifetime" of CO_2 given in the table is a rough indication of the time it would take for the CO_2 concentration to adjust to changes in the emissions.

SOURCE: Intergovernment Panel on Climate Change. 1990. *Climate Change: The IPCC Scientific Assessment,* J. T. Houghton, G. J. Jenkins, and J. J. Ephraums, eds. New York: Cambridge University Press. Reprinted by permission of Cambridge University Press.

CO_2 molecule is small and light in comparison, there are fewer molecules of CFC-12 in each ton of CFC-12 emissions than CO_2 molecules in each ton of CO_2 emissions. Each ton of CFC-12 emissions is about 5,750 times more efficient at trapping heat than each ton of CO_2. The comparatively greater amount of CO_2 in the atmosphere, however, means that it accounts for roughly half of the radiative forcing associated with the greenhouse effect.

9. Do greenhouse gases have different effects over time?

Yes. Figure A.2 shows projected changes in radiative forcing for different greenhouse gases between now and 2030. The potential increase for each

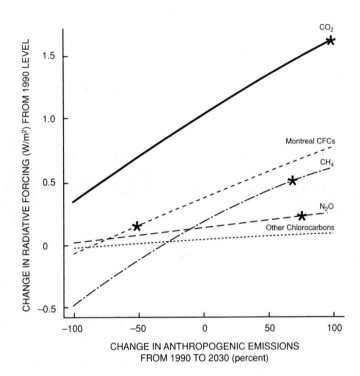

FIGURE A.2 Additional radiative forcing of principal greenhouse gases from 1990 to 2030 for different emission rates. The horizontal axis shows changes in greenhouse gas emissions ranging from completely eliminating emissions (–100 percent) to doubling current emissions (+100 percent). Emission changes are assumed to be linear from 1990 levels to the 2030 level selected. The vertical axis shows the change in radiative forcing in watts per square meter at the earth's surface in 2030. Each asterisk indicates the projected emissions of that gas assuming no additional regulatory policies, based on the Intergovernmental Panel on Climate Change estimates and the original restrictions agreed to under the Montreal Protocol, which limits emissions of CFCs. Chemical interactions among greenhouse gas species are not included.

For CO_2 emissions remaining at 1990 levels through 2030, the resulting change in radiative forcing can be determined in two steps: (1) Find the point on the curve labeled "CO_2" that is vertically above 0 percent change on the bottom scale. (2) The radiative forcing on the surface-troposphere system can be read in watts per square meter by moving horizontally to the left-hand scale, or about 1 W/m^2. These steps must be repeated for each gas. For example, the radiative forcing for continued 1990-level emissions of CH_4 through 2030 would be about 0.2 W/m^2.

SOURCE: Courtesy of Michael C. MacCracken.

gas is plotted for different emissions of each gas compared to 1990 emission levels. The figure shows the impact of different percentage changes in emissions (compared to 1990 emission rates) on the radiative forcing. Figure A.3 extends this to show the impact on equilibrium temperature for different sensitivities of the climatic system (in degrees Celsius).

10. What is meant by a "feedback" mechanism?

One example of a greenhouse warming feedback mechanism involves water vapor. As air warms, each cubic meter of air can hold more water vapor. Since water vapor is a greenhouse gas, this increased concentration of water vapor further enhances greenhouse warming. In turn, the warmer air can hold more water, and so on. This is an example of a positive feedback, providing a physical mechanism for "multiplying" the original impetus for change beyond its initial force.

Some mechanisms provide a negative feedback, which decreases the initial impetus. For example, increasing the amount of water vapor in the air may lead to forming more clouds. Low-level, white clouds reflect sunlight, thereby preventing sunlight from reaching the earth and warming the surface. Increasing the geographical coverage of low-level clouds would reduce greenhouse warming, whereas increasing the amount of high, convective clouds could enhance greenhouse warming. This is because high, convective clouds absorb energy from below at higher temperatures than they radiate energy into space from their tops, thereby effectively trapping energy. Satellite measurements indicate that clouds currently have a slightly negative effect on current planetary temperature. It is not known whether increased temperatures would lead to more low-level clouds or more high, convective clouds.

11. Can the temperature record be used to show whether or not greenhouse warming is occurring?

The estimated warming of between 0.3° and 0.6°C (0.5° and 1.1°F) over the last 100 years is roughly consistent with increased concentrations of greenhouse gases, but it is also within the bounds of "natural" variability for weather and climate. It cannot be proven to a high degree of confidence that this warming is the result of the increased atmospheric concentrations of greenhouse gases. There may be an underlying increase or decrease in average temperature from other, as yet undetected, causes.

12. What is the basis for predictions of global warming?

General circulation models (GCMs) are the principal tools for projecting climatic changes. GCMs project equilibrium temperature increases between 1.9° and 5.2°C (3.4° and 9.4°F) for greenhouse gas concentrations equivalent to a doubling of the preindustrial level of atmospheric CO_2. The midpoint of this range corresponds to an average global climate warmer than

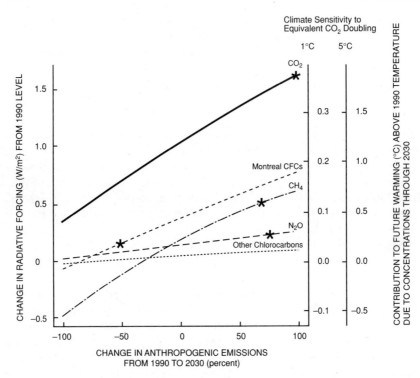

FIGURE A.3 Commitment to future warming. An incremental change in radiative forcing between 1990 and 2030 due to emissions of greenhouse gases implies a change in global average equilibrium temperature (see text). The scales on the right-hand side show two ranges of global average temperature responses. The first corresponds to a climate whose temperature response to an equivalent of doubling of the preindustrial level of CO_2 is 1°C; the second corresponds to a rise of 5°C for an equivalent doubling of CO_2. These scales indicate the equilibrium commitment to future warming caused by emissions from 1990 through 2030. Assumptions are as in Figure A.2.

To determine equilibrium warming in 2030 due to continued emissions of CO_2 at the 1990 level, find the point on the curve labeled "CO_2" that is vertically above 0 percent change on the bottom scale. The equilibrium warming on the right-hand scales is about 0.23°C (0.4°F) for a climate system with 1° sensitivity and about 1.2°C (2.2°F) for a system with 5° sensitivity. For CH_4 emissions continuing at 1990 levels through 2030, the equilibrium warming would be about 0.04°C (0.07°F) at 1° sensitivity and about 0.25°C (0.5°F) at 5° sensitivity. These steps must be repeated for each gas. Total warming associated with 1990-level emissions of the gases shown until 2030 would be about 0.41°C (0.7°F) at 1° sensitivity and about 2.2°C (4°F) at 5° sensitivity.

Scenarios of changes in committed future warming accompanying different greenhouse gas emission rates can be constructed by repeating this process for given emission rates and adding up the results.

SOURCE: Courtesy of Michael C. MacCracken.

any in the last 1 million years. The consequences of this amount of warming are unknown and may include extremely unpleasant surprises.

13. What is "equilibrium temperature"?

The oceans, covering roughly 70 percent of the earth's surface, absorb heat from the sun and redistribute it to the deep oceans slowly. It will be decades, perhaps centuries, before the oceans and the atmosphere fully redistribute the absorbed energy and the currently "committed" temperature rise is actually "realized." The temperature at which the system would ultimately come to rest given a particular level of greenhouse gas concentrations is called the "equilibrium temperature." Since atmospheric concentrations of greenhouse gases are constantly changing, the temperature measured at any time is the "transient" temperature, which lags behind the committed equilibrium warming. The lag depends in part on the sensitivity of the climate system and is believed to be between 10 and 100 years. This phenomenon makes it difficult to use temperature alone to "prove" that greenhouse warming is occurring.

14. How can we know when greenhouse warming is occurring?

The only tools we have for trying to produce credible scientific results are observations combined with theoretical calculation. Detecting additional greenhouse warming will require careful monitoring of temperature and other variables over years or even decades. Further development of numerical models will help characterize the climatic system, including the atmosphere, oceans, and land-based elements like forests and ice fields. However, only careful interpretation of actual measurements can reveal what has occurred and when.

15. How can credible estimates of future global warming be made?

Several approaches can be used. Scientific "first principles" can be used to estimate physical bounds on future trends. GCMs can be used to conduct "what if" experiments under differing conditions. Comparisons can be made with paleoclimatic data of previous interglacial periods. None of these methods is absolutely conclusive, but it is generally agreed that GCMs are the best available tools for predicting climatic changes. Substantial improvements in GCM capabilities are needed, however, for GCM forecasts to increase their credibility.

16. What influences future warming?

The amount of climatic warming depends on several things:

- The amount of sunlight reaching the earth
- Emission rates of greenhouse gases
- Chemical interactions of greenhouse gases in the atmosphere

• Atmospheric lifetimes of greenhouse gases until they decompose or transfer into sinks
• Effectiveness of positive or negative feedback mechanisms that enhance or reduce warming
• Human actions, which affect radiative forcing in both positive and negative directions

17. What are the major "unknowns" in predictions?

Major uncertainties include:

• Future emissions of greenhouse gases
• Role of the oceans and biosphere in uptake of heat and CO_2
• Amount of CO_2 and carbon in the atmosphere, oceans, biota, and soils
• Effectiveness of sinks for CO_2 and other greenhouse gases, especially CH_4
• Interactions between temperature change and cloud formation and the resulting feedbacks
• Effects of global warming on biological sources of greenhouse gases
• Interactions between changing climate and ice cover and the resulting feedbacks
• Amount and regional distribution of precipitation
• Other factors, like variation in solar radiation

18. How can the uncertainties best be handled?

Data can be arrayed to validate components of the models. Increasing the number of data sets can also help. In addition, the variation in GCM results can be compared to provide a sense of their "robustness." A major "intercomparison" of GCMs is being conducted, and has shown large differences in regional precipitation and reduction of snow and ice fields at high latitudes.

19. Are there changes associated with an equivalent doubling of the preindustrial level of atmospheric CO_2 that can be stated with confidence?

Because of the uncertainty in our understanding of various factors, projections reflect different levels of confidence.

Highly plausible: Global average surface warming
                   Global average precipitation increase
                   Reduction in sea ice
                   High-latitude surface winter warming
Plausible: Global sea level rise
                   Intensification of summer mid-latitude, mid-continental drying
                   High-latitude precipitation increase

Highly uncertain: Local details of climate change
                     Regional distribution of precipitation
                     Regional vegetation changes
                     Increase in tropical storm intensity or frequency

20.   What about storms and other extreme weather events?

The factors governing tropical storms are different from those governing mid-latitude storms and need to be considered separately.

One of the conditions for formation of typhoons or hurricanes today is a sea surface temperature of 26°C (79°F) or greater. With higher global average surface temperature, the area of sea with this temperature should be larger. Thus the number of hurricanes could increase. However, air pressure, humidity, and a number of other conditions also govern the creation and propagation of tropical cyclones. The critical temperature for their creation may increase as climate changes these other factors. There is no consistent indication whether tropical storms will increase in number or intensity as climate changes. Nor is there any evidence of change over the past several decades.

Mid-latitude storms are driven by equator-to-pole temperature contrast. In a warmer world, this contrast will probably weaken since surface temperatures in high latitudes are projected to increase more than at the equator (at least in the northern hemisphere). Higher in the atmosphere, however, the temperature contrast strengthens. Increased atmospheric water vapor could also supply extra energy to storm development. We do not currently know which of these factors would be more important and how mid-latitude storms would change in frequency, intensity, or location.

21.   Can projections be improved?

Better computers alone will not solve the problems associated with positive and negative feedbacks. Better understanding of atmospheric physics and chemistry and better mathematical descriptions of relevant mechanisms in the models are also needed, as are data to validate models and their subcomponents. Significant improvements may require decades.

22.   Is it possible to avoid the projected warming?

It is possible only at great expense or by incurring risks not now understood, unless the earth is itself self-correcting. Continued increases in atmospheric concentrations of greenhouse gases would probably result in additional global warming. Avoiding all future warming either would be very costly (if we significantly reduce atmospheric concentrations of greenhouse gases) or potentially very risky (if we use climate engineering). However, a comprehensive action program could slow or reduce the onset of greenhouse warming.

A FRAMEWORK FOR RESPONDING TO ADDITIONAL GREENHOUSE WARMING

23. What kinds of responses to potential greenhouse warming are possible?

Human interventions in natural and economic activities can affect the net rate of change in the radiative forcing of the earth. It is useful to categorize the possible types of intervention into three types:

• Actions to eliminate or reduce emissions of greenhouse gases
• Actions to "offset" such emissions by removing such gases from the atmosphere, blocking solar radiation, or altering the earth's reflectivity or absorption of energy
• Actions to help human and ecologic systems adjust to new climatic conditions and events

In this study the panel analyzes the first two types of action together under the label of "mitigation," since they are aimed at avoiding or reducing greenhouse warming. The third type of action is here called "adaptation."

24. How can response options be evaluated?

The choice of response options to potential greenhouse warming can be guided by a standard cost-benefit approach, augmented to handle some important aspects of the issues involved. The anticipated impacts (both adverse and beneficial) can be arrayed to produce a "damage function" showing the anticipated costs (or benefits) associated with projected climatic changes. The mitigation and adaptation options can be arrayed similarly according to their respective costs and effectiveness to produce an "abatement cost function." Optimal policies involve balancing incremental costs and benefits, which is called cost-benefit balancing. A necessary condition for an optimal policy is that the level of policy chosen should be cost-effective (any step undertaken minimizes costs). Employing such guidelines requires estimating both the anticipated damages and the cost-effectiveness of alternative response options, and choosing a discount rate to use for assessing the current value of future expenditures or returns.

In practice, a full cost-benefit approach can only be approximated. It is impossible to determine in detail the impacts of climatic changes that will not occur for 40 or 100 years. Thus the damage function can be only roughly approximated. Estimation of the abatement cost function is considerably easier.

Responses to greenhouse warming should be regarded as investments in the future. Cost-effectiveness and cost-benefit balancing should guide the selection of options. In general, a mixed strategy employing some investment in many different alternatives will be most effective.

IMPACTS OF ADDITIONAL GREENHOUSE WARMING

25. Can impacts of expected climatic changes be projected?

It currently is not possible to predict regional temperature, precipitation, and other effects of climate change with much confidence. And without quantitative projections of regional and local climatic changes, it is not possible to produce quantitative projections of the consequences of greenhouse warming.

Instead, the degree of "sensitivity" of affected human and natural systems to the projected changes can be estimated. The sensitivity of a particular system to the climate changes expected to accompany different amounts of additional greenhouse warming can be used to estimate the impacts of those changes.

A crucial aspect of the sensitivity of a system is the speed at which it can react. For example, investment decisions in many industries typically have a "life-cycle" of 10 years or less. Climatic changes associated with additional greenhouse warming are expected to emerge slowly enough that these industries may be expected to adjust as climate changes. Some industries, such as electric power production, have longer investment cycles, and might have more difficulty responding as quickly. Natural ecological systems would not be expected to anticipate climate change and probably would not be able to adapt as quickly as climatic conditions change.

The impacts of climate change are thus hard to assess because the response of human and natural systems to climate change must be included.

26. How can the impacts on affected systems be classified?

Likely impacts of climate change can be divided into four categories:

• Low sensitivity. The projected changes would likely have little effect on the system. An example is most industrial production not requiring large quantities of water. Temperature changes of the magnitude projected would not matter much for most industrial processes. These impacts do not give rise to much concern.

• High sensitivity, but adaptation possible at some cost. The system would likely adapt or otherwise cope with the projected changes without completely restructuring the system. An example is American agriculture. Although some crops would likely move into new locations, agricultural scientists and plant breeders would almost certainly develop new crops suitable for changed growing conditions. There would be costs, but food supply would not be interrupted. As a class, these impacts give rise to concern because the affected systems may have difficulty adapting.

• High sensitivity, and adaptation problematic. The system would be seriously affected, and adaptation would probably not be easy or effective. Natural communities of plants and animals would probably lose their current structure, and reformulate with different mixes of species. Some individual species, especially animals, would move to new locations. The natural landscape as we know it today would almost certainly be altered by a climate change at or above the midpoint of the range used in this study. These impacts are of considerable concern because the affected systems may not be able to adapt without assistance.

• Uncertain sensitivity, but cataclysmic consequences. The sensitivity of the system cannot be assessed with certainty, but the consequences would be extremely severe. An example is the possible shifting, slowing, or even stopping of major ocean currents like the Gulf Stream or the Japanese Current. These ocean currents strongly affect weather patterns, and changes in them could drastically alter weather in Europe or the West Coast of the United States. We have no credible way, however, of assessing the conditions that could lead to such shifts.

27. What are the likely impacts of climate change?

Human societies exhibit a wide range of adaptive mechanisms in the face of changing climatic events and conditions. Projected climatic changes, especially at the upper end of the range, may overwhelm human adaptive mechanisms in areas of marginal productivity and in countries where traditional coping mechanisms have been disrupted. In general, natural ecosystems would be much more sorely stressed, probably beyond their capacities for adjustment. For example, even temperature changes at the lower end of the range would result in shifts of local climates at rates faster than the movement of long-lived trees with large seeds.

A comprehensive catalog of beneficial and harmful impacts is not available. Nor is an estimation of the magnitude of the likely impacts of projected climatic changes. Table A.2 summarizes impacts to human and natural systems in the United States according to the sensitivity categories.

28. Can costs be calculated for the various impacts of projected climate changes?

Not directly. The climatic changes likely to occur in the future cannot be directly measured. The costs and benefits associated with some aspects of certain changes can be estimated, however. These can be used to produce very rough estimates of the costs of climatic impacts. However, these must be recognized as very imprecise indicators.

In general, the costs in the United States associated with the first category of sensitivity are low in relation to overall economic activity. The

TABLE A.2 The Sensitivity and Adaptability of Human Activities and Nature

	Low Sensitivity	Sensitive, but Adaptation at Some Cost	Sensitive, Adaptation Problematic
Industry and energy	X		
Health	X		
Farming		X	
Managed forests and grasslands		X	
Water resources		X	
Tourism and recreation		X	
Settlements and coastal structures		X	
Human migration		X	
Political tranquility		X	
Natural landscapes			X
Marine ecosystems			X

NOTE: Sensitivity can be defined as the degree of change in the subject for each "unit" of change in climate. The impact (sensitivity times climate change) will thus be positive or negative depending on the direction of climate change. Many things can change sensitivity, including intentional adaptations and natural and social surprises, and so classifications might shift over time. For the gradual changes assumed in this study, the Adaptation Panel believes these classifications are justified for the United States and similar nations.

costs associated with the second category are higher but still should not result in major disruption of the economy. Appropriate adjustments could probably be accomplished without replacing current systems. Costs associated with the third category are much larger, and the adjustments could involve disruption. Some type of anticipation for meeting them may be justified. The category of extremely adverse impacts would be associated with high potential costs and would disrupt most aspects of the system in question. These outcomes, however, are extremely difficult to assess. Table A.3 summarizes some "benchmark" costs illustrative of impacts similar to those that might be associated with climate change.

TABLE A.3 Illustrative Costs of Impacts and Adaptations

Class	Description	Dollars (1990)	Per
GNP	1985 total U.S.	4015 billion[a]	
	1985 average U.S.	17 thousand	capita
	1985 global average	3 thousand	capita
	2100 global average projected	7-36 thousand	capita
	2100 average U.S.[b]	150 thousand	capita
Climate hazards	1980 U.S. heatwave	20 billion	
	1988 U.S. drought	39 billion	
	1983 Utah heavy snow, floods, and landslide	300 million	
	1985 Ohio and Pennsylvania tornados	500 million	
	1985 West Virginia floods	700 million	
	1989 Hurricane Hugo	5 billion	
Recent annual average U.S. losses[c]	Hurricanes	800-1800 million	
	Floods	3 billion	
	Tornados and thunderstorms	300-2000 million	
	Winter storms and snows	3 billion	
	Drought	800-1000 million	
	1988 budget U.S. Weather Service	323 million	
Farming	Create successful wheat variety	1 million	
	Kansas Agricultural Research Experiment Station	33 million	
	U.S. and state agricultural research	2.3 billion	
	1974-1977 drought, federal expenditures[d]	7 billion	
	1986 U.S. farm GNP	76 billion	
Forestry	Prepare and plant	130	acre
	Treat with herbicide	41	acre
	Fertilize	36	acre
	Thin	55	acre
	Protect from fire for 1 year	1.36	acre
	1983 fire protection on state and private forests[e]	245 million	
	1986 U.S. forestry and fishery GNP	17 billion	
Natural landscape[f]	Preserve a large mammal in zoo	1500-3000	year
	Preserve a large bird in zoo	100-1000	year
	Preserve a plant in botanical garden	500	year
	Recover peregrine falcon	3 million	1970-1990
	Recover all endangered birds of prey	5 million	year
	Preserve an acre in a large reserve	50-5000	acre
	1985 expenditure on wildlife-related recreation, including hunting and fishing	55.4 billion	
	Budget National Park Service	1 billion	year

Water[g]	Delaware River above Philadelphia	51	acrefoot
	Sacramento delta	137	acrefoot
	High flow skimming, Hudson River	555	acrefoot
	Desalting	2200-5400	acrefoot
	Present national average	533	acrefoot
	Present irrigation water in California	15	acrefoot
	Annual water bill for domestic use	60	capita
	Annual cost of water for irrigation	45	acre
	Value of an acre of tomatoes	4000	acre
Industry	Raise offshore drilling platform 1 meter[h]	16 million	
	1986 U.S. manufacturing GNP	824 billion	
Settlement[i]	Raise a Dutch dike 1 meter	3 thousand	m length
	Build seawall, Charleston, South Carolina	6 thousand	m length
	Nourish beach for 1 year, Florida	35-200	m length
	Nourish beach for 1 year, Charleston, South Carolina	300	m length
	Hurricane evacuation	35-50	person
	Strengthen coastal property for 100-mph wind	30-90 billion	U.S. coast
	Floodproof by raising house 3 feet	10-40 thousand	house
	Move house from floodplain	20-70 thousand	house
	Levees, berms, and pumps	17 thousand	1/4 acre
	1986 U.S. state and local services	331 billion	
Migration	Resettle a refugee in 1989, federal contribution	7 thousand	person

[a]National Income in 1985 was $3222 billion.

[b]Assumes 1.9 percent growth per year, which is the annual average growth rate for U.S. GNP from 1800 to 1985.

[c]In an extremely adverse year, climate hazards may cost $40 billion or 1 percent of the $4000 billion U.S. GNP, which is about $160 per capita.

[d]During the drought of the 1970s, annual federal expenditures on drought relief averaged about 3 to 4 percent of GNP.

[e]In 1983, expenditures on about a half billion acres of state and private forest land were $0.50 per acre. Increasing expenditures on all forest land to $1.36 per acre would cost about $500 million or 3 percent of forest and fishery GNP.

[f]The cost of recovering all endangered birds of prey is 1 ten-thousandth and the cost of the National Park Service is 2 percent of the annual expenditures on wildlife-associated recreation.

[g]Doubling the cost of domestic water would cost a person a third of a percent of per capita GNP in the United States. Raising the cost of irrigation water from the present $15 per acre-foot to the $137 per acre-foot for the prospective water from the Sacramento delta would cost 2 percent of the value of the tomatoes on an acre.

[h]The cost of raising an offshore drilling platform 1 m is less than 1 percent of its total cost.

[i]Strengthening coastal properties for 100-mph wind would cost between a tenth and a third of current state and local service budgets for the entire United States. The cost of moving a house would be 1 to 4 times the present U.S. per capita GNP and a tenth to a half of that of 2100.

29. Are there possible consequences of greenhouse warming with highly adverse impacts?

Two have been identified.

- Deep ocean currents could be interrupted. Increased freshwater runoff in the Arctic might alter the salinity of northern oceans, thereby reducing or stopping the vertical flow of water into the deep ocean along Greenland and Iceland. This might interrupt a major deep ocean current running from the North Atlantic around the Cape of Good Hope and through the Indian Ocean to the Pacific. This could affect temperature and precipitation, with repercussions that might be catastrophic. Very little is currently known about the potential of this phenomenon.
- The West Antarctic Ice Sheet could surge. The Antarctic and Greenland ice sheets combined make up the world's largest reservoir of fresh water. The West Antarctic Ice Sheet alone contains enough water to raise global average sea level about 7 meters (23 feet). Warming could affect the speed at which the ice sheet flows to the sea and breaks off into icebergs. A large subsequent influx of fresh water could alter the salinity of the world's oceans, affecting currents and plant and animal populations alike. The ramifications are extreme, and it might lead to disruption of deep ocean currents and all that that entails. The timing of such a possibility is controversial. Current thinking is that it would take centuries, but there is little empirical evidence on which to base estimates.

30. What are appropriate responses to very uncertain, but highly adverse impacts?

Both individuals and societies must decide how to handle events that are very unlikely but which have severe consequences. Homeowners purchase insurance against the very unlikely event of fire. In essence, insurance is a cost today (the insurance premium) to avoid undesirable consequences later (losing one's possessions to fire). If we want to avoid unsure adverse impacts of possible climate change, we might want to spend money now that would reduce the likelihood that those things can happen. In principle, there are two different kinds of "climate insurance." We could do things that reduce the likelihood that the climate will change (mitigation options), or we could do things that reduce the sensitivity of affected human and natural systems to future climate change (adaptation options).

31. Does looking at potential impacts tell us where to set priorities for responding to greenhouse warming?

Partly. The examination of potential impacts can help provide rough estimates of the cost at which adaptation could be accomplished should climate change. This is an approximation of the "damage function" and can be used to assess how much to spend on emission reductions or offsets. However, all estimates are approximations with very little precision. The amount to allocate to prevent additional greenhouse warming depends significantly on the preferred degree of risk aversion.

PREVENTING OR REDUCING ADDITIONAL GREENHOUSE WARMING

32. What are the sources of greenhouse gas emissions?

All of the major greenhouse gases except CFCs are produced by both natural processes and human activity. Table A.4 summarizes the principal sources of greenhouse gases associated with human activity.

33. What interventions could reduce greenhouse warming?

It is useful to examine two different aspects of reducing emissions or offsetting emissions:

  • "Direct" reduction or offsetting of emissions through altering equipment, products, physical processes, or behaviors
  • "Indirect" reduction or offsetting of emissions through altering the behavior of people in their economic or private lives and thus affecting the overall level of activity leading to emissions

It is much easier to estimate potential effectiveness and costs of direct reductions than of indirect incentives on human behavior. This is mostly because of the many factors that affect behavior in addition to the incentives in any particular program.

34. How can specific mitigation options be compared?

Mitigation options can be compared quantitatively in terms of their cost-effectiveness and qualitatively in terms of the obstacles to their implementation and in terms of other benefits and costs.

The standard quantitative unit used to compare mitigation options is the cost per metric ton of carbon emissions reduced or per metric ton of carbon removed from the atmosphere. The amount of carbon can be converted to the amount of CO_2 in the atmosphere by multiplying by 3.67, which is the ratio of the molecular weights of carbon and CO_2. Other greenhouse gases can be "translated" to CO_2 equivalency by using two calculations. First, the amount of radiative forcing caused by a specific concentration of the gas is estimated in terms of the change in energy reaching the surface (in watts per square meter). This estimate accounts for atmospheric chemistry, atmospheric lifetime of the gas, and other relevant factors affecting the total contribution of that gas to greenhouse warming. Second, the amount of

TABLE A.4 Estimated 1985 Global Greenhouse Gas Emissions from Human Activities

	Greenhouse Gas Emissions (Mt/yr)	CO_2-equivalent Emissions[a] (Mt/yr)	
CO_2 Emissions			
Commercial energy	18,800	18,800	(57)
Tropical deforestation	2,600	2,600	(8)
Other	400	400	(1)
TOTAL	21,800	21,800	(66)
CH_4 Emissions			
Fuel production	60	1,300	(4)
Enteric fermentation	70	1,500	(5)
Rice cultivation	110	2,300	(7)
Landfills	30	600	(2)
Tropical deforestation	20	400	(1)
Other	30	600	(2)
TOTAL	320	6,700	(20)[b]
CFC-11 and CFC-12 Emissions			
TOTAL	0.6	3,200	(10)
N_2O Emissions			
Coal combustion	1	290	(>1)
Fertilizer use	1.5	440	(1)
Gain of cultivated land	0.4	120	(>1)
Tropical deforestation	0.5	150	(>1)
Fuel wood and industrial biomass	0.2	60	(>1)
Agricultural wastes	0.4	120	(>1)
TOTAL	4	1,180	(4)
TOTAL		32,880	(100)

NOTE: Mt/yr = million (10^6) metric tons (t) per year. All entries are rounded because the exact values are controversial.

[a]CO_2-equivalent emissions are calculated from the Greenhouse Gas Emissions column by using the following multipliers:

$$CO_2 \qquad 1$$
$$CH_4 \qquad 21$$
$$CFC\text{-}11 \text{ and } \text{-}12 \quad 5,400$$
$$N_2O \qquad 290$$

Numbers in parentheses are percentages of total.
[b]Total does not sum due to rounding errors.

SOURCE: Adapted from U.S. Department of Energy. 1990. *The Economics of Long-Term Global Climate Change: A Preliminary Assessment—Report of an Interagency Task Force.* Springfield, Va.: National Technical Information Service.

CO_2 that would produce the same amount of forcing at the surface is calculated. This is the CO_2 equivalent for that specific concentration of the other greenhouse gas. The respective costs per ton for different options can then be compared directly. It is important to recognize, however, that these calculations allow comparison only of initial contributions. They do not account for changes in energy-trapping effectiveness over the various lifetimes of these gases in the atmosphere.

35. What mitigation options are most cost-effective?

The panel ranks options for reducing greenhouse gas emissions or removing greenhouse gases from the atmosphere according to their cost-effectiveness. Some of these options have net savings or very low net implementation costs compared to other investments. The options range from net savings to more than $100 per metric ton of CO_2-equivalent emissions avoided or removed from the atmosphere. The most cost-effective mitigation options are presented in Table A.5.

36. What are examples of options with large potential to reduce or offset emissions?

The so-called geoengineering options have the potential of substantially affecting atmospheric concentrations of greenhouse gases. They have the ability to screen incoming sunlight, stimulate uptake of CO_2 by plants and animals in the oceans, or remove CO_2 from the atmosphere. Although they appear feasible, they require additional investigation because of their potential environmental impacts.

37. How much would it cost to significantly reduce current U.S. greenhouse gas emissions?

It depends on the level of emission reduction desired and how it is done. The most cost-effective options are those that enhance efficient use of energy: efficiency improvements in lighting and appliances, white roofs and paving to enhance reflectivity, and improvement in building and construction practices.

Figure A.4 compares mitigation options, and Table A.5 gives the panel's estimates of net cost and emission reductions for several options. It must be emphasized that the table presents the panel's estimates of the *maximum* technical potential for each option. The calculation of cost-effectiveness of lighting efficiency, for example, does not consider whether the supply of light bulbs could meet the demand with current production capacities. Nor does it consider the trade-off between expenditures on light bulbs and on health care, education, or basic shelter for low-income families. In addition, there is a danger of some "double counting." For example, in the area of energy supply both nuclear and natural gas energy options assume re-

TABLE A.5 Comparison of Selected Mitigation Options in the United States

Mitigation Option	Net Implementation Cost[a]	Potential Emission Reduction[b] (t CO$_2$ equivalent per year)
Building energy efficiency	Net benefit	900 million[c]
Vehicle efficiency (no fleet change)	Net benefit	300 million
Industrial energy management	Net benefit to low cost	500 million
Transportation system management	Net benefit to low cost	50 million
Power plant heat rate improvements	Net benefit to low cost	50 million
Landfill gas collection	Low cost	200 million
Halocarbon-CFC usage reduction	Low cost	1400 million
Agriculture	Low cost	200 million
Reforestation	Low to moderate cost[d]	200 million
Electricity supply	Low to moderate cost[d]	1000 million[e]

NOTE: Here and throughout this report, tons are metric.

[a]Net benefit = cost less than or equal to zero
Low cost = cost between $1 and $9 per ton of CO$_2$ equivalent
Moderate cost = cost between $10 and $99 per ton of CO$_2$ equivalent
High cost = cost of $100 or more per ton of CO$_2$ equivalent
[b]This "maximum feasible" potential emission reduction assumes 100 percent implementation of each option in reasonable applications and is an optimistic "upper bound" on emission reductions.
[c]This depends on the actual implementation level and is controversial. This represents a middle value of possible rates.
[d]Some portions do fall in low cost, but it is not possible to determine the amount of reductions obtainable at that cost.
[e]The potential emission reduction for electricity supply options is actually 1700 Mt CO$_2$ equivalent per year, but 1000 Mt is shown here to remove the double-counting effect.

placement of the same coal-fired power plants. Table A.5, however, presents only options that avoid double counting. Finally, although there is evidence that efficiency programs can pay, there is no field evidence showing success with programs on the massive scale suggested here. Thus there may be very good reasons why "negative cost options" on the figure are not implemented today.

The United States could reduce its greenhouse gas emissions by between 10 and 40 percent of the 1990 levels at low cost, or perhaps some net savings, if proper policies are implemented.

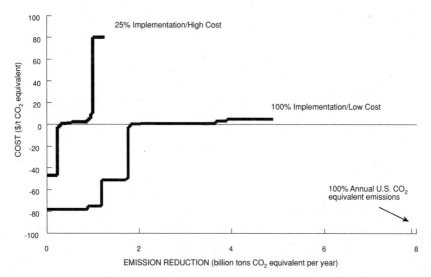

FIGURE A.4 Comparison of mitigation options. Total potential reduction of CO_2-equivalent emissions is compared to the cost in dollars per ton of CO_2 reduction. Options are ranked from left to right in CO_2 emissions according to cost. Some options show the possibility of reductions of CO_2 emissions at a net savings.

ADAPTING TO ADDITIONAL GREENHOUSE WARMING

38. *Will human and natural systems adapt without assistance?*

Farmers adjust their crops and cultivation practices in response to weather patterns over time. Natural ecosystems also adapt to changing conditions. The real issue is the rate at which human and natural systems will be able to adjust.

39. *At what rates can human and natural systems adapt?*

Many human systems have decision and investment cycles that are shorter than the time in which impacts of climate change would become manifest. These systems in the United States should be able to adjust to climate change without governmental intervention, as long as it is gradual and in-formation about the rates of change is widely available. This applies to agriculture, commercial forestry, and most of industry. Industrial sectors with extremely long investment cycles (e.g., transport systems, urban infra-structure, and major structures and facilities) or requiring high volumes of water may require special attention. Coastal urban settlements would be able to react quickly (within 3 to 5 years) if sea level rises. Response would be much more difficult, however, where financial and other resources are limited, such as in many developing countries.

Some natural systems adjust at rates an order of magnitude or more slower than those anticipated for global-scale temperature changes. For example, the observed and theoretical migration of large trees with heavy seeds is an order of magnitude slower than the anticipated change in climate zones. Furthermore, natural ecosystems cannot anticipate climate change but must wait until after conditions have changed to respond.

40.   What is the value of the vulnerable natural ecosystems?

Natural ecosystems contribute commercial products, but their value is generally considered to exceed this contribution to the economy. For example, genetic resources are generally undervalued because people cannot capture the benefits of investments they might make in preserving biodiversity. Many species are unlikely to ever have commercial value, and it is virtually impossible to predict which ones will become marketable.

In addition, some people value natural systems regardless of their economic value. Loss of species, in their view, is undesirable whether or not those species have any commercial value. They generally hold that preservation of the potential for evolutionary change is a desirable goal in and of itself. Humanity, they claim, should not do things that alter the course of natural evolution. This view is sometimes also applied to humanity's cultural heritage—to buildings, music, art, and other cultural artifacts.

41.   How much would it cost to adapt to the anticipated climatic changes?

The panel's analysis suggests that some human and natural systems are not very sensitive to the anticipated climatic changes. These include most sectors of industry. Other systems are sensitive to climatic changes but can be adapted at a cost whose present value is small in comparison to the overall level of economic activity. These include agriculture, commercial forestry, urban coastal infrastructure, and tourism. Some systems are sensitive, and their adaptation is questionable. The unmanaged systems of plants and animals that occupy much of our lands and oceans adapt at a pace slower than the anticipated rate of climatic change. Their future under climate change would be problematic. Poor nations may also adapt painfully. Finally, some possible climatic changes like shifts in ocean currents have consequences that could be extremely severe, and thus the costs of adaptation might be very large. However, it is not currently possible to assess the likelihood of such cataclysmic changes.

No attempt has been made to comprehensively assess the costs of anticipated climatic changes on a global basis.

42. How much should be spent in response to greenhouse warming?

The answer depends on the estimated costs of prevention and the estimated damages from greenhouse warming. In addition, the likelihood and severity of extreme events, the discount rate, and the degree of risk aversion will modify this first-order approximation.

The appropriate level of expenditure depends on the value attached to the adverse outcomes compared to other allocations of available funds, human resources, and so on. In essence, the answer depends on the degree of risk aversion attached to adverse outcomes of climate change. The fact that less is known about the more adverse outcomes makes this a classic example of dealing with high-consequence, low-probability events. Programs that truly increase our knowledge and monitor relevant changes are especially needed.

IMPLEMENTING RESPONSE PROGRAMS

43. What policy instruments could be used to implement response options?

A wide array of policy instruments of two different types are available: regulation and incentives. Regulatory instruments mandate action, and include controls on consumption (bans, quotas, required product attributes), production (quotas on products or substances), factors in design or production (efficiency, durability, processes), and provision of services (mass transit, land use). Incentive instruments are designed to influence decisions by individuals and organizations and include taxes and subsidies on production factors (carbon tax, fuel tax), on products and other outputs (emission taxes, product taxes), financial inducements (tax credits, subsidies), and transferable emission rights (tradable emission reductions, tradable credits). The choice of policy instrument depends on the objective to be served.

44. At what level of society should actions be taken?

Interventions at all levels of human aggregation could effectively reduce greenhouse warming. For example, individuals could reduce energy consumption, recycle goods, and reduce consumption of deleterious materials. Local governments could control emissions from buildings, transport fleets, waste processing plants, and landfill dumps. State governments could restructure electric utility pricing structures and stimulate a variety of efficiency incentives. National governments could pursue action in most of the policy areas of relevance. International organizations could coordinate programs in various parts of the world, manage transfers of resources and technologies, and facilitate exchange of monitoring and other relevant data.

45. Is international action necessary?

The greenhouse phenomenon is global. Unilateral actions can contribute significantly, but national efforts alone would not be sufficient to eliminate the problem. The United States is the largest contributor of CO_2 emissions (with estimates ranging from 17 to 21 percent of the global total). But even if this country were to totally eliminate or offset its emissions, the effect on overall greenhouse warming might be lost if no other countries acted in concert with that aim.

46. What about differences between rich and poor countries?

Poor and developing countries are likely to be the most vulnerable to climate change. In addition, many developing countries today are sorely pressed in a variety of other ways. They may conclude that other issues have more immediate consequences for their citizens. Incentives in all parts of the world for intervention in the area of greenhouse warming may thus draw heavily on the industrialized nations. They may be called upon to help poor countries stimulate economic development and thus become better able to cope with climate change. They may also be asked to provide expertise and technologies to help poor countries adapt to the conditions they face.

ACTIONS TO BE TAKEN

47. Do scientific assessments of greenhouse warming tell us what to do?

Current scientific understanding of greenhouse warming is both incomplete and uncertain. Response depends in part on the degree of risk aversion attached to poorly understood, low-probability events with extremely adverse outcomes. Lack of scientific understanding should not be used as a justification for avoiding reasoned decisions about responses to possible additional greenhouse warming.

48. Is it better to prevent greenhouse warming now or wait and adapt to the consequences?

This complicated question has several parts.

• First, will it be possible to live with the consequences if nothing is done now? The panel's analysis suggests that advanced, industrialized countries will be able to adapt to most of the anticipated consequences of additional greenhouse warming without great economic hardship. In some regions, climate and related conditions may be noticeably worse, but in other regions better. Countries that currently face difficulty coping with extreme climatic events, or whose traditional coping mechanisms are breaking down, may be sorely pressed by the climatic changes accompanying an equivalent doubling of atmospheric CO_2 concentrations. It is important to recognize that there may be dramatic improvement or disastrous deterioration in specific locales. In addition, this analysis applies to the next 30 to 50 years. The situation may be different beyond that time horizon.

Natural communities of plants and animals, however, face much greater difficulties. Greenhouse warming would likely stress such ecosystems sufficiently to break them apart, resulting in a restructuring of the community in any given locale. New species would be likely to gain dominance, with a different overall mix of species. Some individual species would migrate to new, more livable locations. Greenhouse warming would most likely change the face of the natural landscape. Similar changes would occur in lakes and oceans.

In addition, there are possible extremely adverse consequences, such as changing ocean currents, that are poorly understood today. The response to such possibilities depends on the degree of risk aversion concerning those outcomes. The greater the degree of risk aversion, the greater the impetus for preventive action.

• Second, does it matter when interventions are made? Yes, for three different kinds of reasons. Because greenhouse gases have relatively long lifetimes in the atmosphere, and because of lags in the response of the system, their effect builds up over time. These time-dependent phenomena lead to the long-term "equilibrium" warming being greater than the "realized" warming at any given point in time. These dynamic aspects of the climate system show the importance of acting now to change traditional patterns of behavior that we have recently recognized to be detrimental, such as heavy reliance on fossil fuels. In addition, the implications of intervention programs for the overall economy vary with time. Gradual imposition of restraints is much less disruptive to the overall economy than their sudden application. Finally, the length of investment cycles can be crucial in determining the costs of intervention. In addition, some investments can be thought of as insurance, or payments now to avoid undesirable outcomes in the future. The choice is made more complicated by the fact that the outcomes are highly uncertain.

• Third, what discount rate should be used? The selection of a discount rate is very controversial. Macroeconomic calculations for the United States show a return on capital investment of 12 percent. The choice of discount rate reflects time preference. The panel has used discount rates of 3, 6, and 10 percent in its analysis. Finally, consumers often behave as if they have used a discount rate closer to 30 percent. The panel has also included this rate for comparison when options involve individual action.

49. Are there special attributes of programs appropriate for response to greenhouse warming?

Yes. The uncertainties present in all aspects of climate change and our understanding of response to potential greenhouse warming place a high premium on information. Small-scale interventions that are both reversible and yield information about key aspects of the relevant phenomena are especially attractive for both mitigation and adaptation options. Monitoring of emission rates, climatic changes, and human and ecologic responses should yield considerable payoffs.

Perhaps the most important attribute of preferred policies is that they be able to accommodate surprises. They should be constructed so that they are flexible and can change if the nature or speed of stress is different than anticipated.

50. What should be done now?

The panel developed a set of recommended options in five areas: reducing or offsetting emissions, enhancing adaptation to greenhouse warming, improving knowledge for future decisions, evaluating geoengineering options, and exercising international leadership. The panel recommends moving decisively to undertake *all* of the actions described under questions 51 through 55 below.

51. What can be done to reduce or offset emissions of greenhouse gases?

Three areas dominate the panel's analysis of reducing or offsetting current emissions: eliminating CFC emissions and developing substitutes that minimize or eliminate greenhouse gas emissions, changing energy policy, and utilizing forest offsets. Eliminating CFC emissions has the biggest single contribution. Recommendations concerning energy policy are to examine how to make the price of energy reflect all health, environmental, and other social costs with a goal of gradual introduction of such a system; to make conservation and efficiency the chief element in energy policy; and to consider the full range of supply, conversion, end use, and external effects in planning future energy supply. Global deforestation should be reduced, and a moderate domestic reforestation program should be explored.

52. What can be done now to help people and natural systems of plants and animals adapt to future greenhouse warming?

Most of the actions that can be taken today improve the capability of the affected systems to deal with current climatic variability. Options include maintaining agricultural basic, applied, and experimental research; making water supplies more robust by coping with present variability; taking into consideration possible climate change in the margins of safety for long-lived structures; and reducing present rates of loss in biodiversity.

53. What can be done to improve knowledge for future decisions?

Action is needed in several areas. Collection and dissemination of data that provide an uninterrupted record of the evolving climate and of data that are needed for the improvement and testing of climate models should be expanded. Weather forecasts should be improved, especially of extremes, for weeks and seasons to ease adaptation to climate change. The mechanisms that play a significant role in the responses of the climate to changing concentrations of greenhouse gases need further identification, and quantification at scales appropriate for climate models. Field research should be conducted on entire systems of species over many years to learn how CO_2 enrichment and other facets of greenhouse warming alter the mix of species and changes in total production or quality of biomass. Research on social and economic aspects of global change and greenhouse warming should be strengthened.

54. Do geoengineering options really have potential?

Preliminary assessments of these options suggest that they have large potential to mitigate greenhouse warming and are relatively cost-effective in comparison to other mitigation options. However, their feasibility and especially the side-effects associated with them need to be carefully examined. Because the geoengineering options have the potential to affect greenhouse warming on a substantial scale, because there is convincing evidence that some of these cause or alter a variety of chemical reactions in the atmosphere, and because the climate system is poorly understood, such options must be considered extremely carefully. If greenhouse warming occurs, and the climate system turns out to be highly sensitive to radiative forcing, they may be needed.

55. What should the United States do at the international level?

The United States should resume full participation in international programs to slow population growth and contribute its share to their financial and other support. In addition, the United States should participate fully in international agreements and programs to address greenhouse warming, including representation by officials at an appropriate level.

Appendix B

Thinking About Time in the Context of Global Climate Change

The costs, effectiveness, and benefits of policy instruments to mitigate global climate change are influenced by the time at which actions are taken and at which the greenhouse gas emissions and sequestrations occur. Three dimensions are involved. The first is the straightforward matter of the timing of costs and resultant benefits with regard to the discounted present value of resources expended and benefits received. The second is the relative value decision-makers place on different beneficial effects of mitigation; goals are multidimensional, and each aspect may be met to a different degree depending on the timing of changes in greenhouse flows. The cost-benefit ratio of instruments therefore depends on the mix of goals sought. The third dimension is associated with the complex relationship between flows of emissions and sequestrations, and the resultant augmentation of the stock of greenhouse gases in the atmospheric system, inherently a time-dependent phenomenon. Each of these dimensions affects the relative attractiveness of classes of policy instruments and therefore must be taken into account in the design of an optimum system of interventions. It is not a simple matter of minimizing the dollars spent per ton reduced.

TIMING OF COSTS AND EFFECTS (BENEFITS)

The issue of timing of costs and effects is straightforward. The absolute level of the discount rate to be used is a matter of great complexity and no little controversy. However, as long as it is not zero, the earlier that benefits can be received and the longer that costs can be delayed, the better—all other things held equal. The premise behind this conclusion is that resources are fungible and have alternative uses—in satisfying consumption needs and augmenting future production through investment. What makes this a matter of special concern here is that the value placed on the specific mitigation effects of instruments depends crucially on the mix of goals sought.

GOALS OF MITIGATION OF GLOBAL CLIMATE CHANGE

The mitigation of global climate change is not a one-dimensional phenomenon such that all possible benefits of policy actions are achieved simultaneously. This complicates the ranking of instruments on a cost per ton basis. To take different components into account in making rankings, it is first necessary to decompose the bundle of potential desired goals and then to determine how each possible policy instrument furthers or hinders the satisfaction of each. Furthermore, before the instruments can be put on a common basis it is also necessary to form some judgments about the terms of the acceptable trade-offs among mitigation goals. A similar process is required to compare the cost incurred in pursuing the use of a mitigation instrument with the cost of adaptation or of meeting non-climate-change goals such as faster economic growth or increased consumption.

Three component subgoals of global climate change mitigation can be posited. The first is to reduce the rate of change in the stock of greenhouse gases, on the twin premises that the speed of global climate change is sensitive to relatively small changes in the stock and that damage wrought is an increasing function of the rate of change. This goal would stress the avoidance of sudden increases in the flow of greenhouse gases, for example, even at the cost of giving up some reductions in the long-term level of the stock.

The second subgoal is to reduce the total amount of global climate change experienced between now and some future time, with the endpoint defined either arbitrarily or as the point where the global climate system is again in equilibrium. The presumption here is that the damage to be mitigated arises from the integral of global climate change over each year between now and the endpoint selected. This might be loosely termed the "total damage borne" measure, and a proxy for its mitigation is the sum by years of the augmentation of the stock of greenhouse gases avoided.

The third subgoal is to reduce the ultimate level of global climate change at the chosen endpoint. Pursuit of this goal presumes that the time path of global climate change is of little consequence as long as the policy instruments result in an acceptably low level of ultimate change. As a proxy for this goal, the target is the ultimate level of the stock of greenhouse gases. Total benefits of mitigation would presumably be maximized by some optimal combination in achieving all three of these subgoals.

Figure B.1 illustrates these concepts in a schematic way. It shows the stock of greenhouse gases that is taken as a proxy for global climate change.

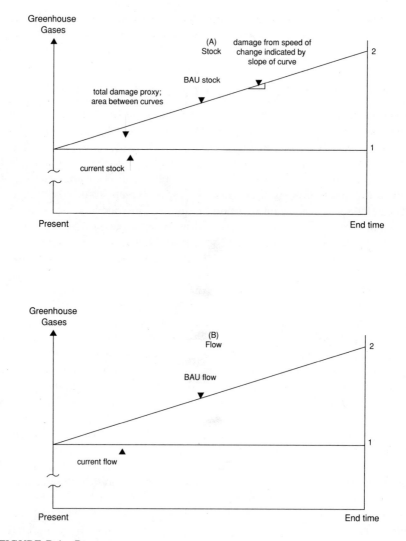

FIGURE B.1   Base case.

Line 2 at the top, business as usual (BAU), illustrates the system without
policy intervention. The slope of this line (for simplicity shown as linear
with time) is a proxy for the speed of global climate change. Line 1 illustrates stabilization of greenhouse gas stocks at the present level. The difference between lines 1 and 2 shows the greenhouse gas stock proxy for the
cumulative exposure to global climate change due to future anthropogenic
augmentation of greenhouse gases. The vertical difference between the

BAU line and line 1 represents a proxy for the level of global climate change introduced to the system at any point in time due to future anthropogenic activity.

It is obvious on inspection that changes in the path of the stock through the use of policy instruments can have different effects on satisfying each of the three subgoals posited. For example, a policy that resulted in severe depression of the line through much of this time, followed by a rapid increase up to and beyond the BAU level, would reduce the total exposure to climate change, but at the cost of rapid change later and of a higher endpoint value. In contrast, a rapid short-term increase of greenhouse gas stocks, in exchange for earlier stabilization and a lower endpoint, would subject the system both to the damage of rapid increase in the short run and to greater cumulative global climate change borne. The point is clear: Realization of components of the bundle of desired mitigation effects may not be achieved simultaneously by policy instruments. Trade-offs among them may be necessary. It follows that three requirements must be met before optimizing policy choices among instruments can be made. First, it is necessary to determine the damage functions associated with the three separate aspects of global climate change—speed, total quantity experienced, and ultimate level. Second, it is necessary to associate these with changes in the stock of greenhouse gases. Third, it is necessary to determine how candidate policy instruments affect the stock and how much they cost. As complex as they are important, these matters are likely to be beyond careful estimation for some time. This does not mean, however, that they are subjects that can rightfully be ignored by policymakers choosing among instruments. On a gross and intuitive level, the trade-offs involved among these goals can be incorporated usefully into decisions about the degree to which different classes of instruments should be pursued.

THE FLOW-STOCK RELATIONSHIP

Greenhouse gases are emitted through both natural and anthropogenic processes and are subsequently sequestered or serve to augment the existing stock in the atmosphere. Sequestration occurs both in unmanaged sinks such as the oceans and in sinks subject to human influence such as forests. Greenhouse gases are also transformed and lose their greenhouse property over time. (This attenuation, which differs in rate among greenhouse gases, is ignored here because it does not affect the essence of this analysis.) The stock is many multiples of the flow and, consequently, exhibits substantial inertia. Further, the portion of the flow that is subject to human management is a fraction of the flow through the system, adding to the inertia of the stock to flows notionally within human control. There are also numerous lags and feedbacks in the system that affect the flow-stock relationship (but these are ignored here as well). Also relevant is the hypothesis that past increases in greenhouse gases have yet to be fully reflected in observed global climate change. This suggests that stabilization of the stock of greenhouse gases would still leave additional global climate change in the system; a reduction of the stock would be required to stabilize the climate itself.

Highly simplified, the basic relationships are illustrated in Figures B.1a and B.1b, which describe stocks and flows, respectively. The vertical scales differ enormously between the two diagrams; in each, the scale is broken to exaggerate the changes relative to the base. Line 2 in Figure B.1b describes the BAU trend of flows of greenhouse gases net of BAU sequestration. It is associated with the BAU trend of greenhouse gas stocks previously described in Figure B.1a. Line 1 of Figure B.1b shows net flows kept constant at current rates, just as line 1 of Figure B.1a shows constant stocks at the current level. The BAU lines of Figure B.1 are used in subsequent diagrams as the base case to which the effects of classes of instruments are compared. Actual future trends, in reality, will probably be nonlinear (i.e., curve) with respect to time, but the trend line is shown here as linear to illustrate the principles involved in characterizing different policy instruments.

CHARACTERIZATION OF CLASSES OF POLICY INSTRUMENTS

The conclusion that follows from the above discussion is that the time dimension is a useful addition to the evaluation criteria used to choose among policy instruments. Their relative attractiveness depends on more than their resource costs and the number of tons removed:

- It depends on when the costs are incurred (the later, the better) and when the benefits are felt (the sooner, the better).
- It depends on the effect of the instrument on the speed with which the climate change occurs (the slower, the better).
- It depends on the effect of the instrument on the total global climate change experienced, as summed over the years from the present to the endpoint (the smaller the total, the better).
- It depends on the effect of the instrument on the ultimate level of global climate change imposed on the future at the chosen endpoint (the lower, the better).

Major classes of policy instruments are discussed below with reference to the above time-related criteria.

Temporary Reduction in Greenhouse Gas Flows: Class 1

One class of instruments yields a temporary reduction of greenhouse gas flows. Different cases are illustrated in Figure B.2. Figure B.2b shows

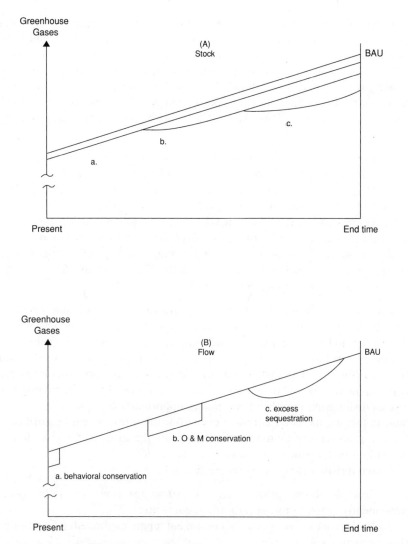

FIGURE B.2   Temporary reduction in flows.

schematically the net change in the flow to the atmosphere by time interval. The effect on the stock is shown (greatly exaggerated for clarity) on Figure B.2a.

The prototypical example of this class would be a public relations campaign that caused thermostat adjustments lasting 1 year (case a). The stock would be permanently reduced, but of course not by much relative to the total. This case is functionally the same as a conservation activity that requires annual operation and management expenditures (case b); the action is simply repeated each year. (For simplicity of presentation, case a is shown as following case b; case c follows both.) In cases a and b the assumption is that contemporaneous economic consumption (defined as including diminished amenities) is foregone to achieve the reduction in greenhouse gas flows and hence stock. The costs of reducing the flows are borne in the year the reduction takes place, but the benefits are experienced (essentially) forever. This class of instruments has the following characteristics:

1. Their costs are borne as the flows of greenhouse gases are reduced.
2. Permanent reduction occurs in the stock, but not in the flow.
3. There is a once-and-for-all decline in stocks that slows the speed of growth of greenhouse gases during the time of the action.
4. Timing affects the total damage borne. To the extent that this consequence is a matter of concern, early conservation is to be preferred.
5. Timing of action does not influence the final level of greenhouse gas stock. It follows that to the extent that the final level of stocks is what matters, conservation now, rather than later, is a poorer bargain.

Case c is a variant of a temporary reduction. An example would be investment in establishing a forest that sequesters greenhouse gases at an increasing and then decreasing rate, with the incremental net quantity sequestered reaching zero when the forest is in long-term carbon sequestration equilibrium. The distinction between this and the previous two cases rests on the timing and the nature of the costs borne. There are investments in establishing the forest and continuing opportunity costs in sustaining the land in forests; the latter continue even after the forest reaches equilibrium. Case c represents a contingent reduction in the greenhouse gas stock— depending on a continuing resource use to secure.
Characteristic of this subclass are the following:

1. Costs are borne prior to any benefit as the flows are reduced and permanently thereafter to sustain the sequestration.
2. The reduction of stock is contingent upon continued expenditures; flow reductions are temporary.
3. The speed of growth of greenhouse gas stocks is slowed steadily as gases are sequestered, but the possibility of later escalation exists.
4. Same as cases a and b.
5. Same as cases a and b.

Permanent Reduction of Greenhouse Gas Flows: Class 2

Another class of policy instrument is one in which a one-time investment leads to a continuous reduction of flows of an equal amount over time. An example would be a change in a long-lived building's envelopes such that less energy was used each year. This class is shown in Figure B.3, with the investment made in the present.

This class of instruments has the following characteristics:

1. Costs are borne before the flows of greenhouse gases are affected.
2. There is a permanent reduction in flows and a cumulative, permanent reduction in stocks.
3. There is a reduction in the speed of change in global climate, which starts at the time of the action.

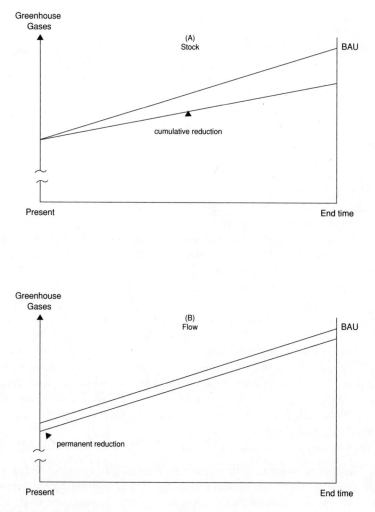

FIGURE B.3   Permanent reduction in flows.

4. Timing of action affects the total damage borne, and the quantity is an increasing function of how soon the instrument is used.

5. Timing of action affects the final level of greenhouse gas stocks. It follows that to the extent the final level of stocks is what is of consequence, action now rather than later is the better bargain.

Temporary Sequestration with Subsequent Release, and Variants: Class 3

This class of policy instruments is characterized by a cycling of greenhouse gases in and out of the atmosphere. It is one that illustrates to a striking degree the importance of different mitigation goals in comparing policy instruments.

The prototypical example of this class is the creation of a forest based on a temporary excess supply of land for agriculture, with that forest subsequently reclaimed to grow food. This example is shown in Figure B.4. The forest is shown as being established in the present. It sequesters greenhouse gases through time, as shown in case a. If the wood were then simply burned, the stock of greenhouse gases at the endpoint would not be affected; the timing of the flow alone is changed, as shown in case b. More to the point, though, the outcome is likely to be that some of the greenhouse gas will remain sequestered in lumber and some of the biomass will be burned to replace fossil fuels, which means that all of the greenhouse gases will not be returned to the atmosphere. This is shown as an alternative case c.

Variants of this cycling process abound. For example, many energy conservation efforts require initial energy-using investments that increase greenhouse gas flows in the short run. Creation of forests from scrubland initially releases greenhouse gases; it may be a substantial time before the initial augmented flow is neutralized.

Timing of flows and of changes in stocks is particularly important in evaluating this class of instruments. An instrument whose costs yielded climate change benefits only with a lag would have a further hurdle to pass if it led to an initial augmentation of greenhouse gas flows. This would be especially true if lessening the total damage borne were an element in the desired outcome. Furthermore, the endpoint against which the final level of stock is judged is crucial. If it occurred as sequestration ended, but before releases occurred, it would give a misleadingly favorable judgment of the instrument; the obverse is also true.

Characteristics of this class of instruments include the following:

1. The timing of costs with respect to effects on stocks is varied; for the forest example, there are up-front investment and continuing maintenance costs, with the latter ending only when the forest is reconverted to its original state.

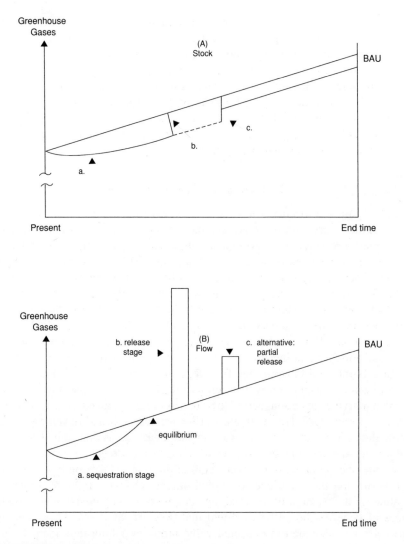

FIGURE B.4 Temporary sequestration and release.

2. Net flows are both positive and negative, depending on the point in the cycle. There may be no effect on the endpoint level of the stock.

3. The effect on the rate of change in greenhouse gas stocks is erratic; because sequestration is typically gradual and release rapid, spurts of increase are possible.

4. Timing of action does not affect the total damage borne over the cycle of sequestration and release.

5. Timing of action does not affect the endpoint level of the stock except insofar as it occurs in a particular part of a sequestration-release cycle.

6. To the extent that the endpoint level is a matter of concern, instruments of this sort are ineffective in principle.

7. The relative standing of instruments of this class is peculiarly dependent on the endpoint chosen. For example, for the forest conversion case, an endpoint sooner than the time of reconversion will give a false signal of excessive effectiveness on all grounds—speed of change, total damage borne, and maximum climate change incurred.

Lagged, Uncertain Reductions in Greenhouse Gas Flows: Class 4

Some policy instruments have effects on greenhouse gas flows substantially in the future, and those effects may be uncertain. An example would be increased research and development directed toward energy-saving technologies and practices in developing countries. These expenditures would precede (perhaps by decades) reductions in flows, but (by assumption) the reductions would then be permanent with the usual effect on stock. The research and development may, of course, be fruitless, because the technology does not work, is superseded by something better, or is not adopted for other reasons. If it were used, however, it would affect all three of the possible policy endpoints by slowing the speed of change, reducing total damage borne, and lowering the final level of global climate change.

A plausible assumption is that neither the cost of the research and development nor the gestation period before flows are reduced is affected by when it is initiated. However, the earlier the research and development is done, the greater is the burden of the costs (measured as discounted present value) and also the time period over which the reductions in greenhouse gas flows are accumulated. Greater accumulation time reduces both total damage borne and the final level of global climate change. It follows that in evaluating the wisdom of undertaking such research and development, both types of benefits should be used and that they are additive. They should, however, be calculated in expected value terms by taking into account the uncertainty of their actually coming to pass. It also follows that any research and development that might be justified in the future is an even better bargain in the present. As noted, this is because the mitigation effect is an increasing function of the time between the introduction of the new technology and the endpoint of the analysis.

A further reason for early rather than later research and development is that it moves forward in time the knowledge about what reductions are possible. This information could increase the time available to plan for needed adaptation and would indicate earlier which additional, more expensive, measures might be necessary and which could be avoided.

This class of instruments has effects on flows and stocks similar to those in Figure B.3 with the reductions displaced into the future (refer to that diagram). The characteristics of such instruments are the following:

1. Costs are borne substantially before any reductions occur, and implementation has further costs. The discount rate used in the decision process has a marked effect on evaluating the instrument.
2. Once reductions begin, there is a permanent effect on flows and a cumulative, permanent reduction in stocks.
3. There is a reduction in the rate of change in global climate, beginning when flows decline.
4. Timing of action affects the total damage borne; the quantity avoided is an increasing function of how soon the instrument is used.
5. Timing of action affects the final level of greenhouse gas stocks. Again, the sooner action is initiated, the better the bargain.
6. The uncertainty of outcomes must be factored into the decision by evaluating the mitigation effects on an expected value basis.
7. Knowledge gained about the prospects for mitigation is a component of the benefits; again, the sooner it is acquired, the greater is its value.

Accelerating Reductions in Greenhouse Gas Flows: Class 5

A class of policy instruments may induce an escalating reduction in greenhouse gas flows. Such instruments have little early consequence but exponentially increasing effects over time. A good example of this class of instrument would be one that reduced population, as described further below. Another example would be investment in infrastructure for research and development on energy conservation. Still another would be expenditures that would lead to a permanent shift in attitudes toward energy-conserving social choices, such as the use of mass transit.

Population reduction is accomplished through reduction in the fertility rate. (Delaying births would only have a once-and-for-all effect.) The immediate result in countries at or near the margin of subsistence is to increase the survival rate of those children born; so in estimating the effects, it is necessary to consider the net change in increased life expectancy. A subsequent effect is to increase per capita income. That effect is strongest in the period immediately after the decline in birthrate because during this period the ratio of employed to nonemployed persons increases—partly because women are freed from child-rearing duties and partly because there are fewer persons (children) not in work force. Another factor is that child-rearing investment and expenditures (schools, medical attention, and so on) are released to other occupations. The issue is to determine how these shifts affect the net emission of greenhouse gases over time.

Conventional wisdom suggests that a declining birthrate would have little effect on net emissions in the short run and that the effect could even be to increase emissions. The latter would occur if the investment, labor, and consumption freed by having a smaller cohort of infants emitted more greenhouse gases than the activities replaced. Over time, however, the expectation is that the effects would be positive and large and would grow exponentially as cohorts of reduced size moved through the demographic cycle. This is because the emission of greenhouse gases is expected to be more responsive to falling population than it is to rising per capita income.

The conclusion that declining population leads to lowered greenhouse gas emissions depends crucially on the amount by which per capita incomes rise. The latter is a matter of fact and depends on particular circumstances. In the poorest countries, for example, declining population may free sufficient resources from basic consumption to allow substantial increases in highly productive investment. This investment could more than compensate for a declining labor force, especially in the early years after the decline in birthrate. Total output could consequently increase, not fall, and added output-related emissions could overshadow the decline in emissions associated with the population drop per se. This is especially true if emissions per person rise more than proportionately with income, which is likely to be the case in a poor country due to shifts in the mix of consumption goods toward those that use more energy. In the long run, after incomes rose sufficiently, countervailing forces would likely dominate, but that long run may be far in the future. This possibility should be taken into account in interpreting the results of the example given below.

The class of instruments that might lead to an accelerated reduction in greenhouse gas flows is illustrated in Figure B.5. The change in BAU flows from a permanent downward shift in fertility rates is shown as positive for a period after the change occurs. It then turns negative and builds in waves over time. The waves are occasioned by the movement of the diminished childbearing cohort through time. The increasing (to some limit) reduction in flows leads to an exponential decline in greenhouse gas stocks as compared to BAU.

The characteristics of instruments of this class (as illustrated in the population example) follow:

1. Expenditures occur well before greenhouse gas emission flows decrease and continue as needed to sustain the drop in fertility rates.

2. The initial impact may be to increase flows and stocks, but this is temporary—though for really poor countries successfully launched on development, it can last a long time.

3. Reductions in flows are permanent because there is a shift downward in population, including that of childbearing age, even if fertility reduction expenditures cease.

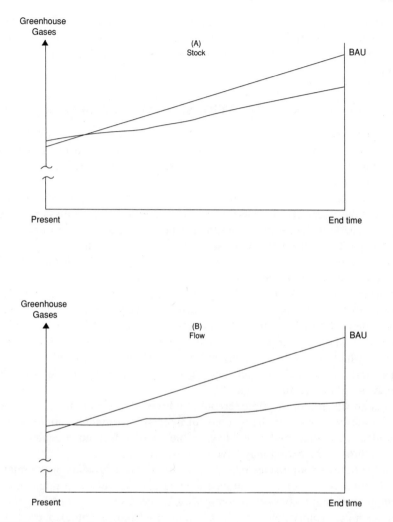

FIGURE B.5   Accelerating reductions in flows.

4. Once begun, there is a cumulative, permanent reduction in greenhouse gas stocks at an exponential rate.

5. The speed of the change in stocks is reduced (at a growing rate) from the time that lower fertility rates result in lower emissions. To the extent that steady movement toward stabilization is a goal, early use of this instrument is more desirable than later.

6. Timing of actions affects the total damage born; thus to the extent that lessening total damage is a goal, the sooner the instrument is used, the better.

7. Timing of actions affects the endpoint level of greenhouse gas stocks as an increasing function of the interval between initiation and endpoint, making early action relatively more valuable than later, all other things held equal.

LESSONS, IMPLICATIONS, AND FURTHER WORK

What has come before suggests that instruments can be divided into classes on the basis of the time at or during which they affect greenhouse gas emissions and stock. Division of this sort is crucial if instruments are to be reasonably compared with each other. This is true on three counts.

First, the relative desirability of instruments depends on their costs related to their benefits. Because the costs of greenhouse gas emission changes may occur at different times and their benefits extend into the future, costs and benefits of different instruments must be put on the same scale with respect to time for their comparison to be meaningful. This is done through the use of a discount rate as discussed in Chapter 20.

Second, the goal of reducing global climate change has at least three dimensions. Instruments can have different effects on the satisfaction of each, depending on the time that effects on greenhouse gas stocks are observed. This is tied to the third matter: the complex relationship between flows (which instruments affect) and stocks (which are the result of changes in flows). It is stocks and changes in them that affect the issue of policy interest—global climate change.

As an illustration of the interconnectedness of these matters, if the final greenhouse gas stock is the outcome of interest, instruments should be measured against that, and those having the same effect on greenhouse gas flows during one period may have very different impacts on greenhouse gas *stocks* at the endpoint selected. This suggests that judgments of the relative cost-effectiveness of different instruments can be very dependent on the temporal endpoint chosen. A ton of flow reduced may be a bad bargain, no matter how cheaply achieved, if it is reinserted into the atmosphere before the endpoint of interest.

Proper treatment of time has another use as well. It can have important consequences for determining the optimal timing and quantity of any intervention. This is true if that decision is based on what society gets in the form of lesser global climate change vis-à-vis what it gives up in terms of current satisfaction and the enhanced ability to accommodate future adaptation. In this, fully accounting for all the positive aspects of mitigation— reduced speed of change, reduced total exposure to damage, and final level of global climate change—is important. Each has separate effects on the consequences of societal interest such as rise in sea level, agricultural productivity, and changes in ecological systems. They can also differ in their effects on the distribution of consequences over time and geography.

The purpose of this appendix is to indicate the role of the time dimension in formulating a global climate change mitigation strategy. It illustrates ways in which different instruments may lead to outcomes that diverge from those expected when only tons reduced and costs are considered. Application of the relationships discussed here requires an understanding of the physical relationships among flows, stock, and global climate change that lies beyond current knowledge. It also requires complex judgments about the trade-offs among sometimes competing policy goals. In illuminating what information is needed to formulate an efficient and effective policy, it suggests potentially fruitful areas for further research. Even before that research is done, however, policymakers can use some of these insights to select the mix of instruments that appears to have the greatest prospect for improving total welfare.

Appendix C

Conservation Supply Curves
for Buildings

Conservation supply curves relate energy savings achieved by implementing a given efficiency measure, to that measure's "cost of conserved energy" (CCE).

$$CCE = \frac{\text{Annualized investment (\$ / yr)}}{\text{Annual energy saved (kWh / yr)}} \tag{1}$$

The initial investment in an efficient technology or program is annualized by multiplying it by the "capital recovery rate" (CRR).

$$CRR = \frac{d}{1 - (1 + d)^{-n}}$$

where d is the real discount rate and n is the number of years over which the investment is written off (i.e., amortized).

Conserved energy is liberated to be "supply" for other energy demands and therefore may be thought of as a resource and plotted on a supply curve. There are two different kinds of conservation supply curves. One shows *technical potential*, based on engineering and economic calculations without concern for the probability of successful implementation. The second type of curve shows *achievable scenarios* based on actual experience; typical utility conservation programs have captured only about 50 percent of the technical potential.

On a conservation supply curve, each measure or step (such as "efficiency improvements to residential refrigerators") is defined as follows:

Height = CCE (cents saved per kilowatt-hour),   (2)
Width = annual kilowatt-hours saved,   (3)
Area under the step = total annualized cost of investment.   (4)

The steps are ranked in order of ascending CCE, with the cheapest options plotted first, causing the curve to be upward-sloping.

To decide whether a step is profitable (and how profitable), its CCE is compared to the "price" of the avoided kilowatt-hour. Table C.1 shows that "price" varies from different viewpoints. The average 1989 price of electricity in buildings (line 1) is 7.5 cents/kWh, whereas industry (line 2) pays only 4.7 cents/kWh. Because one cannot anticipate where a conserved kilowatt-hour will ultimately be used, the societal price is taken to be an all-sector average of 6.4 cents/kWh (line 3). One could then subtract the tax (1.1 cents/kWh), but tax would also have to be subtracted from the cost of conserved energy. However, both the competing utility and the conservation industries pay taxes, and only the difference (if any) in tax rates should be corrected for. To simplify, one will be assumed to cancel the other.

Line 4 addresses the fact that the short-run marginal cost of electricity may be lower than its average price. In some parts of the United States there is still a glut of electric generating capacity, so that the marginal cost of a kilowatt-hour is low. In such areas, the "rock bottom" price of generating a kilowatt-hour from coal and delivering it to the building meter is about 3.5 cents.

Line 5 addresses externalities, although they will not actually be used now. Today, many jurisdictions require a theoretical "environmental adder" of 1 to 3 cents/kWh; that is, they give efficiency an advantage of 1 to 3 cents/kWh over supply during resource planning. For example, New York has recently adopted a point system for evaluating competing resources in which the most environmentally disruptive resource (a new coal plant) under the most unfavorable circumstances is given. This point system provides an "environmental adder" of 1.4 cents/kWh. Desiring to be conventional and conservative in its claims for the profitability of efficiency investments,

TABLE C.1 "Prices" of Electricity at the Meter

	Price (cents/kWh)
1. Residential price (seen by consumer)	7.5
2. Industrial price	4.7
3. All-sector average price	6.4
4. Marginal cost of operating a coal plant and delivering 1 kWh to the meter	3.5
5. Line 3 plus externality cost: 1 to 3 cents/kWh (New York has chosen 1.4 cents/kWh for the worst coal plant)	7.4-9.4

TABLE C.2 Unit Energy Consumption for a New Refrigerator

	Base (kWh/yr)	Target (kWh/yr)
1. Average new 1990 refrigerator consumption "frozen" until year 2000	1000	—
2. Anticipated efficiency resulting from the 1993 National Appliance Standards for refrigerators	700	—
3. Better efficiency in year 2000 achieved by 1980s-type utility efficiency programs	—	600
4. Most efficient refrigerator in year 2000, including all technical improvements with cost of conserved energy (CCE) less than 6 cents/kWh	—	200

the Mitigation Panel has followed the standard sin of setting the adder to zero, but line 5 at least points out that if 1 to 3 cents/kWh is added to the all-sector average price, one arrives at a societal after-tax price of 7.4 to 9.4 cents/kWh, which brackets nicely the present 7.5-cent/kWh price to buildings drawn on all the supply curves in Part Three of this report.

Each of the energy prices above can be drawn as a horizontal line across a supply curve. All steps located below a selected price line are cost-effective, and the rational investor should take each of these steps, stopping where the staircase crosses the line. Of course, different price assumptions drastically alter estimates of dollar savings.

Having addressed the uncertainties in price (y-axis), the panel next addresses the uncertainties in savings (x-axis). To do this, in Table C.2 the unit energy consumption of an average new 1990 refrigerator (1000 kWh/yr) on line 1 is compared with the consumption of an optimal refrigerator (200 kWh/yr) on line 4. From an engineer's point of view, the potential savings from replacing line 1 with line 4 is obviously 800 kWh/yr. However, from the point of view of the utility forecaster or program manager, whose programs never achieve more than one-half to two-thirds of the potential savings, line 3 is more realistic and reflects a sales-weighted average of refrigerator efficiency that is below the optimum. The program manager would target an "achievable" savings of only 400 kWh/yr.

An additional complication should be noted. Many efficiency studies start with a year 2000 base case that has already been reduced by about 30 percent for anticipated efficiency gains, as a result of standards or occurring naturally (see Table C.2, line 2). They then subtract about 300 kWh/yr from their estimates of the savings. The problem with using this "esti-

TABLE C.3 Calculations of Conserved Electricity (using Table C.2 as an example)

	Base	Savings
Line 1 (1000) – line 4 (200) = 800 kWh	Frozen efficiency	Technical potential
Line 1 (1000) – line 3 (600) = 400 kWh	Frozen efficiency	Achievable
Line 2 (700) – line 4 (200) = 500 kWh	Naturally occurring	Technical potential
Line 2 (700) – line 3 (600) = 100 kWh	Naturally occurring	Achievable

NOTE: In its supply curves, the panel has adjusted all curves to "frozen efficiency—technical potential" energy savings and to a real discount rate of 6 percent.

mated" base case is that estimates frequently change, thus muddying cleaner technical potential calculations.

Table C.3 shows how an energy savings of only one efficiency measure on a supply curve can be reported in four ways. In supply curve literature, each of these ways is used, often without explicit distinctions being drawn between types.

Figure C.1 displays the costs and technical potential of the 11-step EPRI conservation supply curve, with an additional first step for white surfaces/ urban trees to save air conditioning. To transform these electrical savings into units of avoided CO_2 as displayed in Figure C.2, two conversions must be made (see Table C.4).

First the x-axis is converted by using the CO_2 produced from the mix of fuels burned by U.S. power plants—estimated to be 500 megatons (Mt) carbon (C) for 1990 electric sales of 2610 billion kilowatt-hours (BkWh) (Edmonds et al., 1989).[1] To get tons of CO_2, multiply by 3.666.

$$1 \text{ kWh} = 0.7 \text{ g } CO_2, \tag{5}$$
$$1 \text{ TWh} = 0.7 \text{ Mt } CO_2.$$

Then the y-axis is divided by 5; so

$$1 \text{ cent/kWh} = \$14.3/\text{Mt } CO_2. \tag{5a}$$

Figure C.1 has two y-axis scales: on the left, *direct* CCE for the investment in efficiency; on the right, *net* CCE, which accounts for the price of avoided electricity. By using equation (5a), net CCE can then be converted to net cost of conserved CO_2 (CC CO_2). The reason is that the ultimate goal is a "grand supply curve" of avoided CO_2 from conserved electricity, oil, natural gas, and so forth. When these fuels are combined, it is no longer possible to track their individual prices; thus one can work only with net savings. Accordingly, Figure C.2 uses the all-sector electric price of 6.4 cents/kWh to create the net scale.

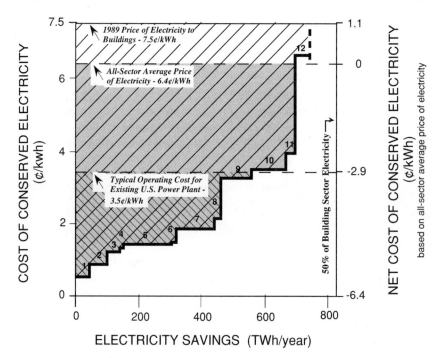

Potential Net Savings:

$ 37 B/yr. - CASE 1: Below 7.5¢/kWh 1989 Price of Electricity to Buildings

$ 29 B/yr. - CASE 2: Below 6.4¢/kWh All-Sector Average Price of Electricity

$ 10 B/yr. - CASE 3: Below 3.5¢/kWh Typical Operating Cost for Existing U.S. Power Plant

FIGURE C.1   Cost of conserved electricity (CCE) for buildings.

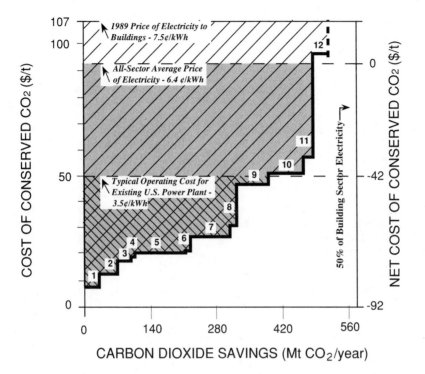

Potential Net Savings:

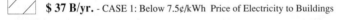 **$ 37 B/yr.** - CASE 1: Below 7.5¢/kWh Price of Electricity to Buildings

$ 29 B/yr. - CASE 2: Below 6.4¢/kWh All-Sector Average Price of Electricity

$ 10 B/yr. - CASE 3: Below 3.5¢/kWh Typical Operating Cost for Existing U.S. Power Plant

FIGURE C.2   Net cost of conserved carbon dioxide (CC CO_2) for electric efficiency in the buildings sector.

TABLE C.4 Worksheet for Conservation Supply Curves for Figures 21.8 and 21.9 (C.1 and C.2) and Table 29.2

Electricity	A	B	C	D
Conservation Measure	Individual TWh Savings	Cumulative TWh Savings	CCE $d=.05$ (¢/kWh)	CCE $d=.06$ (¢/kWh)
1 White surfaces and urban trees	45	45	0.50	0.53
2 Residential lighting	56	101	0.84	0.88
3 Residential water heating	38	139	1.20	1.26
4 Commercial water heating	9	149	1.30	1.37
5 Commercial lighting	167	315	1.38	1.45
6 Commercial cooking	6	322	1.43	1.50
7 Commercial cooling	116	437	1.82	1.91
8 Commercial refrigeration	21	459	2.08	2.18
9 Residential appliances	103	562	3.18	3.34
10 Residential space heating	105	667	3.48	3.65
11 Commercial and industrial space heating	22	689	3.77	3.96
12 Commercial ventilation	45	734	6.50	6.83
Total				
Notes				Figure 21.8 and C.1

Carbon Dioxide	K	L	M
Conservation Measure	Individual Mt CO_2 Savings $(0.7 \times A)$	Cumulative Mt CO_2 Savings $(0.7 \times B)$	CC CO_2 $d=.06$ ($/ton) $(14.3 \times D)$
1 White surfaces and urban trees	32	32	7.6
2 Residential lighting	39	71	12.6
3 Residential water heating	27	97	18.0
4 Commercial water heating	7	104	19.6
5 Commercial lighting	117	221	20.7
6 Commercial cooking	4	225	21.5
7 Commercial cooling	81	306	27.3
8 Commercial refrigeration	15	321	31.2
9 Residential appliances	72	393	47.8
10 Residential space heating	74	467	52.2
11 Commercial and industrial space heating	15	482	56.6
12 Commercial Ventilation	32	514	97.7
Total	514	514	
Notes	Values for Table 29.2		Figures 21.9 and C.2

	E	F	G	H	I	J
	Net CCE – 6.4¢/kWh base			Potential $ Savings (d=.06) $B		
	d=.03 (C × 0.9)–6.4	d=.06 (D–6.4)	d=.10 (C × 1.25)–6.4	(7.5¢/kWh base) [A × (D–7.5)]	(6.4¢/kWh base) [A × (D–6.4)]	(3.5¢/kWh base) [A × (D–3.5)]
1	−5.95	−5.87	−5.78	−3.14	−2.64	−1.34
2	−5.64	−5.52	−5.35	−3.72	−3.10	−1.47
3	−5.32	−5.14	−4.90	−2.36	−1.95	−0.85
4	−5.23	−5.03	−4.78	−0.58	−0.48	−0.20
5	−5.16	−4.95	−4.68	−10.09	−8.26	−3.42
6	−5.11	−4.90	−4.61	−0.38	−0.31	−0.13
7	−4.76	−4.49	−4.13	−6.47	−5.20	−1.84
8	−4.53	−4.22	−3.80	−1.12	−0.89	−0.28
9	−3.54	−3.06	−2.43	−4.29	−3.16	−0.17
10	−3.27	−2.75	−2.05	−4.05	−2.89	0.16
11	−3.01	−2.44	−1.69	-0.78	−0.54	0.10
12	−0.55	0.43	1.72	−0.30	0.20	1.51
				−37.29	−29.41	−9.69
				−37	−29	−10

	N	O	P	Q
	Net CC CO$_2$ – 6.4¢/kWh base			
	d=.03 (14.3 × E)	d=.06 (14.3 × F)	d=.10 (14.3 × G)	d=.30
1	−85	−84	−83	−74
2	−81	−79	−77	−61
3	−76	−74	−70	−49
4	−75	−72	−68	−45
5	−74	−71	−67	−42
6	−73	−70	−66	−40
7	−68	−64	−59	−26
8	−65	−60	−54	−17
9	−51	−44	−35	22
10	−47	−39	−29	33
11	−43	−35	−24	43
12	−8	6.1	25	141

Values for Table 29.2

NOTE

1. Throughout this report, tons (t) are metric; 1 Mt = 1 megaton = 1 million tons.

REFERENCE

Edmonds, J., W. Ashton, H. Cheng, and M. Steinberg. 1989. A Preliminary Analysis of U.S. CO_2 Emissions Reduction Potential from Energy Conservation and the Substitution of Natural Gas for Coal in the Period to 2010. Report DOE/NBB-0085. Washington, D.C.: Office of Energy Research, U.S. Department of Energy.

Appendix D

Conservation Supply Curves for Industrial Energy Use

Relatively little analysis has been undertaken to address systematically the costs of achieving energy savings and consequent CO_2 emission reductions for the industrial sector. This is due in part to the extraordinary heterogeneity of this sector (e.g., in contrast to the buildings or transportation sector) and to the often proprietary nature of industrial process technology. Thus, although technical aspects of industrial energy use have been studied extensively, economic assessments remain largely lacking at this time, especially with regard to fundamental process design changes, which offer some of the potentially most significant energy reduction measures.

ELECTRICITY USE

The economic analyses available focus primarily on the use of electricity in selected manufacturing processes. A key assumption in such analyses is the rate of return, or discount rate, needed to induce capital investments in energy conservation. Empirically, the discount rates required for the industrial sector appear to be on the order of 30 to 50 percent, equivalent to payback periods of only 2 to 3 years (Ross, 1990b). In some cases, the desired rates of return may be as high as 100 percent (Ayres, 1990). Although financial decision-making criteria in industry are not very well understood, U.S. manufacturers appear to be more reluctant to invest in energy-saving equipment than would be suggested by standard financial analyses using more typical rates of return (e.g., 10 to 20 percent). Part of this behavior stems from the fact that energy costs for most industries represent only a small portion of overall expenses. Hence, the reliability of energy supplies is often more critical than energy costs. For the United States, there is little empirical basis to assess investment behavior for substantially higher energy prices than those now prevalent (e.g., electricity prices 2 to 3 times higher).

An estimate of the electricity conservation potential of the overall U.S. manufacturing sector has been developed by Ross (1990a), based on an aggregation of results for aluminum production, fabrication/assembly processes, and other selected process industries, and assuming a capital recovery rate of 33 percent. Figures D.1 to D.3 show the electricity conservation supply curves first developed for individual manufacturing industries. The curve for fabrication and assembly (Figure D.1), developed from studies of the automobile industry, was assumed to apply to a number of other industry groups as well. The results from Figures D.1 to D.3 were then combined by using energy weights based on 1985 electricity consumption (i.e., 1260, 190, and 768 $\times$ 10^{12} Btu for process industries, aluminum, and fabrication/assembly, respectively (Ross, 1990b)). This yielded the overall manufacturing sector curve shown in Figure D.4.

The curve in Figure D.4 can also be transformed into a cost-effectiveness curve for CO_2 reductions similar to those presented in Chapter 21 for residential and commercial buildings. The electricity savings percentages on the x-axis are first converted to kilowatt-hours by employing the total 1985 manufacturing electricity use of 653 billion kilowatt-hours (BkWh) (which was the basis for the estimates of Ross). Current (1989) electricity use is

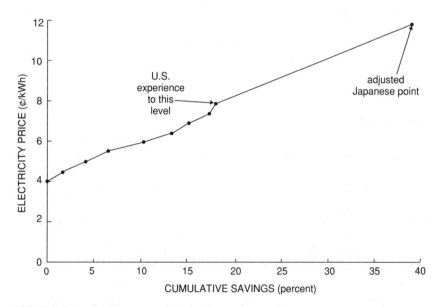

FIGURE D.1   Supply curve: Fabrication and assembly.

Source: Ross (1990b).

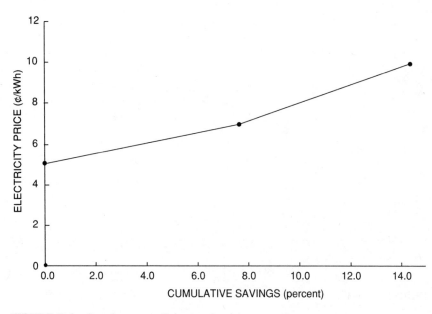

FIGURE D.2   Supply curve: Primary aluminum.

SOURCE: Ross (1990b).

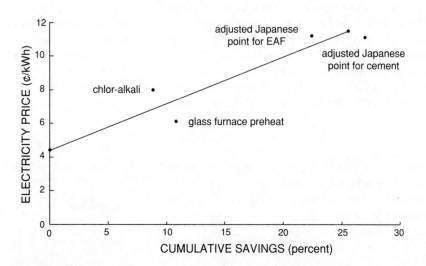

FIGURE D.3   Supply curve: Process industries excluding aluminum.

SOURCE: Ross (1990b).

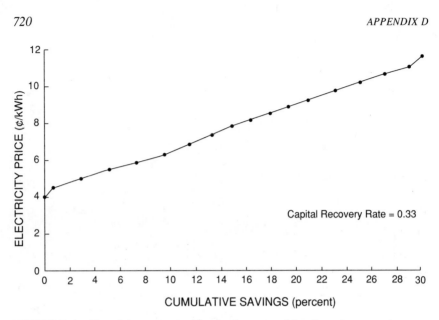

FIGURE D.4   Electricity conservation supply curve: Manufacturing.

SOURCE: Ross (1990a).

roughly comparable in magnitude.   Then, a utility fuel mix must be assumed to convert kilowatt-hours (on both axes) to equivalent CO_2 emissions. Figure D.5 shows the results based on the current U.S. average fuel
mix and carbon content for electricity production (equivalent to 0.7 g CO_2
per kilowatt-hour consumed, as derived in Chapter 21). By using Ross's
original curve for a 33 percent capital recovery factor (which corresponds
to a discount rate of 30 percent over a 10-year project life), curves for real
discount rates of 3, 6, and 10 percent were also developed, based on a 10-
year project life. The capital recovery factors (CRFs) for these three discount rates are 0.117, 0.136, and 0.163, as found from the expression

$$CRF = \frac{d}{1-(1+d)^{-n}} \, ,$$

where d is the discount rate and n is the project life. Because annual
operating and maintenance cost savings are negligible in Ross's cost curve,
the results for a 33 percent CRF can be adjusted to other values by simple
proportion:

$$p_2 = p_1 \frac{(CRF)_2}{(CRF)_1} \, ,$$

where p_1 and p_2 are the equivalent electricity prices of the annualized capital investment.

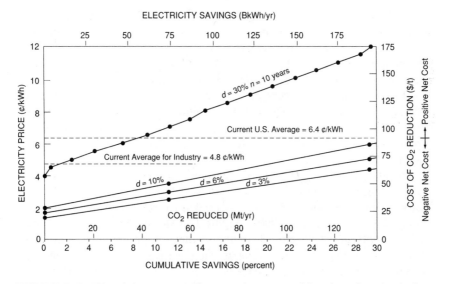

FIGURE D.5 Electricity conservation supply curve: Manufacturing (excluding energy management and co-generation).

As discussed earlier for the buildings sector, the discount rates of 3, 6, and 10 percent do not reflect actual consumer practice. Rather, they are intended to indicate what might be possible if government policies could induce action at these effective rates of return. Thus the maximum electricity savings of 30 percent (200 BkWh) reduces CO_2 emissions by about 140 megatons (Mt) at an average cost of about $175/t CO_2 at a 30 percent discount rate, $85/t at a 10 percent discount rate, and about $60/t at 3 percent.[1]

Offsetting this cost is the savings in electricity use. The value of this savings depends on the price of electricity. By following the method elaborated in Chapter 21, two electricity prices are used to estimate a net cost of CO_2 reduction. For the 30 percent discount rate, reflecting actual industrial practice, the current average price of electricity for the industrial sector (4.8 cents/kWh) is used to reflect typical savings to industry. For the lower discount rates, reflecting a societal perspective, the average U.S. electricity price of 6.4 cents/kWh is used to estimate savings. As discussed in Chapters 21 and 22, the current average electricity prices are implicitly taken to be a long-run marginal cost of supply. To the extent that actual marginal costs are higher in the future, the current estimates of net cost are conservative.

For the maximum electricity savings of 200 BkWh, Figure D.5 shows a net negative cost for the 3, 6, and 10 percent discount rates of –$30, –$20, and $-\$7/t$ CO_2, respectively. For example, at a 6 percent rate of return, the cost of conservation is equivalent to 5 cents/kWh, but the value of electricity saved is 6.4 cents/kWh, leading to a net savings of -1.4 cents/kWh. Dividing by the fuel mix factor of 0.7 kg CO_2/kWh and then adjusting units yield the net savings of $-\$20/t$ CO_2. Similarly, a net positive cost of $\$106/$ t is found for the 30 percent discount rate, based on an actual electricity cost of 4.8 cents/kWh for the industrial sector. Note that significant uncertainty still surrounds all these estimates and that a more refined analysis would also have to consider the fuel mix on a regional basis, as noted in Chapter 22.

The electricity savings and costs derived from Ross (1990a) are comparable to those reported by the Electric Power Research Institute (EPRI) in a study of the maximum technical potential for electricity savings (Electric Power Research Institute, 1990). Figure D.6 shows the composite conservation supply curve developed for the residential, commercial, and industrial sectors. For industry, a maximum electrical savings of about 277 BkWh was estimated for the year 2000, corresponding to 24 to 38 percent of projected industrial electricity use, depending on the assumed growth rate. The technologies considered in the EPRI analysis were largely the same as those considered by Ross: adjustable speed drives for electric motors, high-efficiency motors, waste heat recovery including recouperators, diaphragm and membrane cells in chlor-alkali production, more efficient electrolytic cells in aluminum reduction, and more efficient lighting technologies (Barakat and Chamberlin, Inc., 1990).

Figure D.6 shows the average cost of the energy conservation measures to be about 3 cents/kWh for a 5 percent real rate of return. This is similar to the costs shown in Figure D.5 at a comparable rate of return. Again, however, it must be stressed that significant barriers remain to actually achieving the magnitude of savings suggested by Figures D.5 and D.6.

CO-GENERATION

Rough estimates of the cost and CO_2 reduction potential from increased use of co-generation in the industrial sector are derived based on the assumptions in Table D.1. This approach takes the societal perspective discussed earlier, and reflected in the Chapter 29 results using a 6 percent real discount rate. Thus the fuel savings and investment cost of co-generation are evaluated relative to a reference case where steam and electricity are generated separately using natural gas.

Using the data in Table D.1, the annualized capital cost is $\$87.2$/kW-yr and the levelized annual fuel savings is $\$140.9$/kW-yr, yielding a net cost of $-\$53.7$/kW-yr. With no fuel cost escalation the net cost is $-\$11.4$/kW-yr. The corresponding range of CO_2 reduction costs (based on the carbon con-

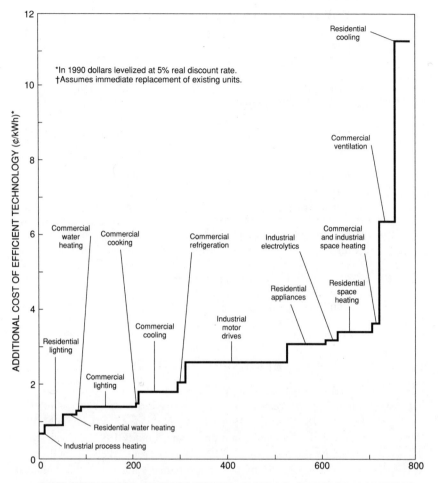

FIGURE D.6   The cost of saving.

SOURCE: Electric Power Research Institute (1990).

tent of natural gas) is –$30 to –$6/t CO_2.   Based on an incremental co-generation capacity of 25,000 MW, the total fuel energy savings would be approximately 0.82 quads.   For natural gas the corresponding overall CO_2 reduction would be 45 Mt.   To the extent that oil rather than gas is the fuel backed out in some co-generation applications, the corresponding CO_2 reduction would be somewhat greater.

TABLE D.1   Assumptions for Co-generation Analysis[a]

Parameter	Value
Energy source	Natural gas
Base case efficiency	10,500 Btu/kWh
Co-generation efficiency	5,500 Btu/kWh
Capital investment	$1000/kW
Current fuel price	$3.00/M Btu
Fuel price escalation	4%/yr (real)[b]
Plant capacity factor	75%
Plant lifetime	20 years
Real discount rate	6%[c]
Total new capacity	25,000 MW

[a]Representative values are based on information from the following sources: California Energy Commission (1990), U.S. Department of Energy (1984), Electric Power Research Institute (1989), Larson and Williams (1985), and RCG (1991).
[b]The 20-year levelization factor is 1.43.
[c]The 20-year capital recovery factor is 0.0872.

OTHER ENERGY SAVINGS

Industrial fuel savings from improvements to current process operations are estimated using the results of three case studies of energy-intensive industries (Ross, 1987; Larsen, 1990; K. C. Nelson, Dow Chemical USA, Plaquemine, Louisiana, personal communication, January 1991). These studies are used to estimate the net cost of achieving different levels of total energy savings.   In the absence of more comprehensive data for the industrial sector, rough estimates of the overall CO_2 reduction potential for the industrial sector are obtained by applying these results to current (1989) CO_2 emission.

1. *Steel Mill (Ross, 1987)*.   From Figure 22.9a (Chapter 22), the most costly project has an incremental cost of $14/t-yr and an energy savings of 3 percent. The reported total specific energy for this plant is 31 MBtu/t; so the energy savings is 0.93 MBtu/t.   Assuming a project life of 10 years and a discount rate of 6 percent (CRF = 0.136),   the project investment cost is $2.05/MBtu saved.   Escalating this cost from 1982 dollars to the present gives a cost of approximately $2.60/MBtu for a 25 percent energy savings. Similarly, using Figure 22.9b for a 15 percent savings, the cost is approximately $1.00/MBtu.

2. *Petroleum Refinery (Larsen, 1990)*.   Use Figure 22.9a and perform the same calculations as above.   The reported total specific energy for this plant

is approximately 1.0 MBtu/bbl. The cost of a 15 percent energy savings is then about $1.80/MBtu, and the cost of a 25 to 30 percent savings is $2.70/MBtu (assuming a 6 percent discount rate).

3. *Petrochemical Plant (Nelson, 1989, personal communication, 1991).* Use the data shown in Table 22.7 (Chapter 22). While no details of cost versus savings are available for specific projects, the data give a rough indication of the capital cost per unit of energy saved. For recent years an approximate figure is $1.25/MBtu assuming a 6 percent discount rate and a 5-year project life. Assume this investment cost applies to an overall energy savings in the neighborhood of 15 percent.

4. *Overall Summary.* Assume the results above apply generally to the industrial sector. Because actual discount rates used for industrial investments are substantially higher than the 6 percent value assumed here, many of the investments that are possible still have not been made (e.g., see Table 29.2 for costs at a 30 percent discount rate). To estimate net costs and CO_2 reductions, use the current fuel-weighted price of industrial energy of approximately $3.00/MBtu and the current total of 1150 Mt CO_2 from industrial fuel combustion (Edmonds and Ashton, 1989). For a 15 percent overall energy savings the average cost for the three cases above is $1.35/MBtu. The fuel-weighted average CO_2 emissions are 0.07 t/MBtu. This yields a net cost of –$24/t at an overall CO_2 reduction of 173 Mt/yr. If a real fuel price escalation were assumed, the net cost savings would be still greater.

For a 30 percent overall energy savings, extend the (nonlinear) steel plant data from 25 to 30 percent and average that cost with the refinery data (which shows a generally linear slope). The average investment cost is then about $3.05/MBtu. Use this as a rough estimate. The net cost is then 5 cents/MBtu, assuming no price escalation for the average fuel mix. This is equivalent to about $1/t CO_2 at an overall reduction level of 345 Mt. With fuel price escalation the net cost would be slightly negative for a 6 percent discount rate, indicating an overall savings from the energy efficiency investments.

NOTE

1. Throughout this report, tons (t) are metric; 1 Mt = megaton = 1 million tons.

REFERENCES

Ayres, R. U. 1990. Energy conservation in the industrial sector. In Energy and the Environment in the 21st Century: Proceedings of a Conference at Massachusetts Institute of Technology. Cambridge, Mass.: MIT Press.

Barakat and Chamberlin, Inc. 1990. Efficient Electricity Use: Estimates of Maximum Energy Savings. Report EPRI CU-6746. Prepared by Barakat and Chamberlin, Inc. for Electric Power Research Institute. Palo Alto, Calif.: Electric Power Research Institute.

California Energy Commission. 1990. Staff Testimony on qualifying Facilities/ Self-Generation Forecast. Docket No. 88-ER-8. Sacramento, Calif.: California Energy Commission.

Edmonds, J., and W. Ashton. 1989. A Preliminary Analysis of U.S. CO_2 Emissions Reduction Potential from Energy Conservation and the Substitution of Natural Gas for Coal in the Period to 2010. Report DOE/NBB-0085. Washington, D.C.: Office of Energy Research, U.S. Department of Energy.

Electric Power Research Institute. 1989. EPRI 1989 Technical Assessment Guide, Electricity Supply. Report EPRI P-6587-L. Palo Alto, Calif.: Electric Power Research Institute.

Electric Power Research Institute. 1990. New push for energy efficiency. EPRI Journal 15(3):4-17.

Larsen, W. G. 1990. Energy Conservation in Petroleum Refining. Ph.D. dissertation. University of Michigan, Ann Arbor.

Larson, E. D., and R. H. Williams. 1985. A Primer on the Thermodynamics and Economics of Steam-Injected Gas Turbine Cogeneration. Report PU/CEES 192. Princeton, N.J.: Princeton University.

Nelson, K. C. 1989. Are there any energy savings left? Chemical Processing (January).

RCG/Hagler, Bailly, Inc. 1991. Industrial Cogeneration Markets. RCG/Hagler, Bailly, Inc., Washington, D.C. January 29. Memorandum to E. Rubin, Carnegie-Mellon University.

Ross, M. 1987. Industrial energy conservation and the steel industry of the United States. Energy 12(10/11):1135-1152.

Ross, M. 1990a. Modeling the energy intensity and carbon dioxide emissions in U.S. manufacturing. In Energy and the Environment in the 21st Century: Proceedings of a Conference at Massachusetts Institute of Technology. Cambridge, Mass.: MIT Press.

Ross, M. 1990b. Conservation supply curves for manufacturing. In Proceedings of the 25th Intersociety Energy Conversion Engineering Conference. New York: American Institute of Chemical Engineers.

U.S. Department of Energy. 1984. Industrial Cogeneration Potential (1980-2000) for Application of Four Commercially Available Prime Movers at the Plant Site. Report DOE/CS/40403-1. Washington, D.C.: U.S. Department of Energy.

Appendix E

Conservation Supply Data for Three Transportation Sectors

This appendix provides information on the calculation method used to determine cost-effectiveness for three transportation sectors: light-duty vehicles, heavy trucks, and aircraft.

LIGHT-DUTY VEHICLES

Light-duty vehicle efficiencies were emphasized in Chapter 23 as the largest and most thoroughly studied transportation sector. Table E.1 shows the amount of fuel used by each type of vehicle for different modes of operation. As discussed in Chapter 23, the long trend to reduce operating costs via technology improvements while maintaining or improving other vehicle attributes is shown in Figure 23.1b. The fuel economy index (FEI), the product of vehicle mass and fuel economy in miles per gallon, controls for the fact that vehicle mass increased throughout the interval shown on the left-hand side of Figure 23.1b. This parameter, used to judge passenger cars for many decades, is a better indicator of powertrain efficiency than fuel economy alone. In the last decade the trend in the FEI, having the same units but measured at a differently specified test condition, is shown increasing at a similar rate. The recent trend was maintained, however, in a period of decreasing car mass and changing market demands for increased performance.

Research on the knocking properties of fuel in 1913 by Ricardo and later by Kettering provided the basis for many of the gains through 1970 (Amann, 1989). In recent times, applications of new computer technology to engine control, and applications of refined design techniques and new materials for weight reduction, have led to improved fuel economy (see Table E.2).

As the hedonic models of Atkinson and Halvorsen (1984, 1990) show,

TABLE E.1   Transportation Energy Use by Mode, 1987

	Energy Use (trillion Btu)	Thousand Barrels per Day Crude Oil Equivalent[a]	Percentage of Total
Highway[b]	16,213.5	7,658.1	73.6
Automobiles	8,862.9	4,186.2	40.3
Motorcycles	24.6	11.6	0.1
Buses	156.8	74.1	0.7
Transit	74.3	35.1	0.3
Intercity	21.6	10.22	—[c]
School	60.9	8.8	0.3
Trucks	7,169.2	3,386.2	32.6
Light trucks[d]	4,031.9	1,904.4	18.3
Other trucks	3,137.3	1,481.8	14.2
Off-Highway[b] (heavy duty)[e]	665.2	314.2	3.0
Construction	209.9	99.1	1.0
Farming	455.3	215.1	2.1
Nonhighway[b]	4,490.6	2,121.0	20.4
Air	1,893.9	894.5	8.6
General aviation[f]	139.1	65.7	0.6
Domestic air carriers	1,564.2	738.8	7.1
International air carriers	190.6[g]	90.0	0.9
Water	1,326.0	626.3	6.0
Freight	1,095.7	517.5	5.0
Domestic trade	370.7	175.1	1.7
Foreign trade	725.0	342.4	3.3
Recreational boats	230.3	108.8	1.0
Pipeline	775.0	366.1	3.5
Natural gas	562.9	265.9	2.6
Crude petroleum	91.0	43.0	0.4
Petroleum product	67.4	31.8	0.3
Coal slurry	3.7	1.7	—[c]
Water	50.0	23.6	0.2

(Table E.1 continues)

consumers choose vehicles as a bundle of attributes that include style, comfort, performance, safety, fuel economy, and price. By definition, externalities associated with pollution and some safety issues are not a component of this bundle. Atkinson and Halvorsen calculate the demand elasticities for the attribute of personal safety, however, and their estimate of the revealed preference for this attribute provides a value of life ranging between $2.4

TABLE E.1 *(continued)*

	Energy Use (trillion Btu)	Thousand Barrels per Day Crude Oil Equivalent[a]	Percentage of Total
Nonhighway—continued			
Rail	495.7	234.1	2.2
Freight[h]	471.9	197.4	1.9
Passenger	77.8	36.7	0.3
Transit	41.0	19.4	0.2
Commuter rail	21.4	10.1	—[c]
Intercity	15.4	7.3	—[c]
Military Operations	647.3	305.7	2.9
TOTAL[i]	22,016.6	10,399.0	100.0

[a]Based on British thermal unit (Btu) content of a barrel of crude oil.
[b]Civilian consumption only; military consumption shown separately.
[c]Negligible.
[d]Two-axle, four-tire trucks.
[e]1985 data.
[f]All aircraft in the U.S. civil air fleet except those operated under CFR parts 121 and 127 (i.e., air carriers larger than 30 seats or having a payload capacity of more than 7500 pounds). General aviation includes air taxis, commuter air carriers, and air travel clubs.
[g]This figure represents an estimate of the energy purchase in the United States for international air carrier consumption.
[h]Includes Class 1, 2, and 3 railroads.
[i]Totals may not include all possible uses of fuels for transportation (e.g., snowmobiles).

SOURCE: Davis et al. (1989).

million and $6 million. Similarly, their results indicate that a significant number of consumers place a great value on performance.

Safety and performance are directly related to the mass and power of a vehicle, and fuel economy is inversely related to these variables. Although the literature on fuel economy (Bleviss, 1988) identifies vehicles having good performance (11 seconds, 0 to 60 mph) and exceptional fuel economy (81 highway miles or 63 city miles per gallon (mpg)), these prototypes are not subject to price or production constraints. Given a price constraint and the laws of physics, the consumer is forced to trade off desired attributes against one another.

TABLE E.2 Comparison of Vehicle Fuel Economy Technology Estimates

Technology	Office of Technology Assessment Fuel Economy Gain (percent)[a]	Domestic Industry Fuel Economy Gain (percent)[a]	Shackson and Leach Fuel Economy Gain (percent)[b]
Front wheel drive	12.0		5.0
Drivetrain efficiency		Nil	
Package weight (1 TWC)		2.0	3.5
Four-cylinder/four-valve	7.5	3.7	Not considered
Four- or five-speed automatic CVT	7.5	3.4	15.0
Electronic transmission control	1.5	0.2	Not considered
Aerodynamics	3.4	3.0	6.0
Tires	0.5	0.5	2.0
Accessories	1.0	1.0	6.0
Engine improvements			
Overhead camshaft	6.0	1.1	
Roller cams	1.5	2.2	
Low-friction rings/pistons	1.5	1.5	7.0
Throttle body fuel injection (over carburetor)	3.0	2.4	
Multiport fuel injection (over TBI)	7.0	1.3	
Technologies proposed in Shackson and Leach study now implemented			
Lubricants			2.0
Design parameters	NA	NA	5.0
Manual transmission improvements			5.0
Material substitutions			13.0

NOTE: TWC = test weight class; NA = not applicable; CVT = continuously variable transmission; TBI = throttle body injection.

[a]Berger et al. (1990).
[b]Shackson and Leach (1980).

When forecasting cost-effective greenhouse gas reductions for future years, several uncertainties should be recognized. Figure E.1 makes clear that, given consumer preferences, the relative sizes of the automobile and light-duty truck markets are highly interactive and there has been a tendency to shift toward less efficient light-duty trucks. In addition, the number of person-miles traveled by each sector depends strongly on fuel price and other product attributes. On-road fuel economies are typically lower than those predicted by the EPA (Environmental Protection Agency) fuel economy test procedure as they depend on differences in highway speed, congestion, urban-rural travel mix, and average trip length. To provide a generous estimate of greenhouse gas reductions, a relatively low composite fuel economy baseline of 19.7 mpg will be used for the combined fleet of automobiles and light-duty trucks. Travel projections from the MOBILE3 Emission Model for the year 2000 were used (the MOBILE3 model is an emissions planning document that has been used by EPA to project vehicle miles traveled, emission levels, and grams per mile).

The CO_2 emitted from the tailpipe of a vehicle must be adjusted for three additional global impacts. The first is the fact that other greenhouse gases such as CH_4 and N_2O often accompany CO_2 emissions from the transportation sector. In addition, the processing and transportation of these fuels introduce greenhouse gases into the atmosphere.

In the case of gasoline, for every 311 g of CO_2 emitted, approximately 78 g of CO_2 equivalent is emitted as CH_4 and 38 g as N_2O. In addition,

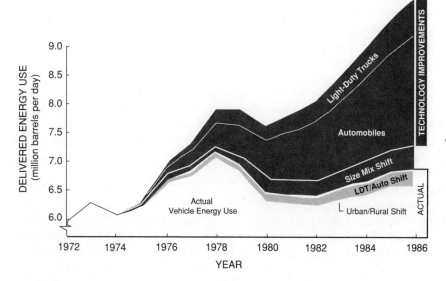

FIGURE E.1 Components of change in light-duty vehicles.

CO_2 emissions and venting during the processing and distribution of gasoline bring the total greenhouse gas emissions to between 455 and 507 g CO_2 equivalent (see Tables 3 and 6 of Unnasch et al., 1989). The CO_2 emission values in each table provided in this appendix are therefore multiplied by 1.55 to obtain CO_2 equivalence for both the cost-effectiveness and the emission reduction axis in each figure.

Ten years ago, a fuel economy technology plan for automobiles and light-duty trucks was designed by the Energy Productivity Center of the Mellon Institute. The data from this study have been used in the calculations summarized in Table E.3 (Shackson and Leach, 1980) and plotted in Figure E.2 using the least-cost supply curve framework proposed by the Lawrence Berkeley Laboratory (Wright et al., 1981).

For each technology, an estimate of consumer purchase cost in 1990 dollars was used as the numerator in the cost-effectiveness ratio. Reductions in fuel consumption produced by each technology were used to estimate the corresponding 10-year benefit stream for the denominator (i.e., reduced greenhouse gas emissions in tons of CO_2 equivalent).[1] Because the benefit stream is directly proportional to vehicle usage, which falls rapidly with age, it is appropriate to discount the benefit terms for each interval between the time of purchase and the time benefits are realized. The effect of discounting is to depreciate future benefits and thereby raise the calculated cost-effectiveness values. For the cost-effectiveness calculations in this study, the CO_2-equivalent emissions avoided were discounted at 3, 6, 10, and 30 percent, and were used in plotting the four curves in Figure E.2. The discount rates of 3, 6, and 10 percent represent a societal perspective, while 30 percent is closer to the discount rate chosen by a consumer when selecting a vehicle.

Because the technologies save fuel, the cost-effectiveness values were credited with $1.00/gal for discount rates of 3, 6, and 10 percent and $1.25/gal for the 30 percent rate—hence the negative values on the conservation supply curves.

The horizontal axis in Figure E.2 represents an estimate of the cumulative annual reductions in greenhouse gas emissions as though each device were employed in the 1989 fleet. These quantities were not discounted (see Table E.3). The 24 technologies analyzed by Shackson and Leach are ordered by their cost-effectiveness in Table E.3—hence the monotonic increase in the curve in Figure E.2.

As mentioned above, many of these most cost-efficient technologies were introduced, in part, during the 1975 to 1982 vehicle production era. The most expensive were not offered on the market by the industry. As the industry moved along the learning curve throughout the decade, old technologies became available at lower cost, and as the cost of fuel increased, new technologies became attractive to the consumer. Furthermore, these

TABLE E.3 Automobile and Light Truck Data (Shackson and Leach, 1980)

Technology[a]	Efficiency Gain (%)	Cost to Consumer (1979 $)	Cost to Consumer (1990 $)	Cost Effectiveness ($/%)	Penetration (%)	Cumulative Improvement (%)	Cumulative Cost (1990 $)	Fleet Fuel Economy (mpg)
1 Weight Reduction	3.50	0.00	0.000	0.000	100.00	3.50	0.00	20.39
2 Aerodynamic Design	4.00	0.00	0.000	0.000	100.00	7.50	0.00	21.18
3 Lubrication	2.00	10.00	17.906	8.953	100.00	9.50	17.91	21.57
4 Access. Ld.	6.00	50.00	89.532	14.922	100.00	15.50	107.44	22.75
5 Red. Roll.	2.00	20.00	35.813	17.906	100.00	17.50	143.25	23.15
6 Impr. Man.	5.00	50.00	89.532	17.906	10.00	18.00	152.20	23.25
7 Front Wheel Drive	5.00	50.00	89.532	17.906	80.00	22.00	223.83	24.03
8 Des. Param.	5.00	50.00	89.532	17.906	70.00	25.50	286.50	24.72
9 TorqLoc.	5.00	60.00	107.438	21.488	40.00	27.50	329.48	25.12
10 Aero. Adds.	2.00	30.00	53.719	26.860	60.00	28.70	361.71	25.35
11 Eng. Des.	5.00	75.00	134.298	26.860	20.00	29.70	388.57	25.55
12 Material Substitution	1.50	25.00	44.766	29.844	100.00	31.20	433.33	25.85
13 4Sp. Auto.	10.00	190.00	340.220	34.022	90.00	40.20	739.53	27.62
14 Material Substitution	8.00	200.00	358.127	44.766	100.00	48.20	1,097.66	29.20
15 Material Substitution	3.50	100.00	179.063	51.161	100.00	51.70	1,276.72	29.88
16 DISC	20.00	600.00	1,074.380	53.719	15.00	54.70	1,437.88	30.48
17 Engine Design	5.00	160.00	286.501	57.300	100.00	59.70	1,724.38	31.46
18 Vehicle Downsizing	12.00	400.00	716.253	59.688	100.00	71.70	2,440.63	33.82
19 Oper. Par.	5.00	175.00	313.361	62.672	100.00	76.70	2,753.99	34.81
20 Vehicle Downsizing	4.00	400.00	716.253	179.063	100.00	80.70	3,470.25	35.60
21 Turbocharging	5.00	650.00	1,163.912	232.782	32.00	82.30	3,842.70	35.91

(Table E.3 continues)

733

TABLE E.3 *(continued)*

Technology[a]	Annual Fuel Savings (million gallons)	Annual Savings (Million Tons CO$_2$ Equivalent)	3% (Marginal Tons CO$_2$ Equivalent)	3% ($/ton CO$_2$ Equivalent) $1.00 credit	6% (Marginal Tons CO$_2$ Equivalent)	6% ($/ton CO$_2$ Equivalent) $1.00 credit	10% (Marginal Tons CO$_2$ Equivalent)
1 Weight Reduction	3,243.08	44.99	2.20	−72.08	1.94	−72.08	1.67
2 Aerodynamic Design	6,690.87	92.82	2.34	−72.08	2.06	−72.08	1.77
3 Lubrication	8,320.31	115.42	1.11	−55.88	0.98	−53.73	0.84
4 Access. Ld.	12,870.04	178.54	3.09	−43.07	2.72	−39.21	2.34
5 Red. Roll.	14,283.36	198.15	0.96	−34.73	0.85	−29.76	0.73
6 Impr. Man.	14,629.20	202.94	0.23	−33.92	0.21	−28.84	0.18
7 Front Wheel Drive	17,293.90	239.91	1.81	−32.46	1.60	−27.18	1.37
8 Des. Param.	19,486.17	270.32	1.49	−29.94	1.31	−24.33	1.13
9 TorqLoc.	20,684.86	286.95	0.81	−19.23	0.72	−12.20	0.62
10 Aero. Adds.	21,386.19	296.68	0.48	−4.33	0.42	4.68	0.36
11 Eng. Des.	21,960.72	304.65	0.39	−3.17	0.34	6.01	0.30
12 Material Substitution	22,806.09	316.38	0.57	5.98	0.51	16.37	0.43
13 4Sp. Auto.	27,498.45	381.47	3.18	24.11	2.81	36.92	2.41
14 Material Substitution	31,190.97	432.70	2.50	70.89	2.21	89.92	1.90
15 Material Substitution	32,683.99	453.41	1.01	104.72	0.89	128.26	0.77
16 DISC	33,909.95	470.42	0.83	121.70	0.73	147.50	0.63
17 Engine Design	35,850.85	497.34	1.32	145.52	1.16	174.49	1.00
18 Vehicle Downsizing	40,047.83	555.56	2.85	179.50	2.51	212.99	2.16
19 Oper. Par.	41,628.32	577.49	1.07	220.20	0.95	259.10	0.81
20 Vehicle Downsizing	42,829.74	594.16	0.81	806.78	0.72	923.77	0.62
21 Turbocharging	43,295.55	600.62	0.32	1,106.65	0.28	1,263.55	0.24

TABLE E.3 *(continued)*

Technology[a]	10% ($/ton CO$_2$ Equivalent) $1.00 credit	30% (Marginal Tons CO$_2$ Equivalent)	30% ($/ton CO$_2$ Equivalent) $1.25 credit	6% Equivalent Fuel Cost ($/gallon)	30% Equivalent Fuel Cost ($/gallon)
1 Weight Reduction	−72.08	0.49	−90.10	0.00	0.00
2 Aerodynamic Design	−72.08	0.52	−90.10	0.00	0.00
3 Lubrication	−50.70	0.25	−17.31	0.16	0.65
4 Access. Ld.	−33.79	0.69	40.24	0.29	1.17
5 Red. Roll.	−22.77	0.21	77.74	0.38	1.50
6 Impr. Man.	−21.70	0.05	81.38	0.39	1.53
7 Front Wheel Drive	−19.77	0.40	87.94	0.40	1.59
8 Des. Param.	−16.45	0.33	99.26	0.43	1.69
9 TorqLoc.	−2.31	0.18	147.38	0.54	2.13
10 Aero. Adds.	17.35	0.11	214.32	0.69	2.72
11 Eng. Des.	18.90	0.09	219.57	0.70	2.77
12 Material Substitution	30.97	0.13	260.66	0.79	3.14
13 4Sp. Auto.	54.91	0.71	342.14	0.98	3.87
14 Material Substitution	116.66	0.56	552.33	1.45	5.75
15 Material Substitution	161.32	0.23	704.33	1.79	7.11
16 DISC	183.74	0.19	780.64	1.97	7.79
17 Engine Design	215.19	0.29	887.67	2.21	8.75
18 Vehicle Downsizing	260.04	0.63	1,040.34	2.55	10.12
19 Oper. Par.	313.77	0.24	1,223.21	2.96	11.75
20 Vehicle Downsizing	1,088.13	0.18	3,853.92	8.91	35.34
21 Turbocharging	1,484.00	0.07	5,206.33	11.95	47.40

(Table E.3 continues)

TABLE E.3 *(continued)*

NOTES: Cost in 1990 = Cost in 1979 × Consumer Price Index (1990)/CPI (1979) = 130/72.6 × D (cost to consumer in 1979).

Cumulative improvement = the sum of (penetrations × efficiency gains).

Cumulative cost = previous cost + new component cost × %penetration.

Fuel economy = (1 + %improvement) × 19.7.

Annual fuel savings = (1,889.28 billion miles traveled in 2000) × [(1/19.7) − (1/mpg)].

Tons of CO_2 equivalent avoided = 0.00895 × 1.55 × annual fuel savings.

At 3%, marginal tons of CO_2 equivalent for change in mpg = .00895 × 1.55 × ten years of vehicle miles traveled (discounted at 3%) × delta reciprocal mpg = .00895 × 1.55 × 92383 × ((1/mpg(i) − 1/mpg (i − 1)).

At 6%, marginal tons of CO_2 equivalent for change in mpg = .00895 × 1.55 × ten years of vehicle miles traveled (discounted at 6%) × delta reciprocal mpg = .00895 × 1.55 × 81530 × ((1/mpg(i) − 1/mpg(i − 1)).

At 10%, marginal tons of CO_2 equivalent for change in mpg = .00895 × 1.55 × ten years of vehicle miles traveled (discounted at 10%) × delta reciprocal mpg = .00895 × 1.55 × 69980 × ((1/mpg(i) − 1/mpg(i − 1)).

At 30%, marginal tons of CO_2 equivalent for change in mpg = .00895 × 1.55 × ten years of vehicle miles traveled (discounted at 30%) × delta reciprocal mpg = .00895 × 1.55 × 20560 × ((1/mpg(i) − 1/mpg(i − 1)).

Corresponding \$/ton of CO_2 = marginal cost/marginal tons of CO_2 equivalent − fuel credit @ \$1.00 per gallon = (change in cumulative cost/marginal tons of CO_2 equivalent) − 111.73/1.55.

[a]Access. Ld. = accessory load reduction; Red. Roll. = reduced rolling resistance; Impr. Man. = improved manual transmission; Des. Param. = engine design parameters; TorqLoc=torque converter lock-up; Aero. Adds = aerodynamic add-on equipment; Eng. Des. = engine design parameters; 4Sp. Auto. = four-speed automatic with torque converter lock-up; DISC = diesel and direct injected stratified charge engines; and Oper. Par. = engine operating parameters.

736

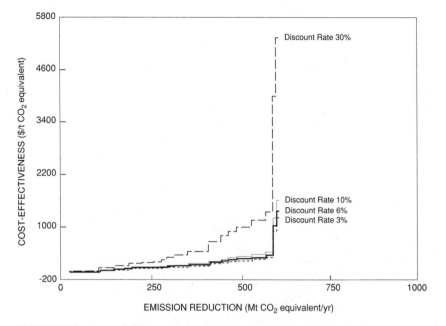

FIGURE E.2   Annual CO_2 reduction (Shackson and Leach (1980) analysis).

technologies became attractive to larger segments of the market and their penetration was increased.

Such a portfolio of technologies, similar to that proposed by Shackson and Leach, has been proposed by DOE (Difiglio et al., 1990). The bulk of the fuel economy gains proposed by DOE are achieved by introducing known technologies to most models in the fleet.

While cautioning the reader on the firmness of the benefits and costs of the DOE portfolio of technologies, Ledbetter and Ross (1989) have also used a supply curve framework for the analysis of these data. The conservation supply curve data (utilizing the cost and fuel economy values for 17 technologies in Table 5 of Ledbetter and Ross) have been used to generate the curve in Figure E.3 for the four different perspectives of this study (see Table E.4).

Comparison of the cost-effectiveness values in Figures E.2 and E.3 shows significant differences. The differences do not result as much from differences in the technology portfolios as from differences in the estimates of the costs and benefits of individual technologies. The disagreement between those who design and build cars and those who have generated the DOE data lies in the estimation, measurement, and aggregation of the fuel economy gain made possible by the technologies themselves when their

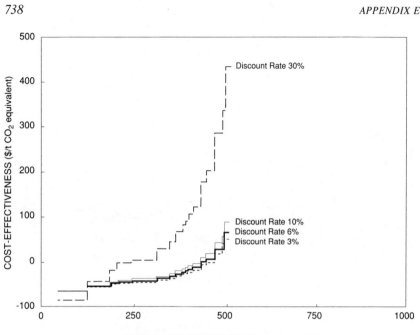

FIGURE E.3   Annual CO_2 reduction (Ledbetter and Ross (1989) analysis).

interactions are taken into account (see Berger et al., 1990). Industry analyses suggest that the potential for fuel economy improvement solely through
diffusion of existing technology is less than one-half that predicted by DOE
(see estimates of technology gains listed in Table E.2).

Specific differences in estimates for engine efficiencies are driven primarily by two factors. The first has to do with performance parameters chosen
by engineers doing the analysis. Although fuel economy at constant horsepower seems like a reasonable criterion for comparison, it turns out that
domestic consumers are more interested in vehicles that deliver torque at
low engine speed. The newer engines being proposed by DOE for introduction will deliver significant gains at constant horsepower; however, the
gains are diminished when compared at constant torque.

The second factor involving engines has to do with how technologies are
bundled and then labeled. While one technology at a time can produce a
gain of a certain magnitude, systems compound in a way that is not always
additive (Berger et al., 1990).

This phenomenon has been demonstrated for vehicles on the market in a
statistical analysis of EPA test data from virtually all of the cars in the
model year 1988 and 1989 fleets (Bussmann, 1989). The statistical study

TABLE E.4 Automobile and Light Truck Data, Department of Energy (Ledbetter and Ross, 1990)

Technology[a]	Efficiency Gain	Cost to Consumer (1987 $)	Cost to Consumer (1990 $)	Cost Effective ($/%)	Penetration (%)	Cumulative Improvement (%)	Cumulative Cost (1990 $)	Fleet Fuel Economy (mpg)
1 4V	6.80	0.00	0.00	0.00	100.00	6.80	0.00	21.04
2 Trans Man	10.00	40.00	45.77	4.58	75.00	14.30	34.33	22.52
3 AERO	4.60	27.00	30.90	6.72	85.00	18.21	60.59	23.29
4 RCF	1.50	11.00	12.59	8.39	37.00	18.77	65.25	23.40
5 Idle-off	11.00	80.00	91.55	8.32	75.00	27.02	133.91	25.02
6 IVC	10.00	80.00	91.55	9.15	75.00	34.52	202.58	26.50
7 Access	1.70	15.00	17.17	10.10	80.00	35.88	216.31	26.77
8 Adv. Fric.	4.00	40.00	45.77	11.44	80.00	39.08	252.93	27.40
9 CVT	4.70	50.00	57.22	12.17	45.00	41.19	278.68	27.81
10 Lub/Tire	1.00	11.00	12.59	12.59	100.00	42.19	291.26	28.01
11 TCLU	3.00	35.00	40.05	13.35	15.00	42.64	297.27	28.10
12 OHC	6.00	74.00	84.68	14.11	69.00	46.78	355.70	28.92
13 FWD	10.00	150.00	171.65	17.17	23.00	49.08	395.18	29.37
14 MPFI	3.50	56.00	64.08	18.31	56.00	51.04	431.07	29.75
15 Wt. Red.	6.60	130.00	148.77	22.54	85.00	56.65	557.52	30.86
16 5AOD	4.70	100.00	114.44	24.35	40.00	58.53	603.30	31.23
17 Tires II	0.50	13.00	14.88	29.75	36.00	58.71	608.65	31.27

(Table E.4 continues)

TABLE E.4 *(continued)*

Technology[a]	Annual Fuel Savings (million gallons)	Annual Savings (Million Tons CO_2 Equivalent)	3% (Marginal Tons CO_2 Equivalent)	3% ($/ton CO_2 Equivalent) $1.00 credit	6% (Marginal Tons CO_2 Equivalent)	6% ($/ton CO_2 Equivalent) $1.00 credit	10% (Marginal Tons CO_2 Equivalent)	10% ($/ton CO_2 Equivalent) $1.00 credit
1 4V	6,106.15	84.71	4.14	-72.08	3.66	-72.08	3.14	-72.08
2 Trans Man	11,998.31	166.45	4.00	-63.49	3.53	-62.35	3.03	-60.74
3 AERO	14,773.58	204.95	1.88	-58.13	1.66	-56.28	1.43	-53.67
4 RCF	15,152.71	210.21	0.26	-53.97	0.23	-51.56	0.19	-48.18
5 Idle-off	20,397.65	282.97	3.56	-52.79	3.14	-50.22	2.70	-46.61
6 IVC	24,607.49	341.37	2.86	-48.04	2.52	-44.84	2.16	-40.34
7 Access	25,321.09	351.27	0.48	-43.72	0.43	-39.94	0.37	-34.63
8 Adv. Fric.	26,945.11	373.80	1.10	-38.84	0.97	-34.42	0.83	-28.20
9 CVT	27,978.08	388.13	0.70	-35.34	0.62	-30.45	0.53	-23.57
10 Lub/Tire	28,455.79	394.75	0.32	-33.24	0.29	-28.07	0.25	-20.00
11 TCLU	28,668.57	397.70	0.14	-30.46	0.13	-24.92	0.11	-17.13
12 OHC	30,564.93	424.01	1.29	-26.66	1.14	-20.61	0.97	-12.12
13 FWD	31,572.96	438.00	0.68	-14.35	0.60	-6.66	0.52	4.14
14 MPFI	32,407.74	449.58	0.57	-8.71	0.50	-0.27	0.43	11.50
15 Wt. Red.	34,681.64	481.12	1.54	9.90	1.36	20.81	1.17	36.14
16 5AOD	35,407.66	491.19	0.49	20.86	0.43	33.23	0.37	50.62
17 Tires II	35,476.26	492.14	0.05	42.99	0.04	58.31	0.04	79.83

TABLE E.4 *(continued)*

Technology[a]	30% (Marginal Tons CO_2 Equivalent)	30% ($/ton CO_2 Equivalent) $1.25 credit	6% Equivalent Fuel Cost ($/gallon)	30% Equivalent Fuel Cost ($/gallon)
1 4V	0.92	−90.10	0.00	0.00
2 Trans Man	0.89	−51.51	0.35	0.09
3 AERO	0.42	−27.42	0.56	0.14
4 RCF	0.06	−8.73	0.73	0.18
5 Idle-off	0.79	−3.39	0.78	0.20
6 IVC	0.64	17.93	0.97	0.24
7 Access	0.11	37.36	1.14	0.29
8 Adv. Fric.	0.25	59.26	1.34	0.34
9 CVT	0.16	75.01	1.48	0.37
10 Lub/Tire	0.07	84.44	1.56	0.39
11 TCLU	0.03	96.92	1.67	0.42
12 OHC	0.29	113.99	1.83	0.46
13 FWD	0.15	169.33	2.32	0.59
14 MPFI	0.13	194.66	2.55	0.64
15 Wt. Red.	0.34	278.26	3.30	0.83
16 5AOD	0.11	327.53	3.74	0.94
17 Tires II	0.01	426.96	4.63	1.17

[a]4V = four valves per cylinder engines, Trans Man = aggressive transmission management (group 2 only), AERO = aerodynamic improvements, RCF = roller cam followers, Idle-off = idle off (group 2 only), IVC = intake valve control, Access = improved accessories, including electric power steering, Adv. Fric. = engine friction reduction, CVT = continuously variable transmission, Lub/Tire = improved lubrication and tires, TCLU = torque converter lockup (group 2 only), OHC = overhead cam engine, FWD = front wheel drive, MPFI = multi-point fuel injection, Wt. Red. = weight reduction, 5AOD = five-speed automatic overdrive transmission, Tires II = advanced tires (improvements beyond that included in LUB/T).

741

predicts a 5.4 percent fuel economy gain with technologies for which the Office of Technology Assessment and DOE predict a 17.3 percent gain. The major difference between these studies is that the 17.3 percent estimate is made by summing the gains from 12 efficiency technologies considered individually and the 5.4 percent estimate is made by a model that considers the system of these same technologies.

Other uncertainties in many parameter estimates lead to significant differences in the cost-effectiveness values in Figures E.2 and E.3. In addition to differing estimates for fuel economy gains, if one allows for technology interactions, differing estimates of consumer preferences and differing methods of allocating costs could underlie the observed uncertainties.

HEAVY-DUTY TRUCKS

Approximately 20 percent of the fuel expended on the U.S. highway system is utilized by heavy trucks and other heavy-duty vehicles, as indicated in Table E.1. The opportunities to conserve fuel and minimize emissions parallel those for light-duty vehicles and light-duty trucks. The method of analysis in this section parallels the methods used in the preceding section. Despite the fact that the data base for these vehicles is relatively meager, it will be possible to create conservation supply curves for three important categories of heavy vehicles.

In a study prepared for the Motor Vehicle Manufacturers Association by Energy and Environmental Analysis (1984), costs and efficiency gains for several technologies were presented for the categories "light-heavy," "medium-heavy," and "heavy-heavy," corresponding to Classes 2B-5, Classes 6-8A, and Class 8 heavy trucks. In most cases the fuel savings and the equipment costs were tabulated directly by analysts from Energy and Environmental Analysis. In others, the level of market penetration corresponding to a break-even mileage for a 2-year payback on the investment cost was provided. Because histograms of the fraction of vehicles traveling each mileage interval were also given for each category, it was possible to calculate the equipment cost using the formula:

$$\text{Fuel savings} = [\text{VMT} \times \text{FP}] \times [1 - (1/(1 + f))] \times [1/\text{FE0}]$$

where VMT = vehicle miles traveled, FP = fuel price, FE0 = base fuel economy before addition of a technology, and f = the fractional improvement in fuel economy. The results of this calculation and other data tabulated in the EEA analysis provide the basis for Tables E.5, E.6, and E.7.

The supply curves resulting from these calculations are presented in Figures E.4, E.5, and E.6. The panel has found no estimates to compare with this analysis for heavy trucks to demonstrate the uncertainties that surely underlie these results.

As is evident from these figures, the tons of CO_2 saved and the cost-effectiveness values vary dramatically for the three categories of trucks.

DOMESTIC AIR CARRIERS

The third most significant component of transportation energy use is domestic airlines, as indicated in Table E.1. The most advanced new jet aircraft are far more efficient than older aircraft still in service. Carlsmith et al. (1990) estimate that on a 1000-mile trip, aircraft produced in the 1960s are capable of between 40 and 50 seat-mpg, while the new Boeing 757 and 767 now in service have a fuel efficiency of 70 seat-mpg. Improvements now being introduced arise from a combination of higher by-pass ratio engines, increased compressor and turbine efficiencies, and more energy-efficient flight planning and operations. Like highway vehicles, aircraft can also benefit from weight reduction and better aerodynamics.

Although some estimate efficiencies approaching 130 to 150 seat-mpg from planned vehicles utilizing fanjets along with other new technologies, personal communication with a participant in that industry would attribute a 20 percent gain to the fanjet technology alone. This same source estimates that an approximately $20 billion investment will be necessary in research, development, training, tooling, and certification for retrofitting the existing fleet with new fanjet technology.

Component costs per vehicle are estimated at $8 million. If a return on investment of 15 percent for retrofitting half of the 4000 transport vehicles in the fleet with this technology, and a 20 percent fuel economy gain, are assumed, 0.016 Gt/yr per year of CO_2 reduction is possible at a cost of $300/t CO_2.

Again, the estimate is based on several unverified assumptions and extrapolations that call for great caution.

SUMMARY

Uncertainties dominate the content of much of this appendix. The first uncertainty is due to disagreements among technologists as to the costs and benefits likely to accrue from a portfolio of devices at various stages of development or implementation. This is revealed in the wide range of values in the conservation supply curves derived above from the Shackson and Leach (1980), Difiglio et al. (1990), and Ledbetter and Ross (1989) data sets.

The second uncertainty relates to disagreements among social scientists as to the relative impact of fuel prices and mandated fuel economy levels on the supply of fuel-efficient vehicles. This is revealed when comparing the results from econometric analyses by Godek (1990), Greene (1989), and

TABLE E.5 Light-Heavy Truck Data (Energy and Environmental Analysis, Inc., 1984)

Technology	Efficiency Gain	Cost to Consumer (1984 $)	Cost to Consumer (1990 $)	Cost-Effectiveness ($/%)	Penetration (%)	Cumulative Improvement (%)	Cumulative Cost (1990 $)	Fleet Fuel Economy (mpg)
1 Accsrys	1.00	10.00	12.51	12.51	100.00	1.00	12.51	12.52
2 Lubric.	1.50	15.00	18.77	12.51	100.00	2.50	31.28	12.71
3 Wt. Red. I	6.60	187.00	233.97	35.45	50.00	5.80	148.27	13.12
4 Wt. Red. II	6.60	187.00	233.97	35.45	50.00	9.10	265.26	13.53
5 ElecTrans	6.00	193.00	241.48	40.25	50.00	12.10	386.00	13.90
6 Radials	8.00	690.00	863.33	107.92	50.00	16.10	817.66	14.40
7 Aerody I	3.40	400.00	500.48	147.20	50.00	17.80	1,067.90	14.61
8 Aerody II	3.40	400.00	500.48	147.20	50.00	19.50	1,318.14	14.82

Technology	Annual Fuel Savings (million gallons)	Annual Savings (million tons CO_2 Equivalent)	3% (Marginal tons CO_2 Equivalent)	3% ($/ton CO_2 Equivalent) $1.00 credit	6% (Marginal tons CO_2 Equivalent)	6% ($/ton CO_2 Equivalent) $1.00 credit	10% (Marginal tons CO_2 Equivalent)	10% ($/ton CO_2 Equivalent) $1.00 credit
1 Accsrys	49.60	0.69	1.02	-59.86	0.90	-58.23	0.78	-55.94
2 Lubric.	122.19	1.70	1.50	-59.55	1.32	-57.88	1.13	-55.54
3 Wt. Red. I	274.63	3.81	3.15	-34.89	2.78	-29.94	2.38	-22.98
4 Wt. Red. II	417.86	5.80	2.95	-32.49	2.61	-27.22	2.24	-19.82
5 ElecTrans	540.74	7.50	2.54	-24.46	2.24	-18.12	1.92	-9.21
6 Radials	694.71	9.64	3.18	63.81	2.80	81.90	2.41	107.31
7 Aerody I	756.98	10.50	1.28	122.70	1.13	148.63	0.97	185.06
8 Aerody II	817.48	11.34	1.25	128.41	1.10	155.10	0.95	192.59

TABLE E.5 *(continued)*

Technology	30% (Marginal tons CO_2 Equivalent)	30% ($/ton CO_2 Equivalent) $1.25 credit
1 Accsrys	0.23	−35.16
2 Lubric.	0.33	−33.79
3 Wt. Red. I	0.70	77.03
4 Wt. Red. II	0.66	87.80
5 ElecTrans	0.56	123.89
6 Radials	0.71	520.51
7 Aerody I	0.29	785.14
8 Aerody II	0.28	810.77

NOTES: Baseline fuel economy – 12.4 mpg. All equations and notes the same as in Table E.3 except for the following:

Cost in 1990 – cost in 1984 × CPI (1990)/CPI(1984) – 130/103.9

Fleet fuel economy – 12.4 × (1 + cumulative improvement/100)

Fuel saved – (62120 million miles traveled in 2000) × (12.4 – 1/mpg), estimate for light trucks in Mobile 3

Marginal tons of CO_2 @ 3% – 92383 miles × .00895 × 1.55 × (1/mpg(i) – 1/mpg(i – 1))

Marginal tons of CO_2 @ 6% – 81530 miles × .00895 × 1.55 × (1/mpg(i) – 1/mpg(i – 1))

Marginal tons of CO_2 @ 10% – 69980 miles × .00895 × 1.55 × (1/mpg(i) – 1/mpg(i – 1))

Marginal tons of CO_2 @ 30% – 20560 miles × .00895 × 1.55 × (1/mpg(i) – 1/mpg(i – 1))

Truck data taken from Table 3-2 of Energy and Environmental Analysis (EEA) (1984). When cost-effectiveness data were not in the EEA report, the mileage at either 50% or 90% of the vehicles providing "cost-effectiveness" was used from the equation on page 3-1 of the EEA report. This "SAVINGS" was then considered at least as great as the cost of technology.

TABLE E.6 Medium–Heavy Truck Data (Energy and Environmental Analysis, Inc., 1984)

Technology	Efficiency Gain	Cost to Consumer (1979 $)	Cost to Consumer (1990 $)	Cost Effectiveness ($/%)	Penetration (%)	Cumulative Improvement (%)	Cumulative Cost (1990 $)	Fleet Fuel Economy (mpg)
1 FanDrive	4.00	142.00	177.67	44.42	100.00	4.00	177.67	9.98
2 Wt. Red.	4.00	142.00	177.67	44.42	100.00	8.00	355.34	10.37
3 BodyAero	4.00	142.00	177.67	44.42	100.00	12.00	533.01	10.75
4 Access.	2.00	72.20	90.34	45.17	100.00	14.00	623.35	10.94
5 Lubric.	1.50	55.20	69.07	46.04	100.00	15.50	692.42	11.09
6 AeroDev.	6.00	400.00	500.48	83.41	15.00	16.40	767.49	11.17
7 Adv.Rad	8.00	690.00	863.33	107.92	30.00	18.80	1,026.49	11.40
8 ShiftInd.	5.00	762.00	953.42	190.68	30.00	20.30	1,312.51	11.55
9 Spd.Cont.	6.00	1,360.00	1,701.64	283.61	15.00	21.20	1,567.76	11.64

Technology	Annual Fuel Savings (million gallons)	Annual Savings (million tons CO_2 Equivalent)	3% (Marginal tons CO_2 Equivalent)	3% ($/ton CO_2 Equivalent) $1.00 credit	6% (Marginal tons CO_2 Equivalent)	6% ($/ton CO_2 Equivalent) $1.00 credit	10% (Marginal tons CO_2 Equivalent)	10% ($/ton CO_2 Equivalent) $1.00 credit
1 FanDrive	186.58	2.59	10.27	-54.79	9.06	-52.48	7.78	-49.24
2 Wt. Red.	359.34	4.98	9.51	-53.40	8.39	-50.91	7.20	-47.42
3 BodyAero	519.75	7.21	8.83	-51.96	7.79	-49.28	6.69	-45.52
4 Access.	595.74	8.26	4.18	-50.48	3.69	-47.61	3.17	-43.57
5 Lubric.	651.01	9.03	3.04	-49.38	2.68	-46.35	2.30	-42.11
6 AeroDev.	683.48	9.48	1.79	-30.08	1.58	-24.49	1.35	-16.64
7 Adv.Rad	767.67	10.65	4.63	-16.19	4.09	-8.75	3.51	1.70
8 ShiftInd.	818.59	11.36	2.80	29.98	2.47	43.57	2.12	62.66
9 Spd.Cont.	848.53	11.77	1.65	82.79	1.45	103.41	1.25	132.37

TABLE E.6 (continued)

Technology	30% (Marginal tons CO_2 Equivalent)	30% ($/tons CO_2 Equivalent) $1.25 credit
1 FanDrive	2.29	-12.36
2 Wt. Red.	2.12	-6.14
3 BodyAero	1.96	0.31
4 Access.	0.93	6.95
5 Lubric.	0.68	11.92
6 AeroDev.	0.40	98.62
7 Adv.Rad	1.03	161.04
8 ShiftInd.	0.62	368.52
9 Spd.Cont.	0.37	605.80

NOTES: Baseline fuel economy = 9.6. All equations and notes the same as in Table E.3 except for the following:

Cost in 1990 = Cost in 1984 × CPI (1990)/CPI (1984) = 130/103.9

Fleet Fuel Economy = 9.6 (1 + Cumulative Improvement/100)

Fuel saved = (46570 million miles traveled in 2000) × (1/9.6 − 1/mpg), estimate for Medium truck in Mobile 3

Marginal tons of CO_2 @ 3% = 2 × 92383 miles × .00895 × 1.55 (1/mpg(i) − 1/mpg(i − 1))

Marginal tons of CO_2 @ 6% = 2 × 81530 miles × .00895 × 1.55 (1/mpg(i) − 1/mpg(i − 1))

Marginal tons of CO_2 @ 10% = 2 × 69980 miles × .00895 × 1.55 (1/mpg(i) − 1/mpg(i − 1))

Marginal tons of CO_2 @ 30% = 2 × 20560 miles × .00895 × 1.55 (1/mpg(i) − 1/mpg(i − 1))

Truck data taken from Table 3-2 of Energy and Environmental Analysis (EEA) (1984). When cost-effectiveness data were not in the EEA report, the mileage at either 50% or 90% of vehicles providing "cost-effectiveness" was used from the equation on page 3-1 of the EEA report. This "SAVINGS" was then considered at least as great as the cost of technology.

747

TABLE E.7 Heavy-Heavy Truck Data (Energy and Environmental Analysis, Inc., 1984)

Technology	Efficiency Gain	Cost to Consumer (1979 $)	Cost to Consumer (1990 $)	Cost Effectiveness ($/%)	Penetration (%)	Cumulative Improvement (%)	Cumulative Cost (1990 $)	Fleet Fuel Economy (mpg)
1 BodyAero	9.00	540.00	675.65	75.07	100.00	9.00	675.65	7.29
2 FanDrives	4.00	252.00	315.30	78.83	100.00	13.00	990.95	7.56
3 Drivetrn	3.00	190.00	237.73	79.24	100.00	16.00	1,228.68	7.76
4 Access.	2.00	128.00	160.15	80.08	100.00	18.00	1,388.84	7.89
5 Lubric.	1.50	97.00	121.37	80.91	100.00	19.50	1,510.20	7.99
6 AeroDev.	6.00	400.00	500.48	83.41	58.00	22.98	1,800.48	8.23
7 Radials	6.00	1,080.00	1,351.30	225.22	70.00	27.18	2,746.39	8.51
8 Spd. Cont.	5.00	1,335.00	1,670.36	334.07	50.00	29.68	3,581.57	8.68
9 Adv. Rad.	6.00	2,070.00	2,589.99	431.67	70.00	33.88	5,394.56	8.96

Technology	Annual Fuel Savings (million gallons)	Annual Savings (million tons CO_2 Equivalent)	3% (Marginal tons CO_2 Equivalent)	3% ($/ton CO_2 Equivalent) $1.00 credit	6% (Marginal tons CO_2 Equivalent)	6% ($/ton CO_2 Equivalent) $1.00 credit	10% (Marginal tons CO_2 Equivalent)	10% ($/ton CO_2 Equivalent) $1.00 credit
1 BodyAero	1,181.39	16.39	98.33	−65.21	83.76	−64.02	71.89	−62.69
2 FanDrives	1,646.04	22.83	38.68	−63.93	32.94	−62.51	28.28	−60.93
3 Drivetrn	1,973.51	27.38	27.26	−63.36	23.22	−61.84	19.93	−60.15
4 Access.	2,182.56	30.28	17.40	−62.88	14.82	−61.28	12.72	−59.49
5 Lubric.	2,334.77	32.39	12.67	−62.50	10.79	−60.84	9.26	−58.98
6 AeroDev.	2,673.57	37.09	28.20	−61.79	24.02	−60.00	20.62	−58.00
7 Radials	3,057.79	42.42	31.98	−42.51	27.24	−37.36	23.38	−31.63
8 Spd. Cont.	3,274.67	45.43	18.05	−25.82	15.38	−17.77	13.20	−8.80
9 Adv. Rad.	3,620.80	50.23	28.81	−9.15	24.54	1.80	21.06	13.99

TABLE E.7 *(continued)*

Technology	30% (Marginal tons CO_2 Equivalent)	30% ($/ton CO_2 Equivalent) $1.25 credit
1 BodyAero	21.12	−59.12
2 FanDrives	8.31	−52.15
3 Drivetrn	5.85	−49.50
4 Access.	3.74	−47.26
5 Lubric.	2.72	−45.50
6 AeroDev.	6.06	−42.18
7 Radials	6.87	47.60
8 Spd. Cont.	3.88	125.29
9 Adv. Rad.	6.19	202.87

NOTES: Average fuel economy = 6.69 mpg. All equations and notes the same as Table D.3 except for the following:

Cost in 1990 = Cost in 1984 × CPI (1990)/CPI(1984)−130/103.9

Fleet fuel economy = 6.69(1 + cumulative improvement/100)

Fuel saved = (95720 million miles traveled in 2000) × (1/6.69−1/mpg), estimate for heavy trucks in Mobile 3

Marginal Tons of CO_2 @ 3% = 6 × 92383 miles × .00895 × 1.55 × (1/mpg(i)−1/mpg(i−1))
Marginal Tons of CO_2 @ 6% = 6 × 81530 miles × .00895 × 1.55 × (1/mpg(i)−1/mpg(i−1))
Marginal Tons of CO_2 @ 10%= 6 × 69800 miles × .00895 × 1.55 × (1/mpg(i)−1/mpg(i−1))
Marginal Tons of CO_2 @ 30%= 6 × 20560 miles × .00895 × 1.55 × (1/mpg(i)−1/mpg(i−1))

Truck data taken from Table 3-1 of Environmental and Energy Analysis (EEA) (1984). When cost-effectiveness data were not in the EEA report, the mileage at either 50% or 90% of vehicles providing "cost-effectiveness" was used from the equation on page 3-1 of the EEA report. This "SAVINGS" was then considered at least as great as the cost of technology.

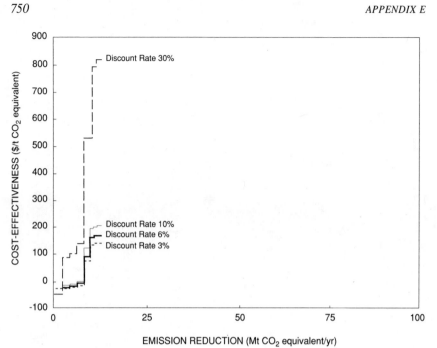

FIGURE E.4   Annual CO_2 reduction (light-heavy trucks).

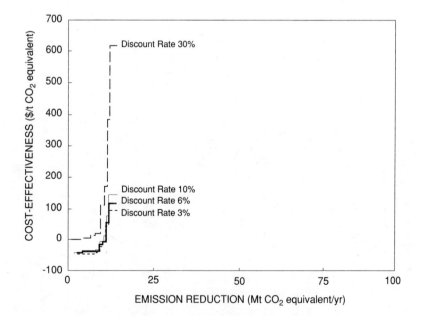

FIGURE E.5   Annual CO_2 reduction (medium-heavy trucks).

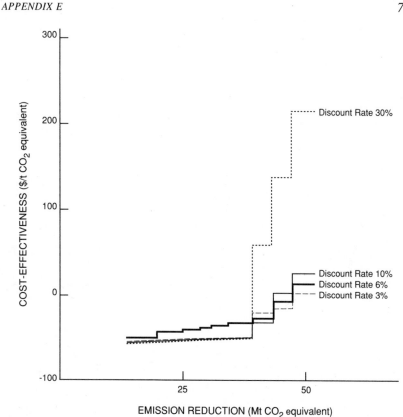

FIGURE E.6   Annual CO_2 reduction (heavy-heavy trucks).

Leone and Parkinson (1990), which differ on the relative importance of market and regulatory mechanisms.

Cross-sectional data sets for several nations are now emerging to provide additional insight into consumer preferences (see Schipper, 1991). Similarly, the wide range of values in the conservation supply curves based on the Shackson and Leach and the Ledbetter and Ross studies may well be reconciled with these emerging data. In light of these remaining uncertainties, it is interesting to examine the automobile and light truck conservation supply curves in the context of fuel prices and consumer preference for new car fuel economy.

To examine the interactions of consumer choice and technology, the panel has plotted conservation supply information in a format that allows a comparison with consumer decision making. Results from Tables E.3, E.4, and E.8 derived from Shackson and Leach (1980), Ledbetter and Ross (1989), and Difiglio et al. (1990), respectively, are plotted in Figure E.7. Values

TABLE E.8 A Supply Curve for Light-Duty Vehicles Fuel Economy Technologies (Difiglio et al., 1990)

Technology Options[a]	Cumulative Cost (1990 $)	Fleet Fuel Economy (mpg)	Annual Fuel Savings (million gallons)	Annual Savings (Million tons CO_2 Equivalent)	3% (Marginal tons CO_2 Equivalent)	3% ($/ton CO_2 Equivalent) $1.00 credit	6% (Marginal tons CO_2 Equivalent)	6% ($/ton CO_2 Equivalent) $1.00 credit
1	0.00	20.77	0.00		0.00	−72.08	0.00	−72.08
2	274.56	24.31	13,241.79	183.70	8.98	−41.52	7.93	−37.45
3	425.57	26.38	19,359.97	268.57	4.15	−35.70	3.66	−30.85
4	562.85	28.00	23,491.05	325.88	2.80	−23.10	2.47	−16.57
5	864.86	30.31	28,628.68	397.15	3.49	14.58	3.08	26.11
6	915.20	31.00	30,020.82	416.46	0.94	−18.78	0.83	−11.69
7	1,121.12	31.77	31,496.47	436.93	1.00	133.63	0.88	161.01
8	1,430.00	32.46	32,764.76	454.53	0.86	286.94	0.76	334.73
9	1,830.40	33.31	34,243.30	475.04	1.00	327.14	0.89	380.28
10	2,516.80	34.00	35,398.27	491.06	0.78	804.02	0.69	920.64
11	3,374.80	34.77	36,627.63	508.12	0.83	956.78	0.74	1,093.74
12	4,919.20	35.62	37,918.59	526.03	0.88	1,691.50	0.77	1,926.26

752

TABLE E.8 *(continued)*

Technology Options[a]	10% ($/ton CO_2 Equivalent) $1.00 credit	30% (Marginal tons CO_2 Equivalent)	30% ($/ton CO_2 Equivalent) $1.25 credit	6% Equivalent Fuel Cost ($/gallon)	30% Equivalent Fuel Cost ($/gallon)
1	−72.08	0.00		1.23	0.31
2	−31.73	2.00	65.26	1.46	0.37
3	−29.30	0.92	388.67	1.97	0.50
4	−25.45	0.62	830.41	3.49	0.88
5	−13.29	0.78	1,042.99	2.14	0.54
6	−12.76	0.21	4,282.57	8.27	2.09
7	−2.81	0.22	4,960.44	14.44	3.64
8	12.85	0.19	7,396.44	16.05	4.05
9	31.94	0.22	8,128.27	35.23	8.68
10	66.28	0.17	14,362.20	41.30	10.43
11	107.23	0.19	18,111.84	70.92	17.89
12	777.68	0.19	20,730.88		

NOTE: Average vehicle fuel economy = 27/1.3 mpg.

[a]Numbers represent combinations of fuel economy technologies phased in as shown in Table 1 and Figure 3 of Difiglio et al. (1990).

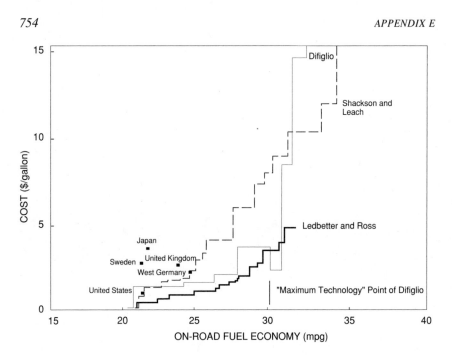

FIGURE E.7   Cost of gasoline and efficiency for a 30 percent discount rate.

for the average new-car fleet efficiencies, along with the average fuel prices for Japan, Sweden, the United Kingdom, the United States, and West Germany, are also plotted as squares on the same figure. The automobile fleet fuel economy values were reduced by a factor of 1.3 since increased urban congestion, higher highway speeds, and a larger fraction of total miles being driven in urban areas are projected to increase the difference between the EPA fuel economy test and actual on-road fuel economy from 15 percent in 1987 to 30 percent in 2010 (Ledbetter and Ross, 1990). Although Difiglio et al. (1990) estimated a 17 percent difference in the year 2000, their fuel economy values were also reduced by the factor 1.3 to be consistent with the other adjustments in Figure E.7. Since the Shackson and Leach (1980) supply curve was for a fleet that included light trucks, no adjustment was made to their base fuel economy of 19.7 mpg.

The perspective in Figure E.7 is that of a consumer expecting a 10-year benefit stream using a 30 percent discount rate on future benefits. If the consumers in these five nations had no preference between purchasing fuel economy technology and avoiding the cost of gasoline, they would choose a set of technologies on one of the three curves. If, on the other hand, consumers valued other attributes in their vehicles sacrificed by fuel economy technologies, they would choose a level of fuel economy lower (i.e., to the left) of the curve in Figure E.7.

If a 30 percent discount rate and a 10-year lifetime are valid assumptions, consumers in the United States and West Germany choose a level of fuel economy appropriate for their fuel prices, provided the Shackson and Leach curve is an accurate indication of the cost of technology. The fact that three other nations lie a significant distance from the steepest supply curve indicates either that their vehicle use patterns are dramatically different or that the technology cost-effectiveness information is inappropriate.

To summarize the relative magnitude of the values along with their uncertainties, a sample of average values from two different regions of two different analyses is presented below.

The discontinuity in the slope of the Difiglio curve at approximately 31 mpg (on-road fuel economy) is the point at which sales shifts in the vehicle mix are required to gain higher average fuel economy levels. Difiglio has labeled this point the "maximum technology" point for the year 2000.[2] The panel has chosen the region beyond this point as the region in which life-style adjustments are incurred. Up to this point, the costs of attributes lost or compromised by fuel efficiency technologies are ignored even though consumers consider them substantial.

The average cost-effectiveness values, as distinct from marginal cost-effectiveness values, which increase significantly as one moves past 25 mpg, are summarized in Table E.9 as a function of the discount rate for the three cost curves (see calculations in Tables E.3 through E.8). The costs are constrained, however, by the fact that the panel has not considered cumulative costs exceeding $3850 (1990 dollars) from the Shackson and Leach study, and Ledbetter and Ross did not go beyond cumulative costs of $609 (1990 dollars).

To provide a visual impression of the relative magnitudes and their uncertainties, Figure E.8 illustrates values derived for the discount rate of 6 percent for light duty vehicles. One should keep in mind that data for the automobile and light truck calculations were from three sources, thereby providing the indication of uncertainty.

NOTES

1. Throughout this report, tons (t) are metric; 1 Mt = 1 megaton = 1 million tons; 1 Gt = 1 gigaton = 1 billion tons.

2. Subsequent to the preparation of these results, K. G. Duleep (co-author with Difiglio and Green) has refined the estimate of the "maximum technology" point. Duleep estimates that in 1996 all available technologies could produce a CAFE mpg of 29.3 (22.5 on-road) and in 2001 all available technologies could produce a CAFE mpg of 36.0 (27.7 on-road) (Plotkin, 1991).

TABLE E.9 Implementation Cost of Vehicle Efficiency Improvements

	Net Implementation Cost ($/t CO_2 equivalent)				Emission Reduction (Mt CO_2 equivalent/yr)
	$d=3\%$	$d=6\%$	$d=10\%$	$d=30\%$	
NO CHANGE IN FLEET MIX					
Full-Cycle Emission Accounting					
Light vehicle, Ledbetter and Ross	−52	−50	−46	−2	379
Light vehicle, Shackson and Leach	−10	−1	+10	+191	389
Light vehicle, Difiglio	−26	−22	−13	+128	397
Heavy truck	−42	−38	−32	+45	61
Aircraft retrofit			+230		13
Consumption Emission Accounting					
Light vehicle, Ledbetter and Ross	−81	−78	−71	−3	245
Light vehicle, Shackson and Leach	−16	−2	+16	+296	251
Light vehicle, Difiglio	−40	−34	−20	+198	256
Heavy truck	−65	−59	−50	+70	39
Aircraft retrofit			+357		8
CHANGE IN FLEET MIX					
Full-Cycle Emission Accounting					
Light vehicle, Ledbetter and Ross	+13	+25	+41	+293	35
Light vehicle, Shackson and Leach	+306	+356	+427	+1,609	108
Light vehicle, Difiglio	+527	+657	+777	+2,820	129
Consumption Emission Accounting					
Light vehicle, Ledbetter and Ross	+20	+39	+64	+454	23
Light vehicle, Shackson and Leach	+474	+552	+663	+2,494	70
Light vehicle, Difiglio	+887	+1,018	+1,204	+4,370	83

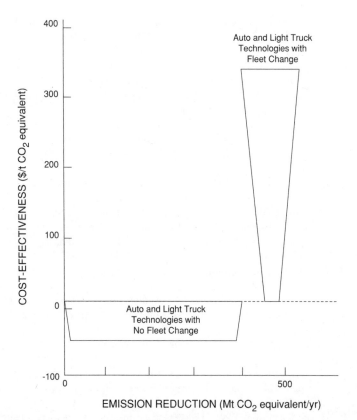

FIGURE E.8   Potential emission reduction from light-duty vehicles.

REFERENCES

Amann, C. A. 1989. The automotive spark-ignition engine—An historical perspective. In History of the Internal Combustion Engine, ICE, Volume 8, Book No. 100294-1989, E. F. C. Somerscales and A. A. Zagotta, eds. American Society of Mechanical Engineers.

Atkinson, S. E., and R. Halvorsen. 1984. A new hedonic technique for estimating attribute demand: An application to the demand for automobile fuel efficiency. Review of Economics and Statistics 66(3):416-426.

Atkinson, S. E., and R. Halvorsen. 1990. Valuation of risks to life: Evidence from the markets for automobiles. Review of Economics and Statistics 72(1):137-142.

Berger, J. O., M. H. Smith, and R. W. Andrews. 1990. A system for Estimating Fuel Economy Potential due to Technology Improvements. Ann Arbor, Mich: The University of Michigan, School of Business Administration.

Bleviss, D. 1988. The New Oil Crisis and Fuel Economy Technologies. New York: Quorum Books.

Bussmann, W. V. 1990. Potential Gains in Fuel Economy: A Statistical Analysis of Technologies Embodied in Model Year 1988 and 1989 Cars. Intra-Industry Analysis of Fuel Economy Efficiencies.

Carlsmith, R. S., W. U. Chandler, J. E. McMahon, and D. J. Santini. 1990. Energy Efficiency: How Far Can We Go? Report ORNL/TM-11441. Prepared for the Office of Policy, Planning and Analysis, U.S. Department of Energy. Oak Ridge, Tenn.: Oak Ridge National Laboratory.

Davis, S. C., D. B. Shonka, G. J. Anderson-Batiste, and P. S. Hu. 1989. Transportation Energy Data Book: Edition 10. Report ORNL-6565 (Edition 10 of ORNL-5198). Prepared for the U.S. Department of Energy. Oak Ridge, Tenn.: Oak Ridge National Laboratory.

Difiglio, C., K. G. Duleep, and D. L. Greene. 1990. Cost effectiveness of future fuel economy improvements. The Energy Journal 11(1):65-86.

Energy and Environmental Analysis (EEA). 1984. Documentation of market penetration forecasts. In Historical and Projected Emissions Conversion Factor and Fuel Economy for Heavy Duty Trucks, 1962-2002. Arlington, Va.: Energy and Environmental Analysis, Inc.

Godek, P. E. 1990. The Corporate Average Fuel Economy Standard 1978-1990. Working Paper, October 1990.

Greene, D. L. 1989. CAFE or Price?: An Analysis of the Effects of Federal Fuel Economy Regulations and Gasoline Price on New Car MPG, 1978-89. Prepared for the Office of Policy Integration, Office of Policy, Planning and Analysis, U.S. Department of Energy. November 1989. Washington, D.C.: U.S. Department of Energy.

Ledbetter, M., and M. Ross. 1989. Supply curves of conserved energy for automobiles. Draft paper prepared for Lawrence Berkeley Laboratory by the American Council for an Energy-Efficient Economy, Washington, D.C.

Leone, R. A., and Parkinson, T. W. 1990. Conserving energy: Is there a better way? Paper prepared for the Association of International Automobile Manufacturers.

Plotkin, S. E. 1991. Testimony before Senate Committee on Energy and Natural Resources. Washington, D.C.: Office of Technology Assessment. March 20, 1991.

Schipper, L. 1991. Energy saving in the U.S. and other wealthy countries: Can the momentum be maintained? Draft. International Energy Studies, Energy Analysis Program, Applied Science Division, Lawrence Berkeley Laboratory.

Shackson, R. H., and H. J. Leach. 1980. Using Fuel Economy and Synthetic Fuels to Compete with OPEC Oil. Pittsburgh, Pa.: Carnegie-Mellon University Press.

Unnasch, S., C. B. Moyer, D. D. Lowell, and M. D. Jackson. 1989. Comparing the Impact of Different Transportation Fuels on the Greenhouse Effect. Prepared by the Acurex Corporation for the California Energy Commission. April 1989. Sacramento: California Energy Commission.

Wright, J., A. Meier, M. Maulhardt, and A. H. Rosenfeld. 1981. Supplying Energy Through Greater Efficiency: The Potential for Conservation in California's Residential Sector. Report LBL-10738, EEB 80-2. January 1981. Berkeley, Calif.: Lawrence Berkeley Laboratory.

Appendix F

Transportation System Management

The basis for the calculation of cost-effectiveness for one possible parking management program is presented here. The program considered would address the CO_2 emissions of some of the 48 million people in U.S. metropolitan areas who drive to work alone (Pisarski, 1987). Currently, three-quarters of them, or 36 million, are provided with free parking by their employers (Pucher, 1988). Under this parking management program, 25 percent, or 9 million, of these spaces would be physically eliminated by the year 1995. Parking fees or surcharges would be imposed on the remaining 75 percent, or 27 million spaces, set at a level designed to reduce the proportion of persons driving alone by 15 percent, from 65 percent (Pisarski, 1987) to 50 percent by 1995.

As calculated below, this proposal would produce an annual CO_2 reduction of 49 megatons (Mt) at a cost of between –$4.75 and $2.59 billion.[1] Cost-effectiveness thus ranges from –$97/t CO_2 to $53/t CO_2, for an average value of –$22/t CO_2.

CALCULATION OF CO_2 EMISSION REDUCTIONS

The first step is to calculate the annual CO_2 emissions attributable to different commuter transportation modes (see Table F.1). Calculations are performed for a 10-mile commuting trip, which is the national average (Pisarski, 1987).

The second step is to calculate the way in which solo commuters will redistribute themselves among alternative transportation modes in response to parking restrictions. This analysis assumes that the percentage of those who use bus, rail, carpool, or vanpool will be proportional to the current "mode split" (excluding pedestrians and those who work at home). Where

TABLE F.1 Carbon Dioxide Emissions by Commuting Mode (tons/year)

Mode	Btu per Passenger Mile[a]	Yearly Energy (MBtu)[b]	Equivalent Gallons Gasoline[c]	Amount of Yearly CO$_2$ Emissions[d]	Difference from Solo Driving
Solo driving	8,333	41.66	333.3	2.98	—
Bus	2,121	14.77	118.2	1.06	1.92
Rail	1,935	13.84	110.7	0.99	1.99
Carpool	3,788	18.94	151.5	1.36	1.62
Vanpool	882	8.58	68.6	0.61	2.37

[a]For solo drivers, the figure is per vehicle-mile for automobile commuting.
[b]Energy use = (Btu per passenger-mile) × (10 miles per commuting trip) × (2 trips per day) × (250 commuting days per year). In addition, for bus, rail, and vanpool modes, it is assumed that commuters drive alone 1 mile (at 8333 Btu/mi) each way per day to get to the transfer point. For rail, energy use for commuter rail is used (rather than the lower energy use for transit rail).
[c]Assumes that 1 gallon of gasoline = 125,000 Btu (Davis et al., 1989).
[d](Gasoline usage) × (19.7 lbs CO$_2$/gal gasoline)/(2200 lb/t).

parking spaces are eliminated, it is assumed that none of the 9 million displaced solo commuters continue to drive alone, and all are divided among the four remaining modes. Where parking spaces are priced to reduce the solo driver mode share to 50 percent, the shares for the remaining modes are proportional to those calculated for elimination of parking spaces. (To account for the remaining solo drivers, the other mode shares add up to 50 percent, rather than 100 percent, of all commuters.) The mode splits for displaced drivers are presented in Table F.2.

These mode splits are then applied to the 9 million solo drivers affected by the parking elimination component and the 27 million solo drivers affected by the parking management component. As shown in Table F.3, the combination of these two measures would produce annual emission reductions of 49 Mt of CO$_2$.

CALCULATION OF COST-EFFECTIVENESS

A parking demand management program of the type described in this appendix would involve several types of costs and savings:

• employees' out-of-pocket costs or savings from the use of alternative transportation modes (a figure that includes fuel savings);
• employers' out-of-pocket operational costs or savings from parking management and provision of transportation alternatives;

TABLE F.2 Calculation of Mode Shares for Multiple Occupancy Vehicle Modes When Parking Spaces Are Eliminated or Restricted

	Current Mode Share (%)	Elimination— Adjusted Mode Share (%)[a]	Surcharge— Adjusted Mode Share (%)[b]
Solo driving	64.4	0.0	50.0
Public transit			
Bus	5.2	19.3	9.6
Rail	2.8	10.4	5.2
Group ride[c]			
Carpool	16.8	62.2	31.1
Vanpool	2.2	8.1	4.1

[a]Assumes no solo driving; share of each mode when considering only the 20.09 million metropolitan commuters currently commuting by bus, rail, and group (carpool and vanpool) ride (Pisarski, 1987).

[b]Assumes 50 percent solo driving; share of other modes calculated by halving adjusted mode shares calculated (in column 2) when all solo driving is eliminated.

[c]Pisarski (1987) gives the "group ride" mode share as 19 percent but does not give separate mode shares for carpooling and vanpooling. The assumed mode shares are based on the proportion of carpooling to vanpooling in Table 3-17 of Pisarski (1987) (20.1 percent carpooling versus 2.6 percent vanpooling) and the census estimate that 1.6 million people used vanpools in 1980.

TABLE F.3 Carbon Dioxide Emission Reductions from Parking Management Program

Mode	New Passenger Trips—Parking Elimination (million trips/yr)[a]	New Passenger Trips—Parking Surcharge (million trips/yr)[b]	Total New Passenger Trips (million trips/yr)[c]	CO_2 Emission Reduction (Mt/yr)
Bus	1.74	2.59	4.33	8.31
Rail	0.94	1.40	2.34	4.66
Carpool	5.59	8.40	13.99	33.16
Vanpool	0.73	1.11	1.84	2.98
TOTAL	9.0	13.5	22.5	49.05

[a]Application of mode shares from Table F.2 to 9 million solo drivers affected by elimination of parking spaces.

[b]Application of mode shares from Table F.2 to 27 million solo drivers affected by surcharges on parking spaces, 13.5 million of them continue to solo commute.

[c]Multiply total new trips for each mode by CO_2 emission reductions, compared to solo driving, from Table F.1.

• employers' capital savings from the avoided costs of constructing parking spaces; and

• monetized costs or savings from changes in the lengths of commuting trips.

The first category—employees' out-of-pocket costs—is calculated by considering costs such as variable automobile operating expenses, bus and train fares, and vanpool fees. The second category—employers' operational costs—involves increased costs for running carpool and vanpool programs, offset by savings from avoiding the annual operating and maintenance costs of providing parking spaces for bus, rail, and some ridesharing commuters. The third category—employers' capital savings—represents the avoided costs of constructing parking spaces at an average investment of $3000 per space. Finally, changes in the length of commuting trips cause productivity losses or gains that can be monetized.

TABLE F.4 Combined Employer/Employee Out-of-Pocket Costs/Savings of Alternative Commuting Modes per Daily Round Trip Commute (1987 dollars)

Mode	Worker Cost ($)	Employer Cost ($)	Total Cost ($)	Difference from Solo Driving ($)
Solo driving	1.44[a]	0.26[b]	1.70	—
Bus	1.24[c]	–0.26[d]	0.98	–0.72
Commuter rail	2.60[e]	–0.26[d]	2.34	0.64
Carpool	0.65[f]	–0.22[g]	0.87	–0.83
Vanpool	2.40[h]	0.04[i]	2.44	0.74

[a]Based on 7.31 cents per mile for 1987 variable operating costs of an automobile (Davis et al., 1989) for 20-mile round trip.

[b]Based on average employer cost of $64 per year to operate a parking space (Wegmann, 1989).

[c]Rounded, based on 1987 average one-way transit trip cost of $0.62 (U.S. DOT, 1989).

[d]Employer savings from not providing a parking space for bus and rail riders.

[e]Based on 1987 average commuter rail fare equivalent to $0.13 per mile (U.S. DOT, 1989) for a 20-mile round trip.

[f]Assumes that an average of 2.2 persons (Pisarski, 1987) splits the cost of solo driving.

[g]Based on providing 1/2.2 (average carpool occupancy) of a parking space and administrative costs of $25 per employee for carpool matching program.

[h]Based on monthly fare of $50 per vanpool rider (Toruemke and Roseman, 1989).

[i]Based on providing 1/10.7 (average vanpool occupancy) of a parking space and employer administrative costs of $4.50 per employee per year for running vanpool program.

TABLE F.5 Out-of-Pocket Employee and Employer Savings from Switching from Solo Driving to Other Commuting Modes

Mode	New Passenger Trips (million)[a]	Commuting Cost Differential ($ billion)[b]
Bus	4.33	−3.12
Rail	2.34	1.50
Carpool	13.99	−11.61
Vanpool	1.84	1.36
TOTAL		−11.87

NOTE: Not counting avoided cost of constructing parking spaces and productivity gains/losses.

[a]From Table F.3.
[b]Number of new passenger trips multiplied by cost differential per trip from Table F.4.

The first two categories of costs are elaborated in Table F.4. Once the cost per commuter trip for each mode is calculated, the total out-of-pocket costs/savings of a parking management program are calculated by multiplying the number of former solo commuters using each alternative mode by the cost differential. The results are presented in Table F.5. Savings to both workers and employers exceed costs, resulting in an overall program savings of −$12 million.

In addition to these savings, employers save money by avoiding the capital costs of providing parking. Constructing a parking space costs between $1,000 and $15,000 (Institute of Transportation Engineers, 1989), with one survey finding an average cost for added spaces of $3,920 (Wegmann, 1988). Even if a space has already been constructed, employers can realize savings from eliminating the use of the space for employee parking and using the space for paid, commercial parking or other purposes. This parking management program would eliminate the need for 16.9 million parking spaces, 9 million directly eliminated and 7.9 million freed when solo commuters shift to less parking-intensive modes. If only 10 percent (or 1.69 million parking spaces) are spaces that would otherwise have been built at an average construction cost of $3000, the total employer capital cost savings is $5.1 billion.

Finally, the program will change the length of commuting trips in two ways. First, traffic congestion will be reduced because 22.5 million solo commuting cars will be replaced by 6.7 million buses, carpools, vanpools,

TABLE F.6 Changes in Annual Commuting Time for Different Modes Relative to Base-Case Solo Commuting Without Parking Management

Mode	Base-Case Speed[a] (mph)	5 Percent Increase in Speed[b]		20 Percent Increase in Speed[c]	
		Speed (mph)	Delay/Savings (hours)[d]	Speed (mph)	Delay/Savings (hours)[d]
Solo driving	32	34	(8)	38	(25)
Bus	13	14	200	16	150
Rail	23	23	58	26	58
Carpool	32	34	(8)	38	(25)
Vanpool	29	30	(8)	35	(17)

[a]Travel speeds for solo driver, bus, and rail are from Table 3-23 in Pisarski (1987). Although Pisarski lists the speed for carpoolers at a faster 34 mph, this was adjusted to 32 mph to account for pickups/drop-offs. The speed for vanpooling was estimated at 10 percent slower than carpooling to account for additional pickups/drop-offs.

[b]This case assumes that travel speeds for highway modes (solo driver, bus, carpool, and vanpool) increase 5 percent relative to the base case due to reduced traffic congestion.

[c]This case assumes that travel speeds for highway modes (solo driver, bus, carpool, and vanpool) increase 20 percent relative to the base case due to reduced traffic congestion.

[d]Time delays/savings are compared to the base case for solo commuters. Annual travel time is based on 250 round-trip commutes annually, with an average trip length of 10 miles each way (Pisarski, 1987).

and solo commuters. With one-third fewer commuter vehicles on the road during peak hours (there are currently 48 million solo commuters in metropolitan areas of the United States), traffic congestion will be reduced and travel speeds increased for all highway modes (solo drivers, carpools, vanpools, buses). This analysis considers two scenarios, one in which travel speed is increased by 5 percent and one in which travel speed is increased by 20 percent.

Trip lengths will also change because shifting to modes such as buses and vanpools will increase commuting times relative to solo automobile travel. Data presented in Pisarski (1987) indicate that commuting by bus and rail is slower than commuting by automobile. Table F.6 calculates the relative changes in annual commuting time accounting for both of these factors. Table F.7 then converts these figures into total commuting time delays/gains and monetizes the resulting productivity changes at values ranging from $5 to $10 per hour. These figures are consistent with values of $5 to

TABLE F.7 Monetized Value of Changes in Trip Lengths Due to Parking Management Program Relative to Base-Case Solo Commuting

Mode	Number of New Passenger Trips (million trips/year)[a]	5 Percent Increase in Speed[b]		20 Percent Increase in Speed[c]	
		Change in Travel Time (hours/persons/yr)[d]	Change in Value of Travel Time (G$/yr)[e]	Change in Travel Time (hours/persons/yr)[d]	Change in Value of Travel Time (G$/yr)[f]
Solo driving	13.50	(8)	(1.08)	(25)	(1.69)
Bus	4.33	200	8.66	150	3.25
Rail	2.34	58	1.36	58	0.68
Carpool	13.99	(8)	(1.12)	(25)	(1.75)
Vanpool	1.84	(8)	(0.15)	(17)	(0.16)
TOTAL			7.67		0.33

[a]From Table F.3.

[b]This case assumes that travel speeds for highway modes (solo driver, bus, carpool, and vanpool) increase 5 percent relative to the base case due to reduced traffic congestion.

[c]This case assumes that travel speeds for highway modes (solo driver, bus, carpool, and vanpool) increase 20 percent relative to the base case due to reduced traffic congestion.

[d]From Table F.6.

[e]Each hour of change in travel is valued at $10, as explained in the text. Total savings is (number of passenger trips) × (hours of delay or savings) × ($10 per hour).

[f]Each hour of change in travel is valued at $5, as explained in the text. Total savings is (number of passenger trips) × (hours of delay or savings) × ($5 per hour).

$7 per hour used by the Federal Highway Administration and transportation researchers to value time spent in traffic delays (U.S. General Accounting Office, 1989; Wegmann, 1989). (Only the upper-bound and lower-bound cases are presented in Table F.7; the lower bound assumes a 20 percent increase in highway speed and values delays at $5 per hour, while the upper bound assumes a 5 percent increase in highway speed and values delays at $10 per hour.)

Thus the total cost of this parking management program is as follows:

Out-of-pocket costs
(employers and employees)   ($0.01 billion)

Avoided parking space   ($5.07 billion)
construction

Productivity gains/ $0.33 billion to $7.67 billion
losses

The total cost thus ranges from –$4.75 billion to $2.59 billion.

NOTE

1. Throughout this report, tons (t) are metric; 1 Mt = 1 megaton = 1 million tons.

REFERENCES

Davis, S. C., D. B. Shonka, G. J. Anderson-Batiste, and P. S. Hu. 1989. Transportation Energy Data Book: Edition 10. Report ORNL-6565 (Edition 10 of ORNL-5198). Prepared for the U.S. Department of Energy. Oak Ridge, Tenn.: Oak Ridge National Laboratory.

Institute of Transportation Engineers. 1989. A Toolbox for Alleviating Traffic Congestion. Washington, D.C.: Institute of Transportation Engineers.

Pisarski, A. 1987. Commuting in America: A National Report on Commuting Patterns and Trends. Westport, Connecticut: Eno Foundation for Transportation.

Pucher, J. 1988. Urban travel behavior as the outcome of public policy: The example of modal split in Western Europe and North America. The Journal of American Planners Association 54(4):509-520.

Toruemke, D., and D. Roseman. 1989. Vanpools: Pricing and market penetration. Transportation Research Record. 122:83-87.

U.S. Department of Transportation. 1989. National Transportation Statistics. Washington, D.C.: U.S. Department of Transportation.

U.S. General Accounting Office (GAO). 1989. Traffic Congestion: Trends, Measures and Effects. Washington, D.C.: U.S. General Accounting Office.

Wegmann, F. 1989. Cost-effectiveness of private employer ridesharing programs: An employer's assessment. Transportation Research Record 1212:88-100.

Appendix G

Nuclear Energy

This appendix discusses the variety of options available for generating energy using either nuclear fission or nuclear fusion. The focus of this appendix is primarily on second-generation nuclear fission reactors, as they are more likely than fusion power plants to be introduced in the near term. Descriptions of some of the proposed new technologies are provided below. These descriptions are not intended to be a comprehensive and critical analysis of the technological options for future development of nuclear power nor an endorsement of particular technologies. Such an analysis will be provided in a forthcoming National Research Council Energy Engineering Board report.

Current advanced nuclear fission reactor development projects world-wide are summarized in Table G.1. Any reactor development project aims to improve performance in the categories of both safety and economics; however, their individual improvement differs substantially—reflecting differing evaluations of which types of improvement are needed most. Reactor development projects can be categorized according to whether they give primary emphasis to economics or safety. The class of goals chosen for emphasis usually guides formulation of the basic reactor concept.

The optimized reactor design is usually very similar to current nuclear reactors, but reflects an approximate attempt to maximize either economics or safety, while attempting to improve performance in the other category of goals to at least the minimal extent required by the safety authorities or the economics of competing technologies.

Reactors emphasizing economic performance attempt to reduce the costs of generating electricity—usually focusing on the cost components of capital and plant operational availability. Reactors emphasizing improved safety performance attempt to gain public acceptance by decreasing the risk of core damage or radioactive release. Reactor safety is improved by increas-

767

TABLE G.1   Worldwide Programs of Nuclear Power Technology
Development as adapted from Golay (1990)

PROGRAMS EMPHASIZING PASSIVE SAFETY

Federal Republic of Germany
- 100-MW$_e$ Modular HTGR (Siemens, Brown Boveri)

United Kingdom and United States
- 300-MW$_e$ Modular PWR (SIR Concept) (Rolls Royce & ABB-Combustion
    Engineering)

United States
- 130-MW$_e$ Modular HTGR (General Atomic)
- 130-MW$_e$ Modular LMR (PRISM Concept, General Electric)
- 600-MW$_e$ LWRs (Semi-Passive Safety)
    ASBWR (BWR, General Electric)
    AP-600 (PWR, Westinghouse)
- 20-MW$_e$ Integral Fast Reactor (IFR Concept, Argonne National
    Laboratory)

Sweden
- 500-MW$_e$ PIUS-PWR (ASEA-Brown Boveri)

PROGRAMS EMPHASIZING ECONOMIC PERFORMANCE

Europe
- Joint European Fast Reactor (France, Germany, United Kingdom)
- European 1400-MW$_e$ PWR (Nuclear Power International: France, Germany)

Canada
- 450-MW$_e$ HWR (CANDU 3) (AECL)
- 900-MW$_e$ HWR (AECL & Ontario Hydro)

France
- 1400-MW$_e$ PWR (N4 Project, Framatome, Electricité de France)
- 1200- to 1450-MW$_e$ LMFBR (Superphenix-1 Project, Novatome, Electricité
    de France)

Federal Republic of Germany
- 500-MW$_e$ HTGR (Successor to 300-MW$_e$ THTR Project)
- 300-MW$_e$ LMR (SNR 300 LMFBR Project)

Japan
- 1250-MW$_e$ LWRs
    ABWR (Tokyo Electric Power, General Electric, Toshiba, Hitachi)
    APWR (Kansai Electric, Mitsubishi, Westinghouse)
- 714-MW$_e$ LMR (Monju LMFBR Project)
- Successor to 148-MW$_e$ FUGEN LWR/HWR Project

United Kingdom
- 1000 to 1400-MW$_e$ PWR (Sizewell-B, Hinkley Point-C Projects)

United States
- LWR Requirements Document Project (Electric Power Research Institute)
- 1250-MW$_e$ ABWR (General Electric)
- 1250-MW$_e$ APWR (Westinghouse)
- System 80+ (ABB-Combustion Engineering)

(Table G.1 continues)

TABLE G.1 *(continued)*

Soviet Union
  • Emphasis upon Passive Safety
        100-MW$_e$ Modular HTGR
        Chernobyl-Type RBMK Reactor Series Discontinued
  • Emphasis upon Economic Performance
        950-MW$_e$ PWR
        1250-MW$_e$ LMR (LMFBR Type)

NOTE: Abbreviations are as follows:
  BWR: Boiling Water Reactor
  CANDU: Canadian Deuterium Uranium, Heavy Water Reactor
  HTGR: High-Temperature Gas-Cooled Reactor
  HWR: Heavy Water Reactor
  IFR: Integral Fast Reactor
  LMFBR: Liquid-Metal-Cooled Fast Breeder Reactor (version of LMR)
  LMR: Liquid-Metal-Cooled Reactor
  LWR: Light Water Reactor
  PIUS: Process Inherent Ultimately Safe (version of LWR)
  PRISM: Power Reactor Inherent Safe Modular (version of LMR)
  PWR: Pressurized Water Reactor
  SIR: Safe Integral Reactor (version of LWR)

ing the mechanical reliability of the post-shutdown reactor cooling and post-fuel damage maintenance of containment integrity functions. However, corresponding reductions in nonmechanical safety function unreliability, subtle common-mode failures, and severe external events (e.g., strong but rare earthquakes) appear to be more difficult to achieve. Thus, from the safety-oriented concepts substantial performance improvements can be expected, but hopes that perfect or idiot-proof technologies will result may be poorly founded.

The term often used for reactor concepts emphasizing safety is passively safe. In a nuclear power plant, passive safety features are those that perform a safety function using only sources of motive force found in nature (e.g., gravity for cooling water instead of pumps). There are developments on concepts that use passive safety features only. In other cases, particularly in light water reactors, a blend of passive and active safety features is being pursued. These concepts could be termed semi-passively safe.

In this appendix, the state of the art for the following three fission concepts are reviewed briefly:

  • Light Water Reactors (LWR)
  • High-Temperature Modular Gas-Cooled Reactors (HTGR)
  • Integral Fast Reactors (IFR)

For the LWR, both passively safe and semi-passively safe developments are included. For HTGR and IFR, only the concepts using passively safe features exclusively are described. As noted earlier, this is not intended to be a comprehensive or critical assessment of all the nuclear technologies available or an endorsement of particular technologies, but a description of a few options to demonstrate some of the nuclear technologies currently being discussed. For example, not all varieties of light water reactors are discussed, nor are heavy water reactors, which are currently not licensed in the United States.

LIGHT WATER REACTORS

In most countries the focus of nuclear fission development activities remains on light water reactors—emphasizing economic-oriented designs. Among the more important elements are plant operational availability and shortening plant construction time. Even for those developments, there is always a serious concern for safety. In the advanced pressurized water reactor (PWR) and boiling water reactor (BWR) designs, automatic mechanical and electronic devices have supplemented human operators in the performance of many emergency duties—making safety systems more redundant.

Light water reactors are divided into two types: large evolutionary light water reactors and mid-sized light water reactors. Large evolutionary light water reactors include the advanced boiling water reactor, advanced pressurized water reactor, and the system 80+ standard design pressurized water reactor. Mid-sized light water reactors with passive safety features include the advanced passive pressurized water reactor and the simplified boiling water reactor. The large evolutionary light water reactors are the most likely to be implemented in the time frame in the Mitigation Panel's analysis. The cost of these reactors is the basis for the calculation described in Appendix J.

One way to reduce risk is to build smaller reactors that contain less radioactive material and, in principle, can be cooled more easily in case of malfunction. The Electric Power Research Institute (EPRI) has encouraged two efforts to develop smaller advanced (LWRs)—the ASBWR and AP-600. These reactors utilize semi-passive safety systems. They are designed to utilize a small number of reliable "active" components to initiate safety operations, but do not require large AC power sources to run the emergency equipment. All water required for heat removal in the primary system drains by gravity to the reactor core. Large volumes of water are stored above the reactor core. Typically, there is sufficient water to flood the reactor containment and reactor system. By so doing, some of the economic penalties of purely passive design may be avoided.

The LWR concept that utilizes exclusively passive safety features is the process inherent ultimately safe (PIUS) reactor conceived by ASEA-Atom in 1979. Their criteria included safety from external events such as earth-quakes and terrorist attack. The intrinsic protection can last a week or more without calling into action any active safety equipment or human actions. Currently, coordinated activities to develop PIUS are under way between ABB and companies in Italy, South Korea, China, and the United States.

HIGH-TEMPERATURE MODULAR GAS-COOLED REACTORS

The high-temperature gas-cooled reactor (HTGR) technology utilizing pebbles for fuel was developed first in West Germany. In the United States, the Fort St. Vrain reactor, which used General Atomic's HTGR technology, was less than successful. The current U.S. reference plant design developed by the Department of Energy's HTGR Program uses four steam generating reactor modules and two steam-turbine-generator sets to achieve a nominal plant rating of 550 MW_e.

The modular gas-cooled reactor (MGR) is predicated on the possibility of building reactors that will not, under any circumstances that can be perceived at this time, release fission products to the environment. In a reactor with localized fuel, this is equivalent to the requirement that the fuel cladding retain its integrity even if all coolant (not just coolant flow) is lost and all control rods are fully withdrawn. This requirement is claimed to be met in the MGR by limiting the power density and reactor size in such fashion that the hottest location in the reactor core never reaches temperatures capable of damaging the fuel. To achieve this, it is essential both that the reactor possess a temperature coefficient of reactivity sufficiently negative for the chain reaction to be quenched before damaging temperatures are reached, and that the processes of conduction and radiation are sufficient to carry the afterheat of the fission products to the environment without exceeding the design basis temperature. The latter requirement imposes important limitations on power density and size.

Although it is possible in principle to meet these requirements with a number of reactor types, the gas-cooled reactor with ceramic-coated fuel has the combination of cladding strength and temperature capability that holds promise in technical feasibility. The challenge of the MGR program is not the usual one of trying to make an economical reactor safe, but rather its inverse—that of making a safe reactor economical. The issues are low power density with its obvious cost penalties and small unit size with its apparent cost in economies of scale. In addition, requiring a containment facility (not in current plans) would increase the cost. There are two different approaches to ameliorating the economic disadvantages of the gas-cooled reactor: the first is based on making the unit size as large as possible and combining the output of several steam-generating units to achieve economies of scale.

Another design concept, developed at the Massachusetts Institute of Technology (MIT), utilizes a high-speed gas turbine in a direct-Brayton cycle and generates electricity at a high frequency—higher than 60 hertz—utilizing power electronics for frequency conversions. The aim is to reduce the size of the balance of plants and thus improve the economics.

The macroscopic properties of gas-cooled reactors are closely coupled to the small-scale properties of the fuel. As a result, incremental improvements in fuel quality can have substantial effects on existing reactors and, more significantly, on the design of commercially improved versions. This requires the most stringent quality control on the fuel manufacturing process. Recent improvements in fuel quality (a two-order-of-magnitude improvement in fission product retention and a method for coating individual pebbles with silicon carbide to render them fireproof) promise more evolutionary improvement.

All modern gas-cooled reactors are based on microencapsulated fuel in which submillimeter spheres of uranium oxide are surrounded by a series of nested spherical shells of pyrolytic carbon and silicon carbide. This fuel was developed by General Atomic and was brought to its current level of capability in the West German nuclear program, where the concept of the passively safe small-scale modular reactor was first developed. In the West German program, intensive series of tests of the fuel under a variety of temperature and radiation environments have been conducted, and several loss of coolant events were tested, and monitored and compared with computer models. Potentially important advances would follow from the development of higher-temperature coatings, which would facilitate the deployment of higher power density systems, with concomitant economic advantage, or the development of 1000°C systems for process heat applications.

INTEGRAL FAST REACTORS

A new fission reactor concept developed at Argonne National Laboratory is the integral fast reactor (IFR). If the IFR, which uses a new formulation of fissile fuel material, performs as claimed, it will breed its own supply of fresh fuel on site and burn up the ultra-long-lived radioactive transuranic fission products (the actinides: elements 89 through 103, including plutonium (94)). This would leave a waste product that could potentially decay in radioactivity to original ore levels in several hundred years. The IFR features a very high fuel burnup and, in two subscale experiments, has demonstrated the ability to survive a total loss of cooling.

The IFR is a sodium-cooled breeder reactor with fuel in the form of a metallic alloy. Conventional reactors employ a ceramic oxide fuel form; the new fuel alloy is a far better conductor of heat, which is one of the factors enhancing the safety of the IFR design. The metallic fuel is reprocessed electrochemically rather than by solvent extraction. Reprocessing may be carried out on site, avoiding long-distance transport.

The utilization of IFR facilities to reduce the radioactivity of used fuel from conventional reactors has been suggested, but this use is still in the early exploratory stage and controversial. Nevertheless, despite all its benefits, one may still expect the IFR concept to display vulnerabilities of its own. For example, disposal of the radioactive inventory in the event of an early reactor shutdown would be no less difficult than for a conventional reactor. Also, loss of sodium coolant, as in an earthquake, could produce a major disaster. Further, the cost for a full-scale reactor is yet to be evaluated and may be quite high.

The safety of the IFR concept was demonstrated in two very interesting experiments, both carried out in the EBR-II Idaho reactor on April 3, 1986. Although small, with just 20 MW of electric generating capacity, the power density of the EBR-II is nevertheless typical of fast reactors. In the first experiment, while the EBR-II was operating at full capacity, power was shut off to the primary coolant pumps. Because of the reactivity feedback characteristics of the IFR, the reactor shut itself down without safety system or operator action. There was no damage to any part of the system. Later that day, the reactor was brought back to full power and a loss-of-heat sink without scram test was carried out. Again, no damage was observed.

In summary, the IFR concept may offer energy and power from nuclear fission while avoiding almost all of the major hazards associated with conventional fission reactors. The reactor breeds its own fresh fuel on site, features high fuel burnup, and burns up the ultra-long-lived radioactive transuranic fission products, leaving a waste product with lower radioactivity. Shipment of large amounts of fissile fuel to and from a reprocessing plant is obviated, as is the need to ship and store, for a geologic time period, a highly pernicious radioactive waste. The on-site fuel is unattractive for diversion to weapons use, and safe recovery in the face of a complete cooling failure has been observed in pilot experiments.

NUCLEAR FUSION

In sharp contrast to the existence of many operating fission reactors, the feasibility of economic controlled nuclear fusion has yet to be demonstrated. Research on this intensely difficult problem has been under way since the very early 1950s, and several orders of magnitude of progress has been made in temperature and confinement time. Temperatures of $300,000,000°C$ have now been achieved in fusion experiments, six times hotter than that necessary for ignition under ideal circumstances. At lower temperatures, confinement of such very hot gases has been extended to periods as long as a second. Densities of these hot gases are also close to those needed for fusion reactor operation.

Fusion experiments may achieve ignition of a deuterium-tritium plasma by the end of this decade and thus provide a definitive demonstration of fusion reactor feasibility. The first third of the twenty-first century may then see a prototype fusion power plant in operation, depending on the energy cost and environmental situation at that time. The cost of nuclear fusion is expected to be very high in comparison with alternative nuclear reactor designs. On the other hand, nuclear fusion offers additional environmental protection compared to nuclear fission. By midcentury, some fraction of energy to the national electrical grids might possibly come from fusion reactors.

The advantages of fusion power with respect to safety and the environment follow:

• No danger from nuclear reactor runaway. The amount of nuclear fuel in the reaction chamber at any given time is minuscule, and a system failure of any sort can lead only to a cooling down of the reacting plasma.

• Enormously reduced amounts of nuclear waste. The nuclear ash from fusion is helium, a stable and totally benign gas. Almost all of the neutrons coming out of the reacting gas will be absorbed in a lithium 6 blanket, generating fresh tritium to replace that used up in the deuterium tritium reactions. Also, although the vacuum-chamber wall is expected to become radioactive due to bombardment by these transiting neutrons, the material of the vacuum chamber can be chosen to reduce the radioactivity level and character of this radioactivity and problems associated with storage or disposal. Further research is needed in this area.

• No production of gases deleterious to the environment such as oxides of carbon and nitrogen; however, there is some concern on the potential leakage of tritium into the water supply.

• No inherent production of fissile materials.

The acid test of fusion power feasibility—achieving nuclear ignition in a confined plasma—is anticipated no earlier than the end of this decade, and a prototype fusion power plant should not be expected before the year 2020. Further progress is clearly needed in the science, technological development, and economics of nuclear fusion before it can actually be implemented. Nevertheless, in view of its minimal impact on atmospheric pollution and greenhouse warming, and the very much reduced level of nuclear hazard, controlled fusion still merits its reputation as a major option for the future generation of electric power.

REFERENCE

Golay, M. W. 1990. Testimony before the U.S. House Committee on Interior and Insular Affairs. Washington, D.C., March 10, 1990.

Appendix H

A Solar Hydrogen System

To convert solar radiation to electricity, one makes use of photovoltaic materials akin to the solar cells used to energize battery-free pocket calculators. However, as an energy source, solar radiation is relatively dilute. Impressive amounts of (desert) land area would have to be devoted to this use in order to replace fossil fuel supplies. For example, it is estimated that the complete replacement of such supplies in the United States would require total collector fields on the order of 50,000 square miles, about 1 percent of the total U.S. land area (Ogden and Williams, 1989). On the other hand, obtaining the same power from biomass grown on energy farms would require more than 10 times that area. Even obtaining synfuels from coal would, in 14 years, use up the 24,000 square miles of land thought to be available for strip mining.

Once the solar energy system generates electricity, the electricity can be used to generate hydrogen. Hydrogen is a transportable, clean-burning fuel that can be used as energy for vehicles, planes, and many other devices. This appendix describes the cost-effectiveness of one such system.

PHOTOVOLTAIC MATERIALS

Prior to 1980 the only commercially available solar cells were those made of high-grade single-crystal silicon. Fabrication of these crystals requires large amounts of time, material, and energy. Much more promising for application to solar power is the later technology of thin-film amorphous (i.e., noncrystalline) silicon cells. The films, typically 1 micron (0.0001 cm) thick, are prepared by deposition from silicon vapor onto a substrate such as glass, plastic, or stainless steel, a process that lends itself easily to mass production. A square meter of cell area would require only 3 g of silicon, a very abundant element. The efficiency of conversion of the power in solar radiation to electricity has increased from 1 percent, for the first cells produced in 1976, to almost 12 percent for modest-area laboratory modules and almost 14 percent in 1987 for small-area laboratory cells. Higher efficiencies, estimated at 18 to 20 percent, may be attained in a few years with multilayer cells, each layer tuned to a different part of the solar spectrum.

COMMERCIAL PHOTOVOLTAICS

The Alabama Power Company has a 100-kW amorphous-silicon generating field in operation at present. Efficiencies of currently available commercial photovoltaics range from 5 to 7 percent. Present-day manufacturing facilities are typically of modest capacity, on the order of 1 MW/yr, at a cost of $1.50 to $1.60 per peak watt. Within a few years, plants of 10-MW capacity per year may be on line. These plants are expected to produce cells of 6 percent efficiency for about $1.00 per peak watt. A 50-MW power plant to sell electricity to the Southern California Edison Company (Chronar Corporation, anticipating a photovoltaic cost of $1.25 per peak watt) and a 70-MW/yr production plant (ARCO Solar, Inc.) are in the planning stage. Looking to the end of the 1990s and the possibility of production levels of many hundreds of megawatts per year, Ogden and Williams (1989) project that costs could drop to the range of $0.20 to $0.40 per peak watt, based on reduced outlays for specialty glass, labor, and depreciation, together with commercial efficiencies increasing to 12 to 18 percent. Allowing for electrical wiring losses and for dirt and dust on the modules would reduce their overall efficiencies by an estimated 15 percent, that is, to 10.2 to 15.3 percent. Land costs, site preparation, array wiring, support structures, and other construction represent additional area-related costs that would come to about $50/m^2 with present technology, but economies of scale might bring these down to $33/m^2.

On the other hand, these figures are pertinent for the U.S. Southwest, and supplying power to other parts of the country means finding means other than electric power lines for energy transport. Also note that these costs are much lower than that used in the Mitigation Panel's analysis as described in Appendix J. Rather than using projections of cost, the panel made a deliberate decision to use only current cost in estimating the cost-effectiveness of different energy options.

HYDROGEN COSTS

The cost for the electrolytic production of hydrogen depends on the capital cost of the electrolyzer and the cost of the DC electricity to run it. There is little economy of scale beyond a hydrogen production rate of 2 MW. Similarly, the scale economies for photovoltaic power disappear beyond levels of 5 to 10 MW. The hydrogen production units could then be highly modularized, with typical unit capacities of 5 to 10 MW and per-unit capital costs of $4 million to $12 million, depending on photovoltaic module costs. Projected costs for solar hydrogen produced in the Southwest would range from $31.80/GJ (equivalent to $3.88 per gallon of gasoline) with 6 percent efficiency for the photovoltaic module producing DC electricity at $0.089/ kWh (1990) to approximately half those costs by 1995 and to $9.10/GJ ($1.11 per gallon of gasoline equivalent) based on 18 percent module efficiency for the year 2000. Compression to 70 atmospheres, for transport through a 1000-mile pipeline, would add another $0.16 to $0.20 to the cost per gallon of gasoline equivalent.

PHASING IN

One of the very attractive features about a solar hydrogen power economy is that it lends itself to a gradual phase-in. Even today, photovoltaic power is very economical for specialized purposes including corrosion protection, spacecraft, navigation buoys, and small remote water pumps or electric power sources. Installations for supplying peak-load daytime power to utilities are marginally economic at the present time. Daytime power for residential use would be economic at solar module costs of $0.70 to $1.50 per peak watt.

Hydrogen-powered transport, although feasible today for lightweight vehicles with modest ranges, would benefit greatly from improvements in the technology for hydrogen storage. One anticipates that hydrogen-powered transportation would be economical first for fleet vehicles and, as such, could be tested initially in major cities in the Southwest without recourse to pipelines for hydrogen transmission.

SUMMARY

Photovoltaic hydrogen power offers a number of advantages. The energy source is radiation from the sun, the materials involved are abundantly available, and the burning of hydrogen fuel is—with the exception of nitrogen oxides—free of polluting or greenhouse gas emissions, including CO, CO_2, volatile organics, SO_2, and particulate matter. The basic technology exists today, and some small-scale applications of solar power are economical even at the present time. Implementation of solar hydrogen power on a larger scale would lend itself to gradual phase-in, and one can expect to see increasingly important applications become economical as improvements are made in solar module efficiency and in hydrogen storage technology.

REFERENCE

Ogden, J. M., and R. H. Williams. 1989. Solar Hydrogen: Moving Beyond Fossil Fuels. Washington, D.C.: World Resources Institute.

Appendix I

Biomass

The economic competitiveness of short-rotation woody crop (SRWC) systems in the United States varies widely depending on a large number of factors such as end-product use, product price, conversion technology, yields, and land costs.[1] Such SRWC systems are considered to be economically viable for production of a stable, secure supply of wood for pulp under some conditions, as evidenced by recent increased interest in these systems by several pulp and paper companies. There are several million acres in the United States on which production of wood for energy feedstocks could be viable today, without subsidies, if there was a market for the wood.

A survey of the literature shows a range of $494 to $780 per hectare in anticipated establishment costs, where establishment includes all site preparation, planting, and weed competition control activities that are necessary to ensure good establishment and survival (Table I.1). The lowest cost per hectare of $494 is very similar to the average cost of establishing loblolly pines in plantations in the Southeast on cropland. It would be relatively rare, however, for the minimal site preparation efforts described by the North Carolina State University (NCSU) Hardwood-Industry Cooperative (Table I.1) to be sufficient to ensure good establishment and survival of hardwood energy crops. Such minimal establishment activity would likely lead to considerable weed competition. Some trees such as sweetgum might survive but exhibit slower growth during the first few years. The estimate provided by Strauss and Wright (1990) of $621 per hectare for establishment of hybrid poplars was developed by obtaining a consensus of several economists and silviculturalists associated with the Short Rotation Woody Crops Program.

Sensitivity analyses have shown that energy crop production costs are most sensitive to yield per hectare, with harvesting costs being the second

779

TABLE I.1 Variations in Establishment Operations and Costs for SRWC Plantations Established on Cropland

	Strauss and Wright (1990)	Campbell (1988)	Lothner et al. (1988)	Heilman et al. (in press)	NCSU Hardwood Co-op[a] Unpublished Report
Fall Site Preparation					
Herbicide	Herbicide	Herbicide	Herbicide	Herbicide	
Non/brush	Non/brush				
Plow	Plow	Plow	Plow/disk	Plow/disk/subsoil	Plow/mark rows
Lime	Lime	Lime		Herbicide	
Spring Site Preparation					
Disk/mark rows	Disk/mark rows	Disk	Disk/mark rows	Disk/mark rows	
Herbicide	Herbicide	Herbicide	Herbicide	Herbicide	
Fertilize	Fertilize	Fertilize			
Planting					
Cuttings (2100/ha)	Cuttings (2100/ha)	Seedlings (2100/ha[b])	Cuttings (1735/ha)	Cuttings (2150/ha)	Seedlings (2150/ha)
Weed Control Year 1					
Herbicide	Herbicide	Herbicide and cultivate	Cultivate and herbicide	Cultivate and herbicide	Herbicide
Weed Control Year 2					
Herbicide	Herbicide	Herbicide and cultivate	Cultivate and herbicide	Cultivate	Herbicide
Weed Control Year 3				Cultivate	
Establishment Cost ($/ha)	621	695	727	780	494

[a]Based on a comparison with data in "Cost and Cost Trends for Forestry Practices in the South" by Straka et al. (1989), these practices and costs are very similar to those required for establishing loblolly pine on old-field sites in the South. Using his estimate of $0.17/seedling, the costs were modified to assume 2100 trees/ha and use of weed control methods for 2 years instead of 1 year.

[b]Campbell chose 6735 trees/ha for evaluation of costs.

most important factor. However, at a given yield, land rental rates can be very important in determining the cost of production, although at higher yields the effect of land rent becomes less pronounced (Figure I.1). Cropland rental rates vary both within region and between regions. Table I.2 indicates some of the land rental estimates and other annual costs assumed by various economists.

None of the establishment or maintenance operations summarized in Tables I.1 and I.2 include the cost of road building, draining, installation of drainage tile, or activities that may be required to prevent damage from large herbivores and small mammals. These are all activities that might be required under some circumstances and might result in SRWC being economically unattractive.

For most analyses, it is assumed that harvest, chipping, and transportation costs will total $20 to $24 per dry megagram (Mg; 1 Mg = 1 million grams). This is based on research by the forest service that showed that smaller-sized feller bunchers, skidders, and chippers were more cost-effective for SRWC when the equipment had to handle a high density of small diameter stems (Stokes et al., 1986). However, if the need for chipping could be eliminated (such as by using the whole-tree burner concept) and

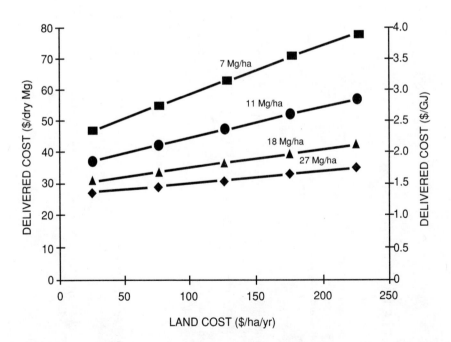

FIGURE I.1 SRWC delivered cost for wood chips harvested on a 6-year rotation as a function of land cost and yield.

TABLE I.2 Variations in SRWC Tending Operations and Other Annual Costs During the First Rotation

Strauss and Wright (1990)	Campbell (1988)	Lothner et al. (1988)	Heilman et al. (in press)	NCSU Hardwood Co-op Unpublished Report
Insecticide/fungicide years 2, 4, 6 at $25/ha/appl.	NA	NA	NA	NA
Fertilizer applied years 3 and 5 at $35/ha/appl.	Fertilizer applied year 2 at $55/ha/appl.	Fertilizer applied year 2 at $99/ha/appl.	NA	NA
Land rent at $85/ha/yr	Land rent at $66/ha/yr	Land rent at $99/ha/yr	Land rent at $123.50/ha/yr	Land rent[a] at $88/ha/yr
Land tax at $13/ha	Land tax at $14/ha	Land tax at $12/ha	Land tax no estimate	Land tax no estimate
Labor and facilities at $35/ha	Labor and facilities at $25/ha	Labor and facilities no estimate	Labor and facilities at $61.75/ha	Labor and facilities no estimate

[a]Based on average 1990 rental rates for cropland in South Carolina, Georgia, Alabama, Mississippi, Arkansas, and Louisiana (USDA/ERS, 1989).

greater efficiencies in harvesting and transportation operations incorporated, it might be possible to reduce that cost to about $14 to $16 per dry ton. Some analysts of SRWC costs have used even lower estimates (Lothner et al., 1988).

The summary of 1989 research status in Table I.3 attempts to draw from the above estimates of cost elements and to evaluate total delivered costs in different regions of the country. Because the recent cost analysis by Strauss and Wright (1990) was based on synthesizing information from a number of SRWC researchers around the country, it was used for basic cost assumptions on establishment, maintenance, and harvesting. A simple cost accounting spreadsheet was used to evaluate the effect of various levels of yield and land rental cost on the final delivered cost with an assumed discount rate of 10 percent. The yield levels used are not the best yields observed in experimental trials in the region, but rather yields that are assumed to be obtainable with currently available plant materials on a variety of cropland conditions in the region.

TABLE I.3 Short Rotation Woody Crops Program 1989 Research Status and Future Research Goals by Region

Regions	1989 Research Status			2010 Research Goals			
	Yield[a] (Mg/ha/yr)	Cost[b] ($/GJ)	Cost ($/Mg)	Yield[c] (Mg/ha/yr)	Cost ($/GJ)	Cost ($/Mg)	2010 Land Resource[d]
Northeast (NE)	9	2.75	54.45	15	1.90	37.62	0.5
South/Southeast (S/SE)	9	2.51	49.70	18	1.90	37.62	5.0
Midwest/Lake (MW/L)	11	2.75	54.45	20	1.90	37.62	21.0
Northwest (NW)	17	2.15	42.57	30	1.90	37.62	1.2
Subtropics	17	2.36	46.73	30	1.90	37.62	0.5

[a] Dry weight, above ground, leafless standing yields at harvest age. Numbers are selected values from production research results considered most representative of current technology in the region. Yield after processing and storage is assumed to be 15 percent less than standing yields.

[b] Delivered costs of chips including production, harvest, in-field chipping, and transportation costs and regional land costs, assuming yields shown in column one and no federal subsidies. Assumed land rental rates of $100/ha in NE, $75/ha in S/SE, $150/ha in MW/L, $150/ha in NW, and $200/ha in subtropics.

[c] Dry weight, above ground, leafless standing yields at harvest age. Numbers are based on projections of possible "average" yields if the best available plant materials were further improved for disease resistance and adaptability.

[d] The potential land base that is estimated to be available and capable of sustaining economically viable energy crop production by 2010, assuming average annual budgets of $10 million or more to allow development of several species. With continued research, up to 77 million ha might produce economically competitive energy crops by 2030.

NOTE

1. The biomass analysis presented in this report is based on work by Wright and Ehrenshaft (1990), who helped in the development of this section.

REFERENCES

Campbell, G. E. 1988. The Economics of Short-Rotation Intensive Culture in Illinois and the Central States. Forestry Research Report 88-12. Urbana: Agricultural Experiment Station, University of Illinois.

Heilman, P. E., R. F. Stettler, D. P. Hanley, and R. W. Gartner. In press. Intensive Culture of High Yield Poplar Plantations in the Pacific Northwest. Puyallup: Washington State University.

Lothner, D. D., E. E. Hansen, and D. A. Netzer. 1988. Growing and utilizing intensively cultured woody crops for energy: Some recent evidence from the north central United States. In Proceedings of the IEA Bioenergy, Task III, Activity 4, Workshop, Economic Evaluations of Biomass Oriented Systems for Fuel, G. Lonner and A. Tornquist, eds. Uppsala: Swedish University of Agricultural Sciences.

North Carolina State University Hardwood Research Cooperative. 1987. Economics and risk of SRWC in the Southeast. Unpublished report submitted to the U.S. Department of Energy's Short Rotation Woody Crops Program. School of Forest Resources, North Carolina State University, Raleigh.

Stokes, B. J., J. Frederick, and D. T. Curtin. 1986. Field trials of a short-rotation biomass feller buncher and selected harvesting systems. North Carolina State University, School of Forest Resources 11(3):185-204.

Straka, T. J., W. F. Watson, and M. Dubois. 1989. Costs and cost trends for forestry practices in the South. Forest Farmer Manual 1989:8-14.

Strauss, C. H., and L. L. Wright. 1990. Woody biomass production costs in the United States: An economic summary of commercial *Populus* plantations systems. Solar Energy 45(2):105-110.

U.S. Department of Agriculture, ERS. 1989. Agricultural Resources: Agricultural Land Values and Markets—Situation and Outlook Report. Report AR-14. Washington, D.C.: U.S. Government Printing Office.

Wright, L. L., and A. R. Ehrenshaft. 1990. Short Rotation Woody Crops Program: Annual Progress Report for 1986. ORNL-6635. Oak Ridge, Tenn.: Oak Ridge National Laboratory.

Appendix J

Cost-Effectiveness of Electrical Generation Technologies

Calculating the cost of electricity is a more complex task than the capital recovery factor calculations used for conservation and efficiency improvement options. In addition to the usual discount rates, one has to be concerned with a number of other parameters in computing the capital component of COE (cost of electricity). These include interest on bonds, minimum acceptable return on equity, depreciation, ad valorem taxes and insurance, and income tax and credits. In addition, there are different accounting procedures: normalized accounting, which uses fast depreciation for income tax calculations but normal depreciation for income statements, and flow-through accounting, in which the actual taxes paid are used in the income statements.

In levelizing the cost of electricity over the life of the plant, different companies may use different depreciation rates and different assumptions on interest rates and inflation. Thus it is quite conceivable that different COEs can be computed for the same technology. In spite of these complications, there is a need to compare different technologies on a consistent basis. The Electric Power Research Institute (1989) has issued a technology assessment guide (TAG), in which they have adopted a set of consistent assumptions. The Mitigation Panel has decided to use EPRI's approach and assumptions on capital cost, fixed charge rate, fixed operating and maintenance costs, variable operating and maintenance costs, and fuel cost. The calculation method used in the panel's analysis is shown in Table J.1, and the assumptions used are shown in Table J.2.

In a few instances, the panel deviates from EPRI's number by broadening the range. This was done for sensitivity comparisons. For example, EPRI's estimate as to the cost of nuclear fission power is presented as the lower of the two figures while the high-end represents a doubling of the

TABLE J.1   An Electricity Cost Calculation Method Used for Energy Supply Options (Constant Dollars)

Capital	$_____	/kW × 0.106 = _____	$/KW-yr
Fixed O&M		= _____	$/kW-yr
		Subtotal = _____	$/kW-yr

$$\text{Subtotal} \times \frac{1 \text{ mill}}{\$0.001} \times \frac{1 \text{ yr}}{8760 \text{ hrs}} \times \frac{1}{\_\text{CF}} = _____ \quad \text{mills/kWh}$$

Variable O&M (total)   = _____   mills/kWh

$$\textit{Fuel Cost} \quad \$\frac{}{10^6 \text{ Btu}} \times \frac{1 \text{ mill}}{\$0.001} \times \frac{\text{Btu}}{\text{kWh}} = _____ \quad \text{mills/kWh}$$

            (fuel cost)   (heat rate)

                                 TOTAL = _____   mills/kWh

NOTE: Capital recovery factor = 0.106 (constant dollar based on EPRI (1989) for a 30-year plant life and 3.6% real discount rate); CF = capacity factor (fraction); mills = 1/10¢ = $0.001; 1 year = 8,760 hours.

EPRI estimate as the cost of building a nuclear power plant varies a great deal for a wide variety of reasons including the time it takes for licensing and construction. Recently built nuclear power plants have cost from just below EPRI's estimate to twice EPRI's figure (U.S. Department of Energy, 1990). If the nuclear power plant construction time in France, Japan, and the United Kingdom can be achieved in the United States, the cost are likely to be in the low end of the range. However, if current experience in the United States as to the licensing and construction time are evidence of what the future will be, nuclear power costs are more likely to be in the high end of the range. Therefore, a range of cost from EPRI's estimate to twice EPRI's estimate was used in the Mitigation Panel's analysis.

Although four discount rates (3, 6, 10, and 30 percent) were used for the conservation options, only one (6 percent) was used in the power generation calculations because utility accounting, as described above, differs from conventional calculation of capital recovery. To use other discount rates, assumptions on acceptable return that the panel was unwilling to make would be needed. Furthermore, in cases such as biomass, only the potential emission reduction and cost could be estimated. In short, the panel has attempted to use what it believed to be the most practical and realistic way of assessing the potential of energy supply options.

TABLE J.2 Assumptions for Energy Supply Option Analysis Based on EPRI (1989), SERI (1990), and Wright and Ehrenshaft (1990)

Technology	Capital Cost ($/kW)	Fixed Operating and Maintenance ($/kW-yr)	Capacity Factor	Variable Operating and Maintenance (mills/kWh)	Fuel Cost[a] ($/10^6 Btu)	Heat Rate (Btu/kWh)	Total (mills/ kWh)
Gas (combined cycle)	518	3.70	0.65	3.70	2.47[b]	7,740	33-45
Nuclear	1,524-3,048[c]	61.1-122.2[c]	0.65	0.6	0.7	10,220	47-86
Solar thermal	2,776	44.4	0.3	0.8	2.47	3,300	143
Biomass	1,500	28.5	0.65	2.7	1-2	12,000	48-60
Wind	1,013	8	0.1-0.3	7.1	0	—	51-139
Solar photovoltaic	2,421	64	0.30	3.1	0	—	103
Geothermal	1,817	58	0.65	4.7	0	—	49
Advanced pulverized coal	1,537	29	0.65	5.7	1.31	9,080	51
Hydroelectric	2,000	0.005	0.45	2.2	0	—	56

[a] Annual average.
[b] The high range estimate for natural gas option assumes fuel price will escalate by 4 percent per year for 30 years.
[c] High cost estimate assumes capital and fixed operating and maintenance cost twice that of EPRI.

COMPARISON OF COSTS, CARBON DIOXIDE EMISSIONS, AND RELATIVE CARBON TAXES

Figure J.1 and Table J.3 summarize costs and CO_2 emissions of electricity generation technologies. In order of increasing cost per kilowatt-hour, the cheapest but dirtiest technology is a fully depreciated coal plant (2.0 to 3.5 cents/kWh), followed by an advanced gas plant (gas turbine combined cycle GTCC), which emits less than half as much CO_2 per kilowatt-hour at 3.3 to 4.5 cents/kWh. Next is geothermal (4.9 cents/kWh), the average 1989 U.S. mix of sources for electricity generation (5 cents/kWh), then advanced coal (5.1 cents/kWh) and nuclear plants (4.7 to 8.6 cents/kWh). The high end of the nuclear energy cost range of 8.6 cents/kWh was for a capital and fixed operating and maintenance cost twice that quoted in the EPRI guide. As discussed earlier, the panel believes this to be more realistic. Last are renewable technologies, ranging from biomass (4.8 to 6 cents/kWh) to hydroelectric (5 to 6 cents/kWh) to solar thermal-gas hybrid (14.3 cents/kWh), all of which have supply or economic limitations.

It is important to note that as the experience with a particular energy technology in the United States increases, so does the reliability of the cost estimate. For example, natural gas plants have been built in the United States for many years and there is a great deal of experience as to their construction and operating costs on a massive scale, so the reliability of these numbers is likely to be higher than that of solar energy where there is

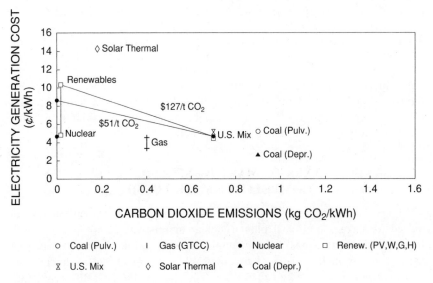

FIGURE J.1 Cost-effectiveness of energy supply options.

TABLE J.3   Cost-Effectiveness of CO_2 Reduction for Different Sources of Electricity Supply

Energy Source	Cost[a] (¢/kWh)	Emissions (kg CO_2/kWh)	CO_2 Tax Needed for Indifference with U.S. Fuel Mix[b] ($/t CO_2)
U.S. mix	5	0.7	0
Coal, advanced pulverized	5.1	0.86	NA
Coal, running cost of depreciated plant	2.0-3.5[c]	0.9	NA
Gas, combined cycle	3.3-4.5[d]	0.41	NA
Nuclear	4.7-8.6[e]	0	NA to 51
Hydroelectric	5.6	0	9
Geothermal	4.9	0	NA
Solar photovoltaic	10.3	0	76
Solar thermal/gas hybrid	14.3	0.18	177
Wind	5.1-13.9	0	1 to 127
Biomass	4.8-6.0	0[f]	NA to 14

NOTE: NA = Not applicable (i.e., cost less than U.S. mix).
[a]Based on assumptions from EPRI (1989), SERI (1990), and Wright and Ehrenshaft (1990).
[b]$/t CO_2 = (Option Cost – U.S. Mix Cost) ($/100¢)(1000 kg/ton)
[c]Assumed by Mitigation Panel.
[d]Assumes 50 percent thermal efficiency and no gas price escalation for low-cost and EPRI efficiency plus 4 percent annual fuel escalation for high-cost estimates.
[e]High estimate assumes capital cost twice EPRI value.
[f]Biomass sequestered CO_2 before it was burned, so the net carbon emission is zero.

only limited experience in the United States. Therefore, cost estimates for industries such as wind and solar power that do not have a developed industry are more speculative. This should be taken into consideration when reviewing any of the estimates presented here.

CARBON TAXES TO MAKE NONFOSSIL GENERATION COMPETITIVE WITH FOSSIL

Figure J.1 allows one to visualize the magnitude of the carbon tax required to make a nonfossil plant (nuclear or renewable) competitive with fossil plants (coal or gas). For example, consider a line sloping down from the top of the nuclear range (8.6 cents/kWh and no CO_2) to advanced coal (5.1 cents/kWh and 0.9 kg CO_2/kWh). The slope is the cost difference (3.5 cents/kWh) divided by the CO_2 difference (0.9 kg), which corresponds to

3.9 cents/kg, or \$39/t.[1] This means that a carbon or CO_2 tax of \$39/t CO_2 would raise the cost of a kilowatt-hour from advanced coal by 3.9 cents, making this fuel exactly competitive with nuclear. Conversely, a "carbon saving" subsidy of \$39/t CO_2 paid to nuclear power would lower its cost and again achieve economic parity with coal.

The overall effect of a carbon tax is shown by drawing a line from each technology to the average point labeled "U.S. Mix." For nuclear power, this line has a slope of \$51/t CO_2. Thus, if current U.S. plants were each taxed at \$51/t CO_2, the average price of electricity would increase the 3.6 cents/kWh needed to make new nuclear plants competitive with the fossil fuels that currently supply the majority of U.S. energy. This would likely encourage utilities to invest in nonfossil forms of energy supply. It is not clear at this point, however, how such complex taxing would affect the cost of electricity and the cost-effectiveness of nuclear power to shareholders. Similar carbon taxes would make renewable technologies competitive. For example, a steeper line joining solar-photovoltaic to the U.S. mix, sloping down at \$127/t CO_2, would raise U.S. electricity to 10.3 cents/kWh and make the hybrid competitive today.

In Table J.3, all fossil and nonfossil technologies are compared with the U.S. mix, and the CO_2 tax needed to make the choice of an alternative economically equivalent to the current U.S. supply is computed. Negative values (which correspond to subsidies for emitting CO_2) make no sense and are labeled not applicable in Table J.3.

NOTE

1. Throughout this report, tons (t) are metric; 1 Mt = 1 megaton = 1 million tons.

REFERENCES

Electric Power Research Institute. 1989. Technical Assessment Guide, Electricity Supply. Report EPRI P-6587-L. Palo Alto, Calif.: Electric Power Research Institute.

Solar Energy Research Institute. 1990. The Potential of Renewable Energy: An Interlaboratory White Paper. Report SERI/TP-260-3674. Golden, Colo.: Solar Energy Research Institute.

U.S. Department of Energy. 1990. An Analysis of Nuclear Power Plant Construction Costs. Report DOE/EIA-0485. Washington, D.C.: U.S. Department of Energy. March/April 1986. Supplemented by Energy Information Administration staff on December 14, 1990.

Wright, L. L., and A. R. Ehrenshaft. 1990. Short Woody Crops Program: Annual Progress Report for 1989. Report ORNL-6625. Oak Ridge, Tenn.: Oak Ridge National Laboratory.

Appendix K

Cost-Effectiveness of Chlorofluorocarbon Phaseout—United States and Worldwide

Tables K.1 and K.2 detail the cost estimates associated with a CFC phaseout in the United States and worldwide, respectively. The analysis considers only the cost of a CFC phaseout and does not include costs associated with the anticipated phaseout of halons. Costs associated with capital obsolescence or taxes are not considered in this analysis. Fluorocarbon substitute costs are assumed to be 2 times and 3 times the present cost of CFCs ($2250/t)[1] for hydrochlorofluorocarbons (HCFCs) and hydrofluorocarbons (HFCs), respectively.

Abatement costs for CO_2 equivalents to CFCs are based on net reductions; that is, the CO_2 equivalents of fluorocarbon substitutes (where applicable) are subtracted from the CO_2 equivalents for the reductions before the cost is calculated. The calculation is based on an estimate of both the present mix of CFCs and an assumed mix of fluorocarbon substitutes.

The CFC reduction (emission) estimates for 1989 were obtained from the Du Pont Company and are based on its market forecasts in 1988.

Details of the assumptions made on each policy option are shown below.

The total cost for a CFC phaseout is approximately $2.0 billion per year in the United States and $6.3 billion per year worldwide (constant 1990 dollars, 6 percent capital recovery rate).

U.S. CFC POLICY OPTIONS

1. *Cleaning and Blowing Agents, Aerosols, Refrigerants, Not-in-Kind Substitutes:* Added equipment costs for these applications are assumed to be $2000/t or $172 million per life. Cost of these substitutes is assumed to be $200/t less than CFCs for an annual operating cost savings of $17 million.

2. *Conservation and Recycling:* A 50-50 split is assumed between con-

792

servation and recycling. Equipment costs for recycling are $1500/t ($750/t for the total category) or $74 million per lifetime. The CFC cost savings of $2250/t will be equaled by the additional costs associated with increased minor annual equipment upgrades and increased manpower efforts for maintenance and recycling.

3. *Cleaning and Blowing Agents, Aerosols, Fluorocarbon Substitutes:* Added equipment costs are assumed to be negligible. The cost of substitutes is assumed to be 2 times the cost of CFCs for an annual increase of $167 million in operating costs.

4. *Refrigerants, Fluorocarbon Substitutes—Chillers:* Each of the present 100,000 chillers now being used is assumed to cost $25,000 additional for retrofit or replacement for a total cost of $2.50 billion per life. Fluorocarbon alternatives are assumed to cost an average of 2.5 times the present cost of CFCs.

5. *Refrigerants, Fluorocarbon Substitutes—Mobile Air Conditioning:* 100 million automobile air conditioners are assumed to be used at present. Each is expected to cost $50 additional when replaced for a total cost of $5.0 billion per life. Fluorocarbon alternatives are assumed to cost 3 times the cost of CFCs.

6. *Refrigerants, Fluorocarbon Substitutes—Other:* Other refrigerant applications (supermarkets, transport, etc.) are estimated to represent $15 billion worth of equipment. Replacement is expected to add 10 percent to this equipment cost. Fluorocarbon alternatives are expected to cost 3 times as much as the current price of CFCs.

7. *Refrigerants, Fluorocarbon Substitutes, Appliance Insulation, Fluorocarbon Substitutes:* Domestic refrigerators are expected to cost $60 additional on replacement for a total cost of $4.8 billion per life for the present 80 million refrigerators. The equipment cost has been allocated to the two uses based on total CFC use. The cost of fluorocarbon substitutes is 3 times and 2 times that of CFCs for refrigerant and insulation, respectively. The high cost of these reductions is due to the small amount of CFCs (approximately 1.0 kg) used in each refrigerator.

WORLDWIDE CFC POLICY OPTIONS

1. *Aerosols, Not-in-Kind Substitutes:* Equipment costs will increase by $100,000 for each aerosol manufacturing line in order to handle flammable CFC replacements. For 250 lines worldwide, the cost will total $25 million. At a present cost of $2.25/kg, CFCs are replaced with hydrocarbons at $0.65/kg. Savings are reduced 10 percent due to lack of availability of suitable hydrocarbons for some aerosol needs. For those applications, substitute costs are assumed equal to CFCs. Savings are also reduced by $100/t for increased costs of handling flammable substitutes.

TABLE K.1   Cost Impact of CFC Phaseout—United States

CFC Policy Option	CFC Reduction (Mt/yr)	CO_2-Equivalent Reduction (Mt/yr)	Capital Cost (M$/life)	Equipment Lifetime (years)	Annual Capital Cost (M$/yr)		
					3%	6%	10%
Cleaning and blowing agents, aerosols, refrigerants, not-in-kind substitutes	0.086	302	172	10	20	23	28
Conservation and recycle	0.098	509	74	5	16	18	20
Cleaning and blowing agents, aerosols, fluorocarbon substitutes	0.074	248	0	10	0	0	0
Refrigerants, fluorocarbon substitutes							
Chillers	0.023	88	2,500	30	128	182	265
Mobile air conditioning	0.030	170	5,000	10	586	679	814
Appliance	0.002	11	1,067	15	89	110	140
Other	0.010	67	1,500	10	176	204	244
Appliance insulation, fluorocarbon substitutes	0.007	14	3,733	15	313	384	491
TOTAL	0.33	1,409	14,046				

NOTE: Mt = megaton = 1 million tons. Tons are metric.

2. *Conservation and Recycling:* A 50-50 split is assumed between conservation and recycling. Equipment costs for recycling are $1500/t ($750/t for the total category) or $202.5 million per lifetime. The CFC cost savings of $2250/t will be equaled by the additional costs associated with minor annual equipment upgrades and increased manpower efforts for maintenance and recycling.

3. *Cleaning and Blowing Agents, Refrigerants, Not-in-Kind Substitutes:* Added equipment cost for these applications is assumed to be $2000/t or $400 million per life. Cost of these substitutes is assumed to be $200/t less than CFCs for an annual operating cost savings of $40 million.

4. *Cleaning and Blowing Agents, Aerosols, Fluorocarbon Substitutes:* Added equipment costs are assumed to be negligible. The cost of substitutes is assumed to be 2 times the cost of CFCs for an annual increase of $472.5 million in operating costs.

5. *Refrigerants, Fluorocarbon Substitutes—Chillers:* Each of the present 150,000 chillers now being used is assumed to cost $25,000 additional for

Operating Cost (M$/yr)	Total Cost (M$/yr)			Abatement Cost ($/t CFC)			Abatement Cost ($/t CO$_2$ Equivalent)		
	3%	6%	10%	3%	6%	10%	3%	%6	%10
−17	3	6	11	35	70	128	0.01	0.02	0.04
0	16	18	20	163	184	204	0.03	0.04	0.04
167	167	167	167	2,250	2,250	2,250	0.67	0.67	0.67
78	206	260	343	8,956	11,304	14,913	2.35	2.97	3.92
135	721	814	949	24,033	27,133	31,633	4.25	4.80	5.60
9	98	119	149	49,000	59,500	74,500	8.67	10.53	13.11
45	221	249	289	22,100	24,900	28,900	3.32	3.74	4.34
16	329	400	507	47,000	57,143	72,429	23.59	28.69	36.36
	1,761	2,033	2,435						

retrofit or replacement for a total cost of $3.75 billion per life. Fluorocarbon alternatives are assumed to have an average of 2.5 times the present cost of CFCs.

6. *Refrigerants, Fluorocarbon Substitutes—Mobile Air Conditioning:* About 200 million automobile air conditioners are assumed to be used at the present time. Each is expected to cost $50 extra when replaced for a total cost of $10 billion per life. Fluorocarbon alternatives are assumed to have 3 times the cost of CFCs.

7. *Refrigerants, Fluorocarbon Substitutes—Other:* Other refrigerant applications (supermarket, transport, etc.) are estimated to represent $35 billion worth of equipment. Replacement is expected to add 10 percent to this equipment cost. Fluorocarbon alternatives are expected to have 3 times the present cost of CFCs.

8. *Refrigerants, Fluorocarbon Substitutes, Appliance Insulation, Fluorocarbon Substitutes:* Domestic refrigerators are expected to cost $60 additional on replacement for a total cost of $30 billion per life for the present

TABLE K.2   Cost Impact of CFC Phaseout—Worldwide

CFC Policy Option	CFC Reduction (Mt/yr)	CO_2- Equivalent Reduction (Mt/yr)	Capital Cost (M$/life)	Equipment Lifetime (years)	Annual Capital Cost (M$/yr)		
					3%	6%	10%
Aerosols refrigerants, not-in-kind substitutes	0.12	492	25	10	3	3	4
Conservation and recycle	0.27	1,402	203	5	44	48	53
Cleaning and blowing agents, refrigerants, not-in-kind substitutes	0.20	701	400	10	47	54	65
Cleaning and blowing agents, aerosols, fluorocarbon substitutes	0.21	705	0	10	0	0	0
Refrigerants, fluorocarbon substitutes							
Chillers	0.04	152	3,750	30	191	272	398
Mobile air conditioning	0.08	452	10,000	10	1,172	1,359	1,628
Appliance	0.013	73	7,800	15	653	803	1,026
Other	0.03	200	3,500	10	410	476	570
Appliance insulation, fluorocarbon substitutes	0.037	74	22,200	15	1,860	2,286	2,919
TOTAL	1.0	4,251	47,878				

NOTE: Mt = megaton = 1 million tons. Tons are metric.

500 million refrigerators. Equipment cost has been allocated to the two uses based on total CFC use. The cost of fluorocarbon substitutes is 3 times and 2 times that of CFCs for refrigerant and insulation, respectively. The high cost of these reductions is due to the small amount of CFCs (approximately 1.0 kg) used in each refrigerator.

NOTE

1. Throughout this report, tons (t) are metric; 1 Mt = 1 megaton = 1 million tons.

Operating Cost (M$/yr)	Total Cost (M$/yr)			Abatement Cost ($/t CFC)			Abatement Cost ($/t CO_2 Equivalent)		
	3%	6%	10%	3%	6%	10%	3%	%6	%10
−161	−158	−157	−157	−1,316	−1,312	−1,307	−0.32	−0.32	−0.32
0	44	48	53	164	178	198	0.03	0.03	0.04
−40	7	14	25	35	72	126	0.01	0.02	0.04
473	473	473	473	2,250	2,250	2,250	0.67	0.67	0.67
135	326	407	533	8,158	10,185	13,320	2.14	2.68	3.49
360	1,532	1,719	1,988	19,154	21,484	24,844	3.39	3.80	4.40
59	712	862	1,084	54,762	66,277	83,385	9.69	11.73	14.76
135	545	611	705	18,177	20,350	23,487	2.73	3.05	3.52
83	1,943	2,369	3,002	52,514	64,027	81,132	26.36	32.14	40.65
	5,424	6,346	7,706						

Appendix L

Agriculture

Some developing countries have reached the limits of land expansion. India's population has more than doubled since 1950, but cropland has only expanded by 15 percent or so. Crop yields have increased, and multiple cropping has increased to enable more than a doubling of agricultural product.

For a number of developing countries, this historical process has not yet been completed, however. In parts of Southeast Asia, most of sub-Saharan Africa, and parts of Latin America, notably Brazil (and Colombia), cropland and pastureland expansion continues.

LAND USE AND CARBON SINKS

Cropland and pastureland constitute significant carbon sinks even though they do not store much carbon in vegetation. The carbon in the soil for cropland and pasture is significant and can actually be higher than for certain woodland types and for semiarid savannah-type lands. Significant carbon is stored in animal stocks as well.

Historically, cropland and pastureland expansion in the temperate zone countries has tended to be "sink-reducing" (expansion against forests) or "sink-neutral" (expansion on prairie lands). In countries still in the expansion process, it is probably on balance sink-reducing, but there is quite considerable expansion that is either sink-neutral or sink-expanding. In addition, most of the expansion on savannah-type land has probably also been sink-expanding. Population change, technology, and government policies affect land use patterns. Typically, as population grows (with constant technology of production) relative to land resources, cropland expands at the expense of other land uses. As land best suited to cropland (and pasture) is settled (i.e., the frontier is closed), various land-saving options are employed. Improved varietal technology (high-yielding varieties) reduces the pressure on resources. The combination of changing economic conditions and new technology brings cropland expansion to a halt in developed countries. Cropland expansion in farms in the United States stopped around 1920, and cropland area has declined in recent years. (Farm production has tripled since 1920.) This is also true for pastureland. The same situation holds in Europe generally.

Large areas of savannah-type land exist in sub-Saharan Africa and in the local Cerrado-Llianos region in Brazil and Colombia (with some in Bolivia and Paraguay). Agricultural research programs in these countries have sought to achieve efficient land use expansion and have been successful in facilitating land expansion in the Cerrado regions in Brazil. This expansion has also been fueled by subsidized credit, which has fueled expansion in the Amazon, where it is sink-reducing. On balance, the agricultural research systems in Brazil and Africa have facilitated expansion on sink-neutral or sink-expanding areas. It is not clear that any policies can materially change some of the land use patterns that will occur in much of Africa over the next few decades. Populations are growing at rapid rates, and few countries have effective family planning. To the extent that improved agricultural technology can be developed, it will alter the ultimate course of expansion of cropped areas. Industrial development and nonfarm employment opportunities for workers will, as well. Much of this expansion will be sink-neutral, however, because savannah lands are not large sinks. The most severe problems will be associated with desertification and the management of shorter fallow systems on savannah soils.

In developed and developing countries alike, however, even if oil prices do not rise appreciably over the next two decades, continued technological improvements are likely to bring some biomass energy options into the competitive range. No major breakthroughs are necessary (although some may be achieved). Continued support for well-established plant breeding and agronomic research programs is required to bring this biomass energy option.

AGRICULTURAL GREENHOUSE GAS MITIGATION

General Options

For purposes of assessing the relative impacts of U.S. emission controls and controls in other countries, the range of emission reduction (million tons of carbon) from a 10 percent reduction in rice production or ruminant production in different regions is used in this analysis.[1] The United States is a minor contributor of CH_4 from rice paddies and contributes virtually nothing from work animals. It is an important source of CH_4 from other ruminant animals (as are other industrialized countries).

The mechanisms by which reductions in CH_4 emissions in the United States and in other countries can be achieved include the following options:

1. Elimination of existing subsidies that stimulate more of the activity than dictated by market equilibrium conditions.

2. Taxation of the CH_4-emitting activity.

3. Quantitative regulation of activities (i.e., through quotas on production and trade) or regulations regarding burning and waste management.

4. Buyouts, either through purchase of assets (e.g., rice paddy land, dairy cows, or pastureland) or payments to induce alternative activities (e.g., paying rice farmers not to produce rice, but allowing them to produce an alternative crop on the land).

These mechanisms vary in effectiveness and cost per unit of CH_4 reduction achieved. The lowest-cost option is generally option 1 because subsidies induce inefficient resource use, and their elimination is actually an economic gain. However, they exist because interest groups have used political power to put them in place. Thus their elimination has political implications.

Option 2 is costly from a consumer's standpoint because it induces inefficient resource use due to market distortions. A producer will produce less of a taxed good than an untaxed good. Therefore from a consumer's standpoint, too little of the taxed good is produced. Calculation of these inefficiency costs is complex and requires estimates of supply and demand responses to a tax.

Option 3 also causes inefficiency losses, and this option, too, requires complex cost calculations.

Option 4 has the seeming merit of being directly calculable. For example, a government agency might pay a rice farmer $100 per acre not to produce paddy rice but allow him to produce an alternative crop on the land. One could then compute the CH_4 emission from an acre of paddy land and arrive at a cost per ton of CH_4 mitigated. Alternatively, a government agency might purchase rice paddy land (for $5000 per acre) and leave it idle (or reforest it). Then the investment could be amortized at alternative interest rates, and a cost per ton of CH_4 reduced can be obtained. The difficulty with this mechanism is that other rice farms might respond to this action by producing more paddy rice.

There are some options associated with farming practices, particularly minimum tillage options, but the scope for extensive adoption of these practices is limited because most farmers are aware of them and have tested them. Where they have been found effective, they have already been adopted.

In addition, as with production practices generally, use of these practices tends to depend on prices—especially the price of energy.

It should be further noted that some options have consequences that may be undesirable. Substitution of tractors for work animals may eliminate CH_4 emissions, but constitutes an increase in fossil fuel use and CO_2 emissions (and some increase in chemical fertilizer use). Swampland drainage has consequences for wildlife and species diversity (Matthews and Fung, 1987).

Options for Rice Paddies

Almost all of the approximately 1 million hectares (ha) of production in the United States is irrigated paddy rice. All water regimes, except upland, produce paddy rice (i.e., rice grown under standing-water conditions). There are no practical options to grow alternative crops in deep- and medium-water rainfed regimes. Perhaps half of the shallow-water-rainfed and irrigated regimes could be shifted to alternative crops but at some cost. Upland rice is not an alternative crop to paddy rice. It is produced under conditions quite different from paddy rice—usually on semiarid land. Even if land is no longer being used for paddy rice, it is highly unlikely to be planted with upland rice.

The United States has a little less than 1 percent of the world's paddy rice land but produces about 1.3 percent of the world's paddy rice. It accounts for approximately 20 percent of world rice exports. Approximately 90 percent of the world's paddy rice production is in Asia, with China, India, Indonesia, Bangladesh, Thailand, Vietnam, and Japan being the leading producers (International Rice Research Institute, 1988).

Several rice-importing countries intervene in rice markets with high tariffs to protect domestic rice producers. The ratio of domestic prices to world prices was over 7 in Japan in 1985. South Korea, Taiwan, and most European economies also protect domestic producers (with ratios of domestic to world prices greater than 2 (World Bank, 1987)). Elimination of this protection in these countries would result in lower domestic prices, decreased domestic production, more imports, and increased domestic consumption. World rice prices would rise in response, and this would reduce consumption marginally in other countries. The net effect of the removal of such protection on global CH_4 emissions would probably be quite small.

Exporting countries, such as the United States, cannot maintain domestic prices at levels above world prices except at high costs to subsidize exports. Consequently, the United States has a relatively modest program of subsidies to rice producers. A price support program is in place, with support prices roughly 30 percent above export prices (Gardner, 1987). Elimination of these subsidy programs would reduce U.S. production and exports, but would be partially offset by increases in production in other countries.

Taxation of paddy rice in the United States could be undertaken, but would be difficult politically because subsidies are now in place. It should be noted, however, that the other major rice-exporting country, Thailand, has used a rice tax (called the rice premium) for years to reduce rice exports, realize a higher export price, and increase government revenues. If such a tax were imposed on U.S. rice farmers (presumably after subsidies had been eliminated) and the supply response elasticity to the tax were significantly negative (Gardner, 1987), a reduction in U.S. production and CH_4 emissions could be achieved. If domestic prices did not change (i.e., were determined by world prices), domestic consumption would not change, so the full effect would be felt in reduced exports. Because the United States is a leading exporter, this could have an impact on world rice prices. The cost of this tax would be loss of the export revenue (10 percent of the value of production) minus the value of other crops that could be produced on land formerly devoted to paddy rice (0.95 × 10 percent of the value of production) (Gardner, 1987). This assumes a demand elasticity of –0.5 and a supply elasticity of 0.5 (see Barker and Herdt, 1985). Thus a 10 percent tax on U.S. paddy production would reduce emissions by 200,000 t C as CH_4/yr (computed as 2 t C/ha). The cost would be 0.005 × 6 Mt × \$300/t, or \$9 million, giving a cost per ton of carbon of \$45 (the cost per ton CH_4 is \$16).

A quota system has been suggested as a way to reduce production and has been used in a number of countries for other products. This could also be applied to paddy rice producers (Johnson, 1990). Licenses might be required to sell paddy rice; these could be traded and the total available licenses to farmers reduced by 10 percent (or some other level). This option would have the same costs as the tax option, provided the licenses were negotiable.

The buyout options for paddy rice in the United States are actually the simplest to analyze. A government agency would have two alternatives:

1. Purchase rice paddy land directly from farmers and convert it to idle land or to some other use (e.g., it could plant trees on the land, although some rice paddy land is probably poorly suited to tree production);

2. Offer a payment to buy the land out of paddy production for 1 or more years and allow farmers to produce an alternative crop.

The option of buying paddy land out of production is the more costly of the two, but it could complement other policies. Paddy land would probably cost \$7,000 to \$10,000/ha. The annualized interest costs at 3 percent would be \$210 to \$300, and approximately 2 t CH_4 (carbon equivalent) would be mitigated. At 6 and 10 percent interest rates the costs would be

$420 to $600, and $700 to $1000. The cost per ton of carbon mitigated would range from $150 to $500.

The option of yearly or multiyear arrangements to pay farmers for not producing paddy rice but allow them to produce alternative crops would depend on the suitability of the land for alternative crops. For land where the substitution could be made easily, payments could be modest (e.g., $100/ha). For land where drainage and other modifications would be required, these payments could rise to the full buyout option costs. Water pricing policies have also affected paddy rice production in California. Farmers have access to water at rates far below the real value of water. If water were priced at market rates, much of the California rice production would be uneconomical. It would be a wise policy for all parties to devise a compensation scheme to enable more efficient water pricing, and this would reduce rice production and CH_4 emissions at little or no cost.

Other countries would incur similar costs if they were to attempt to reduce rice production. It would be difficult to manage the tax options in countries that do not export (where the tax can be levied on the exported goods). Taxation leading to rice price increases could also have severe implications for large low-income populations, where rice is often the staple food. It would also be difficult to manage a coupon or quota system in countries where rice is consumed by the households producing it (most developing countries).

Thus the realistic options in developing countries are the buyout options, and these, if pursued in substantial degree, will have the consequence of raising rice prices, which will induce more conversion of nonrice areas to rice, partially offsetting the effects of the reductions. The options for increasing upland nonpaddy rice are quite limited, in part because little technological progress has been made in upland rice production.

Options for Ruminant Products

A shift from ruminant products (dairy products, beef, and mutton) to cereal-based products would reduce CH_4 emissions. The United States is a major producer and consumer of ruminant products, and several mitigation options are open to it. In fact, a number of these options have been pursued, although not to mitigate CH_4 emissions. The United States, Canada, and the European Economic Community (EEC) countries have been intervening in dairy product markets for many years to achieve prices to producers (and consumers) that are higher than equilibrium market prices. This has been undertaken via import controls in EEC countries and via support prices and regulated trade in milk markets in the United States and in Europe as well (Barichello, 1984).

When prices are supported above market equilibrium levels, consumers wish to consume less and producers wish to produce more than equilibrium levels. This results in the accumulation of surpluses unless supply control measures are taken. Such surpluses have been a common phenomenon in the United States, Canada, and Europe, and in general, these countries have probably produced as much dairy products as would have been the case in an unregulated market even though consumers have consumed less (World Bank, 1987).

Quantitative supply control programs could be employed to reduce both production and consumption further, however. Taxes on dairy products or on meats, except for the normal sales taxes that affect all foods, would also discourage consumption. Political factors, however, produce subsidies and price support systems, not taxes, in the United States and European economies (Johnson, 1990).

Livestock commodities other than dairy products have experienced less government program intervention because of the high costs of surplus storage.

The elimination of existing (costly) dairy support and feed grain support programs (which indirectly support meat production) in the United States (and the EEC) would lead to increased consumption of ruminant products and probably to increased ruminant production and CH_4 emissions. A tax on ruminant consumption and production would probably be politically unacceptable. It could achieve CH_4 mitigation, however. The cost of a tax using standard measurement techniques (see Gardner, 1987) would depend on supply and demand responses to the tax.

Estimates of demand responses (Gardner, 1987) range from -0.4 to -0.7 (i.e., a 10 percent tax would reduce consumption by 4 to 7 percent). Few estimates of supply responses are available, but it is reasonable to postulate a relatively high long-run supply response. Thus a 10 percent tax could reduce consumption by roughly 5 percent (based on medium demand estimates) (Gardner, 1987).

Quota systems have been used to control dairy production in Canada but have generally been costly to monitor and administer. If effective, they have the same efficiency costs as the ruminant tax option but different income options (Barichello, 1984).

Buyout options to reduce dairy product supply have also been used in the United States. These options have generally been ineffective because the compliance of nonparticipants cannot be ensured.

Options for Work Animals

Approximately 300 million of the 970 million cattle and buffalo worldwide are used primarily as work animals. Most south Asian and sub-Saharan African farms are not yet mechanized. It is generally thought that existing subsidy programs, particularly credit subsidies, induce the substitution of machines (tractors) for animals and thus encourage "overmechanization."

Such subsidies could further reduce the world's work animal stock and thus CH_4 emissions; however, fossil fuel use could increase, reducing the greenhouse gas benefit from the subsidies. Thus a trade-off between reduced CH_4 and increased fossil fuel use must be addressed. On balance, it is probably not wise to encourage more mechanization in developing countries (Binswanger, 1986).

Options for Biomass Burning

Biomass burning—to clear land for agricultural production or to carry out general farm management activities—contributes to CH_4 emissions. Burning in sugarcane fields is a low-cost way to reduce trash and facilitate harvest and processing. Rice straw and other plant residues are sometimes burned to lower the cost of plowing and land preparation even though burning reduces the amount of organic matter in soil.

Thus, although some biomass burning by farmers may constitute poor management, most burning by farmers is done for cost considerations. Regulation of this burning (e.g., banning some of the burning in specific situations) is probably not costly and in some cases may actually bring about managerial improvement. Thus selective judicious controls on biomass burning may be cost-effective in CH_4 (and N_2O) mitigation.

Options for Biogas from Animal Waste

Confined animal production systems require special waste management practices and offer some potential for the production of CH_4 biogas. Most cities and counties in developed countries regulate waste management largely for pollution reasons. Waste from animals is used widely as a fuel in many developing countries and as organic fertilizer in most countries. Biogas projects have been implemented in many countries but have not attained widespread use.

Further judicious regulations and technological improvements in biogas production will achieve some mitigation of CH_4 (and replacement of fossil fuel), but these are not likely to be large effects.

Options for Fertilizers

Several studies of fertilizer demand estimate that a 10 percent increase in price (from a tax) would decrease use by roughly 5 percent (Gardner, 1987). The efficiency cost of such a tax would be only 0.0025 percent of the total fertilizer value if farmers were in equilibrium and the long-run supply of fertilizer were perfectly elastic. If such a tax were applied on all nitrogen fertilizer in the United States, it would have an efficiency cost of $25 million and would reduce N_2O emission by 50,000 t N/yr at a cost of $500/t N.

COST-EFFECTIVENESS CALCULATIONS

The cost-effectiveness of the policy measures described above is summarized in Table 25.4. To determine the cost-effectiveness in terms of CO_2 equivalence, the U.S. information in Table 25.4 is used, and CH_4 and N_2O emission reductions are weighted by the global warming potential factor (21 for CH_4 and 190 for N_2O (per discussion of global warming potential in Chapter 19). Therefore

Paddy rice:
$$(3 \times 10^6 \text{ t C as } CH_4)(16 \ CH_4/12 \ C)(21 \ CO_2/1 \ CH_4) = 84 \times 10^6 \text{ t } CO_2 \text{ eq.}$$
$$(\$100/t \text{ C as } CH_4)(12 \ C/16 \ CH_4)(1 \ CH_4/21 \ CO_2) = \$3.6/t \ CO_2 \text{ eq.}$$
Ruminants:
$$(4.5 \times 10^6 \text{ t C as } CH_4)(16 \ CH_4/12 \ C)(21 \ CO_2/1 \ CH_4) = 126 \times 10^6 \text{ t}CO_2 \text{ eq.}$$
$$(\$150/t \text{ C as } CH_4)(12 \ C/16 \ CH_4)(1 \ CH_4/21 \ CO_2) = \$5.4/t \ CO_2 \text{ eq.}$$
Fertilizer:
$$(0.05 \times 10^6 \text{ t N as } N_2O)(44 \ N_2O/28 \ N)(290 \ CO_2/N_2O) = 23 \times 10^6 \text{ t } CO_2 \text{ eq.}$$
$$(\$500/t \text{ N as } N_2O)(28 \ N/44 \ N_2O)(1 \ N_2O/290 \ CO_2) = \$1.1/t \ CO_2 \text{ eq.}$$

NOTE

1. Throughout this report, tons (t) are metric; 1 Mt = 1 megaton = 1 million tons.

REFERENCES

Barichello, R. R. 1984. Analyzing an agricultural marketing quota. Discussion Paper 454. Economic Growth Center, Yale University, New Haven, Conn.

Barker, R., and R. Herdt. 1985. The Rice Economy of Asia. Washington, D.C.: Resources for the Future.

Binswanger, H. 1986. Agricultural Mechanization: A Comparative Historical Perspective. The World Bank Research Observer 1. Washington, D.C.: World Bank.

Gardner, B. 1987. The Economics of Agricultural Policies. New York: Macmillan.

Hayami, Y., and V. W. Ruttan. 1985. Agricultural Development, An International Perspective. Baltimore: John Hopkins Press.

International Rice Research Institute. 1988. World Rice Statistics. Los Ranes, Laguna, Phillipines: International Rice Research Institute.

Johnson, D. G. 1990. World Agriculture in Disarray. Chicago: University of Chicago Press.

Matthews, E., and I. Fung. 1987. Methane emissions from natural wetlands: Global distribution, area and environmental characteristics of sources. Global Biogeochemical Cycles 1:61-86.

World Bank. 1987. World Development Report. Washington, D.C.: World Bank.

Appendix M

Landfill Methane Reduction

As shown in Chapter 25, the potential emission reductions for CH_4 from landfills are given in column 1 of Table 25.8.[1] Under regulatory alternative 2, emissions from existing landfills can be reduced by 60 percent, and new landfills by 65 percent. Multiplying these percentages times the CH_4 emissions in Table 25.7 as shown below yields 11.1 Mt of CH_4 emission reduction per year.

Existing	$18 \times 0.60 = 10.8$
New	$0.53 \times 0.65 = 0.34$
	TOTAL $CH_4 = 11.1$ Mt/yr

Next, this number must be converted to CO_2 equivalence. Information from the IPCC shows that each kilogram of CH_4 is equivalent to 21 times the global warming potential of CO_2 for a 100-yr time horizon. Therefore

$$11.1 \text{ Mt } CH_4/\text{yr} \times 21 \text{ } CO_2 \text{ eq.}/CH_4 = 233 \text{ Mt } CO_2 \text{ eq.}/\text{yr}$$

and

$$(\$22.5/\text{t } CH_4)(1 \text{ } CH_4/21 \text{ } CO_2) = \$1.07/\text{t } CO_2 \text{ eq.}$$

Although these estimates are for 1997, it is assumed that they would be roughly the same for 1990.

NOTE

1. Tons (t) are metric; 1 Mt = 1 megaton = 1 million tons.

Appendix N

Population Growth and Greenhouse Gas Emissions

By utilizing World Bank categories of actual economic growth experience and projected population growth rates, the scenarios for population, per capita income, CO_2 emissions, and family planning (FP) effect are computed and reported in Table N.1. Each group of countries is indexed to 1.00 in 1990. Thus numbers reported for the years 2020, 2050, and 2100 are multiples of the 1990 base.

The rules for calculations include the following:

1. Population is projected for the 1990 to 2020 period by using World Bank projections for 1987 to 2000 for each group. The growth rates (as shown in Table N.1) are from the World Development Report, Table 6. For 2020 to 2050, each group is expected to achieve the population projection for the next highest group in the 1990 to 2020 period (except for the NIEs, who remain at the 1987 to 2000 level). The situation is similar for 2050 to 2100, except that the NIEs have stationary growth.

2. As shown in Table N.1, per capita income for 1990 to 2020 is projected to grow at actual 1965 to 1987 rates (World Bank, 1989, Table 1), except that the NIEs maintain their high growth rates only for 1990 to 2020 and then revert to the upper-middle-income economy growth rates after 2020.

3. Annual CO_2 emissions are calculated from population and income projections. It is assumed that CO_2 emissions increase proportionately with population for all income levels. For low income levels (i.e., multiples below 5), it is assumed that CO_2 emissions additionally increase proportionately with per capita income growth. For higher incomes, CO_2 emissions increase less than proportionately with per capita income growth (i.e., at 0.8 for income multiples between 5 and 10, 0.7 for multiples between 10 and

TABLE N.1   Relationship Between Population and Greenhouse Gas
Emissions

	Low-Income Economies	Lower-Middle-Income Economies	Upper-Middle-Income Economies	Newly Industrialized Economies
Population	(2.6)	(2.1)	(1.7)	(0.8)
1990	1.0	1.0	1.0	1.0
2020	2.16	1.87	1.66	1.27
2050	4.03	3.10	2.10	1.61
2100	9.36	4.62	3.12	1.61
Per capita income	(1.5)	(2.2)	(2.9)	(6.2)
1990	1.0	1.0	1.0	1.0
2020	1.56	1.92	2.35	6.07
2050	2.43	3.69	5.54	14.31
2100	5.11	10.95	23.14	59.75
CO_2 emissions, annual				
1990	1.0	1.0	1.0	1.0
2020	3.37	3.59	3.90	6.17
2050	9.79	11.44	11.63	16.12
2100	47.83	40.47	67.06	57.71
CO_2 emissions, cumulated				
1990	1.0	1.0	1.0	1.0
2020	65.5	68.8	73.5	107.5
2050	262.9	294.3	306.4	441.3
2100	1,703.4	1,591	2,271	2,286
Family planning effect (base = CO_2 emission, cumulated)				
1990				
2020	0.20	0.56	0.49	1.34
2050	2.94	3.43	6.54	7.01
2100	58.71	51.90	34.65	89.09

30, and 0.6 for higher multiples). These estimates are based on World Bank Estimates (Siddayo, 1987).

4. The cumulative CO_2 emissions simply sum up annual emissions to the period indicated.

5. "Family planning" effects are calculated as the difference in population between a given group and the next lower group, multiplied by the income multiples of the group. Thus they represent the amount of increased emissions if the population were as large as it would be with the next lower group's population. For the lowest-income economies, the family planning effect is presumed to be the difference between the actual 2.8 percent growth rate over the 1965 to 1987 period and the 2.6 percent projected for 1987 to 2000.

These calculations are based on actual evidence to a considerable extent. A number of countries in the low-income category are actually experiencing no per capita income growth, and many are experiencing population growth more rapid than 2.6 percent. Construction of scenarios for these cases would not be very realistic.

The major points of this exercise are that family planning impacts on greenhouse gas emissions are important at all levels of development. It is probably not feasible to achieve low population growth rates without moving up the development scale. The reduced population growth associated with higher-income growth (and to a small degree with lower-income elasticities as income rises) offsets in large part the higher greenhouse gas emissions associated with faster economic growth.

The family planning effects indicate that as of the year 2020, carbon emissions will be about 15 percent lower for the lower-middle- and upper-middle-income countries than they would be without family planning. Strong family planning programs are in the interests of all countries for greenhouse gas concerns as well as for broader welfare concerns.

REFERENCES

Siddayo, C. 1987. Petroleum resources in the Pacific rim: The roles played by governments in their development and trade. In The Pacific Rim: Investment, Development, and Trade, P. Nemetz, ed. Vancouver, B.C.: University of British Columbia Press.

World Bank. 1989. 1989 World Development Report. Washington, D.C.: World Bank.

Appendix O

Deforestation Prevention

Assigning an economic cost to preventing deforestation is very difficult, and estimates are based on the cost of providing economic incentives to those who currently deforest the land. This could be done either through providing a cash bonus for those who practice sustainable agriculture or through purchasing land for use as nature preserves.

The first fact needed is the annual rate of deforestation. Based on a World Resources Institute (WRI, 1990) report, this is 20.4 million hectares per year. The arbitrary assumption can then be made that 70 percent of such deforestation could be prevented by using one of these programs.

The carbon content of the soil and vegetation in different ecosystems has been estimated by the Conservation Foundation, World Wildlife Fund, and Fundacion Neotropica (1988). This content, in tons of carbon per hectare (ha),[1] is 256 for an undisturbed forest, 210 for a logged or managed forest, 256 for a 30- to 40-year-old forest plantation, and 75 for land deforested for use as pasture or agriculture. The net carbon saved through forest protection is the difference between a managed forest and pasture land or

net carbon saved = $210 - 75 = 135$ t C/ha,

which would be 495 t CO_2/ha if burned or otherwise oxidized. The carbon release avoided would be

(495 t CO_2/ha)(0.7)(20.4 × 10^6 ha/yr) = 7068 Mt of CO_2 per year.

The cost of preventing this deforestation is based on information from the Conservation Foundation and the World Wildlife Fund. The World Wildlife Fund proposal would create an endowment of $200/ha. Interest from that endowment is used as a financial incentive for those living near a tropical forest to practice sustainable forestry. The community retains ownership of the land and interest from the endowment as long as it practices sustainable forestry. The purpose of the endowment is to compensate the community for the additional income it would have received by using current agricultural techniques. At present, this method is being used in Costa Rica (Conservation Fund et al., 1988).

By using these estimates, a cost-effectiveness of

$$\frac{(\$200 \, / \, \text{ha})(0.7)(20.4 \times 10^6 \, \text{ha} \, / \, \text{yr})}{7068 \, \text{Mt CO}_2 \, / \, \text{yr}} = \$0.40 \, / \, \text{t CO}_2 \text{ at } \$200 \, / \, \text{ha}$$

is obtained.

NOTE

1. Tons (t) are metric; 1 Mt = 1 megaton = 1 million tons.

REFERENCES

Conservation Foundation (CF), World Wildlife Fund (WWF), and Fundacion Neotropica (FN). 1988. The Forestry Fund: An Endowment for Forest Protection, Management, and Reforestation in Costa Rica. Washington, D.C.: World Wildlife Fund.

World Resources Institute. 1990. World Resources 1990-91. New York: Oxford University Press.

Appendix P

Reforestation

The most comprehensive analysis of the potential for sequestering carbon in trees in the United States is that undertaken by Moulton and Richards (1990) of the U.S. Forest Service. This is a detailed analysis of the land available in the United States that could support trees, the carbon uptake that might be expected, and actual costs for each type of land to be managed. The analysis assumes that trees could be planted on economically marginal and environmentally sensitive pasture and croplands and that forest management programs could increase carbon uptake on many nonfederal forestlands. After analyzing the potential carbon uptake and cost per ton for 70 region and land-type classes, Moulton and Richards arrange these in order by cost per ton and assemble a supply curve for carbon sequestering. The analysis concludes that up to 56.4 percent of U.S. emissions could be sequestered in domestic trees at costs ranging from $5.80 to $47.75/t of carbon (C) (there is no adjustment for the small energy and CO_2 cost of implementing such a program).[1]

The analysis has a 40-year time horizon and so does not confront the consequences of declining growth rates as trees approach maturity or of the long-term possibilities for tree maintenance or harvest. Two sets of numbers that heavily influence the numeric results but are likely to elicit some discussion are land rental rates and the ratio between carbon uptake in marketable timber and total ecosystem carbon uptake. Both sets of numbers are carefully laid out in the analysis and could be manipulated by an analyst with different notions. The ecosystem carbon ratios, for example, ranges from 1.8 to 8.4 and include considerable carbon accumulation in soils. The result of using high ecosystem carbon ratios is that average carbon accumulation for the full program amounts to 5.3 t/hectare(ha)/yr. Trexler (1990) suggests that values nearer 3.7 might be more within expectation for a program of this magnitude. Any comparison with current forest growth rates must acknowledge that most of the increased growth envisioned in the Moulton and Richards analysis would be on what is characterized as "marginal cropland" but which would in fact be very good forestland. The analysis does not include a start-up period for tree planting and establishment but assumes "instant trees" with all establishment costs in the first year.

The structure of the Moulton and Richards report is such that one can examine the program incrementally. Table P.1 shows the implications of planting enough trees—in order of increasing dollars per ton of carbon—to sequester carbon at rates of 10 percent, 20 percent, and 56.4 percent of current U.S. total CO_2 emissions. The table shows that at the 10 percent level most of the uptake would be accomplished by changing forest management practices on current forestlands and planting on marginal pasturelands, but that in order to get very much of the maximum potential, large-scale inclusion of marginal croplands would be required.

Recognizing that the Moulton and Richards analysis suggests that 56.4 percent of U.S. CO_2 emissions could perhaps be offset with a massive commitment to a reforestation program, the Mitigation Panel adopts a very conservative approach to estimating the carbon offset that might be envisioned. This analysis accepts that the 10 percent objective described by Moulton and Richards is a reasonable initial target and that reforestation of economically marginal or environmentally sensitive pasture and croplands and nonfederal forestlands to a total 28.7 Mha could take place at costs as described in their analysis. The carbon sequestering rate is then divided by 2 to ensure that only carbon that is truly taken into long-term storage is counted. This baseline then suggests that 240 Mt CO_2 could be sequestered at costs between \$3 and \$10/t CO_2 (average cost is \$7.20/t CO_2). Demonstration projects could verify the lower costs and higher targets for total sequestration projected by some.

TABLE P.1 Reforestation Program Costs by Percentage Reduction

Annual CO$_2$ Offset (%/M short tons)	Land Requirement (M acres)	Total Annual Cost (Billion \$)	Average Cost (\$/t carbon)
5/72	36.9	0.7	9.72
10/143	70.9	1.7	12.02
20/286	138.4	4.5	15.73
30/429	197.6	7.7	17.91

SOURCE: Moulton and Richards (1990).

NOTE

1. Tons (t) are metric; 1 Mt = 1 megaton = 1 million tons.

REFERENCES

Moulton, R. J., and K. R. Richards. 1990. Costs of sequestering carbon through tree planting and forest management in the United States. U.S. Forest Service Report. Draft. U.S. Department of Agriculture, Washington, D.C.

Trexler, M. C. 1990. Minding the carbon store: Weighing U.S. forest strategies to slow global warming. Draft. World Resources Institute, Washington, D.C.

Appendix Q

Geoengineering Options

This appendix is divided into four sections: (1) naval rifle system, (2)-balloon system, (3) multiple balloon system, (4) changing cloud abundance. Each section either describes the system or indicates how the costs were computed.

NAVAL RIFLE SYSTEM

The current cost of a naval projectile weighing 1900 pounds (lb) is $7000 to $8000. The cost of propellant alone (if the shell is furnished) is $900. It seems that a reasonable estimate for a 1-t shell, dust (commercial aluminum oxide can be obtained for $0.25/lb), and a propellant for each shot is $10,000. An efficiency of one-half is assumed: one-half of the shell is dust, and the other half consists of the packaging, dispersal mechanisms, and so on, necessary to make the shell function. Thus the cost of the ammunition for 40 years will be

$$10^{10} \text{ kg} \times \frac{1}{5 \times 10^2 \text{ kg/shot}} \times 10^4 \text{ \$/shot} \times 20 \text{ times} = \$4 \times 10^{12}.$$

The number of shots required in the 40 years is

$$10^{10} \text{ kg} \times 20 \text{ times} \times \frac{1}{5 \times 10^2 \text{ kg/shot}} = \frac{4 \times 10^8 \text{ shots}}{40 \text{ years}} = 10^7 \text{ shots/yr.}$$

If a single rifle can fire 5 shots per hour (naval rifles can fire faster than this, but cooling intervals between shots can lengthen the barrel life) and the rifle operates 250 working days per year, then a rifle can fire 5 shots/hour $\times$ 24 hours/day $\times$ 250 days/yr = 3 $\times$ 10^4 shots/yr per rifle.

Thus

$$\frac{10 \times 10^6}{3 \times 10^4} \approx 350 \text{ rifles working at a time}$$

are required. Therefore, operating inventory of 4×10^2 rifles can be assumed at any time.

A gun barrel will have to be replaced approximately every 1500 shots; thus over the 40 years,

$$\frac{4 \times 10^8 \text{ shots}}{1500 \text{ shots / barrel}} = \frac{4 \times 10^8}{1.5 \times 10^3} \approx 3 \times 10^5 \text{ barrels}$$

will be needed. A gun barrel probably would cost (in continuous production

$$\frac{3 \times 10^5}{40} = \frac{300 \times 10^3}{40} \approx 8000 \text{ barrels / yr})$$

several hundred thousand dollars—say a million dollars. The total cost of rifle barrels is thus

$$3 \times 10^5 \text{ barrels} \times 10^6 \text{ \$/barrel} = \$3 \times 10^{11} \text{ for barrels.}$$

If the rifles are organized into 10-barrel stations, on land or at sea, and a billion dollars is allocated for the capital cost of each station, one might expect to buy 40 10-barrel stations to keep 350 barrels operating at a time, thus giving a cost for stations of

$$40 \text{ stations} \times 10^9 \text{ \$/station} = \$4 \times 10^{10}.$$

This should probably be doubled, at least; to allow for overhead, power, maintenance, replacement, and so on. Multiplying by 5 gives $\$2 \times 10^{11}$ for stations.

Finally, people are needed to operate the system. Although the system would probably be highly automated, assume that it will work like current operations. Then allocate

$$10 \text{ people/barrel} \times 4 \times 10^2 \text{ barrels} \times 3 \text{ shifts} \times \$10^5/\text{person/yr} \times 40 \text{ years}$$
$$= \$48 \times 10^9 \approx \$5 \times 10^{10},$$

which can be doubled to include indirect personnel, overhead, and so on, giving $\$10^{11}$ for operators. Therefore, 24,000 people are assumed to be involved at any time.

To sum up,

Ammunition	$\$4 \times 10^{12} = 4.0 \times 10^{12}$
Rifle barrels	$\$3 \times 10^{11} = 0.3 \times 10^{12}$
Stations	$\$2 \times 10^{11} = 0.2 \times 10^{12}$
People	$\$1 \times 10^{11} = 0.1 \times 10^{12}$
TOTAL	$\$4.6 \times 10^{12} \approx \$5 \times 10^{12}$ for 40 years,

giving an annual undiscounted cost of $\$50/40 \times 10^{11} = \$100$ billion.

Clearly, the cost of the project is dominated by ammunition, and the number of stations and rifles is reasonable, as is the amount of activity, considered on a large industrial scale. The rifles could be deployed at sea or in empty areas (e.g., military reservations) where the noise of the shots and the fallback of expended shells could be managed.

BALLOON SYSTEM

Consider a hydrogen balloon floating at 20 km, using the Archimedes principle and noting that the density of hydrogen gas is one-fourteenth that of air:

$$m_{d(isplaced)} = m_{g(as\ inside\ balloon)} + m_{b(alloon)} + m_{p(ayload)}$$

$$\frac{4}{3}\pi r^3 \rho_o = \frac{4}{3}\pi r^3 \frac{1}{14}\rho_o + 4\pi r^2 \Delta r \rho_{s(kin)} + m_p$$

$$m_p = \frac{4}{3}\pi r^3 \rho_o \frac{13}{14} - 4\pi r^2 \Delta r \rho_s$$

$$= 4\pi r^3 [13/(3\times14)\rho_o - (\Delta r/r)\rho_s]$$

$$= 4\pi[10^2]^3 \left[\frac{13}{3\times14}(8.8\times10^{-2}) - \frac{10^{-3}}{10^2}\times(1.15\times10^3) \right].$$

If

    $r = 100$ m (radius of balloon)

    $\rho_o = 88$ g/m^3 = 8.8 × 10^{-2} kg/m^3 (density of air at 20 km)

    $\Delta r = 1$ mm = 10^{-3} m (thickness of balloon skin)

    $\rho_o = 1.15$ g/cm^3 (nylon) × 10^{-3} kg/g × [10^2 cm/m]^3

        = 1.15 × 10^3 kg/m^3.

Then

    $m_p = 1.26 \times 10^7\ (2.7 \times 10^{-2} - 1.15 \times 10^{-2})$

        = 1.26 × 10^5 (1.55)

        = 1.95 × 10^5 ≈ 2 × 10^5 kg.

The mass of the balloon for a 1-mm thickness is

    $4\pi r^2 \Delta r \rho = 12.6 \times 10^4 \times 10^{-3} \times 1.15 \times 10^3$

                = 1.26 × 1.15 × 10^5 × 10^{-3} × 10^3 kg

                = 1.5 × 10^5 kg.

If the balloon is 2/3-mm-thick (assumed for convenience), its mass from the previous computation is 1.5 × 10^5 kg and the mass of dust lifted, if a 50 percent efficiency factor is used to account for instruments, dust dispenser, container, and so on (this is conservative), is 10^5 kg. Nylon of the appropriate gauge for weaving into a 2/3-mm-thick fabric (1050 denier is about 0.3 mm) costs $2/lb = $4.4/kg. If this is tripled for fabric and balloon manufacture (the cost of parachute fabric is about 3 times the cost of the yarn, based on information from a colleague at Du Pont Industrial Fabrics), cost of controls, dust dispensing, and so on, \$15/kg can be estimated or

$$1.5 \times 10^5 \text{ kg/balloon} \times \$15/\text{kg} = 2.25 \times 10^6 \text{ \$/balloon.}$$

Twenty lifts are necessary in 40 years:

$$\frac{10^{10} \text{ kg}}{10^{10} \text{ kg / balloon}} \times 20 \text{ times} = 2 \times 10^6 \text{ balloons}$$

$$2 \times 10^6 \text{ balloons} \times 2.25 \times 10^6 \text{ \$ / balloon} = \$4.25 \times 10^{12}.$$

Consider the additional costs of infrastructure and support: there will be 2×10^6 lifts in 40 years or

$$\frac{200 \times 10^4}{40} = 5 \times 10^4 \text{ balloon lifts per year.}$$

If there are 100 crews (each responsible for 2 lifts per day on 250 days a year) and each crew has 100 people,

$$10^4 \text{ people} \times 10^5 \text{ \$/person/yr} \times 40 \text{ years} = \$4 \times 10^{10}$$
$$\approx \$10^{11} \text{ with an overhead of 150\%.}$$

If each station is capitalized at $\$10^9$, another $\$10^{11}$ is required, but this infrastructure barely affects costs, as does the cost of dust even at \$0.50/kg or hydrogen at \$10/kg.

Hydrogen can currently be purchased as liquid hydrogen in 1500-gallon lots (equivalent to 169,000 standard cubic feet) for \$2.5/100 ft^3. For conversion, 1 kg of hydrogen = 432.3 standard cubic feet. Thus the cost is

$$\frac{\$2.5}{100 \text{ ft}^3} \times \frac{1}{1 \text{ kg / 423.3 ft}^3} = \$10.6 / \text{kg.}$$

In quantities of 100×10^6 ft^3/day, Ogden and Williams (1989) quote costs lower than \$30/GJ. This is

$$\$30 / \text{GJ} \times \frac{339 \text{ GJ}}{100 \text{ ft}} \times \frac{423.3 \text{ ft}^3}{\text{kg}} = \frac{43 \times 10^5 \text{ \$ / kg}}{10^6} \approx \$4 / \text{kg.}$$

Each balloon has a mass of 4.2×10^6 m$^3 \times 1/14 \times 8.8 \times 10^{-2}$ kg/m$^3 = 2.6 \times 10^4$ kg of hydrogen. At 5×10^4 balloon lifts per year, the annual quantity is

$$13.2 \times 10^8 \text{ kg} \approx 10^9 \text{ kg} = 423 \times 10^9 \text{ ft}^3 \approx 10^9 \text{ ft}^3/\text{day} = 10^2 \times 10^6 \text{ ft}^3/\text{day.}$$

The total mass of hydrogen required for 40 years is

2.6×10^4 kg/balloon $\times 2 \times 10^6$ balloons $= 5.2 \times 10^{10}$ kg.

At \$10/kg, this costs $\$5.2 \times 10^{11} = \$0.52 \times 10^{12}$.

[Design note: The breaking strength of 1200 denier (≈ 0.4 mm) nylon is over 25 lb (Du Pont, 1988). The equatorial circumference of the balloon is

$2\pi r = 6.3 \times 10^2$ m $\times 10^3$ mm/m $= 6.3 \times 10^5$ mm;

therefore, the payload will be suspended from a double (actually 2.5) set of nylon strings 0.4 mm in diameter:

6.3×105 mm $\times [25$ lb/(2.2 lb/kg)] $\times 2 = 142 \times 10^5$ kg.

Because the payload weighs 1.18×10^5 kg, the safety factor $= 121$ times!]
By using hydrogen at \$10/kg, costs may be summarized as

Balloons	$\$4.25 \times 10^{12}$
Infrastructure and personnel	$\$0.10 \times 10^{12}$
Capital for launch stations	$\$0.10 \times 10^{12}$
Hydrogen	$\$0.52 \times 10^{12}$
TOTAL	$\$4.97 \times 10^{12}$
	$\approx \$5 \times 10^{12}$.

This mitigates 10^{12} t of carbon or 4×10^{12} t of CO_2. An undiscounted cost the same as that for the naval rifle system is obtained:

\$5/t C = \$1.25/t CO_2
\$5/40/t C/yr = \$0.125/t C/yr = \$0.03/t CO_2/yr.

All of the above material assumes no reuse of balloons, and no allowance is made for the automation of launch, and so on. The possibility of some reuse, and of automation, probably reduces the total cost. If not controlled to land for reuse, balloons could be "chased" and controlled to land for collection and disposal, or to land in the deep ocean and sink promptly.
Consider hot air balloons. Again by using the Archimedes principle,

$m_{displaced} = m_{gas} + m_{balloon} + m_{payload}$
$V\rho_o = V\rho_i + m_{balloon} + m_{payload}$

Using the perfect gas law

$p_i V_i = m_i R T_i \qquad p_i = R\rho_i T_i$
$p_o V_o = m_o R T_o \qquad p_o = R\rho_o T_o$

where m = mass, V = volume, p_o = outside pressure, p_i = inside pressure, ρ_o = density of air outside, and ρ_i = density of gas inside. At floating equilibrium, $p_o = p_i$, because the balloon is limp. Therefore,

$$\rho_i T_i = \rho_o T_o$$

$$\rho_i = \rho_o \frac{T_o}{T_i}$$

$$\begin{aligned} m_p &= V\rho_o - V\rho_i - m_b \\ &= V\rho_o - V\rho_o(T_o/T_i) - m_b \\ &= V\rho_o(1 - (T_o/T_i)) - m_b \\ &= \rho_o[(T_i - T_o)/T_i]V - m_b \\ &= \rho_o[(T_i - T_o)/T_i]4/3\pi r^3 - 4\pi r^2 \Delta r \rho_s \\ &= 4\pi r^2\{\rho_o[(T - T_o)/T_i)](r/3) - \Delta r \rho_s\} \\ m_p &= 4\pi r^3\{(\rho_o/3)[(T - T_o)/T_i)] - (\Delta r/r)\rho_s\} \end{aligned}$$

If r and Δr are expressed in meters, and ρ_o and ρ_s are in

$$\frac{g}{cm^3} \times \frac{10^{-3} \text{ kg}/g}{10^{-6}[10^{-2} \text{ cm}/m]^3} \ ,$$

each ρ must be multiplied by $1/10^{-3} = 10^3$:

$$\begin{aligned} m_p &= 12.6 \times 10^3 \ r^3 \ \{(\rho_o/3)[(T_i - T_o)/T_i] - (\Delta r/r)\rho_s\} \\ &= 1.26 \times 10^4 \ r^3 \ \{(\rho_o/3)[(T_i - T_o)/T_i] - (\Delta r/r)\rho_s\} \end{aligned}$$

where ρ (specific gravity) is expressed in grams per cubic centimeter, r in meters, and m_p in kilograms. At 20 km,

$$\rho_o = (88 \text{ g/m}^3)(10^2 \text{ cm/m})^3 = 88 \times 10^{-6} \text{ g/cm}^3$$

for

$$\begin{aligned} T_o &= -58.5°C = 217 \text{ K (Kelvin)} \\ T_i &= 104°C = 377 \text{ K (Kelvin)} \\ r &= 102 \text{ m} \\ \Delta r &= 1 \text{ mm} \\ \rho_s &= 1.15 \end{aligned}$$

$$m_p = 1.26 \times 10^{10}\left[2.9 \times 10^{-5}\frac{(377 - 217)}{377} - \frac{10^{-3}}{10^{-2}}(1.15) \right]$$

$$\begin{aligned} &= 1.26 \times 10^{10} (1.23 \times 10^{-5} - 1.15 \times 10^{-5}) \\ &= 0.1 \times 10^5 \text{ kg} = 10^4 \text{ kg}. \end{aligned}$$

If 2/3-mm nylon is used, $m_p = 6 \times 10^4$ kg.

Thus the costs of a hot air balloon system can be expected to be at least 4 to 10 times higher than the cost of a hydrogen balloon system. These costs could be decreased by running the balloon at higher temperature, but to get 10^5 kg of payload per balloon with 1-mm nylon a temperature of 658 K (385°C) is required, and with 2/3-mm nylon 475 K (202°C), which seems difficult to manage. The breaking strength of nylon goes to zero percent of its room temperature value by 250°C. While the skin temperature of a hot air balloon is well below the core gas temperature, the management of temperature to guarantee skin strength with so large a differential between average and skin temperature seems rather difficult, although the skin might be insulated as some weight penalty. The results are sensitive to the factors. Hot air balloons seem to be nearly competitive with hydrogen balloons. This question would have to be explored further before choices between hydrogen and hot air systems could finally be made.

MULTIPLE BALLOON SYSTEM

The mass of a bubble filled with hydrogen is one-fourteenth the mass of the air displaced. The total mass of the hydrogen-filled balloon will be (at any altitude)

$$\frac{1}{14}m_{a(ir)} + 4\pi r^2 \Delta r \rho_{s(kin)} = \frac{1}{14} \cdot \frac{4}{3}\pi r^3 \rho_s + 4\pi r^2 \Delta r \rho_s$$

At floating equilibrium, we have

$$\frac{1}{14} \cdot \frac{4}{3}\pi r^3 \rho_a = 4\pi r^2 \Delta r \rho_s = \frac{4}{3}\pi r^3 \rho_a$$

$$\Delta r \rho_s = \frac{13}{14} r \rho_a$$

$$\Delta r \rho_s = \frac{13}{3 \times 14} r \rho_a = 3 \times 10^{-1} r \rho_a.$$

If plastic with density of 1 g/cm^3 and a skin thickness of

$$\Delta r = 10^{-1} \text{ mm} = 10^{-4} \text{ m} = 10^{-2} \text{ cm}$$

(which is plausible) is used, then

$$r = \frac{10^{-2}}{3 \times 10^{-1} \rho_a} = \frac{10^{-1}}{3\rho_a} = \frac{10 \times 10^{-2}}{3\rho_a} \approx \frac{3 \times 10^{-2}}{\rho_a} \text{ cm.}$$

At 19 km = 12 miles $\approx$ 62,000 feet, $\rho_a \approx 10^{-4}$ and

$$r \approx \frac{3 \times 10^{-2}}{10^{-4}} = 300 \text{ cm} = 3.$$

Such a balloon has a disk area of $\pi r^2 = 9\pi = 28 \text{ m}^2 = 3 \times 10 \text{ m}^2$. Thus,

$$\frac{5 \times 10^{12}}{3 \times 10} \approx 2 \times 10^{11} = 200 \times 10^9 \text{ balloons of 3 - m radius}$$

are required. If the balloon is 10-μm material, a balloon of 3×10^{-1} m (30-cm) radius is obtained and $20{,}000 \times 10^9$ balloons are needed.

Hydrogen will diffuse through the skin of the balloons, which probably means that the system must be refreshed annually. The fall of collapsed balloons might be an annoying form of trash rain. Because the area of the material required for a balloon is $4\pi r^2$, the material requirement is

$$\frac{5 \times 10^{12}}{\pi r^2} \times 4\pi r^2 = 20 \times 10^{12} \text{ m}^2$$

of material for any size balloon. At \$0.10/m^2 (20 m^2 of wrapping plastic can be bought in the supermarket for about \$2), this is \$2 $\times$ 10^{12}. Over 40 years, this amounts to \$80 $\times$ 10^{12}. It offsets 10^{12} t of carbon, so the cost is \$80/t C or \$80/40 = \$2/t C/yr or \$0.50/t CO$_2$/yr. A reasonable cost range of \$0.50 to \$5/t CO$_2$/yr can be assumed.

CHANGING CLOUD ABUNDANCE

A study was undertaken to consider the various factors that would be required to increase the albedo effect of global cloud cover sufficiently to balance the temperature increase that is projected to occur with a doubling of CO$_2$. Toward this end, the temperature sensitivity to different (high, middle, and low) cloud layer properties was calculated by using a radiative-convective atmospheric model. In addition, cost estimates have been made. These amelioration processes are reversible and inexpensive. If they were determined to be deleterious or if cost-competitive programs were developed, these measures could be discontinued immediately.

At the outset it cannot be emphasized too strongly that there are tremendous uncertainties associated with these intellectual exercises. As a case in point, circumstantial evidence teaches that we have a very limited understanding of the role of cloud abundance because a warming accompanied the measured increase in cloud coverage over the past century. Consequently, a much better understanding of the system is necessary before any large-scale operations could reasonably be proposed.

The Climatic Effect of Clouds

Earlier, Reck (1978) studied the effect of increases in cloud cover and, using a radiative-convective atmospheric model, found that a 4 to 5 percent increase in low-level cloud cover would be sufficient to offset the warming predicted from a doubling of preindustrial CO$_2$. This value is in reasonable agreement with Randall et al. (1984), who estimated that a 4 percent increase was required in the amount of marine stratocumulus, which comprises the bulk of the low clouds on a global basis. Unfortunately, many assumptions are contained in these estimates, and to understand those assumptions and the role that clouds could play, cloud sensitivity calculations have been made to illustrate the range of surface temperature for various assumptions of cloud properties.

In these calculations, the Mitigation Panel used the assumed abundances and optical properties shown in Table Q.1 and a global surface albedo of 15.4 percent. The model has three layers of clouds under global average conditions. It is assumed that clouds, once formed, will have the same effects over their entire lifetimes and that they will have optical properties identical to those of current low-level clouds, which are assumed to be unchanging during the seeding process. Unfortunately, these assumptions contain many uncertainties. These sensitivity calculations show that the effects of clouds depend not only on the fraction of a given cloud type, but also on the surface albedo beneath the clouds. The special role of the low-level cloud and its varying effect as the surface albedo changes add considerable complication because the surface albedo varies from about 4 to 20 percent over some water to as high as 90 percent over pure snow or ice (Hummel and Reck, 1979). This means that once a cloud is formed it may start with a cooling effect and end up in an area where it could produce either greater or lesser cooling, with the slight possibility of even a heating effect.

Albrecht (1989) (see also Twomey and Wojciechowski, 1969) suggests that the average low-cloud reflectivity would increase if the abundance of cloud condensation nuclei (CCN) were to increase through emission of SO_2.

TABLE Q.1 Assumed Properties of Average Global Clouds

	Cloud Type		
	High	Middle	Low
Cloud Abundances			
Fraction of shortwave cloud cover	0.181	0.079	0.302
Fraction of longwave cloud cover	0.181	0.079	0.302
Cloud Optical Properties			
Solar albedo of cloud cover	0.21	0.48	0.69
Solar absorptivity of cloud cover	0.005	0.02	0.035
Infrared absorptivity of cloud cover	0.50	1.00	1.00

To test for the sensitivity to this part of the problem, the surface temperature changes with varying optical properties were calculated and are shown in Table Q.2. For comparison purposes the sensitivity of high and middle clouds was also included. Clearly, the estimate depends strongly on the value of assumed low-cloud solar reflectivity. For example, a change of 4 percent in the reflectivity value (low-cloud abundance—see Table Q.2) would be sufficient to cause the calculated surface temperature to change by 3°C. With a sensitivity of this magnitude, clearly a large potential exists for forced changes provided they could be controlled, and provided large regional anomalies and uncontrolled long-distance effects are not created.

There is also a height dependence in the radiation field that varies greatly with latitude and altitude (Ramanathan et al., 1987). The cloud fraction variation with latitude is shown in Table Q.3. In the present environment, there is a greater probability of having clouds over water than over land, with more clouds over land in the afternoon and more clouds over water in the morning. This occurs because cloud height and optical properties are intimately related to humidity and physical conditions. For example, the role of a cloud at a given latitude is controlled by the zenith angle of the sun. If the cloud were to move to a more northern latitude, its cooling effect would be expected to diminish in proportion to the change in the cosine of the sun's zenith angle. As can be noted from the cosines listed in Table Q.3, a cloud at 5° latitude could have about twice as large a contribution as the same cloud at 65° latitude. Many less predictable features are also crucial (such as the degree of evaporation).

Reck (1978, 1979), using a model based on that of Manabe and Wetherald (1967), has also illustrated cloud height effect. These calculations show heating from high-level clouds and cooling from middle- and lower-level

TABLE Q.2 Calculated Surface Temperature Sensitivity to Changes in Cloud Properties

	Cloud Type		
	High	Middle	Low
Sensitivity (°C) per percent change in cloud abundance	0.36	−0.35	−0.66
Sensitivity (°C) per percent change in cloud albedo	−0.16	−0.06	−0.35
Sensitivity (°C) per percent change in cloud absorptivity	−0.062	0.048	0.045

TABLE Q.3 Latitudinal Variation of Assumed Annual Cloud Cover

Latitude (degrees)	Cosine of Zenith Angle	Fraction of Cloud Cover		
		Upper Cloud	Middle Cloud	Lower Cloud
5	0.61	0.225	0.075	0.317
15	0.593	0.181	0.064	0.264
25	0.560	0.160	0.063	0.248
35	0.512	0.181	0.079	0.302
45	0.450	0.210	0.110	0.388
55	0.381	0.242	0.131	0.438
65	0.309	0.254	0.119	0.444
75	0.259	0.252	0.111	0.424
85	0.243	0.205	0.092	0.375

ones. One possible error in the estimates presented here is the assumption of either a fixed cloud altitude or a fixed cloud temperature. Reck (1979) has shown a greater model sensitivity to a fixed cloud temperature. Mixed behavior might be observed in the real atmosphere. Clearly with all the possible heating or cooling effects, the presence of naturally occurring clouds could complicate the analysis of data obtained to test the role of human intervention. See, for example, the cloud experiments suggested below.

With all the above assumptions in mind, it is proposed both that CCN emissions should be done over the oceans at an altitude that will produce an increase in the stratocumulus cloud albedo only, and that the clouds will remain at the same latitudes over the ocean where the surface albedo is relatively constant and low. As noted in Figure Q.1, an increase in surface albedo, should the cloud float over land, would only enhance its cooling effect. This is true provided the latitude of the cloud does not change, as discussed previously.

How Cloud Condensation Nuclei Can Change Climate

Despite the lack of knowledge about cloud processes, the possibility of altering clouds has been considered for a long time. The idea of cloud seeding for agricultural purposes became popular in the 1950s and 1960s, but because of the lack of precision and the litigation that resulted, it has not been very successful (see, for example, Todd and Howell, 1985; and Kerr, 1982). Changes in cloudiness on a regional scale were also proposed some time ago by Russian scientists, who considered decreasing the cloudi-

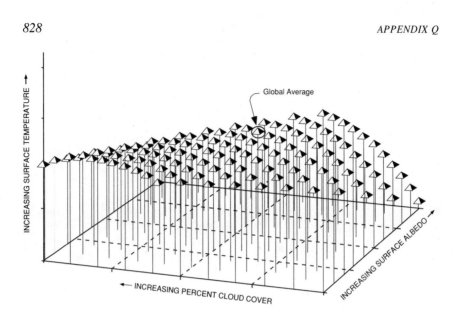

FIGURE Q.1   Calculated surface temperature variation with changes in low-cloud cover and surface albedo.

ness in the arctic region to promote ice melting and improve growing conditions in Siberia.   Before the more recent satellite measurements, most of what was known about cloud processes and how they contribute to the global radiative balance came from climate modeling, and in climate models, most of the details of the cloud processes were not included.   Certainly, no individual clouds were included on the grid scale of the general circulation models (GCM); thus specific details of the microphysics, as it might involve seeding or CCN, could not be studied within the concept of GCMs.

Proposed Change in Low-Cloud Albedo Through Emissions
of Cloud Condensation Nuclei

In a recent paper, Albrecht (1989), following a hypothesis of Twomey and Wojciechowski (1969), grossly estimated the additional CCN that would be necessary to increase the fractional cloudiness or albedo of marine stratocumulus clouds by 4 percent.   He estimates that this increase in low-level fractional cloudiness would be equivalent to that attributed to a 30 percent increase in CCN.   As noted from Table Q.3, this 4 percent increase, if it were strictly in lower-level cloud abundance at global average conditions (35° latitude), would be more or less equivalent to the cloudiness at 4° latitude further north.   Albrecht's idealized stratocumulus cloud, which he argues is typical, has a thickness of 375 m, a drizzle rate of 1 mm per day, and a mean droplet radius of 100 μm; he also assumes that each droplet is formed by the coalescence of 1000 smaller droplets. The rate at which CCN are depleted by this model is 1000/cm^3 per day. Consequently, about 300/cm^3 per day (30 percent of 1000) of CCN would be needed to be discharged at the base of the cloud to maintain a 4 percent increase in cloudiness. This assumes that the perturbed atmosphere would remain sufficiently close to saturation in the vicinity of the CCN that additional cloud cover would be formed every time the number of CCN increased.

Now an extrapolation will be made to the entire globe, while keeping in mind Albrecht's assumption that cloudiness in a typical ocean region is limited by the small number of CCN. On the average, 31.2 percent of the globe is covered by marine stratiform clouds (Charlson et al., 1987). If no high-level clouds are present, the number of CCN that must be added per day is

$= 4\pi \times$ (radius of earth)$^2 \times$ (cloud-layer thickness) $\times$ 31.2 percent $\times$ CCN/volume

$= 4\pi \times (6.37 \times 108$ cm$)^2 \times (3.75 \times 10^4$ cm$) \times 0.312 \times 300$/cm^3/d

$= 1.8 \times 10^{25}$ CCN per day.

The three materials that have been used for cloud seeding are silver iodide (AgI), lead iodide (PbI), and dry ice. Dry ice is not applicable to this situation because it does not create CCN. It is used because of its precipitation-enhancing properties. Lead iodide will not be considered because it was used before full awareness of the environmental problems associated with lead. Although adverse environmental consequences will probably also be associated with AgI, a calculation will be made anyway. Calculations will also be performed using sulfuric acid (H_2SO_4), because most of the CCN that occur naturally over the oceans are believed to be H_2SO_4 CCN arising from the oxidation of dimethyl sulfide (DMS) produced by planktonic algae in the seawater (Charlson et al., 1987).

The mass of a CCN is $(4/3\ \pi r^3 \times$ density), and it is assumed that the mean radius $r = 0.07 \times 10^{-4}$ (Charlson et al., 1987). Because the density of AgI is 5.7 g/cm^3, the CCN mass is

$= 4/3\pi \times (0.07 \times 10^{-4}$ cm$)^3 \times 5.7$ g/cm^3

$= 8.2 \times 10^{-15}$ g.

The total weight of AgI to be added per day is

$= $ (total number to be added) $\times$ (weight of average CCN)

$= 1.8 \times 10^{25}$/day $\times 8.2 \times 10^{-15}$ g

$= 1.5 \times 10^{11}$ g/day or about 1.5×10^5 t per day.

Worldwide silver production in 1985 was 420×10^6 ounces (U.S. Bureau of the Census, 1987). This is converted to metric tons:

420×10^6 oz/yr $\times$ 28.35 g/oz $\times$ 1 t/10^6 g

$= 11.9 \times 10^3$ t/yr of Ag, or

$= 25.5 \times 10^3$ t/yr AgI.

Clearly there is not enough silver or AgI to consider this experiment.

For H_2SO_4, with a density of 1.841 g/cm^3, the total weight to be added per day

$= 1.841/5.7 \times 1.5 \times 10^5$ t/day

$= 48 \times 10^3$ t/day H_2SO_4

$= 31 \times 10^3$ t/day SO_2,

if all the SO_2 is converted to H_2SO_4 CCN. To put this number in perspective, a medium-sized coal-fired U.S. power plant emits about this much SO_2 in a year; the equivalent emissions of 365 U.S. coal-burning power plants (50 percent of present U.S. SO_2 emissions) would produce sufficient CCN. To estimate the value of the sulfur directly, the total weight of SO_2 to be added per day is 32×10^3 t or about 16×10^3 t of sulfur, which is equivalent to about 6 megatons (Mt; 1 Mt = 1 million tons) of sulfur per year. Given the average market price of sulfur for 1983-1987 (f.o.b. mine or plant)—$96.90 (U.S. Bureau of the Census, 1988)—the minimum yearly cost would be at least 580×10^6/yr. Equating this yearly cost to the 300 parts per million by volume (ppmv) of CO_2 necessary for full compensation gives 580×10^6/(2840 Mt C/ppmv $CO_2 \times 300$ ppmv CO_2), or about a fraction of a cent per ton of CO_2. To obtain an equivalence to conserved carbon, known emissions of carbon in 1978, 1979, and 1980 have been compared with the total measured increase of CO_2 to obtain the equivalence: 3890 Mt C $\approx$ 1 ppmv CO_2. A 4 percent increase in cloudiness was then equated to a 300-ppmv CO_2 decrease, which translates into a reduction of 1200 gigatons (Gt; 1 Gt = 1 billion tons) of carbon, or 4400 Gt of CO_2.

The primary cost of this process involves the mechanism for distributing SO_2 in the atmosphere at the correct location. Assume a fleet of ships each carrying sulfur and a suitable incinerator. The ships are dedicated to roaming the subtropical Pacific and Atlantic oceans far upwind of land while they burn sulfur. They are vectored on paths to cloud-covered areas by a control center that uses weather satellite data to plan the campaign. In addition to choosing areas that contain clouds, it is important to distribute the ships and their burning pattern so as not to create major regional changes, or the kind of change with a time or space pattern likely to force unwanted wave patterns. These restrictions (which we may not know how to define) could be a difficult problem for such a system to solve.

From the above, 16×10^3 t/day, or 6 Mt/yr of sulfur must be burned. If 10^2 t per ship per day are allocated, and a ship stays out 300 days each year, roughly 200 ships of 10,000-ton capacity are needed (one reprovisioning stop every 150 days). At a cost of 100×10^6 per ship (surely generous), the capital cost of the fleet is 2×10^{10}. Amortized over 20 years, an annual capital cost of 1×10^9 may be used. The sulfur will cost another 0.6×10^9 per year, and 2×10^6 per ship per year may be allocated for operating costs ($10,000 per operating day), to give a total cost of 2×10^9 annually. Over 40 years (until 2030) this means 8×10^{10}, or 10^{11}. This continuously mitigates ~10^3 Gt = 10^{12} t for a cost of $0.10/t of CO_2. Of course, this continues to be a yearly cost of 1×10^9/yr.

The SO_2 could also be emitted from power plants. These plants could be built in the Pacific Ocean near the equator (hopefully on small deserted islands) and would serve to furnish power for nearby locations (e.g., South America). Transmission or use of the power in the form of refined materials could be considered, or possibly the use of superconducting power transmission systems. It is estimated that eight large power plants using spiked coal would be required (with 4 times the normal amount of sulfur) at a cost of $2 to 2.5×10^6 per plant. Most of the cost would be borne by those buying the power, so the cost might be at most 10 percent per year (the interest on the investment), or a total of 2×10^9 per year (with the above conversion, $2 \times 10^9/3890 \times 10^6 \approx \$0.0005$/t CO_2).

Comparison of the Cloudiness and Proposed Cloud Condensation Nuclei Emissions with Current Estimates in the Real Atmosphere

Total U.S. SO_2 emissions are 65.7×10^3 t per day, which is roughly 2 times the amount calculated in the previous paragraph. Consequently, there should already be some cloud-enhancing effects evident in the northern hemisphere if Twomey and Wojciechowski's hypothesis, as implemented by Albrecht, is correct. An examination of available CCN data shows that the mean CCN concentration at oceanic locations in the northern Atlantic is about 5 times higher than at remote locations in the southern Pacific (see Schwartz (1988), who, however, concludes that there is no discernible contribution of anthropogenic SO_2 emissions to the global cloud cover effect on planetary albedo or temperature). Furthermore, several studies have examined trends in cloudiness in the northern hemisphere and have all come to the same conclusion: The total cloud amount has been increasing in the northern hemisphere (study areas include United States, North America, the North Atlantic, and Europe) since the early 1900s (Henderson-Sellers, 1986, 1989; Changnon, 1981; Angell et al., 1984; Warren et al., 1988). The largest increases in cloudiness in the United States occurred from the 1930s to about 1950 and from the mid-1960s to about 1980. The first period corresponds to a period of rapid growth of U.S. SO_2 emissions after the Depression and extends to the end of World War II; the second period corresponds to the proliferation of tall stacks. From 1965 to 1980 the mean effective stack height (physical height of stack plus plume rise) of SO_2

emissions doubled from about 300 to 600 m. This, of course, increased the lifetime of discharged emissions in the atmosphere and transformed the SO_2 pollution problem from primarily a local issue in many localities to a long-range transport issue.

Between 1900 and 1980 the mean cloud cover over the conterminous United States has increased about 10 percent (Henderson-Sellers, 1989), which should be more than sufficient to compensate for an equivalent doubling of CO_2. Because CO_2 increased only about 12 percent during the same period, the net effect should have been a cooling. However, analyses of temperature data in the northern hemisphere over the same periods consistently indicate that the mean temperature has risen about 0.5° to 0.7°C overall, but no trend was evident in the conterminous United States (Jones et al., 1986; Hansen and Lebedeff, 1987; Hanson et al., 1989). This suggests either that the effects of clouds are not understood, or that other factors, such as the very poor data reliability for cloudiness and the effect of cloud height, need to be considered.

Wigley (1989) presents some crude calculations suggesting that SO_2/ CCN-derived forcing could be large enough to have offset any temperature increase due to CO_2 in the northern hemisphere. Schneider (1972) points out that SO_2 emissions are regionally heterogeneous, which would lead to long-wave forcing anomalies that in turn could lead to long-wave anomalies plus teleconnections. In any event, all of this is quite speculative and underscores the fact that much is yet to be understood about the causes of climate variations during the last century.

Impacts of Enhanced Acid Deposition

One must now consider whether the injection of this much additional SO_2 into the atmosphere will cause an acid deposition problem. It should be kept in mind that the principal component of naturally occurring CCN is sulfate formed from DMS emission from marine algae. Schwartz (1988) quotes estimates of 16 to 40×10^{12} g/yr or perhaps about 25×10^9 kg/yr emitted from this source. The addition about 6×10^9 kg/yr is being considered, approximately 25 percent of the natural amount, although locally much more than 30 percent may be added to the amount naturally present. The oceans have an enormous buffering capacity (Stumm and Morgan, 1970), so the additional rainout of sulfate (especially after dilution through cloud dispersal and droplet coalescence) seems unlikely to have any effect, even locally, although there is clear disagreement on this point. The principal concern is to avoid additional sulfate deposition over land. With a 30 percent rainout per day, this could be ensured to a 90 percent level by operating about a week upwind of land. Such a constraint would have to be added to the others already stated.

Another possible way of dealing with the acid rain concern would be to introduce sulfate in the form of ammonium sulfate or bisulfate, each of which is a neutral salt. This would avoid the acid question from the start. Both salts are used frequently as fertilizers and in the dilutions to be seen here would have a mild fertilizing effect locally. These salts can be made by reacting ammonia with sulfuric acid. The price of ammonia is about $100/t, so the cost of the CCN might double, and there would be an additional cost for equipment to run the reaction at sea. These additional costs might increase the total by as much as 50 percent to $0.15/t of carbon mitigated per year or $0.04/t CO_2.

Necessary Cloud Condensation Nuclei Experiments

If global-scale CCN emissions were to be considered in a serious way a number of fundamental studies would need to be performed. Among these would be the following:

• Exploratory studies of the effectiveness of CCN for enhancing stratocumulus cloud cover, with a full statistical analysis of covariates, and so on.
• Determination of CCN properties: (1) lifetimes of CCN at various altitudes; (2) effectiveness in cloud enhancement; and (3) effect of their precipitation on oceans.
• Determination of the fraction of SO_2 emissions converted to CCN and the resulting particle size distribution.
• Extension of the idea of CCN enhancement from local and regional to global dimensions: a careful study of the scale dependence of the effectiveness of cloud enhancement processes and the interaction of clouds with the radiation field.
• Full confirmatory analysis of the effectiveness of CCN on fractional cloudiness with carefully selected test statistics. A multiplicity of analysis would have to take into account all variables such as the humidity profile, convective processes, and CCN count, along with methods for the study of precipitation processes.

NOTE

1. Throughout this report, tons (t) are metric; 1 Mt = 1 million tons; and 1 Gt = 1 billion tons.

REFERENCES

Albrecht, B. A. 1989. Aerosols, cloud microphysics, and fractional cloudiness. Science 245:1227-1230.
Angell, J. K., J. Korshover, and G. F. Cotton. 1984. Variation in United States

cloudiness and sunshine, 1950-82. Journal of Climatology and Applied Meteorology 23:752-761.

Changnon, S. A. 1981. Midwestern cloud, sunshine and temperature trends since 1901: Possible evidence of jet contrail effects. Journal of Applied Meteorology 20:496-508.

Charlson, R. J., J. E. Lovelock, M. R. Andreae, and S. G. Warren. 1987. Oceanic phytoplankton, atmospheric sulfur, cloud albedo and climate. Nature 326:655-661.

Du Pont. 1988. Properties of Du Pont Industrial Filament Yarns. Du Pont Fibers Technical Information Multifiber Bulletin X-272. Wilmington, Del.: Du Pont.

Hansen, J., and S. Lebedeff. 1987. Global trends of measured surface air temperature. Journal of Geophysical Research 92:13345-13372.

Hanson, K., G. A. Maul, and T. R. Karl. 1989. Are atmospheric "greenhouse" effects apparent in the climatic record of the contiguous US (1895-1987)? Geophysical Research Letters 16:49-52.

Henderson-Sellers, A. 1986. Cloud changes in a warmer Europe. Climatic Change 8:25-52.

Henderson-Sellers, A. 1989. North American total cloud amount variations this century. Palaeogeography, Palaeoclimatology, Palaeoecology 75:175-194.

Hummel, J. R., and R. A. Reck. 1979. A global surface albedo model. Journal of Applied Meteorology 18:239-253.

Jones, P. D., T. M. L. Wigley, and P. B. Wright. 1986. Global temperature variation between 1861 and 1984. Nature 322:430-434.

Kerr, R. A. 1982. Cloud seeding: One success in 35 years. Science 217:519-521.

Manabe, S., and R. T. Wetherald. 1967. Thermal equilibrium of the atmosphere with a given distribution of relative humidity. Journal of the Atmospheric Sciences 24(3):241-259.

Ogden, J. M., and R. H. Williams. 1989. Solar Hydrogen: Moving Beyond Fossil Fuels. Wasington, D.C.: World Resources Institute.

Ramanathan, V., L. Callis, R. Cess, J. Hansen, I. Isaksen, W. Kuhn, A. Lacis, F. Luther, J. Mahlman, R. Reck, and M. Schlesinger. 1987. Climate-chemical interactions and effects of changing atmospheric trace gases. Review of Geophysics 25(7):1441-1482.

Randall, D. A., J. A. Coakley, C. W. Fairall, R. A. Kropfli, and D. H. Lenschow. 1984. Outlook for research on sub-tropical marine stratiform clouds. Bulletin of the American Meteorological Society 65:1290-1301.

Reck, R. A. 1978. Thermal Effects of Cloud Parameter Variations in the Manabe-Wetherald Radiative-Convective Atmospheric Model. Report GMR-2820. Warren, Mich.: General Motors Research Laboratories.

Reck, R. A. 1979. Comparison of fixed cloud-top temperature and fixed cloud- top altitude approximations in the Manabe-Wetherald radiative-convective atmospheric model. Tellus 31:400-405.

Reck, R. A. 1984. Climatic Impact of Jet Engine Distribution of Alumina (Al_2O_3): Theoretical Evidence for Moderation of Carbon Dioxide (CO_2) Effects. Report GMR-4740. Warren, Mich.: General Motors Research Laboratories.

Rowland, F. S. 1987. Can we close the ozone hole? Technology Review 21:51-58.

Schneider, S. H. 1972. Cloudiness as a global climatic feedback mechanism: The effects on the radiation balance and surface temperature of variations in cloudiness. Journal of the Atmospheric Sciences 29:1413-1422.

Schwartz, S. E. 1988. Are global cloud albedo and climate controlled by marine phytoplankton? Nature 336:441-445.

Stumm, W., and J. J. Morgan. 1970. Aquatic Chemistry. New York: Wiley-Interscience.

Todd, C. J., and Howell, W. E. 1985. Weather modification. In Handbook of Applied Meteorology, D. D. Houghton, ed. New York: John Wiley & Sons.

Twomey, S., and T. A. Wojciechowski. 1969. Observations of geographical variation of cloud nuclei. Journal of Atmospheric Sciences 26:1413-1422.

U.S. Bureau of the Census. 1987. Statistical Abstracts of the United States 1988. Washington, D.C.: U.S. Bureau of the Census, U.S. Department of Commerce.

U.S. Bureau of the Census. 1988. Statistical Abstracts of the United States 1989. Washington, D.C.: U.S. Bureau of the Census, U.S. Department of Commerce.

Warren, S. G., C. J. Hahn, J. London, R. M. Chervin, and R. L. Jenne. 1988. Global Distribution of Total Cloud Cover and Cloud Type Amounts over the Ocean. Report DOE/ER-0406. Washington, D.C.: U.S. Department of Energy.

Wigley, T. M. L. 1989. Possible climate change due to SO_2-derived cloud condensation nuclei. Letter. Nature (6223) 339:365-367.

Appendix R

Description of Economic
Estimates of the Cost of Reducing
Greenhouse Emissions

It is useful to compare the estimates of the cost of mitigation derived in this report with those from other studies. One systematic study is a survey (Nordhaus, 1991) that derives from nine different economic modeling families a "cost function" for greenhouse gas emission reductions. The conceptual experiment performed for each model is to estimate the cost of an efficient reduction in CO_2 emissions. For models that assume no externalities or other market imperfections, this is equivalent to estimating the response of greenhouse gas emissions to increasingly stringent carbon taxes. The range of carbon taxes is from zero to around \$100/t CO_2 equivalent.[1]

The methods employed in the nine modeling studies differ considerably. At one extreme are the "econometric" models, which rely largely on behavioral estimates of supply and demand functions. In these studies, estimates are made of the structure of demand and supply on the basis of observed market data on prices and quantities. The models are often energy models that have been extended to include CO_2 emissions. A second generic approach draws on programming or optimization models of the energy sector. In this approach, the energy sector or the economy is represented in terms of technological activities such as demand for space heating or transportation services. By using a mathematical programming or other algorithm, the models then solve for the "optimal" trajectory of prices, outputs, fuel mix, and technologies. It can be shown that, under certain conditions, the optimal trajectory would correspond to the outcome of perfectly competitive markets. Some models are a hybrid of the two approaches.

All studies reviewed here share two important characteristics, however, that differ from the approach of the Mitigation Panel. First, they are all comprehensive energy sector models. That is, they include a consistent accounting of the demand, supply, and resources used in the countries or regions studied. In this respect, they differ from this report, which examines the possibilities for greenhouse gas reductions from individual technologies and attempts to make the estimates mutually consistent by manual calculations.

A second important difference between the Nordhaus (1991) survey and this report is that the survey estimates the cost function for reducing greenhouse gas emissions beginning from the point at which all the "negative-cost" options have been employed. In most economic models, the market equilibrium is this point; in one model, where market failures are allowed, the results have been recast so that the cost estimates begin from the point at which market failures have been allowed for. It is important to note, then, that the negative-cost part of the cost function, should it exist, is excluded from this survey.

The models represented in the survey encompass a wide variety of approaches to energy sector modeling. The studies surveyed (Nordhaus, 1991) were the following, listed roughly in order of their chronological development:

1. A series of mathematical-programming models, developed by Nordhaus and his associates, that use a technological specification for supply and econometric estimates for demand.

2. A purely behavioral or econometric model developed by Nordhaus and Yohe for the 1983 NAS study, *Changing Climate*, with a simplification for estimates of the impact of different taxes.

3. A series of models developed by Edmonds and Reilly, which are a mixture of technological data on the supply side and behavioral assumptions on the demand side.

4. A series of studies by Manne and Richels, which have much the same analytical structure as study 1 but are generally smaller and provide less detail on the demand side.

5. Estimates by Bodlund and associates for Sweden, using largely a mathematical optimization model with many alternative technologies.

6. Studies by Kram and others using a linear programming model of the Netherlands economy with a structure similar to that in study 5.

7. A six-region computable general equilibrium model developed by Whalley and Wigle that includes the energy and nonenergy sectors. The energy sector is purely behavioral and is not econometrically estimated.

8. A series of optimization models developed by the European Community that include both supply and end-use technologies for five European countries. These models allow for market failures in the energy-using sectors.

9. An extension of the Jorgenson approach by Jorgenson and Wilcoxen to include CO_2 emissions. The estimates are purely econometric but are based on extensive data and estimation.

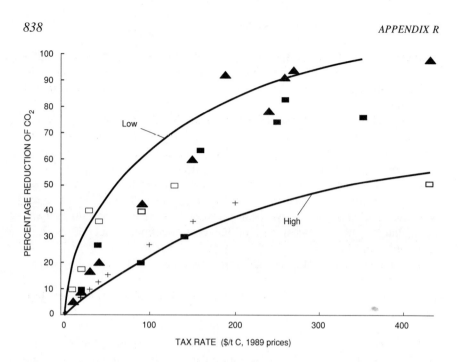

FIGURE R.1 Survey of economic models.

The results of the survey are shown in Figure R.1, with the individual points representing estimates from one of the nine families of models. Figure R.1 also shows a "high" and "low" frontier from the different models. The range has been constructed to include almost all the models, although some of the extreme estimates have been omitted if they appear to have features that are particularly problematic.

Figure R.2 employs a consensus, derived as the central tendency of the different models for CO_2 and alternative estimates for reforestation and CFCs, which shows the "best-guess" estimate of the cost function for reducing greenhouse gas emissions.

Finally, Figure R.3 shows a total cost function derived from the survey. The estimates are the total cost of different reductions of greenhouse gases at 1989 levels of world economic activity and industrial mix.

NOTE

1. Tons (t) are metric.

REFERENCE

Nordhaus, W. D. 1991. The cost of slowing climate change: A survey. The Energy Journal 12(1):37-65.

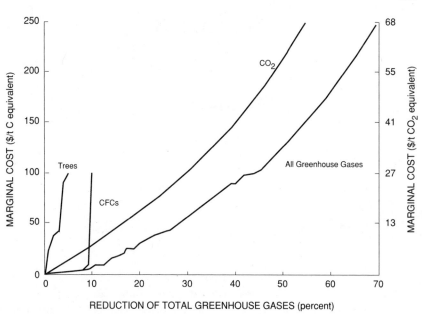

FIGURE R.2   Marginal cost of greenhouse gas reduction.

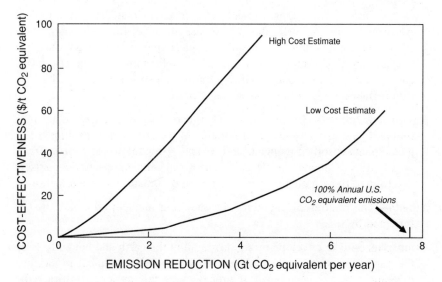

FIGURE R.3   Total cost of greenhouse gas reduction.

Appendix S

Glossary

The climate-based definitions are from the Oak Ridge National Laboratory's (1990) glossary entitled "Carbon Dioxide and Climate." The economic-based definitions are from Sharp, Register, and Leftwich (1988), "Economics of Social Issues," Business Publications, Inc., Plano, Texas.

Adaptation—The adjustment of an organism or population to a new or altered environment through genetic changes brought about by natural selection.

Aerosol—Particulate material, other than water or ice, in the atmosphere ranging in size from approximately 10^{-3} to larger than 10^2 µm in radius. Aerosols are important in the atmosphere as nuclei for the condensation of water droplets and ice crystals, as participants in various chemical cycles, and as absorbers and scatterers of solar radiation, thereby influencing the radiation budget of the earth-atmosphere system, which in turn influences the climate on the surface of the earth.

Airborne fraction—The portion of CO_2 released from all energy consumption and land use activities that remains in the atmosphere as opposed to the amounts absorbed by plants and oceans. How the world's total carbon is partitioned among the oceanic, terrestrial, and atmospheric pools is determined by complex biogeochemical and climatological interactions.

Albedo—The fraction of the total solar radiation incident on a body that is reflected by it.

Atmosphere—The envelope of air surrounding the earth and bound to it by the earth's gravitational attraction. Studies of the chemical properties, dynamic motions, and physical processes of this system constitute the field of meteorology.

840

Biological productivity—The amount of organic matter, carbon, or energy content that is accumulated during a given time period.

Biomass—The total dry organic matter or stored energy content of living organisms that is present at a specific time in a defined unit (community, ecosystem, crop, etc.) of the earth's surface.

Biosphere—The portion of earth and its atmosphere that can support life. The part (reservoir) of the global carbon cycle that includes living organisms (plants and animals) and life-derived organic matter (litter, detritus). The terrestrial biosphere includes the living biota (plants and animals) and the litter and soil organic matter on land, and the marine biosphere includes the biota and detritus in the oceans.

Biota—The animal and plant (fauna and flora) life of a given area.

Carbon-based resources—The recoverable fossil fuel (coal, gas, crude oils, oil shale, and tar sands) and biomass that can be used in fuel production and consumption.

Carbon budget—The balance of the exchanges (incomes and losses) of carbon between the carbon reservoirs or between one specific loop (e.g., atmosphere-biosphere) of the carbon cycle. An examination of the carbon budget of a pool or reservoir can provide information about whether the pool or reservoir is functioning as a source or sink for CO_2.

Carbon cycle—All parts (reservoirs) and fluxes of carbon; usually thought of as a series of the four main reservoirs of carbon interconnected by pathways of exchange. The four reservoirs, regions of the earth in which carbon behaves in a systematic manner, are the atmosphere, terrestrial biosphere (usually includes freshwater systems), oceans, and sediments (includes fossil fuels). Each of these global reservoirs may be subdivided into smaller pools ranging in size from individual communities or ecosystems to the total of all living organisms (biota). Carbon exchanges from reservoir to reservoir by various chemical, physical, geological, and biological processes.

Carbon density—The amount of carbon per unit area for a given ecosystem or vegetation type, based on climatic conditions, topography, vegetative-cover type and amount, soils, and maturity of the vegetative stands.

Carbon dioxide fertilization—Enhancement of plant growth or of the net primary production by CO_2 enrichment that could occur in natural or agricultural systems as a result of an increase in the atmospheric concentration of CO_2.

Carbon sink—A pool (reservoir) that absorbs or takes up released carbon from another part of the carbon cycle. For example, if the net exchange between the biosphere and the atmosphere is toward the atmosphere, the biosphere is the source, and the atmosphere is the sink.

Carbon source—A pool (reservoir) that releases carbon to another part of the carbon cycle.

Chlorofluorocarbons—A family of inert nontoxic and easily liquified chemicals used in refrigeration, air conditioning, packaging, and insulation or as solvents or aerosol propellants. Because they are not destroyed in the lower atmosphere, they drift into the upper atmosphere, where their chlorine components destroy ozone.

Climate—The statistical collection and representation of the weather conditions for a specified area during a specified time interval, usually decades, together with a description of the state of the external system or boundary conditions. The properties that characterize the climate are thermal (temperatures of the surface air, water, land, and ice), kinetic (wind and ocean currents, together with associated vertical motions and the motions of air masses, aqueous humidity, cloudiness and cloud water content, groundwater, lake lands, and water content of snow on land and sea ice), and static (pressure and density of the atmosphere and ocean, composition of the dry air, salinity of the oceans, and the geometric boundaries and physical constants of the system). These properties are interconnected by the various physical processes such as precipitation, evaporation, infrared radiation, convection, advection, and turbulence.

Climate change—The long-term fluctuations in temperature, precipitation, wind, and all other aspects of the earth's climate. External processes, such as solar-irradiance variations, variations of the earth's orbital parameters (eccentricity, precession, and inclination), lithosphere motions, and volcanic activity, are factors in climatic variation. Internal variations of the climate system also produce fluctuations of sufficient magnitude and variability to explain observed climate change through the feedback processes interrelating the components of the climate system.

Cloud—A visible mass of condensed water vapor particles or ice suspended above the earth's surface. Clouds may be classified on their visual appearance, height, or form.

Cloud albedo—Reflectivity that varies from less than 10 to more than 90 percent of the insolation and depends on drop sizes, liquid water content, water vapor content, thickness of the cloud, and the sun's zenith angle. The smaller the drops and the greater the liquid water content, the greater the cloud albedo, if all other factors are the same.

Cloud feedback—The coupling between cloudiness and surface air temperature in which a change in surface temperature could lead to a change in clouds, which could then amplify or diminish the initial temperature perturbation. For example, an increase in surface air temperature could increase the evaporation; this in turn might increase the extent of cloud cover. Increased cloud cover would reduce the solar radiation reaching the earth's surface, thereby lowering the surface temperature. This is an example of negative feedback and does not include the effects of longwave radiation or the advection in the oceans and the atmosphere, which must also be considered in the overall relationship of the climate system.

Cost-benefit analysis—Determination of and comparison of the costs and the benefits of an activity to evaluate its economic worth and the extent, if any, to which it should be carried on.

Deforestation—The removal of forest stands by cutting and burning to provide land for agricultural purposes, residential or industrial building sites, roads, etc., or by harvesting the trees for building materials or fuel. Oxidation of organic matter releases CO_2 to the atmosphere, and regional and global impacts may result.

Demand—The set of quantities of a good or service per unit of time that buyers would be willing to purchase at various alternative prices of the item, other things being equal.

Developed countries—Countries with relatively higher labor quality, relatively large accumulations of capital, and relatively higher levels of technology, all leading to relatively high living standards.

Discount rate—The rate of interest the Federal Reserve banks charge commercial banks when commercial banks borrow from the Fed.

Ecosystem—The interacting system of a biological community and its nonliving environmental surroundings.

Efficiency—The extraction of the greatest possible value of product output from given inputs of resources.

Elasticity of demand, price—The responsiveness of the quantity demanded of a product to changes in its price. Measured by the percentage change in quantity divided by the percentage change in price.

Elasticity of supply, price—The responsiveness of the quantity offered of a product to changes in its price. Measured by the percentage change in quantity divided by the percentage change in price.

Emissions—Materials (gases, particles, vapors, chemical compounds, etc.) that come out of smokestacks, chimneys, and tailpipes.

Emissivity—The ratio of the radiation emitted by a surface to that emitted by a black body at the same temperature.

Externalities—Benefits or costs incurred in the production or consumption of goods and services that do not accrue to the producing or consuming unit, but rather accrue to the remainder of the society.

Feedback mechanisms—A sequence of interactions in which the final interaction influences the original one.

Fossil fuel—Any hydrocarbon deposit that can be burned for heat or power, such as petroleum, coal, and natural gas.

Free riders—Those who receive social spillover benefits without paying the costs of producing the goods or services that yield them.

Full cost pricing—A situation in which the price of a product is equal to its average costs of production.

Geosphere—The solid mass (lithosphere) of the earth as distinct from the atmosphere and hydrosphere or all three of these layers combined.

Greenhouse gases—Those gases, such as water vapor, carbon dioxide, tropospheric ozone, nitrous oxide, and methane, that are transparent to solar radiation but opaque to longwave radiation. Their action is similar to that of glass in a greenhouse.

Gross national product, current—The value of an economy's annual output of goods and services in final form at current prices.

Heat island effect—A "dome" of elevated temperatures over an urban area caused by the heat absorbed by structures and pavement.

Implicit costs—Costs of production incurred by producing a unit for the use of self-owned, self-employed resources.

Infrared radiation—Electromagnetic radiation lying in the wavelength interval from 0.7 μm to 1000 μm. Its lower limit is bounded by visible radiation, and its upper limit by microwave radiation. Most of the energy emitted by the earth and its atmosphere is at infrared wavelength. Infrared radiation is generated almost entirely by large-scale intramolecular processes. The tri-atomic gases, such as water vapor, carbon dioxide, and ozone, absorb infrared radiation and play important roles in the propagation of infrared radiation in the atmosphere.

Investment—The purchase by economic units of such real assets as land, building, equipment, machinery, and raw and semifinished materials.

Lesser developed countries—Countries with relatively low living standards, usually the result of relatively low labor quality, relatively scarce capital, and relatively low levels of technology.

Marginal benefits—The increase or decrease in the total benefits yielded by an activity from a one-unit change in the amount of the activity carried on.

Marginal costs—The change in total costs resulting from a one-unit change in the output of a good or service.

Market—The area within which buyers and sellers of a good or service can interact and engage in exchange.

Modeling—An investigative technique that uses a mathematical or physical representation of a system or theory that accounts for all or some of its known properties. Models are often used to test the effects of changes of system components on the overall performance of the system.

Negative feedback—An interaction that reduces or dampens the response of the system in which it is incorporated.

Nutrient—Any substance assimilated by living things that promotes growth.

Ocean mixing—Processes that involve rates of advection, upwelling/ downwelling, and eddy diffusion and that determine how rapidly excess atmospheric carbon dioxide can be taken up by the oceans.

Ozone—A molecule made up of three atoms of oxygen. In the stratosphere, it occurs naturally and it provides a protective layer shielding the earth from ultraviolet radiation and subsequent harmful health effects on humans and the environment. In the troposphere, it is a chemical oxidant and major component of photochemical smog.

Photosynthesis—The manufacture by plants of carbohydrates and oxygen from carbon dioxide and water in the presence of chlorophyll with sunlight as the energy source. Oxygen and water vapor are released in the process. Photosynthesis is dependent on favorable temperature and moisture conditions as well as on the atmospheric carbon dioxide concentration. Increased levels of carbon dioxide can increase net photosynthesis in many plants.

Phytoplankton—That portion of the plankton community made up of tiny plants (e.g., algae and diatoms).

Planetary albedo—The fraction (approximately 30 percent) of incident solar radiation that is reflected by the earth-atmosphere system and returned to space, mostly by backscatter from clouds in the atmosphere.

Public goods—Goods and services of a collectively consumed nature, usually provided by governmental units.

Soil carbon—A major component of the terrestrial biosphere pool in the carbon cycle. Organic soil carbon estimates, rather than total soil carbon, are generally quoted. The amount of carbon in the soil is a function of historical vegetative cover and productivity, which in turn is dependent upon climatic variables.

Spillover benefits, social—Benefits from consumption or production activities that accrue to persons other than those doing the consuming or producing. Examples include the benefits of education services to those other than the students receiving them. See also, Externalities.

Spillover costs, social—Costs of consumption and production imposed on persons or economic units other than those doing the consuming or producing. See also, Externalities.

Supply—The set of quantities of a good or service per unit of time that sellers would be willing to place on the market at various alternative prices of the item, other things being equal.

Supply curve of a firm—A curve showing the quantities per unit of time a firm will place on the market at alternative price levels, other things being equal. The concept is valid for a competitive firm only, and coincides with its marginal cost curve.

Technology—The know-how and the means and methods available for combining resources to produce goods and services.

Trace gas—A minor constituent of the atmosphere. The most important trace gases contributing to the greenhouse effect are water vapor, carbon dioxide, ozone, methane, ammonia, nitric acid, nitrous oxide, ethylene, sulfur dioxide, nitric oxide, dichlorofluoromethane or Freon 12, trichlorofluoromethane or Freon 11, methyl chloride, carbon monoxide, and carbon tetrachloride.

Upwelling—The vertical motion of water in the ocean by which subsurface water of lower temperature and greater density moves toward the surface of the ocean. Upwelling occurs most commonly among the western coastlines of continents, but may occur anywhere in the ocean. Upwelling results when winds blowing nearly parallel to a continental coastline transport the light surface water away from the coast. Subsurface water of greater density and lower temperature replaces the surface water, and exerts a considerable influence on the weather of coastal regions. Carbon dioxide is transferred to the atmosphere in regions of upwelling. This is especially important in the Pacific equatorial regions, where 1 to 2 Gt C/yr may be released to the atmosphere. Upwelling also results in increased ocean productivity by transporting nutrient-rich waters to the surface layer of the ocean.

Appendix T

Conversion Tables

These conversion factors are from the Oak Ridge National Laboratory's (1990) glossary entitled "Carbon Dioxide and Climate."

International System of Units (SI): Prefixes

Prefix	SI Symbol	Multiplication Factor
exa	E	10^{18}
peta	P	10^{15}
tera	T	10^{12}
giga	G	10^{9}
mega	M	10^{6}
kilo	k	10^{3}
hecto	h	10^{2}
deka	da	10
deci	d	10^{-1}
centi	c	10^{-2}
milli	m	10^{-3}
micro	μ	10^{-6}
nano	n	10^{-9}
pico	p	10^{-12}
femto	f	10^{-15}
atto	a	10^{-18}

Common Conversion Factors

Area-length-volume
  1 acre = 43,560 ft^2 = 4,047 m^2
  1 acre-foot = 1.2335 × 10^3 m^3
  1 cubic foot (ft^3) = 0.0283 m^3
  1 hectare (ha) = 10,000 m^2 = 2.47 acres
  1 square mile (sq mi) = 2.59 × 10^6 m^2

Pressure
  1 atmosphere = 76.0 cm Hg = 1,013 millibars (mbar)
  1 bar = 0.9869 atmosphere
  1 pascal (Pa) = 0.9869 × 10^{-5} atmosphere = 1 × 10^{-2} mbar
              = 10 μbar = 1.4504 × 10^{-4} pounds per square inch (psi)

Carbon and Carbon dioxide
  1 mole C/liter = 12.011 × 10^{-3} Gt C/km^3
  1 ppm by volume of atmosphere CO_2 = 2.13 Gt C
  1 mole CO_2 = 44.009 g CO_2 = 12.011 g C
  1 g C = 0.083 mole CO_2 = 3.664 g CO_2

Energy
  1 quad = 1055 × 10^{15} joules
  1 kcal = 4184 joules
  1 mtce = 29.29 × 10^9 joules
  1 boe = 6119 × 10^6 joules
  1 mtoe = 44.76 × 10^9 joules
  1 m^3 gas = 37.26 × 10^6 joules
  1 TWyr = 31.54 × 10^{18} joules

Appendix U

Prefaces from the Individual
Panel Reports

PREFACE TO SYNTHESIS REPORT

Greenhouse gases and global warming have received increasing attention in recent years. The identification of the antarctic ozone hole in 1985 combined with the hot, dry summer of 1988 to provide the drama that seems to be required for capturing national media coverage. Emerging scientific results, including findings about greenhouse gases other than carbon dioxide, added to the interest.

One consequence was congressional action. The HUD-Independent Agencies Appropriations Act of 1988 (House Report 100-701:26) called for

> [an] NAS study on global climate change. This study should establish the scientific consensus on the rate and magnitude of climate change, estimate the projected impacts, and evaluate policy options for mitigating and responding to such changes. The need for and utility of improved temperature monitoring capabilities should also be examined, as resources permit.

According to subsequent advice received from members of Congress, the study was to focus on radiatively active trace gases from human sources, or "greenhouse warming." This report is one of the products of that study.

The study was conducted under the auspices of the Committee on Science, Engineering, and Public Policy, a unit of the councils of the National Academy of Sciences, the National Academy of Engineering, and the Institute of Medicine. The study involved nearly 50 experts, including scientists as well as individuals with experience in government, private industry, and public interest organizations.

The work of the study was conducted by four panels. The "Synthesis Panel" was charged with developing overall findings and recommendations. The "Effects Panel" examined what is known about changing climatic con-

849

ditions and related effects. The "Mitigation Panel" looked at options for reducing or reversing the onset of potential global warming. The "Adaptation Panel" assessed the impacts of possible climate change on human and ecologic systems and the policies that could help people and natural systems adapt to those changes.

This is the report of the Synthesis Panel. The reports of all four panels will be published by the National Academy Press in a single volume.

The panels conducted their analyses simultaneously between September 1989 and January 1991. The chairmen of the Effects, Mitigation, and Adaptation panels were members of the Synthesis Panel. Several members of the Synthesis Panel also were members of other panels. In its deliberations, however, the Synthesis Panel considered more than just the reports of the other panels. It also heard from experts with a range of views on the policy relevance of computer simulation models, widely held to be the best available tools for projecting climate change, and of economic models used to assess consequences of policies to reduce greenhouse gas emissions. The study also drew upon the report of the Intergovernmental Panel on Climate Change, an international effort released during the course of the study. Several members of the various study panels also contributed to that effort. Finally, the study drew upon other Academy studies. For example, in its examination of sea level, the panel used analyses from the following reports: *Glaciers, Ice Sheets, and Sea Level: Effects of a CO_2-Induced Climatic Change* (National Academy Press, 1985), *Responding to Changes in Sea Level: Engineering Implications* (National Academy Press, 1987), and *Sea-Level Change* (National Academy Press, 1990). The report of the Synthesis Panel is thus much more than a summary of the assessments performed by the other three panels. It contains analysis that goes beyond the topics covered by the other panels.

The report identifies what should be done now to counter potential greenhouse warming or deal with its likely consequences. The recommendations of the Synthesis Panel, if followed, should provide the United States, and the rest of the world, with a rational basis for responding to this very important concern.

> The Honorable Daniel J. Evans, Chairman
> Policy Implications of Greenhouse Warming—Synthesis Panel

PREFACE TO EFFECTS REPORT

Greenhouse gases and global warming have received increasing attention in recent years. The identification of the antarctic ozone hole in 1985 combined with the hot, dry summer of 1988 in North America to provide the drama that seems to be required for capturing national media coverage. Emerging scientific results, including findings about greenhouse gases other than carbon dioxide, added to the interest.

One consequence was congressional action. The HUD-Independent Agencies Appropriations Act of 1988 (House Report 100-701:26) called for

> [an] NAS study on global climate change. This study should establish the scientific consensus on the rate and magnitude of climate change, estimate the projected impacts, and evaluate policy options for mitigating and responding to such changes. The need for and utility of improved temperature monitoring capabilities should also be examined, as resources permit.

According to subsequent advice received from members of Congress, the study was to focus on radiatively active trace gases from man-made sources, or the "greenhouse effect." This report is one of the products of that study.

The study was conducted under the auspices of the Committee on Science, Engineering, and Public Policy, a unit of the councils of the National Academy of Sciences, the National Academy of Engineering, and the Institute of Medicine. The study involved nearly 50 experts, including scientists as well as individuals with experience in government, private industry, and public interest organizations.

The work of the study was conducted by four panels. The Effects Panel examined what is known about changing climatic conditions and related effects. The Mitigation Panel looked at options for reducing or reversing the onset of potential global warming. The Adaptation Panel assessed the impacts of possible climate change on human and ecologic systems and the policies that could help people and natural systems adapt to those changes. The Synthesis Panel was charged with developing overall findings and recommendations.

This is the report of the Effects Panel. The reports of all four panels will be published by the National Academy Press in a single volume under the title *Policy Implications of Greenhouse Warming: Mitigation, Adaptation, and The Science Base.*

The panels conducted their analyses simultaneously between September 1989 and January 1991. The chairmen of the Effects, Mitigation, and Adaptation panels were members of the Synthesis Panel.

> George F. Carrier, Chairman
> Panel on Policy Implications of Greenhouse Warming—Effects Panel

PREFACE TO MITIGATION REPORT

Greenhouse gases and global warming have received increasing attention in recent years. The identification of the antarctic ozone hole in 1985 combined with the hot, dry summer of 1988 to provide the drama that seems to be required for capturing national media coverage. Emerging scientific results, including findings about greenhouse gases other than carbon dioxide, added to the interest.

One consequence was congressional action. The HUD-Independent Agencies Appropriations Act of 1988 (House Report 100-701:26) called for

> [an] NAS study on global climate change. This study should establish the scientific consensus on the rate and magnitude of climate change, estimate the projected impacts, and evaluate policy options for mitigating and responding to such changes. The need for and utility of improved temperature monitoring capabilities should also be examined, as resources permit.

According to subsequent advice received from members of Congress, the study was to focus on radiatively active trace gases from human sources, or "greenhouse warming." This report is one of the products of that study.

The study was conducted under the auspices of the Committee on Science, Engineering, and Public Policy, a unit of the councils of the National Academy of Sciences, the National Academy of Engineering, and the Institute of Medicine. The study involved nearly 50 experts, including scientists as well as individuals with experience in government, private industry, and public interest organizations.

The work of the study was conducted by four panels that did their work in parallel, but with considerable exchange of information and some overlap in membership. The Mitigation Panel looked at options for reducing or reversing the onset of potential global warming. The Effects Panel examined what is known about changing climatic conditions and related effects. The Adaptation Panel assessed the impacts of possible climate change on human and ecologic systems and the policies that could help people and natural systems adapt to those changes. The Synthesis Panel developed overall findings and recommendations.

This is the report of the Mitigation Panel. The report of the Synthesis Panel is currently available as a separate volume entitled *Policy Implications of Greenhouse Warming* (National Academy Press, 1991). In addition, the reports of all four panels will be published in a single volume (National Academy Press, forthcoming).

The charge to the Mitigation Panel was to "examine the range of policy interventions that might be employed to mitigate changes in the earth's radiation balance, assessing these options in terms of their expected impacts, costs, and, at least in qualitative terms, their relative cost-effectiveness." In responding to this charge, the panel developed a methodology for evaluating the cost-effectiveness and greenhouse gas mitigation potential for a wide variety of options. This provided the panel with a priority ranking of these options. Using this methodology, the panel determined that 10 to 40 percent of current U.S. greenhouse gas emissions can be reduced at low cost.

Thomas H. Lee, Chairman
Policy Implications of Greenhouse Warming—Mitigation Panel

PREFACE TO ADAPTATION REPORT

Greenhouse gases and global warming have received increasing attention in recent years. The identification of the antarctic ozone hole in 1985 combined with the hot, dry summer of 1988 to provide the drama that seems to be required for capturing national media coverage. Emerging scientific results, including findings about greenhouse gases other than carbon dioxide, added to the interest.

One consequence was congressional action. The HUD-Independent Agencies Appropriations Act of 1988 (House Report 100-701:26) called for

[an] NAS study on global climate change. This study should establish the scientific consensus on the rate and magnitude of climate change, estimate the projected impacts, and evaluate policy options for mitigating and responding to such changes. The need for and utility of improved temperature monitoring capabilities should also be examined, as resources permit.

According to subsequent advice received from members of Congress, the NAS study was to focus on radiatively active trace gases from human sources, or "greenhouse warming." This report is one of the products of that study.

The study was conducted under the auspices of the Committee on Science, Engineering, and Public Policy, a unit of the councils of the National Academy of Sciences, the National Academy of Engineering, and the Institute of Medicine. The study involved nearly 50 experts, including scientists as well as individuals with experience in government, private industry, and public interest organizations.

The work of the study was conducted by four panels. The Effects Panel examined what is known about changing climatic conditions and related effects. The Mitigation Panel looked at options for reducing or reversing the onset of potential global warming. The Adaptation Panel assessed the impacts of possible climate change on humanity and nature and the policies that could help people and nature adapt to those changes. The Synthesis Panel, chaired by Daniel J. Evans, was charged with weighing effects, mitigation, and adaptation and reaching comprehensive findings and recommendations.

This is the report of the Adaptation Panel. The Adaptation Panel includes experts in terrestrial and marine ecology, agriculture, forestry, population and migration, health, industry, civil engineering, geography, economics, technology, and international relations. The panel began its work by reviewing the literature in the field of impacts and adaptation, stressing studies of the U.S. Environmental Protection Agency (EPA) and the work in progress of the Intergovernmental Panel on Climate Change (IPCC). The panel developed background papers in its fields of concern, several of which have been submitted for publication separately. The panel met five times over the course of 1 year to develop its collective views.

Comments by reviewers helped the panel, and a notable reviewer was Roger R. Revelle. One of the many things Dr. Revelle pioneered was investigation of the impact of climate change. In the National Academy of Sciences 1983 report *Changing Climate*, he reported the impact of climate change on the Colorado River and subsequently initiated and participated in the study that produced the report *Climate Change and U.S. Water Resources.* During the winter of 1990-1991 his thorough review of the present manuscript produced many valuable suggestions. The Adaptation Panel thanks him. As the report was moving to publication, Dr. Revelle died, at age 82.

It is important to stress that the charge to the panel was to develop an assessment of impacts and adaptation to climate change that emphasized consequences and opportunities for the United States. This decision was taken in light of the IPCC effort and the many efforts now under way by individual nations elsewhere in the world to assess their own prospects in light of likely climate change. This report does not claim to speak on behalf of the points of view of all nations.

The report also focuses on the direct effects of greenhouse gases and climate change. It does not attempt to assess all the numerous environmental changes that will be taking place simultaneously, including loss of habitat, destruction of the ozone layer, and marine pollution, to name a few. The panel was not charged with assessing the entire question of "environmentally sustainable development."

The panel immediately recognized that the selection of mitigation strategies for greenhouse gas emissions would also affect adaptation. For example, renewable sources of energy such as solar and wind power that might diminish greenhouse gas emissions also increase sensitivity to climate. In a few places in this report, we allude to interactions between mitigation and adaptation strategies. Although the panel was aware of indirect effects of adaptation to climate change, such as the vitality of schools in a farming community or of wildlife in a neighborhood when irrigation is extended, we naturally concentrated on such direct effects of adaptations as the success of food production. As societies narrow the range of strategies they consider seriously, it will be important to consider these interactions more fully.

The charge to this panel was not primarily to develop a research agenda about the impacts of climate. For a full discussion of research directions, see the 1990 National Research Council report *Research Strategies for the U.S. Global Change Research Program.*

The tasks of the Adaptation Panel were, first, to examine what would happen if climate changed and humanity and nature did not and, second, to find ways to temper any harm and to enhance any benefits of a new climate.

Paul E. Waggoner, Chairman
Policy Implications of Greenhouse Warming, Adaptation Panel

Appendix V

Acknowledgments from the Individual Panel Reports

ACKNOWLEDGMENTS BY THE SYNTHESIS PANEL

The work of the other panels was indispensable in the preparation of this report. George F. Carrier was chairman of the Effects Panel; Thomas H. Lee was chairman of the Mitigation Panel; and Paul E. Waggoner was chairman of the Adaptation Panel.

While this report represents the work of the panel, it would not have been produced without the support of professional staff from the Committee on Science, Engineering, and Public Policy of the National Academy of Sciences, National Academy of Engineering, and Institute of Medicine: Rob Coppock, who drafted the chapters and the question and answers section (Appendix A), and refined them on the basis of the panel's discussions and conclusions, and Deborah Stine, whose work on the Mitigation Panel report is reflected in Chapter 6. Nancy Crowell contributed to preparation of the Adaptation and Mitigation panel reports and the administrative organization of the study. Their resumes are included with those of the panel in Appendix W because of their intellectual contributions, which advanced the committee's efforts throughout the study. The report was greatly improved by the diligent work of its editor, Roseanne Price. In addition, invaluable support was provided by Marion Roberts.

The panel also acknowledges with appreciation presentations made at meetings of the Synthesis Panel by the following persons:

Frederick Bernthal, Assistant Secretary of State
Roger Dower, World Resources Institute
Jae Edmonds, Battelle Northwest Laboratories
James Hansen, Goddard Institute for Space Studies
Dale Jorgenson, Harvard University

Richard Lindzen, Massachusetts Institute of Technology
Gordon MacDonald, MITRE Corporation
Alan Manne, Stanford University
Richard Morgenstern, U.S. Environmental Protection Agency
Veerabhadran Ramanathan, University of Chicago
William Reifsnyder, Yale University
Kevin Trenberth, National Center for Atmospheric Research
Robert Williams, Princeton University
Timothy E. Wirth, United States Senator

ACKNOWLEDGMENTS BY THE EFFECTS PANEL

While this report represents the work of the panel, it would not have been produced without the support of professional staff from the Committee on Science, Engineering, and Public Policy of the National Academy of Sciences, National Academy of Engineering, and Institute of Medicine: Rob Coppock, Deborah Stine, and Nancy Crowell. Their resumes are included with those of the panel because of their intellectual contributions to the study. The report was greatly improved by the diligent work of its editor, Roseanne Price. In addition, invaluable support was provided by Marion Roberts.

The panel acknowledges with appreciation a presentation made to the panel by Donald J. Wuebbles. The panel also wishes to acknowledge contributions to Chapter 8 by Douglas E. Kinnison, Donald J. Wuebbles, and William Emanuel. The analysis in Chapter 5 was partially supported by the U.S. Department of Energy/National Oceanic and Atmospheric Administration Inter-Agency Agreement number DE-AIO5-90ER60592. Analysis presented in Chapter 8 was performed under the auspices of the U.S. Department of Energy Atmospheric and Climate Research Division by the Lawrence Livermore National Laboratory under contract W-7405-ENG-48. The National Research Council's Board on Atmospheric Science and Climate also provided draft documents for the panel's consideration.

ACKNOWLEDGMENTS BY THE MITIGATION PANEL

The panel acknowledges with appreciation the following people, who aided the panel in the analysis of some of the mitigation options: Stephanie Pollack and Robert Russell, both of the Conservation Law Foundation; Ruth Reck, Richard Schwing, and George Wolff, all of General Motors Research; Lynn Wright, Oak Ridge National Laboratory; Edward Lukosius, E.I. du Pont; and Celina Atkinson, Jonathan Koomey, Alan Meier, Robert Mowris, Lynn Price, and Ellen Ward, all of Lawrence Berkeley Laboratory.

While this report represents the work of the Mitigation Panel, it would not have been produced without the support of professional staff from the Committee on Science, Engineering, and Public Policy of the National Academy of Sciences, National Academy of Engineering, and Institute of Medicine, in particular Deborah Stine, who drafted the chapters and refined them based on panel discussions and conclusions. The report was greatly improved by the diligent work of its editor, Roseanne Price. In addition, invaluable support was provided by Marion Roberts and Ruth Danoff.

The panel would also like to thank the following people, who made presentations at panel meetings: Linda Stuntz, Department of Energy; David Montgomery, Congressional Budget Office; and Richard Morgenstern, Alex Cristofore, Mike Shelby, and Paul Schwengels, all of the U.S. Environmental Protection Agency.

ACKNOWLEDGMENTS BY THE ADAPTATION PANEL

While the members of the Adaptation Panel are responsible for this report, it would not have been produced without the support of staff from the Committee on Science, Engineering, and Public Policy. Rob Coppock, Nancy A. Crowell, Lawrence E. McCray, Roseanne Price, and Marion Roberts were indispensable. The panel appreciates the contribution of Scott Becvar of the University of Illinois. It is also grateful for presentations by the following persons: Ronald Benioff and Joel B. Smith of the U.S. Environmental Protection Agency; and Michael D. Bowes, Pierre R. Crosson, Joel Darmstadter, William E. Easterling III, and Kenneth D. Frederick of Resources for the Future.

Appendix W

Background Information on Panel Members and Professional Staff

SYNTHESIS PANEL MEMBERS

The Honorable DANIEL J. EVANS, Chairman, is chairman of Daniel J. Evans & Associates in Seattle, Washington. A registered civil and structural engineer, he served as United States Senator from the State of Washington from 1983 to 1989, and as governor from 1965 to 1977. He was president of The Evergreen State College from 1977 to 1983 and chaired the Pacific Northwest Power and Conservation Planning Council from 1981 to 1983. He is a member of the National Academy of Public Administration.

ROBERT McCORMICK ADAMS is secretary of the Smithsonian Institution in Washington, D.C. An anthropologist and educator, he conducted field research on the history of irrigation and urban settlements. Formerly provost at the University of Chicago, he is a member of the National Academy of Sciences.

GEORGE F. CARRIER is T. Jefferson Coolidge Professor of Applied Mathematics, emeritus, at Harvard University in Cambridge, Massachusetts. He specializes in mathematical modelling of fluid dynamics. He chaired the 1985 Academy Committee on Atmospheric Effects of Nuclear Explosions. He is a member of the National Academy of Sciences and the National Academy of Engineering.

RICHARD N. COOPER is professor of economics at Harvard University in Cambridge, Massachusetts and a director of the Federal Reserve Bank of Boston. He served as a member of the Council of Economic Advisors from 1961 to 1963. From 1972 to 1974 he was provost at Yale University. He was Undersecretary of State for Economic Affairs from 1977 to 1981.

ROBERT A. FROSCH is vice president at General Motors Research Laboratories in Warren, Michigan. He was Assistant Secretary of the Navy for Research and Development from 1966 to 1973. From 1973 to 1975 he was assistant executive director of the United Nations Environment Programme. He was director of the National Aeronautics and Space Administration from 1977 to 1981. He is a member of the National Academy of Engineering.

THOMAS H. LEE is professor emeritus in the Department of Electrical Engineering and Computer Science at Massachusetts Institute of Technology in Cambridge, Massachusetts. He worked at General Electric for 32 years, and from 1978 to 1980 was staff executive and chief technologist. From 1980 to 1984 he directed the Electric Power Systems Engineering Laboratory at Massachusetts Institute of Technology, and was director of the International Institute for Applied Systems Analysis from 1984 to 1987. He is a member of the National Academy of Engineering.

JESSICA TUCHMAN MATHEWS is vice president at the World Resources Institute in Washington, D.C. A molecular biologist and policy analyst, she was a professional staff to the United States Congress House Interior Committee from 1974 to 1975. From 1977 to 1979, she was director of the Office for Global Issues at the National Security Council.

WILLIAM D. NORDHAUS is professor of economics at Yale University in New Haven, Connecticut. He was a member of the Council of Economic Advisors from 1977 to 1979. From 1986 to 1988 he was provost at Yale University.

GORDON H. ORIANS is professor of zoology and was formerly director of the Institute for Environmental Studies at the University of Washington in Seattle, Washington. He specializes in evolution of vertebrate species. He is a member of the National Academy of Sciences.

STEPHEN H. SCHNEIDER is head of Interdisciplinary Climate Systems at the National Center for Atmospheric Research in Boulder, Colorado. He is an expert on global climate change models, and is editor of *Climate Change.*

MAURICE STRONG served on the Panel until February, 1990 when he resigned due to his commitment to serve as secretary general to the 1992 United Nations Conference on Environment and Development. He was director-general of the External Aid Office of the Canadian government, and Undersecretary General of the United Nations with responsibility for environmental affairs. He was chief executive of the 1972 United Nations Conference on the Human Environment.

SIR CRISPIN TICKELL is warden of Green College, Oxford, United Kingdom. He entered the British diplomatic service in 1954. From 1984 to 1987 he was permanent secretary of the Overseas Development Administration in the United Kingdom. From 1987 to 1990 he was permanent representative of the United Kingdom to the United Nations. He is author of *Climate Change and World Affairs* (University Press of America, 1986).

VICTORIA J. TSCHINKEL is senior consultant with Landers, Parsons and Uhlfelder in Tallahassee, Florida. From 1981 to 1987 she was secretary of the Florida Department of Environmental Regulation. An expert on environmental regulation and management, she is a member of the National Academy of Public Administration. She is also a member of the Electric Power Research Institute Advisory Council and the Advisory Committee for Nuclear Facility Safety.

PAUL E. WAGGONER is distinguished scientist at the Connecticut Agricultural Experiment Station in New Haven, Connecticut. He chaired the American Association for the Advancement of Science panel on Climatic Variability, Climate Change, and the Planning and Management of United States Water Resources. He is a member of the National Academy of Sciences.

EFFECTS PANEL MEMBERS

GEORGE F. CARRIER, Chairman, is T. Jefferson Coolidge Professor of Applied Mathematics, emeritus, at Harvard University in Cambridge, Massachusetts. He specializes in mathematical modeling of fluid dynamics. He chaired the 1985 Academy Committee on Atmospheric Effects of Nuclear Explosions. He is a member of the National Academy of Sciences and the National Academy of Engineering.

WILFRIED BRUTSAERT is professor of hydrology at Cornell University in Ithaca, New York. Among other topics, his research includes interactions between microclimate and hydrologic systems, including evaporation, infiltration, and drainage.

ROBERT D. CESS is distinguished service professor of atmospheric sciences at the State University of New York in Stony Brook, New York. He heads an international program to compare atmospheric global circulation models. His research interests include atmospheric radiation and climate modeling.

HERMAN CHERNOFF is professor of statistics at Harvard University in Cambridge, Massachusetts. His research has included statistical problems in econometrics, sequential design of experiments, rational selection of decision functions, large sample theory, and pattern recognition. He is a member of the National Academy of Sciences.

ROBERT E. DICKINSON is professor at the Institute for Atmospheric Research at the University of Arizona in Tucson, Arizona. His interests include atmospheric processes, upper atmosphere radiation and dynamics, and climate effects of land use change. He is a member of the National Academy of Sciences.

JOHN IMBRIE is H. L. Doherty Professor of Oceanography at Brown University in Providence, Rhode Island. He specializes in paleoecology and biometrics. He is a member of the National Academy of Sciences.

THOMAS B. KARL is a meteorologist at the National Climate Data Center in Asheville, North Carolina. His interests include the analysis and reconstruction of the 20th century climate record, and design and management strategies for environmentally sensitive systems.

MICHAEL C. MacCRACKEN is Division Leader of the Atmospheric and Geophysical Sciences Division at the Lawrence Livermore National Laboratory in Livermore, California. His primary interest is in modeling of climate change. He has also served as a scientific advisor to the Department of Energy's Carbon Dioxide Research program since 1978.

BERRIEN MOORE is director of the Institute for Study of Earth, Oceans, and Space at the University of New Hampshire in Durham, New Hampshire. His interests are earth system modeling, with special focus on interactions of biological, geological, and chemical cycles.

MITIGATION PANEL MEMBERS

THOMAS H. LEE, Chairman, is professor emeritus in the Department of Electrical Engineering and Computer Science at Massachusetts Institute of Technology in Cambridge. He worked at General Electric for 32 years, and from 1978 to 1980 was staff executive and chief technologist. From 1980 to 1984 he directed the Electric Power Systems Engineering Laboratory at Massachusetts Institute of Technology, and was director of the International Institute for Applied Systems Analysis from 1984 to 1987. He is a member of the National Academy of Engineering.

PETER BREWER is executive director of the Monterey Bay Aquarium Research Institute in Monterey Bay, California. He was formerly with the Woods Hole Oceanographic Institution in Woods Hole, Massachusetts, and program director of marine chemistry at the National Science Foundation. He also serves as a member of the NRC Oceans Studies Board and is chair of its panel on CO_2.

RICHARD N. COOPER is professor of economics at Harvard University in Cambridge, Massachusetts, and a director of the Federal Reserve Bank of Boston. He served as a member of the Council of Economic Advisors from 1961 to 1963. From 1972 to 1974 he was provost at Yale University. He was Undersecretary of State for Economic Affairs from 1977 to 1981.

ROBERT CRANDALL is a senior fellow at the Brookings Institute in Washington, D.C. From 1977 to 1978 he was deputy director of the Council on Wage and Price Stability. From 1974 to 1974 he was an economic advisor at the Federal Communications Commission. From 1966 to 1974 he was a professor of economics at the Massachusetts Institute of Technology.

ROBERT EVENSON is a professor of economics at Yale University's Economic Growth Center in New Haven, Connecticut. His research is in the area of agricultural development and the economics of science and technology.

DOUGLAS FOY is executive director of the Conservation Law Foundation, Inc., in Boston, Massachusetts. His background is in the area of energy and environmental law.

ROBERT A. FROSCH is vice president at General Motors Research Labs in Warren, Michigan. He was Assistant Secretary of the Navy for Research and Development from 1966 to 1973. From 1973 to 1974 he was assistant executive director of the United Nations Environment Programme. He was director of the National Aeronautics and Space Administration from 1977 to 1981. He is a member of the National Academy of Engineering.

RICHARD GARWIN is a fellow at the Thomas J. Watson Research Center in Yorktown Heights, New York, and an adjunct professor of physics at Columbia University. He is a member of the National Academy of Sciences, National Academy of Engineering, and Institute of Medicine.

JOSEPH GLAS is vice-president and general manager of the Fluorochemicals Division of E.I. du Pont in Wilmington, Delaware. He serves as an executive committee vice-president, member of the board of directors, and vice-chairman of the research committee for the American Refrigeration Institute (ARI). His background is in research, manufacturing, and marketing, with degrees in chemistry and chemical engineering.

KAI N. LEE taught political science and environmental studies at the University of Washington and was a visiting professor at the Institute of Economic Research at Japan's Kyoto University while this study was under way. He is now professor and director of the Center for Environmental Studies at Williams College. He was a member of the Northwest Power Planning Council from 1983 to 1987.

GREGG MARLAND is a scientist with the Environmental Sciences Division of the Oak Ridge National Laboratory in Oak Ridge, Tennessee. From 1975 to 1987 he was a scientist with the Institute for Energy Analysis. His research is in the area of environmental geochemistry, energy options and their environmental implications, and energy resources.

JESSICA TUCHMAN MATHEWS is vice-president at the World Resources Institute in Washington, D.C. A molecular biologist and policy analyst, she was on the professional staff of the United States Congress House Interior Committee from 1974 to 1975. From 1977 to 1979 she was director of the Office for Global Issues at the National Security Council.

ARTHUR H. ROSENFELD is professor of physics, University of California at Berkeley; director, Center for Building Science, Lawrence Berkeley Laboratory (LBL); and acting director, California Institute for Energy Efficiency. Formerly a particle physicist, he established and directed the International Particle Data Group at LBL/CERN (1957 to 1974). Currently, his research is in energy efficiency, and he was founding president of ACEEE (American Council for an Energy-Efficient Economy) from 1979 to 1990.

EDWARD S. RUBIN is professor of mechanical engineering and public policy and director, Center for Energy and Environmental Studies at Carnegie Mellon University in Pittsburgh, Pennsylvania. He also holds a chair as the Alumni Professor of Environmental Engineering and Sciences. From 1985 to 1989 he was a member of the National Air Pollution Control Techniques Advisory Committee of the U.S. Environmental Protection Agency. His research is in the area of environmental impacts of coal conversion and utilization, modeling of energy and environmental systems, air quality management, and technology assessment and public policy.

MILTON RUSSELL is professor of economics at the University of Tennessee in Knoxville and senior economist at Oak Ridge National Laboratory in Oak Ridge, Tennessee. From 1983 to 1987 he was assistant administrator for policy, planning, and evaluation at the Environmental Protection Agency. From 1976 to 1983 he was senior fellow and director of the Center for Energy Policy Research at Resources for the Future. His current research is in the area of environmental policy and policy formation.

STEPHEN H. SCHNEIDER is head of Interdisciplinary Climate Systems at the National Center for Atmospheric Research in Boulder, Colorado. He is an expert on global climate models and serves on the United States National Climate Program Advisory Committee and the Advisory Committee to the World Climate Studies Program.

EUGENE B. SKOLNIKOFF is professor of political science at the Massachusetts Institute of Technology in Cambridge. He is a member of the Department of State OES Advisory Committee. From 1979 to 1985 he was chairman of the board of the German Marshall Fund of the United States and has served in the White House Science Advisor's Office during several administrations. His research is in the area of international science, technology, and public policy.

THOMAS H. STIX is professor of astrophysical sciences and director of the Program in Plasma Physics at Princeton University, Princeton, New Jersey. His research is in the area of controlled fusion, waves and instabilities, and plasma heating and confinement.

EDITH BROWN WEISS of Georgetown University in Washington, D.C., served on the panel until May 1990, when she joined the Environmental Protection Agency. Her background is in international environmental law and policy.

ADAPTATION PANEL MEMBERS

PAUL E. WAGGONER, Chairman, is distinguished scientist at the Connecticut Agricultural Experiment Station in New Haven. He chaired the American Association for the Advancement of Science's Panel on Climatic Variability, Climate Change, and the Planning and Management of United States Water Resources. He is a member of the National Academy of Sciences.

JESSE H. AUSUBEL is a fellow in science and public policy at Rockefeller University in New York City and director of studies for the Carnegie Commission on Science, Technology, and Government. From 1983 through 1988 Mr. Ausubel served as director of the Program Office of the National Academy of Engineering. He has served as a resident fellow at the National Academy of Sciences, and as a research scholar at the International Institute for Applied Systems Analysis in Laxenburg, Austria. From 1981 to 1983 he was a National Research Council staff officer, principally responsible for studies of the greenhouse effect.

CLARK BINKLEY is dean of the faculty of forestry at the University of British Columbia, Vancouver, Canada. From 1979 to 1990 he served in the school of forestry and environmental studies at Yale University.

MARY M. KRITZ is associate director of the population and development program at Cornell University.

JOSHUA LEDERBERG is a university professor of Rockefeller University in New York City, where he served as president from 1978 to 1988. He was on the faculty of the genetics department at the University of Wisconsin from 1947 to 1959 and at Stanford University from 1959 to 1978. He is a member of the National Academy of Sciences and the Institute of Medicine.

WILLIAM LEWIS is a partner with McKinsey and Company in Washington, D.C. Dr. Lewis served as a deputy assistant secretary at the Department of Defense from 1977 to 1979 and as assistant secretary for policy and evaluation at the Department of Energy from 1979 to 1981.

JON C. LIEBMAN is professor of environmental engineering at the University of Illinois in Urbana where he has been on the faculty since 1976. Dr. Liebman earlier was on the faculty of Johns Hopkins University.

JANE LUBCHENCO is professor of zoology at Oregon State University in Corvallis and is a research associate of the Smithsonian Institution. She was on the faculty of Harvard University from 1975 to 1977. She is also a member of the National Research Council's Board on Environmental Studies and Toxicology.

WILLIAM D. NORDHAUS is professor of economics at Yale University. He was a member of the Council of Economic Advisors from 1977 to 1979. From 1986 to 1988 he was provost at Yale University.

GORDON H. ORIANS is professor of zoology and was formerly director of the Institute for Environmental Studies at the University of Washington in Seattle. He specializes in evolution of vertebrate species. He is a member of the National Academy of Sciences.

WILLIAM E. RIEBSAME is director of the Natural Hazards Research and Applications Information Center and assistant professor of geography at the

University of Colorado in Boulder. He served as an A. W. Mellon postdoctoral fellow on the joint SCOPE-UNEP project on "Improving the Science of Climate—Impact Study."

NORMAN J. ROSENBERG is senior fellow and director of the Climate Resources Program at Resources for the Future in Washington, D.C. Dr. Rosenberg was on the faculty of the University of Nebraska, Lincoln, from 1961 to 1987. He has served as a consultant to the National Oceanic and Atmospheric Administration and the Department of the Interior, among others. He was a member of the National Research Council's Board on Atmospheric Sciences and Climate from 1982 to 1985.

DANIEL P. SHEER is president of Water Resources Management in Columbia, Maryland. Previously he served as director of the Cooperative Water Supply Operations on the Potomac, Interstate Commission on the Potomac River Basin, and as executive secretary of the Power Plant Siting Studies Group at John Hopkins University.

SIR CRISPIN TICKELL is warden of Green College, Oxford, United Kingdom. He entered the British diplomatic service in 1954. From 1984 to 1987 he was permanent secretary of the Overseas Development Administration in the United Kingdom. From 1987 to 1990 he was permanent representative of the United Kingdom to the United Nations. He is the author of *Climate Change and World Affairs* (University Press of America, 1986).

PROFESSIONAL STAFF

ROB COPPOCK is staff director for the Panel on Policy Implications of Greenhouse Warming of the Committee on Science, Engineering, and Public Policy of the National Academy of Sciences, the National Academy of Engineering, and the Institute of Medicine in Washington, D.C. From 1976 to 1984 he was a staff scientist at the International Institute for Environment and Society in Berlin, Germany. He has been on the staff at the Academy since 1985. He currently is chairman of the Global Risk Analysis Division of the Society for Risk Analysis.

NANCY A. CROWELL is administrative specialist for the Panel on Policy Implications of Greenhouse Warming of the Committee on Science, Engineering, and Public Policy of the National Academy of Sciences, the National Academy of Engineering, and the Institute of Medicine in Washington, D.C.

DEBORAH D. STINE is staff officer for the Panel on Policy Implications of Greenhouse Warming of the Committee on Science, Engineering, and Public Policy of the National Academy of Sciences, the National Academy of Engineering, and the Institute of Medicine in Washington, D.C. Her specialties are environmental engineering and policy analysis. From 1983 to 1988 she was an air pollution engineer with the Texas Air Pollution Control Board. From 1988 to 1989 she was an air issues manager at the Chemical Manufacturers Association.

Index